# Judgment and Decision Making

Researchers in a growing number of fields – public policy, law, business, medicine, psychology, engineering, and others – are working to understand and improve human judgment and decision making. This book, which presupposes no formal training, brings together a selection of key articles in the area, with careful organization, introductions, and commentaries. Issues include medical diagnosis, weather forecasting, labor negotiations, risk, public policy, business strategy, eyewitness testimony, and more.

This is a revised edition of the 1986 collection of papers, *Judgment and Decision Making*, edited by Hal Arkes and Ken Hammond. The focus of this updated and extended volume is interdisciplinary and applied. The papers selected are scientific in nature, but chosen to appeal to the scholar, student, and layperson alike.

Terry Connolly is FINOVA Professor of Management and Policy in the College of Business and Public Administration at the University of Arizona.

Hal R. Arkes is Professor of Psychology at Ohio University.

Kenneth R. Hammond is Emeritus Professor of Psychology and Director of the Center for Research on Judgment and Policy at the University of Colorado, Boulder.

All three editors are past presidents of the Society for Judgment and Decision Making.

# Cambridge Series on Judgment and Decision Making

The purpose of the series is to convey the general principles of and findings about judgment and decision making to the many academic and professional fields to which these apply. The contributions are written by authorities in the field and supervised by highly qualified editors and the Publications Board. The series will attract readers from many different disciplines, largely among academics, advanced undergraduates, graduate students, and practicing professionals.

# Judgment and Decision Making

## An Interdisciplinary Reader

Second Edition

*Edited by*

Terry Connolly
*University of Arizona*

Hal R. Arkes
*Ohio University*

Kenneth R. Hammond
*University of Colorado*

CAMBRIDGE
UNIVERSITY PRESS

PUBLISHED BY THE PRESS SYNDICATE OF THE UNIVERSITY OF CAMBRIDGE
The Pitt Building, Trumpington Street, Cambridge, United Kingdom

CAMBRIDGE UNIVERSITY PRESS
The Edinburgh Building, Cambridge CB2 2RU, UK    http://www.cup.cam.ac.uk
40 West 20th Street, New York, NY 10011-4211, USA    http://www.cup.org
10 Stamford Road, Oakleigh, Melbourne 3166, Australia
Ruiz de Alarcón 13, 28014 Madrid, Spain

First published 2000

Printed in the United States of America

*Typeface* Palatino 9.75/12 pt.        *System* LATEX $2_\varepsilon$ [TB]

*A catalog record for this book is available from the British Library.*

*Library of Congress Cataloging-in-Publication Data*
Judgment and decision making : an interdisciplinary reader / edited by
Terry Connolly, Hal R. Arkes, Kenneth R. Hammond. – Rev. ed.
p.   cm. – (Cambridge series on judgment and decision making)
Includes bibliographical references and index.
ISBN 0-521-62355-3 (hardcover). – ISBN 0-521-62602-1 (pbk.)
1. Decision making.   2. Judgment.   I. Connolly, Terry.
II. Arkes, Hal R., 1945–   .   III. Hammond, Kenneth R.   IV. Series.
BF441.J79   1999
302.3 – dc21                                                                98-51484
                                                                                    CIP

ISBN  0 521 62355 3  hardback
ISBN  0 521 62602 1  paperback

# Contents

# Series Preface

The Society for Judgment and Decision Making first collaborated with Cambridge University Press in 1986 with the publication of *Judgment and Decision Making: An Interdisciplinary Reader*, edited by Hal R. Arkes and Kenneth R. Hammond. The goals of the reader were to (1) outline the core ideas of the field and (2) illustrate their wide applicability. The purpose of each of the subsequent volumes in the series was to explain in far greater detail the relevance of judgment and decision-making research to particular domains. Thus *Inside the Juror*, edited by Reid Hastie, pertained to law; *Psychological Perspectives on Justice*, edited by Barbara A. Mellers and Jonathan Baron, dealt with economic, legal, and policy issues related to fairness; and *Judgment and Decision-Making Research in Accounting and Auditing*, edited by Robert H. Ashton and Alison H. Ashton, highlighted the burgeoning quantity of research in these two areas. Finally, *Research on Judgment and Decision Making: Currents, Connections, and Controversies*, edited by William M. Goldstein and Robin M. Hogarth, surveyed the field at a more advanced level, including important research ideas and controversies that have emerged as the field has matured.

The present volume returns to the roots of the original *Interdisciplinary Reader*. Though the vast majority of the material is new since the first edition, the aim remains the same: "to provide a general, interdisciplinary introduction that will enable the reader to develop an appreciation of the nature of the new field of judgment and decision making [and] a series of illustrations of the empirical analysis of judgment and decision making in various fields of interest" (from the Editors' preface to the first edition). As in the original collection, examples are drawn from a wide range of application areas, including law, medicine, public policy, business, psychology, and others. The Publications Committee of the Society for Judgment and Decision Making is pleased to present this volume, which offers an introduction to the field for a new generation of readers.

Jon Baron
For the Publications Committee

# Contributors

Hal R. Arkes  *Department of Psychology, Ohio University*

Maya Bar-Hillel  *Department of Psychology, The Hebrew University*

Jonathan Baron  *Department of Psychology, University of Pennsylvania*

Max H. Bazerman  *Kellogg Graduate School of Management, Northwestern University*

Lee Roy Beach  *College of Business and Public Administration, University of Arizona*

Gershon Ben-Shakhar  *Department of Psychology, The Hebrew University*

Catherine Blumer  *Department of Psychology, Ohio University*

Ann Bostrom  *School of Public Policy, Georgia Institute of Technology*

James B. Bushyhead  *Department of Health Services, U.S. Public Service Hospital, Seattle*

Jay J. J. Christensen-Szalanski  *College of Business Administration, University of Iowa*

Terry Connolly  *College of Business and Public Administration, University of Arizona*

Robyn M. Dawes  *Department of Social and Decision Sciences, Carnegie Mellon University*

Carl J. D'Orsi  *University of Massachusetts Medical Center*

Janet Doyle  *School of Communication Disorders, Faculty of Health Sciences, La Trobe University*

Ward Edwards  *Social Science Research Institute, University of Southern California*

Hillel J. Einhorn (Deceased)  *Center for Decision Research, Graduate School of Business, University of Chicago*

David Faust  *Department of Psychology, University of Rhode Island*

Baruch Fischhoff   *Department of Social and Decision Sciences, Carnegie Mellon University*

Robert H. Frank   *Department of Economics, and Johnson Graduate School of Management, Cornell University*

Gary J. Gaeth   *Department of Marketing, University of Iowa*

David J. Getty   *BBN Laboratories Incorporated*

Gerd Gigerenzer   *Max Planck Institute for Psychological Research, Munich*

Thomas Gilovich   *Department of Psychology, Cornell University*

Daniel G. Goldstein   *Department of Psychology, University of Chicago*

Kenneth R. Hammond   *Department of Psychology, University of Colorado*

Lewis O. Harvey, Jr.   *Department of Psychology, University of Colorado*

Reid Hastie   *Department of Psychology, University of Colorado*

Denis J. Hilton   *Department of Psychology, University of Hertfordshire*

Helmut Jungermann   *Institute für Psychologie, Technische Universität Berlin*

Peter Juslin   *Department of Psychology, Uppsala University*

Daniel Kahneman   *Department of Psychology, and Woodrow Wilson School of Public and International Affairs, Princeton University*

Ralph L. Keeney   *Systems Management Department, University of Southern California*

Yong Min Kim   *Kellogg Graduate School of Management, Northwestern University*

Benjamin Kleinmuntz   *Department of Psychology, University of Illinois*

Richard P. Larrick   *Center for Decision Research, Graduate School of Business, University of Chicago*

Elizabeth F. Loftus   *Department of Psychology, University of Washington*

Lola L. Lopes   *College of Business Administration, University of Iowa*

Cynthia M. Lusk   *Center for Research on Judgment and Policy, University of Colorado*

Timothy L. McDaniels   *Westwater Research Center, University of British Columbia*

Barbara J. McNeil   *Department of Radiology, Harvard Medical School*

James N. Morgan   *Department of Psychology, University of Michigan*

Jeryl L. Mumpower   *Center for Policy Research, State University of New York*

Margaret A. Neale   *Graduate School of Business, Stanford University*

J. Robert Newman   *Department of Psychology, California State University at Long Beach*

Richard E. Nisbett   *Department of Psychology, University of Michigan*

Stephen G. Pauker  *Department of Medicine, New England Medical Center Hospital, Boston*

Nancy Pennington  *Department of Psychology, University of Colorado*

Ronald M. Pickett  *Department of Radiology, University of Lowell*

Marilyn Jacobs Quadrel  *Decision Analysis Group, Battelle Pacific Northwest Laboratories*

Dennis T. Regan  *Department of Psychology, Cornell University*

James Shanteau  *Department of Psychology, Kansas State University*

Paul Slovic  *Decision Research, Eugene*

Ben R. Slugoski  *Department of Psychology, Mount Allison University*

Harold C. Sox, Jr.  *Department of Medicine, Stanford University*

Thomas R. Stewart  *Center for Policy Research, State University of New York*

John A. Swets  *BBN Laboratories Incorporated*

Richard H. Thaler  *Center for Decision Research, Graduate School of Business, University of Chicago*

Shane A. Thomas  *School of Behavioural Health Sciences, Faculty of Health Sciences, La Trobe University*

Amos Tversky (Deceased)  *Department of Psychology, Stanford University*

Kathleen L. Valley  *Kellogg Graduate School of Management, Northwestern University*

W. Kip Viscusi  *Department of Economics, Duke University*

Detlof von Winterfeldt  *Social Science Research Institute, University of Southern California*

Edward J. Zajac  *Kellogg Graduate School of Management, Northwestern University*

Richard J. Zeckhauser  *Kennedy School of Government, Harvard University*

Jay Ziskin (Deceased)  *Marina Del Ray, California*

# Preface to the Second Edition

The first edition of this book was, by academic standards, something of a best-seller. It appeared at a time when interest in JDM topics was exploding in a variety of disciplines, and the collection sampled papers from many of those disciplines. The papers it included, though real professional work, were generally accessible to advanced undergraduate and early graduate students without extensive background in psychology, economics, or mathematics. And the editors made a balanced selection of theory, method, and application papers, with brief introductions to each cluster. All this served the "entry-level" student well, and the book became a central resource for many undergraduate and graduate JDM courses. It was universally referred to as "The JDM Reader."

In undertaking a revision of this popular collection, the first need was simply to bring it up to date, while retaining the flavor and breadth of the original. A great deal has happened in the field in the decade or more since "The Reader" was published. New theoretical concerns have emerged, while others seem to have worked themselves out. New applications have been reported in many areas, and computer applications have grown both as a tool for descriptive research and as a decision aid in normative work. Our revision has tried to reflect some of this new work. More than three quarters of the chapters included here did not appear in the first edition – indeed, the vast majority have appeared since the original collection was published. Two chapters were commissioned especially for this volume and have not appeared previously. Several others have been extensively revised and have not previously appeared in the form they take here. All the section introductions have been rewritten to accommodate these changes. The collection, then, is certainly "new"; we hope it is also "improved."

A second challenge in revising the book was simply the enormous growth of the field since the early 1980s. Many of the topics that excited JDM researchers then have now grown into substantial research literatures, and important new topics are added every year. It is increasingly difficult to present even a sampling of both theoretical issues and interdisciplinary applications in a single volume. Fortunately, the Publications Committee of the Society for Judgment and Decision Making has recently added to this series of books a collection edited by William Goldstein and Robin Hogarth (Goldstein & Hogarth, 1997) that does a superb job of reflecting many of the important theoretical ideas in the area. This has allowed us more freedom in the present collection to emphasize chapters whose primary contribution is substantive or methodological. These are, of course, imprecise lines, but the difference in flavor between the two collections will be immediately obvious. Taken together, the companion volumes provide complementary but nonoverlapping introductions to the core ideas of the field and the wide range of their application.

Even with two collections in the place of one, it should be clear that this is a very tiny sampling of the field. When we undertook this revision, we asked for advice from the membership of the Society for Judgment and Decision Making. We received over 500 suggestions of chapters we should add, only two(!) for chapters we should drop – a generous spirit indeed, but not much help in guiding a manageable collection. We thank all who gave their advice, and exonerate all from blame. The final selection, inevitably, has large measures of arbitrariness and, no doubt, others would have made different choices. All we can claim of the chapters included here are that they each seem to us exciting and interesting in one way or another, and that they are drawn from a sufficiently wide range of topics and approaches that they start to suggest the enormous range and interest of JDM research as we approach the year 2000. The field is wide open, highly diverse, full of energy, and fascinating. Its core ideas are deep, and their practical applications of enormous importance. Here is a sampling of papers from the field, intended to whet the appetite and invite the participation of a new generation of researchers and to refresh the interest of those already involved. We look forward to their doing together the work that will force another revision of "The Reader" a decade or so from now!

Terry Connolly
Hal R. Arkes
Kenneth R. Hammond

### References

Arkes, H. R., & Hammond, K. R. (Eds.). (1986). *Judgment and decision making: An interdisciplinary reader*. New York: Cambridge University Press.

Goldstein, W. M., & Hogarth, R. M. (Eds.). (1997). *Research on judgment and decision making: Currents, connections, and controversies*. New York: Cambridge University Press.

# General Introduction

All students like to believe that their particular subject is the center of the universe. Doubtless, students of judgment and decision making are no different, but they may have a good argument for their view. After all, they can claim that the great moments of history all turned on someone's judgment as to what should be done and someone's decision to do it. Moreover, they will claim that although their subject is as old as civilization it has been studied in a scientific, empirical way only within the very last few decades. Indeed, most of the pioneers in this field are still alive and contributing to it. The fact that we are now able to study judgment and decision making in a scientific manner is, these students can claim, an exciting new discovery in and of itself.

Of course, the editors of this book and the authors of the chapters in it firmly believe in this view; judgment and decision making *are* of critical importance, and the fact that it is possible to study them in a scientific, empirical manner *is* a new and exciting event in the recent history of science.

Despite its central importance and long history, however, the field is still so new that it will be useful to turn to the dictionary to discover how these terms have been defined for common use. *Webster's Third New International Dictionary* says that *judgment* is "the mental or intellectual process of forming an opinion or evaluation by discerning and comparing," and the *capacity for judging* is "the power or ability to decide on the basis of evidence." Although the dictionary quotes E. L. Godkin as saying that "judgment is the highest of the human faculties," it also notes that Oliver Wendell Holmes said, "some of the sharpest men in argument are notoriously unsound in judgment." Apparently, we are to understand that the capacity to make sound judgments requires not only intelligence but wisdom and that the former does not guarantee the latter. *Webster's* definition of *decision*, "the act of settling or terminating . . . by giving judgment," suggests that there is little difference between *judgment* and *decision making* in ordinary discourse, so we shall not make a distinction here, although more advanced treatments of the topic do (see, e.g., Goldstein & Hogarth, 1997).

Not only the sources but the nature of sound judgment have fascinated scholars since the beginning of self-reflection; the Greek intellectuals apparently mused about those topics every day. And the discussion continues today among philosophers, psychologists, political scientists, lawyers, management scientists, and others inside and outside of academia, because sound judgment is, of course, of great practical as well as academic concern. No question will be of greater importance to the board of directors of the industrial firm that evaluates candidates for the position of chief executive officer than the soundness of each candidate's judgment. And while members of all the above academic departments debate theories of rational choice (each group in happy ignorance of the activities of the others), members of the board of regents will be exercising their judgment as they select the new president of the university. Indeed, the capacity for sound judgment of every person who desires a high (or even not so high) place in almost every segment of society will be judged by those responsible for selecting them. That is because within both government and industry there is a strong correlation between the prominence and power of one's position, the amount of time that one spends on problems requiring judgment, and the salary one receives. At the other end of the scale, inability to make the simple judgments required in the ordinary circumstances of day-to-day living leads to the diagnosis of mental illness.

In short, judgment and decision making are pervasive, important intellectual activities engaged in by all of us in academic, professional, and social pursuits throughout every day. The ability to form good judgments and make wise and effective decisions generally is considered the mark of a successful person in the smaller as well as the larger matters of living. Apparently, the same has been true of every human society.

What do we know about this salient feature of our lives? This book will not try to answer that question completely, but it will provide a general introduction to our knowledge of judgment and decision making and provide guideposts for those who may wish to pursue their inquiry further. Although the study of judgment and decision making is a field in its own right, it finds application in virtually every known human endeavor. (A recent survey conducted by one of us showed that articles related to judgment and decision making appeared in more than 500 different professional journals.) Therefore, we have chosen to group studies of judgment and decision making within those major fields in which studies of judgment and decision making are currently being conducted. These include judgment and social policy, economics, law, medicine and other fields indicated in the Table of Contents.

It is easy to find examples of the importance of the "intellectual process of forming an opinion or evaluation by discerning or comparing" or "decid[ing] on the basis of evidence." The decision to drop the atomic bomb on Hiroshima without warning is perhaps the most dramatic example of an act of judgment in the 20th century. Other examples include changes in health policy (e.g., the decision to institute a National Health Service in Britain), economic policy (e.g., the deregulation of airlines in the United States), legal policy (e.g., the use of plea bargaining), and environmental policy (e.g., the protection of wildlife and pristine areas, the control of toxic waste), and the reduction of risk (e.g., the nationwide 55-mph speed limit in the United States); all provide examples of the attempt to exercise sound judgment. And in what follows we provide examples of efforts to study such judgments, both in the controlled conditions of the laboratory and in the world outside.

The reader will notice that all of these examples of studies of judgment and decision making are recent. The systematic empirical study of judgment and decision making began to emerge as a discipline in its own right only in the 1960s. This occurred together with a strong surge of interest in the larger, more general field of cognitive psychology, which includes the study of memory, thinking, problem solving, mental imagery, and language. The explosion of research in cognitive psychology marked a sharp shift in interest from the concentration on motivation in psychological research to a concentration on "mental activity." There are two main reasons for this. First, something dropped out; by 1960 strict stimulus – response behaviorism lost credibility among many laboratory scientists, and Freudian psychology based largely on unconscious motivation lost credibility with almost everyone. Second, something dropped in, namely, the electronic computer, which immediately provided a credible metaphor for mental activity. Thus, within a decade of the introduction of the computer, psychologists were talking about and studying "human information processing." As one psychologist (George Miller) put it, "the mind came in on the back of the machine." The arrival of the computer made it possible to carry out research on human information processing (including judgment and decision making) in new and powerful ways. For example, those interested in problem solving were able to build computer models that simulated human information-processing activity, and this led rapidly to the creation of the new field of artificial intelligence. Those interested in constructing mathematical models of the judgment and decision-making process could rapidly test a variety of such models for their ability to represent and/or evaluate the rationality of human judgment and decision making. By the 1980s, work that would have been utterly impossible prior to the computer became commonplace.

Because two types of mathematical representations of judgment and decision-making behavior are frequently used, we present the basic ideas that underlie them in this General Introduction. The mathematical operations of both approaches are easy to grasp; a knowledge of simple algebra is all that is required. We first describe the approach known as *decision analysis* – which involves an a priori decomposition of the decision process – and, second, we describe the approach known as *judgment analysis* – which involves an a posteriori decomposition of the judgment process. Although the distinction between decision and judgment is somewhat arbitrary and need not concern us here, the distinction between a priori and a posteriori decomposition is important and should be kept in mind, for it will be illustrated often in the chapters that follow.

### Decision Analysis: A Priori Decomposition

A priori decomposition refers to separating the decision process into its components *before* the decision is made. Such components include (a) the *probabilities* or likelihood of occurrence of each alternative considered and (b) the *utility* attached to each alternative. The decision process is greatly aided when these concepts are used in the context of a *decision tree*.

Construction of a decision tree prior to making the decision is an easy way of guiding and simplifying the decision process because it *diagrams* the decomposition of the decision process into probabilities and utilities and thus provides a clear picture of the process and its components.

The decision maker needs only four types of information to construct a decision tree:

1. What are my possible courses of action? (Alternatives)
2. What are the events that might follow from those actions? (Outcomes)
3. What is the likelihood of each event?
4. What is the value of each event to me?

Here is a decision-making situation similar to one that actually confronted an elderly man known to us. The man had a very serious medical problem. His physician said that a difficult operation was necessary to remedy the situation. The physician added, however, that, given the man's very advanced age and the nature of the operation, there was a 40% *probability* that the patient would not recover from the operation. If the operation were not performed, the serious medical problem would linger, causing the patient discomfort and impairing his mobility. There was no chance that the problem would "go away," and there was a 20% probability that without the operation the man would die within the next 6 months. What should the man do? Should he have the operation?

Figure I.1 depicts the decision tree for this situation. The box represents a "decision node." The two possible courses of action emanate from this node. They are "operate" and "don't operate," and thus they comprise the first of the four types of information needed to construct a decision tree. The circles are chance nodes. (They are called chance nodes because no decision can be made to cause one of the outcomes to occur rather than the other. Their occurrence is therefore left to chance.) The events emanating from these circles are the possible events that might occur following the courses of action. This is the second type of information needed. Preceding each

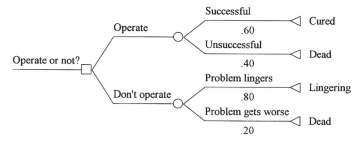

Figure I.1. Decision tree showing probabilities and outcomes associated with alternative actions.

possible event is its probability of occurrence, based on the physician's best estimate. This is the third essential type of information. Finally, we need to know what value the patient places on each of these outcomes.

Because the value of any commodity is judged differently by everyone, the term *utility* rather than *value* is used. This term captures the subjective nature of the evaluation; a particular amount of money may have different utility for me than for you. Even health may have different utilities for different people. To calculate the utility of each outcome, we shall call the worst outcome 0.0 on a utility scale and the best outcome 1.0.

The patient assigned "death" the former value and "complete cure" the latter value. Using this range (0.0–1.0), the patient felt that living in discomfort and having decreased mobility was worth .6 to him. It was a state closer to "complete cure" than to "death," but not by much.

We now have all the information needed to make a decision tree. First, it is necessary to examine each outcome. The utility of each outcome needs to be weighted according to its likelihood. An outcome of 1.0 ("wonderful") that has a high probability of occurring should definitely be preferred to another outcome of utility 0.0 that has very little likelihood of occurring. To accomplish this mathematically, the utility of each outcome is multiplied by its probability of occurrence. This product is the *expected utility* of each outcome. Figure I.2 contains these calculations, which are located at the right edge of each branch of the decision tree.

All that remains now is the process called "folding back," which consists of pruning all but the most preferred course of action at each decision node. There are two possible courses of action: operate and don't operate. For each of these two options we add together all of the expected utilities associated with that option. For example, the option "don't operate" has associated with it two expected utilities of .48 and 0. Their sum, .48, is the expected utility of the "don't operate" course of action. Because the "operate" course of action is higher (.6), the preferred course of action is to operate.

One immense virtue of a decision tree is that it is a wonderfully general decision aid. As long as the four types of information are available, any decision

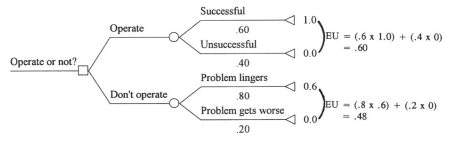

Figure I.2. Calculation of expected utility for each alternative.

can be analyzed by use of the tree. Should I move to Minneapolis to accept this new job? Should I switch insurance policies from X to Y? Should we get a loan to get a new car now, or should we limp along with the one we have?

One difficulty often encountered in constructing a decision tree is that likelihoods and utilities are often not easy to assess. When an expert opinion is available, as in the case of our medical example, reasonable likelihoods can often be provided. Because the helpfulness of a decision tree is based largely on the accuracy of the likelihoods and utilities used, every effort should be made to obtain good estimates.

Occasionally the decision maker is uneasy about the "verdict" of the decision tree. In our medical example, the "operate" option was only .12 superior to the "don't operate" option. "What if I later decide that living with discomfort and decreased mobility isn't so bad? Maybe it's worth a .7 and not a measly .6," thinks the elderly man as the morning of the operation approaches. A quick calculation will reveal that "operate" is *still* the preferred choice, even if .7 is deemed the utility of an uncomfortable and immobile existence. Modifying the probabilities and utilities in this way is called a "sensitivity analysis," because such manipulating of the probabilities and utilities tests how sensitive the final choice is to the numbers initially assigned. Reasonable modifications of the probabilities and utilities often leave the decision unchanged. The decision maker can then rest comfortably with the decision that has been reached.

Concern about the assignment of accurate probabilities, the calculation of expected utilities, and the performance of various arithmetic tasks should not obscure what may be the greatest virtue of a decision tree: It forces the decision maker to make explicit all the bases for the decision. In the tree are contained all the courses of action, all the probabilities, all the utilities, and all the outcomes of which the decision maker is aware – or, at least, those that he or she plans to consider. Every analysis works on a simplified version of the real situation, but the tree at least makes it explicit what is being included, what excluded. It also makes it explicit how far into the future the decision maker is thinking about the consequences of this action. The time-frame issue is important when the utility of an outcome shifts over time. In exercising, for example, a short time-frame stresses negative outcomes like feeling tired, but a longer time-frame stresses more positive ones like good health and vigor. Merely having to generate the information necessary to draw the tree may force the decision maker to confront the situation in a much more organized and thoughtful way than would otherwise be the case.

### Judgment Analysis: A Posteriori Decomposition

If a priori decomposition implies decomposing the decision process *prior* to its occurrence, then a posteriori decomposition obviously implies that decomposition will take place *after* a series of judgments have been made. As we shall see, a person's *judgment policy* can be "captured" after judgments are made regarding hypothetical cases; the policy may then be applied to real cases.

The principal concepts of a judgment analysis are best illustrated by reference to the model of the judgment situation presented in Figure I.3, which indicates that judgment is a cognitive process similar to inductive inference. That is, judgment is a cognitive or intellectual process in which a person draws a conclusion, or an inference ($Y_s$), about something ($Y_e$), which *cannot* be seen, on the basis of data ($X_i$), which *can* be seen. In other words, judgments are made from *tangible* data, which serve as *cues* to *intangible* events and circumstances. The wide-ranging arc connecting $Y_s$ and $Y_e$ (labeled $r_a$ in

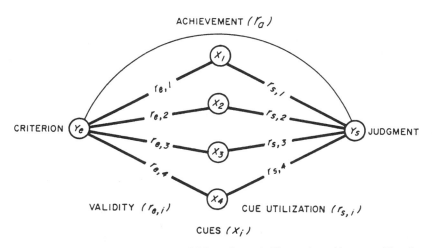

Figure I.3. The "Lens Model," a schematic illustration of how a subject froms a judgment ($Y_s$) of some criterion variable ($Y_e$) on the basis of a set of imperfect cues, $X_i$. Cue validity ($r_{e,i}$) measures the extent to which each cue reflects the value of the criterion; cue utilization ($r_{s,i}$) measures the relation between each cue and the subject's judgment; and achievement, $r_a$, measures how well the subject's judgments correspond to the actual criterion values.

Figure I.3) indicates the degree to which the judgment $Y_s$ was correct, that is, the extent to which the judgment coincides with the actual circumstance to be judged. A rough example can be found in the judgments of the weather forecaster who looks at certain tangible cues ($X_i$) such as wind speed, temperature, and barometric pressure and makes a judgment ($Y_s$) about what tomorrow's weather ($Y_e$) will be. The arc, $r_a$, indicates the degree of accuracy over a series of judgments.

Throughout any ordinary day one frequently encounters similar circumstances. Tangible data (e.g., events in the news, activities of the stock market, actions of friends and neighbors) evoke judgments as to the unperceived events that gave rise to the events perceived. *Causes* ($Y_e$) are frequently being inferred ($Y_s$) from those cue events ($X_i$), or *effects*, that are being observed. And the ability to make correct inferences (indicated by $r_a$) is, of course, an ability in which persons are believed to differ widely. High judgmental accuracy is considered to be an essential attribute of persons with high responsibility; low accuracy indicates persons very likely to be in difficulty with their social or physical surroundings.

The model in Figure I.3 also indicates the concept of *differential weight*. Cues may have differential weight in that they are of differential value in making inferences about events. That is, if a cue has a very strong relation (a high degree of covariation) with an event to be inferred, it will be more useful than one that has a weak relation. Therefore, cues with high degrees of covariation with the event to be inferred have a large degree of *ecological validity*; their weight is greater than those with low degrees of covariation.

The counterpart to the ecological validity ($r_e$) of a cue is its utilization ($r_s$) by the subject (see Figure I.3). Cues also may be used or depended upon to a larger or smaller degree, therefore, with regard to their *subjective utilization*. Thus an observer may compare the differential weights of a set of cues ($r_{e,i}$) in the task with the weights implicitly assigned to them by the person making the inference. Mismatches between ecological validities and subjective utilization of cues are one source of inaccurate judgments. In other words, one source of poor judgment lies in the failure to attach the correct relative weights or importance to cues.

Not only do cues have different task weights, but they may be related to the variable to be inferred ($Y_e$) by means of different functional relations, or *function forms*. These may include positive linear function forms, negative linear function forms, or a variety of curvilinear function forms (see Figure I.4). Of course, cues may be related to judgment ($Y_s$) by means of various function forms also, and the comparison, or match, between task function form and subjective function form will also form the basis for accurate or inaccurate judgments.

Tasks that involve curvilinear functions are apt to be more difficult to learn than those with positive linear function forms, and people's judgments

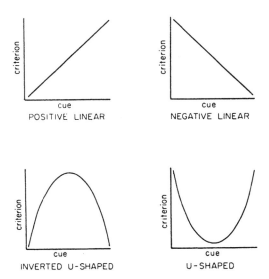

Figure I.4. Four commonly observed function forms between cues and a person's judgment.

related to cues in curvilinear forms are apt to be more difficult for other people to understand. Moreover, people seldom make explicit to others exactly which function form they are employing in a given situation, simply because most people are not aware of this concept. It may appear in colloquial form, however. For example, one way to indicate that another person is using a positive linear function form when he or she should be using a curvilinear one is to say that the person's error lies in believing that "if a little is good, more is better" – a rule that, if followed in the taking of medicine, is apt to lead to disaster. The reader will find it easy to think of other examples of an inappropriate use of linear function forms. One should also consider the difficulties of *changing* a function form to fit the function form of a task, or to fit one preferred by a friend, a teacher, or a therapist.

The principles by which the cue data are organized into a judgment are of considerable importance. Such data may be organized by adding them, $Y_s = X_1 + X_2 + X_3$; by averaging them, $Y_s = (X_1 + X_2 + X_3)/3$; or by making use of some configural or patterning principles, $Y_s = X_1 + X_2 X_3$.

When asked about how they organize information into a judgment, most persons are apt to report that they make use of a pattern or configuration of the data. Physicians who make a diagnosis, experts in investment, and others whose professional judgment is of great importance generally reply to questions about their judgment processes by referring more or less vaguely to their intuitive ability to recognize "patterns." Empirical research, however, in general has not supported these contentions; simpler organizing principles have been found to account for, or at least to predict, judgments from data better than patterns. Although it hardly seems doubtful that human beings *can* organize data by means of patterns, the extent to which they do in fact is unknown; in any event, reports of the use of such principles certainly cannot be taken for granted.

Finally, it is important to consider the *consistency* with which the same judgment is made in response to the same data. Although everyone is apt to assume that they always make the same judgments when confronted with the same facts, it is virtually certain that they will not do so except under the very simplest circumstances. That is, perfect consistency in judgments is apt to occur only when there is no uncertainty whatever in the task situation. Such simple task situations, of course, require little in the way of judgment, inasmuch as a given cue always evokes the same judgment.

The simplest and best way to discover the cues, differential weights, function forms, and consistency of a person's judgment process is to use a computer to present a number of cases to the person making the judgment. After the judgments have been made, a computer program can readily decompose the judgment process into weights, function forms, and consistency. Because this information is extracted *after* a series of judgments have been made, the decomposition is obviously a posteriori. But it is important to observe that, because the judgments can be made with regard to *hypothetical* cases, the person's *judgment policy* (consisting of specific weights and function forms) can then be applied to a real case or a series of real cases. In short, even though the method extracts the various components of the judgment policy after the judgments have been made, the policy may be applied to new cases or to any one judgment problem, just as in the situation where a priori decomposition takes place.

Decision analysis and judgment analysis start at opposite ends of the spectrum of description versus prescription (or advice-giving), but each expands toward the other pole. If one starts with a decision tree, it isn't long before one starts to wonder where these alternatives came from, how the decision maker assessed these probabilities and utilities, chose a time frame, and so on – all interesting descriptive issues. Conversely, if one starts with a descriptive study of, say, a physician attempting to make a diagnosis, it isn't long before one starts to wonder why these cues are being used rather than these others, and how consistently they are being used, and how accurate the diagnoses turn out to be on average, and whether alternative ways of using the available information might be more accurate – all interesting prescriptive issues. Such interplay of description and prescription is deeply woven into JDM research and gives it much of its special interest and value. The central phenomenon, after all, is human efforts to choose actions with some purpose in mind. We are interested in judgment because the thing being judged is of some consequence to us: How sick am I? Will it rain? How strong is this candidate? We are interested in decisions because we believe that some actions are more likely than others to get us where we want to go: Which treatment should I select? Should I take a raincoat? Whom should we hire? These are the sorts of eminently practical concerns that motivate the research sampled in this book.

### Reference

Goldstein, W. M., & Hogarth, R. M. (Eds.). (1997). *Research in judgment and decision making: Currents, connections, and controversies*. New York: Cambridge University Press.

# Part I

# Introduction and Overview

The four chapters in this section lay out some of the topics that have been of central interest to JDM researchers and practitioners. The first, taken from Edwards and Newman's 1982 book, describes in some detail the evaluation process one might go through to select a new office location. The process is explicitly normative in the decision tree approach described in the Introduction: It aims to advise the decision maker what she should do. The problem here is, in fact, simpler in one important sense than in the earlier example, in that no uncertainty is involved. The decision maker knows, for sure, how large, convenient, attractive, and so on each available site is: If she chooses Option 1, she will get a known package of features, if she chooses Option 2, she will get another known package of features, and so on. The problem is in making the trade-offs between the good and bad features of each. The MAUT procedure the authors describe helps the decision maker to set up and make the various judgments required to arrive at a "best" choice. The example is worth following through in detail both to understand what the MAUT technology offers and to better understand the sense in which "best" is used in this approach. Von Winterfeldt and Edwards (1986) describe more complex applications, whereas Edwards and Barron (1994) describe important progress in the weight-assignment problem.

The second chapter, by Tversky and Kahneman, represents an early high-water mark of an important line of research called the "Heuristics and Biases Program." This program, which stimulated an enormous body of research and discussion in the 1970s and 1980s, turned on two fairly simple ideas. First, it is reasonably easy to devise judgment tasks in which many people behave in ways that seem to violate relevant normative standards: They "make mistakes." Second, Tversky and Kahneman proposed an account of many of these errors as manifestations of a small set of cognitive "heuristics" or rules of thumb that, though generally effective enough for most situations, would lead to predictable errors in some carefully constructed tasks. The "error," in this sense, was evidence for the existence of the "heuristic," the existence of which was, in turn, assumed to depend on its general (though not invariable) adequacy. The "representativeness heuristic," for example, is the expectation that a sample of some process will look roughly like the underlying process. However, our intuitions about how closely samples match processes are imperfect, and can sometimes trip up our judgments. Because many of the studies in this line turned on demonstrating deviations between actual behavior and a normative model, many observers interpreted the results as casting a gloomy light on human cognitive abilities – as suggesting, in one memorable reading, that we are "cognitive cripples" subject to dozens of debilitating biases. Counterattacks and reinterpretations (see, for example, Chapter 35, by Gigerenzer & Goldstein; Chapter 36, by Hilton & Slugowski; and Chapter 31, Juslin, in this volume) argued that the models themselves were not compellingly normative or that the tasks were "fixed" in various ways. Some of these counterattacks have tried to make the case that, far from crippled, we are cognitive heroes, tuned by evolution to superb inferential performance. There is, in fact, almost no evidence on which to estimate an overall human judgmental batting average, even if one could define such a number. A balanced view (see, for example, Jungermann, Chapter 33, this volume) would probably conclude that it is not close to either 0 or 1.0.

The third chapter in this section is an extract from a recent book by Hammond. Hammond suggests that much of the argument over the heuristics and biases research can be resolved by considering the two distinct "metatheories" that have underlain JDM research for years. One, the "correspondence" metatheory, focuses on how well someone's judgments and decisions connect to the real world: Does the doctor diagnose the right disease, does the bettor back the winning horse? The other dominant metatheory focuses on the internal "coherence" of someone's judgments and decisions: Do they hang together rationally, are they internally consistent, are they logically reasonable? Obviously, in a finished, mature science, good theories pass both tests. Newtonian physics was, for several centuries, consistent both internally and with the facts of the world as they were known. JDM research, in contrast, is far less developed, and researchers have tended to emphasize one or the other test, reaching opposite conclusions about human competence. Hammond ties the emphasis on coherence or correspondence thinking to a continuum of different ways of thinking, running from purely analytic to purely intuitive.

Regardless of our conclusions about human competence in general, most of us would be grateful for help when we have to make difficult, high-stakes judgments. Swets, in the fourth chapter in this section, sketches one approach, known (for slightly obscure reasons) as the Theory of Signal Detection (TSD). TSD has not been widely used by JDM researchers (though see Getty et al., Chapter 18, this volume, for a fascinating application in radiology), though it provides a powerful framework for integrating judgments and choices. TSD considers situations in which a decision maker must act in some way (for example, to investigate further in face of a suspicious-looking

X-ray, or to abort an airliner landing because of bad weather) on the basis of an uncertain judgment (of the risk of cancer or of windshear). Either action might be mistaken, so the costs of these errors as well as the uncertainty of the underlying judgment must be considered in planning how to act. Note, incidentally, that Connolly (Chapter 14, this volume) takes a decision analytic approach to such a situation in his discussion of reasonable doubt. The two approaches yield exactly equivalent results, despite the apparently quite different frameworks.

### References

Edwards, W., & Barron, F. H. (1994). SMARTS and SMARTER: Improved simple methods for multiattribute measurement. *Organizational Behavior and Human Decision Processes, 60*, 306–325.

Hammond, K. R. (1996). *Human judgment and social policy*. New York, Oxford University Press.

von Winterfeldt, D., & Edwards, W. (1986). *Decision analysis and behavioral research*. New York: Cambridge University Press.

# 1  Multiattribute Evaluation

*Ward Edwards and J. Robert Newman*

The purpose of this chapter is to present one approach to evaluation: Multiattribute Utility Technology (MAUT). We have attempted to make a version of MAUT simple and straightforward enough so that the reader can, with diligence and frequent reexaminations of it, conduct relatively straightforward MAUT evaluations him- or herself. In so doing, we will frequently resort to techniques that professional decision analysts will recognize as approximations and/or assumptions. The literature justifying those approximations is extensive and complex; to review it here would blow to smithereens our goal of being nontechnical.

What is MAUT, and how does it relate to other approaches to evaluation? MAUT depends on a few key ideas:

1. When possible, evaluations should be comparative.
2. Programs normally serve multiple constituencies.
3. Programs normally have multiple goals, not all equally important.
4. Judgments are inevitably a part of any evaluation.
5. Judgments of magnitude are best when made numerically.
6. Evaluations typically are, or at least should be, relevant to decisions.

Some of the six points above are less innocent than they seem. If programs serve multiple constituencies, evaluations of them should normally be addressed to the interests of those constituencies; different constituencies can be expected to have different interests. If programs have multiple goals, evaluations should attempt to assess how well they serve them; this implies multiple measures and comparisons. The task of dealing with multiple measures of effectiveness (which may well be simple subjective judgments in numerical form) makes less appealing the notion of social programs as experiments or quasi-experiments. While the tradition that programs should be thought of as experiments, or at least as quasi-experiments, has wide currency and wide appeal in evaluation research, its implementation becomes more difficult as the number of measures needed for a satisfactory evaluation increases. When experimental or other hard data are available, they can easily be incorporated in a MAUT evaluation.

Finally, the willingness to accept subjectivity into evaluation, combined with the insistence that judgments be numerical, serves several useful purposes. First, it partly closes the gap between the intuitive and judgmental evaluations and the more quantitative kind; indeed, it makes coexistence of judgment and objective measurement within the same evaluation easy and natural. Second, it opens the door to easy combination of complex concatenations of values. For instance, evaluation researchers often distinguish between process evaluations and outcome evaluations. Process and outcome are different, but if a program has goals of both kinds, its evaluation can and should assess its performance on both. Third, use of subjective inputs can, if need be, greatly shorten the time required for an evaluation to be carried out. A MAUT evaluation can be carried out from original definition of the evaluation problem to preparation of the evaluation report in as little as a week of concentrated effort. The inputs to such an abbreviated evaluative activity will obviously be almost entirely subjective. But the MAUT technique at least produces an audit trail such that the skeptic can substitute other judgments for those that seem doubtful, and can then examine what the consequences for the evaluation are. We know of no MAUT social program evaluation that took less than two months, but in some other areas of application we have participated in execution of complete MAUT evaluations in as little as two days – and then watched them be used as the justification for major decisions. Moreover, we heartily approved; time constraints on the decision made haste necessary, and we were very pleased to have the chance to provide some orderly basis for decision in so short a time.

### Steps in a MAUT Evaluation

*Step 1.* Identify the objects of evaluation and the function or functions that the evaluation is intended to perform. Normally there will be several objects of evaluation, at least some of them imaginary, since evaluations are comparative. The functions of the evaluation will often control the choice of objects of evaluation. We have argued that evaluations should help decision makers to make decisions. If the nature of those decisions is known, the objects of evaluation will often be controlled by that knowledge. Step 1 is outside the scope of this chapter. Some of the issues inherent in it have already been discussed in this chapter. The next section, devoted to setting up an example that will be carried through the document, illustrates Step 1 for that example.

*Step 2.* Identify the *stakeholders*. . . .

*Step 3.* Elicit from stakeholder representatives the relevant *value dimensions* or *attributes*, and (often) organize them into a hierarchical structure called a *value tree*. . . .

*Step 4.* Assess for each stakeholder group the *relative importance* of each of the values identified at Step 3. Such judgments can, of course, be expected to vary from one stakeholder group to another; methods of dealing with such value conflicts are important. . . .

*Step 5.* Ascertain how well each object of evaluation serves each value at the lowest level of the value tree. Such numbers, called *single-attribute utilities* or *location measures*, ideally report measurements, expert judgments, or both. If so, they should be independent of stakeholders and so of value disagreements among stakeholders; however, this ideal is not always met. Location measures need to be on a common scale, in order for Step 4 to make sense. . . .

*Step 6.* Aggregate location measures with measures of importance. . . .

*Step 7.* Perform *sensitivity analyses*. The question underlying any sensitivity analysis is whether a change in the analysis, e.g., using different numbers as inputs, will lead to different conclusions. While conclusions may have emerged from Step 6, they deserve credence as a basis for action only after their sensitivity is explored in Step 7. . . .

Steps 6 and 7 will normally produce the results of a MAUT evaluation. . . .

### The Relation between Evaluation and Decision

The tools of MAUT are most useful for guiding decisions; they grow out of a broader methodological field called decision analysis. The relation of evaluation to decision has been a topic of debate among evaluation researchers – especially the academic evaluation researchers who wonder whether or not their evaluations are used, and if so, appropriately used. Some evaluators take the position that their responsibility is to provide the relevant facts; it is up to someone else to make the decisions. "We are not elected officials." This position is sometimes inevitable, of course; the evaluator is not the decision maker as a rule, and cannot compel the decision maker to attend to the result of the evaluation, or to base decisions on it. But it is unattractive to many evaluators; certainly to us.

We know of three devices that make evaluations more likely to be used in decisions. The first and most important is to involve the decision makers heavily in the evaluative process; this is natural if, as is normally the case, they are among the most important stakeholders. The second is to make the evaluation as directly relevant to the decision as possible, preferably by making sure that the options available to the decision maker are the objects of evaluation. The third is to make the product of the evaluation useful – which primarily means making it readable and short. Exhaustive scholarly documents tend to turn busy decision makers off. Of course, nothing in these obvious devices guarantees success in making the evaluation relevant to the decision. However, nonuse of these devices comes close to guaranteeing failure.

By "decisions" we do not necessarily mean anything apocalyptic; the process of fine tuning a program requires decisions too. This chapter unabashedly assumes that either the evaluator or the person or organization commissioning the evaluation has the options or alternative courses of action in mind, and proposes to select among them in part on the basis of the evaluation – or else that the information is being assembled and aggregated because of someone's expectation that that will be the case later on.

### An Example

We now present a fairly simple example of how to use multiattribute utility technology for evaluation. The example is intended to be simple enough to be understandable, yet complex enough to illustrate all of the technical ideas necessary for the analysis. . . . We have invented an example that brings out all the properties of the method, and that will, we hope, be sufficiently realistic to fit with the intuitions of those who work in a social program environment.

*The Problem: How to Evaluate New Locations for a Drug Counseling Center*

The Drug-Free Center is a private nonprofit contract center that gives counseling to clients sent to it by the courts of its city as a condition of their probation. It is a walk-in facility with no beds or other special space requirements; it does not use methadone. It has just lost its lease, and must relocate.

The director of the center has screened the available spaces to which it might move. All spaces that are inappropriate because of zoning, excessive neighborhood resistance to the presence of the center, or inability to satisfy such legal requirements as access for the handicapped have been eliminated, as have spaces of the wrong size, price, or location. The city is in a period of economic recession, and so even after this prescreening a substantial number of options are available. Six sites are chosen as a result of informal screening for serious evaluation. The director must, of course, satisfy the sponsor, the probation department, and the courts that the new location is appropriate, and must take the needs and wishes of both employees and clients into account. But as a first cut, the director wishes simply to evaluate the sites on the basis of values and judgments of importance that make sense internally to the center.

### The Evaluation Process

The first task is to identify stakeholders. They were listed in the previous paragraph. A stakeholder is simply an individual or group with a reason to care about the decision and with enough impact on the decision maker so that the reason should be taken seriously. Stakeholders are sources of *value attributes*. An attribute is something that the stakeholders, or some subset of them, care about enough so that failure to consider it in the decision would lead to a poor decision. . . .

In this case, to get the evaluation started, the director consulted, as stakeholders, the members of the center staff. Their initial discussion of values elicited a list of about 50 verbal descriptors of values. A great many of these were obviously the same idea under a variety of different verbal labels. The director, acting as leader of the discussion, was able to see these duplications and to persuade those who originally proposed these as values to agree on a rephrasing that captured and coalesced these overlapping or duplicating ideas. She did so both because she wanted to keep the list short and because she knew that if the same idea appeared more than once in the final list, she would be "double counting"; that is, including the same value twice. Formally, there is nothing wrong with double counting so long as the *weights* reflect it. But in practice, it is important to avoid, in part because the weights will often not reflect it, and in part because the analysis is typically complex, and addition of extra and unnecessary attributes simply makes the complexity worse.

A second step in editing the list was to eliminate values that, in the view of the stakeholders, could not be important enough to influence the decision. An example of this type of value, considered and then eliminated because it was unimportant, was "proximity to good lunching places." The director was eager to keep the list of values fairly short, and her staff cooperated. In a less collegial situation, elimination of attributes can be much more difficult. Devices that help accomplish it are almost always worthwhile, so long as they do not leave some significant stakeholder feeling that his or her pet values have been summarily ignored.

The director was also able to obtain staff assent to organizing its values into four broad categories, each with subcategories. Such a structure is called a *value tree*. The one that the director worked with is shown in Figure 1.1. We explain the numbers shortly.

Several questions need review at this stage.

Have all important attributes been listed? Others had been proposed and could obviously have been added. The list does not mention number or location of toilets, proximity to restaurants, presence or absence of other tenants

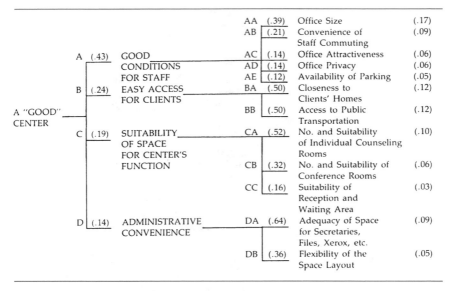

Figure 1.1. A value tree for the Drug-Free Center.

of the same building who might prefer not to have the clients of this kind of organization as frequent users of the corridors, racial/ethnic composition of the neighborhood, area crime rate, and various others. All of these and many more had been included in earlier lists, and eliminated after discussion. Bases for elimination include not only duplication and unimportance, but also that the sites under consideration did not vary from one another on that attribute, or varied very little. That is why racial/ethnic composition and crime rate were eliminated. Even an important attribute is not worth considering unless it contributes to discrimination among sites.

For program evaluation purposes, this principle needs to be considered in conjunction with the purpose of the evaluation. If the function of the evaluation is primarily to guide development of the program, then important attributes should be included even if they serve no discriminative function; in such cases, there may be no discriminative function to serve.

The director was satisfied with the list. It was relatively short, and she felt that it captured the major issues – given the fact that even more major requirements for a new site had been met by prescreening out all options that did not fulfill them.

An obvious omission from the attribute list is cost. For simplicity, we will treat cost as the annual lease cost, ignoring the possibility of other relevant differences among leases.

One possibility would be to treat cost as another attribute, and this is often done, especially for informal or quick evaluations. In such a procedure, one would specify a range of possible costs, assign a weight to that attribute, which essentially amounts to a judgment about how it trades off against other attributes, and then include it in the analysis like any other attribute. We have chosen not to do so in this example, for two reasons. First, some evaluations may not involve cost in any significant way (monitoring, for example), and we wish to illustrate procedures for cost-independent applications of MAUT. Second, we consider the kind of judgment required to trade off cost against *utility points* to be the least secure and most uncomfortable to make of all those that go into MAUT. For that reason, we like to use procedures, illustrated later, that permit extremely crude versions of that judgment to determine final evaluation.

While on the topic, we should discuss two other aspects of trading off dollars against *aggregated utilities*.

The first is budget constraints. If a budget constrains, in this example, the amount of rent the center can pay, then it is truly a constraint, and sites that fail to meet it must be rejected summarily. More common, however, is the case in which money can be used for one purpose or another. A full analysis would require considering also the loss, in this instance, that would result from spending more on rent and so having less to spend on other things. Such considerations are crucial, but we do not illustrate them here. In order to do so, we would have to provide a scenario about what budget cuts the director would need to make in other categories to pay additional rent. At the time she must choose among sites, she may not know what these are. Fairly often, the expansion of the analysis required to evaluate all possible ways in which a program might be changed by budget reallocations is very large indeed – far too large to make an easy example. So we prefer to think of this as a case in which the director's budget is large enough so that, for the range of costs involved, belt-tightening can take care of the difference between smallest and largest. A fuller analysis would consider the programmatic impact of fund reallocation and could explore the utility consequences of alternative reallocations. The circumscription of the analysis in the interest of making it manageable is very common; relevant issues are and should be left out of every analysis. (An equivalent statement: If it can be avoided, no MAUT analysis should include every attribute judged relevant by any stakeholder.) . . . The goal is to enlist stakeholder cooperation in keeping the list of attributes reasonably short.

The other issue having to do with cost but not with the example of this chapter is the portfolio problem. This is the generic name for situations in which a decision maker must choose, not a single option, but a number of options from a larger set. Typically, the limit on the number that can be chosen is specified by a budget constraint. The methods presented in this manual require considerable adaptation to be used formally for portfolio problems, because the decision maker normally wants the portfolio as a whole to have properties such as balance, diversity, or coverage (e.g., of topics, regions, disciplines, problems) that are not attributes of the individual options themselves. Formally, each possible portfolio is an option, and a value tree relevant to the portfolio, not to the individual options, is needed. But such formal complexity is rarely used. A much more common procedure in portfolio problems is to evaluate the individual elements using methods like those of this chapter, choose from the best so identified, and then examine the resulting set of choices to make sure that it meets the budget constraint and looks acceptable as a portfolio.

You will have encountered such terms as benefit-cost analysis. Such analyses are similar in spirit to what we are doing here, but quite different in detail. By introducing into the analysis early assumptions about how nonfinancial values trade off with money, both benefits and costs can be expressed in dollar terms. We see little merit in doing so for social programs, since early translation of nonmonetary effects into money terms tends to lead to underassessment of the importance of nonfinancial consequences. The methods we present in this section . . . are formally equivalent to doing it all in money, but do not require an equation between utility and money until the very end of the analysis, if then.

Back to our example. In the initial elicitation of values from the staff, the orderly structure of Figure 1.1, the value tree, did not appear. Indeed, it took much thought and trial and error to organize the attributes into a tree structure. Formally, only the attributes at the bottom of the tree, which are called *twigs*, are essential for evaluation. Figure 1.1 is a two-level value tree; that is, all second-level values are twigs. More often, different branches of a value tree will vary in how many levels they have. . . . Examples with as many as fourteen levels exist.

Tree structures are useful in MAUT in three ways. First, they present the attributes in an orderly structure; this helps thought about the problem. Second, the tree structure can make elicitation of importance weights for twigs (which we discuss below) much easier than it would otherwise be, by reducing the number of judgments required. . . . Finally, value trees permit what we call *subaggregation*. Often a single number is much too compressed a summary of how attractive an option is. Tree structures permit more informative and less compressed summaries. . . .

Figure 1.1 contains a notational scheme we have found useful in value trees. Main branches of the tree are labeled with capital letters, A, B, and so on. Subattributes under each main branch are labeled with double letters, AA, AB, . . . , BA, BB . . . , and so on. This is a two-level tree, so only double letters are needed.

### Assignment of Importance Weights

The numbers in Figure 1.1 are *importance weights* for the attributes. Note that the weights in Figure 1.1 sum to 1 at each level of the tree. That is, the weights of A, B, C, and D sum to 1. Similarly, the weights of AA through AE sum to 1, as do those of BA and BB and so on. This is a convenient convention, both for elicitation of weights and for their use. The final weights for each attribute at each twig of the tree are easily obtained by "multiplying through the tree." For example, the weight .17 for twig AA (office size) is obtained by multiplying the normalized weight of A (.43) by the normalized weight for AA (.39) to yield .43 × .39 = .17. . . .

The weights presented in Figure 1.1 emerged from a staff meeting in which, after an initial discussion of the idea of weighting, each individual staff member produced a set of weights, using the *ratio method*. . . . Then all the sets of weights were put on the blackboard, the inevitable individual differences were discussed, and afterward each individual once again used the ratio method to produce a set of weights. These still differed, though by less than did the first set. The final set was produced by averaging the results of the second weighting; the average weights were acceptable to the staff as representing its value system.

The director had some reservations about what the staff had produced, but kept them to herself. She worried about whether the weights associated with staff comfort issues were perhaps too high and those associated with appropriateness to the function of the organization were perhaps too low. (Note that she had no serious reservations about the relative weights within each major branch of the value tree; her concerns were about the relative weights of the four major branches of the tree. This illustrates the usefulness of organizing lists of twigs into a tree structure for weighting.) The director chose to avoid argument with her staff by reserving her concerns about those weights for the sensitivity analysis phase of the evaluation.

Although a common staff set of weights was obtained by averaging (each staff member equally weighted), the individual weights were not thereafter thrown away. Instead, they were kept available for use in the later sensitivity analysis. In general, averaging may be a useful technique if a consensus position is needed, especially for screening options, but it is dangerous, exactly because it obliterates individual differences in weighting. When stakeholders disagree, it is usually a good idea to use the judgments of each separately in evaluation; only if these judgments lead to conflicting conclusions must the sometimes difficult task of reconciling the disagreements be faced. If it is faced, arithmetic is a last resort, if usable at all; discussion and achievement of consensus is much preferred. Often such discussions can be helped by a sensitivity analysis; it will often turn out that the decision is simply insensitive to the weights.

### The Assessment of Location Measures or Utilities

With a value tree to guide the choice of measures to take and judgments to make, the next task was to make detailed assessments of each of the six sites that had survived initial screening. Such assessments directly lead to the utilities in multiattribute utility measurement. The word "utility" has a 400-year-old history and conveys a very explicit meaning to contemporary decision analysts. The techniques for obtaining such numbers that we present in this manual deviate in some ways from those implicit in that word. So we prefer to call these numbers *location measures*, since they simply report the location or utility of each object of evaluation on each attribute of evaluation.

Inspect Figure 1.1 again. Two kinds of values are listed on it. Office size is an objective dimension, measurable in square feet. Office attractiveness is a subjective dimension; it must be obtained by judgment. Proximity to public transportation might be taken in this example as measured by the distance from the front door of the building to the nearest bus stop, which would make it completely objective. But suppose the site were in New York. Then distance to the nearest bus stop and distance to the nearest subway stop would both be relevant and probably the latter would be more important than the former. It would make sense in that case to add another level to the value tree, in which the value "proximity to public transportation" would be further broken down into those two twigs.

As it happens, in Figure 1.1 all attributes are monotonically increasing; that is, more is better than less. That will not always be true. For some attributes, less is better than more; if "crime rate in the area" had survived the process of elimination that led to Figure 1.1, it would have been an example. On some attributes, intermediate values are preferable to either extreme; such attributes have a peak inside the range of the attribute. If "racial composition of the neighborhood" had survived as an attribute, the staff might well have felt that the site would score highest on that attribute if its racial/ethnic mix matched that of its clients. If only two racial/ethnic categories were relevant, that would be expressed by a twig, such as "percentage of whites in the neighborhood" that would have a peak at the percentage of whites among the center's clients and would tail off from there in both directions. If more than two racial/ethnic categories were relevant, the value would have been further broken down, with percentage of each relevant racial/ethnic category in the neighborhood as a twig underneath it, and for each of those twigs, the location measure would have a peak at some intermediate value. . . .

Figure 1.1 presented the director with a fairly easy assessment task. She chose to make the needed judgments herself. If the problem were more complex and required more expertise, she might well have asked other experts to make some or all of the necessary judgments.

Armed with a tape measure and a notebook, she visited each of the sites, made the relevant measures and counts, and made each of the required judgments. Thus she obtained the raw materials for the location measures.

However, she had to do some transforming on these raw materials. It is necessary for all location measures to be on a common scale, in order for the assessment of weights to make any sense. Although the choice of common scale is obviously arbitrary, we like one in which 0 means horrible and 100 means as well as one could hope to do.

Consider the case of the office size expressed in square feet. It would make no sense to assign the value 0 to 0 sq. ft.; no office could measure 0 sq. ft. After examining her present accommodations and thinking about those of other similar groups, the director decided that an office 60 sq. ft. in size should have a value of 0, and one of 160 sq. ft. should have a value of 100. She also decided that values intermediate between those two limits should be linear in utility. This idea needs explaining. It would be possible to feel that you gain much more in going from 60 to 80 sq. ft. than in going from 140 to 160 sq. ft., and consequently that the scale relating square footage to desirability should be nonlinear. Indeed, traditional utility theory makes that assumption in almost every case.

Curved functions relating physical measurements to utility are probably more precise representations of how people feel than straight ones. But fortunately, such curvature almost never makes any difference to the decision. If it does, the fact that the difference exists means that the options are close enough so that it scarcely matters which is chosen. For that reason, when an appropriate physical scale exists, we advocate choosing maximum and minimum values on it, and then fitting a straight line between those boundaries to translate those measurements into the 0 to 100 scale. . . . Formal arguments in support of our use of linearity are far too technical for this chapter. . . .

The director did the same kind of thing to all the other attributes for which she had objective measures. The attribute "proximity to clients' homes" presented her with a problem. In principle, she could have chosen to measure the linear distance from the address of each current client to each site, average these measures, choose a maximum and minimum value for the average, and then scale each site using the same procedure described for office size. But that would have been much more trouble than it was worth. So instead she looked at a map, drew a circle on it to represent the boundaries of the area that she believed her organization served, and then noted how close each site was to the center of the area. It would have been possible to use radial distance from that center as an objective measure, but she chose not to do so, since clients' homes were not homogeneously distributed within the circle. Instead, she treated this as a directly judgmental attribute, simply using the map as an aid to judgment.

Of course, for all judgmental dimensions, the scale is from 0 to 100. For both judgmental and objective attributes, it is important that the scale be realistic. That is, it should be easy to imagine that some of the sites being considered might realistically score 0 to 100 on each attribute.

In this example, since the six sites were known, that could have been assured by assigning a value of 0 to the worst site on a given attribute and a value of 100 to the best on that attribute, locating the others in between. This was not done, and we recommend that it not be done in general. Suppose one of the sites had been rented to someone else, or that a new one turned up. Then if the evaluation scheme were so tightly tied to the specific options available, it would have to be revised. We prefer a procedure in which one attempts to assess realistic boundaries on each relevant attribute with less specific reference to the actual options available. Such a procedure allows the evaluation scheme to remain the same as the option set changes. And the procedure is obviously necessary if the option set is not known, or not fully known, at the time the evaluation scheme is worked out.

It can, of course, happen that a real option turns up that is more extreme than a boundary assigned to some attribute. If that happens, the evaluation scheme can still be used. Two possible approaches exist. Consider, for example, the attribute "access to public transportation" operationalized as distance to the nearest bus stop. One might assign 100 to half a block and 0 to four blocks. Now, suppose two new sites turn up. For one, the bus stop is right in front of the building entrance; for the other, it is five blocks away. The director might well judge that it scarcely matters whether the stop is in front of the building entrance or half a block away, and so assign 100 to all distances of half a block or closer. However, she might also feel that five blocks is meaningfully worse than four. She could handle the five-block case in either of two ways. She might simply disqualify the site on the basis of that fact. Or, if she felt that the site deserved to be evaluated in spite of this disadvantage, she could assign a negative score (it would turn out to be −29 . . . ) to that site on that attribute. While such scores outside the 0 to 100 range are not common, and the ranges should be chosen with enough realism to avoid them if possible, nothing in the logic or formal structure of the method prevents their use. It is more important that the range be realistic, so that the options are well spread out over its length, than it is to avoid an occasional instance in which options fall outside it.

Table 1.1 represents the location measures of the six sites that survived initial screening, transformed onto the 0 to 100 scale. As the director looked at this table, she realized an important point. No matter what the weights,

Table 1.1. *Location Measures for Six Sites*

| | Twig Label | | | | | | | | | | | |
|---|---|---|---|---|---|---|---|---|---|---|---|---|
| Site Number | *AA* | *AB* | *AC* | *AD* | *AE* | *BA* | *BB* | *CA* | *CB* | *CC* | *DA* | *DB* |
| 1 | 90 | 50 | 30 | 90 | 10 | 40 | 80 | 10 | 60 | 50 | 10 | 0 |
| 2 | 50 | 30 | 80 | 30 | 60 | 30 | 70 | 80 | 50 | 40 | 70 | 40 |
| 3 | 10 | 100 | 70 | 40 | 30 | 0 | 95 | 5 | 10 | 50 | 90 | 50 |
| 4 | 100 | 80 | 10 | 50 | 50 | 50 | 50 | 50 | 10 | 10 | 50 | 95 |
| 5 | 20 | 5 | 95 | 10 | 100 | 90 | 5 | 90 | 90 | 95 | 50 | 10 |
| 6 | 40 | 30 | 80 | 30 | 50 | 30 | 70 | 50 | 50 | 30 | 60 | 40 |

site 6 would never be best in utility. The reason why is that site 2 is at least as attractive as site 6 on all location measures, and definitely better on some. In technical language, site 2 *dominates* site 6. But Table 1.1 omits one important issue: cost. Checking cost, she found that site 6 was in fact less expensive than site 2, so she kept it in. If it had been as expensive as site 2 or more so, she would have been justified in summarily rejecting it, since it could never beat site 2. No other option dominates or is dominated by another. (Although she might have dropped site 6 if it had not been cheaper than site 2, she would have been unwise to notify the rental office of site 6 that it was out of contention. If for some reason site 2 were to become unavailable, perhaps because it was rented to someone else, then site 6 would once more be a contender.)

### Aggregation of Location Measures and Weights

The director now had weights provided by her staff and location measures provided either directly by judgment or by calculations based on measurements. Now her task was to aggregate these into measures of the aggregate utility of each site. The aggregation procedure is the same regardless of the depth of the value tree. Simply take the final weight for each twig, multiply it by location measure for that twig, and sum the products. This is illustrated in Table 1.2 for site 1. In this case, the sum is 48.79, which is the aggregate utility of site 1. It would be possible but tedious to do this for each site. All calculations like that in Table 1.2 were done with hand calculator programs;

Table 1.2. *Calculation of the Aggregate Utility of Site 1*

| Twig Label | Weight | Location Measure | Weight × Location Measure |
|---|---|---|---|
| AA | .168 | 90 | 15.12 |
| AB | .090 | 50 | 4.50 |
| AC | .060 | 30 | 1.80 |
| AD | .060 | 90 | 5.40 |
| AE | .052 | 10 | 0.52 |
| BA | .120 | 40 | 4.80 |
| BB | .120 | 80 | 9.60 |
| CA | .099 | 10 | .99 |
| CB | .061 | 60 | 3.66 |
| CC | .030 | 50 | 1.50 |
| DA | .090 | 10 | 0.90 |
| DB | .050 | 0 | 0.00 |
| *Sums* | 1.000 | | 48.79 |

Table 1.3. *Aggregate Utilities and Rents*

| Site | Utility | Cost (rent per year) |
|------|---------|----------------------|
| 1 | 48.80 | $48,000 |
| 2 | 53.26 | 53,300 |
| 3 | 43.48 | 54,600 |
| 4 | 57.31 | 60,600 |
| 5 | 48.92 | 67,800 |
| 6 | 46.90 | 53,200 |

the discrepancy between the 48.79 for site 1 of Table 1.2 and the 48.80 of Table 1.3 is caused by a rounding process in the program. Table 1.3 shows the aggregate utilities and the costs for each of the six sites. The costs are given as annual rents.

Now a version of the idea of dominance can be exploited again. In Table 1.3, the utility values can be considered as measures of desirability and the rents are costs. Obviously, you would not wish to pay more unless you got an increase in desirability. Consequently, options that are inferior to others in both cost and desirability need not be considered further.

On utility, the rank ordering of the sites from best to worst is 425163. On cost, it is 162345. Obviously sites 1 and 4 will be contenders, since 4 is best in utility (with these weights) and 1 is best in cost. Site 5 is dominated, in this aggregated sense, by site 4, and so is out of the race. Sites 3 and 6 are dominated by site 1, and are also out. So sites 1, 2, and 4 remain as *contenders*; 2 is intermediate between 1 and 4 in both utility and cost. This result is general. If a set of options is described by aggregated utilities and costs, and dominated options are removed, then all of the remaining options, if listed in order of increasing utility, will turn out also to be listed in order of increasing cost. This makes the decision problem simpler; it reduces to whether each increment in utility gained from moving from an option lower to one higher in such a list is worth the increase in cost. Note that this property does *not* depend on any numerical properties of the method that will eventually be used to aggregate utility with cost.

A special case arises if two or more options tie in utility, cost, or both. If the tie is in utility, then the one that costs least among the tied options dominates the others; the others should be eliminated. If they tie in cost, the one with the greatest utility dominates the others; the others should be eliminated. If they tie in both utility and cost, then only one of them need be examined for dominance. If one is dominated, all are; if one is undominated, all are. So either all should be eliminated or all should survive to the next stage of the analysis. Note that a tie in aggregate utility can occur in two

Table 1.4. *Incremental Utilities and Costs for the Siting Example*

| Site No. | Utility Differences (increment) | Cost Differences (increment) | Cost Incr./ Utility Incr. |
|----------|--------------------------------|------------------------------|---------------------------|
| 1        | 0                              | 0                            |                           |
| 2        | 4.46                           | $5300                        | $1188                     |
| 4        | 4.05                           | $7300                        | $1802                     |

different ways: by accident of weighting, or because all location measures are equal. If all location measures are equal, the lower cost will always be preferable to the higher one regardless of weights, so the higher cost can be eliminated not only from the main analysis, but from all sensitivity analyses. If they tie in aggregate utility by accident of weighting, changes in weight will ordinarily untie them, and so the tied options must be included in the sensitivity analysis.

If the option that represents the tie emerges from the next stage of the analysis looking best, the only way to discriminate it from its twins is by sensitivity analysis, by considering other attributes, or both.

Nothing guarantees that the dominance analysis we just performed will eliminate options. If the ordering in utility had been 123456 and the ordering in cost had been 654321 (just the opposite) no option would have dominated any other, and none could have been eliminated. Such perfect relationships between cost and utility are rare, except perhaps in the marketplace, in which dominated options may be eliminated by market pressure.

The decision about whether to accept an increase in cost in order to obtain an increase in utility is often made intuitively, and that may be an excellent way to make it. But arithmetic can help. In this example, consider Table 1.4. It lists the three contending sites, 1, 2, and 4, in order of increasing utility and cost. In the second column, each entry is the utility of that site minus the utility of the site just above it. Thus, for example, the 4.05 utility difference associated with site 4 is obtained by subtracting the aggregate utility of 2 from that of 4 in Table 1.3: $57.31 - 53.26 = 4.05$. Similarly, the cost difference of $7,300 for site 4 is obtained from Table 1.3 in the same way: $60,600 - 53,300 = $7,300$. The other numbers in the second and third columns are calculated similarly. The fourth column is simply the number in the third column divided by the number in the second.

The numbers in the fourth column increase from top to bottom. This means that all three sites are true contenders. This is not necessarily the case. ...

The last column of Table 1.4 also serves another purpose. Since it is the increase in cost divided by the increase in utility, it is a dollar value for one utility point. Specifically, it is the dollar value for one utility point that would be just enough to cause you to prefer the higher cost site to the lower cost one. If the dollar value of a utility point is less than $1188, you should choose site 1; if it is between $1188 and $1802, you should choose site 2; and if it is above $1802, you should choose site 4.

But how can you know the dollar value of a utility point, for yourself or for other stakeholders? The judgment obviously need not be made with much precision – but it is, if formulated in that language, an impossible judgment to make. But it need not be formulated in that language. Consider instead the following procedure. Refer back to Figure 1.1. First pick a twig that you have firm and definite opinions about. Suppose it is DA, availability and suitability of space for secretaries, files, Xerox, and the like. Now, ask of yourself and of the other stakeholders, "How much money would it be worth to improve that twig by so many points?" The typical number of points to use in such questions is 100, so the question becomes: "How much would it be worth to improve the availability and suitability of space for secretaries, files, Xerox, and the like from the minimum acceptable state, to which I have assigned a location measure of 0, to a state to which I would assign a location measure of 100?"

Such a question, asked of various stakeholders, will elicit various answers; a compromise or agreed-on number should be found. Suppose, in this example, that it turned out to be $13,500. Now, refer to Table 1.2 and note that the twig weight for DA is .090. Consequently, a 100-point change in DA will change aggregate utility by $100 \times .090 = 9$ points – for this particular set of weights. Note, incidentally, that while the 9-point number depends on the weights, the judgment of the dollar value of a 100-point change in DA does not. Consequently, if you choose to change weights . . . you will need to recalculate the value of a utility point, but will not need to obtain a new dollar value judgment of this kind from anyone.

If a 9-point change in utility is worth $13,500, then a 1-point change in utility is worth $13,500/9 = $1500$. So, using the weights on which this chapter is based, site 2 is clearly preferable to sites 1 and 4 since $1500 is between $1188 and $1802.

Let us verify that statement. One way to do so is to penalize the more expensive sites by a number of utility points appropriate for their increase in cost. Thus, if utility is worth $1500 per point, and site 2 costs $5300 more than site 1, then site 2 should be penalized $5300/1500 = 3.53$ utility points in order to make it comparable to site 1. Similarly, if utility is worth $1500 per point, then site 4 should be penalized by the increment in its costs over site 1, $5300 + $7300 = $12,600, divided by the dollar value of a point; $12,600/1500 = 8.40$ utility points. This makes all three sites comparable, by correcting each of the more expensive ones by the utility equivalent of the additional expense. So now the choice could be based on utility alone.

Table 1.5 makes the same calculation for all three sites and for three different judgments of how much a 9-point swing in aggregate utility is worth: $9000, $13,500, and $18,000; these correspond, with the weights used in this

Table 1.5. *Aggregate Utilities after Subtracting Penalties for Excess Cost*

| Site No. | Value of a 100 Point Swing in DA (weight = .09) | | |
| --- | --- | --- | --- |
| | *$9,000* | *$13,500* | *$18,000* |
| 1 | 48.80 | 48.80 | 48.80 |
| 2 | 47.96 | 49.73 | 50.61 |
| 4 | 44.71 | 48.91 | 51.01 |

chapter, to utility values per point of $1000, $1500, and $2000, respectively. Table 1.5 is included here not because it is a calculation that the director would ever need to make, but because it demonstrates that the choices made on the basis of Table 1.4, which is a calculation she might well need to make, are appropriate.

As illustrated in Table 1.5, a utility value of $1000 per point makes site 1 best, a utility value of $1500 per point makes site 2 best, and a utility value of $2000 per point makes site 4 best. Note, however, that the differences in corrected utilities are relatively small. This is normal, and is one reason why we make no strong case for using such calculations to go from Table 1.3 to Table 1.5. Elimination of noncontenders is usually both more important and easier to do than selection among those that survive the elimination process, since the survivors are likely to be close enough to one another in attractiveness so that no choice will be disastrous.

### Sensitivity Analysis

The director of the center had some doubt about the weights her staff had given her. She therefore considered various other weights. She found a set of weights that make site 5 best in utility, and another for which site 2 is best.

... The director was relatively well satisfied with the location measures she was using, and felt no need to change them – and she also felt that there were so many that she was unsure which ones to change.

At this point the director felt she had enough information and analysis to make her recommendation of site 2. ...

### Summary

This section presents an example in detail. A social service center needs to move; six sites are available. Using staff weights applied to a value tree with twelve twigs, the director of the center is able to eliminate three of the six sites and to reach a conclusion among the other three.

Various technical problems arise and are discussed in presentation of the example. One is cost. The analysis treats cost as an evaluative attribute but keeps it separate from all other attributes until the end. Dominance techniques are used to eliminate options based on aggregated utilities and cost. An illustration is given of how judgments or trade-offs between cost and all other attributes can be used as a basis for a single multiattributed evaluation of what option is best. A second problem is how the nature of the context affects detailed definitions of values. A third is how to deal with options that fall outside anticipated ranges on one or more values. A fourth is how to go about operationalizing some values in order to obtain location measures. The last is what to do about ties in value, cost, or both.

### Reference

Edwards, W. (1980). Multiattribute utility for evaluation: structures, uses, and problems. In M. W. Klein & K. S. Teilman (Eds.), *Handbook of criminal justice evaluation* (pp. 177–215). Beverly Hills, CA: Sage.

# 2 Judgment under Uncertainty: Heuristics and Biases

*Amos Tversky and Daniel Kahneman*

Many decisions are based on beliefs concerning the likelihood of uncertain events such as the outcome of an election, the guilt of a defendant, or the future value of the dollar. These beliefs are usually expressed in statements such as "I think that ... ," "chances are ... ," "it is unlikely that ... ," and so forth. Occasionally, beliefs concerning uncertain events are expressed in numerical form as odds or subjective probabilities. What determines such beliefs? How do people assess the probability of an uncertain event or the value of an uncertain quantity? This chapter shows that people rely on a limited number of heuristic principles which reduce the complex tasks of assessing probabilities and predicting values to simpler judgmental operations. In general, these heuristics are quite useful, but sometimes they lead to severe and systematic errors.

The subjective assessment of probability resembles the subjective assessment of physical quantities such as distance or size. These judgments are all based on data of limited validity, which are processed according to heuristic rules. For example, the apparent distance of an object is determined in part by its clarity. The more sharply the object is seen, the closer it appears to be. This rule has some validity, because in any given scene the more distant objects are seen less sharply than nearer objects. However, the reliance on this rule leads to systematic errors in the estimation of distance. Specifically, distances are often overestimated when visibility is poor because the contours of objects are blurred. On the other hand, distances are often underestimated when visibility is good because the objects are seen sharply. Thus, the reliance on clarity as an indication of distance leads to common biases. Such biases are also found in the intuitive judgment of probability. This chapter describes three heuristics that are employed to assess probabilities and to predict values. Biases to which these heuristics lead are enumerated, and the applied and theoretical implications of these observations are discussed.

### Representativeness

Many of the probabilistic questions with which people are concerned belong to one of the following types: What is the probability that object A belongs to class B? What is the probability that event A originates from process B? What is the probability that process B will generate event A? In answering such questions, people typically rely on the representativeness heuristic, in which probabilities are evaluated by the degree to which A is representative of B, that is, by the degree to which A resembles B. For example, when A is highly representative of B, the probability that A originates from B is judged to be high. On the other hand, if A is not similar to B, the probability that A originates from B is judged to be low.

For an illustration of judgment by representativeness, consider an individual who has been described by a former neighbor as follows: "Steve is very shy and withdrawn, invariably helpful, but with little interest in people, or in the world of reality. A meek and tidy soul, he has a need for order and structure, and a passion for detail." How do people assess the probability that Steve is engaged in a particular occupation from a list of possibilities (for example, farmer, salesman, airline pilot, librarian, or physician)? How do people order these occupations from most to least likely? In the representativeness heuristic, the probability that Steve is a librarian, for example, is assessed by the degree to which he is representative of, or similar to, the stereotype of a librarian. Indeed, research with problems of this type has shown that people order the occupations by probability and by similarity in exactly the same way (Kahneman & Tversky, 1973). This approach to the judgment of probability leads to serious errors, because similarity, or representativeness, is not influenced by several factors that should affect judgments of probability.

### Insensitivity to Prior Probability of Outcomes

One of the factors that have no effect on representativeness but should have a major effect on probability is the prior probability, or base-rate frequency, of the outcomes. In the case of Steve, for example, the fact that there are many more farmers than librarians in the population should enter into any reasonable estimate of the probability that Steve is a librarian rather than a farmer. Considerations of base-rate frequency, however, do not affect the similarity of Steve to the stereotypes of librarians and farmers. If people evaluate probability by representativeness, therefore, prior probabilities will be neglected. This hypothesis was tested in an experiment where prior probabilities were manipulated (Kahneman & Tversky, 1973). Subjects were shown brief personality descriptions of several individuals, allegedly sampled at random from a group of 100 professionals – engineers and lawyers. The subjects were asked to assess, for each description, the probability that it belonged to an engineer rather than to a lawyer. In one experimental condition, subjects were told that the group from which the descriptions had been drawn consisted of 70 engineers and 30 lawyers. In another condition, subjects were told that the group consisted of 30 engineers and 70 lawyers. The odds that any particular description belongs to an engineer rather than to a lawyer should be higher in the first condition, where there is a majority of engineers, than in the second condition, where there is a majority of lawyers. Specifically, it can be shown by applying Bayes' rule that the ratio of these odds should be $(.7/.3)^2$, or 5.44, for each description. In a sharp violation of Bayes' rule, the subjects in the two conditions produced essentially the same probability judgments. Apparently, subjects evaluated the likelihood that a particular description belonged to an engineer rather than to a lawyer by the degree to which this description was representative of the two stereotypes, with little or no regard for the prior probabilities of the categories.

The subjects used prior probabilities correctly when they had no other information. In the absence of a personality sketch, they judged the probability that an unknown individual is an engineer to be .7 and .3, respectively, in the two base-rate conditions. However, prior probabilities were effectively ignored when a description was introduced, even when this description was totally uninformative. The responses to the following description illustrate this phenomenon:

Dick is a 30 year old man. He is married with no children. A man of high ability and high motivation, he promises to be quite successful in his field. He is well liked by his colleagues.

This description was intended to convey no information relevant to the question of whether Dick is an engineer or a lawyer. Consequently, the probability that Dick is an engineer should equal the proportion of engineers in the group, as if no description had been given. The subjects, however, judged the probability of Dick being an engineer to be .5 regardless of whether the stated proportion of engineers in the group was .7 or .3. Evidently, people respond differently when given no evidence and when given worthless evidence. When no specific evidence is given, prior probabilities are properly utilized; when worthless evidence is given, prior probabilities are ignored (Kahneman & Tversky, 1973).

### Insensitivity to Sample Size

To evaluate the probability of obtaining a particular result in a sample drawn from a specified population, people typically apply the representativeness heuristic. That is, they assess the likelihood of a sample result, for example, that the average height in a random sample of ten men will be 6 feet (180 centimeters), by the similarity of this result to the corresponding parameter (that is, to the average height in the population of men). The similarity of a sample statistic to a population parameter does not depend on the size of the sample. Consequently, if probabilities are assessed by representativeness, then the judged probability of a sample statistic will be essentially independent of sample size. Indeed, when subjects assessed the distributions of average height for samples of various sizes, they produced identical distributions. For example, the probability of obtaining an average height greater than 6 feet was assigned the same value for samples of 1000, 100, and 10 men (Kahneman & Tversky, 1972). Moreover, subjects failed to appreciate the role of sample size even when it was emphasized in the formulation of the problem. Consider the following question:

A certain town is served by two hospitals. In the larger hospital about 45 babies are born each day, and in the smaller hospital about 15 babies are born each day. As you know, about 50 percent of all babies are boys. However, the exact percentage varies from day to day. Sometimes it may be higher than 50 percent, sometimes lower.

For a period of 1 year, each hospital recorded the days on which more than 60 percent of the babies born were boys. Which hospital do you think recorded more such days?

▶ The larger hospital (21)
▶ The smaller hospital (21)
▶ About the same (that is, within 5 percent of each other) (53)

The values in parentheses are the number of undergraduate students who chose each answer.

Most subjects judged the probability of obtaining more than 60 percent boys to be the same in the small and in the large hospital, presumably because these events are described by the same statistic and are therefore equally representative of the general population. In contrast, sampling theory entails that the expected number of days on which more than 60 percent of the babies are boys is much greater in the small hospital than in the large one, because a large sample is less likely to stray from 50 percent. This fundamental notion of statistics is evidently not part of people's repertoire of intuitions.

A similar insensitivity to sample size has been reported in judgments of posterior probability, that is, of the probability that a sample has been drawn from one population rather than from another. Consider the following example:

Imagine an urn filled with balls, of which $2/3$ are of one color and $1/3$ of another. One individual has drawn 5 balls from the urn, and found that 4 were red and 1 was white. Another individual has drawn 20 balls and found that 12 were red and 8 were white. Which of the two individuals should feel more confident that the urn contains $2/3$ red balls and $1/3$ white balls, rather than the opposite? What odds should each individual give?

In this problem, the correct posterior odds are 8 to 1 for the 4:1 sample and 16 to 1 for the 12:8 sample, assuming equal prior probabilities. However, most people feel that the first sample provides much stronger evidence for the hypothesis that the urn is predominantly red, because the proportion of red balls is larger in the first than in the second sample. Here again, intuitive judgments are dominated by the sample proportion and are essentially unaffected by the size of the sample, which plays a crucial role in the determination of the actual posterior odds (Kahneman & Tversky, 1972). In addition, intuitive estimates of posterior odds are far less extreme than the correct values. The underestimation of the impact of evidence has been observed repeatedly in problems of this type (Edwards, 1968; Slovic & Lichtenstein, 1971). It has been labeled "conservatism."

### Misconceptions of Chance

People expect that a sequence of events generated by a random process will represent the essential characteristics of that process even when the sequence is short. In considering tosses of a coin for heads or tails, for example, people regard the sequence H-T-H-T-T-H to be more likely than the sequence H-H-H-T-T-T, which does not appear random, and also more likely than the sequence H-H-H-H-T-H, which does not represent the fairness of the coin (Kahneman & Tversky, 1972). Thus, people expect that the essential characteristics of the process will be represented, not only globally in the entire sequence, but also locally in each of its parts. A locally representative sequence, however, deviates systematically from chance expectation: it contains too many alternations and too few runs. Another consequence of the belief in local representativeness is the well-known gambler's fallacy. After observing a long run of red on the roulette wheel, for example, most people erroneously believe that black is now due, presumably because the occurrence of black will result in a more representative sequence than the occurrence of an additional red. Chance is commonly viewed as a self-correcting process in which a deviation in one direction induces a deviation in the opposite direction to restore the equilibrium. In fact, deviations are not "corrected" as a chance process unfolds, they are merely diluted.

Misconceptions of chance are not limited to naive subjects. A study of the statistical intuitions of experienced research psychologists (Tversky & Kahneman, 1971) revealed a lingering belief in what may be called the "law of small numbers," according to which even small samples are highly representative of the populations from which they are drawn. The responses of these investigators reflected the expectation that a valid hypothesis about a population will be represented by a statistically significant result in a sample – with little regard for its size. As a consequence, the researchers put too much faith in the results of small samples and grossly overestimated the replicability of such results. In the actual conduct of research, this bias leads to the selection of samples of inadequate size and to overinterpretation of findings.

*Insensitivity to Predictability*

People are sometimes called upon to make such numerical predictions as the future value of a stock, the demand for a commodity, or the outcome of a football game. Such predictions are often made by representativeness. For example, suppose one is given a description of a company and is asked to predict its future profit. If the description of the company is very favorable, a very high profit will appear most representative of that description; if the description is mediocre, a mediocre performance will appear most representative. The degree to which the description is favorable is unaffected by the reliability of that description or by the degree to which it permits accurate prediction. Hence, if people predict solely in terms of the favorableness of the description, their predictions will be insensitive to the reliability of the evidence and to the expected accuracy of the prediction.

This mode of judgment violates the normative statistical theory in which the extremeness and the range of predictions are controlled by considerations of predictability. When predictability is nil, the same prediction should be made in all cases. For example, if the descriptions of companies provide no information relevant to profit, then the same value (such as average profit) should be predicted for all companies. If predictability is perfect, of course, the values predicted will match the actual values and the range of predictions will equal the range of outcomes. In general, the higher the predictability, the wider the range of predicted values.

Several studies of numerical prediction have demonstrated that intuitive predictions violate this rule, and that subjects show little or no regard for considerations of predictability (Kahneman & Tversky, 1973). In one of these studies, subjects were presented with several paragraphs, each describing the performance of a student teacher during a particular practice lesson. Some subjects were asked to *evaluate* the quality of the lesson described in the paragraph in percentile scores, relative to a specified population. Other subjects were asked to *predict*, also in percentile scores, the standing of each student teacher 5 years after the practice lesson. The judgments made under the two conditions were identical. That is, the prediction of a remote criterion (success of a teacher after 5 years) was identical to the evaluation of the information on which the prediction was based (the quality of the practice lesson). The students who made these predictions were undoubtedly aware of the limited predictability of teaching competence on the basis of a single trial lesson 5 years earlier; nevertheless, their predictions were as extreme as their evaluations.

*The Illusion of Validity*

As we have seen, people often predict by selecting the outcome (for example, an occupation) that is most representative of the input (for example, the description of a person). The confidence they have in their prediction depends primarily on the degree of representativeness (that is, on the quality of the match between the selected outcome and the input) with little or no regard for the factors that limit predictive accuracy. Thus, people express great confidence in the prediction that a person is a librarian when given a description of his personality which matches the stereotype of librarians, even if the description is scanty, unreliable, or outdated. The unwarranted confidence which is produced by a good fit between the predicted outcome and the input information may be called the illusion of validity. This illusion persists even when the judge is aware of the factors that limit the accuracy of his predictions. It is a common observation that psychologists who conduct selection interviews often experience considerable confidence in their predictions, even when they know of the vast literature that shows selection interviews to be highly fallible. The continued reliance on the clinical interview for selection, despite repeated demonstrations of its inadequacy, amply attests to the strength of this effect.

The internal consistency of a pattern of inputs is a major determinant of one's confidence in predictions based on these inputs. For example, people express more confidence in predicting the final grade-point average of a student whose first-year record consists entirely of B's than in predicting the grade-point average of a student whose first-year record includes many A's and C's. Highly consistent patterns are most often observed when the input variables are highly redundant or correlated. Hence, people tend to have great confidence in predictions based on redundant input variables. However, an elementary result in the statistics of correlation asserts that, given input variables of stated validity, a prediction based on several such inputs can achieve higher accuracy when they are independent of each other than when they are redundant or correlated. Thus redundancy among inputs decreases accuracy even as it increases confidence, and people are often confident in predictions that are quite likely to be off the mark (Kahneman & Tversky, 1973).

### Misconceptions of Regression

Suppose a large group of children has been examined on two equivalent versions of an aptitude test. If one selects ten children from among those who did best on one of the two versions, he will usually find their performance on the second version to be somewhat disappointing. Conversely, if one selects ten children from among those who did worst on one version, they will be found, on the average, to do somewhat better on the other version. More generally, consider two variables $X$ and $Y$ which have the same distribution. If one selects individuals whose average $X$ score deviates from the mean of $X$ by $k$ units, then the average of their $Y$ scores will usually deviate from the mean of $Y$ by less than $k$ units. These observations illustrate a general phenomenon known as regression toward the mean, which was first documented by Galton more than 100 years ago.

In the normal course of life, one encounters many instances of regression toward the mean, in the comparison of the height of fathers and sons, of the intelligence of husbands and wives, or of the performance of individuals on consecutive examinations. Nevertheless, people do not develop correct intuitions about this phenomenon. First, they do not expect regression in many contexts where it is bound to occur. Second, when they recognize the occurrence of regression, they often invent spurious causal explanations for it (Kahneman & Tversky, 1973). We suggest that the phenomenon of regression remains elusive because it is incompatible with the belief that the predicted outcome should be maximally representative of the input, and, hence, that the value of the outcome variable should be as extreme as the value of the input variable.

The failure to recognize the import of regression can have pernicious consequences, as illustrated by the following observation (Kahneman & Tversky, 1973). In a discussion of flight training, experienced instructors noted that praise for an exceptionally smooth landing is typically followed by a poorer landing on the next try, while harsh criticism after a rough landing is usually followed by an improvement on the next try. The instructors concluded that verbal rewards are detrimental to learning, while verbal punishments are beneficial, contrary to accepted psychological doctrine. This conclusion is unwarranted because of the presence of regression toward the mean. As in other cases of repeated examination, an improvement will usually follow a poor performance and a deterioration will usually follow an outstanding performance, even if the instructor does not respond to the trainee's achievement on the first attempt. Because the instructors had praised their trainees after good landings and admonished them after poor ones, they reached the erroneous and potentially harmful conclusion that punishment is more effective than reward.

Thus, the failure to understand the effect of regression leads one to overestimate the effectiveness of punishment and to underestimate the effectiveness of reward. In social interaction, as well as in training, rewards are typically administered when performance is good, and punishments are typically administered when performance is poor. By regression alone, therefore, behavior is most likely to improve after punishment and most likely to deteriorate after reward. Consequently, the human condition is such that, by chance alone, one is most often rewarded for punishing others and most often punished for rewarding them. People are generally not aware of this contingency. In fact, the elusive role of regression in determining the apparent consequences of reward and punishment seems to have escaped the notice of students of this area.

### Availability

There are situations in which people assess the frequency of a class or the probability of an event by the ease with which instances or occurrences can be brought to mind. For example, one may assess the risk of heart attack among middle-aged people by recalling such occurrences among one's acquaintances. Similarly, one may evaluate the probability that a given business venture will fail by imagining various difficulties it could encounter. This judgmental heuristic is called availability. Availability is a useful clue for assessing frequency or probability, because instances of large classes are usually recalled better and faster than instances of less frequent classes. However, availability is affected by factors other than frequency and probability. Consequently, the reliance on availability leads to predictable biases, some of which are illustrated below.

### Biases due to the Retrievability of Instances

When the size of a class is judged by the availability of its instances, a class whose instances are easily retrieved will appear more numerous than a class of equal frequency whose instances are less retrievable. In an elementary demonstration of this effect, subjects heard a list of well-known personalities of both sexes and were subsequently asked to judge whether the list contained more names of men than of women. Different lists were presented to different groups of subjects. In some of the lists the men were relatively more famous than the women, and in others the women were relatively more famous than the men. In each of the lists, the subjects erroneously judged that the class (sex) that had the more famous personalities was the more numerous (Tversky & Kahneman, 1973).

In addition to familiarity, there are other factors, such as salience, which affect the retrievability of instances. For example, the impact of seeing a house burning on the subjective probability of such accidents is probably greater than the impact of reading about a fire in the local paper. Furthermore, recent occurrences are likely to be relatively more available than earlier occurrences. It is a common experience that the subjective probability of traffic accidents rises temporarily when one sees a car overturned by the side of the road.

### Biases due to the Effectiveness of a Search Set

Suppose one samples a word (of three letters or more) at random from an English text. Is it more likely that the word starts with r or that r is the third letter? People approach this problem by recalling words that begin with r (road) and words that have r in the third position (car) and assess the relative frequency by the ease with which words of the two types come to mind. Because it is much easier to search for words by their first letter than by their third letter, most people judge words that begin with a given consonant to be more numerous than words in which the same consonant appears in the third position. They do so even for consonants, such as r or k, that are more frequent in the third position than in the first (Tversky & Kahneman, 1973).

Different tasks elicit different search sets. For example, suppose you are asked to rate the frequency with which abstract words (thought, love) and concrete words (door, water) appear in written English. A natural way to answer this question is to search for contexts in which the word could appear. It seems easier to think of contexts in which an abstract concept is mentioned (love in love stories) than to think of contexts in which a concrete word (such as door) is mentioned. If the frequency of words is judged by the availability of the contexts in which they appear, abstract words will be judged as relatively more numerous than concrete words. This bias has been observed in a recent study (Galbraith & Underwood, 1973) which showed that the judged frequency of occurrence of abstract words was much higher than that of concrete words, equated in objective frequency. Abstract words were also judged to appear in a much greater variety of contexts than concrete words.

### Biases of Imaginability

Sometimes one has to assess the frequency of a class whose instances are not stored in memory but can be generated according to a given rule. In such situations, one typically generates several instances and evaluates frequency or probability by the ease with which the relevant instances can be constructed. However, the ease of constructing instances does not always reflect their actual frequency, and this mode of evaluation is prone to biases. To illustrate, consider a group of 10 people who form committees of $k$ members, $2 \leq k \leq 8$. How many different committees of $k$ members can be formed? The correct answer to this problem is given by the binomial coefficient $\binom{10}{k}$ which reaches a maximum of 252 for $k = 5$. Clearly, the number of committees of $k$ members equals the number of committees of $(10 - k)$ members, because any committee of $k$ members defines a unique group of $(10 - k)$ nonmembers.

One way to answer this question without computation is to mentally construct committees of $k$ members and to evaluate their number by the ease with which they come to mind. Committees of few members, say 2, are more available than committees of many members, say 8. The simplest scheme for the construction of committees is a partition of the group into disjoint sets. One readily sees that it is easy to construct five disjoint committees of 2 members, while it is impossible to generate even two disjoint committees of 8 members. Consequently, if frequency is assessed by imaginability, or by availability for construction, the small committees will appear more numerous than larger committees, in contrast to the correct bell-shaped function. Indeed, when naive subjects were asked to estimate the number of distinct committees of various sizes, their estimates were a decreasing monotonic function of committee size (Tversky & Kahneman, 1973). For example, the median estimate of the number of committees of 2 members was 70, while the estimate for committees of 8 members was 20 (the correct answer is 45 in both cases).

Imaginability plays an important role in the evaluation of probabilities in real-life situations. The risk involved in an adventurous expedition, for example, is evaluated by imagining contingencies with which the expedition is not equipped to cope. If many such difficulties are vividly portrayed, the expedition can be made to appear exceedingly dangerous, although the ease with which disasters are imagined need not reflect their actual likelihood. Conversely, the risk involved in an undertaking may be grossly underestimated if some possible dangers are either difficult to conceive of, or simply do not come to mind.

### Illusory Correlation

Chapman and Chapman (1967, 1969) have described an interesting bias in the judgment of the frequency with which two events co-occur. They presented naive judges with information concerning several hypothetical mental patients. The data for each patient consisted of a clinical diagnosis and a drawing of a person made by the patient. Later the judges estimated the frequency with which each diagnosis (such as paranoia or suspiciousness) had been accompanied by various features of the drawing (such as peculiar eyes). The subjects markedly overestimated the frequency of co-occurrence of natural associates, such as suspiciousness and peculiar eyes. This effect was labeled illusory correlation. In their erroneous judgments of the data to which they had been exposed, naive subjects "rediscovered" much of the common, but unfounded, clinical lore concerning the interpretation of the draw-a-person test. The illusory correlation effect was extremely resistant to contradictory data. It persisted even when the correlation between symptom and diagnosis was actually negative, and it prevented the judges from detecting relationships that were in fact present.

Availability provides a natural account for the illusory-correlation effect. The judgment of how frequently two events co-occur could be based on the strength of the associative bond between them. When the association is strong, one is likely to conclude that the events have been frequently paired. Consequently, strong associates will be judged to have occurred together frequently. According to this view, the illusory correlation between suspiciousness and peculiar drawing of the eyes, for example, is due to the fact that suspiciousness is more readily associated with the eyes than with any other part of the body.

Lifelong experience has taught us that, in general, instances of large classes are recalled better and faster than instances of less frequent classes; that likely occurrences are easier to imagine than unlikely ones; and that the associative connections between events are strengthened when the events frequently co-occur. As a result, man has at his disposal a procedure (the availability heuristic) for estimating the numerosity of a class, the likelihood of an event, or the frequency of co-occurrences, by the ease with which the relevant mental operations of retrieval, construction, or association can be performed. However, as the preceding examples have demonstrated, this valuable estimation procedure results in systematic errors.

### Adjustment and Anchoring

In many situations, people make estimates by starting from an initial value that is adjusted to yield the final answer. The initial value, or starting point, may be suggested by the formulation of the problem, or it may be the result of a partial computation. In either case, adjustments are typically insufficient (Slovic & Lichtenstein, 1971). That is, different starting points yield different estimates, which are biased toward the initial values. We call this phenomenon anchoring.

#### Insufficient Adjustment

In a demonstration of the anchoring effect, subjects were asked to estimate various quantities, stated in percentages (for example, the percentage of African countries in the United Nations). For each quantity, a number between 0 and 100 was determined by spinning a wheel of fortune in the subjects' presence. The subjects were instructed to indicate first whether that number was higher or lower than the value of the quantity, and then to estimate the value of the quantity by moving upward or downward from the given number. Different groups were given different numbers for each quantity, and these arbitrary numbers had a marked effect on estimates. For example, the median estimates of the percentage of African countries in the United Nations were 25 and 45 for groups that received 10 and 65, respectively, as starting points. Payoffs for accuracy did not reduce the anchoring effect.

Anchoring occurs not only when the starting point is given to the subject, but also when the subject bases his estimate on the result of some incomplete computation. A study of intuitive numerical estimation illustrates this effect. Two groups of high school students estimated, within 5 seconds, a numerical expression that was written on the blackboard. One group estimated the product

$$8 \times 7 \times 6 \times 5 \times 4 \times 3 \times 2 \times 1$$

while another group estimated the product

$$1 \times 2 \times 3 \times 4 \times 5 \times 6 \times 7 \times 8$$

To rapidly answer such questions, people may perform a few steps of computation and estimate the product by extrapolation or adjustment.

Because adjustments are typically insufficient, this procedure should lead to underestimation. Furthermore, because the result of the first few steps of multiplication (performed from left to right) is higher in the descending sequence than in the ascending sequence, the former expression should be judged larger than the latter. Both predictions were confirmed. The median estimate for the ascending sequence was 512, while the median estimate for the descending sequence was 2250. The correct answer is 40,320.

### Biases in the Evaluation of Conjunctive and Disjunctive Events

In a recent study by Bar-Hillel (1973) subjects were given the opportunity to bet on one of two events. Three types of events were used: (i) simple events, such as drawing a red marble from a bag containing 50 percent red marbles and 50 percent white marbles; (ii) conjunctive events, such as drawing a red marble seven times in succession, with replacement, from a bag containing 90 percent red marbles and 10 percent white marbles; and (iii) disjunctive events, such as drawing a red marble at least once in seven successive tries, with replacement, from a bag containing 10 percent red marbles and 90 percent white marbles. In this problem, a significant majority of subjects preferred to bet on the conjunctive event (the probability of which is .48) rather than on the simple event (the probability of which is .50). Subjects also preferred to bet on the simple event rather than on the disjunctive event, which has a probability of .52. Thus, most subjects bet on the less likely event in both comparisons. This pattern of choices illustrates a general finding. Studies of choice among gambles and of judgments of probability indicate that people tend to overestimate the probability of conjunctive events (Cohen, Chesnick, & Haran, 1972) and to underestimate the probability of disjunctive events. These biases are readily explained as effects of anchoring. The stated probability of the elementary event (success at any one stage) provides a natural starting point for the estimation of the probabilities of both conjunctive and disjunctive events. Since adjustment from the starting point is typically insufficient, the final estimates remain too close to the probabilities of the elementary events in both cases. Note that the overall probability of a conjunctive event is lower than the probability of each elementary event, whereas the overall probability of a disjunctive event is higher than the probability of each elementary event. As a consequence of anchoring, the overall probability will be overestimated in conjunctive problems and underestimated in disjunctive problems.

Biases in the evaluation of compound events are particularly significant in the context of planning. The successful completion of an undertaking, such as the development of a new product, typically has a conjunctive character: for the undertaking to succeed, each of a series of events must occur. Even when each of these events is very likely, the overall probability of success can be quite low if the number of events is large. The general tendency to overestimate the probability of conjunctive events leads to unwarranted optimism in the evaluation of the likelihood that a plan will succeed or that a project will be completed on time. Conversely, disjunctive structures are typically encountered in the evaluation of risks. A complex system, such as a nuclear reactor or a human body, will malfunction if any of its essential components fails. Even when the likelihood of failure in each component is slight, the probability of an overall failure can be high if many components are involved. Because of anchoring, people will tend to underestimate the probabilities of failure in complex systems. Thus, the direction of the anchoring bias can sometimes be inferred from the structure of the event. The chain-like structure of conjunctions leads to overestimation, the funnel-like structure of disjunctions leads to underestimation.

### Anchoring in the Assessment of Subjective Probability Distributions

In decision analysis, experts are often required to express their beliefs about a quantity, such as the value of the Dow-Jones average on a particular day, in the form of a probability distribution. Such a distribution is usually constructed by asking the person to select values of the quantity that correspond to specified percentiles of his subjective probability distribution. For example, the judge may be asked to select a number, $X_{90}$, such that his subjective probability that this number will be higher than the value of the Dow-Jones average is .90. That is, he should select the value $X_{90}$ so that he is just willing to accept 9 to 1 odds that the Dow-Jones average will not exceed it. A subjective probability distribution for the value of the Dow-Jones average can be constructed from several such judgments corresponding to different percentiles.

By collecting subjective probability distributions for many different quantities, it is possible to test the judge for proper calibration. A judge is properly (or externally) calibrated in a set of problems if exactly $n$ percent of the true values of the assessed quantities falls below his stated values of $Xn$. For example, the true values should fall below $X_{01}$ for 1 percent of the quantities and above $X_{99}$ for 1 percent of the quantities. Thus, the true values should fall in the confidence interval between $X_{01}$ and $X_{99}$ on 98 percent of the problems.

Several investigators (Alpert & Raiffa, 1982; von Holstein, 1971; Winkler, 1967) have obtained probability distributions for many quantities from a large number of judges. These distributions indicated large and systematic departures from proper calibration. In most studies, the actual values of the assessed quantities are either smaller than $X_{01}$ or greater than $X_{99}$ for about 30 percent of the problems. That is, the subjects state overly narrow confidence intervals which reflect more certainty than is justified by their knowledge about the assessed quantities. This bias is common to naive and to sophisticated subjects, and it is not eliminated by introducing proper scoring rules, which provide incentives for external calibration. This effect is attributable, in part at least, to anchoring.

To select $X_{90}$ for the value of the Dow-Jones average, for example, it is natural to begin by thinking about one's best estimate of the Dow-Jones and to adjust this value upward. If this adjustment – like most others – is insufficient, then $X_{90}$ will not be sufficiently extreme. A similar anchoring effect will occur in the selection of $X_{10}$, which is presumably obtained by adjusting one's best estimate downward. Consequently, the confidence interval between $X_{10}$ and $X_{90}$ will be too narrow, and the assessed probability distribution will be too tight. In support of this interpretation it can be shown that subjective probabilities are systematically altered by a procedure in which one's best estimate does not serve as an anchor.

Subjective probability distributions for a given quantity (the Dow-Jones average) can be obtained in two different ways: (i) by asking the subject to select values of the Dow-Jones that correspond to specified percentiles of this probability distribution and (ii) by asking the subject to assess the probabilities that the true value of the Dow-Jones will exceed some specified values. The two procedures are formally equivalent and should yield identical distributions. However, they suggest different modes of adjustment from different anchors. In procedure (i), the natural starting point is one's best estimate of the quantity. In procedure (ii), on the other hand, the subject may be anchored on the value stated in the question. Alternatively, he may be anchored on even odds, or 50-50 chances, which is a natural starting point in the estimation of likelihood. In either case, procedure (ii) should yield less extreme odds than procedure (i).

To contrast the two procedures, a set of 24 quantities (such as the air distance from New Delhi to Peking) was presented to a group of subjects who assessed either $X_{10}$ or $X_{90}$ for each problem. Another group of subjects received the median judgment of the first group for each of the 24 quantities. They were asked to assess the odds that each of the given values exceeded the true value of the relevant quantity. In the absence of any bias, the second group should retrieve the odds specified to the first group, that is, 9:1. However, if even odds or the stated value serves as an anchor, the odds of the second group should be less extreme, that is, closer to 1:1. Indeed, the median odds stated by this group, across all problems, were 3:1. When the judgments of the two groups were tested for external calibration, it was found that subjects in the first group were too extreme, in accord with earlier studies. The events that they defined as having a probability of .10 actually obtained in 24 percent of the cases. In contrast, subjects in the second group were too conservative. Events to which they assigned an average probability of .34 actually obtained in 26 percent of the cases. These results illustrate the manner in which the degree of calibration depends on the procedure of elicitation.

## Discussion

This chapter has been concerned with cognitive biases that stem from the reliance on judgmental heuristics. These biases are not attributable to motivational effects such as wishful thinking or the distortion of judgments by payoffs and penalties. Indeed, several of the severe errors of judgment reported earlier occurred despite the fact that subjects were encouraged to be accurate and were rewarded for the correct answers (Kahneman & Tversky, 1972; Tversky & Kahneman, 1973).

The reliance on heuristics and the prevalence of biases are not restricted to laymen. Experienced researchers are also prone to the same biases – when they think intuitively. For example, the tendency to predict the outcome that best represents the data, with insufficient regard for prior probability, has been observed in the intuitive judgments of individuals who have had extensive training in statistics (Kahneman & Tversky, 1973; Tversky & Kahneman, 1971). Although the statistically sophisticated avoid elementary errors, such as the gambler's fallacy, their intuitive judgments are liable to similar fallacies in more intricate and less transparent problems.

It is not surprising that useful heuristics such as representativeness and availability are retained, even though they occasionally lead to errors in prediction or estimation. What is perhaps surprising is the failure of people to infer from lifelong experience such fundamental statistical rules as regression toward the mean, or the effect of sample size on sampling variability. Although everyone is exposed, in the normal course of life, to numerous examples from which these rules could have been induced, very few people discover the principles of sampling and regression on their own. Statistical principles are not learned from everyday experience because the relevant instances are not coded appropriately. For example, people do not discover that successive lines in a text differ more in average word length than do successive pages, because they simply do not attend to the average word length of individual lines or pages. Thus, people do not learn the relation between sample size and sampling variability, although the data for such learning are abundant.

The lack of an appropriate code also explains why people usually do not detect the biases in their judgments of probability. A person could conceivably learn whether his judgments are externally calibrated by keeping a tally of the proportion of events that actually occur among those to which he assigns the same probability. However, it is not natural to group events by their judged probability. In the absence of such grouping it is impossible for an individual to discover, for example, that only 50 percent of the predictions to which he has assigned a probability of .9 or higher actually came true.

The empirical analysis of cognitive biases has implications for the theoretical and applied role of judged probabilities. Modern decision theory (de Finetti, 1968; Savage, 1954) regards subjective probability as the quantified opinion of an idealized person. Specifically, the subjective probability of a given event is defined by the set of bets about this event that such a person is willing to accept. An internally consistent, or coherent, subjective probability measure can be derived for an individual if his choices among bets satisfy certain principles, that is, the axioms of the theory. The derived probability is subjective in the sense that different individuals are allowed to have different probabilities for the same event. The major contribution of this approach is that it provides a rigorous subjective interpretation of probability that is applicable to unique events and is embedded in a general theory of rational decision.

It should perhaps be noted that, while subjective probabilities can sometimes be inferred from preferences among bets, they are normally not formed in this fashion. A person bets on team A rather than on team B because he believes that team A is more likely to win; he does not infer this belief from his betting preferences. Thus, in reality, subjective probabilities determine preferences among bets and are not derived from them, as in the axiomatic theory of rational decision (Savage, 1954).

The inherently subjective nature of probability has led many students to the belief that coherence, or internal consistency, is the only valid criterion by which judged probabilities should be evaluated. From the standpoint of the formal theory of subjective probability, any set of internally consistent probability judgments is as good as any other. This criterion is not entirely satisfactory, because an internally consistent set of subjective probabilities can be incompatible with other beliefs held by the individual. Consider a person whose subjective probabilities for all possible outcomes of a coin-tossing game reflect the gambler's fallacy. That is, his estimate of the probability of tails on a particular toss increases with the number of consecutive heads that preceded that toss. The judgments of such a person could be internally consistent and therefore acceptable as adequate subjective probabilities according to the criterion of the formal theory. These probabilities, however, are incompatible with the generally held belief that a coin has no memory and is therefore incapable of generating sequential dependencies. For judged probabilities to be considered adequate, or rational, internal consistency is not enough. The judgments must be compatible with the entire web of beliefs held by the individual. Unfortunately, there can be no simple formal procedure for assessing the compatibility of a set of probability judgments with the judge's total system of beliefs. The rational judge will nevertheless strive for compatibility, even though internal consistency is more easily achieved and assessed. In particular, he will attempt to make his probability judgments compatible with his knowledge about the subject matter, the laws of probability, and his own judgmental heuristics and biases.

## Summary

This article described three heuristics that are employed in making judgments under uncertainty: (i) representativeness, which is usually employed when people are asked to judge the probability that an object or event A belongs to class or process B; (ii) availability of instances or scenarios, which is often employed when people are asked to assess the frequency of a class or the plausibility of a particular development; and (iii) adjustment from an anchor, which is usually employed in numerical prediction when a relevant value is available. These heuristics are highly economical and usually effective, but they lead to systematic and predictable errors. A better understanding of these heuristics and of the biases to which they lead could improve judgments and decisions in situations of uncertainty.

### References

Alpert, M., & Raiffa, H. (1982). A progress report on the training of probability assessors. In D. Kahneman & A. Tversky (Eds.), *Judgment under uncertainty: Heuristics and biases*. Cambridge: Cambridge University Press.

Bar-Hillel, M. (1973). On the subjective probability of compound events. *Organizational Behavior and Human Performance, 9*, 396–406.

Chapman, L. J., & Chapman, J. P. (1967). Genesis of popular but erroneous psychodiagnostic observations. *Journal of Abnormal Psychology, 72*, 193–204.

Chapman, L. J., & Chapman, J. P. (1969). Illusory correlation as an obstacle to the use of valid psychodiagnostic signs. *Journal of Abnormal Psychology, 74*, 271–280.

Cohen, J., Chesnick, E. I., & Haran, D. (1972). A confirmation of the intertial-$\Psi$ effect in choice and decision. *British Journal of Psychology, 63*, 41–46.

De Finetti, B. (1968). Probability: Interpretations. In D. E. Sills (Ed.), *International encyclopedia of the social sciences* (Vol. 12, pp. 496–504). New York: MacMillan.

Edwards, W. (1968). Conservatism in human information processing. In B. Kleinmuntz (Ed.), *Formal representation of human judgement*. New York: Wiley.

Galbraith, R. C., & Underwood, B. J. (1973). Perceived frequency of concrete and abstract words. *Memory and Cognition, 1*, 56–60.

Kahneman, D., & Tversky, T. (1972). Subjective probability: A judgment of representativeness. *Cognitive Psychology, 3*, 430–454.

Kahneman, D., & Tversky, T. (1973). On the psychology of prediction. *Psychological Review, 80*, 237–251.

Savage, L. J. (1954). *The foundations of statistics*. New York: Wiley.

Slovic, P., & Lichtenstein, S. (1971). Comparison of Bayesian and regression approaches to the study of information processing in judgment. *Organizational Behavior and Human Performance, 6*, 649–744.

Tversky, A., & Kahneman, D. (1971). Belief in the law of small numbers. *Psychological Bulletin, 76*, 105–110.

von Holstein, C. A. S. (1971). Two techniques for assessment of subjective probability distributions: An experimental study. *Acta Psychologica, 35*, 478–494.

Winkler, R. L. (1967). Assessment of prior distributions in Bayesian analysis. *Journal of the American Statistical Association, 62*, 776–800.

# 3    Coherence and Correspondence Theories in Judgment and Decision Making

*Kenneth R. Hammond*

Two grand metatheories have been persistent rivals in the history of science in general and in the history of research in judgment and decision making in particular. Research programs in judgment and decision making can easily and usefully be classified into one of these two well-established types of scientific endeavor, namely, the correspondence metatheory of judgment and decision making and the coherence metatheory of judgment and decision making. Because the reader is likely to be unfamiliar with these terms, I offer here a brief explanation.

The goal of a correspondence metatheory is to describe and explain the process by which a person's judgments achieve *empirical accuracy*. The goal of a coherence metatheory of judgment, in contrast, is to describe and explain the process by which a person's judgments achieve logical, or mathematical, or statistical *rationality*. Thus, the word "correspondence" can be roughly translated into *accuracy*: Did the interest rates go up, as the banker predicted? Did it rain, as the weather forecaster predicted? The word "coherence" can be roughly translated into *rationality*: Did the argument for that conclusion meet the test of logical or mathematical consistency?

It may come as a surprise to the reader that rationality does not directly imply accuracy and vice versa, but brief reflection shows that this is the case. Rationality always operates in a closed system; given the premises, certain conclusions always follow *if* a rational reasoning process is followed. When the reasoning process satisfies a logical test, the system is termed coherent, and that is all it is and all it claims to be. Many people, for example, believe that every word in the Bible is true. It would be rational for these people to believe that the world is flat, for the Bible indicates that that is the case. Historically, however, the empirical question of whether the earth is flat has been largely ignored; medieval scholars spent their time arguing about the

This chapter originally appeared in Hammond, K. R. (1996), *Human Judgment and Social Policy*. New York: Oxford University Press. Copyright © 1996 by Oxford University Press. Reprinted by permission.

*rationality*, the logical coherence, of various theological propositions. The correspondence of any theological statement with empirical observations was beside the point. It was Galileo, with his stubborn insistence on empirical facts, who created the tension between truth based on coherent dogma and truth based on the correspondence of ideas with facts. The church resolved this tension by arresting and imprisoning Galileo and then denying his conclusions for more than three hundred years. It takes very, very strong empirical contradictions to overturn a highly coherent theory in which a great deal has been invested on the assumption that it is true. Religion is not unique in its stubbornness. Coherence, in and of itself, is a very powerful organizing principle. It is seldom given up easily.

Scientific research seeks both coherence and correspondence but gets both only in advanced, successful work. Most scientific disciplines are forced to tolerate contradictory facts and competitive theories. Researchers must, therefore, live with the tension created by those who wish to pursue the reconciliation of facts and those who wish to resolve the contradictions of theories. But policymakers find it much harder than researchers to live with this tension because they are expected to *act* on the basis of information. Here is an example of how the implicit use of a coherence theory led to one policy recommendation and the implicit use of a correspondence theory led to another.

At the Science and Public Policy Seminar sponsored by the Federation of Behavioral, Psychological, and Cognitive Sciences in July 1994, Nancy Adler addressed congressional staff members on the question of the cognitive competence of adolescents to decide whether to engage in sexual behavior. Her criterion for competence is rationality, and her criterion for rationality is coherence: "Insofar as people are consistent in their reasoning, insofar as they are making the choice that maximizes their perceived benefits and minimizes their perceived costs, we can consider them rational."[1]

The same sort of argument that is applied to the judgment that the earth is flat—if you believe that every word in the Bible is true and if the Bible indicates that the earth is flat, then it is rational to believe the earth is flat—is thus also used to defend adolescents' judgment that "if you think that you can't get pregnant it may be perfectly rational not to use a contraceptive."[2] If you believe that adolescents are capable of rational cognition, therefore, then it is the adolescents' perceptions of reality that should be changed and it should be the goal of social policy to provide better, more accurate information that would change those perceptions. For on the assumption that rationality will prevail—that is, accurate information will be used in a rational, coherent manner—then rational behavior will follow ("you can affect . . . [the] behavior if you can correct the information"[3]).

Adler's conclusion flies in the face of the results obtained by coherence researchers over the past twenty years, which have emphasized exactly the opposite conclusion. . . . Irrespective of the tenuous basis of Adler's conclusion, it is implicitly based on the coherence theory of truth.

But it is not difficult to find exactly the opposite conclusions drawn from researchers who employ a correspondence theory. G. Loewenstein and F. Furstenberg indicate that merely offering correct information is insufficient to affect behavior: "Imparting knowledge . . . [is] unlikely to be successful in affecting either sexual activity or contraception. Once we controlled for other variables, the effect of knowledge virtually disappeared."[4]

The implications of these two sets of conclusions for public policy could hardly be more pronounced. One researcher tells us that adolescents are rational information processors who simply need better information in order for their decisions to become rational ones; the other researchers tell us the opposite. The fact that these conclusions rest on the use of different methods derived from different theories of truth (and thus different methodologies) was not acknowledged, however. Therefore, the policies they advocate will be based on an implicit choice of methodology as well as explicit choice of result. The coherence approach was introduced to psychologists interested in judgment and decision making by Ward Edwards in 1954 in an article entitled, "The Theory of Decision Making."[5] The next year, I introduced a correspondence approach to judgment in an article titled "Probabilistic Functionalism and the Clinical Method."[6] Fifteen years later there was a sufficient accumulation of research to allow P. Slovic and S. Lichtenstein to publish a review article describing the research conducted within both approaches.[7]

W. Edwards and his colleague Detlof von Winterfeldt have emphasized that the goal of decision analysis is the achievement of *rationality*.[8] This is evidenced in a subhead on the first page of their book: "What this book is about: rationality." On page two they state: "Explicitly, this book is intended to help people be rational in making inferences and decisions. . . . The notion of rationality is prescriptive: In any version it explicitly says that some thoughts and actions are appropriate and others are not." Von Winterfeldt and Edwards do not claim that readers of their book will become more *empirically* accurate in their inferences and decisions. Accuracy is not under discussion; it isn't even indexed. In parallel fashion, correspondence theorists, such as myself, ignore the question of coherence to focus on empirical accuracy; the rationality of the process is hardly addressed.

Until the present little has been said in the field of judgment and decision making about the distinction between coherence and correspondence metatheories. And what little has been said has largely been ignored. Although R. Hastie and K. A. Rasinski treat the matter in some detail,[9] their article has seldom been cited. J. F. Yates's textbook on judgment and decision making does, however, make use of the correspondence-coherence distinction.[10] (He uses the term "accuracy" rather than "correspondence," but the distinction is the same.) His chapter on accuracy begins with a treatment of the empirical accuracy of weather forecasting, and his chapter on coherence begins with "coherence and probability theory," thus demonstrating the different reference points for each topic. Yates makes a further contribution by raising the question of the "practical significance of coherence,"[11] a matter I will discuss later in this chapter.

In 1990 I contrasted what I called "functionalism" and "illusionism" in judgment and decision making research as a way of introducing the distinction between correspondence (functionalism) and coherence (illusionism). I suggested that those researchers who focused on errors and cognitive illusions in judgment and decision making were working within the context of the coherence theory, whereas those who focused on accuracy (functionalism) were working within the correspondence theory of truth. In an effort to show the complementarity of the two approaches, I stated:

> In sum, the theories derived from functionalism and illusionism are not competing theories about judgment and decision making; rather, they are complementary theories about cognition that takes place under different conditions, conditions that induce subjects to employ different theories of truth. Because both types of inducement frequently occur in human ecologies, it is costly for *persons* to deny truth to either theory; it is, however, highly beneficial to be able to employ either, particularly when one knows which theory to apply under which conditions. Additionally it is costly for *researchers* to deny that subjects can employ either or both forms of cognition, but it is beneficial to learn the consequences of their application in various circumstances. It is this argument that leads me to believe that integration [of these approaches] could strengthen the research effort to understand human judgment and decision making.[12]

D. Frisch and R. T. Clemen have presented a similar point of view. In the course of their argument they note that L. J. Savage, one of the prominent early students of the topic, saw that the standard Subjective Expected Utility theory was based on coherence: "To use the preference [utility] theory is to search for incoherence among potential decisions. . . . The theory itself does not say which way back to coherence is to be chosen."[13] And Frisch and Clemen add: "Thus, violations of S[ubjective] E[xpected] U[tility] imply internal inconsistency. . . . This is known as the *coherence argument*."[14] They conclude that utility theory not only fails as a descriptive theory; it "does not provide an adequate standard for this [the decision] process."[15]

Frisch and Clemen thus find coherence to be the basic criterion for this bedrock theory and then dismiss the theory as *neither* descriptively nor normatively useful. Their "alternative framework" offers three features to be included as "part of good decision making": (1) consequences, (2) thorough structuring, and (3) trade-offs. Thus, these authors come close to the correspondence metatheory but do not embrace it. Their dismissal of (coherent) *utility theory* may well be justified on grounds of irrelevance. But that dismissal should not cause one to overlook the value of coherence as a criterion for rationality – where rationality may be demanded. Coherence remains an essential feature of certain mathematically oriented theories, which then have to meet the additional test emphasized by Frisch and Clemen – namely, relevance to the process of interest. Correspondence theory does not, of course, propose to meet the test of coherence, but it does propose to describe the process by which empirical accuracy is achieved.

The three features of good decision making offered by Frisch and Clemen may well be related to correspondence theory. As they note, "In our view the ultimate justification of a standard of decision making is empirical. This is in contrast to the SEU approach, which is based on the premise that the justification of a normative model is logical or mathematical,"[16] that is, coherence.

Herbert Simon's remarks about SEU theory make the distinction between coherence and correspondence clear:

> Conceptually, the SEU model is a beautiful object deserving a prominent place in Plato's heaven of ideas. But vast difficulties make it impossible to employ it in any literal way in making actual human decisions. . . .
>
> The SEU model assumes that the decision maker contemplates, in one comprehensive view, everything that lies before him. He understands the range of alternative choices open to him, not only at the moment but over the whole panorama of the future. He understands the consequences of each of the available choice strategies, at least up to the point of being able to assign a joint probability distribution to future states of the world. He has reconciled or balanced all his conflicting partial values and synthesized them into a single utility function that orders, by his preference for them, all these future states of the world. . . .
>
> When these assumptions are stated explicitly, it becomes obvious that SEU theory has never been applied, and never can be applied – with or without the largest computers – in the real world.[17]

Striking the final blow, he says: "I hope I have persuaded you that, in typical real-world situations, decision makers, no matter how badly they want to do so, simply cannot apply the SEU model."[18]

Having indicated how the coherence and correspondence theories provide a context for understanding judgment and decision making research, I now use them as a framework for discussing *competence*.

Finally, there is new evidence from the field of neuroscience that the coherence/correspondence distinction may well have a counterpart in the architecture and function of the brain. Vilayanur Ramachandran, a neurologist, has studied brain function in stroke victims, paying particular attention to the different forms of cognitive activity carried out by the left and right hemispheres of the brain. His studies – some of which are quite remarkable – lead him to conclude: "The left [hemisphere's] job is to create a model and maintain it at all costs"[19]; that is, the left hemisphere seeks coherence ("create[s] a model") from the information it has been provided and "maintains" the coherence of that model "at all costs." Although the latter phrase may be an exaggeration, we have all observed persons who hold firmly to a model (theory, ideology), and continue to maintain its truth despite all the evidence against it. Ramachandran goes on to say that "the right [hemisphere's] job is to detect anomalies," to discover instances in which the model is empirically erroneous. And "when anomalous information reaches a certain threshold, its job is to force the left hemisphere to revise the entire model and start from scratch."[20] A difficult task as we all know only too well. Without the left hemisphere to organize all the information in a coherent form, we would be hopelessly confused by all the information we receive from the world around us. As Ramachandran puts it: "At any given moment in our waking lives, . . . our brains are flooded with a bewildering variety of sensory inputs, all of which must be incorporated into a coherent perspective. . . . To act, the brain must have some way of selecting [and organizing detail into] . . . a story that makes sense."[21]

No wonder students of the history of science have found a persistent tension between coherence and correspondence. That tension appears to be built into our brains.

### A Framework for Evaluation of the Competence of Human Judgment

The principal components of the framework for our investigation of the competence of human judgment are the correspondence metatheory and the coherence metatheory; both have persisted in the history of science, and both persist today in the field of judgment and decision making. Although largely unrecognized by researchers, the great majority of studies in the field take place within one or other of these metatheories, and research results are obtained by virtue of their different methodologies. Once this is recognized, it becomes possible to understand – and to reconcile – conflicting and contradictory conclusions.

Correspondence theory focuses on the *empirical* accuracy of judgments, irrespective of whether the cognitive activity of the judge can be justified or even described. Although correspondence researchers may be interested in describing the processes that produce the judgment, they rarely inquire into the question of whether these processes are *rational*, that is, conform to some normative, or prescribed, model of how a judgment ought to be reached. They are interested, however, in the extent to which the experiments represent the conditions to which the results are generalized.

Coherence theorists have opposite interests; they examine the question of whether an individual's judgment processes meet the test of rationality – internal consistency – irrespective of whether the judgment is empirically accurate. Indeed, no test of empirical accuracy may be available in principle or fact. Thus, for example, if a problem is offered to a subject that is susceptible to a solution by a standard statistical model, the coherence theorist first compares the subject's answer with that produced by the statistical model, declares the answer to be correct or incorrect, tests (if possible) the process by which the answer is produced, and then evaluates the rationality of the cognitive process(es) involved. In addition, if the answer is incorrect, the research tradition has been to offer a description of the incorrect cognitive process, thus not only demonstrating irrationality but offering a description of the irrational "heuristic" that produced the "bias" that led to the wrong answer.

In short, correspondence theorists are interested in the way the mind works in relation to the way the world works, while coherence theorists are interested in the way the mind works in relation to the way it ought to work. That description is useful because it suggests immediately that each approach to the evaluation of competence in judgment has its own criteria. Correspondence researchers are interested in the empirical accuracy of judgments; coherence researchers are interested in the intentional rationality of judgments. What conclusions has each set of researchers drawn?

## Current Conclusions about the Competence of Human Judgment

Although the question of competence was present in the 1950s, it gained prominence in 1974 when A. Tversky and D. Kahneman[22] published research results and conclusions that led to what are now widely accepted negative views about the competence of human judgment. It may come as a surprise to some readers, but most students of judgment and decision making now regard the situation as "bleak"; human judgment, they believe, has been clearly demonstrated to be irrational, badly flawed, and generally not only wrong but overconfident; in a word, untrustworthy.[23]

### Coherence Theorists' Conclusions

The gestalt psychologists, prominent during the 1930s and 1940s, provide a natural background for the coherence theorists of today. The gestaltists' emphasis on "good figure," "completeness," "wholes," and pattern illustrates their interest in coherence rather than correspondence. In addition, their interest in perceptual illusions was a forerunner of modern judgment and decision-making coherence theorists' interest in "cognitive illusions."[24] Today's coherence theorists generally have little to say about the empirical accuracy of judgments; they also have little to say about adaptation, or functionalism, and, surprisingly, nothing to say about the relation of their work to that of the earlier coherence theorists, the gestalt psychologists. Current coherentists are more concerned with the rationality, that is, the prescriptive, logical, mathematical coherence of a person's cognitive activity and the description of the "cognitive illusions," labeled "heuristics."

Heuristics are precisely those cognitive activities that deceive us (thus "illusions") and prevent the achievement of coherence, and thus rationality. This work extends the gestalt psychologists' interest in perception to higher-level cognitive functions (albeit from a perspective different from that of the gestaltists).

Beginning in the 1970s Daniel Kahneman and Amos Tversky initiated a series of studies that described in detail the lack of coherence and therefore rationality in human judgment. Their anthology brings together an impressive body of evidence that supports their generally negative views of the competence of human judgment and the "cognitive illusions" or "biases" that, they argued, decrease it. Their work has resulted in the widespread use of these terms in the judgment and decision-making literature and beyond, a usage that reflects the authors' emphasis on error. Although these authors deny the charge that they have denigrated the rationality and competence of human judgment (e.g., "the focus on bias and illusion . . . neither assumes nor entails that people are perceptually or cognitively inept"[25]), the charge remains, for the denial seems disingenuous in view of the persistent demonstration – and celebration – of ineptness.[26]

The negative demonstrations of errors in probabilistic judgment by Kahneman and Tversky have become so widely accepted that by 1994 R. L. Klatzky, J. Geiwitz, and S. C. Fischer, writing in a book titled *Human Error in Medicine*, used them almost exclusively to illustrate physicians' errors in statistical reasoning.[27] Physicians and researchers reading this chapter on "using statistics" therefore learn only that a failure to achieve coherence in their judgments will lead to error and that achievement of coherence is enough to achieve competence. Avoiding "cognitive illusions" and achieving coherence came to exhaust the meaning of competence.

The negative conclusions regarding competence have been cited and quoted thousands of times by researchers and textbooks in a variety of disciplines, as well as in the popular literature, not only because of their significance but because of the simple and compelling nature of the demonstrations that produced them. For example, D. N. Kleinmuntz and D. A. Schkade state: "Two decades of research have emphasized the shortcomings of human judgment and decision-making processes,"[28] an emphasis that has rarely been disputed by psychologists (but frequently disputed by economists who believe that it contradicts fundamental premises of the "rational expectations" school in economics). The generally accepted pessimistic view of the quality of human judgment by researchers in this field should be given very serious consideration by those who must rely on it – and that means most of us most of the time. Because this conclusion is now accepted outside the narrow circle of judgment and decision making researchers, it may well turn out that research on judgment and decision making will provide the empirical support for Freud's third blow to our self-esteem that neither he nor his followers were able to offer.

Specifically, human judgments under uncertainty – probability judg-ments – are claimed to be subject to numerous "biases"; when we are asked to make probability judgments, our answers are biased and thus wrong. Here is an example that has been cited on numerous occasions:

Problem 1 ($N = 152$): Imagine that the U.S. is preparing for the outbreak of an unusual Asian disease, which is expected to kill 600 people. Two alternative pro-grams to combat the disease have been proposed. Assume that the exact scientific estimates of the consequences of the programs are as follows:

If Program A is adopted, 200 people will be saved. (72%)

If Program B is adopted, there is a one-third probability that 600 people will be saved and a two-thirds probability that no people will be saved. (28%)

Which of the two programs would you favor?[29]

Kahneman and Tversky report the responses to this question but first explain why the question is formulated as it is:

The formulation of Problem 1 implicitly adopts as a reference point a state of affairs in which the disease is allowed to take its toll of 600 lives. The outcomes of the programs include the reference state and two possible gains, measured by the number of lives saved. As expected, preferences are risk averse: A clear majority of respondents prefer saving 200 lives for sure over a gamble that offers a one-third chance of saving 600 lives. Now consider another problem in which the same cover story is followed by a different description of the prospects associated with the two programs:

Problem 2 ($N = 155$): If Program C is adopted, 400 people will die. (22%)

If Program D is adopted, there is a one-third probability that nobody will die and a two-thirds probability that 600 people will die. (78%)[30]

Kahneman and Tversky explain the nature of this problem as follows:

It is easy to verify that options C and D in Problem 2 are indistinguishable in real terms from options A and B in Problem 1, respectively. The second version, however, assumes a reference state in which no one dies of the disease. The best outcome is the maintenance of this state and the alternatives are losses measured by the number of people that will die of the disease. People who evaluate options in these terms are expected to show a risk seeking preference for the gamble (option D) over the sure loss of 400 lives. Indeed, there is more risk seeking in the second version of the problem than there is risk aversion in the first.[31]

When people are given the problem they do not see the numerical equiv-alence of the options; they do not see that options C and D are, as the authors put it, "indistinguishable in real terms" from options A and B. (Did the reader see this? If not, take another look at the problem and do the arithmetic.)

Similar errors have been demonstrated many times over a wide variety of problems. As a result, most students of judgment and decision making have attributed these errors to a fundamental flaw in the reasoning capacity of human beings.[32]

Thus, in the short space of twenty years Kahneman and Tversky and their colleagues have turned the field of judgment and decision making in a new direction. Moreover, they have given it a degree of visibility and prestige it never before enjoyed. Both authors received the Distinguished Scientist Award from the American Psychological Association and other prizes for their work. The publication of the anthology in 1982, barely ten years after their initial contributions were made, constituted a landmark in the field. The entire theme of this anthology is that human judgment under uncertainty is error-ridden and resistant to improvement and that a new approach to the study of human judgment is on its way. The anthology contains convincing evidence for all three points. Subsequent research has driven home the argument time and again. The recent textbook by S. Plous is an example of the enthusiasm with which the negative views of competence are presented; the text offers 252 pages of undiluted reports of studies that discover incompetence in virtually all aspects of judgment and decision making. (The alternative view gets five pages.)

But there has been serious dissent from these negative conclusions. Not every researcher in this field has accepted them, and some have bitterly resented them.[33]

### Correspondence Theorists' Conclusions

Correspondence theorists commit themselves, implicitly if not explicitly, to a Darwinian approach. They use either the term "adaptive"[34] or "functional,"[35] terms used in psychology since the early twentieth century to signify a Darwinian approach. The common research aim among these theorists is to examine the correspondence between a person's judgments and a specific state of the world to which those judgments are supposed to correspond (how often does it rain when the weather forecaster says it will?). They also share a common presumption, derived from their Darwinian commitment, namely, that a high degree of correspondence will in fact be found, for competence in the form of correspondence is fundamental to survival. It is natural to ask: How could human beings have been so successful in their survival if they did not make accurate judgments of the world around them?

The modern origin of the correspondence view of competence in judgment and decision making can be found in the classical treatment of perception by Egon Brunswik.[36] Brunswik challenged the gestalt psychologists' emphasis on perceptual illusions (which after all are perceptual inaccuracies) by presenting evidence for the high degree of accuracy of perception regarding events in the natural world outside the psychologists' artificial laboratory conditions. Brunswik's general theory of perception was introduced into the topic of judgment in 1955 by the present author[37] and has been further developed by many researchers (e.g., Björkman, Brehmer, Cooksey,

Doherty, Einhorn, Funder, Gigerenzer, Gillis, Holzworth, Joyce, Klayman, and Stewart[38]).

Correspondence theorists found competence to be largely determined by task conditions. In general, however, judgments mediated by perception (e.g., the visual perception of objects and events) have been found to be remarkably good but to become less so as judgment moves from *perceptual* to *conceptual* tasks and materials. That is, perceptual judgments of physical attributes such as size and color under a wide variety of conditions in the natural environment are excellent, but judgments and predictions about the behavior of objects and events (people, weather, economic conditions) that are complicated by considerable irreducible uncertainty, as well as by conceptual confusion, are often far from accurate. The central feature of the correspondence theory of judgment is its emphasis – inherited from Darwin – on the flexibility of the organism in its adaptive efforts, its multiple strategies, its ability to rely on various intersubstitutable features – what are called *multiple fallible indicators* – in the environment.

Thus, it is not surprising that the differences in viewpoint between those pursuing the question of competence within the frameworks of correspondence and coherence theories has produced tension between them.

### References and Notes

1  N. Adler. (1994). *Adolescent sexual behavior looks traditional – But looks are deceiving.* Washington, DC: Federation of Behavioral, Psychological, and Cognitive Sciences, p. 6.

2  Adler, p. 7.

3  Adler, p. 7.

4  G. Lowenstein & F. Furstenberg. (1991). Is teenage sexual behavior rational? *Journal of Applied Social Psychology, 21*, p. 983.

5  W. Edwards. (1954). The theory of decision making. *Psychological Bulletin, 41*, 380–417.

6  K. R. Hammond. (1955). Probabilistic functioning and the clinical method. *Psychological Review, 62*, 255–262.

7  P. Slovic & S. Lichtenstein. (1971). Comparison of Bayesian and regression approaches to the study of information processing in judgment. *Organizational Behavior and Human Performance, 6*, 649–744; P. Slovic & S. Lichtenstein. (1973). Comparison of Bayesian and regression approaches to the study of information processing in judgment. In L. Rappoport & D. A. Summers (Eds.), *Human judgment and social interaction* (pp. 16–108). New York: Holt, Rinehart, & Winston.

8  D. von Winterfeldt & W. Edwards. (1986). *Decision analysis and behavioral research.* Cambridge: Cambridge University Press.

9  R. Hastie & K. A. Rasinski. (1988). The concept of accuracy in social judgment. In D. Bar-Tal & A. W. Kruglanski (Eds.), *The social psychology of knowledge* (pp. 193–208). Cambridge: Cambridge University Press.

10  J. F. Yates. (1990). *Judgment and decision making.* Englewood Cliffs, NJ: Prentice-Hall.

11  Yates, pp. 137–139.

12  K. R. Hammond. (1990). Functionalism and illusionism: Can integration by usefully

achieved? In R. M. Hogarth (Ed.), *Insights in decision making: A tribute to Hillel J. Einhorn* (pp. 227–261). Chicago: University of Chicago Press, p. 256.

13  L. J. Savage. (1954). *The foundations of statistics*. New York: Wiley, p. 308.

14  D. Frisch & R. T. Clemen. (1994). Beyond expected utility: Rethinking behavioral decision research. *Psychological Bulletin, 116*, p. 48.

15  Frisch & Clemen, p. 49.

16  Frisch & Clemen, p. 52.

17  H. A. Simon. (1983). *Reason in human affairs*. Stanford, CA: Stanford University Press, pp. 13–14.

18  Simon, pp. 16–17. Despite the sharply worded argument by Simon, it is doubtful that the SEU theory is headed for extinction. In 1991, for example, Baron and Brown, two prominent researchers in the field of judgment and decision making, reprinted an article published in the *Washington Post* in 1988 in which they used SEU theory to demonstrate the value of teaching decision making to adolescents; see J. Baron & R. Brown. (1991). Prologue. In J. Baron & R. Brown (Eds.), *Teaching decision making to adolescents* (pp. 1–6). Hillsdale, NJ: Erlbaum.

19  Vilayanur Ramachandran quoted by S. Blakeslee. (1996, January 23). Figuring out the brain from its acts of denial. *New York Times*, p. B7.

20  Blakeslee, p. B7.

21  Blakeslee, p. B7.

22  See A. Tversky & D. Kahneman. (1974). Judgment under uncertainty: Heuristics and biases. *Science, 185*, 1124–1131; et seq.

23  For example, see R. M. Dawes. (1988). *Rational choice in an uncertain world*. San Diego: Harcourt, Brace, Jovanovich.

24  See D. Kahneman, P. Slovic, & A. Tversky. (Eds.). (1982). *Judgment under uncertainty: Heuristics and biases*. Cambridge: Cambridge University Press; et seq.

25  A. Tversky & D. Kahneman. (1983). Extensional versus intuitive reasoning: The conjunction fallacy in probability judgment. *Psychological Review, 90*, p. 313.

26  For example, see W. Edwards. (1992). Discussion: Of human skills. *Organizational Behavior and Human Decision Processes, 53*, 267–277; D. Funder. (1987). Errors and mistakes: Evaluating the accuracy of social judgment. *Psychological Bulletin, 101*, 75–90; G. Gigerenzer. (1991). From tools to theories: A heuristic of discovery in cognitive psychology. *Psychological Review, 98*, 254–267; G. Gigerenzer. (1991). How to make cognitive illusions disappear: Beyond "heuristics and biases." *European Review of Social Psychology, 2*, 83–115; G. Gigerenzer. (1991). On cognitive illusions and rationality. In E. Eells & T. Maruszewski (Eds.), *Probability and rationality: Studies on L. Jonathan Cohen's philosophy of science* (pp. 225–249). Amsterdam: Rodopi; G. Gigerenzer, U. Hoffrage, & H. Kleinbölting. (1991). Probabilistic mental models: A Brunswikian theory of confidence. *Psychological Review, 98*, 506–528.

27  R. L. Klatzky, J. Geiwitz, & S. C. Fischer. (1994). Using statistics in clinical practice: A gap between training and application. In M. S. Bogner (Ed.), *Human error in medicine* (pp. 123–140). Hillsdale, NJ: Erlbaum.

28  D. N. Kleinmuntz & D. A. Schkade. (1993). Information displays and decision processes. *Psychological Science, 4*, p. 221.

29  D. Kahneman & A. Tversky. (1984). Choices, values, and frames. *American Psychologist, 39*, p. 343.

30  Kahneman & Tversky, p. 343.

31  Kahneman & Tversky, p. 343.

32  For examples, see H. R. Arkes & K. R. Hammond. (Eds.). (1986). *Judgment and decision making: An interdisciplinary reader*. Cambridge: Cambridge University Press;

Kahneman, Slovic, & Tversky. For a textbook completely devoted to this point of view, see especially S. Plous. (1993). *The psychology of judgment and decision making*. Philadelphia: Temple University Press.

33 For example, see Edwards, Discussion.

34 J. R. Anderson. (1990). *The adaptive character of thought*. Hillsdale, NJ: Erlbaum.

35 B. Brehmer. (1994). The psychology of linear judgement models. *Acta Psychologica, 87*, 137–154; E. Brunswik. (1952). The conceptual framework of psychology. In *International encyclopedia of unified science* (Vol. 1, no. 10, pp. 4–102). Chicago: University of Chicago Press; E. Brunswik. (1956). *Perception and the representative design of psychological experiments* (2nd ed.). Berkeley, CA: University of California Press; S. Epstein. (1994). Integration of the cognitive and the psychodynamic unconscious. *American Psychologist, 49*, 709–724; K. R. Hammond. (Ed.). (1966). *The psychology of Egon Brunswik* (2nd ed.). New York: Holt, Rinehart, and Winston; K. R. Hammond, R. M. Hamm, J. Grassia, & T. Pearson. (1986). Direct comparison of the efficacy of intuitive and analytical cognition in expert judgment. *IEEE Transactions on Systems, Man, and Cybernetics, 17*, 753–770.

36 Brunswik, The conceptual framework; *Perception and the representative design*.

37 Hammond, Probabilistic functioning.

38 For an anthology of studies, see B. Brehmer & C. R. B. Joyce. (Eds.). (1988). *Human judgment: The SJT view*. Amsterdam: Elsevier. For a detailed application of the theory, see R. Cooksey. (1996). *Judgment analysis: Theory, methods, and applications*. San Diego: Academic Press. Bruner, Goodnow, & Austin's classic *The study of thinking* was dedicated to Brunswik: J. S. Bruner, J. Goodnow, & G. A. Austin. (1956). *A study of thinking*. New York: Wiley.

# 4    Enhancing Diagnostic Decisions

*John A. Swets*

## Is It There, or Is It Not? That Is the Diagnostic Question

My research interest is in discrimination and decision making in diagnostic situations and particularly in improving those processes in practice. A simple definition of a diagnostic situation is that it is one in which repetitive choices must be made between two competing alternatives. There are more detailed definitions, but most situations are adequately characterized by the simple definition. A doctor reading mammograms to determine if they are indicative or not indicative of breast cancer is an example. Looking at available weather data to determine whether or not a storm is on its way is another example. The common thread that ties these diagnostic situations together is that they are all instances in which information is used to decide whether or not a specified condition – cancer, stormy weather, and so on – is present (Swets, 1996, 1997; Swets & Pickett, 1982). In the jargon of my research specialty, this is called signal detection. The question held in common across diagnostic situations is this: Is the signal present or not? Or in the extension to recognition: Is it signal A or signal B?

My thesis is that there are diagnostic support techniques available that can greatly enhance the ability of diagnosticians to correctly detect the signal and, further, that these techniques are largely unknown to diagnosticians and are rarely applied in many very important diagnostic settings. These neglected opportunities for application include diagnostic arenas that are important to us as individuals and as a society.

The techniques I am going to describe are well tested. They have been used in enough diagnostic settings to have proven their worth. I will give several

A version of this chapter was presented orally at the Seminar on Science and Public Policy organized by the Federation of Behavioral, Psychological and Cognitive Sciences, and held at the Rayburn House Office Building in Washington, D.C. on September 6, 1991. The author would like to thank Dr. David Johnson, Executive Director of the Federation, for permission to include the presentation in this book of readings.

examples of those applications. However, the techniques are not widely practiced, with the result that accuracy levels across a variety of diagnostic settings are substantially less than they could be. So a professional and public policy question arises: What can be done to see that these techniques come into use in the settings where they ought to be used? This policy question is unlike many others in that the solution exists. The science is there. The problem lies in achieving widespread implementation.

Before proceeding, I'll give some other examples of diagnostic questions whose answers could be improved by application of these techniques: Is this aircraft fit to fly? Is that plane intending to attack this ship? Is this nuclear power plant malfunctioning? Is this assembly line item flawed? Does this patient have the AIDS virus? Is this person lying? Is this football player using drugs? Will this school, or job, applicant succeed? Does this tax return justify an audit? Is there oil beneath this ground? Will the stock market advance? Will this prisoner vindicate a furlough or a parole? Are there explosives in this luggage? Does this document contain the information that I need?

## Evidence Is a Matter of Degree in Diagnostic Situations

What all these examples highlight is that diagnostic evidence for a positive decision is a matter of degree. The information is probabilistic. It is not cut and dried. If it were, there would not be a diagnostic problem. Such evidence can be thought of as lying along a probabilistic scale. It is evident that, to make a decision based on such information, a decision threshold must be set somewhere along that scale. A cutoff point is needed. That is, one must decide how much evidence (how high a probability) is needed to warrant a positive decision. There are good ways and bad ways to set that threshold, as I shall discuss.

A second thing the examples illustrate is that diagnostic tests are not perfectly accurate. We would not call them diagnostic tests if they could guarantee total accuracy. So our decision support systems need to accomplish two tasks. They need to help us determine a threshold of evidence that is sufficient to make a decision in a given situation; they need to help us set a decision threshold. I will call this a type 1 decision support system. They also need to help us determine what information will make it most likely that we will make an accurate decision. I will call this a type 2 decision support system.

First I wish to show you through examples how to set the decision threshold in the right place. Then I want to show how diagnostic accuracy can be substantially improved. Setting the decision threshold and making an accurate diagnosis are not the same thing. Decision thresholds and accuracy must each be considered in their own right.

## The Challenge of a Type 1 System Is to Balance Hits and False Alarms

As a device for helping us think about these two aspects of diagnostic decision making, I have two graphs. I will build my discussion of the type 1, or threshold setting, decision support system around the first graph (Figure 4.1). Then I will use the second graph (see Figure 4.2) to illustrate my explanation of the type 2 decision support system, which has to do with enhancing accuracy.

To understand both graphs, it is necessary to know that, in any two-alternative or yes–no decision-making situation, there are four possible decision outcomes. You can say "yes" and be right or wrong or you can say "no" and be right or wrong. In medicine, we talk about these outcomes as true and false positives and true and false negatives. In signal detection theory, we refer to true and false positives as hits and false alarms, and to true and false negatives as peace-and-quiet and misses.

When you analyze a diagnostic situation, however, you need to look at only two of the possible outcomes because the other two are their complements. Both graphs plot true positives – or hits – verses false positives – or false alarms. The way these two vary together, as the decision threshold

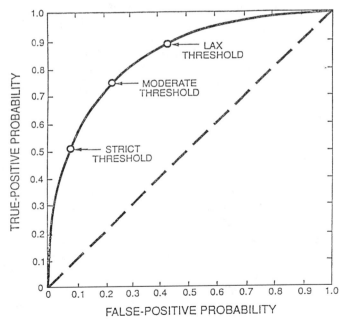

Figure 4.1. Decision thresholds.

varies, tells us essentially all we need to know about where the decision threshold is set and how accurate the diagnostic test is.

The curve of Figure 4.1 represents the fact that true and false positives go up or down together. This is the same as saying that if we want more hits, or true positives, with a given diagnostic system, we are going to have to accept more false alarms as well. There is no free lunch. If we want fewer false alarms, we must go down that curve in terms of the probability of true positives. What we want to do is set a decision threshold that constitutes a reasonable, rational, desirable balance between those two kinds of outcomes.

Figure 4.1 shows at the upper part of the curve a lax, or lenient, decision threshold. At that threshold, one would say yes often. In other words, one would not require very strong evidence to say yes. Both true and false positives are quite probable under the lax threshold, and that stands to reason: If we say yes a lot, we are going to get many hits and many false alarms. There are situations where you would want a lax threshold. Such might be the case if you are predicting a serious storm. You would rather risk a false alarm than a miss. An error of commission is no fun, but an error of omission is a lot less fun in this case. Your audience might be inconvenienced in preparing for a storm that does not come, but not nearly as inconvenienced as it would be if the storm battered them unexpectedly. Therefore, you would not require much evidence to say the storm is coming. Breast cancer presents a similar example. Radiologists reading mammograms will recommend follow-up of some kind at the slightest indication of a malignancy. It makes little sense to do anything less because doing tests that turn out to be unnecessary may cost money and duress, but not doing tests that needed to be done may cost a life.

Figure 4.1 also illustrates a strict threshold, at the lower left side of the curve. At this decision threshold, one says yes rarely. We have fewer false positives in this case than at the lax threshold, but we also have fewer true positives. Since the case of Willie Horton, which you may recall from a former presidential campaign, I understand the country's governors have become much more conservative about permitting furloughs and paroles. They have moved to a stricter threshold on such decisions, requiring more evidence of rehabilitation before agreeing to a parole or furlough of a possibly dangerous prisoner.

Another classic case of a strict threshold, and of changed thresholds, has to do with a military response to an enemy attack. In peacetime at least, one does not want to retaliate against a supposed threat that is not real. One wants strong evidence that there is an attack before launching a counterattack. To make a mistake could cause an international incident, maybe even a war. Let me remind you of the Navy ships, the *Stark* and the *Vincennes*. The crew of the *Stark* could not decide for sure that their ship was being attacked by an enemy plane. It turned out that it was attacked, and damaged, and there was loss of life. The crew had too strict a threshold for making a positive decision about the attack. The crew of the *Vincennes*, on the other hand, thought that their ship was being attacked. As a result, they shot down a passenger plane, causing the loss of hundreds of innocent lives. The decision threshold for the *Vincennes* crew was too lax. Between those two incidents, I can imagine the Navy shifting the threshold. Before the *Stark* incident, Navy officials may have felt it was most important not to respond to a false alarm. But such a dramatic miss as the *Stark* attack changes things. After the *Stark*, it may have seemed more reasonable to risk a false alarm since it would prevent another *Stark* incident. Then the *Vincennes* came along and demonstrated that too lax a threshold can be as unfortunate as too strict a threshold.

### Base Rate, Analysis of Costs and Benefits, and the Decision Threshold

In the ideal situation, two kinds of information are needed to calculate the best decision threshold: base rates and an analysis of costs and benefits. Base rate refers to the probability or frequency of occurrence of the event in question. A base rate question is, How often does breast cancer occur among women in the 25- to 35-year-old age range? The answer will have an impact on where one chooses to set a decision threshold. The other consideration that matters most is a measurement of relative cost against relative benefit of a given decision. Again, you can think of breast cancer. To first order, the benefit of a correct positive diagnosis may be that a life is saved. The costs of an incorrect positive diagnosis are the anguish of the person who believes for a time that she has cancer, the discomfort of the biopsy, and the cost of the tissue sample tests.

If, in a given diagnostic situation, the base rate is high and the cost of a miss is also high, then you would be inclined to set a lax threshold. Alternatively, if an event occurs rarely, and the cost of deciding that the event is occurring when it is not is high, then you would be inclined toward a stricter threshold. That is the lesson to be derived from the *Vincennes* incident. In repetitive diagnoses, the base rate and costs and benefits can be taken into account mathematically, with the result that the best point at which to place the decision threshold may be determined with some precision for a given diagnostic situation. From the technical point of view, we use the values for base rate, and costs and benefits in a formula to determine a slope for the curve (of Figure 4.1) at the point that is the best threshold. So, for example, if the formula yields a slope of $\frac{1}{2}$, then we can draw a line with such a slope, see where it touches the curve, and set the decision threshold at that point (Swets, 1992).

Base rates and costs and benefits provide the strongest means for determining the best decision threshold, but they are not the only factors that may be taken into account to establish the best decision threshold for a given diagnostic situation. In some cases, they may not be the most appropriate factors to take into account. It may be the case that it is very difficult to estimate costs and benefits in a particular diagnostic situation. Say, for example, that human lives are concerned. It is very difficult to set a value on life. You may not want to put something like that into a mathematical formula. You need not do so. There are softer ways to set the threshold that do not require an explicit definition of benefit or cost in terms of dollars.

As an alternative, for example, you might decide that you want your false alarm rate to stay below a certain rate. Consider again the case of breast cancer. In this case, you may want a certain number of your positive predictions to be correct. At question here is whether or not you recommend a biopsy based on your prediction. You want a certain number of those biopsy recommendations to have been justified. You can't set an extremely lax threshold such that the great majority of biopsies come back negative. There are not enough surgeons and pathologists to go around. The procedure is not easy on the patient, and there is growing concern in the medical community and among patients about doing unnecessary tests. By the same token, you can't set a strict threshold because you do not want to tell people who have cancer that they do not have it. You might say, for example, that you want three of ten biopsies to be positive, that is, you want the yield of biopsies to be three out of ten. That, in fact, is about what the current yield of biopsy is in the United States. In England the yield is closer to five out of ten. They are more conservative in recommending biopsy than we are. At any rate, determining the desired yield is a second way to set a reasonable decision threshold, and it does not require explicit definition of all the benefits and costs and probabilities. There are other means to determine proper thresholds; suffice it to say that they are all aimed at determining the best slope at which to intersect the curve. They are all aimed at setting the best decision threshold for each diagnostic situation (Swets, 1992).

## The Challenge of a Type 2 System Is to Maximize Accuracy

Now let us look at Figure 4.2 to help us consider the type 2 decision support system, that having to do with maximizing the accuracy of diagnoses. Figure 4.2 is, again, a plot of the true-positive probability against the false-positive probability. Incidentally, such a graph is called a "relative operating characteristic" and is known as an "ROC" graph (Swets, 1988, 1996). Figure 4.2 illustrates three nominal systems having either low, medium, or high accuracy. The first thing this graph tells you is that each diagnostic system has its own inherent accuracy. Some are more accurate than others. The closer the curve representing the accuracy of a diagnostic system comes to the dashed line, the less accurate the system. That line represents chance accuracy, a situation in which there are, on the average, as many hits as false alarms. As the curve moves up toward the northwest corner of the graph, the accuracy of the system approaches perfection. That is, it approaches a

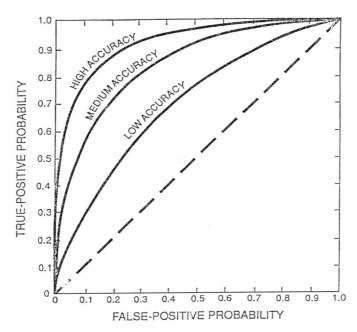

Figure 4.2. Decision accuracy.

situation in which each decision is a hit; there are no false alarms. A system with all hits and no false alarms is a perfect system. Systems come in all degrees of accuracy. Thus, the graph gives you two essential pieces of information. It tells you where the decision threshold actually is. You can go beyond that threshold by deciding where the threshold ought to be. The graph also tells you how accurate the system is. Again, you can improve the accuracy by certain procedures I'll discuss next.

The accuracy of a diagnostic system may be increased by improving the quality of the evidence that one is working with. There are systematic ways to do that, and those methods are known to psychologists, psychometricians, and statisticians. The task is to find the features of the available evidence that are truly diagnostic. You would identify, for example, the perceptual features of the mammogram that are most often associated with true-positive diagnoses, that is, with a correct diagnosis of cancer. Of course radiologists try to do this for every kind of imaging technique and disease. What I am suggesting, however, is that this process of identifying diagnostic features can be gone about in a systematic way, such that the diagnostically most relevant features can be defined much more precisely than they would be otherwise (Swets, 1997).

The relative importance of each item in a set of diagnostically relevant features may also be determined in this systematic way. The idea is to find the dozen or so most important perceptual features out of the many dozens of possible perceptual features and then to order these important features in terms of their relative importance. In the case of the mammogram, there may be a mass apparent. It may have spiculation, that is, a spiky border, or otherwise the border may be smooth. The question is, What features are important, and, among those features, which are more important and which are less important?

### Methods to Improve Diagnoses Are Available but Often Go Unused

To anticipate, I'll mention some critically important diagnostic situations in which the decision support techniques are used and others in which they are not. Weather forecasters are very conscious of accuracy and decision thresholds. In fact, you know that when weather forecasters predict rain they do not tell you it is going to rain. They tell you the probability that it will rain, and they leave it to you to set your own decision threshold. You decide what level of probability is sufficient to warrant your taking your umbrella with you to work. You know the personal costs and benefits associated with your decision. More seriously in this same domain, you might have to decide whether or not to protect your crop against frost. You have to look at the risk, the probability that the cold weather will come, and then weigh the cost of taking protective measures against the cost of losing the crop. The forecaster tells you the probability that the frost will occur. You provide the cost–benefit analysis. Performance and aptitude testing is another area where attention is paid to decision thresholds and accuracy. Test theorists worry a lot about the length of their test, the validity of their items, and so forth, and employers and colleges determine cutoff scores. The IRS is getting rather sophisticated about deciding whether or not to audit your tax return. They look at lots of pieces of information and assign them relative weights to determine whether to have a look at you. Geologists looking for oil are also sophisticated in the methods they use for determining whether or not to drill.

### Decision Thresholds Could Improve AIDS Diagnoses

Consider two examples where these techniques ought to be, but are not being, applied. The first area is testing for the human immunodeficiency virus (HIV) of AIDS and the second is looking for cracks in airplane wings. In both of these critical areas, there is little sophistication in deciding where to set the decision threshold, and there is little attention paid to improving the accuracy of the judgments. I think you will be surprised at how poorly these two diagnostic tasks are done. I am sure you will grant me that these are situations of importance both for individuals and for society (Swets, 1992).

First, let us look at testing for HIV. What are some of the factors that would influence where the decision threshold should be set? One consideration is the domain in which the decision is made. Are you deciding whether a donated pint of blood contains the virus or are you making the decision about a real live patient sitting in front of you? You ought to set your decision threshold in a different place for each of these diagnostic domains. Destroying a good batch of blood is one thing, but mistakenly telling a person he or she has AIDS is quite another. The costs and benefits present in each of these two situations are quite different from each other. It is also important to understand that the base rate probability of presence of HIV varies tremendously in different samples of the population. In low-risk populations, the probability of occurrence is about 30 in 100,000. Higher risk populations have occurrences in the 95 to 100 per 100,000 range. Among military recruits, the incidence is about 150 per 100,000. Among individuals seen in methadone clinics, the incidence is about 50,000 per 100,000. So the base rate varies across different populations from .0003 to .5.

As I have said, the frequency of occurrence should have a bearing on where you set the decision threshold. If the likelihood that HIV is present is high, then you want a decision threshold that is going to assure that you will spot it. But if you use a lax threshold with a low-frequency population, the results could be terrible. You could be telling thousands of people erroneously that they have the AIDS virus. There are other considerations that should be taken into account, for example, whether the test is mandatory or not, and mandatory for whose benefit? You would want to set the threshold differently for those who must take the test because their insurance company requires it, or because they travel internationally, than you would for someone who comes to you and requests the test. Whether or not there is effective therapy available is another factor that can bear on how inclined you might be to say that a person does or does not have the AIDS virus. Those are a few of the considerations that should go into setting decision thresholds for diagnosis of HIV.

What happens in practice? The decision thresholds are set and remain fixed, with one exception that I will describe. There is no attention paid to these very different diagnostic settings. The HIV test manufacturers set the decision threshold to get the test approved by the Food and Drug Administration, and the test is used at that decision threshold. Surprising to me is that the thresholds for certain tests – the so-called EIA or enzyme-linked immunoassay tests, which are the most used tests for screening for HIV – were designed to sample blood, and then, when those tests came to be used for human patients, the threshold was not changed. A couple of friends of mine who work in decision analysis at Massachusetts General Hospital went to one of the EIA test manufacturers and offered to cooperate with them to write some software that would help doctors decide, based on the characteristics of their diagnostic situation, what decision threshold to set. (The fact is that it is very easy to quantify any given decision threshold in HIV testing. It is nowhere near as difficult as quantifying decision thresholds in the reading of mammograms. In the HIV case, the output of the EIA test is a number issued by a machine, corresponding to an optical density. The output is scaled along a continuum of numbers, and so it is easy to quantify a cutoff level. Moreover, it is easy to design software for the physician who would then select the diagnostic situation – as represented by the probability of occurrence and the costs and benefits – and then the program would give back the decision threshold indicated by those selections.) But the drug company was not interested. The test had already been approved. It appeared that revisiting threshold levels was too touchy a thing to do.

Now, it is the case in human HIV testing that if the screening test is taken to be positive, then another presumably more conclusive test, the Western blot test, is given. In the case of that test, however, the decision threshold is set in a given place depending on some chemical considerations, without explicit reference to the costs and benefits and the probabilities that vary by diagnostic situation. It is also the case that using two tests does not guarantee perfect accuracy by any means. Consider a firm of 100,000 employees that wants to set up testing for the entire firm. With the two tests for HIV operating at their estimated ideal performance, if the prevalence probability is 12 in 100,000 in the firm's population of employees, then the tests would find the 12 and would mistakenly identify 5 additional people. If, however, the tests were operating at only their estimated actual efficiency level, they would find the 12 but they would erroneously identify another 80 as having the virus (Bloom & Glied, 1991). So having two tests is certainly a precaution, but it does not solve the whole problem. It is desirable to adjust the thresholds in the two tests taking into account, among other things, that the threshold set for the second test should be partially dependent on the particular quantitative result of the first test.

I should mention that there are actually three popular, and much used, EIA tests for HIV. Two of them have about the same decision threshold. But one is on the high accuracy curve and the other is on the medium accuracy curve of Figure 4.2. The third one has a decision threshold that is much more lenient than either of those two (Swets, 1992). The question is, why are these three tests in such different places with respect to accuracy and decision threshold? And why are they all approved and used? For example, the one that is most lenient relative to the stricter one of the same accuracy picks up 95% rather than 92% of the positive cases at a cost of going from .05 to .17 on the false-positive probability scale. Maybe that more lenient threshold is rational and maybe it is not. My argument is that the FDA should be self-conscious about what the accuracies are and where the decision thresholds are when approving tests.

Testing for HIV seems to be a situation in which test developers and test approvers seem to have little interest in taking the steps that would lead to improved accuracy. Just a word about the issue of getting these diagnostic decision improvement techniques used: How might it be accomplished? It seems clear that one would have to concentrate on working with the user communities – the physicians, the directors of counseling and testing centers – to arrive at appropriate thresholds. Here a difficulty is that physicians, initially at least, have very different ideas about what those thresholds ought to be. I'll give a few pieces of data regarding that point. A survey of directors of counseling and testing centers asked the directors, How probable would the presence of HIV in one of your patients have to be before you would discuss decreased life expectancy with that patient? Twenty-five percent of the physicians gave a probability less than .15. So the probability that the patient had the virus would have to be only 15% before those physicians would discuss decreased life expectancy with the patient. On the other hand, 50% of the respondents to the survey said they would require a probability of .95 before they would have such a discussion with the patient. Thus, there is tremendously wide variation of opinion among physicians on this matter. They were also asked at what probability of infection they would advise the patient against pregnancy. Forty-three percent said a probability no greater than 15% would be enough to advise against it. Thirty percent would not discuss it unless the probability were 95%. Clearly, one would have to get the decision theory advocates together with the users to work out how these decision aids would be used.

## Diagnostic Aids Can Improve Accuracy of Cancer Diagnoses

The AIDS example had to do with improving the decision threshold. Next is an example of improving the accuracy of diagnosis. The work of my colleagues and me in this area, as you have probably gathered, has concerned improving the accuracy of breast cancer diagnoses based on mammograms. As I suggested earlier, what we have done is to identify the visual features of mammograms that have predictive value. This determination can be made in various ways. One can interview specialists. They might identify 50 features. They did in our case. Those lists are pruned. Different radiologists, for example, call the same thing by different names. Two items may be different but are so highly correlated that there is no need to keep track of both of them. So we prune the list to a necessary and sufficient set. We also do perceptual tests. We have radiologists judge the similarity of two images, and we do multidimensional scaling analysis to derive the dimensions of the perceptual space. These dimensions are candidates for perceptual features to consider for the final set. We might have 30 features at that point. Then we do a multivariate statistical analysis to determine which of those features are worth keeping. That gets us down to about a dozen critical features. We take those 12 features and devise a checklist for them; usually with a 10-point scale for each feature. For example, the radiologist can scale how fuzzy the border of the mass is or how clustered the microcalcifications are. There are also scales for shape and size and each of the other critical features. We put those scale ratings into a computer program to aid the radiologist in practice. The program merges the ratings, assigns an appropriate relative weight to each feature, and turns out a probability of malignancy.

Thus, we have given two aids to the radiologist. One is the checklist. The other is the computer-based pattern analyzer that uses the information from the checklist to give back a probability that cancer is present. The radiologist might enter the rating information and get back a .78. This means that, based on the scaling of the 12 critical features, the likelihood the patient has cancer is 78%. At that point the radiologist can say, "I think the probability is more like .85 because I saw some other things not accounted for in the checklist." That is fine. The radiologist can consider the aids to be advisory.

We find that when we give radiologists these two aids they make substantially more accurate diagnoses. They move approximately from the level of medium accuracy on Figure 4.2 to the level of high accuracy. That means they are gaining about .15 in their true-positive probability. Out of 100 patients with cancer they diagnose, they are accurately spotting 15 more cancers than they were before. You can look at that the other way around, too. That is, in terms of what in medical circles is called "specificity" or the relative number of false positives. The aids are reducing the number of people told erroneously that they probably have cancer by about 15 in 100. These are fairly sizable numbers of additional cases correctly identified as the result of these decision aids (Getty et al., 1988; Swets et al., 1991).

The radiologists we have worked with have been pleased to see this. They have been very cooperative. They are, of course, interested in doing better. They are also interested in standardizing their techniques across radiologists. If these aids are approved by the American College of Radiologists (ACR), and if all radiologists use the aids, then there should be a substantial improvement in the accuracy of breast cancer diagnoses from mammograms. We have worked with the ACR to develop the set of features, as well as a lexicon for those features, that mammographers now use widely, though without the computer aid. If all this is successful, there will be enhanced motivation to use the aids. Not only will they afford enhanced accuracy, but they will also afford standardization.

The National Cancer Institute, the Food and Drug Administration, the Centers for Disease Control, and the American College of Radiologists are working together to standardize mammographic reports. These are the reports to the clinician, to the surgeon. Surgeons have been complaining that the reports are not standardized and that the radiologists are not being very committal in their diagnoses. The surgeons claim the national flower of the radiologists is the hedge. The idea now is to standardize the reports and make them more informative. Our technique is a way of doing this, not just in terms of the language used in the reports, but also in terms of the perceptual features that lie behind the words that are used to tell the surgeon what the probability of cancer is (D'Orsi et al., 1992). The point I want to make is that, in some areas of medicine – mammography, for example – these techniques are being used in at least a preliminary way, and, in some areas – AIDS screening, for example – they are not even being considered.

### An Effort to Improve Staging Diagnoses for Prostate Cancer

Another cancer project in my laboratory concerns the staging of prostate cancer by magnetic resonance imaging (MRI). Staging means to determine whether the disease is extensive or confined to the gland; in the former case, treatments are often merely palliative; in the latter case, surgical removal may be possible. We have found enhancements of MRI accuracy in this situation similar to those described above for breast cancer (Seltzer et al., 1997). MRI can be used effectively in cases for which the common clinical tests are inconclusive.

### How Often Do Experts Spot Cracks in Airplane Wings?

As mentioned earlier, images are also used to detect metal fatigue in aircraft. I have some data from an Air Force study in which 150 metal specimens were assembled – some with cracks, some without – and taken to 17 different Air Force bases. Technicians at each of the bases were asked to examine images of the specimens (acquired by ultrasound and eddy current) and determine which specimens had cracks and which did not. On a graph like those of Figures 4.1 and 4.2, the proportions of decisions of approximately 125 technicians were plotted with respect to their accuracy and their decision threshold, that is, one point per observer. The graph of their overall performance looked like a picture of measles. The scores of the 125 technicians were spread over the entire usable space (the upper diagonal half) of the graph. They varied from chance accuracy to very good accuracy. They varied from being very strict in calling a crack in an airplane wing to being very lax. Again, they varied over the whole usable space of the graph, under no apparent control (Swets, 1992).

The data show that the accuracies of people at a given base were similar. That is, at a good base, all the technicians were good. At a bad base, all the technicians were bad. It was clear, therefore, that one could go to the best base and fruitfully study what those really expert technicians were doing. That is, one could capture it in terms of the visual features they were looking at, bottle that wisdom, so to speak, and carry it to the other bases so technicians there could be good as well. I have been trying for several years to get people to become interested in trying some of these techniques to improve the diagnosis of cracks in airplane wings. So far, I have had no success. For the moment, one has to hope that any plane one flies on was checked at a good facility rather than a poor one (Swets, 1983).

## NASA Wants to Improve Diagnoses of Dangerous Flight Conditions

Meanwhile, on a more positive note, we have been working with NASA lately to look at their diagnostic systems for providing warnings in the cockpit: collision avoidance and wind shear detection, for example. They are getting very interested in deciding how to enhance these detection accuracies and in determining where to set the decision threshold. They are concerned about the positive predictive value of an alert. If, out of 10 alerts, one of them is a true alert and 9 of them are false alerts, that is bad. The busy pilot is going to stop paying attention to the alerts, or at least delay a response. NASA wants to know what false alarm rate people will tolerate. The accuracy is important as well. Take wind shear detection as an example. There are instruments on the plane and instruments on the ground that provide data on wind shear. The data from all the instruments are fused into a diagnostic probability. It is a technique similar to fusing features in a mammogram evaluation. The trick is to put the right weights on the various detectors depending on how reliable each is. You also have to put the threshold in the right place, however, because the cost for not doing so can be very high. I am told, for example, that if a pilot flying into Chicago is told to go around because of wind shear, then it takes three hours for the air traffic control system to get back to some semblance of normalcy. That means that a false positive can interrupt the system for three hours. On the other hand, of course, if wind shear is there, you would not want a plane to fly into it. It is a tough problem, but one that can be approached with some of the quantitative techniques I have mentioned (Getty et al., 1995).

## Other Benefits of Decision Support Techniques

Beyond immediate improvements in accuracy and decision threshold, the decision support techniques can bring improvements in other facets of diagnostics that carry with them the assurance of greater quality. I mentioned the standardization of radiologists' reports. Communication among radiologists, for example, second opinions, is another example where quantitative assessments of image features would help. Building a quantitative feature-oriented data base could have several ramifications. It could be used to construct (automatically) individualized tutoring programs that are tailored to the difficulties a given radiologist may have with particular perceptual features. It could also be used to help adjust decision thresholds so that, for example, the yield of biopsy in breast-cancer diagnosis would be in a desired range (D'Orsi et al., 1992).

## The Public Policy Question

Let me close by returning to what I think of as a practical question this work raises. How can we get these techniques used, or at least considered, in situations where they would be useful? It is very difficult for an individual who is working in the behavioral or information or decision sciences to go to a regulatory agency like the Food and Drug Administration or the Federal Aviation Administration and say, "Hey, we have some good ideas." I say it is difficult because those agencies have front-line responsibilities that severely challenge their resources. They have problems that seem more pressing than the problems that we are offering to solve. It is not easy to go to medical societies either. It is not easy to tell physicians how to run their business. (The radiologists have been an exception. They have been receptive, but they may be a different breed. They are quantitatively trained, whereas most other physicians are not.) The question for us is how, as scientists and citizens, can we improve the situation. How can the diffusion of knowledge and technology be hastened when lives are at stake? There are no easy answers, but the problem deserves the consideration of those us interested in applications of research.

### References

Bloom, D. E., & Glied, S. (1991). Benefits and costs of HIV testing. *Science, 252,* 1798–1804.

D'Orsi, C. J., Getty, D. J., Swets, J. A., et al. (1992). Reading and decision aids for improved accuracy and standardization of mammographic diagnosis. *Radiology, 184,* 619–622.

Getty, D. J., Swets, J. A., Pickett, R. M., & Gonthier, D. (1995). System operator response to warnings of danger: A laboratory investigation of the effects of the predictive value of a warning on human response time. *Journal of Experimental Psychology: Applied, 1,* 19–33.

Getty, D. J., Pickett, R. M., D'Orsi, C. J., & Swets, J. A. (1988). Enhanced interpretation of diagnostic images. *Investigative Radiology, 23,* 240–252.

Seltzer, S. E., Getty, D. J., Tempany, C. M. C., et al. (1997). Staging prostate cancer with MR imaging: A combined radiologist-computer system. *Radiology, 202,* 219–226.

Swets, J. A. (1983). Assessment of nondestructive-testing systems – Part I: The relationship of true and false detections; Part II: Indices of performance. *Materials Evaluation, 41,* 1294–1303.

Swets, J. A. (1988). Measuring the accuracy of diagnostic systems. *Science, 240,* 1285–1293.

Swets, J. A. (1992). The science of choosing the right decision threshold in high stakes diagnostics. *American Psychologist, 47,* 522–532.

Swets, J. A. (1996). *Signal detection theory & ROC analysis in psychology and diagnostics: Collected papers*. Mahwah, NJ: Erlbaum.

Swets, J. A. (1997). Separating discrimination and decision in detection, recognition, and matters of life and death: Vol. 4. *Methods, models, and conceptual issues*. In D. N. Osherson (Series Ed.), J. D. Scarborough, & S. Sternberg (Vol. Eds.), *An invitation to cognitive science*. Cambridge, MA: MIT Press,

Swets, J. A., Getty, D. J., Pickett, R. M., et al. (1991). Enhancing and evaluating diagnostic accuracy. *Medical Decision Making, 11*, 9–18.

Swets, J. A., & Pickett, R. M. (1982). *Evaluation of diagnostic systems: Methods from signal detection theory*. New York: Academic Press.

# Part II

# Applications in Public Policy

Since decisions in the public policy arena have the largest potential to affect many people, they have been of special interest to JDM researchers. Power plant siting, medical reimbursement, educational innovation, crime policy, even war and peace: Most of the really huge decisions fall under the heading of public policy. If these decisions are defective, the consequences of the errors are enormous. Should we be concerned? Several of the authors whose work is sampled in this section suggest that we should. Thaler, in the first chapter, suggests that our thinking about public policy issues is likely to be clouded by what he terms "illusions and mirages" – cognitive phenomena that can be readily demonstrated in the laboratory and which, if generalizable to real-world settings, would seem to produce undesirable results. (The link to the heuristics and biases ideas and coherence metatheories will be apparent). Thaler's wit and gift for the vivid example makes such generalization plausible.

A more detailed development of the lab-to-policy path is provided by Arkes and Blumer, in the second chapter of the section. The authors here review a series of experiments on the sunk cost effect, the tendency (universally deplored by economists) to increase investment of time, money, or effort once one has made an initial investment in a project – to "throw good money after bad." What makes the sunk cost effect so interesting is the ease with which most of us are lured into the trap, despite our ready agreement that sunk costs should not count. Still more alarming is to hear senior public officials (such as the two senators quoted in the reading) arguing in favor of sunk cost thinking to maintain their own pet projects. Staw (1976) has argued that the effect was sufficiently powerful to draw the United States into the disastrous Vietnam War after the first few casualties had been incurred, and Dawes (1997) quotes similar evidence in connection with the Desert Storm invasion of 1991. Obviously, we don't fall into, or stay in, sunk cost traps in every case. Equally obviously, we do fall sometimes and, judging from the associated rhetoric, not infrequently at huge cost.

The third chapter, by Keeney and McDaniels, outlines a clearly prescriptive approach to major public policy decisions. Keeney has made important contributions in several areas of decision analysis, but the line of his work sampled here comes from his interest in what he calls "value-focused thinking," an approach to decision making that takes as its point of departure the decision maker's values and objectives rather than the alternatives he or she faces. This approach, developed in more detail in Keeney (1992), frequently surfaces issues that more conventional decision analysis approaches do not – for example, how complex and intertwined our values and objectives are in significant choice domains (see, for example, the "objectives network" sketched in Figure 7.1). The work involved in tracing out this network and then reducing it to a usable utility function is a major part of Keeney's approach.

The final chapter in this section, by Hammond, Harvey, and Hastie, provides examples of application of the theory of signal detection and of judgment analysis to important public policy issues. A central theme of these authors is that we currently muddle together factual and value judgments concerning important policy decisions in unhelpful ways. These decisions demand a blending of both scientific and political expertise, but the process used to achieve the blending is crucial. As one of their examples makes clear, a ballistics expert can offer solid scientific evidence on a number of technical characteristics of alternative weapons and bullets, but have nothing useful to say as to which is the right choice for a particular police department. The value trade-offs, they argue, are appropriately the function of the political, rather than the scientific, process (though we, as decision analysts, may be able to offer some technical assistance in making these trade-off processes.) The short essay reprinted here is intended both to illustrate the interweaving of judgment and decision making and to whet the reader's appetite for the details of the public policy applications he uses as examples (forecasting severe weather, assessing professional polygraph operators, selecting a bullet for the Denver Police Department, designing a major water project in Central Arizona).

### References

Dawes, R. M. (1997). Behavioral decision making and judgment. In D. Gilbert, S. Fiske, & G. Lindzey (Eds.), *Handbook of social psychology*. Boston: McGraw-Hill.

Keeney, R. L. (1992). *Value-focused thinking*. Cambridge, MA: Harvard University Press.

Staw, B. M. (1976). Knee-deep in the big muddy: A study of escalating commitment to a chosen course of action. *Organizational Behavior and Human Performance, 16*, 27–44.

# 5 Illusions and Mirages in Public Policy

*Richard H. Thaler*

Like most people, I have always found optical illusions fascinating. Figure 5.1 is a scale drawing of the world's largest man-made optical illusion – the Gateway Arch in St. Louis. Although it appears to be at least 50 percent taller than it is wide, the height and width are actually equal. This optical illusion is an example of what I will call "judgmental illusions": Somehow the mind is fooled into making an error of judgment. We all erroneously judge the arch's height to be greater than its width.

Another type of optical illusion is the mirage. We have all experienced the illusion of "seeing" water on a perfectly dry highway on a hot day. Such mirages on the desert are commonplace. Mirages, like judgmental illusions, fool the mind. We are fooled into believing that an object exists when it does not.

The subject of this chapter is not optical illusions, but rather the related concept of cognitive illusion. Like optical illusions, cognitive illusions can be of two types. Judgmental cognitive illusions induce people to mis-estimate magnitudes, and in a specific direction. Other cognitive illusions are like mirages: A situation is structured such that we are fooled into thinking we have many choices when in fact only one really exists. Both kinds of cognitive illusions have powerful influences on how people make choices – in their private lives and in the realm of public policy.

## Four Illusions

The following example of a judgmental cognitive illusion will be familiar to anyone who has taken a course in probability theory:

A class has 25 students in it. What is the chance that at least two students will have a common birthday?

This chapter originally appeared in *The Public Interest*, 1983, *73*, 60–74. Copyright © 1983 by National Affairs, Inc. Reprinted by permission.

Figure 5.1.   The Gateway Arch in St. Louis (scale drawing).

Most people guess that the chance of a match is pretty small, perhaps one in 10 or one in 20. In fact, the chance of at least one pair of students having the same birthday is better than 50–50.

The interesting thing about this problem is that it affects almost everyone the same way. We all judge the chance of a match to be smaller than it really is. This is the defining characteristic of a judgmental cognitive illusion: The problem induces predictable errors in a particular direction.

Can such cognitive illusions that create errors in judgment also create errors in contemporary public policy debates? Yes – and to illustrate this I have selected several examples that relate to our perceptions of risk and uncertainty. The first tests one's ability to estimate magnitudes:

What is the relative frequency of homicides and suicides in the United States?

Most people think homicides are much more common, when in fact suicides are more common – in one recent year there was 27,300 suicides and 20,400 homicides. (This is true in spite of the fact that the official statistics understate the true level of suicides. Many suicides are classified as accidental deaths.) Why do we guess that homicides are more common? Well, often when we have to estimate the frequency of an event or class of events we do so by judging the ease with which we can recall instances of it. Psychologists Daniel Kahneman and Amos Tversky call this the *availability heuristic* (Kahneman, Slovic, & Tversky, 1982). The availability heuristic is usually a good way to estimate frequency because ease of recall is usually highly correlated with actual frequency. Sometimes, however, availability and frequency diverge. Since homicides receive more publicity than suicides, they are more available, and thus are erroneously judged to be more common.

The next example, first devised by Daniel Ellsberg, consists of an imaginary lottery:

You are shown three urns, each containing 100 balls. Urn A has 50 red and 50 black balls, urn B has 80 red and 20 black balls, and urn C has 20 red and 80 black balls. You are given a choice between two lotteries. You can take lottery A, in which a ball will be picked at random from urn A. If the ball picked is red you win $100, otherwise you win nothing. Alternatively, you can take lottery BC. In this case the lottery has two stages. The first step is to flip a coin. If it comes up heads you must choose a ball from urn B. If it comes up tails you must choose from urn C. The second step is to pick a ball from the urn determined by the coin flip. Again, if the ball is red you win $100, otherwise you win nothing. Which lottery do you prefer?

Simple multiplication will confirm that the chance of winning either lottery is 50 percent, yet most people say that they prefer lottery A. Why? Two characteristics of the BC lottery make it unattractive. First, lottery A is simpler. Complexity itself is aversive. Second, the chance of winning the BC lottery is more ambiguous: Depending on the outcome of the coin flip it might be 80 percent or 20 percent. This ambiguity is also aversive. The moral is that most people – if forced to gamble – would prefer a simple, well-defined risk to a complex, ambiguous risk (Ellsberg, 1961).

The next set of three situations relates to the value people place on their lives. How much would someone pay to avoid a risk to his life? How much would he charge to take an additional risk?

Risk Situation 1: While attending the movies last week you inadvertently exposed yourself to a rare, fatal disease. If you contract the disease, you will die a quick and painless death in one week. The chance that you will contract the disease is exactly .001 – that is, one chance in 1000. Once you get the disease there is no cure, but you can take an innoculation now which will prevent you from getting the disease. Unfortunately there is only a limited supply of innoculation, and it will be sold to the highest bidders. What is the most you would be willing to pay for this innoculation? (If you wish, you may borrow the money to pay at a low rate of interest.)

Risk Situation 2: This is basically the same as situation 1 with the following modifications. The chance you will get this disease is now .004 – that is, four in 1000. The innoculation is only 25 percent effective – that is, it would reduce the risk to .003. What is the most you would pay for the innoculation in this case? (Again, you may borrow the money to pay.)

Risk Situation 3: Some professors at a medical school are doing research on the disease described above. They are recruiting volunteers who would be required to expose themselves to a .001 (one chance in 1000) risk of getting the disease. No innoculations would be available, so this would entail a .001 chance of death. The 20 volunteers from this audience who demand the least money will be taken. What is the least amount of money you would require to participate in this experiment?

I have asked these questions to numerous groups. The typical median responses are that people would pay $800 in Situation 1; pay $250 in Situation 2; and charge $100,000 in Situation 3. Obviously, people treat these as three quite different questions. Yet economists would argue that the answers should all be about the same. (They would allow for a small difference between Situation 3 and the other two, but nothing like the magnitude observed.) Essentially each situation presents the subject with a choice between more money or a greater chance of living. If Situations 1 and 2 are compared, we can see that people will pay over three times as much to reduce a risk from .001 to zero than to reduce a risk from .004 to .003. While the increase in the chance of living is the same in each case, the change is more attractive in Situation 1 because the risk is eliminated altogether. Generally, people will pay more to eliminate a risk than to achieve an equivalent reduction of a risk. Daniel Kahneman and Amos Tversky call this the *certainty effect* (Tversky & Kahneman, 1981).

If we compare the responses to Situation 3 with those given to Situations 1 and 2, we see that the median response to Situation 3 is several times larger. Yet this implies that a typical individual would refuse to pay $5000 to eliminate a risk, *and* would refuse to take $5000 to accept the same risk. How can $5000 be both better and worse than bearing some risk?

This comparison illustrates another behavioral regularity, which I have called the *endowment effect* (Thaler, 1980). The endowment effect stipulates that an individual will demand much more money to give something up than he would be willing to pay to acquire it. The endowment effect can be observed in cases that do not involve any risk. Suppose you won a ticket to a sold-out concert that you would love to attend, and the ticket is priced at $15. Before the concert you are offered $50 for the ticket. Do you sell? Alternatively, suppose you won $50 in a lottery. Then, a few weeks later, you are offered a chance to buy a ticket to the same concert for $45. Do you buy? Many people say they would not sell for $50 in the first case and would not buy for $45 in the second case. Such responses are logically inconsistent.

### Policy Deceptions

These illusions can affect policy decisions in many ways. Take the endowment effect: Essentially it says that once people have something it is very hard to take it away. Residents of communities with declining school populations know how this has created problems for their school boards. People who would be unwilling to pay for a tax increase to add a school in their neighborhood nevertheless become incensed if an existing school in their neighborhood is closed in order to avoid a tax increase.

Similarly, most people know that when social security benefits were indexed, the formula used was inadvertently generous. The result has been that benefits have grown much faster than wages in recent years – clearly an unintended outcome. Nevertheless, any politician who dared to suggest a reduction in the rate at which benefits increase was considered an enemy of senior citizens. Just because it was a mistake to give people something does not mean it can be easily taken away. Even the most recent solution to this problem – a one-time postponement of cost of living increases for six months – is a curious sort of deception. We did not take anything away – we just postponed it!

An issue that is particularly interesting in the present context is nuclear power, the debate over which involves all of the illusions discussed so far. The specific question I wish to discuss is: Why is nuclear power so unpopular? I do not intend to evaluate the advantages and disadvantages of nuclear and conventional power plants, since I have no particular insights to offer. The question is why nuclear power generates so much vocal, emotional opposition. This *is* a puzzle, since the experts seem at least evenly divided. Yet how many demonstrations do we see opposing coal-fired plants? Surely it is not because conventional power sources are without risk to humans or to the environment. Coal mining accidents could be (but are not) attributed indirectly to coal-fired power plants. And acid rain is partly attributed to conventional power plants, but nuclear power is rarely suggested as a solution to the problems of acid rain. So why is nuclear power so unpopular? The four cognitive illusions each play a role:

### Availability

As with homicide, the risks from nuclear power are widely publicized, while as with suicides, the risks from conventional sources are not as well known. The Three Mile Island incident and the popular movie *The China Syndrome* have helped keep the nuclear risks very "available," even though, so far as we know, there has not been a single death related to nuclear power.

### Complexity and Ambiguity

As with the Ellsberg urn, the risks from nuclear power are complex and ambiguous. People are not confident that they have been estimated correctly. Future risks, such as those related to waste disposal, are especially ambiguous. The Ellsberg effect shows that such risks are particularly aversive. (It is rather ironic that Ellsberg is now so active in the anti-nuclear power movement. Has he fallen into his own trap?)

### The Certainty Effect and the Endowment Effect

The responses to the three risk situations demonstrated that people are least willing to pay to decrease an existing risk (Situation 2) and demand great compensation for the introduction of a new risk (Situation 3). The way the nuclear power issue is generally discussed, replacing a conventional power plant with a nuclear power plant would reduce an existing risk and add a new risk – the least attractive combination possible.

I am not saying that opposition to nuclear power is silly or irrational. Rather, I have just tried to show how four cognitive illusions all happen to be working to make nuclear power seem highly unattractive, which may help explain why opposition to nuclear power is so widespread.

There is a good book on optical illusions by Stanley Coren and Joan Girgus called *Seeing is Deceiving*. That title might be applied to thinking: Seeming is deceiving. But like optical illusions, cognitive illusions can be overcome. We can measure the height and width of the Gateway Arch; similarly, we can look in the almanac to find out how many homicides and suicides there are. Nevertheless, there is no practical way of preventing cognitive illusions from influencing policy decisions. Cognitive illusions influence representatives, senators, presidents – even so-called experts are not immune. A physicist may fall for a cognitive illusion just as easily as an economist might fall for an optical illusion. But since informed judgment and explicit analysis can in principle mitigate the effects of illusions, we must encourage the use of scientific research, cost-benefit and cost-effectiveness analyses, and expert commissions in the making of policy decisions.

## Mirages

The second class of policy problems involves mirages. Rather than illusory objects, these mirages are illusory choices, choices we perceive that do not really exist.

Economists tell us that we should keep our options open, and that we should prefer having more choices to having fewer. This is good advice, like "buy low and sell high," but like all good advice it has exceptions. One exception would arise when the costs of deciding are exceptionally high, in which case any decision may be better than more costly pondering.

A second, more interesting, exception is illustrated by the following true story. A group of economists was sitting around having cocktails, awaiting the arrival of dinner. A large bowl of cashews was placed on the cocktail table, and within 90 seconds one half of the cashews were gone. A simple linear extrapolation would have predicted the total demise of the cashews and our appetites in another 90 seconds. Leaping into action, I grabbed the bowl and (while stealing a few more nuts on the way) hid it in the kitchen. Everyone seemed relieved, yet puzzled. How could removing the bowl, and thus removing a choice, have made us better off? Let us analyze this case with the help of the simple decision tree shown in Figure 5.2.

At time 1 we have a decision: to have the bowl or to remove it. If we remove the bowl, we have no further choices to make, and no more nuts to eat. We obtain Option C. If we leave the bowl, we must then decide how many more nuts to eat. Suppose we would most like to eat a few nuts (Option A) but that we would prefer to stop (Option C) rather than to end up eating the whole bowl (Option B). Given these preferences the rational thing would be to leave the bowl and pick Option A. But it is rational only so long as Option A is really feasible. At the dinner party, Option A was a mirage. As much as we might have liked at time 1 to eat only a few more nuts, at time 2 we would have devoured the whole can. If Option A is a mirage, then

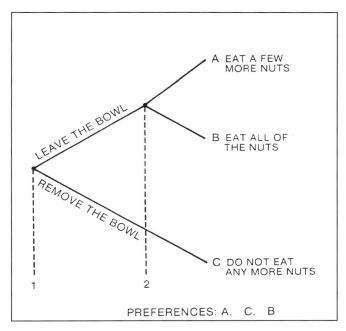

Figure 5.2. Cashew nut decision tree.

Option C becomes the rational choice. I will call taking Option C an act of *precommitment*: commiting oneself to a particular choice in advance.

The first recorded act of precommitment was that taken by Ulysses in his encounter with the Sirens, a popular singing group in Ulysses's time whose songs were highly addictive. Anyone on the seas who heard their songs would feel compelled to draw ever nearer to land, inevitably crashing on the rocks near shore. Ulysses's strategy was to have himself tied to the mast so he could not alter the course of his ship.

Ulysses's method of dealing with the Sirens and my act of removing the cashews were both acts of *rational precommitment*. They both satisfy the two conditions that are necessary for precommitment to be rational: (1) a change of preferences is anticipated; and (2) the change will be for the worse. Ulysses knew that he would alter the course of his ship if he had the option, and that the change of course would be for the worse.

A common precommitment institution is the Christmas club. Christmas clubs have three distinguishing features: They pay little or no interest; they require weekly deposits at some inconvenience; and they do not allow the customer to withdraw any money before Thanksgiving. This institution clearly seems inefficient. But is it irrational? The decision tree in Figure 5.3 shows once again that C is a rational choice only if A is a mirage. But for the individuals or families on a tight budget who would otherwise not save enough,

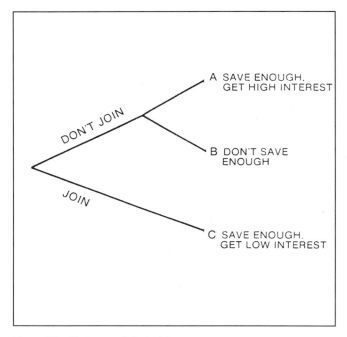

Figure 5.3.  Christmas club decision tree.

a Christmas club could be rational. The fundamental point is that a rule (which is what a precommitment strategy is) must *necessarily* be crude and inflexible, and may also be inefficient. Nevertheless, these drawbacks, in and of themselves, should not lead us to the conclusion that a particular rule is undesirable. To evaluate a rule we must compare it with the alternatives. Normally a rule specifying that the captain of the ship may not alter the ship's course would be judged unacceptable. But for Ulysses, that rule was better than any other feasible alternative.

### Public Uses of Precommitment

Rational precommitment is highly important in the domain of public policy. Take terrorism or airplane hijacking, for example: As all airline passengers know, we spend millions of dollars and countless hours of time screening airline passengers for bombs, guns, keys, lighters, and calculators. Film is ruined, people miss planes, and we all pay more for plane tickets. What do we gain from this? Since any security system can be beaten, planes are still occasionally hijacked. As an alternative to all the equipment I propose we adopt the following rule: "Never make concessions to hijackers." Hijackers would be given a choice: Give up or be shot. One might say, "Won't that be a dangerous rule? Won't many innocent people be hurt or killed?" The answer is no. First, if no one ever gets anything from hijacking a plane, then the incidence will fall almost to zero. Second, there is no defense against a crazed terrorist. If someone wants to kill himself and a lot of other people he can do it, and we cannot stop him. Anyone can hijack a bus or blow up an office building at will.

A different criticism of this rule is that there might be situations in which society would want to make concessions. Suppose someone hijacks a caravan of school buses – would we not want to make concessions in this case? But such examples simply illustrate the value of the rule: If an exception is made for a school bus once, no school bus would ever be safe again. To enforce this rule we could decide now that anyone not personally at risk who grants a concession to a hijacker would be guilty of a felony. (A jail sentence would be mandatory, of course.)

Another example of rational precommitment is mandatory retirement. Mandatory retirement rules normally have two separate provisions. First, an organization will announce that it is under no obligation, moral or legal, to keep a worker past the age of 60 (or 65, or 70). One reason organizations adopt such a policy is that for most workers, though not all, productivity reaches its peak some time before retirement. Wages, on the other hand, usually rise throughout a worker's employment. These two factors together suggest that just before retirement most workers are earning more than they produce. Clearly a firm would not want to allow that state of affairs to go on indefinitely (Lazear, 1979).

The second provision, while not universal, frequently accompanies the first. It provides that no worker may remain employed after the normal retirement age; this might be called "mandatory mandatory retirement" (or MMR for short). Since the adoption of MMR eliminates some future options for an organization, it qualifies as precommitment. But is it rational? It is easy to criticize an MMR rule since it might force a university to lose a Nobel laureate who is still active. Nevertheless, I believe such rules make good sense because it is so difficult to tell anyone he is no longer productive. Thus the option to keep some people can, and will, become a practice of keeping almost anyone who wants to stay on. So for every Nobel laureate who is kept for an extra couple of years, the organization must retain several others who are no longer productive.

I am not advocating any particular age for mandatory retirement; clearly that should differ across jobs. What I do oppose is the recent federal law that declared mandatory retirement illegal for ages under 70. I believe this is an unnecessary and ill-advised intrusion into private organizations' affairs. In many cases these rules were arrived at through an explicit process of collective bargaining. The abolition of mandatory retirement is sometimes posed, improperly, as a civil rights issue. But old age is a state we all hope to attain. Young people benefit when mandatory retirement creates new openings, but those same young people will face those rules later. Mandatory retirement makes sense for some organizations, and they should be given the freedom to enforce their own rules.

### The Federal Budget as Dinner Check

I would also encourage the federal government to impose some precommitment rules on itself, in particular fiscal caps such as Proposition 13 in California. Several proposed constitutional amendments would impose such rules on the federal government either by restricting future growth of spending to no more than the growth rate of real GNP, and/or by requiring a balanced federal budget. Such ideas are not new. In 1798 Thomas Jefferson wrote, "I wish it were possible to obtain a single amendment to our Constitution. I would be willing to depend on that alone for the reduction of the administration of our government to the genuine principles of its Constitution; I mean an additional article, taking from the government the power of borrowing."

Since these proposed amendments would greatly restrict the government's flexibility (though exceptions are made for declarations of war), it must be demonstrated that such precommitment would be rational. Though the growth in government's share of GNP in the last 55 years should be evidence enough, let me describe some of the mirages that led to this explosion.

Suppose we consider the behavior of a hypothetical group of 500 people going to an expensive restaurant for drinks and dinner. Compare their expected behavior under two different rules: Each person pays his own bill; or, the total bill is divided evenly. Under which rule will people spend more? The latter of course. If I order a shrimp cocktail for $5.00 and it is split 500 ways, I pay only one cent. I am more likely to order a shrimp cocktail at one cent than at $5.00. This "check-splitting effect" is what leads to so-called pork barrel legislation (Buchanan & Tullock, 1962). The amount a district will pay toward a particular local project can be very small indeed, so it is in the interest of every Representative to get many projects into his district – just as it is my interest to order dessert if everyone else is chipping in.

Suppose the larger dinner party comes up with a clever idea: The check will still be divided evenly, but to save time, the ordering will be done by committee. There will be separate committees for drinks, appetizers, entrees, salads, and desserts. Each person can serve on the committee of his choice. How will people allocate themselves to committees? You guessed it – the lushes will be on the drinks committee, the vegetarians on salad committee, the sweet-tooths on the dessert committee, etc. (After all, we do want the people with expertise on the relevant committees.) Of course such an arrangement will exacerbate the tendency toward over-ordering. The lushes will have a bottle of wine with each course, the sweet-tooths two rounds of dessert, and if by chance a lush finds himself on the dessert committee we can be sure that rum cake will be served. Unfortunately, this metaphor closely resembles the structure of the U.S. Congress, where the committee process reinforces the tendency toward excessive spending (Niskanen, 1971).

Suppose further that each of our diners can put his bill on a credit card – a special credit card that does not have to be paid if the diner loses his job or retires. This rounds out the story nicely. To a Representative more concerned with getting re-elected than with posterity, "buy now, pay later (maybe)" is a very appealing process.

How can we control the budget? I advocate random committee assignments, but that is probably politically infeasible. Failing that, we need both a limit on the rate at which government spending can grow, and an enforced balanced budget.

Such rules have been criticized on numerous grounds: They are rightly described as crude and inflexible, and the definition of a balanced budget is far from obvious. Nonetheless, the spirit of such amendments is worth supporting, and the criticisms are not persuasive. The issue is not whether such rules are perfect, but rather whether they are an improvement over the current situation. As Richard Wagner and Robert Tollison recently wrote:

Annual budget balance is a good idea because it places useful and meaningful constraints on political choice. This is not to say that it is a *perfect* rule for the conduct of government, for there are no perfect rules for the conduct of something as massive as our government. The problem is to search for feasible, workable rules that encourage political decision makers to act as if they had good common sense. A rule of annual budget balance and careful up-front monitoring of the viability of long-term government projects seems to be the wisest course of action (Wagner, Tollison, Rabuska, & Noonan, 1982).

### No Thyself

By definition, precommitment must be done in *advance*, before we actually face temptation. We always resolve to go on a diet – next week. "Lord give me strength – but not now." So we should not be surprised to find that we, or our organizations, want to break rules that were established earlier, even if the rules are desirable. Indexation of the federal income tax is a good illustration of this principle.

Because we have a progressive income tax with marginal rates that increase with income, inflation automatically produces real tax increases. In 1981, Congress passed a law that instituted indexing of the personal income tax beginning in 1985. The way the law works, the personal exemption (now $1000), the zero-tax bracket (now $3400), and all other bracket levels would automatically rise with inflation. This would be particularly helpful to lower income families, since the brackets are much closer together at lower levels. Not surprisingly, some in Congress now want the law repealed. As Martin Feldstein, chairman of the President's Council of Economic Advisors, argues in a recent *Wall Street Journal*:

If tax revenue must be raised, the repeal of indexing isn't a satisfactory substitute for an explicit tax increase. Because the repeal of indexing is a *hidden* way of increasing taxes, it removes the pressure to choose between spending cuts and more taxes. And unlike voting an explicit tax increase, repealing indexing doesn't provide a fixed amount of additional tax revenues but starts a money machine that will squeeze more and more money from taxpayers in years ahead. The repeal of indexing is politically *tempting* to many in Congress because it increases revenue without explicitly increasing taxes. But it is the very opposite of responsible budgeting [emphasis added].

Feldstein's choice of language is quite apt. First, he describes the tax increases in the absence of indexation as *hidden*. This is right on target. To keep government spending under control we should want tax increases to be visible, not hidden. Second, he says the repeal of indexation would be *tempting* to Congress. Congress recognized its addiction to hidden tax increases and resolved to break the addiction – starting in four years. It is important that this resolution be kept. Indexation is particularly important in the absence of spending restrictions or a balanced budget amendment, since it will help keep government from growing.

My proposal can perhaps best be summarized in the dictum Thomas Schelling set down in these pages several years ago: "No Thyself." This is good advice for individuals, organizations, and governments. If we make rules to enforce the "no," we must remember that all rules are imperfect, and that they must not be lightly abandoned. Not even Ulysses could count on self-restraint.

### References

Buchanan, J., & Tullock, G. (1962). *The calculus of consent.* Ann Arbor: University of Michigan Press.

Ellsberg, D. (1961). Risk, ambiguity, and the Savage axioms. *Quarterly Journal of Economics, 75,* 642–699.

Kahneman, D., Slovic, P., & Tversky, A., (Eds.). (1982). *Judgment under uncertainty: Heuristics and biases.* Cambridge: Cambridge University Press.

Lazear, E. (1979). Why is there mandatory retirement? *Journal of Political Economy, 87,* 1261–1284.

Niskanen, W. (1971). *Bureaucracy and representative government.* Chicago: Aldine-Atherton.

Thaler, R. H. (1980). Toward a positive theory of consumer choice. *Journal of Economic Behavior and Organization, 1,* 39–60.

Tversky, A., & Kahneman, D. (1981). The framing of decisions and the rationality of choice. *Science, 221,* 453–458.

Wagner, R., Tollison, R., Rabuska, A., & Noonan, J. T. Jr. (1982). *Balanced budgets, fiscal responsibility, and the Constitution.* Washington, DC: Cato Institute.

# 6 The Psychology of Sunk Cost

*Hal R. Arkes and Catherine Blumer*

> To terminate a project in which $1.1 billion has been invested represents an unconscionable mishandling of taxpayers' dollars.
> Senator Denton, November 4, 1981

> Completing Tennessee–Tombigbee [Waterway Project] is not a waste of taxpayer dollars. Terminating the project at this late stage of development would, however, represent a serious waste of funds already invested.
> Senator Sasser, November 4, 1981

The purpose of the present chapter is to attempt to explain an irrational economic behavior, which will be termed the sunk cost effect. This effect is manifested in a greater tendency to continue an endeavor once an investment in money, effort, or time has been made. The prior investment, which is motivating the present decision to continue, does so despite the fact that it objectively should not influence the decision. We will provide evidence that the psychological justification for this maladaptive behavior is predicated on the desire not to appear wasteful.

As an example of the sunk cost effect, consider the following example.[1] A man wins a contest sponsored by a local radio station. He is given a free ticket to a football game. Since he does not want to go alone, he persuades a friend to buy a ticket and go with him. As they prepare to go to the game, a terrible blizzard begins. The contest winner peers out his window over the arctic scene and announces that he is not going, because the pain of enduring the snowstorm would be greater than the enjoyment he would derive from watching the game. However, his friend protests, "I don't want to waste the twelve dollars I paid for the ticket! I want to go!" The friend who purchased the ticket is not behaving rationally according to traditional economic theory.

This chapter originally appeared in *Organizational Behavior and Human Decision Processes*, 1985, *35*, 124–140. Copyright © 1985 by Academic Press, Inc. Reprinted by permission.

Only incremental costs should influence decisions, not sunk costs. If the agony of sitting in a blinding snowstorm for three hours is greater than the enjoyment one would derive from trying to see the game, then one should not go. The $12 has been paid whether one goes or not. It is a sunk cost. It should in no way influence the decision to go. But who among us is so rational?

Examples of the sunk cost effect exist in great quantity and for great quantities. During late 1981 the funding for the immensely expensive Tennessee–Tombigbee Waterway Project was scheduled for Congressional review. As the above quotes indicate, proponents of the project insisted that to stop the project after a great deal had already been spent would represent a waste of taxpayers' money. In other words, the sunk cost provided a strong impetus to continue the project.

Those who are aware of the fact that sunk costs are difficult to ignore can turn this realization to their advantage. When discussing why he thought the nuclear energy program would prevail, one nuclear industry executive explained:

When it comes down to it, no one with any sense would abort a $2.5 billion construction project. And, by extension, no administration would abort a $200 billion national investment in nuclear energy. So the trick for the industry is to get more new plants under construction without the (anti-nuclear) movement knowing about it. By the time they get around to demonstrating and challenging the license, we'll have a million tons of steel and concrete in the ground, and no one in their right mind will stop us. (Dowie, 1981, p. 23)

The executive's final assertion may be correct if what he means by "right mind" is a typical line of reasoning. However, such reasoning is irrational, no matter how compelling it may seem. To repeat: sunk costs are irrelevant to current decisions.[2]

These economic examples should not obscure the fact that there are numerous nonmonetary sunk costs. Should I continue this unhappy relationship? I have already put so much into it. Should I continue with this terrible job? I spent a year in training to get this position. We suspect that many bad movies are seen to their completion simply because once the viewer realizes how poor the movie is, several minutes and dollars have already been invested. This sunk cost promotes lingering until the bitter end. During the Viet Nam War some people counseled against ending the hostilities before total victory had been achieved because to do so would have meant the waste of those lives already lost. Teger (1980) summarized this phenomenon by suggesting that we often feel we have too much invested to quit.

Our analysis of the sunk cost effect will be presented in three stages. First, demonstrations of the effect will be presented. Second, some possible explanations of the effect will be offered. Third, the relation between the sunk cost effect and several areas of social psychological research will be examined.

## Demonstrations of the Sunk Cost Effect

All of our questionnaire studies were done with Ohio and Oregon college students as subjects. No subject responded to more than one question. The number of subjects giving each answer is indicated after every question.

*Experiment 1*

Assume that you have spent $100 on a ticket for a weekend ski trip to Michigan. Several weeks later you buy a $50 ticket for a weekend ski trip to Wisconsin. You think you will enjoy the Wisconsin ski trip more than the Michigan ski trip. As you are putting your just-purchased Wisconsin ski trip ticket in your wallet, you notice that the Michigan ski trip and the Wisconsin ski trip are for the same weekend! It's too late to sell either ticket, and you cannot return either one. You must use one ticket and not the other. Which ski trip will you go on?

$100 ski trip to Michigan   33
$50 ski trip to Wisconsin   28

An axiom of traditional economic theory is that decisions should be based on the costs and benefits that are expected to arise from the choice of each option. Based on this axiom we would expect everyone to choose the trip thought to be more enjoyable – the trip to Wisconsin. However, only 46% of the subjects chose the Wisconsin trip. The 99% confidence interval around this datum is 30 to 62%. We therefore conclude that the prediction of traditional economic theory that 100% of the subjects would choose the Wisconsin trip is disconfirmed. Obviously the larger sunk cost of the Michigan trip is influencing many subjects' choice.

*Experiment 2*

Experiment I was a questionnaire study. Actual money was obviously not involved. While a number of experiments have shown that the results of questionnaire studies replicated when real monetary stakes were introduced (e.g., Grether & Plott, 1979; Lichtenstein, 1973), we felt it would be desirable to demonstrate the sunk cost effect in a more realistic setting. We decided to provide discounts to some subscribers to a theater series. We predicted that those who paid less for the privilege to see as many plays as they liked would choose to see fewer plays than those who had paid more. Those who had paid more would have a greater sunk cost.

*Method.* The first 60 people who approached the ticket window to purchase season tickets to the Ohio University Theater's 1982–1983 season were

included in the experiment. After the person announced his or her intention to buy a season ticket, the ticket seller sold the purchaser one of three
types of tickets, which had been randomly ordered beforehand. One type
was the normal price ticket ($15); the second was a ticket selling at a $2 discount; the third was selling at a $7 discount. The seller explained to the latter
two groups that the discount was being given as part of a promotion by the
theater department.

As we sold the three types of tickets, we immediately decided not to
use the forthcoming data from three $7 discount subjects, one $2 discount
subject, and two no-discount subjects. This was because these six people
were buying tickets as couples. If the two members of a couple had tickets
with different discounts, their joint decision whether or not to attend a play
would render their data nonindependent. Our final sample thus had eighteen
no-discount, nineteen $2 discount, and seventeen $7 discount subjects. Since
the ticket stubs were color coded, we were able to collect the stubs after each
performance and determine how many persons in each group had attended
each play. Each season ticket package contained one ticket labeled with the
name of one play plus two unlabeled extra tickets which could be used to
bring a guest to any play.

*Results.* We divided the theater season into halves – the first five plays and
the last five plays – because we felt that the experimental manipulation might
be of different strength during the two halves of the season. We performed a 3
(discount: none, $2, $7) × 2 (half of season) analysis of variance on the number
of tickets used by each subject. The latter variable was a within-subjects factor.
It was also the only significant source of variance, $F(1, 51) = 32.32$, $MS_e =$
1.81, $p < .001$. More tickets were used by each subject on the first five plays
(3.57) than on the last five plays (2.09). We performed a priori tests on the
number of tickets used by each of the three groups during the first half
of the theater season. The no-discount group used significantly more tickets
(4.11) than both the $2 discount group (3.32) and the $7 discount group (3.29),
$t = 1.79, 1.83$, respectively, $p$'s $< .05$, one tailed. The groups did not use significantly different numbers of tickets during the last half of the theater season
(2.28, 1.84, 2.18, for the no-discount, $2 discount, and $7 discount groups,
respectively).

*Conclusion.* Those who had purchased theater tickets at the normal price
used more theater tickets during the first half of the season than those who
purchased tickets at either of the two discounts. According to rational economic theory, after all subjects had their ticket booklet in hand, they should
have been equally likely to attend the plays. Since the discounts were assigned randomly, the groups should not have differed on the costs and benefits they could have anticipated by attending each play. The groups did
differ, however, because they had different sunk costs.[3]

We consider this demonstration of the sunk cost effect to be particularly noteworthy, because the effect lasted for 6 months following the purchase of the tickets. The effect was not manifested, however, during the second half of the theater series (6 to 9 months following the purchase).

Experiments 1 and 2 are relatively pure examples in that other explanations of the results are not readily available. Many of the following studies are less pure. They involve much more complex economic decisions than are required in the first two experiments. As a result of using more complex stories, we are creating a stimulus situation in which some explanations of the data other than the sunk cost effect may exist. It is virtually impossible to rule out every alternate explanation in every such story. However, the consistent pattern of results found in all of the stories plus the demonstration of the sunk cost effect in the purer stories lead us to feel confident in our explanation of the data.

The next three experiments differ from the prior two in that pairs of scenarios are presented in each experiment. One member of each pair is as similar to the other member in as many financial aspects as possible. They differ, however, in that only one member of each pair has a sunk cost. In this way we can assess the impact of the sunk cost component of the scenario.

*Experiment 3*

*Question 3A.* As the president of an airline company, you have invested 10 million dollars of the company's money into a research project. The purpose was to build a plane that would not be detected by conventional radar, in other words, a radar-blank plane. When the project is 90% completed, another firm begins marketing a plane that cannot be detected by radar. Also, it is apparent that their plane is much faster and far more economical than the plane your company is building. The question is: should you invest the last 10% of the research funds to finish your radar-blank plane?

Yes 41
No 7

*Question 3B.* As president of an airline company, you have received a suggestion from one of your employees. The suggestion is to use the last 1 million dollars of your research funds to develop a plane that would not be detected by conventional radar, in other words, a radar-blank plane. However, another firm has just begun marketing a plane that cannot be detected by radar. Also, it is apparent that their plane is much faster and far more economical than the plane your company could build. The question is: should you invest the last million dollars of your research funds to build the radar-blank plane proposed by your employee?

Yes    10
No     50

Question A vs B: $\chi^2(1, N = 108) = 50.6$, $p < .001$.

The difference between these stories is that in question A millions have already been invested, while in question B nothing has been invested yet. Whereas the large majority of the question B respondents think the project is a bad idea, question A respondents overwhelmingly endorse continuing construction. There is no obvious economic reason to complete the project. Yet there appears to be a compelling psychological one: sunk cost.

While 3A respondents thought that continued spending was a much better idea than 3B respondents did, we did not know if this would be accompanied by an inflated certainty among 3A respondents that a completed project would be a financial success. It may be that 3A respondents grimly decide to spend despite desperate odds. On the other hand, perhaps their willingness to throw good money after bad is due to the fact that they do not perceive the situation as a lost cause. In Experiment 4 we sought the answer to this question.

*Experiment 4*

Questions 4A and 4B were identical to questions 3A and 3B. At the end of each story subjects were told "Use the following 0 to 100 scale. Write in the box the number between 0 and 100 that reflects what you think your plane's chance of financial success really is. You can use any number." The scale had five likelihood labels varying from "no chance" at 0 to "sure thing" at 100.

The seventy-six 4A subjects' mean probability estimate was 41.0. The eighty-two 4B subjects' mean probability estimate was 34.0, $t(156) = 2.02$, $p < .05$. We conclude that subjects in a sunk cost situation have an inflated estimate of the likelihood that the completed project will be a success. We do not know if this inflated estimate helps foster continued investment, is a consequence of the decision to continue investing, or both.

A possible flaw in Experiments 3 and 4 is that in questions 3A and 4A the completed plane would be a 10 million dollar product. In questions 3B and 4B the plane would cost only 1 million. Perhaps 3B respondents were unwilling to spend because they knew that a 1 million dollar plane was likely to be a cheap, inferior product. Question A respondents would not have such fears and therefore would be more likely to continue. In Experiment 5 we tested this explanation of Experiments 3 and 4 by changing the plane in question B to a 10 million dollar product.

*Experiment 5*

The story used in Experiment 5 was identical to that used in question 3B except that "1 million" was changed to "10 million." Respondents' decisions whether or not to build the plane were

Yes   10
No    50

Since the data from Experiment 5 were identical to those of 3B, we conclude that the overwhelming decision not to build the radar-blank plane in question 3B was not due to the smaller final price of the plane compared to the price in 3A. We conclude that the critical difference in questions 3A and 3B was that in the former the investor had incurred a sunk cost.

### Explanation of the Sunk Cost Effect

Thaler's (1980) explanation of the sunk cost effect is based on prospect theory (Kahneman & Tversky, 1979). Two features of prospect theory seem particularly pertinent to the analysis of the sunk cost effect. The first of the features is depicted in Figure 6.1, which contains prospect theory's value function. This function represents the relation between objectively defined gains and losses (e.g., measured in dollars) and the subjective value a person places on such gains and losses.

When an initial investment is being considered, the investor is at point A. After a substantial unsuccessful investment has been made, the investor is at point B. At point B further losses do not result in large decreases in value; however, comparable gains do result in large increases in value. Therefore an investor at point B in Figure 6.1 will risk small losses in order to obtain

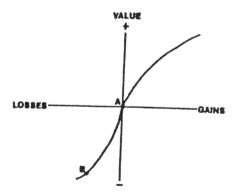

Figure 6.1. The value function of prospect theory (after Kahneman & Tversky, 1979).

possible large gains. Point B is the location of a person who has paid a sunk cost. Compared to a person at point A, a person at B is more likely to make a risky investment, i.e., to continue adding funds to the sunk cost. This analysis is consistent with a finding by McGlothlin (1956) that long shots at a race track are most popular during the final race of the day. At that time many bettors are at point B and are more risk prone than they were before any losses occurred.

Thaler (1980) has used prospect theory's value function (Figure 6.1) to explain the snowstorm example presented earlier. The value of going to the game is $v(g)$. The value of losing \$12 is $\bar{v}(-12)$, where $\bar{v}$ is the value function for losses. The cost of enduring a snowstorm is $c$. We set the enjoyment of the game equal to the cost of enduring the snowstorm, i.e., $v(g) = -\bar{v}(-c)$; therefore someone who received the tickets for free would be indifferent about going to the game in a snowstorm. However, the person who has already paid \$12 will want to go since

$$v(g) + \bar{v}(-(c + 12)) > \bar{v}(-12).$$

The terms to the left of the "greater than" sign represent the net gain/loss should the person go to the game. The term to the right of the "greater than" sign represents the loss of \$12 – the result of not going to the game. Call the ticket price $p$. Due to the convexity of $\bar{v}$, the second term in the equation $(\bar{v}(-(c + p)))$ will always be smaller (i.e., closer to zero) than $(\bar{v}(-c) + \bar{v}(-p))$ for all $p > 0$. Thus the person who had paid for the ticket will want to go.

A second feature of prospect theory pertinent to sunk costs is the certainty effect. This effect is manifested in two ways. First, absolutely *certain* gains ($p = 1.0$) are greatly overvalued. By this we mean that the value of certain gains is higher than what would be expected given an analysis of a person's values of gains having a probability less than 1.0. Second, certain losses ($p = 1.0$) are greatly undervalued (i.e., further from zero). The value is more negative than what would be expected given an analysis of a person's values of losses having a probability less than 1.0. In other words, certainty magnifies both positive and negative values.

Note that in question 3A the decision not to complete the plane results in a certain loss of the amount already invested. Since prospect theory states that certain losses are particularly aversive, we might predict that subjects would find the other option comparatively attractive. This is in fact what occurred. Whenever a sunk cost dilemma involves the choice of a certain loss (stop the waterway project) versus a long shot (maybe it will become profitable by the year 2500), the certainty effect favors the latter option.

However, prospect theory does not specify the psychological basis for the findings that sure losses are so aversive and sunk costs are so difficult to ignore. One reason why people may wish to throw good money after bad is that to stop investing would constitute an admission that the prior money was wasted. The admission that one has wasted money would seem to be an aversive event. The admission can be avoided by continuing to act as if the prior spending was sensible, and a good way to foster that belief would be to invest more. Staw (1976) showed that when business school students felt responsible for a financially unsuccessful prior decision, they continued to invest more money into that option than if their prior decision was successful. This result seems to contradict the commonsense notion that negative consequences will cause a change in one's course of action. Instead, Staw showed that negative consequences fostered further commitment to the chosen alternative. This unusual behavior is consistent with our own notion that sunk costs are difficult to write off because to do so would appear wasteful.

We examined this proposed explanation in Experiment 6 – another of our relatively pure cases.

*Experiment 6*

On your way home you buy a tv dinner on sale for $3 at the local grocery store. A few hours later you decide it is time for dinner, so you get ready to put the tv dinner in the oven. Then you get an idea. You call up your friend to ask if he would like to come over for a quick tv dinner and then watch a good movie on tv. Your friend says "Sure." So you go out to buy a second tv dinner. However, all the on-sale tv dinners are gone. You therefore have to spend $5 (the regular price) for the tv dinner identical to the one you just bought for $3. You go home and put both dinners in the oven. When the two dinners are fully cooked, you get a phone call. Your friend is ill and cannot come. You are not hungry enough to eat both dinners. You cannot freeze one. You must eat one and discard the other. Which one do you eat?

| | |
|---|---|
| $3 dinner | 2 |
| $5 dinner | 21 |
| No preference | 66 |

Since the costs and benefits of choosing either dinner are precisely equal, we would expect, based on traditional economic theory, that everyone would choose "no preference." Sunk cost considerations, however, heighten the attractiveness of the $5 dinner. Since the choice of the $3 dinner is based on unknown factors, we deleted these respondents. Of the remaining 87 subjects, 76% chose "no preference." The 99% confidence interval around this datum is 64 to 88%. We therefore conclude that the prediction of traditional economic theory that 100% of the subjects would have no preference is disconfirmed. We suggest that the choice of the $5 dinner is made by many subjects because discarding it would appear more wasteful than discarding the $3 dinner.

Another way to examine the role of wastefulness in the psychology of sunk cost would be to write two stories that differ in that further expenditures would appear to be wasteful in only one of the two stories. Subjects should then demonstrate a greater willingness to spend in the other story. For example, to buy a new printing press that is far better than one's present press would seem to be an excellent choice. But what if one's present press is rather new? To purchase another press – no matter how superior – might then seem wasteful. Would the excellent choice therefore be forsaken?

### Experiment 7

*Question 7A.* As the owner of a printing company, you must choose whether to modernize your operation by spending $200,000 on a new printing press or on a fleet of new delivery trucks. You choose to buy the trucks, which can deliver your products twice as fast as your old trucks at about the same cost as the old trucks. One week after your purchase of the new trucks, one of your competitors goes bankrupt. To get some cash in a hurry, he offers to sell you his computerized printing press for $10,000. This press works 50% faster than your old press at about one-half the cost. You know you will not be able to sell your old press to raise this money, since it was built specifically for your needs and cannot be modified. However, you do have $10,000 in savings. The question is should you buy the computerized press from your bankrupt competitor?

Yes   49
No    15

*Question 7B.* As the owner of a printing company, you must choose whether to modernize your operation by spending $200,000 on a new printing press or on a fleet of new delivery trucks. You choose to buy the press, which works twice as fast as your old press at about the same cost as the old press. One week after your purchase of the new press, one of your competitors goes bankrupt. To get some cash in a hurry, he offers to sell you his computerized printing press for $10,000. This press works 50% faster than your new press at about one-half the cost. You know you will not be able to sell your new press to raise this money, since it was built specifically for your needs and cannot be modified. However, you do have $10,000 in savings. The question is should you buy the computerized press from your bankrupt competitor?

Yes   43
No    38

Question A vs B: $\chi^2(1, N = 145) = 7.51. p < .01.$

Despite the fact that buying the printing press would result in the same proportion of improvement in printing capability in questions 7A and 7B, subjects in 7A were significantly more likely to buy the press. When asked at the bottom of their questionnaires to give reasons for their choice, the subjects in 7B who opted not to buy the press gave such remarks as "I already have a good, new press that cost a lot of money." Subjects were less likely to buy if the purchase appeared to duplicate an immediately prior one and therefore appeared to render it wasteful.[4]

Our explanation based on the appearance of wastefulness has an interesting implication: if one's own money is at stake or if one is personally responsible for the initial investment (Staw, 1976), then wastefulness should be more aversive than if someone else's money is involved or if someone else was responsible for the original investment decision. In support of this conjecture Staw (1976) and Staw and Fox (1977) found that personal responsibility for the situation did tend to increase further financial allocations to a foundering investment.

In Experiment 8 we modified the questions used in Experiment 3 in order to examine the role of personal involvement. In Experiment 3 *you* are the president of an airline company. In Experiment 8 we described a company in the third person.

*Experiment 8*

*Question 8A.* The Acme Airline Company has invested 10 million dollars of the company's money into a research project. The purpose was to build a plane that would not be detected by conventional radar, in other words, a radar-blank plane. When the project is 90% completed, another firm begins marketing a plane that cannot be detected by radar. Also, it is apparent that their plane is much faster and more economical than the plane Acme is building. The question is should Acme Airlines invest the last million dollars of its research funds to finish the radar-blank plane?

Yes    37
No      21

*Question 8B.* The Acme Airlines Company has received a suggestion from one of its employees. The suggestion is to use the last 1 million dollars of research funds to build a plane that would not be detected by conventional radar, in other words, a radar-blank plane. However, another firm has just begun marketing a plane that cannot be detected by radar. Also, it is apparent that their plane is much faster and far more economical than the plane your company could build. The question is should you invest the last million dollars of your research funds to build the radar-blank plane proposed by your employee?

Yes    2
No    35

Answers to question 8A differed significantly from those in 3A, $\chi^2(1, N = 106) = 5.25$, $p < .05$. When you were the president of the company, you were more likely to be a victim of the sunk cost effect than if you were rendering judgment in general. Even when one's general opinion was solicited, however, the sunk cost effect was still very powerful (8A vs 8B: $\chi^2(1, N = 95) = 29.5$, $p < .01$).

In Experiment 9 we attempted to manipulate the personal involvement present in Experiment 1. In the original experiment, you had paid for the Michigan and Wisconsin ski trips. Would the sunk cost effect be diluted if you had paid for neither trip?

*Experiment 9*

As you are listening to the radio one morning, the disk jockey from 95XIL[5] calls you. He informs you that you have won a free ski trip to either Michigan or Wisconsin the last weekend of skiing season (which happens to be next weekend). You think you will prefer the trip to Wisconsin rather than the trip to Michigan. You call a travel agent and find out that the value of the Michigan ski trip is $100, and the value of the Wisconsin ski trip is $50. You must decide which trip to take. Which trip will you go on?

$100 ski trip to Michigan    44
$50 ski trip to Wisconsin    42

The $\chi^2$ test comparing Experiment 1 (personal money at stake) to Experiment 9 (no personal money at stake) did not approach significance. The analogous comparison between 8A and 3A had been significant. In questionnaire studies such as these it is difficult to manipulate personal commitment. Since in Experiments 8 and 9 we detected only equivocal support for the hypothesis that personal involvement heightens the sunk cost effect, we can draw no firm conclusions as yet on this point.

*Experiment 10*

We made one effort to ascertain whether economically sophisticated subjects are less susceptible to the sunk cost effect. Fischhoff (1982) has concluded that many attempts to debias people of their judgment errors have not been successful. However, some of these debiasing efforts have been of rather

Table 6.1. *Frequency of Choosing Each Trip as a Function of Economics Background*

| | Student Characteristic | | |
| --- | --- | --- | --- |
| | *Economics Students* | *Psychology Students with no Economics* | *Psychology Students with Economics* |
| $100 trip | 20 | 22 | 19 |
| $50 trip | 41 | 39 | 40 |

short duration, such as one experimental session. We sought to determine if a college level economics course (or two) might prove to be of value in lessening the sunk cost effect.

*Method.* One hundred twenty introductory psychology students were divided into two groups based on whether or not they had ever taken a college economics course. Fifty-nine students had taken at least one course; sixty-one had taken no such course. All of these students were administered the Experiment 1 questionnaire by a graduate student in psychology. A third group comprised 61 students currently enrolled in an economics course, who were administered the Experiment 1 questionnaire by their economics professor during an economics class. Approximately three fourths of the students in this group had also taken one prior economics course. All of the economics students had been exposed to the concept of sunk cost earlier that semester both in their textbook (Gwartney & Stroup, 1982, p. 125) and in their class lectures.

*Results.* Table 6.1 contains the results. The $\chi^2$ analysis does not approach significance. Even when an economics teacher in an economics class hands out a sunk cost questionnaire to economics students, there is no more conformity to rational economic theory than in the other two groups. We conclude that general instruction in economics does not lessen the sunk cost effect.

### Relation to Other Theories

*Cognitive Dissonance Theory*

The sunk cost effect would appear to be related to cognitive dissonance theory (Festinger, 1957). Numerous studies have shown that once a subject is induced to expend effort on an onerous task, the task is revalued upward (e.g., Aronson & Mills, 1959). Such revaluation would presumably result in increased willingness to expend further resources on the task compared to the resources which would be voluntarily allocated by a subject not having made a prior expenditure. This generally corresponds to the sunk cost effect.

There are differences, however, between dissonance experiments and the research presented here. First, in dissonance research subjects who have no sufficient justification for performing an onerous task improve their attitude toward the task. In the sunk cost situation, on the other hand, it is unlikely that investors begin to enjoy their foundering investments. Investors may pour good money after bad, but it is doubtful that the bad money engenders positive feelings. Poor investments typically engender substantial distress.

Second, cognitive dissonance theory would predict that a person who endures suffering in order to attend the football game will enjoy the game more than those who do not suffer. However, cognitive dissonance theory does not predict who will be more motivated to *attend* the snowy game (the contest winner or the ticket purchaser) unless we assume that the act of paying for the ticket engendered suffering. This is most unlikely. A more sensible assumption is that a person who has paid for the ticket goes to the game because one knows that if one does not, one will *later* suffer. The reason suffering will later occur if one does not go to the game is that one will feel regret for having wasted the admission price. The cognitive dissonance analysis is mute on the question, "What causes the later suffering," which is answered directly by our wastefulness explanation. We therefore feel that cognitive dissonance theory adds little to our understanding of the sunk cost effect.

### Entrapment

Another area that would seem to be relevant to the sunk cost effect is the research on entrapment (e.g., Brockner, Shaw, & Rubin, 1979). Subjects in entrapment situations typically incur small, continuous losses as they seek or wait for an eventual goal. Brockner et al. cite the example of waiting for a bus. After a very long wait, should you decide to take a cab, thereby nullifying all the time you have spent waiting for the bus? This is analogous to a sunk cost situation: time already spent waiting is the sunk cost. Reluctance to call a cab represents the desire to invest further in waiting.

In a recent analysis of entrapment experiments, Northcraft and Wolf (1984) concluded that continued investment in many of them does not necessarily represent an economically irrational behavior. For example, continued waiting for the bus will increase the probability that one's waiting behavior will be rewarded. Therefore there is an eminently rational basis for continued patience. Hence this situation is not a pure demonstration of the sunk cost effect.

However, we believe that *some* sunk cost situations do correspond to entrapment situations. The subjects who "owned" the airline company would have endured continuing expenditures on the plane as they sought the eventual goal of financial rescue. This corresponds to the Brockner et al. entrapment situation. However, entrapment is irrelevant to the analysis of all our other studies. For example, people who paid more money last September for the season theater tickets are in no way trapped. They do not incur small continuous losses as they seek an eventual goal. Therefore we suggest that entrapment is relevant only to the subset of sunk cost situations in which continuing losses are endured in the hope of later rescue by a further investment.

### Foot-in-the-Door and Low-Ball Techniques

Freedman and Fraser (1966) demonstrated that a person who first complies with a small request is more likely to comply with a larger request later. When the large and small requests are for *related* activities that differ in their cost to the complying person, the phenomenon is called the foot-in-the-door technique. An example would be first having people sign a petition to encourage legislators to support safe driving laws. Later, the petition signers are asked to display on their lawn a large sign that reads, "Drive safely."

When the small and large requests are for the *same* target behavior, the technique is called the "low-ball" procedure (Cialdini, Cacioppo, Bassett, & Miller, 1978). An example would be getting someone to agree to buy a car at a discounted price and then removing the discount. The initial decision to buy heightens willingness to buy later when the car is no longer a good deal.

Both the foot-in-the-door and low-ball techniques bear some similarity to the sunk cost phenomenon in that an investment which is unlikely to be made (question 3B) will be more likely if a prior commitment has occurred (3A). A major difference between the sunk cost effect and the two techniques is that compliance is the dependent variable with the two techniques. Compliance typically plays no role in the sunk cost effect.

Most explanations of the foot-in-the-door technique are couched in terms of self-perception theory (Bem, 1967). A person observes himself or herself complying with a request to support good driving or a charitable organization. The person then concludes, "I'm the sort of person who supports that cause." This conclusion based on self-observation then results in a high level of compliance when the larger request is made later (Snyder & Cunningham, 1975).

We do not see how a self-perception explanation could readily be applied to the sunk cost effect. We very much doubt that people continue investing because they conclude they are the sort of person who continues some particular investment. We suggest that the foot-in-the-door technique applies largely to compliance and not the domain of the sunk cost effect.

We believe that the low-ball procedure bears even less similarity to the sunk cost effect. In the latter, a prior investment has occurred. In the low-ball procedure, no prior investment has occurred, only a verbal commitment. The buyer has not actually paid money to obtain the discounted car. Therefore, in the sunk cost situation, an investment can be lost, while in the low-ball procedure, there are no funds to be forfeited.

### Epilogue

We have presented evidence which suggests that the sunk cost effect is a robust judgment error. According to Thomas (1981), one person who recognized it as an error was none other than Thomas A. Edison. In the 1880s Edison was not making much money on his great invention, the electric lamp. The problem was that his manufacturing plant was not operating at full capacity because he could not sell enough of his lamps. He then got the idea to boost his plant's production to full capacity and sell each extra lamp below its total cost of production. His associates thought this was an exceedingly poor idea, but Edison did it anyway. By increasing his plant's output, Edison would add only 2% to the cost of production while increasing production 25%. Edison was able to do this because so much of the manufacturing cost was sunk cost. It would be present whether or not he manufactured more bulbs. Edison then sold the large number of extra lamps in Europe for much more than the small *added* manufacturing costs. Since production increase involved negligible new costs but substantial new income, Edison was wise to increase production. While Edison was able to place sunk costs in proper perspective in arriving at his decision, our research suggests that most of the rest of us find that very difficult to do.

### Notes

1   This example is adapted from Thaler (1980).
2   We are aware that the senators who supported the Tennessee – Tombigbee Waterway Project and those who supported or opposed nuclear power may have had motives other than sunk cost considerations. It is instructive that Senators Denton and Sasser used sunk cost arguments in defending the project's continuation. Apparently they felt that sunk cost was a more compelling rationale than others that might have been offered.
3   In this analysis we are ignoring "income effects." While it is true that the discount groups had more disposable income with which to seek nontheater entertainment during the year, we contend that this extra income was not the reason they attended fewer plays. The $2 discount group, whose members manifested the sunk cost effect, had only an extra 10¢ or so of disposable income per week during the course of the experiment.
4   A possible problem with Experiment 7 is that even though the purchase of a press would result in an increase of 50% in printing capability in both stories, the purchase in 7A would result in a slower machine than would the corresponding purchase in 7B. We ran another experiment in which this difference in absolute printing speed was eliminated. The results of this study replicated the results of Experiment 7.
5   95XIL is a local radio station.

## References

Aronson, E., & Mills, J. (1959). The effect of severity of initiation on liking for a group. *Journal of Abnormal and Social Psychology, 59*, 177–181.

Bem, D. (1967). Self-perception: An alternative interpretation of cognitive dissonance phenomenon. *Psychological Review, 74*, 183–200.

Brockner, J., Shaw, M. C., & Rubin, J. Z. (1979). Factors affecting withdrawal from an escalating conflict: Quitting before it's too late. *Journal of Experimental Social Psychology, 15*, 492–503.

Cialdini, R. B., Cacioppo, J. T., Bassett, R., & Miller, J. A. (1978). Low-ball procedure for procuring compliance: Commitment then cost. *Journal of Personality and Social Psychology, 36*, 463–476.

Dowie, M. (1981). Atomic psyche-out. *Mother Jones, 6*, 21–23, 47–55.

Festinger, L. (1957). *A theory of cognitive dissonance.* Stanford: Stanford University Press.

Fischhoff, B. (1982). Debiasing. In D. Kahneman, P. Slovic, & A. Tversky (Eds.), *Judgment under uncertainty: Heuristics and biases.* New York: Cambridge University Press.

Freedman, J. L., & Fraser, S. (1966). Compliance without pressure: The foot-in-the-door technique. *Journal of Personality and Social Psychology, 4*, 195–202.

Grether, D. M., & Plott, C. R. (1979). Economic theory of choice and the preference reversal phenomenon. *American Economic Review, 69*, 623–638.

Gwartney, J. D., & Stroup, R. (1982). *Microeconomics: Private and public choice.* New York: Academic Press.

Kahneman, D., & Tversky, A. (1979). Prospect theory: An analysis of decision under risk. *Econometrica 47*, 263–291.

Lichtenstein, S. (1973). Response-induced reversals of preference in gambling: An extended replication in Las Vegas. *Journal of Experimental Psychology, 101*, 16–20.

McGlothlin, W. H. (1956). Stability of choices among uncertain alternatives. *American Journal of Psychology, 69*, 604–615.

Northcraft, G. B., & Wolf, G. (1984). Dollars, sense, and sunk costs: A life-cycle model of resource-allocation decisions. *Academy of Management Review, 9*, 225–234.

Snyder, M., & Cunningham, M. R. (1975). To comply or not comply: Testing the self-perception explanation of the "foot-in-the-door" phenomenon. *Journal of Personality and Social Psychology, 31*, 64–67.

Staw, B. M. (1976). Knee-deep in the big muddy: A study of escalating commitment to a chosen course of action. *Organizational Behavior and Human Performance, 16*, 27–44.

Staw, B. M., & Fox, F. (1977). Escalation: Some determinants of commitment to a previously chosen course of action. *Human Relations, 30*, 431–450.

Teger, A. I. (1980). *Too much invested to quit.* New York: Pergamon.

Thaler, R. (1980). Toward a positive theory of consumer choice. *Journal of Economic Behavior and Organization, 1*, 39–60.

Thomas, R. P. (1981). *Microeconomic applications: Understanding the American economy.* Belmont. CA: Wadsworth.

# 7 Value-Focused Thinking about Strategic Decisions at BC Hydro

*Ralph L. Keeney and Timothy L. McDaniels*

British Columbia Hydro and Power Authority (BC Hydro) is a large hydro-electric-based, publically owned, integrated electric utility supplying power to over 90 percent of the British Columbia population. As a major corporation with billions of dollars in annual sales (and one of Canada's 10 largest corporations in terms of assets), BC Hydro naturally faces many complex strategic decisions in the coming decades. These decisions involve such issues as adding resources to generate electricity, siting and constructing transmission lines, negotiating international power agreements and arrangements with independent power producers, mitigating the environmental effects of facilities, communicating with the public and interest groups, and addressing such actual or perceived public risks as electromagnetic fields and global warming [BC Hydro 1990]. Such decisions should be made using quality information and sound logic in a coordinated manner that can be clearly justified and openly communicated to stakeholders.

Many individuals have key decision-making roles at BC Hydro. One department has responsibility for dams and dam safety, another for high voltage transmission, a third for pricing policies, and others for electricity exports to the United States. To facilitate the coordination of their decisions, L. I. Bell, the chairman and CEO of BC Hydro, appointed Ken Peterson as BC Hydro's director of planning. In simple but profound terms, Peterson's assignment was to make BC Hydro the best planned electric utility in North America. To help fulfill this responsibility, Peterson created a planning committee composed of senior managers from departments with major decision-making roles at BC Hydro.

Peterson realized that all the decisions at BC Hydro should contribute to achieving a set of long-range objectives, which could be called the strategic objectives of the organization. BC Hydro has published a mission statement and broad goals, but these are very general, as is usually the case. Peterson

This chapter originally appeared in *Interfaces*, 1992, 22, 94–109. Copyright © 1992 by The Institute of Management Sciences (currently INFORMS). Reprinted by permission.

realized that they were too general to provide guidance for coordinating decisions, although they would be useful in articulating strategic objectives that would provide insight for a range of decisions.

In early 1989, we were invited to present a one-day seminar at BC Hydro to discuss the role of analysis in facilitating and coordinating strategic decisions. Subsequently, we began working with Peterson and other members of the planning committee to make a preliminary attempt to identify, structure, and quantify BC Hydro's strategic objectives.

### Defining Strategic Objectives

Objectives are widely recognized as essential for informed decision making. All organizations and individuals have objectives, either implicit or explicit, that guide their decisions to some extent. Authorities on strategic management often discuss the need for objectives, sometimes cast in terms of mission statements, organizational goals, or value credos, as a key step in developing strategic approaches (for example, Pearce and Robinson [1985]). This step can be difficult for those not experienced in clarifying unstructured problems: they often confuse ends with means or objectives with targets or constraints, they fail to see the relationships between different objectives, and they easily misconstrue the concept of priorities within objectives [Keeney 1988a]. How then does value-focused thinking differ from other ways to define objectives, and what advantages does it offer?

In simple terms, most approaches emphasize the need for objectives but pay remarkably little attention to how objectives should be developed. There is a need for greater depth, clearer structure, a sound conceptual base, and better practice in developing objectives for strategic decisions.

Because the terms *strategic* and *objectives* are widely used, but often with different meanings, some definitions are in order. We define an objective as a statement of something that one wants to achieve. It is characterized by three features: a decision context, an objective, and a direction of preference [Keeney 1992]. For example, one objective of siting a dam is to "minimize environmental impacts." With this objective, the decision context is siting a dam, the objective is environmental impact, and less impact is preferred to more.

We distinguish between *fundamental objectives* and *means objectives*. Fundamental objectives are concerned with ends rather than means. Ends are the fundamental objects of value that stakeholders care about in a specific decision context, while means objectives are methods to achieve ends. Fundamental objectives provide a basis for making value trade-offs and developing a utility function that mathematically represents how subobjectives contribute to broader objectives and how much of one objective a decision maker should be willing to forgo to achieve better performance on another objective.

Thus, fundamental objectives provide a structure for clarifying the values of interest in a given decision context and provide a basis for evaluating alternatives. Fundamental objectives can be developed for a specific decision context, such as choosing a new technology [Keeney, Lathrop, and Sicherman 1986], or they can be used to provide insight for a whole class of decisions or strategies. We define the fundamental objectives for strategic decisions, the broadest class of decisions facing an organization, as strategic objectives.

Strategic objectives should have the following characteristics. They should be relevant to a wide range of decision contexts, to a long time period, and to many levels in an organization. Strategic objectives should be deep, in the sense that they should clarify the fundamental objects that are important to all aspects of an organization's activities. Strategic objectives should be structured to provide insight into how analysis should proceed in applied decision contexts. Finally, strategic objectives should be deliberately general to enhance flexibility, which comes at the cost of detail. Thus, strategic objectives can provide a basis for more detailed fundamental objectives that would be appropriate for specific decisions.

The basic process for developing and quantifying strategic objectives should involve the following steps:

1. Hard thinking by key decision makers, guided by analysts, to identify what factors are fundamentally important for the organization's decisions. The analyst ensures that important objectives are not omitted.
2. Structuring the strategic objectives into a hierarchy that clarifies the differences between ends and means and eliminates redundancies.
3. Defining attributes for the objectives to clarify exactly what the objectives mean and to measure possible consequences.
4. Developing a utility function over the strategic objectives that indicates value trade-offs among the objectives. The utility function should reflect the viewpoints of various groups within the organization and could possibly consider the viewpoints of other stakeholders as well.

Keeney [1988b] discusses in detail the steps involved in identifying and structuring fundamental objectives for public policy decisions. Many of these methods are relevant in the organizational context of BC Hydro as well, with one major difference. Because strategic objectives are intended to be used across a wide variety of decision contexts, one must build consensus at every step in the process. Consensus on the relevance of the objectives and their structure is a precursor to successful implementation.

## Identifying and Structuring Strategic Objectives for BC Hydro

The first step in identifying and structuring objectives is to list the objectives that individuals from the organization judge important. For this purpose, we separately met with Victor de Buen, senior systems studies engineer, Zak El-Ramly, manager of policy development, and Ken Peterson, director of planning, to obtain their views on BC Hydro objectives for the next decade. The general procedure we used to obtain information about objectives was an open discussion. Each discussion lasted about three hours and began with a short introduction. We made no attempt to structure the discussion further, as such measures tend to limit its breadth.

We used two devices to enhance the likelihood that objectives would not be limited to the context of business as usual but also cover unusual situations. We inquired about particularly undesirable alternatives and asked why they were so undesirable or what could have gone wrong to make them undesirable. We also asked about particularly undesirable consequences, such as a government inquiry being convened to investigate BC Hydro, and then pursued what grounds could have led to such a situation. Both of these devices led to discussions that helped identify objectives that might otherwise have been omitted.

Keeney [1992] discusses these interviews extensively, focusing on the sequential and iterative nature of the questioning we used to clarify what particular objectives meant and how they related to more fundamental objectives. In brief, we clarified what the three individuals each meant when they mentioned particular objectives by pursuing means-ends relationships among the objectives and specifying the details of the objectives. The process is intended to get beyond the motherhood-and-apple-pie objectives to which everyone can agree but which serve no operational purpose. But even after these ambiguities are eliminated, a range of interpretations could still be given to any of the stated objectives. The process of structuring these objectives, identifying attributes to indicate the degree to which they are achieved, and quantifying values for objectives all substantially reduce the remaining ambiguity.

### Hierarchy of Strategic Objectives

Our initial discussions with these three individuals resulted in two main products. One was a preliminary hierarchy of strategic objectives, which is a comprehensive list of the objectives that should be used to evaluate alternatives. In such a hierarchy, major objectives are specified by subobjectives to render the set more useful for analysis. The second product was a network of preliminary objectives that relates all the fundamental objectives specified in the objectives hierarchy to all the other objectives identified in our

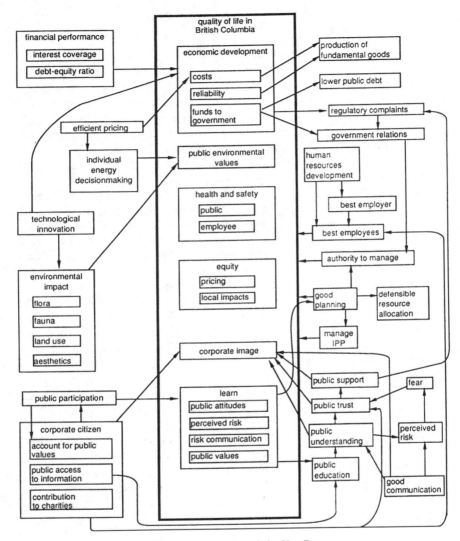

Figure 7.1. The initial objectives network for Ken Peterson.

discussion. The objectives network also indicates the relationships among the various objectives by indicating how the achievement of certain objectives influences the achievement of other objectives (Figure 7.1). Keeney [1992] provides examples and discussion of objective networks, including those for the individuals interviewed from BC Hydro.

After the initial discussions, we developed the material regarding preliminary objective hierarchies and objective networks for each of the three individuals. A few weeks later, we again met with Peterson to review his initial set of strategic objectives and to specify attributes for the objectives. The objectives stated by de Buen and El-Ramly and the process of specifying attributes both suggested improvements for Peterson's list of strategic objectives.

The result of our meeting was a revised version of Peterson's hierarchy of strategic objectives, together with a preliminary set of attributes. We documented the changes to the strategic objectives and gave Peterson an opportunity to review them. We met again to finalize the set of strategic objectives and attributes and to quantify Peterson's values. Prior to the meeting, we had done a little background work to help identify potentially better attributes for some of the strategic objectives. Based on our discussions with Peterson, we felt we understood his values reasonably well, certainly well enough to make productive suggestions for changes. This meeting again led to a few alterations to the strategic objectives.

Table 7.1 summarizes the final version of Ken Peterson's views on strategic objectives for BC Hydro planning over the next decade. His overall strategic objective is to maximize BC Hydro's contribution to quality-of-life in British Columbia, an overall objective common among all three individuals interviewed. This reflects the fact that BC Hydro is a Crown corporation and its activities affect many dimensions of economic, social, and environmental well-being in British Columbia. This overall objective is broken into six major objectives, most of which have several subobjectives. The major objectives include maximizing contribution to economic development in British Columbia, which is further disaggregated into minimizing cost of electricity, maximizing funds transferred to the British Columbia government, and minimizing the economic implications of natural resource losses due to BC Hydro generation and transmission facilities. The subobjectives clarify what the higher level objective means; in this case, the subobjectives clarify three kinds of economic values that BC Hydro activities could affect.

Another major objective is to act consistently with the public's environmental values, which clearly is distinct from simply attempting to minimize environmental effects. This objective is disaggregated into local environmental impacts and global environmental impacts. Other major objectives include minimizing the adverse health and safety effects of BC Hydro activities, promoting equitable business arrangements, and maximizing the quality of service, which has four subobjectives. Two of these deal with reliability issues, while two others concern customer service responsiveness. A final objective is to be recognized as public-service oriented. This set of strategic objectives was viewed as comprehensive, in that it addresses factors that are important at the strategic level of BC Hydro decision making over the next 10 years, and fundamental, in that it addresses the ends rather than means.

Table 7.1. *The Final Version of Peterson's Strategic Objectives Hierarchy, with Attributes*

1. Maximize contribution to economic development
    11. Minimize cost of electricity use (mills per kilowatt-hour in 1989 Canadian dollars)
    12. Maximize funds transferred to government (annualized dividend payable)
    13. Minimize economic implications of resource losses (cost of resource losses in 1989 Canadian dollars)
2. Act consistently with the public's environmental values
    21. About local environmental impacts
        211. To flora (hectares of mature forest lost)
        212. To fauna (hectares of wildlife habitat lost of Spatzizi Plateau quality)
        213. To wildlife ecosystems (hectares of wilderness lost of the Stikine Valley quality)
        214. To limit recreational use (hectares of high quality recreational land lost)
        215. To aesthetics (annual person-years viewing high voltage transmission lines in quality terrain)
    22. About global impacts (generation capacity in megawatts that results in "fossil fuel" pollution)
3. Minimize detrimental health and safety impacts
    31. To the public
        311. Mortality (public person-years of life lost)
        312. Morbidity (public person-years of disability equal in severity to that causing employee lost work time)
    32. To employees
        321. Mortality (employee person-years of life lost)
        322. Morbidity (employee person-years of lost work time)
4. Promote equitable business arrangements
    41. Equitable pricing to different customers (constructed scale, see text)
    42. Equitable compensation for concentrated local impacts (number of individuals who feel they are inequitably treated)
5. Maximize quality of service
    51. To small customers
        511. Minimize outages (expected number of annual outages to a small customer annually)
        512. Minimize duration of outages (average hours of outage per outage to small customers)
    52. To large customers
        521. Minimize outages (expected number of annual outages to a large customer annually)
        522. Minimize duration of outages (average hours of outage per outage to large customers)
    53. Improve new service (elapsed time until new service is installed)
    54. Improve response to telephone inquiries (time until human answers the telephone)
6. Be recognized as public service oriented (constructed scale, see text)

Numbers 1–6 refer to major objectives; two digit numbers (for example, 11–13) refer to subobjectives for a given major objective; three digit numbers (for example, 211–215) refer to components of subobjectives. Attributes are in parentheses. Numbering could refer to either objectives or attributes (for example, objective 311 and attribute 311).

## Attributes to Measure the Strategic Objectives

For each of the lowest level objectives in the hierarchy, we needed to specify an attribute to measure the degree to which the objective is achieved. Specifying attributes is the most effective way to make the objectives hierarchy useful for subsequent analysis of strategic decisions. Without attributes, there are two dangers: (1) confusion could arise over what the objectives mean and (2) the objectives might be of no more relevance than principles that were generally important to the organization. With attributes, the objectives can be used as a framework to evaluate alternatives.

Attributes must clearly capture and reflect the intent of a particular objective. For example, objective 11, to minimize cost of electricity use, is measured by the levelized cost of energy for new sources as it enters the local transmission network. Thus, attribute 11 in Table 7.1 is mills per kilowatt-hour in 1989 Canadian dollars, which addresses possible transmission losses by calculating their effect on the levelized cost of electricity. The annual dividend paid to the provincial government increases the cost of electricity, when all other things are held equal. Thus, objective 12, to maximize funds transferred to the government, conflicts with objective 11, which is always the case when there are multiple objectives. If there is no conflict, then by definition there is only a single objective.

The details of the attributes for objective 2, to act consistently with the public's environmental values, would ideally be generated from values expressed by the public or by stakeholder groups within that public. The attributes listed below address the subobjectives of the environmental objective and are intended to give the range over which the public might assess their values. This range is also sufficient for setting priorities among the major six objectives.

With each of the attributes 211 through 215, we had to address environmental impacts of a different quality and type. For example, with objective 211, we translated different impacts to flora into an equivalent amount of acres of mature forest lost. Also, to assess this attribute we needed a clear understanding of precisely what is meant by "mature forest." For our purposes, we assumed it was densely wooded but not highly valued old-growth forest.

For health and safety impacts, we used the same attributes for mortality and morbidity for both the public and employees. The mortality attributes weight the death of a younger person more than the death of an older person, since the younger person loses more expected lifetime. To be more precise, a 15-year-old who is electrocuted may have had an expected life-time of 80. The electrocution would result in the loss of 65 person-years of life.

The morbidity could result from either injuries due to accidents or illnesses induced by emissions from power plants, for example. By specifying the level of severity as that causing employees lost work time, we mean to evaluate only the significant morbidity. It would be natural to assume that less important cases of morbidity would be correlated with more important cases. Hence, in any evaluation of alternatives, it may be appropriate in sensitivity analysis to overweight this attribute measuring serious morbidity to also account for cases of lesser morbidity that might be correlated.

With attribute 41, equitable pricing to different customers, we are concerned with three types of customers: residential, commercial, and industrial. The input to the constructed scale for equity would use the price of electricity to each of the groups relative to its cost of service delivered to the premises. The most equitable situation is when all three types of customers have the exact same ratio. The constructed scale is to measure the sum of the differences between the ratios of each group and the average of those ratios. Thus, if $r_i$, $i = 1, 2, 3$ is the price to cost ratio for the three types of customers, and if $\bar{r}$ is the average of $r_1$, $r_2$, and $r_3$, then the measure of equity is $\sum_i |r_i - \bar{r}|$.

The attribute for public-service orientation is a constructed scale with five levels of impact. An individual may perceive BC Hydro as very public-service oriented (level 4), as moderately public-service oriented (level 3), as somewhat public-service oriented (level 2), as minimally public-service oriented (level 1), or not public-service oriented at all (level 0). The extremes of this scale would correspond to situations in which everyone felt that BC Hydro was very public-service oriented or that the organization was not at all public-service oriented.

### Strategic Utility Function Assessment

At this stage, we (and Peterson) felt that Table 7.1 represented a good initial set of strategic objectives for BC Hydro over the next decade. It would have been useful to conduct this in-depth qualitative identification of objectives with additional members of management and then aggregate the lists, which we did not do in this preliminary study. We did quantify the values that Peterson felt were appropriate for BC Hydro to pursue. Such a quantitative exercise represents only one individual's view of the value trade-offs pertinent to BC Hydro decisions. Nevertheless, it demonstrates the process for others and indicates the types of insights that might be gained from the effort expended.

### Ranges of Impacts for the Attributes

Having defined the objectives and attributes, our next step was to specify a range for each of the attributes, over which the utility function was to be assessed (Table 7.2). These ranges were essential so that we could set priorities among the objectives in a way that made sense and had a meaningful interpretation. We selected these attributes to broadly reflect the range of the potential impacts of policies BC Hydro may consider over the next decade.

Table 7.2. *A List of Objectives, Attributes, and Ranges for Assessment*

|  | Worst Level | Best Level |
|---|---|---|
| 11. Levelized cost of energy from new sources at grid (1989 mills/kWh) | 55 | 35 |
| 12. Annualized dividend payable (1989 dollars in millions) | 0 | $200 |
| 13. Economic cost of resource losses (1989 dollars in millions) | $20 | 0 |
| 211. Flora (hectares of mature forest) | 10,000 | 0 |
| 212. Fauna (hectares of wildlife habitat – Spatzizi Plateau quality) | 10,000 | 0 |
| 213. Wilderness ecosystem (hectares of wilderness loss – Stikine Valley quality) | 10,000 | 0 |
| 214. Recreation (hectares of recreational land lost – provincial park quality) | 10,000 | 0 |
| 215. Aesthetic (annual person-years viewing high voltage transmission line in quality terrain) | 500,000 | 0 |
| 22. Global environmental impact (megawatts of fossil pollutants) | 1,000 | 0 |
| 311. Public mortality (annual person-years of life lost) | 100 | 0 |
| 312. Public morbidity (annual person-years "severe" disability) | 1,000 | 0 |
| 321. Worker mortality (annual person-years life lost) | 100 | 0 |
| 322. Worker morbidity (annual person-years lost work time) | 1,000 | 0 |
| 41. Equitable pricing (constructed scale) | 0.5 | 0 |
| 42. Equitable compensation (annual average number of individuals who suffer significant impact, such as property loss, felt to be inequitably treated) | 500 | 0 |
| 511. Small customer outages (annual number/customer) | 2 | 0 |
| 512. Small customer outage duration (hours/outage) | 24 | 0 |
| 521. Large customer outages (annual number/customer) | 2 | 0 |
| 522. Large customer outage duration (hours/outage) | 24 | 0 |
| 53. New service (hook up time in work days) | 20 | 1 |
| 54. Inquiries (time until personal response in minutes) | 1 | 0 |
| 6. Recognized as acting in public's interest (constructed scale) | 0 | 4 |

Numbering follows that of Table 7.1. Attributes are in parentheses. Worst and best refer to levels of the attribute.

### The Strategic Utility Function

Even though the strategic utility function has 22 attributes, it is of a rather simple form. The main reason is that when fundamental objectives (the strategic objectives in this case) are quantified by a value assessment, the form of the utility function should be additive, or multiplicative [Keeney 1980]. Typically, the functional forms become more unwieldy when values are assessed over means. The software "Logical Decision" [Smith 1989] was used to determine the utility function implied by the value assessment.

The overall utility function has six major components concerning (1) economics, (2) environment, (3) health and safety, (4) equity, (5) service, and (6) public-interest perception. After verifying the appropriate assumptions [Fishburn 1965], we found the overall utility function $u$ to be additive, so

$$u(u_1, \ldots, u_6) = k_1 u_1 + k_2 u_2 + \cdots + k_6 u_6, \tag{1}$$

where $u$ and the major-objective utility functions $u_i$, $i = 1, \ldots, 6$ are scaled from 0 to 1 over the ranges in Table 7.2 and $k_i$, $i = 1, \ldots, 6$ are scaling constants for the major objectives.

Most of the major-objective utility functions and the utility functions of subobjectives were also additive with a few notable exceptions. The economic utility function was not additive because the three economic subobjectives are in a sense substitutes for each other. There was an overall risk aversion for this component, indicating an aversion to bad performance on all three subobjectives simultaneously. We verified preferential independence for pairs of three economic attributes, and each attribute was utility independent of others. Hence, a multiplicative utility function was appropriate for the subobjectives of the economic objective [Keeney and Raiffa 1976]. The utility functions for possible outages for small and large customers are also not additive. The dependence here concerns the inclusion of both quality (duration) and quantity (number) of outages in the same function. If either dimension is very low in terms of extent of outages, the decision maker would not be as concerned about the other dimension. Both quality and quantity are utility independent of each other, implying that the subobjective utility functions are multiplicative.

### Assessed Value Trade-offs and Risk Attitudes

To illustrate the types of judgments necessary to determine a utility function, we present some examples of value trade-offs and risk attitudes provided by Ken Peterson.

To quantify value trade-offs, one needs to determine pairs of consequences that vary in the achievement of two attributes and that are indifferent to each other. A relatively easy value trade-off to make concerns two economic attributes. Using procedures discussed in Keeney [1980], we found that Peterson was indifferent between consequences ($x_{11} = 48$, $x_{13} = 20$) and ($x_{11} = 55$, $x_{13} = 0$). This meant that it was just worth a change in levelized cost from 48 to 55 mills per kilowatt-hour to obtain a drop in resource cost from $20 million to $0. Resource costs are defined as direct economic costs due to the loss of such resources as productive forests or commercial fisheries.

Impacts on wildlife ecosystems turned out to be the most heavily weighted environmental attribute, given the ranges. The assessed value trade-off indicated that ($x_{13} = 0$, $x_{213} = 10{,}000$) is indifferent to ($x_{13} = 20$, $x_{213} = 2{,}000$), meaning that eliminating a $20 million direct resource cost would be indifferent to reducing the loss of quality wilderness from 10,000 to 2,000 hectares. Because the economic utility function is not additive, the exact value trade-off depends on where the other two economic attributes are fixed. For this value trade-off, they were set at $x_{11} = 40$ and $x_{12} = 100$.

Regarding risk attitudes, most of the component utility functions were linear as should be expected for most fundamental objectives. Two were not, and they illustrate both risk-averse and risk-prone attitudes. For attribute 12, the annual government dividend, a payment of $50 million was felt to be indifferent to a half chance of paying either $200 million or $0. To pay nothing might be misinterpreted as an emergency. This indicates risk aversion.

For attribute 522, the duration of power outages to large customers, a duration of eight hours was indifferent to equal chances at zero or 24 hours outage. Here the feeling was that part of the damage occurs rather quickly as shifts of workers may have to be sent home and as some equipment cannot immediately be started up again after a shutdown. This is an example of a risk prone attitude.

### The Scaling Constants

Perhaps the most interesting results of the value assessment involve the scaling constants. The value trade-offs just outlined were used to calculate the scaling constants in the overall utility function (1) for the six major objectives. The results of the calculations provided the following scaling constants:

$k_1 = 0.395$ (economics),
$k_2 = 0.250$ (environment),
$k_3 = 0.089$ (health and safety),
$k_4 = 0.012$ (equity),
$k_5 = 0.250$ (quality of service), and
$k_6 = 0.004$ (perceived public-service orientation).

These scaling constants must be interpreted using the ranges in Table 7.2. Each scaling constant indicates the relative importance, in terms of overall contribution to quality of life in British Columbia, of moving the corresponding attributes from their worst to their best levels in Table 7.2.

By multiplying the constants $k_1$ through $k_6$ by the individual scaling constants determined for the utility functions we could determine priorities for the corresponding strategic objectives, again recognizing the ranges for those objectives in Table 7.2. The resulting priorities, both in terms of weights and ranks, are given in Table 7.3. Because the component utility function for economic objectives was not additive, we used normalized scaling constants in the calculations. Also, with the quality of service utility function, we assumed there were 1.2 million small customers and 20,000 large customers.

Table 7.3. *Calculated Priorities among the Strategic Objectives*

|  | Weight | Rank |
|---|---|---|
| 11. Levelized cost | 0.253 | 1 |
| 12. Annualized government dividend | 0.053 | 6 |
| 13. Resource cost | 0.088 | 5 |
| 211. Flora | 0.023 | 11 |
| 212. Fauna | 0.046 | 7 |
| 213. Wilderness | 0.093 | 4 |
| 214. Recreation | 0.046 | 7 |
| 215. Aesthetic | 0.023 | 11 |
| 22. Global impact | 0.019 | 13 |
| 31. Public health and safety | 0.045 | 9 |
| 32. Employee health and safety | 0.045 | 9 |
| 41. Equitable compensation | 0.008 | 15 |
| 42. Equitable pricing | 0.004 | 17 |
| 51. Small customer service | 0.111 | 3 |
| 52. Large customer service | 0.125 | 2 |
| 53. New customer service | 0.010 | 14 |
| 54. Inquiries response | 0.005 | 16 |
| 6. Public impact perception | 0.004 | 17 |

### Insights from the Value Assessment

From the scaling constants calculated above, it is clear that the major strategic objectives that matter concern economics, the environment, health and safety, and quality of service. The combined weight on equity and perceived public-service orientation, given their ranges, is less than two percent. Moreover, parts of two of the four important objectives are also relatively insignificant. Global environmental impact accounts for only seven percent of the environmental impact (as a consequence of the ranges considered in Table 7.2) and is less important than any of the five separate local environmental impact categories. Within service quality, the impacts of outages accounted for 94 percent of the concern, whereas the impacts on new service and inquiries together accounted for the other six percent. Collectively, the implication is that 95 percent of the utility from achievement of objectives is associated with economic impacts, local environmental impacts, health and safety, and possible service outages. The other six objectives, those ranked 13 and below in Table 7.3, contribute only five percent.

It is interesting to review the insight provided by the assessment for the values associated with specific impacts. Given the utility function (1), we can calculate for any specified impact on one attribute an equivalently valued impact on another attribute. In practice, a useful way to examine value trade-offs is in terms of economic impacts because we usually have a common experience in comparing dollar values. One interesting value trade-off concerned system reliability, a dimension of quality of service, and economics. Peterson's value judgments indicated that, in his view, two outages per year of two hours duration each to 20,000 large customers (either commercial or industrial accounts) were equivalent to an increase of 1.7 mills/kWh for system energy costs. A 1.7 mills/kWh increase in cost is effectively equivalent to $83,300,000 in net earnings potentially available for transfer to the provincial government as a dividend. Thus, if BC Hydro had opportunities to reduce expected outages of that nature at a cost less than $83 million, those opportunities would be good investments from the utility's perspective, based on Peterson's value trade-offs.

## Potential Uses

The assessed utility function and the potential insights that it provides could be used in a variety of strategic decision contexts at BC Hydro: to clarify complex decisions, to improve communication within the organization, to facilitate stakeholder input and regulatory review, and to identify decision opportunities. In simple words, the structured and quantified values promote and provide the basis for value-focused thinking.

## Clarifying Complex Decisions

The objectives and utility function are potentially useful to BC Hydro in all its major decisions over the next decade. The objectives can clarify the basic structure of value trade-offs that should be considered in any decision context, even though further specification of the objectives could be needed for many specific decisions. Virtually any major decision, ranging from selecting new supply sources to siting facilities, to determining the roles of independent power producers or demand-side management, to setting policies regarding the environmental effects of projects, to making investments in health and safety (such as dam safety or electromagnetic fields) could be clarified and structured using these objectives.

BC Hydro has used versions of this multiobjective structure in various contexts since we did this work. In one example the planning committee was charged with determining how an overall percentage reduction in capital expenditures should be allocated across the range of capital expenditures planned for coming years. A typical approach for such restraint programs would be to simply reduce all capital expenditures by a fixed percentage. That approach makes no allowance for differences in the importance of the budget items in terms of effects on the organization's objectives. The planning committee elected instead to develop a scoring model approach with a multiple objective structure reflecting the considerations outlined here. It used this scoring model approach to help clarify how the capital budget reductions should be allocated.

In another example, BC Hydro is also using a multiple objective approach in developing the utility's integrated electricity plan. This plan will clarify how new electrical loads will be served over the coming decade. BC Hydro intends to use a multiple objective structure, rather than a cost-minimizing or social-benefit-cost-analysis approach as the analytical basis for selecting among alternatives. In a third example, BC Hydro is using a multiple objective approach to reliability planning. It is developing an explicit multiple objective structure, in this case involving two major objectives (cost and reliability), as a basis for evaluating investment options to improve reliability.

## Improving Communication within the Organization

One of the key issues facing senior management in BC Hydro, as in many other organizations, is effective management and implementation of organizational change. The utility is using new approaches to planning, and managers must translate strategic direction from senior management into ongoing operational practice. One of the most effective means to facilitate this task is to clarify objectives that are important for organizational decision making. A number of writers (for example, Peters [1987]) have stressed the importance of "empowered" employees who are given responsibility for making and implementing decisions within a particular area. One of the best ways to facilitate empowerment is to provide employees with a structured set of objectives, accompanied by an organizational utility function, that makes it easier for them to make appropriate decisions within their realms of responsibility.

## Facilitating Stakeholder Input and Regulatory Review

Electric utilities must respond to the interests of a wide variety of stakeholder groups. Because BC Hydro is a Crown corporation rather than an investor-owned utility, the importance of stakeholder groups is perhaps even greater than in most other utilities. Its concern for stakeholder input is indicated by its increasing reliance on public involvement programs in its planning activities. Those who implement public involvement programs and attempt to interpret their findings must find a way to represent stakeholder views in analytical terms. The multiple objective structure and utility function is an excellent vehicle for clarifying to stakeholders the strategic issues of importance to BC Hydro and for structuring stakeholder views in analytical terms.

Utility functions for stakeholder groups have been used in a variety of contexts to foster communication, to clarify differences, and to build consensus on the full range of objectives important in a planning problem [Edwards and von Winterfeldt 1987]. Such an approach could be implemented for BC Hydro planning as an explicit means of clarifying the value trade-offs that interest groups feel are appropriate for the organization's activities. By explicitly outlining a set of objectives and a preliminary statement of value trade-offs between these objectives, the organization would facilitate informed debate by illustrating that all policies have benefits and costs associated with them and that value trade-offs are unavoidable.

An approach that encourages informed debate about desired value trade-offs for the utility's activities would also be beneficial for regulatory contexts. It makes the organization's objectives and value trade-offs for any decision clear. Regulators or government agencies can then easily examine the implications of different value trade-offs.

### Identifying Decision Opportunities

The set of objectives and the utility function we outlined are useful for identifying potential decision opportunities. A decision opportunity is the natural result of thinking about what is important and how to get there [Keeney 1992]. Each of the tasks comprising the BC Hydro value assessment suggests potential decision opportunities that may be worthwhile for BC Hydro to pursue.

Some of the decision opportunities available to BC Hydro pertain to gathering information about values that might help make decisions later. These opportunities include: investigating the relationship between natural resource losses (objective 13) and overall economic activity; determining values associated with environmental losses associated with potential hydroelectric developments (objectives 212 and 213); obtaining complete data regarding public and employee fatalities associated with BC Hydro equipment and activities (objectives 311 and 321); developing a more detailed utility function for equitable pricing (objective 41); and refining the quality of service utility function (objectives 511–514).

Other decision opportunities involve significant decisions in themselves. These include: examining consumer decisions about demand-side management; clarifying opportunities for involvement of independent power producers; and clarifying strategies regarding electromagnetic fields.

### References

British Columbia Hydro and Power Authority 1990, *Corporate Business Plan*, Management Services Division, Vancouver, British Columbia, Canada.

Edwards, W. and von Winterfeldt, D. 1987, "Public values in risk debates," *Risk Analysis*, Vol. 7, No. 2, pp. 141–158.

Fishburn, P. C. 1965, "Independence in utility theory with whole product sets," *Operations Research*, Vol. 13, No. 1, pp. 28–45.

Keeney, R. L. 1980, *Siting Energy Facilities*, Academic Press, New York.

Keeney, R. L. 1988a, "Building models of values," *European Journal of Operational Research*, Vol. 37, No. 1, pp. 149–157.

Keeney, R. L. 1988b, "Structuring objectives for problems of public interest," *Operations Research*, Vol. 36, No. 3, pp. 396–405.

Keeney, R. L. 1992, *Value-Focused Thinking*. Harvard University Press, Cambridge, Massachusetts.

Keeney, R. L.; Lathrop, J.; and Sicherman, A. 1986, "An analysis of Baltimore Gas and Electric Company's technology choice," *Operations Research*, Vol. 34, No. 1, pp. 18–39.

Keeney, R. L. and Raiffa, H. 1976, *Decisions with Multiple Objectives*, John Wiley & Sons, New York.

Pearce, J. and Robinson, R. 1985, *Strategic Management: Strategy Formulation and Implementation*, Richard Irwin, Homewood, Illinois.

Peters, T. 1987, *Thriving on Chaos: A Handbook for a Management Revolution*, Harper and Row, New York.

Smith, G. R. 1989, *Logical Decision: Multi-Measure Decision Analysis Software*, Logical Decisions, Inc., Golden, Colorado.

# 8    Making Better Use of Scientific Knowledge: Separating Truth from Justice

*Kenneth R. Hammond, Lewis O. Harvey, Jr., and Reid Hastie*

In a recent (February 15, 1991) address to the American Association for the Advancement of Science, George E. Brown, Jr., chair of the House Committee on Science, Space, and Technology, and well-known for his long-standing interest in and support of science, put scientists on notice that their conventional lobbying approach lacks "uniqueness" (Brown, 1991, p. 2). After mentioning an appeal from "250 university physicists, biologists, and chemists, who reflected on the state of funding for research with great pain and discouragement," he pointed out that "one could easily document a similar level of despair among 250 Medicare recipients, 250 disabled veterans, 250 soldiers in Saudi Arabia, or even among 250 members of Congress" (p. 2). He further noted that "all the basic science funding in the world will have no positive effect on the well-being of our nation if the research is not carried out within a system that can effectively digest and apply the results" (p. 3). He then urged scientists to "view your own efforts as part of a complex system" and to "justify the need for Federal support in the context of a broader vision" (p. 4) – broader, that is, than merely pleading that science is more deserving than other money-starved segments of society. Thus, he noted that current "fiscal constraints can lead to divisiveness, and encourage the proliferation of lobbying efforts," a situation that he believes "is already occurring" and that "in the eyes of many members of Congress . . . relegates scientists to the level of every other special interest group" (p. 4).

Had Brown's speech been scheduled a month later, he could have offered his audience an example of how research is presently conducted within a system that cannot "effectively digest and apply the results," for he could have cited the acknowledged failure of the National Acid Precipitation Assessment Program (NAPAP), described in *Science*, March 15, 1991. *Science*'s Leslie Roberts (1991) reported that the project, carried out over a 10-year period and

This chapter originally appeared in *Psychological Science*, 1992, 3, 80–87. Copyright © 1992 by the American Psychological Society. Reprinted by permission.

consuming $500 million, involved "some 2000 scientists" who "studied everything from lake sediments to atmospheric processes to damage to chain link fences" (p. 1302). But, "when Congress and the Bush Administration were haggling over the president's acid rain bill ... NAPAP was nowhere to be found" (p. 1302). What was the reason for this failure? Roberts reported Milton Russell's (chair of NAPAP's oversight committee) explanation that "in 1980, there were no models for doing this: NAPAP was the first big effort at marrying science and public policy" (p. 1302). Worse still, the prospects for learning from this failed effort seem dim, for Roberts noted that the people associated with NAPAP "warn that the scenario is already repeating itself in the new federal climate change program" (p. 1305), a matter we discuss below.

However one judges the effectiveness and moral justification of special interest lobbying, it is our purpose to show that scientists – particularly psychologists – have the potential to make a special contribution to the difficult cognitive process of integrating current scientific information and social values by employing current research methods and concepts.

The Carnegie Corporation of New York also thinks the problem deserves attention. Its Committee on Science, Technology, and Congress, guided by a Congressional Advisory Council, issued its report in 1991 in response "to a sense of concern and frustration among Senators and Representatives, and leaders both within and outside the federal government, that the S&T [science and technology] system in the United States is not working as well as it should. Senators and Representatives are finding it increasingly difficult to address science and technology issues effectively" (p. 8). The committee then issued a set of recommendations to which we shall return. First, however, we observe that in April of 1990, D. Allan Bromley, assistant to the President for science and technology and director of the Office of Science and Technology Policy, organized a White House Conference on Science and Economics Research Related to Global Change. The purpose of this conference was for "delegations from 17 countries and from the European Community and the Organization for Economic Cooperation and Development ... to explore what we know and what we do not know about the scientific, economic, and policy questions surrounding global [climate] change" (Bromley, 1990, p. 59). According to Bromley, the conference "was organized around a straightforward but *surprisingly unexplored* [italics added] question: How best can the results of scientific and economic research be integrated into the policy making process" (p. 59). What was the outcome? Bromley noted with apparent satisfaction, "Several promising proposals on international cooperation" were made (p. 59).

This dubious outcome supports our view that integration of scientific knowledge into policy making is indeed a process in need of examination and improvement. Smith's (1990) review of science policy since World War II led him to a similar conclusion, namely, that "the difficulty ... of separating science and technology from the wider social ends to which they are but means" is "still a source of conceptual confusion" (p. 1).

## Uncertainty in Expert Judgment

We believe that one major obstacle to the effective utilization of scientific results in science-related policy derives from a common inability to manage uncertainty or, perhaps, even to recognize its inevitable presence in policy decisions. Although strict, fully determined, causal relations in many scientific disciplines have long been well understood, the application of such knowledge to widely varying circumstances outside the laboratory inevitably requires the judgment of experts. No matter how well informed the expert, field conditions almost always produce uncertainty – sometimes more, sometimes less – in the application of his or her knowledge.

### Inevitable Error: The Consequence of Uncertainty

Under circumstances of irreducible uncertainty, two forms of error are inevitable: the false positive (action taken when it should not have been) and the false negative (action not taken when it should have been). Because these errors are inextricably inversely linked, they offer policy makers agonizing choices; risk of one error or the other must be assigned to some constituents. But most laypersons (and many scientists) have yet to grasp the implications of false positive and false negative errors – let alone their linkage. Thus, it is not surprising that no consensus has arisen regarding the value question of what the appropriate relation between these two kinds of error ought to be. Yet this relation is a precise definition of the allocation of risk to different segments of society and, therefore, is as much a matter of distributive justice as is the widely discussed problem of the differential allocation of resources (MacLean, 1986).

### Traditional Methods for Coping with Uncertainty: More Funding, More Equipment

The wide recognition of the potential threat of global warming has made the need for effective integration of science and policy glaringly obvious. But scientific information will apparently be used in this case much as it has been in the past. That is, there will be sharp disagreement and bitter disputes among scientists, uncertainty will be acknowledged, and scientists will then ask for more funding to resolve the disputes. For example, Hansen, an outspoken expert in this field, together with Rossow and Fung, recently observed that "scientific warnings have generated rancorous political debate" (Hansen, Rossow, & Fung, 1990, p. 62), thus indicating once more what has become typical for policy problems involving science. As would be expected, Hansen et al. further observed that "the debate is fueled by scientific uncertainties" and predicted that "until [the scientific] questions can be answered, legislators are unlikely to agree on a policy response" (p. 62). Also to be expected, Hansen et al. claimed that uncertainty must be reduced by further research, for "policy makers cannot even weigh the various options rationally until the climate system is better understood" (p. 62). Their conclusion was that what is needed to resolve the problem of global warming is more scientific information, produced by more science funding.

The cynic will observe that the solutions advocated always require that more resources be supplied to the persons offering the solutions. Is such a conclusion overly cynical? Misguided? Uninformed? Few scientists have ever spoken with the candor of Stephen Schneider (1989), also an authority on global climate, who not only noted that scientific consensus "crumbles over the value question of whether present information is sufficient to generate a societal response stronger than more scientific research on the problems," but also observed that this is "self-serving . . . advice which we scientists, myself included, somehow always manage to recommend" (p. 778).

Schneider not only wrote with candor about scientific uncertainties and the inevitable suggestion from scientists that more science and more funding are needed to resolve them, he noted that action is impeded by the difficulties of integrating factual material and social values: "Whether the uncertainties are large enough to suggest delaying policy responses is not a scientific question per se, but a value judgment" (p. 771). He added, "Of course, whether to *act* [italics added] is not a scientific judgment, but a value-laden political choice" (p. 778). He then made the barrier explicit: "Value-laden political choice[s] . . . cannot be resolved by scientific methods" (p. 778).

In short, the confusion of scientific issues of fact and policy matters of value is a serious impediment to the effective management of uncertainty.

### Separating Fact and Value: Should It Be Done? Can It Be Done?

A psychologist-lawyer team, Thibaut and Walker (1978), thought the separation of fact and value to be essential to alleviate the confusion that so frequently arises in policy decision processes. In pursuit of that aim, they drew a distinction between the aim of sciences (truth) and the aim of policy (justice) and urged a "two-tiered solution": "The first stage should resolve issues of fact with the objective of determining truth; the second stage should resolve policy questions in a *wholly separate procedure* [italics added]" (p. 563).

But separation has recently been challenged, both as an ideal and as a fact of policy formation. In a guest editorial for *Risk Analysis*, Jasanoff (1989), under the heading of "The Separatist Fallacy," stated, "The separatists . . . argued that the line between science and policy could be sharply drawn, and they proposed that all decision-making on the scientific side should be left to scientists" (pp. 271–272). But, Jasanoff argued, this ideal cannot be attained; the very practice of science includes social policy considerations. Therefore, "if the findings of regulatory science rest upon such a mix of technical and nontechnical considerations" (and she argued that they do), "then the notion of separating science from policy when assessing uncertainty makes very little sense" (p. 272). In Jasanoff's recent (1990) comprehensive study of the contemporary use of scientific information, she not only found a "blurring of the boundaries between science and policy" (p. 177) in practice, but indicated that such blurring of boundaries was to be preferred to the traditional ideal of the separation of science and policy. For example, discussing the practices of the Food and Drug Administration (FDA), she reported that "advisory proceedings, moreover, are structured in ways that leave the line of demarcation between FDA's decisionmaking authority and that of its scientific advisers ill defined" (p. 178). Jasanoff believes that blurred boundaries allow the FDA "to construe science and to make policy in ways that may in the end serve the public better than an overly rigid commitment to separating science from policy" (p. 179).

We agree that the demarcation of science and policy is blurred in practice – that is where the trouble lies – but disagree emphatically with the conclusion that this practice will serve the public better than the separatist ideal expressed, for example, by Smith (1990) and by Thibaut and Walker (1978). The admonition by Koshland (1990), the editor of *Science*, that "scientists are the servants of society, not its masters and we should remain so" (p. 9) would become very hollow rhetoric indeed, should the traditional separation not be maintained.

Therefore, in what follows, we demonstrate that psychological research methods can – and should – make possible a more appropriate and effective use of scientific knowledge in the pursuit of social policy.

## Examples

### Signal Detection Theory

*Social Policy Unknowingly Created and Changed by Weather Forecasters.* Signal detection theory provides a mathematical model and summary of weather forecasters' performance based on the frequencies of forecast-outcome events, traditionally labeled hits, false alarms, misses, and correct rejections. The important contribution of signal detection theory for present purposes is that it provides a practically applicable method of precisely analyzing judgment policies into a scientific component (accuracy) and a value component (decision criterion).

In this example, we illustrate how psychological factors – in this case, stress – can change the location of decision criteria and thus influence policy, without the knowledge of any of the participants in the decision process. The experts in this example were research weather forecasters who were predicting severe weather at approaches to Stapleton International Airport in Denver (see Mueller, Wilson, & Heckman, 1988, for further details). The predictions considered here are in the form of probabilities that a severe weather event will occur 15 min from the time of the forecast. The prior probability of severe weather was .098.

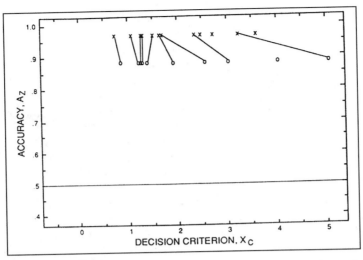

Figure 8.1. Accuracy, $A_z$, as a function of the signal detection theory decision criterion, $X_c$, for high-stress ($x$) and low-stress ($o$) days for the 15-min forecasting period. Criterion points that separate the same response categories (forecasts) in the high- and low-stress data sets are connected by solid lines. The solid horizontal line represents chance accuracy. (Some of the $x$s and one $o$ are not connected because the subject did not use exactly the same response categories in the two conditions. Only criteria that separate two identical response categories in the two conditions are connected with lines.)

Forecasters' performance was analyzed separately for high-stress (high activity, high cognitive demand) and low-stress days. As Figure 8.1 shows, stress influenced forecasting performance in two ways: It (a) increased accuracy ($A_z$) and (b) caused a shift in the location of the decision criteria ($X_c$). The location of $X_c$ reflects the allocation of risks, that is, of increasing and decreasing false positives and false negatives, independent of the accuracy of the forecasting system. In the case of aviation weather forecasting, for example, it should be the policy makers who decide to what extent the passengers, pilots, aircraft controllers, and operators of airlines should suffer differentially (a) the risks and consequences of unnecessary changes in approaches (false positives, i.e., false warnings of dangerous convection) and (b) the risks and consequences of failures to warm of dangerous convection (false negatives).

These two roles – determining and improving accuracy, on the one hand, and specifying the location of $X_c$, on the other – can be separated in the manner society expects them to be separated by means of signal detection theory because it separates accuracy ($A_z$) and the location of the decision criterion ($X_c$). In short, the use of signal detection theory makes this separation of function obvious and direct and therefore of practical significance.

*Social Policy Disguised as Scientific Information.* Because the polygraph is a derivative of scientific research, largely from psychology, and because its use has been debated at length by policy makers in Congress, we chose the use of the polygraph "lie detector" to illustrate how social policy is created by the scientist or technician. The studies of professional polygraph operators by Kleinmuntz and Szucko (Kleinmuntz & Szucko, 1984; Szucko & Kleinmuntz, 1981) provide our basic data. Operators rendered judgments about whether persons were lying based on their polygraph responses while answering questions during an interview. Half of the persons were lying and half were not. When judging whether or not each person was lying, the operators used a confidence scale from 1 to 8, with 1 meaning confident "no" and 8 meaning confident "yes."

The signal detection model provided an excellent description of the behavior of the operators (assessed by chi-square goodness-of-fit measures; $p > .05$). Tables 8.1 and 8.2 display several parameters that provide a definitive description of two of the experts in terms of the model. The $d_a$ and $A_z$ measures summarize the experts' ability to discriminate between liars and truth-tellers; both show that Expert B was more accurate than Expert A (see Swets, 1986.) The critical hit rate (unlike the two "pure" measures of accuracy) depends on the prior probability of a critical event's (lying) occurrence. It is the hit rate (the proportion of actual liars who are caught) achieved when a decision criterion is selected to produce a posterior hit probability of .90 (i.e., the probability that a person was actually lying, given that the expert said the person was lying). In terms of this index, the performance of neither operator was very good. Expert B had a critical hit rate of .23, and Expert A had one of only .07. In other words, both operators would miss more than half the liars if they used a decision criterion that had a high credibility, corresponding to a legal standard of "beyond reasonable doubt."

Table 8.1. *Measures of the Performance of Two Professional Polygraph Operators*

| Performance Index | Expert A | Expert B |
| --- | --- | --- |
| $m_s$ | 0.7142 | 1.2345 |
| $s_s$ | 1.1482 | 0.9621 |
| $d_a$ | 0.6634 | 1.2584 |
| $A_z$ | 0.6805 | 0.8132 |
| $HR_{90}$ | 0.0669 | 0.2260 |

*Note:* The table shows the best-fitting parameters of the dual-Gaussian, variable-criterion signal detection model, $m_s$ and $s_s$; two accuracy indices, $d_a$ and $A_z$; and the critical hit rate performance index, $HR_{90}$.

Table 8.2. *Miss-to-False-Alarm Ratios for Two Professional Polygraph Operators*

| Judgment Boundary | Expert A | | Expert B | |
|---|---|---|---|---|
| | Decision Criterion ($X_c$) | Miss-to-False-Alarm Ratio | Decision Criterion ($X_c$) | Miss-to-False-Alarm Ratio |
| 1–2 | −2.1825 | 0.006 | −2.0703 | 0.000 |
| 2–3 | −1.7103 | 0.018 | −1.1990 | 0.006 |
| 3–4 | −0.9062 | 0.097 | −0.0392 | 0.180 |
| 4–5 | 0.3001 | 0.940 | 0.3743 | 0.524 |
| 5–6 | 1.0691 | 4.361 | 0.5907 | 0.907 |
| 6–7 | 1.9083 | 36.34 | 1.5039 | 9.204 |
| 7–8 | — | — | 2.2447 | 68.80 |

*Note:* The miss-to-false-alarm ratio is conceptually related to the ratio of "incorrectly exonerated perpetrators" to "innocents falsely accused," the focus of many discussions of the "standard of proof" required to take various legal actions. The $X_c$ values represent locations of the boundary thresholds corresponding to the rating scale responses for each expert in terms of the signal detection model.

To what use can the consumer of the polygraph operator's expert judgment put the information in the tables? It will depend on the consumer's value system. If the consumer has a value system consistent with the policy that "it is better that ten guilty persons escape than one innocent suffer" (Blackstone, 1765–1769/1966), the operator's ratio of misses to false alarms should be 10. This ratio may be formally expressed:

$$\frac{(1 - P(Y|s))P(s)}{P(Y|n)P(n)} = \frac{1 - P(Y|s)}{P(Y|n)} \cdot \frac{P(s)}{P(n)} = 10 \tag{1}$$

where

$P(Y|s)$ is the hit rate,
$P(Y|n)$ is the false alarm rate,
$P(s)$ is the prior probability of lying, and
$P(n)$ is the prior probability of not lying.

The two conditional probabilities of Equation 1 were computed for each decision criterion, and the miss-to-false-alarm ratios (using a prior event probability of .5) for the two experts are listed in Table 8.2, next to the corresponding decision criteria.

Neither polygraph expert used a decision criterion that achieved the 10-to-1 ratio, although Expert B came close. If Expert B's judgment of 7 or higher were used as the basis for taking some action against the accused person, 9.2 liars would be missed for each nonliar falsely accused. If action were taken when Expert A gave a judgment of 7 or higher, 36.3 liars would be missed for each nonliar falsely accused, a number far from the goal of 10, but if action were taken when A gave a judgment of 6 or higher, 4.4 liars would be missed for each nonliar falsely accused.

Despite lengthy congressional hearings conducted during the preparation of the Employee Protection Act of 1988, no one ever explained the distinction between *accuracy* and a *decision criterion* to the legislators. Thus, the policy makers never learned about a polygrapher's predilection to err on the side of false positives or false negatives, constancy in the location of his or her decision criterion, or ability to change his or her decision criterion. Individual differences among polygraphers with respect to their decision criteria thus remain unknown, and persons appearing before a polygrapher are – unknowingly – up against the "luck of the draw."

We turn now to a description of two cases that illustrate how fact and value determinations were separated and how the judgments of scientists and technologists were integrated with those of policy makers to choose a course of action.

### Judgment Analysis

*Community Chaos: Choice of a Bullet for the Police.* In 1974, the Denver Police Department, among others, decided to replace the traditional round-nosed bullet used in officers' handguns with a hollow-point bullet on the ground that the latter provided more "stopping power"; that is, the hollow-point bullet reduced the capacity of a person who was shot to fire back. This decision was challenged by a number of groups who alleged the hollow-point bullet was nothing other than the already outlawed "dum-dum" bullet. Roughly 1 year later, after bitter accusations from both sides, and a police officers' march on the city hall and state capitol, an impasse was acknowledged, and the Center for Research on Judgment and Policy at the University of Colorado was asked to help resolve the dispute. The center employed theory and research on conflict resolution based on the lens model approach to human judgment (Hursch, Hammond, & Hursch, 1964; see Brehmer & Joyce, 1988; Hammond & Grassia, 1985). The schematic model illustrated in Figure 8.2 was implemented (details may be found in Hammond & Adelman, 1976).

As may be seen from the diagram, facts and values were separately ascertained and combined analytically by a straightforward, if simple, method. Value judgments were obtained from the public, a number of interest groups, the mayor of Denver, and the Denver City Council; scientific judgments were obtained from experts (ballistics scientists).

Social value judgments and scientific judgments were combined by means of the equation in Figure 8.2, which makes explicit the separation and combination of the judgments of policy makers and scientists-technologists. We

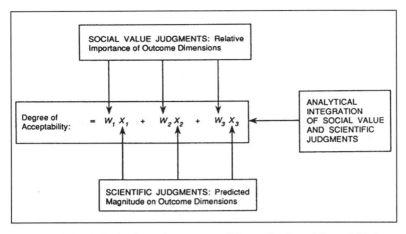

Figure 8.2.  A schematic summary of the application of the social judgment theory framework to separate, estimate, and then systematically recombine value and scientific judgments in the formation of a public policy.

used the following algebraic form of this equation:

$$Y_s = W_1 X_1 + W_2 X_2 + W_3 X_3 \tag{2}$$

where $Y_s$ is the overall acceptability of a bullet; $W$ represents the weight, or relative importance, policy makers placed on stopping effectiveness (1), injury (2), and threat to bystanders (3); and $X$ represents the experts' judgments regarding stopping effectiveness (1), injury (2), and threat to bystanders (3).

The bullet providing the greatest overall acceptability ($Y_s$) was identified and was accepted by the city council and all other parties concerned. It has been used ever since by the Denver Police Department.

*The Central Arizona Water Control Study.* Our second example, the Central Arizona Water Control Study (CAWCS), is intended to illustrate the effectiveness of the schematic model (Figure 8.2) in its application to a more complex and difficult case than the Denver police bullet study (details of the CAWCS study may be found in Brown, 1984). CAWCS was more difficult and complex because it was far wider in the scope of its political, economic, and physical consequences. Yet the procedure was essentially the same, and the outcome was equally successful.

In 1976, the Bureau of Reclamation proposed that the Orme Dam be constructed at the confluence of the Salt and Verde rivers a few miles upstream from Phoenix to hold water during periods of low demand and then release it during periods of peak demand in the summer. Enthusiasm for the construction of the dam increased considerably after three major floods caused approximately \$200 million in damages and the loss of seven lives.

Opposition to the dam was also vigorous, and CAWCS was formed to study alternative solutions.

Value identification was carried out through the distribution of a factbook and a series of public meetings. Representatives from 60 public groups and organizations assigned "importance weights" to 14 factors to reflect their own values. The representatives were divided into seven clusters sharing similar views, and a values profile based on the self-ratings was developed and approved by each cluster.

The scientific-technical phase of the analysis was initiated after the value importance analysis was completed. The performance of eight plans as measured on the 14 factors was assessed by scientists from a variety of disciplines. The importance weights were combined with the performance predictions to produce global acceptability ratings of the eight plans for each of the seven clusters.

The results of the analysis were striking. None of the plans involving Orme Dam was rated high, not even by the groups representing water development concerns or by the two clusters most concerned with flood control. In spite of long-standing public promotion of Orme Dam by these groups, other alternatives that fit more closely with their value positions were available.

On October 2, 1981, the Governor's Advisory Committee voted 19 to 1 to develop an alternative to the Orme Dam ("Governor's Panel," 1981), and soon after, many public groups and politicians, longtime supporters of Orme Dam, chose to support the alternative (the Waddell Dam Plan). Said Senator Barry Goldwater, "I don't know why someone didn't dream up the Waddell Dam a long time ago" ("Cost and Indian Opposition," 1981). And Congressman Morris Udall reflected, "The Orme Dam was a critically important issue to Arizona. . . . But we finally ended up, to my utter amazement, with the whole Arizona establishment agreeing we really didn't want the [Orme] dam" (Gendlin, 1982, p. 25).

It cannot be argued that just any type of study would have succeeded – a previous study had produced only conflict.

It is essential to observe that in both types of examples – those involving signal detection theory and those involving social judgment analysis – the approach taken was based on psychological theory tested by empirical research, in the laboratory as well as in the field. In both cases, the methods used were supported by a long history of research.

### Conclusion

The growing threat to the status of scientists through their identification as simply one more interest group should encourage scientists to consider developing the "broader vision" now asked for by Congressman Brown, rather than merely to pursue the tradition of competing vigorously for more support. We argue that the major impediment to more effective use of scientific information lies not in the absence of scientific research, but in the "conceptual confusion" noted by Smith (1990) and documented by Jasanoff (1990) regarding the separation of science and policy.

As we have shown through examples, however, that conceptual confusion can be removed through the use of psychological research methods. Our two examples of the application of signal detection theory show that it is capable of implementing the "separatist" approach, that is, empirically disentangling, within a single expert's judgment, scientific decisions of fact from value decisions to act. Our two examples of the use of social judgment analysis also demonstrate the separation of fact and value, but through the specification of different judgment tasks for partisan policy makers and scientists, together with an analytical, observable method of combining the two sets of separated judgments.

Can such procedures as signal detection theory and judgment analysis be applied to the acid rain problem, the greenhouse problem, and problems of similar magnitude and complexity? Yes. But whatever procedures are used, the acquisition and organization of scientific information must be related to the social values that are to guide the formation of policy. That is, specification of social values by one means or another should occur prior to the acquisition and organization of scientific information. Once these separate tasks are accomplished, integration of fact and value must be accomplished, if not by the means indicated here, then by some other public method.

If not the separatist approach to a broader vision, then which? The Carnegie Commission's Committee on Science, Technology, and Congress (1991) recommends (a) a bicameral legislative service organization, (b) improved efforts by Congress to obtain science and technology analyses, (c) direct requests for studies by the National Academies of Science (NAS), (d) more frequent use of the NAS scientific merit review process, and (e) making scientific and technical information developed at hearings more readily available to scientists and the public. These suggestions, while perhaps administratively useful, fail to recognize the fundamental problem – uncertainty in expert judgment and the need to cope with uncertainty in ways both scientifically and morally justifiable.

It is time for policy makers and scientists to acknowledge that judgments of value, judgments of fact, and their integration are as amenable to scientific inquiry as any other cognitive activity, such as memory, learning, or perception – as, indeed, we have shown here and as the corpus of existing research already shows (see, e.g., Arkes & Hammond, 1986).

### References

Arkes, H. R., & Hammond, K. R. (Eds.). (1986). *Judgment and decision making: An interdisciplinary reader*. Cambridge, England: Cambridge University Press.
Blackstone, W. (1966). *Commentaries on the Laws of England*. New York: Oceana. (Original work published 1765–1769)

Brehmer, B., & Joyce, C. R. B. (1988). *Human judgment: The SJT view*, Amsterdam: North-Holland.

Bromley, D. A. (1990). The making of a greenhouse policy. *Issues in Science and Technology, 7*, 55–61.

Brown, C. A. (1984). The Central Arizona Water Control Study: A case of multiobjective planning and public involvement. *Water Resources Bulletin, 20*, 331–337.

Brown, G. E., Jr. (1991). *Federation News Special Supplement: Address by Congressman George E. Brown, Jr.* Washington, DC: Federation of Behavioral, Psychological and Cognitive Sciences.

Committee on Science, Technology, and Congress. (1991). *Science, technology, and Congress: Expert advice and the decision-making process.* New York: Carnegie Commission on Science, Technology, and Government.

Cost and Indian opposition may halt Arizona dam plans. (1981, November 4). *New York Times.*

Gendlin, F. (1982). A talk with Mo Udall, Chair of the House Interior Committee. *Sierra, 67*(4), 23–27.

Governor's panel backs Waddell Dam over Orme. (1981, October 3). *Phoenix Gazette.*

Hammond, K. R., & Adelman, L. (1976). Science, values, and human judgment. *Science, 194*, 389–396.

Hammond, K. R., & Grassia, J. (1985). The cognitive side of conflict: From theory to resolution of policy disputes. In S. Oskamp (Ed.), *Applied social psychology annual: Vol. 6. International conflict and national public policy issues* (pp. 233–254). Beverly Hills, CA: Sage.

Hansen, J., Rossow, W., & Fung, I. (1990). The missing data on global climate change. *Issues in Science and Technology, 7*, 62–69.

Hursch, C. J., Hammond, K. R., & Hursch, J. L. (1964). Some methodological considerations in multiple-cue probability studies. *Psychological Review, 71*, 42–60.

Jasanoff, S. (1989). Norms for evaluating regulatory science. *Risk Analysis, 9*, 271–273.

Jasanoff, S. (1990). *The fifth branch: Science advisors as policy makers.* Cambridge, MA: Harvard University Press.

Kleinmuntz, B., & Szucko, J. J. (1984). A field study of the fallibility of polygraphic lie detection. *Nature, 308*, 449–450.

Koshland, D. E., Jr. (1990). To see ourselves as others see us. *Science, 247*, 9.

MacLean, D. (1986). Social values and the distribution of risk. In D. MacLean (Ed.), *Values at risk* (pp. 75–93). Totowa, NJ: Rowman & Allenheld.

Mueller, C. K., Wilson, J. W., & Heckman, B. (1988). Evaluation of the TDWR aviation nowcasting experiment. In *Preprints, Third International Conference on the Aviation Weather System* (pp. 212–216). Boston: American Meteorological Society.

Roberts, L. (1991). Learning from an acid rain program. *Science, 251*, 1302–1305.

Schneider, S. H. (1989). The greenhouse effect: Science and policy. *Science, 243*, 771–781.

Smith, B. (1990). *American science policy since World War II.* Washington, DC: Brookings Institute.

Swets, J. A. (1986). Form of empirical ROCs in discrimination and diagnostic tasks: Implications for theory and measurement of performance. *Psychological Bulletin, 99*, 181–198.

Szucko, J. J., & Kleinmuntz, B. (1981). Statistical versus clinical lie detection. *American Psychologist, 36*, 488–496.

Thibaut, J., & Walker, L. (1978). A theory of procedure. *California Law Review, 66*, 541–566.

# Part III

# Applications in Economics

Ideas of individuals making rational choices are central to economic theorizing. Economists have usually assumed that humans are not only rational decision makers but fully informed consumers who want to maximize their happiness and well-being through careful allocation of their limited resources and who are capable of acquiring and processing vast amounts of information in pursuit of this goal. In the 1950s Herbert Simon started to explore the implications of making the psychologically more plausible assumption that people are "boundedly rational" and are forced to "satisfice" (make do with acceptable options) because they lack the wits or resources to "maximize" (find the best possible option) (Simon, 1955). In one sense the JDM research interest in human cognitive shortcomings is a detailed unpacking and spelling out of Simon's "bounded rationality" idea. Economic rationality has provided the impetus (and often the straw man) for any number of JDM studies.

The first chapter in this section, by Kahneman and Tversky (Chapter 9), suggests some of the stimulation that comes from putting together formal theory in the economic tradition and modern psychological experimentation. One part of their essay reports a series of tiny experimental findings – for example, that we respond differently to choices when equivalent outcomes are described in terms of "lives saved" rather than "lives lost." (See also Chapter 17 for a similar demonstration in a medical context.) The other part of the essay modifies such standard devices of economic theory as utility functions to try to account for such behavior. Note that their original formulation of this effort, which they labeled "Prospect Theory" (Kahneman & Tversky, 1979) was published in a leading journal of *economic* theory. Their interest, plainly, was in uniting economic and psychological work on rationality. Tversky & Kahneman (1992) provides the most recent attempt.

Larrick, Nisbett, and Morgan, in Chapter 10 take up the issue of whether or not economic principles of sound decision making (e.g., select on net benefit, ignore sunk costs, consider only opportunity costs) are actually used by smart people and, if so, whether they lead to better life outcomes. Their evidence, based on samples of students and faculty, suggests that these factors are positively correlated with one another (though, of course, it is difficult to infer what is causing what). Further, the data suggest that those who take more economics classes are more likely to employ these principles, and to enjoy better GPAs (students) or salaries (faculty). This in turn raises questions as to how fixed people's tendencies are toward sunk cost thinking (cf. Arkes & Blumer, Reading, Chapter 6, this volume), and whether they can be changed by a few college courses (see Nisbett, 1993, for a review of evidence for these training effects in statistical, logical, and economic reasoning). All in all, the Larrick et al. chapter provides a strong rationale for taking more economics.

Frank, Gilovich, and Regan (Chapter 11) are not so sure. Their concern is with settings in which cooperation is called for if individual outcomes are going to be achieved – experimental games such as prisoner's dilemma and ultimatum, real-world choices like contributions to charities and other public goods. Their evidence suggests that economics students are more self-interested than noneconomists. As the authors note, economics students have had ". . . repeated and intensive exposure to a model whose unequivocal prediction is that people will defect whenever self-interest dictates" (p. 193), and they seem to follow this prediction. Note that this may leave them better off in situations like charitable giving (where the altruist gives up what the recipient gains), but may lead to self-inflicted injuries in settings where both benefit from cooperation (and self-interest is thus self-punishing).

### References

Kahneman, D., & Tversky, A. (1979). Prospect theory: An analysis of decision under risk. *Econometrica, 47*, 263–291.

Nisbett, R. E. (ed.) (1993). *Rules for Reasoning*. Hillsdale, NJ: Erlbaum.

Tversky, A., & Kahneman, D. (1992). Advances in prospect theory: Cumulative representation of uncertainty. *Journal of Risk and uncertainty, 5*, 297–323.

Simon, H. A. (1955). A behavioral model of rational choice. *Quarterly Journal of Economics, 69*, 99–118.

# 9    Choices, Values, and Frames

*Daniel Kahneman and Amos Tversky*

Making decisions is like speaking prose – people do it all the time, knowingly or unknowingly. It is hardly surprising, then, that the topic of decision making is shared by many disciplines, from mathematics and statistics, through economics and political science, to sociology and psychology. The study of decisions addresses both normative and descriptive questions. The normative analysis is concerned with the nature of rationality and the logic of decision making. The descriptive analysis, in contrast, is concerned with people's beliefs and preferences as they are, not as they should be. The tension between normative and descriptive considerations characterizes much of the study of judgment and choice.

Analyses of decision making commonly distinguish risky and riskless choices. The paradigmatic example of decision under risk is the acceptability of a gamble that yields monetary outcomes with specified probabilities. A typical riskless decision concerns the acceptability of a transaction in which a good or a service is exchanged for money or labor. In the first part of this article we present an analysis of the cognitive and psychophysical factors that determine the value of risky prospects. In the second part we extend this analysis of transactions and trades.

### Risky Choice

Risky choices, such as whether or not to take an umbrella and whether or not to go to war, are made without advance knowledge of their consequences. Because the consequences of such actions depend on uncertain events such as the weather or the opponent's resolve, the choice of an act may be construed as the acceptance of a gamble that can yield various outcomes with different probabilities. It is therefore natural that the study of decision making under risk has focused on choices between simple gambles with monetary outcomes and specified probabilities, in the hope that these simple problems will reveal basic attitudes toward risk and value.

We shall sketch an approach to risky choice that derives many of its hypotheses from a psychophysical analysis of responses to money and to probability. The psychophysical approach to decision making can be traced to a remarkable essay that Daniel Bernoulli published in 1738 (Bernoulli 1738/1954) in which he attempted to explain why people are generally averse to risk and why risk aversion decreases with increasing wealth. To illustrate risk aversion and Bernoulli's analysis, consider the choice between a prospect that offers an 85% chance to win $1000 (with a 15% chance to win nothing) and the alternative of receiving $800 for sure. A large majority of people prefer the sure thing over the gamble, although the gamble has higher (mathematical) expectation. The expectation of a monetary gamble is a weighted average, where each possible outcome is weighted by its probability of occurrence. The expectation of the gamble in this example is .85 × $1000 + .15 × $0 = $850, which exceeds the expectation of $800 associated with the sure thing. The preference for the sure gain is an instance of risk aversion. In general, a preference for a sure outcome over a gamble that has higher or equal expectation is called risk averse, and the rejection of a sure thing in favor of a gamble of lower or equal expectation is called risk seeking.

Bernoulli suggested that people do not evaluate prospects by the expectation of their monetary outcomes, but rather by the expectation of the subjective value of these outcomes. The subjective value of a gamble is again a weighted average, but now it is the subjective value of each outcome that is weighted by its probability. To explain risk aversion within this framework, Bernoulli proposed that subjective value, or utility, is a concave function of money. In such a function, the difference between the utilities of $200 and $100, for example, is greater than the utility difference between $1200 and $1100. It follows from concavity that the subjective value attached to a gain of $800 is more than 80% of the value of a gain of $1000. Consequently, the concavity of the utility function entails a risk averse preference for a sure gain of $800 over an 80% chance to win $1000, although the two prospects have the same monetary expectation.

It is customary in decision analysis to describe the outcomes of decisions in terms of total wealth. For example, an offer to bet $20 on the toss of a fair coin is represented as a choice between an individual's current wealth W and an even chance to move to W + $20 or to W − $20. This representation appears psychologically unrealistic: People do not normally think of relatively small outcomes in terms of states of wealth but rather in terms of gains, losses, and neutral outcomes (such as the maintenance of the status quo). If the effective carriers of subjective value are changes of wealth rather than ultimate states of wealth, as we propose, the psychophysical analysis of outcomes should

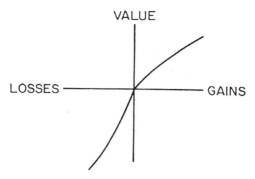

Figure 9.1.  A hypothetical value function.

be applied to gains and losses rather than to total assets. This assumption plays a central role in a treatment of risky choice that we called prospect theory (Kahneman & Tversky, 1979). Introspection as well as psychophysical measurements suggest that subjective value is a concave function of the size of a gain. The same generalization applies to losses as well. The difference in subjective value between a loss of $200 and a loss of $100 appears greater than the difference in subjective value between a loss of $1200 and a loss of $1100. When the value functions for gains and for losses are pieced together, we obtain an S-shaped function of the type displayed in Figure 9.1.

The value function shown in Figure 9.1 is (a) defined on gains and losses rather than on total wealth, (b) concave in the domain of gains and convex in the domain of losses, and (c) considerably steeper for losses than for gains. The last property, which we label *loss aversion*, expresses the intuition that a loss of $X is more aversive than a gain of $X is attractive. Loss aversion explains people's reluctance to bet on a fair coin for equal stakes: The attractiveness of the possible gain is not nearly sufficient to compensate for the aversiveness of the possible loss. For example, most respondents in a sample of undergraduates refused to stake $10 on the toss of a coin if they stood to win less than $30.

The assumption of risk aversion has played a central role in economic theory. However, just as the concavity of the value of gains entails risk aversion, the convexity of the value of losses entails risk seeking. Indeed, risk seeking in losses is a robust effect, particularly when the probabilities of loss are substantial. Consider, for example, a situation in which an individual is forced to choose between an 85% chance to lose $1000 (with a 15% chance to lose nothing) and a sure loss of $800. A large majority of people express a preference for the gamble over the sure loss. This is a risk seeking choice because the expectation of the gamble (−$850) is inferior to the expectation of the sure loss (−$800). Risk seeking in the domain of losses has been confirmed by several investigators (Fishburn & Kochenberger, 1979; Hershey & Schoemaker, 1980;

Payne, Laughhunn, & Crum, 1980; Slovic, Fischhoff, & Lichtenstein, 1982). It has also been observed with nonmonetary outcomes, such as hours of pain (Eraker & Sox, 1981) and loss of human lives (Fischhoff, 1983; Tversky, 1977; Tversky & Kahneman, 1981). Is it wrong to be risk averse in the domain of gains and risk seeking in the domain of losses? These preferences conform to compelling intuitions about the subjective value of gains and losses, and the presumption is that people should be entitled to their own values. However, we shall see that an S-shaped value function has implications that are normatively unacceptable.

To address the normative issue we turn from psychology to decision theory. Modern decision theory can be said to begin with the pioneering work of von Neumann and Morgenstern (1947), who laid down several qualitative principles, or axioms, that should govern the preferences of a rational decision maker. Their axioms included transitivity (if A is preferred to B and B is preferred to C, then A is preferred to C), and substitution (if A is preferred to B, then an even chance to get A or C is preferred to an even chance to get B or C), along with other conditions of a more technical nature. The normative and the descriptive status of the axioms of rational choice have been the subject of extensive discussions. In particular, there is convincing evidence that people do not always obey the substitution axiom, and considerable disagreement exists about the normative merit of this axiom (e.g., Allais & Hagen, 1979). However, all analyses of rational choice incorporate two principles: *dominance* and *invariance*. Dominance demands that if prospect A is at least as good as prospect B in every respect and better than B in at least one respect, then A should be preferred to B. Invariance requires that the preference order between prospects should not depend on the manner in which they are described. In particular, two versions of a choice problem that are recognized to be equivalent when shown together should elicit the same preference even when shown separately. We now show that the requirement of invariance, however elementary and innocuous it may seem, cannot generally be satisfied.

### Framing of Outcomes

Risky prospects are characterized by their possible outcomes and by the probabilities of these outcomes. The same option, however, can be framed or described in different ways (Tversky & Kahneman, 1981). For example, the possible outcomes of a gamble can be framed either as gains and losses relative to the status quo or as asset positions that incorporate initial wealth. Invariance requires that such changes in the description of outcomes should not alter the preference order. The following pair of problems illustrates a violation of this requirement. The total number of respondents in each problem is denoted by *N*, and the percentage who chose each option is indicated in parentheses.

*Problem 1 (N = 152)*

Imagine that the U.S. is preparing for the outbreak of an unusual Asian disease, which is expected to kill 600 people. Two alternative programs to combat the disease have been proposed. Assume that the exact scientific estimates of the consequences of the programs are as follows:

If Program A is adopted, 200 people will be saved. (72%)

If Program B is adopted, there is a one-third probability that 600 people will be saved and a two-thirds probability that no people will be saved. (28%)

Which of the two programs would you favor?

The formulation of Problem 1 implicitly adopts as a reference point a state of affairs in which the disease is allowed to take its toll of 600 lives. The outcomes of the programs include the reference state and two possible gains, measured by the number of lives saved. As expected, preferences are risk averse: A clear majority of respondents prefer saving 200 lives for sure over a gamble that offers a one-third chance of saving 600 lives. Now consider another problem in which the same cover story is followed by a different description of the prospects associated with the two programs:

*Problem 2 (N = 155)*

If Program C is adopted, 400 people will die. (22%)

If Program D is adopted, there is a one-third probability that nobody will die and a two-thirds probability that 600 people will die. (78%)

It is easy to verify that options C and D in Problem 2 are indistinguishable in real terms from options A and B in Problem 1, respectively. The second version, however, assumes a reference state in which no one dies of the disease. The best outcome is the maintenance of this state and the alternatives are losses measured by the number of people that will die of the disease. People who evaluate options in these terms are expected to show a risk seeking preference for the gamble (option D) over the sure loss of 400 lives. Indeed, there is more risk seeking in the second version of the problem than there is risk aversion in the first.

The failure of invariance is both pervasive and robust. It is as common among sophisticated respondents as among naive ones, and it is not eliminated even when the same respondents answer both questions within a few minutes. Respondents confronted with their conflicting answers are typically puzzled. Even after rereading the problems, they still wish to be risk averse in the "lives saved" version; they wish to be risk seeking in the "lives lost" version; and they also wish to obey invariance and give consistent answers in the two versions. In their stubborn appeal, framing effects resemble perceptual illusions more than computational errors.

The following pair of problems elicits preferences that violate the dominance requirement of rational choice.

*Problem 3 (N = 86)*

Choose between:
E. 25% chance to win $240 and
   75% chance to lose $760                                    (0%)

F. 25% chance to win $250 and
   75% chance to lose $750                                    (100%)

It is easy to see that F dominates E. Indeed, all respondents chose accordingly.

*Problem 4 (N = 150)*

Imagine that you face the following pair of concurrent decisions. First examine both decisions, then indicate the options you prefer.

Decision (i) Choose between:
A. a sure gain of $240                                        (84%)
B. 25% chance to gain $1000 and
   75% chance to gain nothing                                 (16%)

Decision (ii) Choose between:
C. a sure loss of $750                                        (13%)
D. 75% chance to lose $1000 and
   25% chance to lose nothing                                 (87%)

As expected from the previous analysis, a large majority of subjects made a risk averse choice for the sure gain over the positive gamble in the first decision, and an even larger majority of subjects made a risk seeking choice for the gamble over the sure loss in the second decision. In fact, 73% of the respondents chose A and D and only 3% chose B and C. The same pattern of results was observed in a modified version of the problem, with reduced stakes, in which undergraduates selected gambles that they would actually play.

Because the subjects considered the two decisions in Problem 4 simultaneously, they expressed in effect a preference for A and D over B and C. The preferred conjunction, however, is actually dominated by the rejected one. Adding the sure gain of $240 (option A) to option D yields 25% chance to win $240 and 75% to lose $760. This is precisely option E in Problem 3. Similarly, adding the sure loss of $750 (option C) to option B yields a 25% chance to win $250 and 75% chance to lose $750. This is precisely option F in Problem 3. Thus, the susceptibility to framing and the S-shaped value function produce a violation of dominance in a set of concurrent decisions.

The moral of these results is disturbing: Invariance is normatively essential, intuitively compelling, and psychologically unfeasible. Indeed, we conceive only two ways of guaranteeing invariance. The first is to adopt a procedure that will transform equivalent versions of any problem into the same canonical representation. This is the rationale for the standard admonition to students of business, that they should consider each decision problem in terms of total assets rather than in terms of gains or losses (Schlaifer, 1959). Such a representation would avoid the violations of invariance illustrated in the previous problems, but the advice is easier to give than to follow. Except in the context of possible ruin, it is more natural to consider financial outcomes as gains and losses rather than as states of wealth. Furthermore, a canonical representation of risky prospects requires a compounding of all outcomes of concurrent decisions (e.g., Problem 4) that exceeds the capabilities of intuitive computation even in simple problems. Achieving a canonical representation is even more difficult in other contexts such as safety, health, or quality of life. Should we advise people to evaluate the consequence of a public health policy (e.g., Problems 1 and 2) in terms of overall mortality, mortality due to diseases, or the number of deaths associated with the particular disease under study?

Another approach that could guarantee invariance is the evaluation of options in terms of their actuarial rather than their psychological consequences. The actuarial criterion has some appeal in the context of human lives, but it is clearly inadequate for financial choices, as has been generally recognized at least since Bernoulli, and it is entirely inapplicable to outcomes that lack an objective metric. We conclude that frame invariance cannot be expected to hold and that a sense of confidence in a particular choice does not ensure that the same choice would be made in another frame. It is therefore good practice to test the robustness of preferences by deliberate attempts to frame a decision problem in more than one way (Fischhoff, Slovic, & Lichtenstein, 1980).

### The Psychophysics of Chances

Our discussion so far has assumed a Bernoullian expectation rule according to which the value, or utility, of an uncertain prospect is obtained by adding the utilities of the possible outcomes, each weighted by its probability. To examine this assumption, let us again consult psychophysical intuitions. Setting the value of the status quo at zero, imagine a cash gift, say of $300, and assign it a value of one. Now imagine that you are only given a ticket to a lottery that has a single prize of $300. How does the value of the ticket vary as a function of the probability of winning the prize? Barring utility for gambling, the value of such a prospect must vary between zero (when the chance of winning is nil) and one (when winning $300 is a certainty).

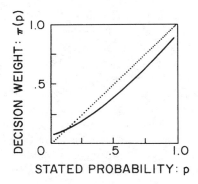

Figure 9.2.  A hypothetical weighting function.

Intuition suggests that the value of the ticket is not a linear function of the probability of winning, as entailed by the expectation rule. In particular, an increase from 0% to 5% appears to have a larger effect than an increase from 30% to 35%, which also appears smaller than an increase from 95% to 100%. These considerations suggest a category-boundary effect: A change from impossibility to possibility or from possibility to certainty has a bigger impact than a comparable change in the middle of the scale. This hypothesis is incorporated into the curve displayed in Figure 9.2, which plots the weight attached to an event as a function of its stated numerical probability. The most salient feature of Figure 9.2 is that decision weights are regressive with respect to stated probabilities. Except near the endpoints, an increase of .05 in the probability of winning increases the value of the prospect by less than 5% of the value of the prize. We next investigate the implications of these psychophysical hypotheses for preferences among risky options.

In Figure 9.2 decision weights are lower than the corresponding probabilities over most of the range. Underweighting of moderate and high probabilities relative to sure things contributes to risk aversion in gains by reducing the attractiveness of positive gambles. The same effect also contributes to risk seeking in losses by attenuating the aversiveness of negative gambles. Low probabilities, however, are overweighted, and very low probabilities are either overweighted quite grossly or neglected altogether, making the decision weights highly unstable in that region. The overweighting of low probabilities reverses the pattern described above: It enhances the value of long shots and amplifies the aversiveness of a small chance of a severe loss. Consequently, people are often risk seeking in dealing with improbable gains and risk averse in dealing with unlikely losses. Thus, the characteristics of decision weights contribute to the attractiveness of both lottery tickets and insurance policies.

The nonlinearity of decision weights inevitably leads to violations of invariance, as illustrated in the following pair of problems:

*Problem 5 (N = 85)*

Consider the following two-stage game. In the first stage, there is a 75% chance to end the game without winning anything and a 25% chance to move into the second stage. If you reach the second stage you have a choice between:

A. a sure win of $30 (74%)
B. 80% chance to win $45 (26%)

Your choice must be made before the game starts, i.e., before the outcome of the first stage is known. Please indicate the option you prefer.

*Problem 6 (N = 81)*

Which of the following options do you prefer?

C. 25% chance to win $30 (42%)
D. 20% chance to win $45 (58%)

Because there is one chance in four to move into the second stage in Problem 5, prospect A offers a .25 probability of winning $30, and prospect B offers .25 × .80 = .20 probability of winning $45. Problems 5 and 6 are therefore identical in terms of probabilities and outcomes. However, the preferences are not the same in the two versions: A clear majority favors the higher chance to win the smaller amount in Problem 5, whereas the majority goes the other way in Problem 6. This violation of invariance has been confirmed with both real and hypothetical monetary payoffs (the present results are with real money), with human lives as outcomes, and with a nonsequential representation of the chance process.

We attribute the failure of invariance to the interaction of two factors: the framing of probabilities and the nonlinearity of decision weights. More specifically, we propose that in Problem 5 people ignore the first phase, which yields the same outcome regardless of the decision that is made, and focus their attention on what happens if they do reach the second stage of the game. In that case, of course, they face a sure gain if they choose option A and an 80% chance of winning if they prefer to gamble. Indeed, people's choices in the sequential version are practically identical to the choices they make between a sure gain of $30 and an 85% chance to win $45. Because a sure thing is overweighted in comparison with events of moderate or high probability (see Figure 9.2) the option that may lead to a gain of $30 is more attractive in the sequential version. We call this phenomenon the *pseudo-certainty* effect because an event that is actually uncertain is weighted as if it were certain.

A closely related phenomenon can be demonstrated at the low end of the probability range. Suppose you are undecided whether or not to purchase earthquake insurance because the premium is quite high. As you hesitate, your friendly insurance agent comes forth with an alternative offer: "For half the regular premium you can be fully covered if the quake occurs on an odd day of the month. This is good deal because for half the price you are covered for more than half the days." Why do most people find such probabilistic insurance distinctly unattractive? Figure 9.2 suggests an answer. Starting anywhere in the region of low probabilities, the impact on the decision weight of a reduction of probability from $p$ to $p/2$ is considerably smaller than the effect of a reduction from $p/2$ to 0. Reducing the risk by half, then, is not worth half the premium.

The aversion to probabilistic insurance is significant for three reasons. First, it undermines the classical explanation of insurance in terms of a concave utility function. According to expected utility theory, probabilistic insurance should be definitely preferred to normal insurance when the latter is just acceptable (see Kahneman & Tversky, 1979). Second, probabilistic insurance represents many forms of protective action, such as having a medical checkup, buying new tires, or installing a burglar alarm system. Such actions typically reduce the probability of some hazard without eliminating it altogether. Third, the acceptability of insurance can be manipulated by the framing of the contingencies. An insurance policy that covers fire but not flood, for example, could be evaluated either as full protection against a specific risk (e.g., fire), or as a reduction in the overall probability of property loss. Figure 9.2 suggests that people greatly undervalue a reduction in the probability of a hazard in comparison to the complete elimination of that hazard. Hence, insurance should appear more attractive when it is framed as the elimination of risk than when it is described as a reduction of risk. Indeed, Slovic, Fischhoff, and Lichtenstein (1982) showed that a hypothetical vaccine that reduces the probability of contracting a disease from 20% to 10% is less attractive if it is described as effective in half of the cases than if it is presented as fully effective against one of two exclusive and equally probable virus strains that produce identical symptoms.

### Formulation Effects

So far we have discussed framing as a tool to demonstrate failures of invariance. We now turn attention to the processes that control the framing of outcomes and events. The public health problem illustrates a formulation effect in which a change of wording from "lives saved" to "lives lost" induced a marked shift of preference from risk aversion to risk seeking. Evidently, the subjects adopted the descriptions of the outcomes as given in the question and evaluated the outcomes accordingly as gains or losses. Another formulation effect was reported by McNeil, Pauker, Sox, and Tversky (1982). They found that preferences of physicians and patients between hypothetical therapies for lung cancer varied markedly when their probable outcomes were described in terms of mortality or survival. Surgery, unlike radiation therapy, entails a risk of death during treatment. As a consequence, the surgery option was relatively less attractive when the statistics of treatment outcomes were described in terms of mortality rather than in terms of survival.

A physician, and perhaps a presidential advisor as well, could influence the decision made by the patient or by the President, without distorting or suppressing information, merely by the framing of outcomes and contingencies. Formulation effects can occur fortuitously, without anyone being aware of the impact of the frame on the ultimate decision. They can also be exploited deliberately to manipulate the relative attractiveness of options. For example, Thaler (1980) noted that lobbyists for the credit card industry insisted that any price difference between cash and credit purchases be labeled a cash discount rather than a credit card surcharge. The two labels frame the price difference as a gain or as a loss by implicitly designating either the lower or the higher price as normal. Because losses loom larger than gains, consumers are less likely to accept a surcharge than to forgo a discount. As is to be expected, attempts to influence framing are common in the marketplace and in the political arena.

The evaluation of outcomes is susceptible to formulation effects because of the nonlinearity of the value function and the tendency of people to evaluate options in relation to the reference point that is suggested or implied by the statement of the problem. It is worthy of note that in other contexts people automatically transform equivalent messages into the same representation. Studies of language comprehension indicate that people quickly recode much of what they hear into an abstract representation that no longer distinguishes whether the idea was expressed in an active or in a passive form and no longer discriminates what was actually said from what was implied, presupposed, or implicated (Clark & Clark, 1977). Unfortunately, the mental machinery that performs these operations silently and effortlessly is not adequate to perform the task of recoding the two versions of the public health problem or the mortality-survival statistics into a common abstract form.

### Transactions and Trades

Our analysis of framing and of value can be extended to choices between multiattribute options, such as the acceptability of a transaction or a trade. We propose that, in order to evaluate a multiattribute option, a person sets up a mental account that specifies the advantages and the disadvantages associated with the option, relative to a multiattribute reference state. The overall value of an option is given by the balance of its advantages and its disadvantages in relation to the reference state. Thus, an option is acceptable if the value of its advantages exceeds the value of its disadvantages. This analysis assumes psychological – but not physical – separability of advantages and disadvantages. The model does not constrain the manner in which separate attributes are combined to form overall measures of advantage and of disadvantage, but it imposes on these measures assumptions of concavity and of loss aversion.

Our analysis of mental accounting owes a large debt to the stimulating work of Richard Thaler (1980, 1985), who showed the relevance of this process to consumer behavior. The following problem, based on examples of Savage (1954) and Thaler (1980), introduces some of the rules that govern the construction of mental accounts and illustrates the extension of the concavity of value to the acceptability of transactions.

### Problem 7

Imagine that you are about to purchase a jacket for $125 and a calculator for $15. The calculator salesman informs you that the calculator you wish to buy is on sale for $10 at the other branch of the store, located 20 minutes' drive away. Would you make a trip to the other store?

This problem is concerned with the acceptability of an option that combines a disadvantage of inconvenience with a financial advantage that can be framed as a *minimal, topical,* or *comprehensive* account. The minimal account includes only the differences between the two options and disregards the features that they share. In the minimal account, the advantage associated with driving to the other store is framed as a gain of $5. A topical account relates the consequences of possible choices to a reference level that is determined by the context within which the decision arises. In the preceding problem, the relevant topic is the purchase of the calculator, and the benefit of the trip is therefore framed as a reduction of the price, from $15 to $10. Because the potential saving is associated only with the calculator, the price of the jacket is not included in the topical account. The price of the jacket, as well as other expenses, could well be included in a more comprehensive account in which the saving would be evaluated in relation to, say, monthly expenses.

The formulation of the preceding problem appears neutral with respect to the adoption of a minimal, topical, or comprehensive account. We suggest however, that people will spontaneously frame decisions in terms of topical accounts that, in the context of decision making, play a role analogous to that of "good forms" in perception and of basic-level categories in cognition. Topical organization, in conjunction with the concavity of value, entails that the willingness to travel to the other store for a saving of $5 on a calculator should be inversely related to the price of the calculator and should be independent of the price of the jacket. To test this prediction, we constructed another version of the problem in which the prices of the two items were interchanged. The price of the calculator was given as $125 in the first store and $120 in the other branch, and the price of the jacket was set at $15. As predicted, the proportions of respondents who said they would make the trip differed sharply in the two problems. The results showed that 68% of the respondents ($N = 88$) were willing to drive to the other branch to save $5 on a $15 calculator, but only 29% of 93 respondents were willing to make the same trip to save $5 on a $125 calculator. This finding supports the notion of topical organization of accounts, since the two versions are identical both in terms of a minimal and a comprehensive account.

The significance of topical accounts for consumer behavior is confirmed by the observation that the standard deviation of the prices that different stores in a city quote for the same product is roughly proportional to the average price of that product (Pratt, Wise, & Zeckhauser, 1979). Since the dispersion of prices is surely controlled by shoppers' efforts to find the best buy, these results suggest that consumers hardly exert more effort to save $15 on a $150 purchase than to save $5 on a $50 purchase.

The topical organization of mental accounts leads people to evaluate gains and losses in relative rather than in absolute terms, resulting in large variations in the rate at which money is exchanged for other things, such as the number of phone calls made to find a good buy or the willingness to drive a long distance to get one. Most consumers will find it easier to buy a car stereo system or a Persian rug, respectively, in the context of buying a car or a house than separately. These observations, of course, run counter to the standard rational theory of consumer behavior, which assumes invariance and does not recognize the effects of mental accounting.

The following problems illustrate another example of mental accounting in which the posting of a cost to an account is controlled by topical organization:

*Problem 8 ($N = 200$)*

Imagine that you have decided to see a play and paid the admission price of $10 per ticket. As you enter the theater, you discover that you have lost the ticket. The seat was not marked, and the ticket cannot be recovered.

Would you pay $10 for another ticket?
    Yes (46%)      No (54%)

*Problem 9 ($N = 183$)*

Imagine that you have decided to see a play where admission is $10 per ticket. As you enter the theater, you discover that you have lost a $10 bill.

Would you still pay $10 for a ticket for the play?
    Yes (88%)      No (12%)

The difference between the responses to the two problems is intriguing. Why are so many people unwilling to spend $10 after having lost a ticket, if they would readily spend that sum after losing an equivalent amount of cash? We attribute the difference to the topical organization of mental accounts. Going to the theater is normally viewed as a transaction in which the cost of the ticket is exchanged for the experience of seeing the play. Buying a second ticket increases the cost of seeing the play to a level that many respondents apparently find unacceptable. In contrast, the loss of the cash is not posted to the account of the play, and it affects the purchase of a ticket only by making the individual feel slightly less affluent.

An interesting effect was observed when the two versions of the problem were presented to the same subjects. The willingness to replace a lost ticket increased significantly when that problem followed the lost-cash version. In contrast, the willingness to buy a ticket after losing cash was not affected by prior presentation of the other problem. The juxtaposition of the two problems apparently enabled the subjects to realize that it makes sense to think of the lost ticket as lost cash, but not vice versa.

The normative status of the effects of mental accounting is questionable. Unlike earlier examples, such as the public health problem, in which the two versions differed only in form, it can be argued that the alternative versions of the calculator and ticket problems differ also in substance. In particular, it may be more pleasurable to save $5 on a $15 purchase than on a larger purchase, and it may be more annoying to pay twice for the same ticket than to lose $10 in cash. Regret, frustration, and self-satisfaction can also be affected by framing (Kahneman & Tversky, 1982). If such secondary consequences are considered legitimate, then the observed preferences do not violate the criterion of invariance and cannot readily be ruled out as inconsistent or erroneous. On the other hand, secondary consequences may change upon reflection. The satisfaction of saving $5 on a $15 item can be marred if the consumer discovers that she would not have exerted the same effort to save $10 on a $200 purchase. We do not wish to recommend that any two decision problems that have the same primary consequences should be resolved in the same way. We propose, however, that systematic examination of alternative framings offers a useful reflective device that can help decision makers assess the values that should be attached to the primary and secondary consequences of their choices.

### Losses and Costs

Many decision problems take the form of a choice between retaining the status quo and accepting an alternative to it, which is advantageous in some respects and disadvantageous in others. The analysis of value that was applied earlier to unidimensional risky prospects can be extended to this case by assuming that the status quo defines the reference level for all attributes.

The advantages of alternative options will then be evaluated as gains and their disadvantages as losses. Because losses loom larger than gains, the decision maker will be biased in favor of retaining the status quo.

Thaler (1980) coined the term "endowment effect" to describe the reluctance of people to part from assets that belong to their endowment. When it is more painful to give up an asset than it is pleasurable to obtain it, buying prices will be significantly lower than selling prices. That is, the highest price that an individual will pay to acquire an asset will be smaller than the minimal compensation that would induce the same individual to give up that asset, once acquired. Thaler discussed some examples of the endowment effect in the behavior of consumers and entrepreneurs. Several studies have reported substantial discrepancies between buying and selling prices in both hypothetical and real transactions (Gregory, 1983; Hammack & Brown, 1974; Knetsch & Sinden, 1984). These results have been presented as challenges to standard economic theory, in which buying and selling prices coincide except for transaction costs and effects of wealth. We also observed reluctance to trade in a study of choices between hypothetical jobs that differed in weekly salary (S) and in the temperature (T) of the workplace. Our respondents were asked to imagine that they held a particular position $(S_1, T_1)$ and were offered the option of moving to a different position $(S_2, T_2)$, which was better in one respect and worse in another. We found that most subjects who were assigned to $(S_1, T_1)$ did not wish to move to $(S_2, T_2)$, and that most subjects who were assigned to the latter position did not wish to move to the former. Evidently, the same difference in pay or in working conditions looms larger as a disadvantage than as an advantage.

In general, loss aversion favors stability over change. Imagine two hedonically identical twins who find two alternative environments equally attractive. Imagine further that by force of circumstance the twins are separated and placed in the two environments. As soon as they adopt their new states as reference points and evaluate the advantages and disadvantages of each other's environments accordingly, the twins will no longer be indifferent between the two states, and both will prefer to stay where they happen to be. Thus, the instability of preferences produces a preference for stability. In addition to favoring stability over change, the combination of adaptation and loss aversion provides limited protection against regret and envy by reducing the attractiveness of forgone alternatives and of others' endowments.

Loss aversion and the consequent endowment effect are unlikely to play a significant role in routine economic exchanges. The owner of a store, for example, does not experience money paid to suppliers as losses and money received from customers as gains. Instead, the merchant adds costs and revenues over some period of time and only evaluates the balance. Matching debits and credits are effectively cancelled prior to evaluation. Payments made by consumers are also not evaluated as losses but as alternative purchases. In accord with standard economic analysis, money is naturally viewed as a proxy for the goods and services that it could buy. This mode of evaluation is made explicit when an individual has in mind a particular alternative, such as "I can either buy a new camera or a new tent." In this analysis, a person will buy a camera if its subjective value exceeds the value of retaining the money it would cost.

There are cases in which a disadvantage can be framed either as a cost or as a loss. In particular, the purchase of insurance can also be framed as a choice between a sure loss and the risk of a greater loss. In such cases the cost-lost discrepancy can lead to failures of invariance. Consider, for example, the choice between a sure loss of $50 and a 25% chance to lose $200. Slovic, Fischhoff, and Lichtenstein (1982) reported that 80% of their subjects expressed a risk-seeking preference for the gamble over the sure loss. However, only 35% of subjects refused to pay $50 for insurance against a 25% risk of losing $200. Similar results were also reported by Schoemaker and Kunreuther (1979) and by Hershey and Schoemaker (1980). We suggest that the same amount of money that was framed as an uncompensated loss in the first problem was framed as the cost of protection in the second. The modal preference was reversed in the two problems because losses are more aversive than costs.

We have observed a similar effect in the positive domain, as illustrated by the following pair of problems:

*Problem 10*

Would you accept a gamble that offers a 10% chance to win $95 and a 90% chance to lose $5?

*Problem 11*

Would you pay $5 to participate in a lottery that offers a 10% chance to win $100 and a 90% chance to win nothing?

A total of 132 undergraduates answered the two questions, which were separated by a short filler problem. The order of the questions was reversed for half the respondents. Although it is easily confirmed that the two problems offer objectively identical options, 55 of the respondents expressed different preferences in the two versions. Among them, 42 rejected the gamble in Problem 10 but accepted the equivalent lottery in Problem 11. The effectiveness of this seemingly inconsequential manipulation illustrates both the cost-loss discrepancy and the power of framing. Thinking of the $5 as a payment makes the venture more acceptable than thinking of the same amount as a loss.

The preceding analysis implies that an individual's subjective state can be improved by framing negative outcomes as costs rather than as losses. The possibility of such psychological manipulations may explain a paradoxical form of behavior that could be labeled the *dead-loss effect*. Thaler (1980) discussed the example of a man who develops tennis elbow soon after paying the membership fee in a tennis club and continues to play in agony to avoid wasting his investment. Assuming that the individual would not play if he had not paid the membership fee, the question arises: How can playing in agony improve the individual's lot? Playing in pain, we suggest, maintains the evaluation of the membership fee as a cost. If the individual were to stop playing, he would be forced to recognize the fee as a dead loss, which may be more aversive than playing in pain.

### Concluding Remarks

The concepts of utility and value are commonly used in two distinct senses: (a) *experience value*, the degree of pleasure or pain, satisfaction or anguish in the actual experience of an outcome; and (b) *decision value*, the contribution of an anticipated outcome to the overall attractiveness or aversiveness of an option in a choice. The distinction is rarely explicit in decision theory because it is tacitly assumed that decision values and experience values coincide. This assumption is part of the conception of an idealized decision maker who is able to predict future experiences with perfect accuracy and evaluate options accordingly. For ordinary decision makers, however, the correspondence of decision values and experience values is far from perfect (March, 1978). Some factors that affect experience are not easily anticipated, and some factors that affect decisions do not have a comparable impact on the experience of outcomes.

In contrast to the large amount of research on decision making, there has been relatively little systematic exploration of the psychophysics that relate hedonic experience to objective states. The most basic problem of hedonic psychophysics is the determination of the level of adaptation or aspiration that separates positive from negative outcomes. The hedonic reference point is largely determined by the objective status quo, but it is also affected by expectations and social comparisons. An objective improvement can be experienced as a loss, for example, when an employee receives a smaller raise than everyone else in the office. The experience of pleasure or pain associated with a change of state is also critically dependent on the dynamics of hedonic adaptation. Brickman and Campbell's (1971) concept of the hedonic treadmill suggests the radical hypothesis that rapid adaptation will cause the effects of any objective improvement to be short-lived. The complexity and subtlety of hedonic experience make it difficult for the decision maker to anticipate the actual experience that outcomes will produce. Many a person who ordered a meal when ravenously hungry has admitted to a big mistake when the fifth course arrived on the table. The common mismatch of decision values and experience values introduces an additional element of uncertainty in many decision problems.

The prevalence of framing effects and violations of invariance further complicates the relation between decision values and experience values. The framing of outcomes often induces decision values that have no counterpart in actual experience. For example, the framing of outcomes of therapies for lung cancer in terms of mortality or survival is unlikely to affect experience, although it can have a pronounced influence on choice. In other cases, however, the framing of decisions affects not only decision but experience as well. For example, the framing of an expenditure as an uncompensated loss or as the price of insurance can probably influence the experience of that outcome. In such cases, the evaluation of outcomes in the context of decisions not only anticipates experience but also molds it.

### References

Allais, M., & Hagen, O. (Eds.). (1979). *Expected utility hypotheses and the Allais paradox.* Hingham, MA: Reidel.

Bernoulli, D. (1954). Exposition of a new theory on the measurement of risk. *Econometrica, 22,* 23–36. (Original work published 1738.)

Brickman, P., & Campbell, D. T. (1971). Hedonic relativism and planning the good society. In M. H. Appley (Ed.), *Adaptation-level theory: A symposium.* New York: Academic Press.

Clark, H. H., & Clark, E. V. (1977). *Psychology and language.* New York: Harcourt, Brace Jovanovich.

Eraker, S. E., & Sox, H. C. (1981). Assessment of patients' preferences for therapeutic outcomes. *Medical Decision Making, 1,* 29–39.

Fishburn, P. C., & Kochenberger, G. A. (1979). Two-piece von Neumann–Morgenstern utility functions. *Decision Sciences, 10,* 503–518.

Fischhoff, B. (1983). Predicting frames. *Journal of Experimental Psychology: Learning, Memory and Cognition, 9,* 103–116.

Fischhoff, B., Slovic, P., & Lichtenstein, S. (1980). Knowing what you want: Measuring labile values. In T. Wallsten (Ed.), *Cognitive processes in choice and decision behavior.* Hillsdale, NJ: Erlbaum.

Gregory, R. L. (1983). *Measures of consumer's surplus; Reasons for the disparity in observed values.* Keene, NH: Keene State College.

Hammack, J., & Brown, G. M. Jr. (1974). *Waterfowl and wetlands: Toward bioeconomic analysis.* Baltimore: Johns Hopkins University Press.

Hershey, J. C., & Schoemaker, P. J. H. (1980). Risk taking and problem context in the domain of losses: An expected-utility analysis. *Journal of Risk and Insurance, 47,* 111–132.

Kahneman, D., & Tversky, A. (1979). Prospect theory: An analysis of decision under risk. *Econometrica, 47,* 263–291.

Kahneman, D., & Tversky, A. (1982). The simulation heuristic. In D. Kahneman, P. Slovic, & A. Tversky (Eds.), *Judgment under uncertainty: Heuristics and biases.* Cambridge: Cambridge University Press.

Knetsch, J. L., & Sinden, J. A. (1984). Willingness to pay and compensation demanded: Experimental evidence of an unexpected disparity in measures of value. *Quarterly Journal of Economics, 99,* 507–521.

March, J. G. (1978). Bounded rationality, ambiguity, and the engineering of choice. *Bell Journal of Economics, 9,* 587–608.

McNeil, B. J., Pauker, S., Sox, H. Jr., & Tversky, A. (1982). On the elicitation of preferences for alternative therapies. *New England Journal of Medicine, 306,* 1259–1262.

Payne, J. W., Laughhunn, D. J., & Crum, R. (1980). Translation of gambles and aspiration level effects in risky choice behavior. *Management Science, 26,* 1039–1060.

Pratt, J. W., Wise, D., & Zeckhauser, R. (1979). Price differences in almost competitive markets. *Quarterly Journal of Economics, 93,* 189–211.

Savage, L. J. (1954). *The foundations of statistics.* New York: Wiley.

Schlaifer, R. (1959). *Probability and statistics for business decisions.* New York: McGraw-Hill.

Schoemaker, P. J. H., & Kunreuther, H. C. (1979). An experimental study of insurance decisions. *Journal of Risk and Insurance, 46,* 603–618.

Slovic, P., Fischhoff, B., & Lichtenstein, S. (1982). Response mode, framing, and information-processing effects in risk assessment. In R. Hogarth (Ed.), *New directions for methodology of social and behavioral science*: No.11. *Question framing and response consistency.* San Francisco: Jossey-Bass.

Thaler, R. H. (1980). Toward a positive theory of consumer choice. *Journal of Economic Behavior and Organization, 1,* 39–60.

Thaler, R. H. (1985). Mental accounting and consumer choice. *Management Science, 4,* 199–214.

Tversky, A. (1977). On the elicitation of preferences: Descriptive and prescriptive considerations. In D. Bell, R. L. Keeney, & H. Raiffa (Eds.), *Conflicting objectives in decisions: International series on applied systems analysis.* New York: Wiley.

Tversky, A., & Kahneman, D. (1981). The framing of decisions and the rationality of choice. *Science, 221,* 453–458.

von Neumann, J., & Morgenstern, O. (1947). *Theory of games and economic behavior* (2nd ed.). Princeton: Princeton University Press.

# 10 Who Uses the Cost-Benefit Rules of Choice? Implications for the Normative Status of Microeconomic Theory

*Richard P. Larrick, Richard E. Nisbett,*
*and James N. Morgan*

A basic distinction is made in the field of decision making between normative and descriptive models of choice behavior. A normative model is one that depicts how people ought to make decisions in order to maximize their personal outcomes and a descriptive model is one that depicts how people actually make decisions. The maximization model of microeconomic theory, a set of principles governing appropriate choice given the decision maker's assessment of costs and benefits (Mishan, 1976; Morgan & Duncan, 1982), has been advanced as both a normative and a descriptive model (Becker, 1976; see also Hirshleifer, 1985), but it has fared better as a normative model than as a descriptive one. A large accumulation of empirical evidence indicates that certain aspects of the microeconomic model do not describe people's ordinary decision processes (Arkes & Blumer, 1985; Hoskin, 1983; Tversky & Kahneman, 1986). The fact that the model often fails descriptively raises the question, If people do not commonly use cost-benefit reasoning, why should we believe that it is normative? Why should it guide our choices?

Different methods are typically used to evaluate the normative versus the descriptive strength of a model. Normative adequacy has usually been tested by formal, mathematical proof, whereas descriptive adequacy has been tested by empirical means. To defend the normative adequacy of microeconomic models of choice, economists have argued that the model is based on a few assumptions about consistency that most people agree are intuitively reasonable criteria for good decision making. If one assents to the assumptions, economists argue, then one assents to the model because it is mathematically implied by the assumptions.

But there is also a tradition of justifying, and amending, normative models in response to empirical considerations. March (1978), for example, argues that the fact that clients are willing to purchase the services of experts with

This chapter originally appeared in *Organizational Behavior and Human Decision Processes*, 1993, 56, 331–347. Copyright © 1993 by Academic Press, Inc. Reprinted by permission.

skills in the decision sciences speaks positively to the normativeness of the model employed by the experts. And Simon (1955) argued that "satisficing" due to time and energy constraints more nearly describes people's choice behavior than the optimizing posited by the normative model. Simon and others have reasoned that this suggests that a model is normative only if it is practicable.

Some people might be inclined to think that empirical arguments are not appropriately raised in connection with considerations of normativeness, viewing this as an instance of the *naturalistic fallacy*, or moving from an "is" to an "ought." But in fact there is a long-standing tradition in epistemology of treating pragmatic considerations as prior to purely reflective ones. Hume held that "reason is and ought to be the slave of passion," by which he meant that human needs and their most efficient means of solution dictate the mental procedures that underlie inference and choice. The modern inheritors of the Hume tradition in epistemology describe their position as *consequentialism*, by which they mean that the appropriate gauge of a putatively normative cognitive procedure is whether it produces consequences that are beneficial for the individual (Goldman, 1978, 1986; Stich, 1990; see also Stich & Nisbett, 1980; Thagard, 1982; Thagard & Nisbett, 1983).

A second respect in which empirical considerations affect normative assumptions concerns whether people's behavior is *corrigible* by a putatively normative model. Goldman (1978, 1986) has argued that a rule system cannot be held to be normative if people cannot actually use it, or be taught to use it. Applying these considerations to microeconomic, cost-benefit choice theory, we can generate three easily tested predictions that would reflect on the normativeness of the theory.

First, it should be the case that the consequences of using putatively normative rules ought to be superior. Economists claim that using the cost-benefit rules of choice will maximize (or at least improve) outcomes and lead to greater life success. The argument is that use of the rules makes people more efficient in their use of scarce resources such as time and effort. As a result, one would expect that people who use cost-benefit rules would be more productive and thereby receive greater returns in school or work. We measured outcomes in two different ways – by grade point averages in the case of undergraduates and by salaries and raises in the case of professional academics. Of course, other explanations for a positive relationship would be plausible. Perhaps productive people seek optimal rules to help them manage their time and energy, or a third factor, such as motivation, leads to both greater productivity and the use of economic reasoning. Whatever the explanation, the finding is relevant to questions of normativeness. If it were to turn out *not* to be the case that people who use the rules have better outcomes, this would throw doubt on the claims of the model to normativeness.

A second expectation from present considerations is that intelligent people would be more likely to use cost-benefit reasoning. Because intelligence is generally regarded as being the set of psychological properties that makes for effectiveness across environments (Baron, 1985, p. 15; Sternberg, 1985, 1988), intelligent people should be more likely to use the most effective reasoning strategies than should less intelligent people. Evidence for a link between intelligence and use of normative inferential rules has been obtained by Jepson, Krantz, and Nisbett (1983) in the statistical reasoning domain. They found that, in a sample of untrained undergraduates, use of presumably normative statistical rules to solve problems drawn from everyday life was positively correlated with verbal and mathematical skills as measured by standardized test scores. In this chapter, we examine the relationship between the use of economic reasoning and intelligence as measured by undergraduates' scores on the Scholastic Aptitude Test.

A third implication is that people ought to be trainable by the cost-benefit rules in the sense of coming to use them in everyday life choices once they have been exposed to them. If use of the rules leads to more desirable outcomes, people should be increasingly likely to use them both because they see the superiority of the rules in principle and because they experience improved outcomes when they use them. We have shown in a previous paper (Larrick, Morgan, & Nisbett, 1990) that professional training in economics is positively correlated with cost-benefit reasoning and that naive subjects who have been given brief training in one of the cost-benefit rules (the sunk cost rule) subsequently use the rule outside the laboratory. In this chapter we attempt to extend the finding by examining the relationship between taking university economics courses and the use of cost-benefit reasoning. Once again, of course, we cannot assess the causal relationship between training in economics and the use of cost-benefit rules. Nonetheless, if people who were well-versed in economics failed to employ their knowledge, it would undermine our confidence that the cost-benefit rules were normative.

## Cost-Benefit Rules

We envision microeconomics as a set of rules that can be used to maximize the outcomes of choices. We depict the model as a set of rules because the rule-based approach to reasoning has been influential in cognitive psychology and has received substantial empirical support in a range of reasoning domains (Holland, Holyoak, Nisbett, & Thagard, 1986; Newell & Simon, 1972; Smith, Langston, & Nisbett, 1992). The particular rules we consider serve as general guides for maximizing the benefits of a course of action (Mishan, 1976; Morgan & Duncan, 1982). When a person is confronted with a set of possible actions each of which can lead to some set of outcomes, the person should convert the benefits and costs of all possible outcomes to a single scale and adjust them for the probabilities that the outcomes will occur. In this calculation, the following three rules apply.

1. *The net benefit rule.* The action that has the greatest expected net benefit should be chosen from a set of possible actions.
2. *The sunk cost rule.* Only future benefits and costs should be considered in current decisions. Past costs and benefits are not relevant, unless they predict future benefits and costs.
3. *The opportunity cost rule.* The cost of engaging in a given course of action is the loss of the benefits of the next-best course of action.

We will attempt to distinguish use of rules such as these from mere preference or value differences. The question of whether different kinds of people are using different rules or simply hold different values arises in several contexts. One has to do with alleged differences between men and women in their use of economic rules of choice. There is a well-established finding in the literature on the teaching of economics that men perform better than women in economics classes and on tests of economic knowledge (Heath, 1989; Watts & Lynch, 1989). The most common explanations refer to the well-documented differences in socialization between boys and girls with respect to mathematics ability. Boys are more likely to be encouraged to be interested in math in general and financial matters in particular, whereas girls may be actively discouraged from such interests, or at least made to doubt their abilities. We propose that the difference between men and women in their use of economic rules may not be entirely due to differences in math socialization. It may be due at least in part to differences in moral reasoning between the sexes. This topic has received attention in the literature on moral development, following Gilligan's (1982) work, which holds that women tend to value compassion for others more than do men, whereas men tend to value justice more than do women. In the studies described below, we examined subjects' use of microeconomic rules both when they conflicted with humanitarian values and when they did not. If women differ from men in their values rather than in their understanding of microeconomic rules of choice, their answers should differ from those of men primarily when the rules of choice conflict with a humanitarian value.

We also examined a second issue concerning values. It is sometimes contended that formal exposure to economics makes people more selfish or more concerned with money (Frank, 1988) or, alternatively, that more selfish people choose to make themselves familiar with economics. To examine this possibility, we measured the extent to which subjects were concerned with money, pleasure, and other benefits.

We present two studies in which we examined correlates of cost-benefit reasoning. In the first study, we administered an economic reasoning survey to a random sample of University of Michigan seniors and obtained information on economics training (number of economics classes), academic effectiveness (grade point average), intellectual skills (standardized aptitude test scores), and gender. In the second study, we surveyed University of Michigan faculty from three disciplines (economics, biology, and humanities) and obtained information on career effectiveness (salary and raises), gender, and age. Some of the discipline results from the second study have been reported previously in a paper on the effect of training (Larrick et al., 1990).

## Study 1

In Study 1, we examined whether academic effectiveness, intellectual aptitude, economics training, and gender of college students are related to economic reasoning. We surveyed seniors because they had had a greater opportunity for their reasoning about everyday choices to affect their academic performance.

We constructed four types of questions – questions about people's own behavior and choices, questions reflecting a recognition of what rules are recommended by economics, questions about social policy that involved a conflict between cost-benefit rules and other values, and questions about the salience of money and pleasure. If cost-benefit rules are normative, we would expect academic effectiveness, intellectual ability, and economics training to be associated with use of the rules in subjects' personal choices. If economics training is effective, we would expect that it would be positively related to the recognition of cost-benefit reasoning. Because we argue that it is reasoning about costs and benefits and not the sheer pursuit of money or pleasure that underlies the use of cost-benefit reasoning, we expected that the predictor variables would not be related to salience of money and enjoyment.

### Method

*Subjects.* One hundred students who were listed as seniors at the beginning of the 1989–1990 academic year were randomly selected from the student directory (56 men, 44 women). Near the end of the 1989–1990 academic year, they were contacted by mail and offered 5 dollars for filling out and returning a short questionnaire on decision making. Three follow-up contacts were made to encourage people who had not returned it to complete the survey. Eighty-six subjects completed and returned the questionnaire (48 men, 38 women).

*Materials.* Four measures were created by averaging the scores for each of several types of question. All questions were scored on a 0 to 1 scale, with 0 indicating reasoning counter to cost-benefit rules and 1 indicating reasoning in line with the rules. A lack of preference was assigned an intermediate score of .5. Questions were designed to cover a wide range of behaviors and opinions. The questions for each index were similar in that each contained a response that reflected the use of cost-benefit rules, although of course reasons for giving a particular response to a particular question may have been due in part to other considerations as well. Indices were constructed based on a priori, commonsense considerations about what sort of question was best regarded as a reflection of actual behavior, of recognizing economic principles, and so on. We took the precaution, however, of eliminating any items that were negatively correlated with the other items on the index.

1. *Own behavior and decisions (6 items).* The first set of questions was about reasoning subjects used in their own decisions and behaviors. These questions were intended to measure the extent to which subjects ignored sunk costs and attended to opportunity costs in their day-to-day decisions. An example of a question about decisions they had actually made was "In the past 3 years, have you ever started one of the following but not finished it?" The question was followed by a list of activities, such as a restaurant meal, a movie at a theater, or attendance at an athletic event. The item score consisted of the average across all of the questions.

Subjects were also asked open-ended questions about some common decisions they might make in their everyday lives. One question read, "You and a friend have each spent $5 to see a movie that is turning out to be pretty bad. What are good reasons for staying to see the end? What are good reasons for leaving?" Stating that the spent money was a good reason for staying was scored as a failure to ignore sunk costs. Stating that the movie was a waste of time was scored as partial attendance to opportunity costs, and stating that there might be better things to do was scored as full attendance to opportunity costs. (All of the open-ended questions were coded by two coders who agreed on 90 percent of the classifications. The remaining 10 percent were coded through consensus.)

2. *Recognition of economic reasoning (3 items).* The second set of questions measured whether subjects could correctly identify the sort of reasoning that would be endorsed by economists. An example of a sunk cost recognition problem is the following. The multiple choice responses represented different combinations of behavior (continuing vs. discontinuing an activity that involved a sunk cost) and rationale for the behavior (attending to sunk costs vs. ignoring sunk costs):

> Imagine that you have paid $5 for a movie that is turning out to be pretty bad. If the movie had been free, you probably wouldn't stay. What do you think an economist would recommend doing?
> (0.00)____Stay, even though it's bad, because you've spent the $5 on it. Otherwise, you're wasting your money. (Sunk cost trap behavior, sunk cost trap rationale.)
> (0.50)____Leave, because the boredom of a bad movie is worse than the $5 you lose by leaving. It's more costly to stay than to leave. (Cost-benefit behavior, sunk cost trap rationale.)
> (1.00)____Leave, because the movie is bad and the $5 doesn't matter anymore. If you wouldn't stay for free, you shouldn't stay because it cost $5. (Cost-benefit behavior, cost-benefit rationale.)

(0.50)——Stay, because the movie might get better. You should think of the $5 as a gamble that might pay off. (Sunk cost trap behavior, cost-benefit rationale.)

The cost-benefit combination was given the highest score, the trap combination the lowest score, and the mixed combinations were given the same intermediate score.

3. *Value conflict (8 items)*. The third set of questions was about university and government policy issues for which cost-benefit reasoning led to a conflict with a salient humanitarian consideration. The following (from Larrick et al., 1990) is an example of a net-benefit problem in which the cost-benefit answer conflicts with values against exploitation of another's weakness.

> As you may know, there are continuing problems with assuring that blood supplies for patients are free of all viruses. The suggestion has recently been made to purchase blood from Asians for use in the West, on the grounds that many of the most dangerous viruses, including AIDS, are less common there. Many citizens of relatively poor Asian countries would be happy to have the extra cash; however, others have argued that such a practice would be an inappropriate form of exploitation. Do you tend to:
> (1.00)——favor the idea strongly
> (0.75)——favor it somewhat
> (0.50)——have no preference
> (0.25)——oppose the idea somewhat
> (0.00)——oppose it strongly

The following is an example of an opportunity cost problem in which the economic answer conflicts with the knowledge of certain harm to individuals resulting from the choice.

> The state of Michigan is anticipating a large budget deficit and is trying to find budget items on which it can reduce spending. One program that has recently been mentioned is funding for road and bridge repair. Experts estimate that a $200 million cut in the highway fund would lead to only 5 to 10 more people dying each year in automobile accidents than do at the present. Many legislators have argued that it is morally wrong to let people die due to the state's negligence. Others have argued that this large savings would keep more beneficial programs funded. Do you tend to favor:
> (0.00)——spending the money to repair the state's highways and bridges
> (1.00)——spending the money on other programs
> (0.50)——no preference

4. *Salience of money or enjoyment (5 items)*. The fourth set of questions was about the importance of money or enjoyment in the person's own decisions and behaviors. This index was used to measure the pursuit of self-interest. For example, an open-ended question asked "Of the careers that you have decided not to pursue, what is the career that you liked the best? Why did you decide not to pursue it?" and was coded for (a) mention of pay or financial stability and (b) mention of anticipated enjoyment.

Questions about gender and number of economics classes taken were included at the end of the questionnaire. In addition, subjects were asked for permission to contact the University for college grade point average (GPA) and standardized test scores, which were either Scholastic Aptitude Test (SAT) or American College Test (ACT) verbal and mathematics aptitude scores.

### Results and Discussion

The four cost-benefit reasoning measures were correlated with GPA, SAT Verbal score, SAT Math score, number of economics classes, and gender, which was coded as a dummy variable with males as 1 and females as 0. In these analyses, ACT scores were converted to SAT score form for subjects who had not taken the SAT.[1] SAT Verbal and SAT Math scores had zero-order correlations with the economic reasoning measures that were similar except that in every case the Verbal scores were more highly positively correlated with the reasoning measures than were the Math scores, in most cases substantially so. The same relationship held when the analyses were repeated using ordinary least squares multiple regression. The zero-order correlations are reported in Table 10.1 and the standardized regression coefficients are

Table 10.1. *Zero-Order Correlation Coefficients among Measures of Economic Reasoning and Grade Point Average, Verbal Score, Number of Economics Classes, and Gender*

| Predictor Variables | Own Behavior and Decisions | Recognition of Economists' Position | Value Conflict | Salience of Money and Enjoyment |
|---|---|---|---|---|
| Grade point average | .40*** | .20 | .14 | −.02 |
| Verbal score | .13 | .39*** | .36** | −.12 |
| Economics classes | .10 | .27** | .33** | −.20 |
| Gender | .25* | .14 | .32** | −.24* |

*Note:* All *p*-values are two-tailed.
* $p < .05$.
** $p < .01$.
*** $p < .001$.

Table 10.2. *Standardized Regression Coefficients for Measures of Economic Reasoning Regressed on Grade Point Average, Verbal Score, Number of Economics Classes, and Gender*

| Predictor Variables | Own Behavior and Decisions | Recognition of Economists' Position | Value Conflict | Salience of Money and Enjoyment |
|---|---|---|---|---|
| Grade point average | .50*** | .18 | .15 | −.06 |
| Verbal score | .03 | .39** | .50*** | −.06 |
| Economics classes | .15 | .32** | .39** | −.09 |
| Gender | .25* | .15 | .43*** | −.19 |

*Note:* Analyses also control for Math score. All $p$-values are two-tailed.
* $p < .05$.
** $p < .01$.
*** $p < .001$.

reported in Table 10.2 for all the predictor variables except SAT Math score. It may be seen that the two analyses yield very similar results.

The measure of academic effectiveness, grade point average, was positively related to choosing the cost-benefit response for own behaviors and decisions. Intelligence, as measured by SAT Verbal score, was positively related to recognition of economists' position on various economic problems. The SAT Verbal measure was also positively related to choosing the economic response for policy choices in which there was a conflict with humanitarian values. A similar pattern was found for the number of economics classes taken. The more economics classes the student had taken, the more likely the student was to recognize what the economists' position is on a variety of problems and to prefer the economic response in policy choices that had a value conflict.

Gender was related to choice of economic responses in own behavior and in choices on policy issues in which there was a conflict between cost-benefit rules and humanitarian values. Because the value conflict effect was of a larger magnitude than the behavior effect and there was no relationship between gender and recognition of economists' reasoning, we believe that the gender difference in behavior may be due to value differences that arise in everyday decisions rather than to differences in the understanding of economic rules. This interpretation is supported by results reported for Study 2, indicating that the gender difference for behavior is nonsignificant except when there is a value conflict.

None of the variables was related to our measure of the salience of money and enjoyment. What this indicates most notably is that we find no evidence that economics training is associated with an enhanced concern with money or pleasure. Thus the preference of economically trained students for economic answers to problems is probably related to their preference for the rule system and not to a greater concern with money or with maximizing pleasure.

It is important to note that the regression coefficients in Table 10.2 are in general quite similar to the zero-order correlations between predictor and outcome variables in Table 10.1. An interesting exception is the correlation between GPA and the own behavior and decisions index, which was .50 – higher than the zero-order correlation of .40. What this discrepancy suggests is the conclusion that students who obtain higher GPAs than would be predicted by their intelligence are particularly likely to use cost-benefit rules in their own behaviors and decisions. The only zero-order correlation that loses significance in the regression analysis is the correlation between gender and salience of money and pleasure (a significant −.24). Female subjects are more concerned with money and pleasure than male subjects, although not, for reasons we do not pretend to understand, when their levels on the other predictor variables are taken into consideration.

Our major predictions are well supported by the data. The behavior and decisions of students with higher GPAs were more consistent with cost-benefit rules, and particularly so for students whose GPA exceeded what would be expected on the basis of ability measures. Cost-benefit reasoning was recognized more by more intelligent students and by students with training in economics, reflecting a better understanding of rules endorsed by economists. Cost-benefit reasoning was endorsed more by more intelligent students and more by students with training in economics when there was a policy choice in which there was a conflict between cost-benefit rules and humanitarian considerations. This pattern of results suggests that there may actually be separate behavioral and attitudinal components underlying the use of economic rules that do not necessarily intersect (a distinction similar to the one Wagner and Sternberg (1985) make between practical intelligence and formal knowledge). Neither economics training nor the other predictor variables was associated with greater salience of money or pleasure in decision-making. Finally, the data supported our supposition that females' adherence to economic rules differs from that of males primarily in that it simply takes a backseat to humanitarian values. Females were significantly less likely to give answers in line with economic rules for problems for which the rules gave an answer in conflict with such values.

## Study 2

In Study 2, we reexamined data collected in a survey of economic reasoning administered to University of Michigan faculty. Professors of economics, biology, and the humanities were asked two types of questions, one type measuring behavior reflecting economic choices and the other type measuring reasoning about university and international policy.

The other variables studied were salary, academic discipline, gender, and age. The study allows us to replicate the training and gender findings of Study 1 and to attempt a conceptual replication of the life consequences finding by examining salary instead of grade point average.

### Method

*Subjects.* All of the professors in the economics, biology, art history, and modern languages departments at the University of Michigan were contacted by telephone and asked to participate in a 20 min telephone survey on university policy choices and personal choices. Overall, 88% of the professors agreed to participate, yielding a sample of 125 subjects.

*Materials.* Two types of reasoning questions were included on the faculty survey: reasoning about university policy and about international policy. Several of the questions were identical to those asked of the university seniors. For example, one of the policy questions was the one concerning buying blood from poor Asians. Policy questions were also asked in which economic reasoning led to the same conclusion as would the consideration of a humanitarian value. An example of an opportunity cost problem of this type (from Larrick et al., 1990) is

> Some financial planners for the university anticipate that jobs for young people may soon be much more plentiful than in the recent past, for the simple reason that a much smaller fraction of the population is in the younger age group. One implication is that pay will increase for entry level jobs in all kinds of industries. The argument has been made that the university should respond to this situation by offering more money for scholarships in order to lure low income students away from starting work and toward continuing their education. Do you feel:
> (1.00)____scholarships should be kept competitive with salaries
> (0.00)____scholarships should simply maintain pace with inflation and not respond to competitive inducements
> (0.50)____or you do not have an opinion?

An analysis of opportunity cost indicates that if students are expected to forgo jobs in an improving market, universities will have to increase their financial aid in order to maintain their attractiveness to students. In this case, the cost-benefit recommendation is consistent with the salient humanitarian consideration that low income students should receive financial assistance for their education.

The policy questions were followed by questions about consumer and time-use choices that subjects had actually made. For instance, the faculty were asked a question similar to the one asked of the university seniors in Study 1: "In the past 5 years, have you ever started one of the following items and then not finished it?" This was followed by a list of seven consumer items. Discontinuing an activity for which one has already paid is an indication that one is willing to ignore sunk costs. Faculty were also asked, "Have you ever dropped a research project that was not proving worthwhile?" which measures willingness to ignore a sunk cost and to attend to opportunity costs. They were also asked about attempts to save time: "Do you own a microwave? A dishwasher? A VCR?" Freeing up time for other activities by investing in time-saving appliances was considered a measure of attending to opportunity costs.

The questions were subsequently reclassified into three types: no conflict with humanitarian values (for example, the scholarship question), conflict with humanitarian values (for example, the blood purchase question), and money and enjoyment maximization (for example, "do you own a microwave?"). It should be noted that the last index is not directly comparable to the salience of money and enjoyment index used in Study 1. The Study 1 index included questions asking subjects to describe the considerations that would enter into different decisions they might make, and then the responses were coded for the mention of financial or of enjoyment concerns. The Study 2 index consisted of questions that asked subjects about how they managed their money and about whether they owned creature comforts.

Subjects also provided demographic information regarding gender and age. Six years of salary data were obtained from published sources at the university.

### Results and Discussion

The behavior and policy choice indices were correlated with salary, economics training, gender, and age, and are reported in the left side of Table 10.3.[2] In addition, the analyses were repeated using ordinary least squares multiple regression to assess the independent effects of the predictors. It may be seen that the standardized multiple regression coefficients in Table 10.4 yield very similar conclusions as the correlations, with the zero-order correlations being in general higher.

The results show that higher salaries were significantly related to economic behavior and policy choices. It is important to note that all of these relationships also held when the salary-sensitive items were removed from the indices. In addition, the salary results were actually stronger when the economists were omitted from the sample. When the sample included only biologists and humanists, the standardized salary coefficients were .28 for behavior and .43 for combined policy choices. There was no effect of discipline among the noneconomists for any of the indices. The salary relationships were of a similar magnitude when examined entirely within a discipline, although the significance levels suffered due to the smaller sample size.

Table 10.3. *Zero-Order Correlation Coefficients among Measures of Economic Reasoning and Salary, Economics Training, Gender, and Age*

|  | Behavior and Policy Indices | | Value Indices | | |
|---|---|---|---|---|---|
|  | Own Behavior and Decisions | Combined Policy Choices | No Value Conflict Items | Value Conflict Items | Money- and Enjoyment-directed Behavior |
| Salary | .32*** | .32*** | .29*** | .27** | .35*** |
| Economics | .43** | .45** | .36*** | .49*** | .27** |
| Gender | .19* | .24** | .09 | .21* | .26** |
| Age | −.11 | −.21* | −.06 | −.23** | .04 |

*Note:* The behavior and policy indices and the value indices are different ways of indexing the same items. They are not independent findings. All *p*-values are two-tailed.
* *p* < .05.
** *p* < .01.
*** *p* < .001.

The variables on the right side of Tables 10.3 and 10.4 are recategorizations of the variables on the left. It may be seen that higher salaries were significantly related to cost-benefit reasoning both when it was and when it was not in conflict with humanitarian values. And, as might be expected, salary

Table 10.4. *Standardized Regression Coefficients for Economic Reasoning Regressed on Salary, Economics Training, Gender, and Age*

|  | Behavior and Policy Indices | | Value Indices | | |
|---|---|---|---|---|---|
|  | Own Behavior and Decisions | Combined Policy Choices | No Value Conflict Items | Value Conflict Items | Money- and Enjoyment-directed Behavior |
| Salary | .26* | .33*** | .26* | .26** | .30** |
| Economics | .32*** | .27** | .24* | .34*** | .16 |
| Gender | .11 | .20** | .02 | .19* | .17* |
| Age | −.16 | −.30** | −.12 | −.27** | −.08 |

*Note:* The behavior and policy indices and the value indices are different ways of indexing the same items. They are not independent findings. All *p*-values are two-tailed.
* *p* < .05.
** *p* < .01.
*** *p* < .001.

was positively related to money- and enjoyment-directed behavior, which included such measures as owning labor-saving devices. The relationships were once again somewhat stronger when the economists were excluded from the sample (standardized regression coefficients of .30 for salary for all three value indices).

Another measure of effectiveness is the average size of raise, which may be regarded as reflecting changes in the rate of effectiveness. Average raise over the past 5 years, measured as an annual percentage change in salary, was (weakly) related to cost-benefit reasoning for policy choices (regression coefficient = .15, $p = .07$) when it was added to the full regression model. Again, the relationship is stronger – although not more statistically significant because of the smaller sample size – when the economists are excluded (coefficient = .19, $p = .11$).

As has been reported previously by Larrick et al. (1990), economics training was significantly related to economic reasoning and behavior. It may be seen from the right sides of Tables 10.3 and 10.4 that economics training was significantly related to cost-benefit reasoning both when it did and when it did not conflict with humanitarian values. Economists, however, were not significantly more likely to engage in the pursuit of money and enjoyment when the other predictors were controlled in the analysis.

Gender was not related to behavior when the other predictors were held constant. Men were more likely to endorse cost-benefit reasoning for the policy index than were women, but this was due entirely to differences when there was a value conflict. It may be seen that men and women showed no difference on the no-conflict items, but a significant difference on the conflict items. Men were more concerned with money- and enjoyment-related behavior, and this remained significant when the other variables were controlled.

Age was not related to economic behavior but was significantly related to economic reasoning such that younger subjects employed more cost-benefit reasoning. This difference was confined to problems in which cost-benefit reasoning conflicted with humanitarian values. Younger subjects were more likely to employ cost-benefit reasoning only for problems for which there was such a conflict. We cannot tell whether this is a developmental effect, leading us to expect that the younger subjects will eventually come to resemble older subjects, or a cohort effect, reflecting what may be a stable preference in the younger generation for cost-benefit reasoning even when its conclusions conflict with other values. An answer will have to await the arrival of another generation or two of academics.

### General Discussion

The present results greatly expand the empirically based case for the normativeness of cost-benefit rules. As microeconomic theory predicts, the people who use these rules are more likely to have successful life outcomes. The college seniors who used cost-benefit reasoning in their everyday decisions had higher grade point averages, including higher averages net of their aptitude, and the faculty who used cost-benefit reasoning in their everyday behaviors had higher salaries. These data cannot answer questions of causality and tell us whether use of the rules leads to greater success, greater success leads to use of the rules, or some third factor causes both. However, Study 1 shows at least that the relationship between cost-benefit reasoning and academic effectiveness is independent of intelligence and of economics training.

Additional evidence for the normative claim of cost-benefit reasoning comes from the fact that it was positively related to intelligence in Study 1. As Baron (1985) and others have defined it, intelligence is the set of psychological properties that enables a person to achieve his or her goals effectively. On this view, intelligent people will be more likely to use rules of choice that are effective in reaching their goals than will less intelligent people.

Finally, our results show that people who are familiar with the economic rules use them to a large extent in the way they behave and think in their everyday lives. We found in Study 1 that the number of economics classes taken was positively correlated with cost-benefit reasoning and in Study 2 that economists were more likely to use the rule system in both behavior and expressed choices than noneconomists. Unfortunately, we cannot assess whether these results are due to the effect of training, to self-selection, or some other combination of factors. But it should be recalled that we have elsewhere shown that laboratory-training in the cost-benefit rules has effects on behavior outside the laboratory.

The fact that effectiveness, intelligence, and training were related to cost-benefit reasoning even when it conflicted with certain humanitarian values raises interesting normative questions concerning the conflict between maximizing material well-being for society as a whole and concern with rules of fairness and compassion. These findings suggest that many of the people who know and use the rules in their own decisions believe that they are beneficial when applied to a larger social context, even when there are costs involving important values. On the other hand, the women in both studies and the older faculty in Study 2 tended to favor humanitarian considerations when they conflicted with the economic rules. Younger men seemed to be concerned with issues of maximizing material well-being to society in general. Women and older men seemed to be more concerned with avoiding inegalitarian or debasing outcomes for groups or individuals.

There is some evidence indicating that the age difference reflects at least in part a cohort effect. A fair amount of survey data indicates that members of the present younger generation hold more conservative values related to humanitarian concerns than their elder colleagues, who were often found taking action to uphold those values when they were younger (Inglehart & Flanagan, 1987; American Council on Education, 1973–1986). But we also suspect, in this case in the absence of supporting data, that people become more concerned with individual welfare and more dubious of abstract utilitarian principles as they grow older. We believe that a complete set of normative rules for choice must include rules that can adjudicate between cost-benefit reasoning and moral questions reflecting such considerations as the rights of particular individuals and the avoidance of exploitation.

### Notes

1   There were no records of standardized test scores for seventeen subjects who had transferred to the university after their first year. We ran two regressions to test whether the complete sample of 86 was different from the sample of 69 for whom we had scores on all the predictor variables. We excluded the test scores from these regressions to determine whether the remaining predictors had the same relationship to the outcome measures in both samples. The results were essentially the same, so we report the analyses for the sample of 69 subjects for which we have values for all of the predictors.

2   Some of the items in the behavior index (e.g., discontinuing an activity for which a sunk cost was incurred) could be affected by consumption opportunities (e.g., how often the person sees movies, plays, concerts, and so on), so the analysis was repeated with consumption opportunities included as an additional predictor variable. It was not significant ($p > .20$) and did not change the significance levels of any of the predictor variables.

### References

American Council on Education (1973–1988). *The American freshman: National norms.* Annual report issued by the Cooperative Institution Research Program, Graduate School of Education, University of California.

Arkes, H. R., & Blumer, C. (1985). The psychology of sunk cost. *Organizational Behavior and Human Decision Processes, 35,* 124–140.

Baron, J. (1985). *Rationality and intelligence.* Cambridge: Cambridge University Press.

Becker, G. (1976). *The economic approach to human behavior.* Chicago: University of Chicago Press.

Frank, R. (1988). *Passions within reason: The strategic role of the emotions.* New York: Norton.

Gilligan, C. (1982). *In a different voice: Psychological theory and women's development.* Cambridge, MA: Harvard University Press.

Goldman, A. I. (1978). Epistemics: The regulative theory of cognition: *Journal of Philosophy, 75,* 509–523.

Goldman, A. I. (1986). *Epistemology and cognition.* Cambridge, MA: Harvard University Press.

Heath, J. (1989). An econometric model of the role of gender in economic education. *American Economic Review, 79,* 226–230.

Hirshleifer, J. (1985). The expanding domain of economics. *American Economic Review, 75,* 53–68.

Holland, J. H., Holyoak, K. J., Nisbett, R. E., & Thagard, P. R. (1986). *Induction: Processes of inference, learning, and discovery.* Cambridge, MA: MIT Press.

Hoskin, R. E. (1983). Opportunity cost and behavior. *Journal of Accounting Research, 21,* 78–95.

Inglehart, R., & Flanagan, S. C. (1987). Value change in industrial societies. *American Political Science Review*, *81*, 1288–1322.

Jepson, C., Krantz, D. H., & Nisbett, R. E. (1983). Inductive reasoning: Competence or skill? *Behavioral and Brain Sciences*, *6*, 494–501.

Larrick, R. P., Morgan, J. N., & Nisbett, R. E. (1990). Teaching the use of cost-benefit reasoning in everyday life. *Psychological Science*, *1*, 362–370.

March, J. G. (1978). Bounded rationality, ambiguity, and the engineering of choice. *Bell Journal of Economics*, *9*, 587–608.

Mishan, E. J. (1976). *Cost-benefit analysis*. New York: Praeger.

Morgan, J. N., & Duncan, G. J. (1982). *Making your choices count: Economic principles for everyday decisions*. Ann Arbor: University of Michigan Press.

Newell, A., & Simon, H. A. (1972). *Human problem solving*. Englewood Cliffs, NJ: Prentice-Hall.

Nisbett, R. E., Fong, G. T., Lehman, D. R., & Cheng, P. W. (1987). Teaching reasoning. *Science*, *238*, 625–631.

Simon, H. A. (1955). A behavioral model of choice. *Quarterly Journal of Economics*, *69*, 99–118.

Smith, E. E., Langston, C., & Nisbett, R. E. (1992). The case for rules in reasoning. *Cognitive Science*, *16*, 99–102.

Sternberg, R. J. (1985). *Beyond IQ: A triarchic theory of human intelligence*. New York: Cambridge University Press.

Sternberg, R. J. (1988). *The triarchic mind: A new theory of human intelligence*. New York: Viking.

Stich, S. P. (1990). *The fragmentation of reason: Preface to a pragmatic theory of cognitive evaluation*. Cambridge, MA: MIT Press.

Stich, S. P., & Nisbett, R. E. (1980). Justification and the psychology of human reasoning. *Philosophy of Science*, *47*, 188–202.

Thagard, P. R. (1982). From the descriptive to the normative in science. *Philosophy of Science*, *49*, 24–42.

Thagard, P. R., & Nisbett, R. E. (1983). Rationality and charity. *Philosophy of Science*, *50*, 250–267.

Tversky, A., & Kahneman, D. (1986). Rational choice and the framing of decisions. *Journal of Business*, *59*, 251–278.

Wagner, R. K., & Sternberg, R. J. (1985). Practical intelligence in real world pursuits: The role of tacit knowledge. *Journal of Personality and Social Psychology*, *49*, 436–458.

Watts, M., & Lynch, G. J. (1989). The principles courses revisited. *American Economic Review*, *79*, 236–241.

# 11    Does Studying Economics Inhibit Cooperation?

*Robert H. Frank, Thomas Gilovich, and Dennis T. Regan*

From the perspective of many economists, motives other than self-interest are peripheral to the main thrust of human endeavor, and we indulge them at our peril. In Gordon Tullock's (1976) words (as quoted by Mansbridge, 1990, p. 12), "the average human being is about 95 percent selfish in the narrow sense of the term."

In this chapter we investigate whether exposure to the self-interest model commonly used in economics alters the extent to which people behave in self-interested ways. The chapter is organized into two parts. In the first, we report the results of several empirical studies – some our own, some by others – that suggest economists behave in more self-interested ways. By itself, this evidence does not demonstrate that exposure to the self-interest model *causes* more self-interested behavior, since it may be that economists were simply more self-interested to begin with, and this difference was one reason they chose to study economics. In the second part of the chapter, we present preliminary evidence that exposure to the self-interest model does in fact encourage self-interested behavior.

## Do Economists Behave Differently?

*Free-Rider Experiments*

A study by Gerald Marwell and Ruth Ames (1981) found that first-year graduate students in economics are much more likely than others to free-ride in experiments that called for private contributions to public goods. In their experiments, groups of subjects were given initial endowments of money, which they were to allocate between two accounts, one "public," the other "private." Money deposited in the subject's private account was returned

This chapter originally appeared in *Journal of Economic Perspectives*, 1993, 7, 159–171. Copyright © 1993 by American Economic Association. Reprinted by permission.

dollar-for-dollar to the subject at the end of the experiment. Money deposited in the public account was pooled, multiplied by some factor greater than one, and then distributed equally among all subjects. Under these circumstances, the socially optimal behavior is for all subjects to put their entire endowment in the public account. But from an individual perspective, the most advantageous strategy is to put everything in the private account. Marwell and Ames found that economics students contributed an average of only 20 percent of their endowments to the public account, significantly less than the 49 percent average for all other subjects.

To explore the reasons for this difference, the authors asked their subjects two follow-up questions. First, what is a "fair" investment in the public good? Of the noneconomists, 75 percent answered "half or more" of the endowment, and 25 percent answered "all." Second, are you concerned about "fairness" in making your investment decision? Almost all noneconomists answered "yes." The corresponding responses of the economics graduate students were more difficult to summarize. As Marwell and Ames wrote,

> More than one-third of the economists either refused to answer the question regarding what is fair, or gave very complex, uncodable responses. It seems that the meaning of "fairness" in this context was somewhat alien for this group. Those who did respond were much more likely to say that little or no contribution was "fair." In addition, the economics graduate students were about half as likely as other subjects to indicate that they were "concerned with fairness" in making their decisions.

The Marwell and Ames study can be criticized on the grounds that their noneconomist control groups consisted of high school students and college undergraduates, who differ in a variety of ways from first-year graduate students in any discipline. Perhaps the most obvious difference is age. As we will see, however, criticism based on the age difference is blunted by our own evidence that older students generally give greater weight to social concerns like the ones that arise in free-rider experiments. It remains possible, however, that more mature students might have had a more sophisticated understanding of the nuances and ambiguities inherent in concepts like fairness, and for that reason gave less easily coded responses to the follow-up questions.

Yet another concern with the Marwell and Ames experiments is not easily dismissed. Although the authors do not report the sex composition of their group of economics graduate students, such groups are almost always preponderantly male. The authors' control groups of high school and undergraduate students, by contrast, consisted equally of males and females.[1] As our own evidence will later show, there is a sharp tendency for males to behave less cooperatively in experiments of this sort. So while the Marwell and Ames findings are suggestive, they do not clearly establish that economists behave differently.

*Economists and the Ultimatum Bargaining Game*

Another study of whether economists behave differently from members of other disciplines is by John Carter and Michael Irons (1991). These authors measured self-interestedness by examining behavior in an ultimatum bargaining game. This simple game has two players, an "allocator" and a "receiver." The allocator is given a sum of money (in these experiments, $10), and must then propose a division of this sum between herself and the receiver. Once the allocator makes this proposal, the receiver has two choices: (1) he may accept, in which case each player gets the amount proposed by the allocator; or (2) he may refuse, in which case each player gets zero. The game is played only once by the same partners.

Assuming the money cannot be divided into units smaller than one cent, the self-interest model unequivocally predicts that the allocator will propose $9.99 for herself and the remaining $0.01 for the receiver, and that the receiver will accept on the grounds that a penny is better than nothing. Since the game will not be repeated, there is no point in the receiver turning down a low offer in the hope of generating a better offer in the future.

Other researchers have shown that the strategy predicted by the self-interest model is almost never followed in practice: 50–50 splits are the most common proposal, and most highly one-sided offers are rejected in the name of fairness (Guth et al., 1982; Kahneman et al., 1986). Carter and Irons found that in both roles (allocator and receiver) economics majors performed significantly more in accord with the predictions of the self-interest model than did nonmajors.[2]

As always, questions can be raised about experimental design. In this case, for example, Carter and Irons assigned the allocator and receiver roles by choosing as allocators those who achieved higher scores on a preliminary word game.[3] Allocators trained in the marginal productivity theory of wages (that is, economics majors) might thus be more likely than others to reason that they were entitled to a greater share of the surplus on the strength of their earlier performance. But while not conclusive, the Carter and Irons results are again suggestive.

*Survey Data on Charitable Giving*

The free-rider hypothesis suggests that economists might be less likely than others to donate to private charities. To explore this possibility, we mailed questionnaires to 1245 college professors randomly chosen from the professional directories of 23 disciplines, asking them to report the annual dollar amounts they gave to a variety of private charities. We received 576 responses with sufficient detail for inclusion in our study. Respondents were grouped into the following disciplines: economics ($N = 75$); other social sciences ($N = 106$); math, computer science, and engineering ($N = 48$);

natural sciences ($N = 98$); humanities ($N = 94$); architecture, art, and music ($N = 68$); and professional ($N = 87$).[4] The proportion of pure free riders among economists – that is, those who reported giving no money to any charity – was 9.3 percent. By contrast, only 1.1 percent of the professional school respondents gave no money to charity, and the share of those in the other five disciplines who reported zero donations ranged between 2.9 and 4.2 percent.[5] Despite their generally higher incomes, economists were also among the least generous in terms of their median gifts to large charities like viewer-supported television and the United Way.[6]

On a number of other dimensions covered in our survey, the behavior of economists was little different from the behavior of members of other disciplines. For example, economists were only marginally less likely than members of other disciplines to report that they would take costly administrative action to prosecute a student suspected of cheating. Economists were slightly above average for the entire sample in terms of the numbers of hours they reported spending in "volunteer activities." And in terms of their reported frequency of voting in presidential elections, economists were only slightly below the sample average.[7]

### *Economists and the Prisoner's Dilemma*

One of the most celebrated and controversial predictions of the self-interest model is that people will always defect in a one-shot prisoner's dilemma game. Figure 11.1 shows the monetary payoffs in dollars to two players, $X$ and $Y$, in a standard prisoner's dilemma. The key feature of such a game is that for each player, defection has a higher payoff irrespective of the choice made by the other player. Yet if both players follow this self-interested logic and defect, both end up with a lower payoff than if each cooperates. The game thus provides a rich opportunity to examine self-interested behavior.

We conducted a prisoner's dilemma experiment involving both economics majors and nonmajors. All groups were given an extensive briefing on the

| | | Player *X* | |
|---|---|---|---|
| | | Cooperate | Defect |
| You | Cooperate | 2 for *X*<br>2 for *Y* | 3 for *X*<br>0 for *Y* |
| | Defect | 0 for *X*<br>3 for *Y* | 1 for *X*<br>1 for *Y* |

Figure 11.1. Monetary payoffs for a Prisoner's Dilemma game.

prisoner's dilemma at the start of the experiment and each subject was required to complete a questionnaire at the end to verify that he or she had indeed understood the consequences of different combinations of choices; in addition, many of our subjects were students recruited from courses in which the prisoner's dilemma is an item on the syllabus. Our subjects met in groups of three and each was told that he or she would play the game once only with each of the other two subjects. The payoff matrix, shown in Figure 11.1, was the same for each play of the game. Subjects were told that the games would be played for real money, and that confidentiality would be maintained so that none of the players would learn how their partners had responded in any play of the game.

Following a period in which subjects were given an opportunity to get to know one another, each subject was taken to a separate room and asked to fill out a form indicating a response (cooperate or defect) to each of the other two players in the group. After the subjects had filled out their forms, the results were tallied and the payments disbursed. Each subject received a single payment that was the sum of three separate amounts: the payoff from the game with the first partner; the payoff from the game with the second partner; and a term that was drawn at random from a large list of positive and negative values. None of these three elements could be observed separately, only their sum. The purpose of this procedure was to prevent subjects from inferring both individual and group patterns of choice. Thus, unlike earlier prisoner's dilemma experiments,[8] ours did not enable the subject to infer what happened even when each (or neither) of the other players defected.

In one version of the experiment (the "unlimited" version), subjects were told that they could make promises not to defect during the time they were getting to know each other, but they were also told that the anonymity of their responses would render such promises unenforceable. In two other versions of the experiment (the "intermediate" and "limited" versions), subjects were not permitted to make promises about their strategies. The latter two versions differed from one another in terms of the length of pre-game interaction, with up to 30 minutes permitted for the intermediate groups and no more than ten minutes for the limited groups.

For the sample as a whole there were a total of 267 games, which means a total of 534 choices between cooperation and defection. For these choices, the defection rate for economics majors was 60.4 percent, as compared to only 38.8 percent for nonmajors. This pattern of differences strongly supports the hypothesis that economics majors are more likely than nonmajors to behave self-interestedly ($p < .005$).[9]

One possible explanation for the observed differences between economics students and others is that economics students are more likely to be male, and males have lower cooperation rates. To control for possible influences of sex, age, and experimental condition, we performed the ordinary least squares regression reported in Figure 11.2.[10] Because each subject played

*Dependent Variable: Cooperate (0) or Defect (1)*

| Variable | Coefficient | s.e. | $t$-ratio |
|---|---|---|---|
| Constant | 0.579127 | 0.1041 | 5.57 |
| econ | 0.168835 | 0.789 | 2.16 |
| limited | 0.00 | — | — |
| intermediate | −0.091189 | 0.0806 | −1.13 |
| unlimited | −0.329572 | 0.0728 | −4.53 |
| sex | 0.23994 | 0.0642 | 3.74 |
| class | −0.065363 | 0.0303 | −2.16 |

$R^2 = 22.2\%$    $R^2(\text{adjusted}) = 20.3\%$
$s = 0.4402$    with $207 - 6 = 201$ degrees freedom

| Source | Sum of Squares | $df$ | Mean Square | $F$-ratio |
|---|---|---|---|---|
| Regression | 11.1426 | 5 | 2.229 | 11.5 |
| Residual | 38.9540 | 201 | 0.193801 | |

Figure 11.2. Whole-sample regression.

the game twice, the individual responses are not statistically independent. To get around this problem, we limited our sample to the 207 subjects who either cooperated with, or defected from, each of their two partners. The 60 subjects who cooperated with one partner and defected on the other were deleted from the sample. The dependent variable is the subject's choice of strategy, coded as 0 for "cooperate" and 1 for "defect." The independent variables are "econ" which takes the value 1 for economics majors, 0 for all others; "unlimited," which is 1 for subjects in the unlimited version of the experiment, 0 for all others; "intermediate," which is 1 for subjects in the intermediate version, 0 for all others; "limited," which is the reference category; "sex," coded as 1 for males, 0 for females; and "class," coded as 1 for freshmen, 2 for sophomores, 3 for juniors, and 4 for seniors.

Consistent with a variety of other findings on sex differences in cooperation,[11] we estimate that, other factors the same, the probability of a male defecting is almost 0.24 higher than the corresponding probability for a female. But even after controlling for the influence of gender, we see that the probability of an economics major defecting is almost 0.17 higher than the corresponding probability for a nonmajor.

The coefficients for the unlimited and intermediate experimental categories represent effects relative to the defection rate for the limited category. As expected, the defection rate is smaller in the intermediate category (where subjects have more time to interact than in the limited category), and falls sharply further in the unlimited category (where subjects are permitted to make promises to cooperate).[12]

Note, finally, that the overall defection rate declines significantly as students progress through school. The class coefficient is interpreted to mean that with the passage of each year the probability of defection declines, on the average, by almost 0.07. This pattern will prove important when we take up the question of whether training in economics is the cause of higher defection rates for economics majors.

For subjects in the unlimited subsample, we found that the difference between economics majors and nonmajors virtually disappears once subjects are permitted to make promises to cooperate. For this subsample, the defection rate for economics majors is 28.6 percent, compared to 25.9 percent for nonmajors. Because the higher defection rates for economics majors are largely attributable to the no-promises conditions of the experiment, the remainder of our analysis focuses on subjects in the limited and intermediate groups. The conditions encountered by these groups are of special significance, because they come closest to approximating the conditions that characterize social dilemmas encountered in practice. After all, people rarely have an opportunity to look one another in the eye and promise not to litter on deserted beaches or disconnect the smog control devices on their cars.

When the choices are pooled for the limited and intermediate groups, both economics majors and nonmajors defect more often, but the effect is considerably larger for economists. In those groups, the defection rate was 71.8 percent for economics majors and just 47.3 percent for nonmajors, levels that differ significantly at the .01 level.

As part of the exit questionnaire that tested understanding of the payoffs associated with different combinations of choices, we also asked subjects to state reasons for their choices. We hypothesized that economists would be more inclined to construe the objective of the game in self-interested terms, and therefore more likely to refer exclusively to features of the game itself, while noneconomists would be more open to alternative ways of interpreting the game, and would refer more often to their feelings about their partners, aspects of human nature, and so on. Indeed, among the sample of economics students, 31 percent referred only to features of the game itself in explaining their chosen strategies, compared with only 17 percent of the noneconomists. The probability of obtaining such divergent responses by chance is less than .05.

Another possible explanation for the economists' higher defection rates is that economists may be more likely to expect their partners to defect. The self-interest model, after all, encourages such an expectation, and we know from other experiments that most subjects defect if they are told that their partners are going to defect. To investigate this possibility, we asked students in an upper division public finance course in Cornell's economics department whether they would cooperate or defect in a one-shot prisoner's dilemma if they knew *with certainty* that their partner was going to cooperate. Most of these students were economics majors in their junior and senior years. Of the 31 students returning our questionnaires, 18 (58 percent) reported that they would defect, only 13 that they would cooperate. By contrast, just 34 percent of noneconomics Cornell undergraduates who were given the same questionnaire reported that they would defect from a partner they knew would cooperate ($p < .05$). For the same two groups of subjects, almost all respondents (30 of 31 economics students and 36 of 41 noneconomics students) said they would defect if they knew their partner would defect. From these responses, we conclude that while expectations of partner performance play a strong role in predicting behavior, defection rates would remain significantly higher for economists than for noneconomists even if both groups held identical expectations about partner performance.

## Why Do Economists Behave Differently?

Economists appear to behave less cooperatively than noneconomists along a variety of dimensions. This difference in behavior might result from training in economics; alternatively, it might exist because people who chose to major in economics were different initially; or it might be some combination of these two effects. We now report evidence on whether training in economics plays a causal role.

### Comparing Upperclassmen and Underclassmen

If economics training causes uncooperative behavior, then defection rates in the prisoner's dilemma should rise with exposure to training in economics, all other factors held constant. Recalling our earlier finding that defection rates for the sample as a whole fall steadily between the freshman and senior years, the question is thus whether defection rates fall to the same degree over time for economists as for noneconomists. We found that the pattern of falling defection rates holds more strongly for noneconomics majors than for economics majors in the no-promises subsample. For noneconomics underclassmen in this group (freshmen and sophomores), the defection rate is 53.7 percent, compared to only 40.2 percent for upperclassmen. By contrast, the trend toward lower defection rates is virtually absent from economics majors in the no-promises subsample (73.7 percent for underclassmen, 70.0 percent for upperclassmen). In other words, students generally show a pronounced tendency toward more cooperative behavior with movement toward graduation, but this trend is conspicuously absent for economics majors.[13]

Naturally, we are in no position to say whether the trend for noneconomists reflects something about the content of noneconomics courses. But the fact that this trend is not present for economists is at least consistent with the hypothesis that training in economics plays some causal role in the lower observed cooperation rates of economists.

*Honesty Surveys*

In a further attempt to assess whether training in economics inhibits cooperation, we posed a pair of ethical dilemmas to students in two introductory microeconomics courses at Cornell University and to a control group of students in an introductory astronomy course, also at Cornell. In one dilemma, the owner of a small business is shipped ten microcomputers but is billed for only nine; the question is whether the owner will inform the computer company of the error. Subjects are first asked to estimate the likelihood that the owner would point out the mistake; and then, on the same response scale, to indicate how likely *they* would be to point out the error if they were the owner. The second dilemma concerns whether a lost envelope containing $100 and bearing the owner's name and address is likely to be returned by the person who finds it. Subjects are first asked to imagine that they have lost the envelope and to estimate the likelihood that a stranger would return it. They are then asked to assume that the roles are reversed and to indicate the likelihood that they would return the money to a stranger.

Students in each class completed the questionnaire on two occasions: during the initial week of class in September, and then during the final week of class in December. For each of the four questions, each student was coded as being "more honest" if the probability checked for that question rose between September and December; "less honest" if it fell during that period; and "no change" if it remained the same.

The first introductory microeconomics instructor (instructor A) whose students we surveyed is a mainstream economist with research interests in industrial organization and game theory. In class lectures, this instructor placed heavy emphasis on the prisoner's dilemma and related illustrations of how survival imperatives often militate against cooperation. The second microeconomics instructor (instructor B) is a specialist in economic development in Maoist China who did not emphasize such material to the same degree, but did assign a mainstream introductory text. On the basis of these differences, we expected that any observed effects of economics training should be stronger in instructor A's class than in instructor B's.

The results for these two classes, plus the class of noneconomists, are summarized in Figure 11.3, which shows the proportion of each class reporting a "less honest" result at the end of the semester than at the beginning. As the figure indicates, one semester's training was accompanied by greater movement toward more cynical ("less honest") responses in instructor A's introductory economics class than in instructor B's. Subjects in instructor B's class, in turn, showed greater movement toward less honest responses than did those in our control group of introductory astronomy students.

It may seem natural to wonder whether some of the differences between the two economics classes might stem from the fact that students chose their instructors rather than being randomly assigned. Perhaps the ideological

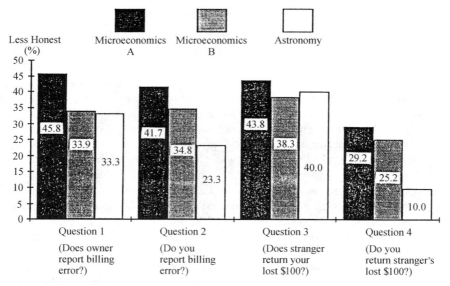

Figure 11.3. Freshman honesty survey results.

reputations of the two professors were known in advance to many students, with the result that a disproportionate number of less cynical students chose to take instructor B's course. However, the average values of the initial responses to the four questions were virtually the same for both classes. Moreover, even if students had differed across the two classes, this would not alter the interpretation of our findings, since the entries in Figure 11.3 record not the *level* of cynicism but the *change* in that level between the beginning and end of the course. Even if the students in Microeconomics A were more cynical to begin with, they became still more so during the course of the semester. This finding is consistent with the hypothesis that emphasis on the self-interest model tends to inhibit cooperation.

### Discussion

A variety of evidence suggests a large difference in the extent to which economists and noneconomists behave self-interestedly. We believe our survey of charitable giving and our prisoner's dilemma results lend additional support to the hypothesis that economists are more likely than others to free-ride.

Both of these exercises, however, also produced evidence that economists behave in traditionally communitarian ways under at least some circumstances. For example, economists reported spending as much time as others in volunteer activities, and were only marginally less likely than others to vote in presidential elections. Moreover, in the unlimited version of our prisoner's dilemma experiments, where subjects were allowed to promise to cooperate, economists were almost as likely to cooperate as noneconomists.

We also found evidence consistent with the view that differences in cooperativeness are caused in part by training in economics. This evidence is clearly less compelling than the evidence for a difference in cooperativeness. But it would be remarkable indeed if none of the observed differences in behavior were the result of repeated and intensive exposure to a model whose unequivocal prediction is that people will defect whenever self-interest dictates.

Should we be concerned that economics training may inhibit cooperation? Some might respond that while society would benefit if more people cooperated in social dilemmas, economists cannot be faulted for pointing out the unpleasant truth that self-interest dictates defection. One difficulty with this response is that it may be wrong. Several researchers have recently suggested that the ultimate victims of noncooperative behavior may be the very people who practice it (see, for example, Akerlof, 1983; Frank, 1988; Hirshleifer, 1987; and the essays in Mansbridge, 1990). Suppose, by way of illustration, that some people always cooperate in one-shot prisoner's dilemmas while others always follow the seemingly dominant strategy of defecting. If people are free to interact with others of their own choosing, and if there are cues that distinguish cooperators from defectors, then cooperators will interact selectively with one another and earn higher payoffs than defectors. Elsewhere we have shown that even on the basis of brief encounters involving strangers, experimental subjects are adept at predicting who will cooperate and who will defect in prisoner's dilemma games (Frank, 1988, ch. 7; Frank, Gilovich, and Regan, 1992). If people are even better at predicting the behavior of people they know well – a reasonable enough presumption – then the direct pursuit of material self-interest may indeed often be self-defeating.

In an ever more interdependent world, social cooperation has become increasingly important – and yet increasingly fragile. With an eye toward both the social good and the well-being of their own students, economists may wish to stress a broader view of human motivation in their teaching.

### Notes

1   This was the case, in any event, for the groups whose sex composition the authors reported.

2   Kahneman, Knetsch, and Thaler (1986) report findings similar to those of Carter and Irons: commerce students (the term used to describe business students in Canadian universities) were more likely than psychology students to make one-sided offers in ultimatum bargaining games.

3   This allocation procedure is described in a longer, unpublished version of the Carter and Irons paper (1990).

4   The "other social sciences" category includes psychology, sociology, political science, and anthropology: "natural sciences" includes physics, chemistry, biology, and geology: "humanities" includes philosophy, history, English, foreign languages, and religion; and "professional" includes education, business, and nursing.

5   Although we do not have data on the gender of each survey respondent, gender differences by discipline do not appear to account for the observed pattern of free-ridership. For example, the natural sciences, which are also preponderantly male, had only one-third as many free riders as did economics.

6   The annual median gift of economists to charities is actually slightly larger, in absolute terms, than the median for all disciplines taken as a whole. But because economists have significantly higher salaries than do the members of most other disciplines, the median gift overstates the relative generosity of economists. To correct for income differences by discipline, we proceeded as follows: First, we estimated earnings functions (salary vs. years of experience) for each discipline using data from a large private university. We then applied the estimated coefficients from these earnings functions to the experience data from our survey to impute an income for each respondent in our survey. Using these imputed income figures, together with our respondents' reports of their total charitable giving, we estimated the relationship between income and total giving. (In the latter exercise, all economists were dropped from the sample on the grounds that our object was to see whether the giving pattern of economists deviates from the pattern we see for other disciplines.) We then calculated our measure of a discipline's generosity as the ratio of the average value of gifts actually reported by members of the discipline to the average value of gifts expected on the basis of the members' imputed incomes. The computed ratio for economists was 0.91, which means that economists in our sample gave 91 percent as much as they would have been expected to give on the basis of their imputed incomes.

7   In fairness to the self-interest model, we should note that there may be self-interested reasons for volunteering or contributing even in the case of charities like the United Way and public television. United Way campaigns, for example, are usually organized in the workplace and there is often considerable social pressure to contribute. Public television fund drives often make on-the-air announcements of donors' names and economists stand to benefit just as much as the members of any other discipline from being hailed as community-minded citizens. In the case of smaller, more personal charitable organizations, there are often even more compelling self-interested reasons for giving or volunteering. After all, failure to contribute in accordance with one's financial ability may mean outright exclusion from the substantial private benefits associated with membership in religious groups, fraternal organizations, and the like.

8   For an extensive survey, see Dawes (1980).

9   Because each subject responded twice, the 534 choices are not statistically independent, and so the most direct test of statistical significance, the chi-square test, is inappropriate for the sample as a whole. To overcome this problem, we performed a chi-square test on the number of subjects who made the same choice – cooperate or defect – in both of their games. There were 207 such subjects (78 percent of the sample). The pattern of results observed in this restricted sample is essentially the same as the one observed for the sample as a whole.

10  Because the conventional assumptions regarding the distribution of the error term

are not satisfied in the case of linear models with dichotomous dependent variables, the standard ordinary least squares significance tests are not valid. In an appendix available on request from the authors, we report the results of models based on the probit and logit transformations. The statistical significance patterns shown by the coefficients from these transformed models are the same as for the ordinary least squares model. Because the coefficients of the ordinary least squares model are more easily interpreted, we report the remainder of our results in that format only.

11   See, for example, the studies cited in Gilligan (1982).

12   With the permission of subjects, we tape-recorded the conversations of several of the unlimited groups, and invariably each person promised each partner to cooperate. There would be little point, after all, in promising to defect.

13   A regression similar to the one shown in Figure 11.2 confirms that this pattern continues to hold even when controlling for other factors that might influence defection rates.

### References

Akerlof, George, "Loyalty Filters," *American Economic Review*, March, 1983, 73:1, 54–63.

Carter, John, and Michael Irons, "Are Economists Different, and If So, Why?" *Journal of Economic Perspectives*, Spring 1991, 5.2, 171–177.

Carter, John, and Michael Irons, "Are Economists Different, and If So, Why?" working paper, College of the Holy Cross, December 1990.

Dawes, Robyn, "Social Dilemmas," *Annual Review of Psychology*, 1980, *31*, 163–193.

Frank, Robert H., *Passions Within Reason*. New York: W. W. Norton, 1988.

Frank, Robert H., Thomas Gilovich, and Dennis T. Regan, "The Evolution of Hardcore Cooperation." In *Ethology and Sociobiology*, forthcoming 1993.

Gilligan, Carol, *In a Different Voice*. Cambridge: Harvard University Press, 1982.

Guth, Werner, Rolf Schmittberger, and Bernd Schwarze, "An Experimental Analysis of Ultimatum Bargaining," *Journal of Economic Behavior and Organization*, December 1982, 3:4, 367–388.

Hirshleifer, Jack, "On the Emotions as Guarantors of Threats and Promises." In Dupre, John, ed., *The Latest and the Best: Essays on Evolution and Optimality*. Cambridge: The MIT Press, 1987, 307–326.

Kahneman, Daniel, Jack Knetsch, and Richard Thaler, "Fairness and the Assumptions of Economics," *Journal of Business*, Part 2, October 1986, *59*, S285–S300.

Mansbridge, Jane J., *Beyond Self-Interest*. Chicago: University of Chicago Press, 1990.

Marwell, Gerald, and Ruth Ames, "Economists Free Ride, Does Anyone Else?: Experiments on the Provision of Public Goods, IV," *Journal of Public Economics*, June 1981, *15*:3, 295–310.

Tullock, Gordon, *The Vote Motive*. London: Institute for Economic Affairs, 1976.

# Part IV

# Legal Applications

In a California criminal case in 1968 (*People* v. *Collins*), a robbery victim testified that the robber was a woman with a blond ponytail who left the scene of the crime in a yellow convertible driven by a black male with a beard and mustache. All these characteristic matched the accused and her supposed accomplice. A prosecution expert testified, on the basis of some rather casual assessments of the frequency of each characteristic in the population, and multiplying all these probabilities together, that the probability of finding all the characteristics in a given couple drawn at random was one in 12 million. Therefore, he argued, the accused were guilty with probability close to 1.0!

The Collins argument is plainly nonsense (since it gave no attention to the nonindependence of the characteristics chosen or to the pool of possible matches from which they were drawn), but the elements of the problem are real. Courtroom testimony is rarely of the overwhelming, smoking-gun sort; and humans are known to cope poorly with complex statistical inferences. Is there anything decision research of either the normative or descriptive sort can do to help?

A number of researchers have tried. Important research dating from the 1970s (Ebbesen & Konečni, 1975; Carroll, 1978) has attempted to describe the causes and outcomes of what happens in the courtroom when a judge sets bail or a parole board decides whether or not to release an offender. In an early paper reprinted here (Loftus, Chapter 12) from a long and influential line of research (see Loftus, 1992, for a review), Loftus has examined the question of just how good we are as eyewitnesses in legal contexts. Her overall conclusion is that we are not very good (though we are often impressively confident!). Our memories, on her evidence, are not the neutral, accurate videocameras they seem. We seem to be active, error-prone reconstructors of the past, not passive retrievers of it.

An important landmark in thinking about decision research in trial settings was the 1971 paper of Tribe's entitled "Trial by Mathematics." Tribe, a major legal scholar, reviewed a substantial body of theory and research up to that date, concluding generally against any large role for such innovations as expert testimony helping the jury to make Bayesian revisions to their probability estimates. Many of Tribe's claims are challenged by studies such as Smith et al. (1996), which report experiments with real potential jurors reacting to videotapes of realistic courtroom testimony and argument. A contrasting approach is taken by the jury studies of Hastie and Pennington (Chapter 13 presents a recent review), in which the underlying model is not Bayes' Theorem but the narrative discipline of the storyteller. In their view, evidence is convincing to a juror not because it shifts his conditional probability of guilt but because it fits into a convincing story of how the crime happened.

The final chapter in this section (Connolly, Chapter 14) draws on a simple expected utility model to examine the legal notion of reasonable doubt. Jurors, he assumes, are aware that they might make a mistake, voting either to convict the truly innocent, or to acquit the truly guilty. How sure would a prudent person want to be? Presumably the answer turns on a balance of how undesirable the juror judges each error to be, compared to the two correct outcomes. Interestingly, his analysis leads to the conclusion that a juror setting a high threshold for conviction (e.g., a probability of guilt higher than .9) must hold a very rosy view of erroneous acquittals – which most citizens deny. Ancient verbal discussions of "reasonable doubt" are brought into much sharper focus when turned into numerical form in this way – and the conclusions appear paradoxical.

**References**

Carroll, J. S. (1978). Causal theories of crime and their effect upon expert parole decisions. *Law and Human Behavior, 2*(4), 377–388.

Ebbesen, E. B., & Konečni, V. J. (1975). Decision making and information integration in the courts: The setting of bail. *Journal of Personality and Social Psychology, 32*, 805–821.

Loftus, E. F. (1992). When a lie becomes the truth: Memory Distortion after exposure to misinformation. *Current Directions in Psychological Science, 1*, 121–123.

Smith, B. C., Penrod, O. D., Otto, O. L., & Park, R. C. (1996). Jurors' use of probabilistic evidence. *Law and Human Behavior, 20*, 49–82.

Tribe, L. H. (1971). Trial by mathematics: Precision and ritual in the legal process. *Harvard Law Review, 84*, 1329–1393.

# 12 Leading Questions and the Eyewitness Report

*Elizabeth F. Loftus*

Although current theories of memory are derived largely from experiments involving lists of words or sentences, many memories occurring in everyday life involve complex, largely visual, and often fast-moving events. Of course, we are rarely required to provide precise recall of such experiences – though as we age, we often volunteer them – but on occasion such recall is demanded, as when we have witnessed a crime or an accident. Our theories should be able to encompass such socially important forms of memory. It is clearly of concern to the law, to police and insurance investigators, and to others to know something about the completeness, accuracy, and malleability of such memories.

When one has witnessed an important event, one is sometimes asked a series of questions about it. Do these questions, if asked immediately after the event, influence the memory of it that then develops? This chapter first summarizes research suggesting that the wording of such initial questions can have a substantial effect on the answers given, and then reports four new studies showing that the wording of these initial questions can also influence the answers to different questions asked at some later time. The discussion of these findings develops the thesis that questions asked about an event shortly after it occurs may distort the witness's memory for that event.

## Answers Depend on the Wording of Questions

An example of how the wording of a question can affect a person's answer to it has been reported by Harris (1973). His subjects were told that "the experiment was a study in the accuracy of guessing measurements, and that they should make as intelligent a numerical guess as possible to each question" (p. 399). They were then asked either of two questions such as, "How tall was the basketball player?", or, "How short was the basketball player?"

Presumably the former form of the question presupposes nothing about the height of the player, whereas the latter form involves a presupposition that the player is short. On the average, subjects guessed about 79 and 69 in. (190 and 175 cm), respectively. Similar results appeared with other pairs of questions. For example, "How long was the movie?", led to an average estimate of 130 min, whereas, "How short was the movie?" led to 100 min. While it was not Harris's central concern, his study clearly demonstrates that the wording of a question may affect the answer.

The phenomenon has also been demonstrated in two other contexts: past personal experiences and recently witnessed events.

### Past Personal Experiences

In one study (Loftus, unpublished), 40 people were interviewed about their headaches and about headache products under the belief that they were participating in market research on these products. Two of the questions were crucial to the experiment. One asked about products other than that currently being used, in one of two wordings:

> 1a. In terms of the total number of products, how many other products have you tried? 1? 2? 3?
> 1b. In terms of the total number of products, how many other products have you tried? 1? 5? 10?

The 1/2/3 subjects claimed to have tried an average of 3.3 other products, whereas the 1/5/10 subjects claimed an average of 5.2; $t(38) = 3.14, \sigma = .61, p < .01$.

The second key question asked about frequency of headaches in one of two ways:

> 2a. Do you get headaches frequently, and, if so, how often?
> 2b. Do you get headaches occasionally, and, if so, how often?

The "frequently" subjects reported an average of 2.2 headaches/wk, whereas the "occasionally" group reported only 0.7/wk; $t(38) = 3.19, \sigma = .47, p < .01$.

### Recently Witnessed Events

Two examples from the published literature also indicate that the wording of a question put to a person about a recently witnessed event can affect a person's answer to that question. In one study (Loftus, 1974; Loftus & Zanni, 1975), 100 students viewed a short film segment depicting a multiple-car accident. Immediately afterward, they filled out a 22-item questionnaire which contained six critical questions. Three of these asked about items that had appeared in the film whereas the other three asked about items not present in the film. For half the subjects, all the critical questions began with the words, "Did you see a. . ." as in, "Did you see a broken headlight?" For the remaining half, the critical questions began with the words, "Did you see the. . ." as in, "Did you see the broken headlight?"

Thus, the questions differed only in the form of the article, *the* or *a*. One uses "the" when one assumes the object referred to exists and may be familiar to the listener. An investigator who asks, "Did you see the broken headlight?" essentially says, "There was a broken headlight. Did you happen to see it?" His assumption may influence a witness's report. By contrast, the article "a" does not necessarily convey the implication of existence.

The results showed that witnesses who were asked "the" questions were more likely to report having seen something, whether or not it had really appeared in the film, than those who were asked "a" questions. Even this very subtle change in wording influences a witness' report.

In another study (Loftus & Palmer, 1974), subjects saw films of automobile accidents and then answered questions about the accidents. The wording of a question was shown to affect a numerical estimate. In particular, the question, "About how fast were the cars going when they smashed into each other?" consistently elicited a higher estimate of speed than when "smashed" was replaced by "collided," "bumped," "contacted," or "hit."

We may conclude that in a variety of situations the wording of a question about an event can influence the answer that is given. This effect has been observed when a person reports about his own experiences, about events he has recently witnessed, and when answering a general question (e.g., "How short was the movie?") not based on any specific witnessed incident.

## Question Wording and Answers to Subsequent Questions

Our concern in this chapter is not on the effect of the wording of a question on its answer, but rather on the answers to other questions asked some time afterward. We will interpret the evidence to be presented as suggesting a memorial phenomenon of some importance.

In the present experiments, a key initial questions contains a *presupposition*, which is simply a condition that must hold in order for the question to be contextually appropriate. For example, the question, "How fast was the car going when it ran the stop sign?" presupposes that there was a stop sign. If a stop sign actually did exist, then in answering this question a subject might review, strengthen, or make more available certain memory representations corresponding to the stop sign. This being the case, the initial question might be expected to influence the answer to a subsequent question about the stop sign, such as the question, "Did you see the stop sign?" A simple extension of the argument of Clark and Haviland (1975) can be made here: When confronted with the initial question, "How fast was the car going when it ran the stop sign?", the subject might treat the presupposed information as if it were an address, a pointer, or an instruction specifying where information related to that presupposition may be found (as well as where new information is to be integrated into the previous knowledge). In the process the presupposed information may be strengthened.

What if the presupposition is false? In that case it will not correspond to any existing representation, and the subject may treat it as new information and enter it into his memory. Subsequently, the new "false" information may appear in verbal reports solicited from the subject.

To explore these ideas, subjects viewed films of complex, fast-moving events. Viewing of the film was followed by initial questions which contained presuppositions that were either true (Experiment 1) or false (Experiments 2–4). In Experiment 1, the initial questions either did or did not mention an object that was in fact present in the film. A subsequent question, asked a few minutes later, inquired as to whether the subject has seen the existing object. In Experiments 2–4, the initial questions were again asked immediately after the film, whereas the subsequent questions were asked after a lapse of 1 wk.

## Experiment 1

### Method

One hundred and fifty University of Washington students, in groups of various sizes, were shown a film of a multiple-car accident in which one car, after failing to stop at a stop sign, makes a right-hand turn into the main stream of traffic. In an attempt to avoid a collision, the cars in the oncoming traffic stop suddenly and a five-car, bumper-to-bumper collision results. The film lasts less than 1 min, and the accident occurs within a 4-sec period.

At the end of the film, a 10-item questionnaire was administered. A diagram of the situation labeled the car that ran the stop sign as "A," and the cars involved in the collision as "B" through "F." The first question asked about the speed of Car A in one of two ways:

1. How fast was Car A going when it ran the stop sign?
2. How fast was Car A going when it turned right?

Seventy-five subjects received the "stop sign" question and 75 received the "turned right" question. The last question was identical for all subjects: "Did you see a stop sign for Car A?" Subjects responded by circling "yes" or "no" on their questionnaires.

### Results and Discussion

Fifty-three percent of the subjects in the "stop sign" group responded "yes" to the question, "Did you see a stop sign for Car A?", whereas only

35% in the "turn right" group claimed to have seen the stop sign; $\chi^2(1) = 4.98$, $p < .05$. The addition of a presupposition in a question about an event, asked immediately after that event has taken place, can influence the answer to a subsequent question concerning the presupposition itself, asked a very short time later, in the direction of conforming with the supplied information.

There are at least two possible explanations of this effect. The first is that when a subject answers the initial stop sign question, he somehow reviews, or strengthens, or in some sense makes more available certain memory representations corresponding to the stop sign. Later, when asked, "Did you see a stop sign . . . ?", he responds on the basis of the strengthened memorial representation.

A second possibility may be called the "construction hypothesis." In answering the initial stop sign question, the subject may "visualize" or "reconstruct" in his mind that portion of the incident needed to answer the question, and so, if he accepts the presupposition, he introduces a stop sign into his visualization whether or not it was in memory. When interrogated later about the existence of the stop sign, he responds on the basis of his earlier supplementation of the actual incident. In other words, the subject may "see" the stop sign that he has himself constructed. This would not tend to happen when the initial question refers only to the right turn.

The construction hypothesis has an important consequence. If a piece of true information supplied to the subject after the accident augments his memory, then, in a similar way, it should be possible to introduce into memory something that was not in fact in the scene, by supplying a piece of false information. For example, Loftus and Palmer (1974, Expt. 2) showed subjects a film of an automobile accident and followed it by questions about events that occurred in the film. Some subjects were asked "About how fast were the cars going when they smashed into each other?", whereas others were asked the same question with "hit" substituted for "smashed." On a retest 1 wk later, those questioned with "smashed" were more likely than those questioned with "hit" to agree that they had seen broken glass in the scene, even though none was present in the film. In the present framework, we assume that the initial representation of the accident the subject has witnessed is modified toward greater severity when the experimenter uses the term "smashed" because the question supplies a piece of new information, namely, that the cars did indeed *smash* into each other. On hearing the "smashed" question, some subjects may reconstruct the accident, integrating the new information into the existing representation. If so, the result is a representation of an accident in memory that is more severe than, in fact, it actually was. In particular, the more severe accident is more likely to include broken glass.

The presupposition that the cars smashed into each other may be additional information, but it can hardly be said to be false information. It is important to determine whether it is also true that false presuppositions can affect a witness's answer to a later question about that presupposition. Such a finding would imply that a false presupposition can be accepted by a witness, that the hypothesis of a strengthening of an existing memorial representation is untenable (since there should be no representation corresponding to nonexistent objects), and that the construction hypothesis discussed above is supported. Experiment 2 was designed to check this idea.

## Experiment 2

### Method

Forty undergraduate students at the University of Washington, again in groups of various sizes, were shown a 3-min videotape taken from the film *Diary of a Student Revolution*. The sequence depicted the disruption of a class by eight demonstrators; the confrontation, which was relatively noisy, resulted in the demonstrators leaving the classroom.

At the end of the videotape, the subjects received one of two questionnaires containing one key and nineteen filler questions. Half of the subjects were asked, "Was the leader of the four demonstrators who entered the classroom a male?", whereas the other half were asked, "Was the leader of the twelve demonstrators who entered the classroom a male?" The subjects responded by circling "yes" or "no."

One week later, all subjects returned and, without reviewing the videotape, answered a series of 20 new questions about the disruption. The subjects were urged to answer the questions from memory and not to make inferences. The critical question here was, "How many demonstrators did you see entering the classroom?"

### Results and Discussion

Subjects who had previously been asked the "12" question reported having seen an average of 8.85 people 1 wk earlier, whereas those asked the "4" question recalled 6.40 people, $t(38) = 2.50$, $\sigma = .98$, $p < .01$. The actual number was, it will be recalled, eight. One possibility is that some fraction of the subjects remembered the number 12 or the number 4 from the prior questionnaire and were responding to the later question with that number, whereas the remainder had the correct number. An analysis of the actual responses given reveals that 10% of the people who had been interrogated with "12" actually responded "12," and that 10% of those interrogated with "4" actually responded with "4." A recalculation of the means, excluding those subjects in the "12" condition who responded "12" and those in the "4" condition who responded "4," still resulted in a significant difference between the two conditions (8.50 versus 6.67), $t(34) = 1.70$, $p < .05$. This analysis demonstrates that recall of the specific number given in the initial questionnaire is not an adequate alternative explanation of the present results.

The result shows that a question containing a false numerical presupposition can, on the average, affect a witness' answer to a subsequent question about that quantitative fact. The next experiment was designed to test whether the same is true for the existence of objects when the false presupposition concerns one that did not actually exist.

## Experiment 3

### Method

One hundred and fifty students at the University of Washington, in groups of various sizes, viewed a brief videotape of an automobile accident and then answered ten questions about the accident. The critical one concerned the speed of a white sports car. Half of the subjects were asked, "How fast was the white sports car going when it passed the barn while traveling along the country road?", and half were asked, "How fast was the white sports car going while traveling along the country road?" In fact, no barn appeared in the scene.

All of the subjects returned 1 wk later and, without reviewing the videotape, answered ten new questions about the accident. The final one was, "Did you see a barn?" The subjects responded by circling "yes" or "no" on their questionnaires.

### Results and Discussion

Of the subjects earlier exposed to the question containing the false presupposition of a barn, 17.3% responded "yes" when later asked, "Did you see a barn?", whereas only 2.7% of the remaining subjects claimed to have seen it; $\chi^2(1) = 8.96$, $p < .01$. An initial question containing a false presupposition can, it appears, influence a witness's later tendency to report the presence of the nonexistent object corresponding to that presupposition.

The last experiment not only extends this finding beyond the single example, but asks whether or not the effect is wholly due to the word "barn" having occurred or not occurred in the earlier session. Suppose an initial question merely asks about, instead of presupposing, a nonexistent object; for example, "Did you see a barn?," when no barn existed. Presumably subjects will mostly respond negatively to such questions. But, what if that same question is asked again some time later? It is possible that a subject will reflect to himself, "I remember something about a barn, so I guess I must have seen one." If this were the case, then merely asking about a nonexistent object could increase the tendency to report the existence of that object at some later time, thereby accounting for the results of Experiment III.

## Experiment 4

*Method*

One hundred and fifty subjects from the University of Washington, run in groups of various sizes, viewed a 3-min 8 mm film clip taken from inside of an automobile which eventually collides with a baby carriage being pushed by a man. Following presentation of the film, each subject received one of three types of booklets corresponding to the experimental conditions. One hundred subjects received booklets containing five key and 40 filler questions. In the "direct" version, the key questions asked, in a fairly direct manner, about items that were not present in the film. One example was, "Did you see a school bus in the film?" All of these questions are listed in Table 12.1, under the column labeled "Direct questions." In the "False presupposition" version, the key questions contained false presuppositions referring to an item that did not occur in the film. The corresponding example was, "Did you see the children getting on the school bus?" All of these questions are listed in Table 12.1, under the column labeled "False presupposition questions." The third group of 50 subjects received only the 40 filler questions and no key questions. The goal of using so many filler items was to minimize the possibility that subjects would notice the false presuppositions.

All subjects returned 1 wk later and, without reviewing the film clip, answered 20 new questions about the incident. Five of these questions were critical: They were direct questions, shown in Table 12.1, that had been asked a week earlier in identical form, of only one of the three groups of subjects. The subjects responded to all questions by circling "yes" or "no" on their questionnaires.

*Results and Discussion*

The percentage of subjects responding "yes" to each of the key questions during the final experimental session is shown in Table 12.1. Overall, of those who had been exposed to questions including a false presupposition, 29.2% said "yes" to the key nonexistent items; of those who had been exposed to the direct questions, 15.6% said "yes" and of those in the control group, 8.4% said "yes."

For each question individually, the type of prior experience significantly influenced the percentage of "yes" responses, with all chi-square values having $p < .05$. Additional chi-square tests were performed to test for the significance of the differences between the pairs of groups. For each of the five questions, the differences were all significant between the control group and the group exposed to false presuppositions, all chi-square values having $p < .025$. Summing over all five questions, a highly significant chi-square resulted, $\chi^2(5) = 40.79$, $p < .001$. Similarly, over all five questions, the

Table 12.1. *Percentage of "Yes" Responses to Direct Questions Asked 1 Wk After the Film, for the Control Group (C), the Direct Group (D), and the False Resupposition Group (F). All Questions Referred to Items That Were Not Present*

| Direct Questions | False Presupposition Questions | Percentage of "Yes" Responses to Direct Question 1 Wk Later[a] | | | Chi-square | p |
|---|---|---|---|---|---|---|
| | | C | D | F | | |
| Did you see a school bus in the film? | Did you see the children getting on the school bus? | 6 | 12 | 26 | 8.44 | .025 |
| Did you see a truck in the beginning of film? | At the beginning of the film, was the truck parked beside the car? | 0 | 8 | 22 | 26.01 | .01 |
| Did you see a center line on the country road? | Did another car cross the center line on the country road? | 8 | 14 | 26 | 6.26 | .05 |
| Did you see a woman pushing the carriage? | Did the woman who was pushing the carriage cross into the road? | 26 | 36 | 54 | 8.52 | .025 |
| Did you see a barn in the film? | Did you see a station wagon parked in front of the barn? | 2 | 8 | 18 | 7.66 | .05 |

[a] Means: C, 8.4; D, 15.6; F, 29.2.

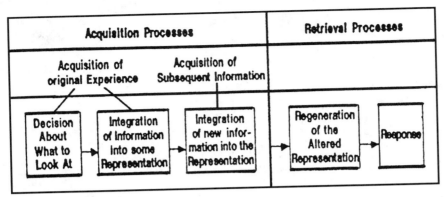

Figure 12.1.  Schematic diagram of the memorial processes.

difference between the group exposed to direct questions and the group exposed to false presuppositions was significant, $\chi^2(5) = 14.73$, $p < .025$. The difference between the control group and the group exposed to direct questions failed to reach significance, $\chi^2(5) = 9.24$, $p > .05$.

### General Discussion

We saw that either a strength hypothesis or a construction hypothesis would account for the results of the first experiment in which the presupposition of a true event increased the later assertion that the event had occurred. But only the construction hypothesis explains the comparable results which occur when the presupposition is of false information, as in Experiments 2–4.[1]

We need, therefore, to consider the form of a theory of memory for complex visual experiences in which a constructive mechanism plays an integral role. Figure 12.1 presents a skeleton of this theory that has three major components. The first two components involve acquisition processes, and the third involves retrieval processes.

#### Acquisition Processes

*Acquisition of the Original Experience.*  When a complex event is experienced, we assume that some of the features of that experience are extracted for arriving at action decisions and/or storage. Early on, the observer must decide to which aspects of the visual stimulus he should attend. Our visual environment typically contains a vast amount of information, and the proportion of information that is actually perceived is very small. The process of deciding to what we attend must consist of a series of decisions, each corresponding to where the next eye fixation should be.

*The Form of the Representation.* Into what form of representation is the newly acquired information integrated? Many views have been suggested. A prominent view is that when a person experiences an event, he organizes and retains knowledge about that event in the form of statements or propositions that can be treated as a labeled graph structure (e.g., Anderson & Bower, 1973; Rumelhart, Lindsay & Norman, 1972). In this view, experience might appear as a collection of points or nodes representing particular concepts or objects, with links between the nodes representing labeled semantic relationships between the particular objects.

Other hypotheses about the representation of knowledge are stated in terms of decision routines (e.g., Winograd, 1972); features (e.g., Selfridge & Neisser, 1963); or "mental images" that are isomorphic to the original event (Shepard, 1966). At present, the issue is clearly unresolved. One appealing resolution, however, is that people may use more than one form of representation, they may be sufficiently flexible to store information in whichever form is most appropriate to the situation, and they may transform information from one form to another at will. So, for example, human beings may be able to store information in terms of propositions which are then transformed into mental images at the time the information is retrieved.

*Acquisition of Subsequent Information.* However an event may be represented, there is little reason to believe that the representation is accurate; in fact, it may be quite malleable by occurrences other than the event it is supposed to represent. Events or information occurring subsequent (and probably prior) to the original event may alter the representation of that event. One way this might be accomplished is by simply influencing the process of entering new information into the existing memory structure, thereby enhancing, enriching, or otherwise altering that structure. We will refer to the added information as "external" to distinguish it from the information acquired during the initial experience.

### Retrieval Processes

Some time after both the initial visual experience and the first interrogation about it, a witness may be quizzed again. For example, after being questioned by the police, a witness may have to testify in court. At this point he must "re-create" from long-term memory, at least that portion of the experience needed to answer a specific question. Thus, the image may be based both on information acquired during the original experience and external information acquired subsequently. This regenerated image has some internal structure, which may or may not be "visual," but must contain information as to the spatial structure of its referent. Any response which a witness makes is based on this regenerated image.

To reiterate, we suggest that information acquired during a complex experience is apparently integrated into some overall memory representation. Subsequent information about that event – for example, that introduced inadvertently via questions containing true or false presuppositions – is also integrated, and can alter the initial representation. When the person is later queried about the original experience, he forms a regenerated image based on the altered memorial representation, and bases his response on that image.

In thinking about the present work in relation to some of the existing literature on reconstructive memory, Bartlett's (1932) notions come immediately to mind. Bartlett was one of the first to argue that the way we represent experiences in memory is determined by our permanent knowledge about objects, events, and processes of our experiences. In this view, the new experience is somehow assimilated into the framework of prior experiences. Since Bartlett's work, there has been a lasting interest in the interaction of prior knowledge and present input experiences (cf. Bransford & Johnson, 1972; Dooling & Lachman, 1971). The belief that a person's prior knowledge can wield considerable influence over his recollection of a specific experience is expressed in the recent articles of several noted cognitive psychologists. For example, Rumelhart and Norman (1973) make the point that the "retrieval of an experience from memory is usually a reconstruction which is heavily biased by the person's general knowledge of the world" (p. 450), while Tulving and Thomson (1973) regard "remembering" as "a joint product of information stored in the past and information present in the immediate cognitive environment of the rememberer" (p. 352).

The present work extends these notions to include the influence on a to-be-remembered experience of information acquired subsequent to that experience. In the present experiments, the subsequent information was introduced via presuppositions in questions, a technique which is effective in introducing information without calling attention to it. Obviously, there are many other ways to introduce new information. The experimental manipulation of subsequent information may constitute a useful technique for investigating the interaction of a person's specific experiences and subsequent knowledge related to those experiences.

### Note

1   It should be emphasized that even though Experiments 2–4 demonstrate support for a construction hypothesis, a strength hypothesis is not necessarily excluded as an explanation for Experiment 1.

### References

Anderson, J. R., & Bower, G. H. *Human Associative Memory*. Washington, DC: Winston, 1973.

Bartlett, F. C. *Remembering: A study in experimental and social psychology.* London: Cambridge University Press, 1932.

Bransford, J. D., & Johnson, M. K. Contextual prerequisites for understanding: Some investigations of comprehension and recall. *Journal of Verbal Learning and Verbal Behavior,* 1972, *11,* 717–726.

Clark, H. H., & Haviland, S. E. Psychological processes as linguistic explanation. In D. Cohen (Ed.), *The nature of explanation in linguistics.* Milwaukee: University of Wisconsin Press, 1975.

Dooling, D. J., & Lachman, R. Effects of comprehension on retention of prose. *Journal of Experimental Psychology,* 1971, *88,* 216–222.

Harris, R. J. Answering questions containing marked and unmarked adjectives and adverbs. *Journal of Experimental Psychology,* 1973, *97,* 399–401.

Loftus, E. F. Reconstructing memory. The incredible eyewitness. *Psychology Today,* 1974, *8,* 116–119.

Loftus, E. F., & Palmer, J. C. Reconstruction of automobile destruction: An example of the interaction between language and memory. *Journal of Verbal Learning and Verbal Behavior,* 1974, *13,* 585–589.

Loftus, E. F., & Zanni, G. Eyewitness testimony: The influence of the wording of a question. *Bulletin of the Psychonomic Society,* 1975, *5,* 86–88.

Rumelhart, D. E., Lindsay, P. H., & Norman, D. A. A process model of long-term memory. In E. Tulving & W. Donaldson (Eds.), *Organization of memory.* New York: Academic Press, 1972.

Rumelhart, D. E. & Norman, D. A. *Active semantic networks as a model of human memory.* Proceedings of the Third International Joint Conference on Artificial Intelligence, Stanford University, 1973.

Shepard, R. N. Learning and recall as organization and search. *Journal of Verbal Learning and Verbal Behavior,* 1966, *5,* 201–204.

Selfridge, O. G., & Neisser, U. Pattern recognition by machine. In E. A. Feigenbaum & J. Feldman (Eds.), *Computers and thought.* New York: McGraw Hill, 1963.

Tulving, E., & Thomson, D. M. Encoding specificity and retrieval processes in episodic memory. *Psychological Review,* 1973, *80,* 352–373.

Winograd, T. Understanding natural language. *Cognitive Psychology,* 1972, *3,* 1–191.

# 13    Explanation-Based Decision Making

*Reid Hastie and Nancy Pennington*

The theory of explanation-based decision making is a psychologically realistic description of how people make many important decisions in law, engineering, medicine, politics, diplomacy, and everyday life. These decisions are made under conditions in which a large base of implication-rich, conditionally dependent pieces of evidence must be evaluated as a preliminary to choosing an alternative from a set of prospective courses of action (Hastie & Pennington, 1993, 1995, 1996; Pennington, 1981; Pennington & Hastie, 1981, 1986, 1988, 1991, 1993a, 1993b). According to the explanation-based approach, decision makers begin their decision process by constructing a causal model to explain the available facts. This stage of the decision process is more like "comprehension" than like judgment or choice (indeed, models of text and situation comprehension were the sources for many elements of the theory).

Concomitant with or subsequent to the construction of a causal model of the evidence, the decision maker is engaged in a separate activity to learn or to create a set of alternatives from which an action will be chosen. Frequently, this process focuses on the construction of a single plan for one course of action, including its preconditions and consequences (see current psychological theories of planning and problem solving, e.g., Anderson, 1990; Wilensky, 1983). A decision is made when the causal model of the evidence is successfully matched to an alternative in the choice set. Of course, in many cases the outcome of the "decision" process is really the adjustment of an ongoing course of action or the proposal of one course of action, with a "choose or reject" frame on the single option (Figure 13.1).

The distinctive assumption in the explanation-based approach to decision making is the hypothesis that decision makers construct an intermediate summary representation of the evidence and that this representation, rather than the original "raw" evidence, is the basis of the final decision.

This chapter was specially prepared for this book.

212

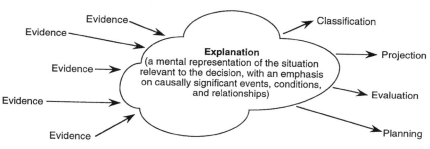

Figure 13.1. An overview of the explanation-based framework for judgments and decisions.

This intermediate mental model of the decision situation facilitates evidence comprehension, directs inferencing, enables the decision maker to reach a decision, and determines the confidence assigned to the accuracy or expected success of the decision. The essence of our claim is a synthesis of the rule-based (Rips, 1994) and mental models (Johnson-Laird, 1983) views of reasoning: We believe that decision makers use inference rules to construct mental models of decision situations. This means that the locus of theoretical accounts for differences in decisions rendered by different individuals, systematic biases exhibited by many individuals, and the effects of most variations in decision task characteristics will usually lie in the evidence evaluation stage of the decision process.

The fundamental difference between our explanation-based approach and traditional algebraic approaches (e.g., Cognitive Algebra: Anderson, 1981; the Lens Model: Hammond, Stewart, Brehmer, & Steinmann, 1975; Utility Theory: von Neumann & Morgenstern, 1947) is that we view *reasoning about the evidence* to be a central process in decision making, in contrast to an emphasis on the computation that occurs once evidence has been selected and evaluated. Our approach parallels recent work demonstrating the role of explanations and the insufficiency of similarity computations to account for categorization behavior (Murphy & Medin, 1985; Rips, 1989), category learning (e.g., Schank, Collins, & Hunter, 1986), planning (Wilensky, 1983), and learning by generalization from examples (e.g., Lewis, 1988).

The structure of the causal model constructed to explain the evidence will be specific to the decision domain. In the legal judgment domain that we have studied most extensively, we found that jurors use narrative story structures to organize and interpret evidence in criminal and civil trials. Since most of the causal, explanatory relationships that "glue" together events in these cases involve human actions in social contexts, we found that most of the critical relationships concern human motives, goals, and intentions. But different causal rules and structures will underlie a physician's causal model of a patient's physiological condition (Joseph & Patel, 1990; Pople, 1982), an

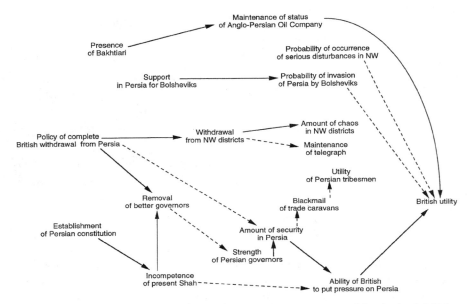

Figure 13.2. Summary of part of a cognitive map generated by Axelrod (1976) representing the views of the British Ambassador concerning British policy in Persia after World War I. (Solid lines show direct causal relations; broken lines show indirect causal relations.)

epidemiologist's or citizen's model of the physical and biological factors that are relevant to a natural health hazard (Bostrom, Fischhoff, & Morgan, 1992), an engineer's mental model of an electrical circuit (de Kleer & Brown, 1983), an operator's cognitive model of the mechanical, chemical, and electrical processes in a nuclear power plant (Rasmussen, 1986), a manager's or politician's image of the economic factors in a city or a country (Barr, Stimpert, & Huff, 1992; Hogarth, Michaud, & Mery, 1980; Sevón, 1984), and diplomats' or politicians' causal maps of the military and political forces in political theatre (Figure 13.2; this figure is based on Figure 4–2, pp. 88–89 in Axelrod, 1976, a seminal and influential analysis of explanations in decision making; see also Bonham, Shapiro, & Trumble, 1979; and Voss, Greene, Post, & Penner, 1983). Thus, a primary task for the researcher studying explanation-based decision making is the identification of the type of intermediate summary structure that is imposed on evidence by decision makers in a specific domain of decision making. This is in contrast with earlier process-oriented calculational models in which the theoretical focus was on attentional processes and the computations whereby separate sources of information were integrated into a unitary numerical value or utility (Anderson, 1981; Edwards, 1954; Kahneman & Tversky, 1979).

## Explanation-Based Processes in Legal Decisions

The juror's decision task is a prototype of the tasks to which the explanation-based model should apply: First, a massive "database" of evidence is presented at trial, frequently comprising several days of testimony, exhibits, and arguments. Second, the evidence comes in a scrambled sequence; usually many witnesses and exhibits convey pieces of the historical puzzle in a a jumbled temporal sequence. Third, the evidence is piecemeal and gappy in its depiction of the historical events that are the focus of reconstruction: event descriptions are incomplete, usually some critical events were not observed by the available witnesses, and information about personal reactions and motivations is not presented (often because of the rules of evidence). Finally, subparts of the evidence (e.g., individual sentences or statements) are interdependent in their probative implications for the verdict. The meaning of one statement cannot be assessed in isolation because it depends on the meanings of several other related statements.

We call our application of the explanation-based approach to legal decision making the "Story Model" because the central cognitive process in juror decision making is *story construction*: the construction of a narrative summary of the events under dispute in a legal trial. Our first application of the Story Model to criminal judgments identified three component processes: (a) evidence evaluation through story construction, (b) representation of the decision alternatives (verdicts) by learning their attributes or elements, and (c) reaching a decision through the classification of the story into the best fitting verdict category (see Figure 13.4).

These latter processes are likely to vary with the demands of different decision tasks. Some tasks involve a classification response, some an estimate or judgment of a magnitude, some a projection to future events, and so on. Even the shift from criminal judgments, in which categorical verdicts play a prominent role, to civil judgments, in which degrees of liability play the analogous role, changes these last stages. Our fundamental assumption, however, is that many decisions involve the explanation process allocated to our first stage. Thus, a central claim of the model is that the story the juror constructs *determines* the juror's decision.

An example of this focus on the critical role of (narrative) evidence summaries is provided by our interpretation of the dramatic differences between White and African American reactions to the verdict in the O. J. Simpson murder trial (there even appeared to be racial differences on the jury and within the defense team; Mixon, Foley, & Orme, 1995; Toobin, 1995). We hypothesized that race made a difference in the construction and acceptance of the "defense story" in which a racist police detective (Mark Fuhrman) planted incriminating evidence (Hastie & Pennington, 1996). African Americans, compared to White Americans, have much larger "memory stores" of beliefs *and experiences* that support the plausibility of stories of police misconduct and police bigotry (Gates, 1995). Most African Americans or members of their immediate families have had direct negative, and possibly racist encounters with justice system authorities. African Americans know of many more stories (some apocryphal) of police racism and police brutality directed against members of their race than do White Americans. This background of experience, beliefs, and relevant stories made it easy to construct a story in which a police officer manufactured and planted key incriminating evidence and made the constructed story more plausible to an African American compared to a White person.

### Evidence Summary

Empirical research on both criminal and civil jury decisions has demonstrated that the juror's "explanation" of legal evidence takes the form of a "story" in which causal and intentional relations among events are prominent (Bennett & Feldman, 1981; Pennington, 1981; Pennington & Hastie, 1986). The story is constructed from information explicitly presented at trial and from background knowledge possessed by the juror. Two kinds of knowledge are critical: expectations about what makes a complete story and knowledge about events similar in content to those that are the topic of dispute.

General knowledge about the structure of human purposive action sequences, characterized as an episode schema, serves to organize events according to the causal and intentional relations among them as perceived by the juror. An episode schema specifies that a story should contain initiating events, goals, actions, consequences, and accompanying states, in a particular causal configuration (Mandler, 1980; Pennington & Hastie, 1986; Rumelhart, 1977; Stein & Glenn, 1979; Trabasso & van den Broek, 1985). Each component of an episode may also consist of an episode so that the story the juror constructs can be represented as a hierarchy of embedded episodes. The highest level episode characterizes the most important features of "what happened." Knowledge about the structure of stories allows the juror to form an opinion concerning the *completeness* of the evidence, the extent to which a story has all its parts. In practice, gaps in stories are usually readily apparent to the comprehender because events subjectively "stand out" when they are disconnected or "unexplained" in the context of the rest of the developing story. Figure 13.3 depicts a story structure that was extracted from the think-aloud protocols of mock-jurors who judged the defendant in a murder trial to be guilty of first degree murder (Pennington & Hastie, 1986). Briefly, the "story" is that a quarrel between two men left the defendant angry and vengeful, in a premediated manner he obtained a knife and the assistance of a friend, then went searching for the man with whom he had quarreled, found him, initiated a fight, and deliberately stabbed him to death.

More than one story may be constructed by the juror, but one story will usually be accepted as more coherent than the others. *Coherence* combines

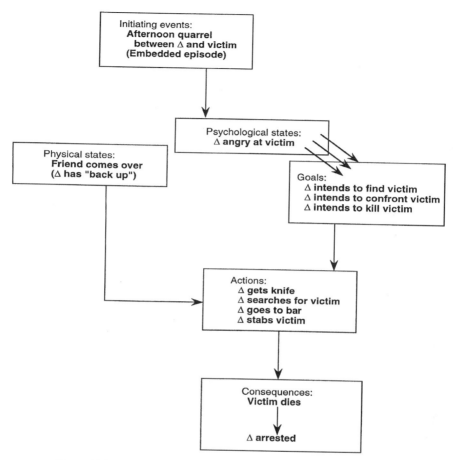

Figure 13.3.  Example of a story representation of evidence extracted from think-aloud protocols of mock jurors rendering guilty verdicts. (Arrows represent various forms of causal influence; box labels show components of general episode schema.)

judgments of completeness, consistency, and plausibility. If more than one story is judged to be coherent, then both stories will lack uniqueness and uncertainty will result. If there is one coherent story, this story will be accepted as the explanation of the evidence and will be instrumental in reaching a decision.

### Choice Set

The decision maker's second major task is to learn or to create a set of potential solutions or action alternatives that constitute the choice set. In some decision tasks the potential actions are given to the decision maker (instructions from the trial judge on verdict alternatives) or known before-hand (diagnostic options available to a physician or psychotherapist). In others, creation of alternatives is a major activity of the decision maker (for example, drafting alternate regulations for industrial waste disposal, plan-ning alternate marketing strategies, or negotiating alternate acceptable trade contracts). These solution design tasks may invoke their own (embedded) decision tasks.

In criminal trials the information for this processing stage is given to jurors at the end of the trial in the judge's instructions on the law. The pro-cess of learning the verdict categories is a one-trial learning task in which the material to be learned is very abstract. We hypothesize that the concep-tual unit is a category (frame) defined by a list of criterial features referring to identity, mental state, circumstances, and actions linked conjunctively or disjunctively to the verdict alternative (Kaplan, 1978). Smith (1991; see also Finkel & Groscup, 1997) provides evidence that verdict categories are rep-resented as prototype feature lists and that preconceptions as well as the judge's instructions are combined in the juror's verdict representation.

*Match Process*

The final stage in the global decision process in a criminal trial involves matching solution alternatives to the summary evidence representation to find the most successful pairing. Confidence in the final decision will be partly determined by the goodness of fit of the evidence–solution pairing selected and the uniqueness of the winning combination when compared to alternative pairings. Because verdict categories are unfamiliar concepts, the classification of a story into an appropriate verdict category is likely to be a deliberate process. For example, a juror may have to decide whether a circumstance in the story such as "pinned against a wall" constitutes a good match to a required circumstance, "unable to escape," for a verdict of Not Guilty by Reason of Self Defense. The story classification stage involves the application of the judge's procedural instructions on the presumption of in-nocence and the standard of proof. That is, if not all of the verdict attributes for a given verdict category are satisfied "beyond a reasonable doubt" by events in the accepted story, then the juror should presume innocence and return a default verdict of not guilty (again, Smith, 1991, provides empiri-cal evidence for the validity of the story–verdict match process in criminal judgments).

In a typical civil trial, where the central legal question concerns the defen-dant's liability for damages to the plaintiff, the final stages of the decision process concentrate more on the implications of the focal story, rather than on category classification. Conscientious jurors attempt to follow the judge's instruction by comparing the focal story to alternate "counterfactual" stories about the defendant to determine if the defendant's actions were a cause of the damage and if the defendant's actions were a gross deviation from proper behavior in the situation. For example, the judge's instruction on legal causation usually admonishes the juror to determine if the harmful consequence would have occurred had the defendant acted differently, what we might call a counterfactual, causal necessity evaluation (cf., McGill & Klein, 1993; Roese & Olson, 1995).

### Confidence in Decisions

Several aspects of the decision process influence the juror's level of certainty about the final decision. First, the accepted story is judged to be the most *coherent*, but the degree of coherence will affect confidence. Thus, if the story is incomplete, parts of the story are inconsistent or contradictory, or the plausibility of the story is low in the context of other stories and background knowledge, confidence in the story and therefore in the verdict will be diminished. Second, people are sensitive to the *coverage* of the evidence by the explanation; the more unexplained facts there are, the less confidence the decision maker will have that a decision based on the story is correct. Third, if a story lacks *uniqueness*, that is, there is more than one coherent story, then certainty concerning the accuracy of any one explanation will be lowered (Einhorn & Hogarth, 1986). Finally, in criminal trials the *goodness of fit* between the accepted story and the best-fitting verdict category will influence confidence in the verdict decision. Figure 13.4 depicts the Story Model.

In summary, our application of the general explanation-based decision model to legal decisions is based on the hypothesis that jurors impose a narrative story organization on trial information, in which causal and intentional relations between events are central (Bennett & Feldman, 1981; Pennington & Hastie, 1986). Meaning is assigned to trial evidence through the incorporation of that evidence into one or more plausible accounts or stories describing "what happened" during events testified to at the trial. The story organization facilitates evidence comprehension and enables jurors to reach a predeliberation verdict decision. In a criminal trial, the ultimate stage of the decision process involves classifying the story into one of the verdict categories provided by the judge. Confidence in the verdict is based on the coherence, coverage, uniqueness, and goodness of fit of the story in the verdict category.

### Empirical Research

Our initial research on the Story Model elicited descriptions of mental representations of evidence and verdict information at one point in time during the legal decision process (Pennington & Hastie, 1986). In the first studies we established that evidence summaries constructed by jurors had a narrative story structure (and not other plausible structures, such as a pro-versus-con

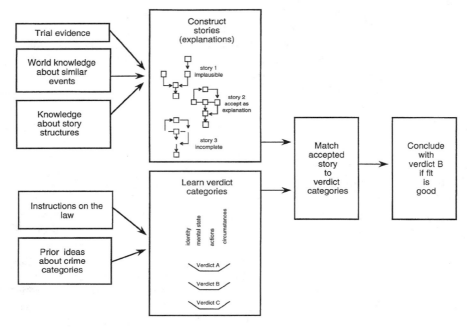

Figure 13.4. An overview of the "story model" for juror decision making.

argument structure) and that verdict representations looked like feature lists (or simple frames). Jurors who chose different verdicts had constructed different stories such that there was a distinct causal configuration of events that constituted a story corresponding to each verdict category. Moreover, jurors choosing different verdicts did not have systematically different verdict representations, nor did they apply different classification criteria. Thus, verdict decisions covary with story structures but do not covary with verdict learning or story classification. However, the highly directive interview method used in this research precluded strong inferences concerning the spontaneity of story construction and the functional role of stories in the decision phase.

In a second empirical study we established that decision makers spontaneously constructed causal accounts of the evidence in the legal decision task (Pennington & Hastie, 1988). In this study, subjects' responses to sentences presented in a recognition memory task were used to draw conclusions about subjects' postdecision representations of evidence. Subjects were expected to "recognize" as having been presented as trial evidence sentences from the story associated with their decision with a higher probability than to recognize sentences from stories associated with other (rejected) verdicts. This implies that hit rates (correct recognitions) and false alarm rates (false recognitions) for sentences from each story can be predicted from subjects' verdicts. These predictions were confirmed; verdict decisions predicted the hit and false alarm rates found for sentences within the subjects' stories. Thus, differences in method, subject population, and stimulus materials yielded results converging with the interview study conclusions about the correlation between memory structure and decision outcome. Even though we concluded that story representations were constructed *spontaneously*, the causal role of stories in decisions was still not established because subjects could decide on a verdict and then (spontaneously) justify it to themselves by constructing a coherent story.

A third experiment was conducted to study the effects of variations in the order of evidence presentation on judgments. Our primary goal was to test the claim that the construction of stories in evidence evaluation *causes* decisions. A secondary goal was to determine whether story coherence and uniqueness influence judgments of confidence in the correctness of verdicts. The "logic" of the experiment was summarized in our hypothesis that (manipulated) ease of story construction would influence verdict decisions; easy-to-construct stories would result in more decisions in favor of the corresponding verdicts.

Stories were considered easy to construct when the evidence was ordered in a temporal and causal sequence that matched the occurrence of the original events (Story Order; Baker, 1978). Stories were considered difficult to construct when the presentation order did not match the sequence of the original events. We based the non-story order on the sequence of evidence as conveyed by witnesses in the original trial (Witness Order). Mock-jurors listened to a tape recording of a 100-sentence summary of the trial evidence (50 prosecution statements and 50 defense statements), followed by a judge's charge to choose between a Murder verdict and a Not Guilty verdict. The contents of the materials were identical across all experimental conditions, only the order of presentation was varied. The 50 prosecution statements, constituting the First Degree Murder story identified in our initial interview study (Pennington & Hastie, 1986), were presented either in a Story Order or a Witness Order. Similarly, the defense statements, the Not Guilty story, were presented in one of the two orders creating a four-cell factorial design. In all four order conditions the prosecution evidence preceded the defense evidence as per standard legal procedure. After listening to the tape recorded trial materials, the subjects completed a questionnaire indicating their verdict, confidence in the verdict, and their perceptions of the strengths of the prosecution and defense cases.

As predicted, subjects were likeliest to convict the defendant when the prosecution evidence was presented in Story Order and the defense evidence was presented in Witness Order (78% chose guilty) and they were least likely to convict when the prosecution evidence was in Witness Order and defense was in Story Order (31% chose guilty). Conviction rates were intermediate in conditions where both sides of the case were in Story Order (59% convictions) or both were in Witness Order (63% convictions). Furthermore, the perceived strength of one side of the case depended on both the order of evidence for that side *and for the other side* of the case. This finding supports our claim that the *uniqueness* of the best-fitting story is one important basis for confidence in the decision.

Subsequent research has addressed some practical questions from the legal trial domain. For example, many criminal cases involve the presentation of only one story, by the prosecution, and the defense tactic is to "raise reasonable doubts" by attacking the plausibility of that story. In these one-sided cases, jurors construct only one story and confidence in the verdict is determined by coherence and fit of the single story to the verdict category. In this situation, a weak defense story is worse than no story at all; in fact, a weak prosecution story is bolstered and more guilty verdicts are rendered when a weak defense story is presented versus no defense story at all. This again demonstrates the importance of the comparative *uniqueness* factor, when more than one story has been constructed. Another observation, which reinforces the lore of trial tactics, is that when a narrative rhetorical strategy is used to argue a case, anticipating the story in the attorney's opening statement is an effective tactic. The probability of obtaining a verdict consistent with a story is increased when the story is "primed" in the opening statement, all other factors remaining equal.

We have also extended the research program to include civil cases, specifically an application of the explanation-based model to jurors' reasoning about liability for compensatory and punitive damages (Hastie, Schkade, & Payne, 1997). A typical set of elements to conclude that a defendant's conduct was reckless enough to warrant punitive damages includes: a judgment that the conduct was a cause of real damages sustained by the plaintiff; plus subjective consciousness of a foreseeable grave danger by the defendant, and conduct that was a gross deviation from an ordinary level of care. Mock-jurors were asked to, "Think aloud as you make your decision on the verdict," and then they were asked to respond to specific questions about each of the legal elements underlying the punitive damages judgment. The contents of these verbal reports were scored to assess the extent to which the mock-jurors considered each of the elements and as to the nature of the reasoning that they applied to evaluate the elements that they did consider.

We found that, just as in criminal cases, the juror's first step was to construct a narrative summary of the evidence. This summary included the major events from evidence that the juror believed occurred, ordered in a temporal sequence. This narrative included causal linkages, many of them inferred, that served as "glue" holding the story of the credible evidence together. Content analyses showed that, for these cases, the explanatory "glue" usually took the form of inferences about the defendants' motives. Since the defendants were all businesses or corporations, "corporate greed" was a common ingredient in the explanations for "Yes, liable for punitive damages" decisions.

After constructing an explanatory story, the jurors focused on key actions of the defendant, the actions that were alleged to be the causes of the plaintiffs' injuries. Consistent with the relevant legal conceptions, this assessment of causal importance emphasized the "necessity" of the defendant's alleged causal action. Typically, the jurors "mutated" the candidate causal event and then "counterfactually" inferred the probability that the harmful effect would still have occurred, *if the causal event (defendant's action) had not occurred.* (If there had been additional guards in the shopping mall, would the plaintiff have been assaulted? If there had been a recall program with registered letters mailed to boat owners, would the plaintiff's boat have sunk?) When the jurors judged there was a large difference in the probabilities of the effect, as a function of mutating the cause, then they concluded the candidate cause was truly a cause of the effect (cf., Roese & Olson, 1995; Wells & Gavanski, 1989).

If the defendant's action was deemed causally important, the jurors attempted to apply the judge's instructions on elements of negligence and recklessness: Could the defendant foresee that the harmful outcome was a possibility? Jurors who did consider this issue attended to evidence, summarized in their stories, that there were tangible "warnings" that the situation was risky (Had there been other violent crimes at the mall where the assault occurred? Had similar boats had problems with seaworthiness?). Did the defendant deliberately choose between courses of action, while subjectively conscious of the foreseeable harmful outcome? Here jurors looked for evidence that an explicit choice (an "act of commission"; Spranca, Minsk, & Baron, 1991) had been made by the defendant (e.g., a security company asked the defendant to hire additional guards, but the defendant refused; the defendant made a choice between a recall campaign or a warning campaign). And did the defendant's conduct exhibit a gross deviation from ordinary care or reasonable conduct? Here jurors who considered the issue often reasoned by (counterfactually) imagining themselves in the situation and then inferring what they might have done. When their postdiction of their own behavior was highly discrepant from the defendant's action, they were likely to conclude the defendant's action was a "gross deviation" (cf. Pennington & Hastie, 1993a, at p. 152, on jurors' "self analogies" in reasoning about the motives of criminal defendants). Mock-jurors often "imported" personal beliefs and criteria to justify their judgment that the defendant's action was reckless (e.g., "The company was greedy, cutting corners, that's 'reckless'"; "They weren't thinking ahead, anyone would've known the ship was going to sink"; "Everyone knew it was dangerous, but they didn't take proper care, that's 'callous disregard'").

In our explanation-based model the decision process is divided into three stages: construction of a summary explanation; determination of decision alternatives; mapping the explanation onto a best-fitting decision alternative. This subtask framework is in contrast to the uniform on-line updating computation or the unitary memory-based calculation hypothesized in most alternative approaches (cf. Hastie & Park, 1986). Furthermore, we diverge sharply from traditional approaches with our emphasis on the structure of memory representations as the key determinant of decisions. We also depart from the common assumption that, when causal reasoning is involved in judgment, it can be described by algebraic, stochastic, or logical computations that lead directly to a decision (e.g., Anderson, 1974; Einhorn & Hogarth, 1986; Kelley, 1973). In our model causal reasoning plays a subordinate but critical role by guiding inferences in evidence evaluation and construction of the intermediate explanation.

## Concluding Comments

Our approach to the problem of how to generalize conclusions from our research to new settings, tasks, and subject populations is to begin by assuming that the establishment of a phenomenon, such as a cause–effect relationship, in one setting is a prima facie argument for its generality. Then the projectability of the result should be evaluated by examining each conceptual dimension along which variation occurs from one setting to the other. Our program of empirical research relies on simulations of the juror's decision task in laboratory and field settings. We believe that this combination of low- and high-fidelity methods has yielded a strong foundation for a theory of actual jurors' decisions.

We do *not* claim that explanation-based decision making is the only decision making strategy available to decision makers, nor do we claim it will be applied everywhere. For example, in the popular laboratory research tasks in which subjects are asked to assess the attractiveness of lottery gambles, it is unlikely that a subject would construct an explanatory causal model of the evidence or reason about causal relations concerning outcomes that are explicitly determined by random mechanisms such as game spinners or bingo cages.

In other laboratory tasks in which a decision is made among a relatively small set of options, the evidence items are independent of one another, and the evaluative dimensions are simple and known prior to hearing evidence, algebraic models such as those based on linear additive, anchor-and-adjust updating processes should provide good summaries of the judgment process (Anderson, 1981; Einhorn & Hogarth, 1986; Hammond et al., 1975; Lopes, 1982). Even in some complex judgments, such as diagnostic tasks that are made routinely and the configurations of evidence that have been seen many times before, explanation-based decision making will not occur. For example, in many medical diagnoses a familiar pattern will be recognized immediately without much intermediate reasoning or interpretation (e.g., Brooks, Norman, & Allen, 1991).

In "consumer" choice tasks in which a person chooses which car to buy, which videotape to rent, or which entree to order, where attributes of the choice alternatives are simple and unambiguous and the choice is one that has been made before, we would not expect interpretation of the evidence (attributes) to play a large role (see Goldstein & Weber, 1995, for a similar view). However, for nonroutine choices in which the person is a relative novice – the important dimensions are unknown and the choice is made for the first time (e.g., the first time a house is purchased, the first time a job offer is accepted) – we expect that explanation-based strategies would come into play. There is also a great deal of evidence that explanatory situation models play a central role in nonroutine expert decisions in many natural settings (cf. many contributions in Chi, Glaser, & Farr, 1988; and in Klein, Orasanu, Calderwood, & Zsambok, 1993).

If there is one characteristic of our program of research that distinguishes it from the many recent efforts to study the manner in which complex knowledge structures serve as mediators for relationships among evidence, goals, and decisions, it is our intense focus on the specific structure of the hypothesized mediating representation. Critics of the "mental models" approach to reasoning, planning, and decision making processes have noted that many theorists have failed to clearly specify the nature of these knowledge representations and, thus, their theories are vacuous and untestable (Rips, 1986; Rouse & Morris, 1986). We hope that our research can provide one example of a rigorous approach to these issues that yields a useful theory of important decision-making phenomena.

### References

Anderson, J. R. (1990). *The adaptive character of thought.* Hillsdale, NJ: Erlbaum.

Anderson, N. H. (1974). Cognitive algebra: Integration theory applied to social attribution. In L. Berkowitz (Ed.), *Advances in experimental social psychology* (Vol. 7, pp. 1–101). New York: Academic Press.

Anderson, N. H. (1981). *Foundations of information integration theory.* New York: Academic Press.

Axelrod, R. (Ed.). (1976). *Structure of decision: The cognitive maps of political elites.* Princeton: Princeton University Press.

Baker, L. (1978). Processing temporal relationships in simple stories: Effects of input sequences. *Journal of Verbal Learning and Verbal Behavior, 17,* 559–572.

Barr, P. S., Stimpert, J. L., & Huff, A. S. (1992). Cognitive change, strategic action, and organizational renewal. *Strategic Management Journal, 13,* 15–36.

Bennett, W. L., & Feldman, M. (1981). *Reconstructing reality in the courtroom.* New Brunswick, NJ: Rutgers University Press.

Bonham, G. M., Shapiro, M. J., & Trumble, T. L. (1979). The October War: Changes in cognitive orientation toward the Middle East conflict. *International Studies Quarterly, 23,* 3–44.

Bostrom, A., Fischhoff, B., & Morgan, M. G. (1992). Characterizing mental models of hazardous processes: A methodology and an application to radon. *Journal of Social Issues, 48,* 85–100.

Brooks, L. R., Norman, G. R., & Allen, S. W. (1991). Role of specific similarity in a medical diagnostic task. *Journal of Experimental Psychology: General, 120,* 278–287.

Chi, M. T. H., Glaser, R., & Farr, M. J. (Eds.). (1988). *The nature of expertise.* Hillsdale, NJ: Erlbaum.

deKleer, J., & Brown, J. S. (1983). Assumptions and ambiguities in mechanistic mental models. In D. Gentner & A. L. Stevens (Eds.), *Mental models.* Hillsdale, NJ: Erlbaum.

Edwards, W. (1954). The theory of decision making. *Psychological Review, 51,* 380–417.

Einhorn, H. J., & Hogarth, R. M. (1986). Judging probable cause. *Psychological Bulletin, 99,* 3–19.

Finkel, N. J., & Groscup, J. L. (1997). Crime prototypes, objective versus subjective culpability, and a commonsense balance. *Law and Human Behavior, 21,* 209–230.

Gates, H. L., Jr. (1995, October 23). Thirteen ways of looking at a black man. *New Yorker,* pp. 56–60, 62–65.

Goldstein, W. M., & Weber, E. U. (1995). Content and discontent: Indications and implications of domain specificity in preferential decision making. In J. Busemeyer, R. Hastie, & D. L. Medin (Eds.), *Decision making from a cognitive perspective.* Vol. 32. *The psychology of learning and motivation* (pp. 83–136). San Diego: Academic Press.

Hammond, K. R., Stewart, T. R., Brehmer, B., & Steinmann, D. (1975). Social judgment theory. In M. Kaplan & S. Schwartz (Eds.), *Human judgment and decision processes.* New York: Academic Press.

Hastie, R., & Park, B. (1986). The relationship between memory and judgment depends on whether the judgment task is memory-based or on-line. *Psychological Review, 93,* 258–268.

Hastie, R., & Pennington, N. (1993). The story model of juror decision making. In R. Hastie (Ed.), *Inside the juror* (pp. 192–221). New York: Cambridge University Press.

Hastie, R., & Pennington, N. (1995). Cognitive approaches to judgment and decision making. In J. Busemeyer, R. Hastie, & D. L. Medin (Eds.), *Decision making from a cognitive perspective.* Vol. 32. *The psychology of learning and motivation* (pp. 1–31). San Diego: Academic Press.

Hastie, R., & Pennington, N. (1996). The O. J. Simpson stories: Behavioral scientists' reflections on *The People of the State of California* v. *Orenthal James Simpson. University of Colorado Law Review, 67,* 957–976.

Hastie, R., Schkade, D., & Payne, D. (1997, June). *Juror judgments in civil cases: Assessing punitive damages* (Rep. No. 371). Boulder: University of Colorado, Center for Research on Judgment and Policy.

Hogarth, R. M. Michaud, C., & Mery, J. L. (1980). Decision behavior in urban development: A methodological approach and substantive considerations. *Acta Psychologica, 45,* 95–117.

Huff, A. S. (Ed.). (1990). *Mapping strategic thought.* New York: Wiley.

Johnson-Laird, P. N. (1983). *Mental models: Towards a cognitive science of language, inference, and consciousness.* Cambridge, MA: Harvard University Press.

Joseph, G.-M., & Patel, V. L. (1990). Domain knowledge and hypothesis generation in diagnostic reasoning. *Medical Decision Making, 10,* 31–46.

Kahneman, D., & Tversky, A. (1979). Prospect theory: An analysis of decision under risk. *Econometrica, 47,* 263–291.

Kaplan, J. (1978). *Criminal justice: Introductory cases and materials* (2nd ed.). Mineola, NY: Foundation Press.

Kelley, H. H. (1973). The processes of causal attribution. *American Psychologist, 28,* 107–128.

Klein, G. A., Orasanu, J., & Calderwood, R., & Zsambok, C. E. (Eds.). (1993). *Decision making in action: Models and methods.* Norwood, NJ: Ablex.

Lewis, C. H. (1988). Why and how to learn why: Analysis-based generalization of procedures. *Cognitive Science, 12,* 211–256.

Lopes, L. L. (1982). *Toward a procedural theory of judgment* (Rep. No. 17). Madison: Wisconsin Human Information Processing Program.

Mandler, J. M. (1980). Categorical and schematic organization in memory. In C. R. Puff (Ed.), *Memory organization and structure*. New York: Academic Press.

McGill, A. L., & Klein, J. G. (1993). Contrastive and counterfactual thinking in causal judgment. *Journal of Personality and Social Psychology, 64*, 897–905.

Mixon, K. D., Foley, L. A., & Orme, K. (1995). The influence of racial similarity on the O. J. Simpson trial. *Journal of Social Behavior and Personality, 10*, 481–490.

Murphy, G. L., & Medin, D. L. (1985). The role of theories in conceptual coherence. *Psychological Review, 92*, 289–316.

Pennington, N. (1981). *Causal reasoning and decision making: The case of juror decisions.* Unpublished doctoral dissertation, Harvard University.

Pennington, N., & Hastie, R. (1981). Juror decision making models: The generalization gap. *Psychological Bulletin, 89*, 246–287.

Pennington, N., & Hastie, R. (1986). Evidence evaluation in complex decision making. *Journal of Personality and Social Psychology, 51*, 242–258.

Pennington, N., & Hastie, R. (1988). Explanation-based decision making: The effects of memory structure on judgment. *Journal of Experimental Psychology: Learning, Memory, and Cognition, 14*, 521–533.

Pennington, N., & Hastie, R. (1991). A cognitive theory of juror decision making: The Story Model. *Cardozo Law Review, 13*, 519–557.

Pennington, N., & Hastie, R. (1993a). Reasoning in explanation-based decision making. *Cognition, 49*, 123–163.

Pennington, N., & Hastie, R. (1993b). A theory of explanation-based decision making. In G. A. Klein, J. Orasanu, R. Calderwood, & C. E. Zsambok (Eds.), *Decision making in action: Models and methods* (pp. 188–201). Norwood, NJ: Ablex.

Pople, H. E., Jr. (1982) Heuristic methods for imposing structure on ill-structured problems: The structuring of medical diagnostics. In P. Szolovits (Ed.), *Artificial intelligence in medicine*. Boulder, CO: Westview Press.

Rasmussen, J. (1986). *Information processing and human-machine interaction: An approach to cognitive engineering*. Amsterdam: North-Holland.

Rips, L. J. (1986). Mental muddles. In M. Brand & R. M. Harnish (Eds.), *The representation of knowledge and belief* (pp. 258–286). Tucson: University of Arizona Press.

Rips, L. J. (1989). Similarity, typicality, and categorization. In S. Vosniadu & A. Ortony (Eds.), *Similarity and analogy*. Cambridge, UK: Cambridge University Press.

Rips, L. J. (1994). *The psychology of proof: Deductive reasoning in human thinking*. Cambridge, MA: MIT Press.

Roese, N. J., & Olson, J. M. (1995). Counterfactual thinking: A critical overview. In N. J. Roese & J. M. Olson (Eds.), *What might have been: The social psychology of counterfactual thinking* (pp. 1–56). Mahwah, NJ: Erlbaum.

Rouse, W. B., & Morris, N. M. (1986). On looking into the black box: Prospects and limits on the search for mental models. *Psychological Bulletin, 100*, 349–363.

Rumelhart, D. E. (1977). Understanding and summarizing brief stories. In D. LaBerge & S. J. Samuels (Eds.), *Basic processes in reading: Perception and comprehension*. Hillsdale, NJ: Erlbaum.

Sevón, G. (1984). Cognitive maps of past and future economic events. *Acta Psychologica, 56*, 71–79.

Schank, R. C., Collins, G. C., & Hunter, L. E. (1986). Transcending inductive category formation in learning. *Behavioral and Brain Sciences, 9*, 639–686.

Smith, V. L. (1991). Prototypes in the courtroom: Lay representations of legal concepts. *Journal of Personality and Social Psychology, 61*, 857–872.

Spranca, M., Minsk, E., & Baron, J. (1991). Omission and commission in judgment and choice. *Journal of Experimental Social Psychology, 27*, 76–105.

Stein, N. L., & Glenn, C. G. (1979). An analysis of story comprehension in elementary school children. In R. O. Freedle (Ed.), *New directions in discourse processing* (Vol. 2., pp. 83–107). Norwood, NJ: Ablex.

Toobin, J. (1995, October 23). A horrible human event. *New Yorker*, 40–46, 48–49.

Trabasso, T., & van den Broek, P. (1985). Causal thinking and the representation of narrative events. *Journal of Memory and Language, 24*, 612–630.

von Neumann, J., & Morgenstern, O. (1947). *Theory of games and economic behavior* (2nd ed.). Princeton: Princeton University Press.

Voss, J. F., Greene, T. R., Post, T. A., & Penner, B. C. (1983). Problem-solving skill in the social sciences. In G. H. Bower (Ed.), *The psychology of learning and motivation* (Vol. 17, pp. 165–213). New York: Academic Press.

Wells, G. L., & Gavanski, I. (1989). Mental simulation of causality. *Journal of Personality and Social Psychology, 56*, 161–169.

Wilensky, R. (1983). *Planning and understanding: A computational approach to human reasoning*. Reading, MA: Addison-Wesley.

# 14 Decision Theory, Reasonable Doubt, and the Utility of Erroneous Acquittals

*Terry Connolly*

Efforts to apply the tools of formal Decision Theory to the analysis of legal procedure appear to have generated at least as much controversy as clarification (see Milanich (1981: p. 87), for a sampling of references to this debate). Opponents of these applications such as Tribe (1971) tend to argue for the inherent inappropriateness of decision thoretic methods in the legal context. However, as we shall argue below, much of the earlier literature is flawed by technical weakness or overambitious intent, so that the real contributions Decision Theory offers may have been obscured.

The intent of this chapter is a modest one. We first present a simple model of the individual criminal-trial juror's decision as to a vote of convict or acquit. The only novelty in this development is in paying a little more attention than have earlier derivations to the precise meanings of and relationships between terms. The yield is a rather specific set of meanings embracing the notion of reasonable doubt, the juror's evaluation of the possible consequences of his vote, and the sense in which these elements might be subjected to tests of mutual consistency. As it turns out, such consistency tests appear to fail rather often in practice: direct and indirect measures of an individual's interpretation of "reasonable doubt" are widely divergent. The final part of the chapter considers some implications of this divergence.

## The Basic Model

The model we wish to explore here represents the cognitive processes of the trier of fact in a criminal trial in terms of two "degrees of belief": $P_g$, the trier's degree of belief that the accused is actually guilty of the crime; and $P^*$, the degree of belief the trier requires before deciding to vote for a conviction. If, at the conclusion of the trial, $P_g$ exceeds $P^*$, the trier votes to convict, if not

This chapter originally appeared in *Law and Human Behavior*, 1987, *11*, 101–112. Copyright © 1987 by Plenum Publishing Corporation. Reprinted by permission.

to acquit. We shall, without detailed defense, treat $P_g$ and $P^*$ as "subjective probabilities," bounded at zero (no degree of belief in the proposition, a certainty of its falsity) and one (a certainty of the truth of the proposition). We shall not be concerned here with the mechanisms by which $P_g$ reaches its final value over the course of the trial. Our concern is solely with the choice of $P^*$, the threshold probability which the trier holds as minimal for conviction – that is, his or her personal standard of what constitutes "reasonable doubt."

Judicial efforts at clarifying the meaning of "reasonable doubt" by verbal paraphrase and metaphor are plentiful (see, for example, references cited in Nagel et al., 1981: p. 365), though McCormick (1972: p. 800) argues that little is gained by such efforts. Empirical research suggests that normal English is an exceedingly imprecise language for expressing uncertainty. For example, Behn and Vaupel (1982: p. 76) report that their students interpreted the phrase "There is a possibility that. . ." as meaning somewhere between a 5% and a 70% chance; "There is a good chance. . ." was interpreted between 30% and 90%; and so on (See also Beyth-Marom 1982; Bryant & Norman, 1980; Lichtenstein & Newman, 1967). It is thus unsurprising that huge ranges are reported by researchers who have asked judges, potential jurors, and others what probability they associate with "reasonable doubt" (for example, Dane, 1985; Simon & Mahan, 1971). Typical values seem to fall above 90% in direct questioning, though responses range from 50% to 100% (see also Champagne & Nagel, 1982).

Such simple direct questioning presupposes that people have both a well-developed sense of their own threshold degree of belief, and a facility for expressing such a sense in probabilistic terms. These presuppositions seem rather strong, and a prudent decision analyst would probably wish to probe and check the responses in various ways. For example, he might ask the decision maker to contemplate urns filled with different mixtures of balls labeled "Guilty" and "Innocent" representing subpopulations of defendants, and reflect on the verdict he would wish to pronounce on any single element drawn randomly from each urn. A modest technology exists for probability elicitations of this sort (see, for example, Hogarth, 1980; Iversen, 1971).

A second approach to clarifying the decision maker's $P^*$ is to assume that it is chosen, not in a vacuum, but in contemplation of its consequences. That is, the decision maker, while hoping to acquit the innocent and convict the guilty, is presumed to be aware of the possibility of the other two outcomes (erroneous convictions and erroneous acquittals), and to have some feelings (presumably negative) about them. If the decision maker responds to a series of hypothetical questions about these outcomes in a way that meets certain strict but perfectly plausible requirements (see Coombs, Dawes, & Tversky, 1970, for an excellent nontechnical discussion of these requirements), then it is possible to associate with each of the four outcomes a number known as a "utility." From these utilities, in turn, it is possible to derive an unambiguous value of $P^*$ for the decision maker providing the original assessments. The hypothetical choices determining the utilities of the four outcomes thus provide a powerful indirect method of estimating an individual's $P^*$ in a specific setting. The method has formed the basis for several efforts to measure individuals' values of reasonable doubt (e.g., Dane, 1985; Nagel, 1979; Nagel, Lamm, & Neef, 1981).

Leaving aside for the moment the matter of establishing the relevant utilities, the derivation of $P^*$ is straightforward (and, indeed, familiar: see Cullison, 1971; Fried, Kaplan, & Klein, 1975; Grofman, 1981; Kaplan, 1968; Tribe, 1971). A fundamental result in utility theory (e.g., Luce & Raiffa, 1957) shows that consistent decision makers will prefer options that maximize the "expectation" (i.e., payoff times probability of attainment) of their utilities, even in one-shot, never-to-be-repeated choices. [Such counterexamples as those proposed by Allais (1953) are of considerable technical interest, but need not concern us here, for reasons discussed by, for example, MacCrimmon (1967).] $P^*$ is, by definition, the value of $P_g$ at which the decision maker is "indifferent to" (i.e., exactly balanced between) a vote to convict and one to acquit, and thus the value at which the expected utilities of these two verdicts are precisely equal. That is

Expected utility of convict = expected utility of acquit

or

$$P^* U_{cg} + (1 - P^*)U_{ci} = P^* U_{ag} + (1 - P^*)U_{ai} \qquad (1)$$

where $U_{cg}$ is the utility of convicting a guilty defendant, $U_{ci}$ is the utility of convicting an innocent defendant, $U_{ag}$ is the utility of acquitting a guilty defendant, and $U_{ai}$ is the utility of acquitting an innocent defendant. It will be clear that, given numerical values for the four utilities, Equation (1) can be rearranged to yield a numerical value for $P^*$.

## Assigning Numerical Values

The assignment of numerical values to the terms in Equation (1) is a nontrivial problem, and has been the source of numerous technical errors and misunderstandings in efforts to apply the model. Tribe (1971), for example, selects correct conviction ($cg$) as the best, and incorrect conviction ($ci$) as the worst possible outcomes, assigning them the utility values 1.0 and 0.0, respectively – an unexceptionable procedure, since utility scales can always be transformed to run from zero to one. (As will be shown later, this rescaling has the effect of setting up a utility scale that runs from zero, the worst possible outcome of the decision, to one, the best possible outcome. There is no implication that undesirable outcomes have "positive utility" in the sense of being gains, simply that desirable outcomes will score close to one, undesirable outcomes close to zero.) Tribe then assigns, "for the sake of illustration" (1971: p. 1380), the values of $\frac{1}{2}$ to $U_{ag}$, and $\frac{2}{3}$ to $U_{ai}$, and correctly calculates the corresponding $P^*$ as $\frac{4}{7}$, or .571. However, within less than a page he uses this numerical result to impugn the model itself, arguing "...a threshold probability of $\frac{4}{7}$ as much too low" (1971: p. 1381). The indictment seems manifestly unfair, since the unacceptable (to Tribe) value of $P^*$ is simply the result of the arbitrary utilities he selected for illustration.

Tribe is sternly taken to task on this by Milanich (1981), who argues that the ordering and, in fact, the approximate numerical values of the four utilities are dictated by "... certain established social values which the legal system is designed to promote and protect" (1981: p. 91), and that Tribe's valuations are "extremely unintuitive" (1981: p. 90). She proposes instead that acquitting the innocent, $ai$, is the highest valued outcome (hence $U_{ai} = 1.0$); $U_{ci}$ remains at zero; $U_{cg}$ is assigned a small range of high values ($\frac{9}{10}-\frac{7}{8}$); and $U_{ag}$ a small range of low values ($\frac{1}{9}-\frac{1}{10}$). The ordering is forcefully presented, and it is clearly assumed that these "corrected" utility values will yield a suitably high value of $P^*$ – perhaps above .9, since Milanich refers to a value of .8 as "much too weak" (1981: p. 92). Unfortunately, they do not. Substituted into Equation (1), above, Milanich's "corrected" utility guesses yield a range of $P^*$ from .556 to .567 – embarrassingly close to, and below, Tribe's "unintuitive result" of .571!

Some scholars (e.g., Nagel et al., 1981) have attempted to resolve the utility assignment problem by use of "Blackstone's ratio," drawing on Sir William Blackstone's frequently quoted remark that "It is better than ten guilty persons escape than that one innocent suffer." Other commentators have proposed other ratios: Hale (1678/1972) proposed 5:1, Fortescue (1567/1969) 20:1, and so on. Such proposals certainly suggest that erroneous convictions should be treated much more seriously than erroneous acquittals. They do not, however, resolve the crucial numerical issue of the utilities that should be associated with these two undesirable outcomes.

The error is readily demonstrated. Suppose that a given trial system receives some number, $N_g$, of truly guilty defendants, and some number, $N_i$, of defendants who are, in truth, innocent. The procedures of the court are such that even the truly guilty have some nonzero probability, $P(A/G)$, of being acquitted; and the truly innocent have a nonzero probability, $P(C/I)$, of being convicted. In the long run, the number of guilty who escape is then $N_g \times P(A/G)$, and the number of innocent who suffer is $N_i \times P(C/I)$. Blackstone's ratio is the first product divided by the second. While the court may well have some control over the two probabilities (for example, by the value of $P^*$ it adopts), it does not control the numbers of innocent and guilty with whom it deals. Other things equal, a doubling of the ratio of guilty to innocent defendants brought before the court will double Blackstone's ratio, while leaving unchanged the balance of utilities used in setting $P^*$.

Suppose, for example, that, of the defendants appearing before a particular court, half are truly innocent, half truly guilty. Support further that the court operates to a standard of proof such that only one innocent in a hundred is convicted; and that this standard has the incidental consequence that one guilty in ten goes free. Though the court cannot, of course, observe these error rates for itself, an omniscient observer might well approve the court's procedures, and the utilities they imply, in that Blackstone's ratio is satisfied. Imagine, however, that, as a result of improved police procedure, decline of professional skills among the criminal class, or other circumstance beyond the court's control, the mix of defendants changes to include 60% guilty, 40% innocent. With no change whatsoever in the court's standards, the ratio of false acquittals to false convictions is now 15:1. This ratio is jointly determined by the court's standards and the mixture of defendants with whom it deals. Blackstone's comment is thus only indirectly related to the assignment of utilities to the two erroneous outcomes. It can be fairly read as urging that one type of error be treated as much more serious than the other; it cannot be read as establishing the numerical ratio of their utilities.

### The Nature of Utilities

Since utility theory has, in the present context, been more often disparaged then explained, a brief technical digression will be useful here. To a modern utility theorist a utility is not an explanation of a choice, but a representation of a set of consistent choices (cf. Luce & Raiffa, 1957: p. 32). The basic measurement procedure is to ask a decision maker to choose, not to invite him or her to provide a number. Specifically, let us suppose that there are three possible outcomes, $A$, $B$, and $C$ flowing from a given decision, and that the decision maker values them in the order given. It is axiomatic (i.e., assumed) in utility theory, and apparently plausible in fact, that some lottery involving $A$ and $C$ as prizes can always be constructed such that the decision maker would be as happy or unhappy with a ticket to that lottery as (s)he would be with the intermediate outcome, $B$. This equivalent lottery offers prize A with some probability $p$, and prize C with probability $(1 - p)$, and is represented by the notation $(A, p, C)$.

In general if $B$ is close in value to $A$ (i.e., is on the high end of the scale), we would expect the decision maker to demand high values of $p$ before the lottery became attractive. If, on the other hand, $B$ is closer to $C$ in value, then low values of $p$ would make the lottery acceptable. In this sense, $p$ provides a measure of value for $B$, on a scale bounded by the value of $A$ and that of $C$. If a utility value of 1.0 is assigned to $A$, the best outcome, and 0.0 to $C$, the worst outcome, then $p$ is the utility of the intermediate outcome $B$ (all valuations being, of course, from the perspective of the focal decision maker). It is thus somewhat misleading to describe, as does Milanich (1981), a utility of $\frac{1}{2}$ as indicating that the outcome "...does not matter one way or the other – not in favor, not opposed" (p. 91) or as indicating "no preference" (p. 92). If, for example, $A$ were a large gift ($1,000) and $C$ a small one ($100), then a utility value of $\frac{1}{2}$ might be associated with an intermediate gift ($200? $300?) which the decision maker finds exactly as attractive as the lottery ($1,000, .5, $100). It seems unlikely that the decision maker would feel neither in favor of, nor opposed to, receipt of this intermediate gift.

A crucial and surprising result, noted earlier, is that a decision maker for whom a certain outcome is associated with a utility $p$ will, if consistent, treat an option that offers that outcome with probability $q$ as having utility $pq$. This result can be read as either descriptive of an idealized consistent decision maker, or as prescriptive for an ordinary muddled human, but it should be emphasized that the axioms upon which it rests are perfectly plausible elements of what one might mean by sensible choice. This result opens the way for Decision Analysis' "divide and conquer" strategy for complex problems: preferences can be established for elementary outcomes of the choice, and then "folded back" using the rules of probability to determine preferred decision options (see Behn & Vaupel, 1982, Raiffa, 1968; for elementary introductions to the technique).

### Assessing Utilities for Trial Outcomes

Returning now to the criminal trial context, let us sketch the procedure by which a trier's utilities for the four possible outcomes might be established. We might ask the trier to imagine that, after the verdict of convict or acquit has been irrevocably cast, the defendant turns at the courtroom door and rips back the veil of ignorance that has so far obscured the proceedings and reveals, with absolute veridicality, whether he was really guilty or innocent. The four possible trial outcomes are thus, in this imagining, made vivid, and the trier is asked to reflect on how desirable or undesirable each seems in the particular circumstances of this trial.

With the four outcomes clearly delineated, the trier would be led through a thought experiment of the following kind. First, choose which of the four represents the best, and which the worst, possible outcome. Suppose, purely for illustration, that the trier follows Milanich, rather than Tribe, and that $ai$ (acquitting the innocent) is rated best, $ci$ (convicting the innocent) worst. For the two intermediate outcomes $cg$ (convicting the guilty) and $ag$ (acquitting the guilty), the trier would now be led through a series of choices comparing the intermediate outcome with various lotteries offering these "best" and "worst" outcomes as possible payoffs. This procedure would continue until the trier decides on two numbers: the value $P_1$ that makes the lottery (Best, $P_1$, Worst) as attractive or unattractive as the outcome $cg$; and the value $P_2$ that makes the lottery (Best, $P_2$, Worst) as attractive or unattractive as $ag$. This labor yields values for the four utilities of Equation

(1): $U_{cg} = P_1; U_{ag} = P_2; U_{ai} = 1.0$; and $U_{ci} = 0.0$. Equation (1) now provides the value of $P^*$ that these four utilities imply.

The procedure may seem clumsy, especially at first use, but it has crucial advantages. Most important it yields numbers with specific, identifiable meaning, in a way that questions of the kind "How much more do you like A than B?" do not. A metric of "intensity of liking or disliking" is difficult to provide with concrete referents: the response to "How much do you like A?" must surely be "Compared to what?" In the utility assessment procedure sketched above, the comparison is quite explicit: "How much do you like A, compared to a lottery which you will play only once, and in which you will get a specific, better outcome with probability $P$, or a specific, worse outcome with probability $(1 - P)$?" The value of $P$ at which the respondent finds the question impossible to answer – that is, at which A and the lottery seem equally appealing – is a precise statement of his or her utility for A.

## Consistent Utility and Probability Assignments

The purpose of the apparatus erected to this point is to allow us to move freely between the four outcome utilities and $P^*$, the threshold probability implied by these utilities. That is, we can try tentative values for the four utilities and see what value of $P^*$ they imply; or we can select a value of $P^*$ and explore what ranges of utility valuations are consistent with it. To facilitate such two-way explorations, two graphs (Figures 14.1(a) and (b)) will be useful. Figure 14.1(a) assumes a Milanich-type decision maker, who treats acquitting the innocent as the best possible outcome, and convicting the innocent as the worst. The curves then represent the values of $P^*$ implied by choosing values of $U_{cg}$ and $U_{ag}$, the utilities assigned to convicting the guilty and acquitting the guilty, respectively. The sample point marked $X$ thus represents the views of an individual who has a utility of .9 (i.e., very high) for convicting the guilty, and a utility of .4 (moderate to low) for acquitting the guilty. These utilities imply a value of $P^*$ of about .65, read from the left-hand scale. Other combinations can be read off in the same way. Figure 14.1(b) assumes a Tribe-type decision maker, who values conviction of the guilty above all else, while retaining conviction of the innocent as the worst possible outcome. The curves now represent the $P^*$ values that correspond to various combinations of utilities for $ag$ and $ai$.

The general shapes of these curves seem to accord with intuitions. In Figure 14.1(a), for example, the curves slope downward to the right, indicating that the more desirable one feels the conviction of the guilty to be, the lower the value of $P^*$ for which one will settle. Similarly, for any value of $U_{cg}$, lower utilities for acquitting the guilty dictate lower values of $P^*$. In Figure 14.1(b), the curves slope upward to the right, reflecting the demand for more convincing evidence (high $P^*$) as higher utilities are assigned to acquitting the innocent; and, again, lower values of $P^*$ are acceptable to those

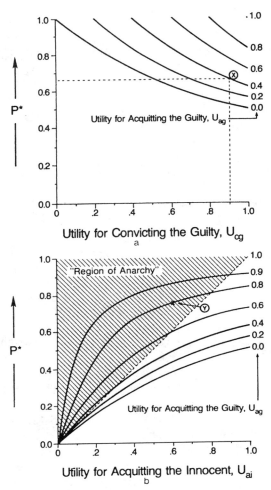

Figure 14.1. (a) Critical probability, $P^*$, vs. utilities for correct conviction ($U_{cg}$) and for erroneous acquittal ($U_{ag}$) for jurors rating correct acquittal as the best outcome (i.e., $U_{ai} = 1.0$). (b) Critical probability, $P^*$, vs. utilities for correct acquittal ($U_{ai}$) and for erroneous acquittal ($U_{ag}$) for jurors rating correct conviction as the best outcome (i.e., $U_{cg} = 1.0$).

who feel acquitting the guilty to be more undesirable. The shaded, upper left-hand portion of Figure 14.1(b) represents a "region of anarchy," in which acquitting the guilty is seen as more desirable than acquitting the innocent. The point marked $Y$, for example, represents an individual who places a higher value (0.8) on acquitting the guilty than he does on acquitting the innocent (0.6). Such a preference ordering seems clearly to violate Milanich's "established social values" that the legal system is designed to uphold.

If the shapes of these curves accord with intuition, the numerical values do not. Consider, for example, the utility assignments that correspond to $P^*$ values of .90 – a common response in efforts to establish "reasonable doubt" by direct questioning (e.g., Dane, 1985; Nagel et al., 1981; Simon & Mahan, 1971). Given Milanich-type ordering [Figure 14.1(a)], the only allowable values of $U_{cg}$ and $U_{ag}$ are those that differ by less than .11 – for example, $U_{cg} = .91$, $U_{ag} = .80$; or $U_{cg} = .31$, $U_{ag} = .20$. Neither pairing seems very satisfactory. For the first, the values seem reasonable for $U_{cg}$ – convicting the guilty seems a high-value outcome – but $U_{ag}$ seems much too high. Conversely, the second pair seems reasonable for $U_{ag}$, intuitively a rather undesirable outcome, but much too low for $U_{cg}$. Nor is the problem resolved by adopting a Tribe-type ordering [Figure 14.1(b)]. The tiny region above $P^* = .9$ can be reached by assigning a very high value to $U_{ai}$ (reasonably enough), but only if one is also prepared to assign a very high value to $U_{ag}$ – that is, if acquittals of both sorts are valued almost as much as the best outcome, convicting the guilty. Valuations of this sort may be defensible, but it is difficult to imagine how.

We are now brought, at last, to the central puzzle of this analysis. We have argued that Decision Theory offers ways of assigning unambiguous meanings to the notions of "reasonable doubt" (as a subjective probability, $P^*$), "desirability of outcomes" (as the four utilities), and "consistency" [centrally the argument leading to Equation (1)]. If we now apply this sense of "consistency" to link our judgment of outcome desirability with our sense of reasonable doubt, we find a very large gap. If we start with a reasonable $P^*$, we end up with odd utilities; if we start with reasonable utilities, we end up with an odd $P^*$.

The quandary can be presented still more forcefully if, like the present author, one is unable to decide whether correct convictions or correct acquittals are preferable and is thus prepared to assign them both the designation "best," with a utility of 1.0. In this simplified case, there is only one problematic utility to assign, $U_{ag}$, and assigning a value for it determines $P^*$, and vice versa. The relationship is plotted in Figure 14.2. If one feels, for example, that a false acquittal is as bad as a false conviction, then $U_{ag} = U_{ci} = 0.0$, and one sets $P^*$ at .50. (These values, and this $P^*$, appear to reflect the "preponderance of evidence" burden of proof required for civil cases; see, for example, Kaplan, 1968: p. 1072; Tribe, 1971: p. 1381). On the other hand a $P^*$ of .9 can be sustained only if one is prepared to assign $U_{ag}$ a value of .89 or higher, which seems outrageously high. For, recall, such a utility indicates that one finds a false acquittal to be so highly valued that, to match it, one would require odds of better than 8:1 in a lottery between making the correct decision and making the other kind of error (false conviction). Does such an evaluation really reflect what one imagines feeling as the acquitted, irrevocably freed, turns smirking at the courtroom door and reveals himself unambiguously as guilty?

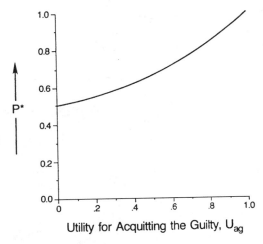

Figure 14.2. Critical probability, $P^*$, vs. utility for erroneous acquittal ($U_{ag}$) for jurors rating conviction of the guilty and acquittal of the innocent as joint best outcome (i.e., $U_{ai} = U_{cg} = 1.0$).

## Toward a Possible Resolution

The analysis to this point suggests that there is a clear conflict between the value of $P^*$ we give when asked directly (typically .90 or higher) and the value (typically .5–.6) that is readily derived from the utilities we express for trial outcomes, whether the latter are found by assertion (Milanich, Tribe) or by measurement (Dane, Nagel et al.). How is this conflict to be resolved? One possibility is to deny the need for resolution, as Tribe (1971) appears to argue in his emphasis on the need for necessary unclarity and vagueness in the "rich fabric of ritual" (p. 1393) that constitutes a criminal trial. A second possibility is to attack, at either conceptual or operational levels, one or more of the three elements – probability, utilities, and consistency framework – that comprise the conflict. We shall not attempt to rebut either argument here, beyond noting that, whatever the virtues of public vagueness and unclarity, they are unlikely to justify private confusion; and that the normative power of modern utility theory, if not beyond question, is certainly not to be lightly dismissed in such simple choice contexts as those examined here.

The third resolution, and the one that we wish to propose, is to conclude that the conflict between direct and indirect determinations of $P^*$ reflects human muddle, the confrontation of which will force us to examine more deeply the values we hold and thus the evidentiary standards we will demand of criminal prosecutions. In this view the divergent $P^*$ values obtained by direct and indirect assessments are simply examples of the common observation that decision problems are treated differently when differently presented or "framed" (see, for example, Kahneman & Tversky, 1984). Perhaps the direct assessment of $P^*$ focuses the respondent's attention on one specific trial outcome, the false acquittal, giving that outcome special salience. The indirect assessment, in contrast, calls attention equally to all four possible outcomes, but fails to provide the respondent with any help in integrating the resulting evaluations into an overall $P^*$ value. Either or both $P^*$ assessments might thus be flawed, in the sense of imperfectly representing the decision rule an individual would arrive at after careful, reflective analysis.

Nagel et al. (1981), commenting on the disparity between direct and indirect determinations of $P^*$, suggest that there is a "fundamental question of which of those two measures is a more valid reflection of a respondent's true standard for convicting" (1981: p. 364), proposing that the two measures be simply averaged. Such a procedure seems to us to dismiss rather lightly a disparity large enough to raise a "fundamental question." Disagreement about shades of grey may be usefully averaged out; but it seems unlikely that truth is well served by averaging together two reports, one of "black," the other "white," into a composite "grey." We would propose instead that the disparity be used as a stimulus to discussion and clarification. Dane's (1985) data suggest that the indirect measure provides a somewhat better predictor of the verdict an individual will actually reach than does the direct measure, but it is significant that neither measure predicts very well. Such findings strengthen the conclusion that, for many people, utility assessments for trial outcomes and threshold probabilities for conviction are not well developed and closely articulated. From this perspective one would look, not for a victory of one method of assessment over another, but for a decision aid that can help clarify the individual's thinking.

There appears to be a significant contradiction here between the consistency demands of the model and the inconsistent views implied by the numerical values of one's utilities and one's $P^*$. One escape is to abandon the model and adopt an alternative scheme for assessing the consistency of actions and consequences. This will not be an easy task. If the model is preserved, one or both of the enumerations must give significant ground. It may well be that, after careful reflection, one would want to cling to a $P^*$ of .9; but if one does, one must be prepared to hold the acquittal of the guilty as highly desirable, at least in comparison to the other available outcomes. If, on the other hand, one finds false acquittals repugnant, there is no escaping the direct implication of a low $P^*$. Decision Theory has nothing to say as to which values to hold; it simply tries to spell out the implications of the values one does hold. In this light, it would seem to have a place, not as a rival, but as a modest adjunct, to the serious rational ritual of the criminal trial.

### References

Allais, M. (1953). Le comportement de l'homme rationnel devant le risque: Critique des postulats et axiomes de l'école américaine. *Econometrica*, *21*, 503–546.

Behn, R. D., & Vaupel, J. W. (1982). *Quick analysis for busy decision makers*. New York: Basic Books.

Beyth-Marom, R. (1982). How probable is probable? A numerical translation of verbal probability expressions. *Journal of Forecasting, 1*, 257–269.

Bryant, G. D., & Norman, G. R. (1980). Expression of probability with words and numbers. *New England Journal of Medicine, 302*, 411.

Champagne, A., & Nagel, S. (1982). The psychology of judging. In N. L. Kerr & R. M. Bray (Eds.) *The psychology of the courtroom*. New York: Academic Press.

Coombs, C. H., Dawes, R. M., & Tversky, A. (1970). *Mathematical psychology: An elementary introduction*. Englewood Cliffs, NJ: Prentice-Hall.

Cullison, A. (1971). The model of rules and the logic of decision. In S. Nagel (Ed): *Modeling the criminal justice system*. Beverly Hills, CA: Sage.

Dane, F. C. (1985). In search of reasonable doubt: A systematic examination of selected quantification approaches. *Law and Human Behavior, 9*, 141–158.

Fortescue, J. (1969). *A learned communication on the laws of England* (reprint of 1567 ed.). New York: W. J. Johnson.

Fried, M., Kaplan, K. J., & Klein, K. W. (1975). Juror selection: An analysis of voir dire. In R. J. Simon (Ed.), *The jury system in America: A critical overview*. Beverley Hills, CA: Sage.

Grofman, B. (1981). Mathematical models of juror and jury decision-making: The state of the art. In B. D. Sales (Ed.), *The trial process*. New York: Plenum.

Hale, M. (1972). *Pleas of the Crown* (reprint of 1678 ed.). Oxford: Professional Books.

Hogarth, R. M. (1980). *Judgement and choice*. New York: Wiley.

Iversen, G. R. (1971). Operationalizing the concept of probability in legal-social science research. *Law and Society Review, 5*, 331–333.

Kahneman, D., & Tversky, A. (1984). Choices, values, and frames. *American Psychologist, 39*(4), 341–350.

Kaplan, J. (1968). Decision theory and the factfinding process. *Stanford Law Review, 20*, 1065–1092.

Lichtenstein, S., & Newman, J. R. (1967). Empirical scaling of common verbal phrases associated with numerical probability. *Psychonomic Science, 10*, 563–564.

Luce, R. D., & Raiffa, H. (1957). *Games and decisions*. New York: Wiley.

McCormick, C. (1972). *Handbook of the law of evidence* (2nd ed.). St. Paul, MN: West Publishing.

MacCrimmon, K. R. (1967). Descriptive and normative implications of the decision theory postulates. In K. Borch (Ed.), *Risk and uncertainty*. New York: Macmillan.

Milanich, P. G. (1981). Decision theory and standards of proof. *Law and Human Behavior, 5*, 87–96.

Nagel, S. (1979). Bringing the values of jurors in line with the law. *Judicature, 63*, 189–195.

Nagel, S., Lamm, D., & Neef, M. (1981). Decision theory and juror decision-making. In B. D. Sales (Ed.), *The trial process*. New York: Plenum.

Raiffa, H. (1968). *Decision analysis*. Reading. MA: Addison-Wesley.

Simon, R. J., & Mahan, L. (1971). Quantifying burdens of proof: A view from the bench, the jury, and the classroom. *Law and Society Review, 5*, 319–330.

Tribe, L. H. (1971). Trial by mathematics: Precision and ritual in the legal process. *Harvard Law Review, 84*, 1329–1393.

# Part V

# Medical Applications

Decision research has flourished in the medical arena for several reasons. First, this is a world in which decisions and decision makers can be readily found: A specific person (the doctor or the patient) at a specific point in time reviews some identifiable information (tests, symptoms, history), decides on a course of action (an operation, a drug), and acts. Second, it is often possible to assess the consequences of the action chosen: the patient recovers, remains sick, or gets worse. Third, physicians routinely make judgments and decisions about large numbers of similar patients (e.g., arthritics, cancer patients), so it is possible to use powerful statistical tools such as multiple regression to explore their thought processes, and (sometimes) to assess their success rates. Finally, the decisions matter: to the individual patient in terms of health, suffering, functioning, or life itself; and to the larger society, in terms of the astonishingly large percentage of our national budget that goes to health care. Studying medical decisions thus provides researchers with an opportunity to get out of the laboratory and into a world where the decisions are real, the stakes are high, and the rewards for improvement are large.

As long ago as the 1940s and 1950s researchers such as Meehl (1954) studied the clinical judgment of physicians. Clinical judgment refers to the process by which a skilled professional (such as a physician or a clinical psychologist) reviews a large amount of clinical information about a patient and arrives at an overall diagnosis (an inference about what's wrong) or prognosis (a prediction about what will happen in the future). Researchers attempted to understand the judgment process by building mathematical models of how each item of information influenced the expert's overall judgments. The consistent, and amazing, finding of this work was that ridiculously simple models – really, simple weighted averages – did as well in study after study as sophisticated, experienced clinicians. The explanation for, and implications of, this result are still hotly debated (see, for example, Goldberg, 1968; Dawes, Chapter 23, this volume), but it has yielded the useful technique of "policy capturing" in judgment studies. Chapter 15, by Doyle and Thomas, reprinted in this section, illustrates the technique. Note particularly the care these authors devoted to making realistic the "paper patients" whom their audiologists evaluated. As Brunswikians emphasize, "representative design" requires experimental tasks that closely mimic real-world tasks.

The realism issues shows up in different ways in the other three chapters in this section. Christensen-Szalanski and Bushyhead (Chapter 16) used a large sample of real patients at an Army base clinic. The physicians' task was to estimate the probability that each patient had pneumonia. Echoing numerous laboratory studies, the physicians were hugely overconfident, giving their highest subjective probabilities (near certainly) to groups of patients of whom only 20% actually had pneumonia. They were, however, somewhat sensitive to the predictive value of the presence and absence of symptoms (in a task where there are many symptoms, most having small but real predictive value), and to the overall base rate of pneumonia (about 3% in this sample).

The chapter by McNeil, Pauker, Sox, and Tversky (Chapter 17) seems, at first glance, less realistic, but has worrying implications. It is a paper-and-pencil study of whether people's preferences for different treatments change when the treatments are described in different, but seemingly equivalent, ways – for example, as having a 90% survival rate versus a 10% mortality rate. The results suggest that these apparently trivial verbal changes do, in fact, elicit very different preferences for many people – including doctors as well as students and patients. The results are especially alarming in the context of the growing efforts to involve patients as active decision makers in their own treatment decisions. How does one best inform them about the choices they face? (The concern is reflected in the fact that this paper was published in the prestigious *New England Journal of Medicine*.)

The final chapter in this section, (by Getty, Pickett, D'Orsi, and Swets, Chapter 18), provides a fascinating glimpse of the perceptual judgments and decisions made by radiologists when they "read" X-ray film and other medical images. As Getty has noted elsewhere, "Radiologists bring impressive perceptual and cognitive skills to the task of reading and interpreting medical images. Nonetheless, there are several general and fundamental weaknesses in the way human observers read complex images and make diagnostic decisions based on what they see. As a result, the diagnostic accuracy realized in practice is almost always lower than that which could be achieved if these weaknesses were not present" (Getty, 1996:2). The large research project described by Getty et al. has led to significant improvements in the use of mammography to diagnose breast cancer. It could serve as a model for decision-aiding efforts in many areas. It also illustrates the power of the signal detection approach described earlier by Swets in Chapter 4.

### References

Getty, D. J. (1996). Assisting the radiologist to greater accuracy. *Proceedings of SPIE, 2708*, 2–15.

Goldberg, L. R. (1968). Simple models or simple processes? Some research on clinical judgments. *American Psychologist, 23,* 483–496.

Meehl, P. E. (1954). *Clinical versus statistical prediction: A theoretical analysis and a review of the evidence.* Minneapolis: University of Minnesota Press.

# 15    Capturing Policy in Hearing-Aid Decisions by Audiologists

*Janet Doyle and Shane A. Thomas*

In audiology the hearing-aid rehabilitation of hearing-impaired individuals is an ill-defined and complex task,[1] in which processes and outcomes may be suboptimal[2–7] and in the process of which the influence of audiologist behavior is almost unknown. The question of whether or not to recommend hearing aid(s) in a given case is a common decision problem for audiologists.[8] The present chapter describes research in which the social judgment theory approach to decision analysis was applied to this decision problem.

Social judgment theory (SJT) has been used in many fields to investigate the decision rules employed by expert decision makers.[9] The SJT approach is particularly relevant for the study of complex judgment and decision situations in which there is usually no unambiguously "correct" or optimal decision, and in which it is important to describe the behaviors of individual decision makers. Such decision situations are common in clinical settings.[10]

The focus of SJT is the description of how decision makers weight and combine informational cues in forming judgments. The policy-capturing techniques typical of the SJT approach to judgment analysis[11] rely on the assumption that all of the salient cues or predictors used by the judge(s) are known to the researcher and included in the cases presented to the judges for decision.[12,13] The identification of cues (cue elicitation) is thus a crucial part of policy capturing and analysis.[11,14]

The process of identifying salient cues typically comprises formal and/or informal interviews or surveys of persons familiar with the problem, who are asked to generate a list of possible cues and then assist with the selection of a subset of the most relevant of those cues.[11] The principal risk with this process is that it relies on verbal reports of the decision makers' interpretations of their cue use, rather than observation of the natural decision behavior. It is possible that important cues will be omitted, and/or distracting unimportant cues included, in the cue array.

This chapter originally appeared in *Medical Decision Making*, 1995, 15, 58–64. Copyright © 1995 by Hanley & Belfus, Inc. Reprinted by permission.

An additional problem with some policy-capturing studies is that the selection of cue values may proceed in a manner designed to satisfy experimental and statistical requirements (such as the minimization of cue intercorrelations), rather than to reflect naturally occurring cue values.[11] This practice runs counter to one of the theoretical underpinnings of SJT, that is, Brunswik's principle of representative design, which advocates that the cue combinations encountered by judges be representative of those found in the natural judgment environment.[15] When researching decision problems associated with complex natural clinical situations, the generalizability of findings concerning the judges' policies and cue utilization may be threatened if this principle is violated.

A further aspect of representative design is the experience of the judges with the decision task in question. Brehmer and Brehmer[16] argue that if a judge has no experience of making judgments associated with a particular decision task, then there may be no policy to capture. The corollary of this is that some policy-capturing studies may in fact investigate aspects of learning of a new "unrealistic" decision task, rather than natural decision behavior. This is particularly likely if students are used as judges.[17]

Much has also been written about the importance of task presentation in policy-capturing studies. Again, representativeness is desired in the format employed.[16,18,19] Dawes[18] described the interaction between the task demands and presentation and its underlying logical structure, and argued that performance on problem isomorphs is substantially affected by task presentation. Dawes made some interesting and still pertinent points concerning exactly what is being modeled in some decision research.

It follows that if high external validity in clinical decision research is to be achieved, particular attention must be paid to the four aspects of policy-capturing studies already mentioned: cue identification, the assignment of cue values to be used in the presented cases, the selection of judges representative of those who normally make such decisions, and the presentation and demands of the task. It is proposed that researchers who take care to address these issues will be rewarded by robust findings likely to represent the ways clinical practitioners behave in their natural environments. Further, the "problems of entangled task dimensions"[10] sometimes associated with ecological representativeness may be reduced by particular attention to the first step of cue identification. In other words, if the policy-capturing experiment in all aspects is designed with a high degree of representativeness, then an adequate degree of precision in statistical descriptions of policy will follow.

The present research aims to investigate cue use by clinical audiologists faced with the question of whether or not to recommend hearing-aid amplification. The initial phase of the present research was aimed at the identification of salient cues. The second phase of the research studied the decision policies of individual audiologists using the cues derived from the first study.

The cue values were selected with particular attention to naturally occurring values and to realistic combinations of cue values. The judges used were practicing audiologists, and the task presentation involved realistic stimuli.

## Study 1: Cue Identification

The process of cue identification began with observations of actual audiology practice. This strategy acknowledged that the cues available to clinicians depend on the activity of the clinicians[20] and that clinicians' self-reports of the cues they use are not necessarily accurate.[21]

### Method

*Subjects.* Subjects of the study were 10 audiologists who were employed full-time in Melbourne metropolitan government–funded hearing-aid clinics and who normally worked with adult clients. Such centers account for 80% of hearing-aid fittings in Australia.

*Procedures.* Fifty initial consultations, comprising a consecutive series of five consultations from each of the 10 audiologist subjects, were audiotaped and transcribed. The transcripts were examined to determine the items of information (cues) most frequently sought by the audiologists in the questions they asked and the types of assessment procedures carried out.

The 10 audiologists whose consultations were observed were also asked, in individual interviews conducted after the recording of their five consultations, "What information do you use when deciding whether or not to recommend hearing-aid fitting?" Their responses were transcribed verbatim and analyzed for cue content.

### Results

The audiologists' questions across the 50 consultations indicated four broad categories of information sought: (1) symptoms and causes of hearing loss (43% of total questions); (2) clients' potential ability to participate in testing and to manage hearing aids if fitted (12% of total questions); (3) clients' opinions and knowledge of hearing aids (26% of total questions); and (4) details of communication difficulties (19% of total questions). Study of these questions yielded six general informational cues that were relevant to the decision to recommend aiding. These cues are shown in the top box of Figure 15.1.

The assessment procedures carried out by the audiologists in the 50 consultations were noted, since the diagnostic information yielded was likely to contain cues significant to audiologists' decisions to recommend aiding. Apart from simple auroscopic inspection, the most common procedures were

CUES ELICITED FROM QUESTIONS ASKED IN CONSULTATION

**1**

Signs/symptoms of ear disease
Etiology of hearing loss
Manual dexterity
Client experience/knowledge of hearing aids
* Client report of listening difficulties
* Client attitude to aiding

CUES ELICITED FROM ASSESSMENT PROCEDURES

**2**

* Average pure-tone threshold sensitivity
Threshold sensitivity at 250 Hz
Threshold sensitivity at 500 Hz
Threshold sensitivity at 1,000 Hz
* Threshold sensitivity at 2,000 Hz
Threshold sensitivity at 4,000 Hz
Threshold sensitivity at 8,000 Hz
* Slope of threshold configuration
* Speech discrimination scores

CUES ELICITED FROM VERBAL REPORTS OF AUDIOLOGISTS

**3**

* Average pure-tone threshold sensitivity
* Threshold sensitivity at 2,000 Hz
* Slope of threshold configuration
* Speech discrimination scores
Most comfortable listening level
* Client report of listening difficulties
* Client attitude to aiding
Suitability for other devices
Client expectations

COMMON CUES

**4**

Cue 1 * Average pure-tone threshold sensitivity
Cue 2 * Threshold sensitivity at 2,000 Hz
Cue 3 * Slope of threshold configuration
Cue 4 * Speech discrimination scores
Cue 5 * Client report of listening difficulties
Cue 6 * Client attitude to aiding

Figure 15.1. Cue identification procedure.

air-conduction threshold audiometry [carried out in 49 (98%) of the 50 consultations] and some form of speech discrimination audiometry [performed in 43 (86%) of the 50 consultations]. These procedures yield a range of data relating to hearing sensitivity, type of hearing loss, and the effect of hearing loss on speech perception. The nine cues embedded in those data are shown in the second box of Figure 15.1.

The audiologists' responses to the interview question "What information do you use when deciding whether or not to recommend hearing-aid fitting?" were analyzed for mentions of specific cues. The third box in Figure 15.1 shows the nine cues most commonly mentioned.

The three lists of cues were then examined to determine which cues were reported by audiologists to be important (box 3, Figure 15.1) and also observed to be sought by them via questions (box 1) or audiometric procedures (box 2). This process of checking audiologists' reports against empirical elicitation evidence of their behaviors yielded a list of six cues (box 4 of Figure 15.1): (1) pure-tone sensitivity loss; (2) threshold at 2,000 Hz; (3) slope of hearing loss; (4) speech discrimination score; (5) client report of hearing difficulty; and (6) client attitude toward aiding.

It was hypothesized that these six cues would be most salient to the decision to recommend aiding, and that if this were so, it would be evidenced by the derivation of judgment policies from which classification of cases would be highly successful. This hypothesis was tested in study 2.

### Study 2: Cue Use

The six potentially salient cues identified in study 1 were employed in a policy-capturing experiment that addressed the yes/no decision task of recommending, or not recommending, hearing-aid amplification.

*Method*

*Subjects.* Sixteen practicing audiologists (eight male, eight female), participated in the experiment. The subjects were randomly selected from a variety of practice settings. No subject had participated in study 1 of this investigation.

*Selection of Cue Values for Potential Judgment Cases.* One hundred potential judgment cases were constructed using the six identified cues. The assignment of cue values was as follows. The representation of cues 1 (pure-tone sensitivity loss), 2 (threshold at 2,000 Hz), and 3 (slope of hearing loss) was achieved by taking audiograms from real clients in the Speech and Hearing Clinic of the School of Communication Disorders at La Trobe University and from the private practice of the senior author. These audiograms each contained naturally occurring values of these three cues. Cue 4 (speech discrimination score) was presented as a percentage correct score for each ear, as is usually recorded. The cue values for cue 4 were selected randomly, with the constraint that no score was less than 30% (since in reality such poor scores are very unusual) and that there was no more than 5% difference between ears (since the audiograms all showed essentially symmetrical losses and significant interaural discrimination ability would be unusual in such losses). The latter requirement was met by randomly selecting the score for one ear, then randomly selecting a second score until a value for the second ear within 5% of the first was obtained. Cue 5 (client report of hearing difficulty) and cue 6 (client attitude toward aiding) were each represented by statements reflecting one point on a five-point scale. The statements were typical of those seen in clinical reports. For example, values for cue 5 (client report of hearing difficulty) ranged from 1, "The client reports that he never experiences problems hearing," to 5, "The client is always aware of hearing difficulties, especially in background noise." Cue values for cues 5 and 6 were randomly selected for each case.

Values for cue 1 (pure-tone sensitivity loss) ranged from 0 to 70 (mean 30.49, SD 13.53). For cue 2 (threshold at 2,000 Hz), the range was 0 to 72.5 (mean 39.09, SD 16.49). Cue 3 (slope of hearing loss) had values ranging from −0.004 to 1.41 (mean 0.026, SD 0.168). Values for cue 4 (speech discrimination score) ranged from 41 to 100 (mean 79.8, SD 16.72). Cue 5 (client report of hearing difficulty) had values ranging from 1 to 5 (mean 3.33, SD 1.36). Cue 6 (client attitude toward aiding) had values ranging from 1 to 5 (mean 3.26, SD 1.35).

*Format.* Each of the 100 potential-judgment cases was presented in the form of a single sheet on which the data were displayed in a format typical of case notes. The format had been determined after study of typical record forms from three different audiology clinics.

*Realism Assessment of the Potential-judgment Cases.* The 100 cases constructed in the manner described above were then independently judged for realism by two audiologists, each with over 20 years of clinical experience. Of the original 100 cases, 30 were rejected in this process. Twelve cases were rejected by both audiologists as representing clearly unrealistic combinations of cues, and a further 18 cases were rejected because they were judged to be questionable by one or the other of the judges.

Cue values for the 70 cases that passed the realism assessment were analyzed for cue intercorrelations. In each case a single value for each cue was entered, this representing the mean values from left and right ears in the case of audiometric information. These intercorrelations are shown in Table 15.1. It can be seen that there was a high correlation between cues 1 and 2. These two cues are naturally intercorrelated because cue 2 (threshold at 2,000 Hz) is always included in the computation of cue 1 (pure-tone average). Since

Table 15.1. *Intercorrelation Matrix for Cues Used by 16 Audiologists in the Decision for or against Recommending a Hearing Aid*

|  | Cue | | | | | |
|---|---|---|---|---|---|---|
|  | *1* | *2* | *3* | *4* | *5* | *6* |
|  | Pure-tone Average | 2 kHz Threshold | Slope of Hearing Loss | Speech Discrimination Score | Client Report of Hearing Difficulty | Client Attitude toward Aiding |
| Pure-tone average |  |  |  |  |  |  |
| 2 kHz threshold | 0.795 |  |  |  |  |  |
| Slope of hearing loss | 0.040 | 0.014 |  |  |  |  |
| Speech discrimination score | 0.078 | 0.020 | −0.201 |  |  |  |
| Client report of hearing difficulty | 0.071 | 0.233 | 0.155 | −0.211 |  |  |
| Client attitude toward aiding | −0.220 | −0.257 | −0.108 | 0.095 | −0.189 |  |

the judgment task was designed with the aim of high fidelity, it was decided to proceed despite the fact that high cue intercorrelation is known to reduce the stability of statistical estimates in judgment analysis.[11] It was considered that this risk was balanced by the use of 70 cases. The distribution of the cue values of the 70 cases was then assessed by the same two experienced audiologists and judged to represent the natural distribution.

*Procedures.* Each subject participated in two judgment sessions. Two sessions were used to avoid possible fatigue effects and to allow for the assessment of test–retest reliability. In the first session, judgments of 40 cases were made. In a second session approximately one week later, the subjects provided judgments on the remaining 30 cases and on 10 repeated cases randomly selected from the set of 70. The same 10 repeated cases were used for each of the 16 subjects. The subjects were asked to record either a "yes" or a "no" response to the question: "Would you recommend hearing aid(s)?" in each case.

### Analysis and Results

*Discriminant-function Analysis.* Discriminant-function analysis[22–24] was employed to analyze the data, in order to determine the importance of each of the six cues to the yes-or-no hearing-aid judgment. Discriminant-function analysis was appropriate because of the categorical nature of the judgments required ("yes" or "no" hearing aid) and is formally equivalent to linear regression in this situation. For each audiologist, estimates of the standardized discriminant coefficients were calculated with the six cues as the discriminating variables and the yes/no hearing-aid recommendation as the criterion variable. The calculations were performed using SPSS.[25]

Table 15.2 shows the standardized discriminant function coefficients for the six cues for each audiologist. Nine of the audiologists used four cues at statistically significant levels and seven of them used three cues. This is consistent with previous findings that judges often use relatively small subsets of the available cues[11,16] and that the numbers typically vary between one and five cues.[16]

Examination of the audiologists' standardized discriminant function coefficients shows that of the six available cues, cue 2 (2-kHz threshold) was the most important discriminating variable for the recommendations of 9 of the 16 audiologists. Although the same four cues (pure-tone average, 2-kHz threshold, client report, and client attitude) tended to be more heavily weighted for all of the 16 judges, there was substantial individual variation in their weightings. For example, audiologist 11, who recommended aiding in 55 cases (79%) (Table 15.3) had a decision policy dominated by cue 2 (2-kHz threshold). In contrast, audiologist 12 had a decision policy in which cues 1 (pure-tone average), 2 (2-kHz threshold), and 6 (client attitude) interacted

Table 15.2. *Standardized Discriminant Function Coefficients for the Judgment Cues Used by 16 Audiologists in the Decision for or against Recommending a Hearing Aid*

| | Pure-tone Average | 2 kHz Threshold | Slope of Hearing Loss | Speech Discrimination Score | Client Report of Hearing Difficulty | Client Attitude toward Aiding |
|---|---|---|---|---|---|---|
| Audiologist 1 | 0.40573 | 0.39373 | 0.08212 | −0.03289 | 0.38748 | −0.53281 |
| Audiologist 2 | −0.42598 | −0.57532 | 0.02330 | 0.48327 | 0.11636 | 0.41898 |
| Audiologist 3 | 0.44732 | 0.45263 | 0.09631 | 0.07485 | −0.01130 | −0.64250 |
| Audiologist 4 | −0.11984 | 1.03781 | 0.06710 | −0.05794 | 0.02834 | −0.22561 |
| Audiologist 5 | 0.04020 | 0.83323 | 0.01949 | −0.18647 | 0.57289 | −0.08584 |
| Audiologist 6 | 0.19160 | 0.87474 | 0.10924 | −0.16406 | −0.08907 | −0.12914 |
| Audiologist 7 | 0.05142 | 0.48066 | −0.08496 | 0.12464 | 0.88089 | −0.34551 |
| Audiologist 8 | 0.07032 | 0.91362 | 0.05259 | −0.33148 | −0.08500 | −0.22129 |
| Audiologist 9 | −0.09846 | 0.93606 | 0.01689 | 0.03107 | 0.59053 | 0.16070 |
| Audiologist 10 | 0.21373 | −0.58749 | −0.01680 | 0.02001 | −0.16698 | 0.87141 |
| Audiologist 11 | −0.04677 | 0.97282 | 0.05971 | −0.06532 | 0.16111 | −0.22139 |
| Audiologist 12 | 1.48515 | −0.84557 | −0.28671 | −0.10670 | 0.18838 | −0.34628 |
| Audiologist 13 | −0.12367 | 0.95520 | −0.01013 | −0.14080 | 0.35265 | −0.35495 |
| Audiologist 14 | −0.32679 | 0.89558 | 0.01931 | −0.01569 | 0.37650 | −0.69859 |
| Audiologist 15 | 0.47770 | 0.02033 | −0.14068 | −0.30489 | 0.55652 | −0.60312 |
| Audiologist 16 | 0.59132 | 0.45346 | 0.17251 | 0.10975 | 0.35282 | 0.06977 |

Table 15.3. *Classification Results of Discriminant-function Analyses for 16 Audiologists' Decisions for and against Recommending Hearing Aids*

| | Classification Result (%) | Base Rate of Classifications[a] | |
|---|---|---|---|
| | | 0 | 1 |
| Audiologist 1 | 85.7 | 34 | 36 |
| Audiologist 2 | 87.4 | 17 | 53 |
| Audiologist 3 | 88.6 | 27 | 43 |
| Audiologist 4 | 95.7 | 12 | 58 |
| Audiologist 5 | 87.1 | 22 | 48 |
| Audiologist 6 | 94.3 | 21 | 49 |
| Audiologist 7 | 95.7 | 11 | 59 |
| Audiologist 8 | 94.3 | 23 | 47 |
| Audiologist 9 | 90.0 | 9 | 61 |
| Audiologist 10 | 84.3 | 24 | 46 |
| Audiologist 11 | 94.3 | 15 | 55 |
| Audiologist 12 | 91.4 | 55 | 15 |
| Audiologist 13 | 94.3 | 14 | 56 |
| Audiologist 14 | 88.6 | 24 | 46 |
| Audiologist 15 | 81.4 | 11 | 59 |
| Audiologist 16 | 85.7 | 33 | 37 |

[a] 0 = hearing aid not recommended; 1 = hearing aid recommended.

to result in only 15 (21%) recommendations for aiding. These individual differences have important implications for audiology practice.[26] Of primary interest here is the achievement of the classification functions in predicting the audiologists' hearing-aid recommendations.

*Classification Analysis.* In the classification process, the likely group membership of each case (i.e., hearing-aid group or no-hearing-aid group) is identified by the discriminant function derived from those cases, using each case's values on the discriminating cues. This predicted group membership is then compared with actual group membership (i.e., the group to which the audiologist judge assigned the case) to yield the proportion of correct classifications.[25] Table 15.3 shows the classification performances of the discriminant-function analyses for each audiologist. The correct-classification percentage performances ranged from 81.4% to 95.7% ($\bar{x} = 89.9\%$). These are remarkable given the wide variations in the base rates of the hearing-aid recommendations of the individual judges. The recommendation rates ranged from 21.4% to 87.1% ($\bar{x} = 68.6\%$). Each of the judges' derived equations demonstrated a statistically significant discriminating advantage over this base rate at the 0.05 level.

*Audiologist Reliability.* Intraaudiologist reliability was assessed by comparison of initial and second judgments for the 10 cases that were repeated. Reliabilities ranged from 0.75 to 0.96. Eleven of the 16 audiologists recorded the same judgments in at least 9 of the 10 repeat cases. Certain cases were common among audiologists who recorded different judgments in repeated cases. Across audiologists, initial and repeat judgments differed for 18 (11%) of 160 repeat cases (10 cases × 16 audiologists). In 17 of these instances the same six cases were involved, suggesting that these cases had particular characteristics that increased the difficulty of interpreting the available cues.

### General Discussion

The major findings in the research were:

1. With the rigorous protocol employed in the identification of the salient cues, the correct percentage classification rates for the hearing-aid-recommendation criterion variable for all judges were very high, with an average correct rate of 89.9%. In other words, the policy-capturing process achieved high model performance.
2. The high correct percentage classification rates were maintained even across judges with widely divergent base rates in their hearing-aid recommendations. These recommendation rates ranged from 21.4% to 87.1% and are indicative of considerable differences in the audiologists' decision behaviors. This represents substantial outcome differences if the same patients were to see different audiologists.
3. Examination of the standardized discriminant-weight profiles or policies of the judges reveals substantial individual differences in such weightings consistent with the large individual differences in aid-decision behaviors.
4. Most of the judges had high test–retest reliability in their decisions, but some judges showed variability in their aid decisions.

Thus, the judges were individualistic in their recommendations for hearing-aid fitting, individualistic in their application of weights in their policies although they used the same cues, and consistent in their hearing-aid recommendations for the same cases. In short, they were reliably idiosyncratic.

One of the notable features of this investigation is the rigorous cue-protocol elicitation. Rather than relying solely on clinician descriptions of salient cues, behavioral observations of actual clinician behaviors while making such decisions were employed. It is suggested that these procedures provide a useful means of cue elicitation that, in this instance, has been rewarded with powerful predictive models for individual clinicians' decision behaviors. An important aspect of the principle of representative design is the necessity for all the salient cues to be included in the task. Omission of such cues, as may occur without preliminary study of decision behavior in a real-world context, could lead to diminution in model predictive performance and biased estimates of cue weights. While there is substantial work involved in the approach to cue elicitation demonstrated here, we are convinced that this strategy is very useful in studies of clinical decision making. From the detailed observation of the real-world behaviors of a limited number of representative clinicians, it is possible to design judgment tasks that have the potential to capture clinicians' policies without sacrificing external validity.

From the perspective of clinical audiology practice, we make two additional points with regard to the present research findings. First, the varying judgment policies of the 16 audiologists in study 2 reflect the lack of a universally agreed-upon method for making the decision whether or not to recommend hearing-aid amplification to clients. Given that there is no obviously "correct" decision for the yes/no hearing-aid question (as there would be in many diagnostic decisions), the relative merits of audiologists' different judgment policies cannot easily be evaluated. The many possible reasons for audiologist differences in judgment policy include cognitive style, influence of practice setting, educational background, particular clinical experience, and various interactions among these factors. Whatever the reasons, the present findings suggest that individual audiologists reliably use cue information in manners consistent with their own representations of the problem, but these representations can differ to the extent that many clients may be unlikely to receive consistent advice from different audiologists. This situation requires further study of audiologist decisions in the light of client outcomes.

The second point in relation to clinical practice is that the present study addressed audiologist judgment for a common and fundamental decision that must be made in order for the audiologist to provide the client with a professional opinion. The research focused on audiologist thinking. Related issues (such as whether the client would follow the recommendation, or whether audiologist judgment would change following discussion of the recommendation with the client) were not addressed. These are questions that will be explored in planned investigations of decision making and client outcomes in natural clinical situations.

### References

1   Demorest ME. Problem solving: stages, strategies and stumbling blocks. J Acad Rehabil Audiol 1986;19:13–26.
2   Brooks DN. Use of post aural hearing aids by NHS patients. Br J Audiol 1981;15:79–86.

3   Brooks DN. Factors relating to the under-use of post aural hearing aids. Br J Audiol 1985;19:211–7.

4   Gates GA, Cooper JC, Kannel WB, Miller NB. Hearing in the elderly: the Framingham cohort 1983–1985. Ear Hear. 1990;11:247–56.

5   Gray-Thompson M, Richards S. A computer program for hearing aid selection: its trial and development. Aust J Audiol. 1987;9:19–23.

6   Upfold LJ, Wilson DA. Hearing aid distribution and use in Australia: the Australian Bureau of Statistics 1978 survey. Aust J Audiol. 1980;2:31–6.

7   Upfold LJ, Smither MF. Hearing aid fitting protocol. Br J Audiol. 1981;15:181–8.

8   Doyle J. A survey of Australian audiologists' clinical decision-making. Aust J Audiol. 1989;11:75–88.

9   Hammond KR, Stewart TR, Brehmer B, Steinmann DO. Social judgment theory. In Arkes HR, Hammond KR (eds). Judgment and Decision Making: An interdisciplinary Reader. New York: Cambridge University Press, 1986, pp 56–76.

10  Cooksey RW. Social judgment theory in education: current and potential applications. In Brehmer B, Joyce CRB (eds). Human Judgment: The SJT View. Amsterdam: North-Holland, 1988, 273–315.

11  Stewart TR. Judgment analysis procedures. In Brehmer B, Joyce CRB (eds). Human Judgment: The SJT View. Amsterdam: North Holland, 1988, pp 41–74.

12  Elstein AS, Holmes MM, Ravitich MM, Rovner DR, Holtzman GB, Rothbert ML. Medical decisions in perception: applied research in cognitive psychology. Perspect Biol Med. 1983;26:486–501.

13  Schwartz S, Griffin T. Medical Thinking: The Psychology of Medical Judgment and Decision-making. New York: Springer-Verlag, 1986.

14  Hammond KR, Joyce CRB (eds). Psychoactive Drugs and Social Judgments. New York: Wiley Interscience, 1975.

15  Brunswik E. Perception and the Representative Design of Psychological Experiments. Berkeley, CA: University of California Press, 1956.

16  Brehmer A, Brehmer B. What have we learnt about human judgment from thirty years of policy capturing? In Brehmer B, Joyce CRB (eds). Human Judgment: The SJT View. Amsterdam: North-Holland, 1988, pp 75–114.

17  Thomas SA, Doyle J, Browning C. Clinical decision making: what do we know about real world performance? In Loke WH (ed). Judgment and Decision Making. Chicago: Scarecrow Press, 1994.

18  Dawes RM. The mind, the model and the task. In Restle F, Shiffrin RM, Castellan NJ, Lindman HR, Pisoni DB (eds). Cognitive Theory, vol. 1. Hillsdale. NJ: Lawrence Erlbaum Associates, 1975, pp 119–29.

19  Hayes JR, Simon HA. Psychological differences among problem isomorphs. In Castellan NJ, Pisoni DB, Potts GR (eds). Cognitive Theory, vol. 2. Hillsdale, NJ: Lawrence Erlbaum Associates, 1977, pp 21–41.

20  Brehmer B. The development of social judgment theory. In Brehmer B, Joyce CRB (eds). Human Judgment: The SJT View. Amsterdam: North-Holland, 1988, pp 13–40.

21  Wigton RS. Applications of judgment analysis and cognitive feedback to medicine. In Brehmer B, Joyce CRB (eds). Human Judgment: The SJT View. Amsterdam: North-Holland, 1988, 227–245.

22  Kerlinger FN, Pedhazur EJ. Multiple Regression in Behavioral Research. New York: Holt Rinechart Winston, 1973.

23  Schuerman JR. Multivariate Analysis in the Human Services. Boston: Kluwer-Nijhoff, 1983.

24    Tatsuska MM. Multivariate Analysis: Techniques for Educational and Psychological Research. New York: John Wiley & Sons, 1971.
25    SPSS Inc. SPSS-X User's Guide, 3rd ed. Chicago: SPSS, 1988.
26    Doyle J. Audiologists' decisions about hearing aid candidacy: charters and chatters. Presented at the 10th National Conference of the Audiological Society of Australia, Barossa Valley, S. A., May 1–3, 1992. (Available from the Audiological Society of Australia, C/ – National Acoustics Laboratories, 126 Greville Street, Chatswood, NSW 2067.)

# 16    Physicians' Use of Probabilistic Information in a Real Clinical Setting

*Jay J. J. Christensen-Szalanski and James B. Bushyhead*

Past researchers have identified biased heuristics that people use when processing probabilistic information in a laboratory setting (Fischhoff, 1975; Kahneman & Tversky, 1972; Lichtenstein, Fischhoff, & Phillips, 1977; Tversky & Kahneman, 1974). These biases are commonly assumed to be inherent in a person's information-processing abilities. However, articles by Slovic on stockbrokers (1969), Murphy and Winkler on weather forecasters (1974), Ebbesen and Konečni on court judges (1975), and Phelps and Shanteau on livestock judges (1978) have suggested that experts in a real-life setting are often not subject to the same cognitive limitations found in laboratory studies. This investigation studied a group of physicians managing possible pneumonia patients in an outpatient clinic. It examined their methods of using probabilistic information when estimating a patient's probability of pneumonia and a symptom's diagnostic value.

## General Method

### Participants

Nine physicians participated in this study. Each physician was either board-eligible or board-certified in internal or adolescent medicine. Board-eligible physicians have completed specialized training beyond medical school. Board-certified physicians are board-eligible and have passed a national certification board examination.

### Procedure

*Clinical Information Available to Physicians.* To standardize the type of information obtained from different patients over the course of the study, research

This chapter first appeared in *Journal of Experimental Psychology: Human Perception and Performance*, 7 (1981), 928–35. © 1981 American Psychological Association Inc. Reprinted by permission.

assistants used a checklist to collect a standard medical history from each patient. The physicians then completed the checklist to obtain the predefined physical examination and reviewed the historical data, supplementing it with their own questions when they saw fit. The physicians examined 1,531 first-time patients with a cough of less than 1 mo. duration at the walk-in clinic at Brooke Army Medical Center in San Antonio, Texas. The majority of patients were either retired military personnel, their dependents, or dependents of active service members. Each patient was examined by only one physician.

*Assignment of Pneumonia Probability.* After completing the history and physical examination, physicians were required to estimate the probability that the patient had pneumonia. Probability estimates were made on a scale that ranged from 0 (certain that the patient does not have pneumonia) to 100 (certain that the patient does have pneumonia) for all patients in the study. Because the patients could have diseases other than pneumonia, an assigned probability of pneumonia of $p = .00$ does not necessarily imply that the physician was certain that the patient was well. It could also mean that the physician was certain that the patient had a disease other than pneumonia. Probability estimates were made without knowledge of chest X-ray results.

*Assignment of Pneumonia Status.* Because most physicians consider the chest X-ray to be the definitive test for pneumonia, chest X-rays were taken of all patients in the study. Radiologists then examined each patient's X-ray and decided whether the patient had pneumonia. The radiologist made the diagnosis without knowledge of the patient's history and physical findings (except that all patients had an acute cough) or the examining physician's probability estimates.

### Experiment 1

*Validity of Probability Estimates*

Although the physician's ability to estimate probability may be important for correct patient management (Elstein, Shulman, & Sprafka, 1978; Christensen-Szalanski & Bushyhead, Note 1), there are no published studies that report on the validity of physicians' probability estimates. "Degree of calibration" is a frequently used measure of validity in the psychological and meteorological literature (Lichtenstein & Fischhoff, 1977; Lichtenstein et al., 1977; Murphy & Winkler, 1974): It indicates the ability to evaluate a *set* of probability estimates. A physician would be considered to be "perfectly calibrated" if he or she assigned a pneumonia probability of $N$ to patients of whom $N\%$ really did have pneumonia.

Lichtenstein et al. (1977) have reviewed the experimental calibration literature. They found that people normally either overestimate how much they know or overestimate how often an event will occur. However, participants in the studies they reviewed were usually required to answer two-alternative multiple choice questions and indicate their confidence in the selected alternative. (E.g., What is absinthe? (a) a liqueur; (b) a precious stone.) Participants in this task probably judged the cost of selecting alternative (a) and being wrong as equal to the cost of selecting alternative (b) and being wrong; The payoff matrix was the same regardless of the alternative they selected (Lichtenstein et al., 1977). Physicians in a clinical setting might be using a different payoff matrix – one that assigns a greater cost to a false negative diagnosis than to a false positive diagnosis (Scheff, 1963).

This study reports on physician's degree of calibration when judging a patient's probability of pneumonia and the payoff matrix associated with the physicians' decision to assign a pneumonia diagnosis.

### Method

*Obtaining a Calibration Curve.* The calibration curve was constructed by the common process of first grouping (across physicians) the probability estimates into probability ranges to ensure stability of the calibration estimates (Lichtenstein & Fischhoff, 1977). Six ranges were used for this study (0%, 1%–20%, 21%–40%, 41%–60%, 61%–80%, 81%–100%). The mean assigned probability for each range was plotted against the percentage of radiographically diagnosed pneumonia cases within each range to yield the calibration curve.

*Obtaining Personal Outcome Values.* Several months after all the patients were examined, physicians received a questionnaire that listed the possible outcomes for the pneumonia diagnosis decision: (a) Assign a pneumonia diagnosis to a patient who does have pneumonia. (b) Assign a pneumonia diagnosis to a patient who does not have pneumonia. (c) Assign a nonpneumonia diagnosis to a patient who does have pneumonia. (d) Assign a nonpneumonia diagnosis to a patient who does not have pneumonia. Physicians were asked to assign a value rating for each outcome using a balanced scale that ranged from −50 (worst thing I could do) to +50 (best thing I could do). All questionnaires were completed anonymously and sent to the experimenter by mail. One physician who was transferred to another Army base before the questionnaire was sent left no forwarding address. Therefore, the value data are based on eight physicians' responses.

### Results

*Physicians' Calibration.* Previous research on the physicians participating in this study (Christensen-Szalanski & Bushyhead, Note 1) showed that their

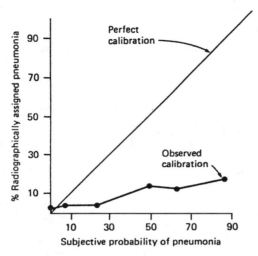

Figure 16.1. Relationship between physicians' subjective probability of pneumonia and the actual probability of pneumonia.

subjective probability estimate of a patient having pneumonia was significantly correlated with their decision to give a patient a diagnostic chest X-ray ($r = .99$, $p < .05$) and to assign a pneumonia diagnosis ($r = .99$, $p < .05$). This suggests that physicians have internally valid probability estimates. The present study, however, suggests that physicians' probability estimates are not externally valid. The observed physicians' calibration is compared with perfect calibration in Figure 16.1. A binomial test was used to compare the percentage of diagnosed pneumonia cases for each probability range to the percentage expected for perfect calibration. For each probability range greater than zero, the observed number of pneumonia diagnoses was significantly less than that expected if physicians were perfectly calibrated ($p < .001$). Thus, physicians expressed an overestimation bias when assigning the probability that a patient had pneumonia.

*Payoff Matrix of Pneumonia Diagnosis Decision.* The physicians' mean values reported for the possible outcomes of a pneumonia diagnosis decision are shown in Figure 16.2. Two Wilcoxon signed rank tests were used to compare the values assigned to the different outcomes for each physician. There was no difference between the physicians' values for a correct pneumonia diagnosis and a correct nonpneumonia diagnosis ($T = 13$, $z = 1.43$, $p > .15$). Nor was there a difference between the values for an incorrect pneumonia diagnosis and an incorrect nonpneumonia diagnosis ($T = 17$, $z = .14$, $p > .80$). These data suggest that in this setting the payoff matrix was the same for the two diagnoses. By implication, the overestimation bias is cognitive and not motivational.

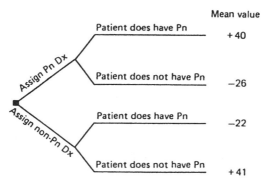

Figure 16.2. Physicians' mean values for outcomes of pneumonia diagnosis (Pn Dx) decision.

## Experiment 2

*Base Rate Information and the Absence of a Cue*

Medical schools teach students the frequency of symptoms or test results, given a particular disease. In practice, however, the opposite relationship is more important: How frequent is the disease, given a symptom or test result? For example, suppose the physician was informed of the following hypothetical relationship: Ninety percent of all patients who have pneumonia have chills. Ninety percent of all patients who do not have pneumonia do not have chills.

A patient with chills entering the physician's office does not necessarily have a 90 percent chance of having pneumonia. Suppose 70 percent of the patients who visit a certain clinic have pneumonia. A physician seeing patients in that setting should be more than 95 percent certain that a patient with chills has pneumonia. However, if only .1 percent of the patients who visit another clinic have pneumonia, a physician seeing patients in the second clinic setting should recognize that there is not a 95 percent chance but less than a 1 percent chance that a patient with chills has pneumonia.

The symptom, patient, and physician are identical in the two settings. The difference in the posterior probabilities is caused by the different prior probabilities or base rates of pneumonia in the two patient populations. This result can be explained by using Bayes' Theorem as given below (also see Table 16.1):

$$\frac{P(\text{Pn}|\text{Chills})}{P(\text{No Pn}|\text{Chills})} = \frac{P(\text{Chills}|\text{Pn})}{P(\text{Chills}|\text{No Pn})} \times \frac{P(\text{Pn})}{P(\text{No Pn})}. \tag{1}$$

These calculations can be simplified if we substitute, $a$, $b$, $c$, $d$, and $N$ from Table 16.1(A) into the equation where $a$, $b$, $c$, and $d$ correspond to the number

Table 16.1. *Hypothetical Relationship between Chills and Pneumonia*

| Pneumonia | A. Prior $P(\text{Pn}) = (a+b)/N$ | | | B. Prior $P(\text{Pn}) = .70^a$ | | | C. Prior $P(\text{Pn}) = .001^b$ | | |
|---|---|---|---|---|---|---|---|---|---|
| | Chills | | | Chills | | | Chills | | |
| | Present | Absent | Total | Present | Absent | Total | Present | Absent | Total |
| Present | $a$ | $b$ | $a+b$ | 6,300 | 700 | 7,000 | 9 | 1 | 10 |
| Absent | $c$ | $d$ | $c+d$ | 300 | 2,700 | 3,000 | 999 | 8,991 | 9,990 |
| Total | $a+c$ | $b+d$ | $N$ | 6,600 | 3,400 | 10,000 | 1,008 | 8,992 | 10,000 |

Prior probability of pneumonia is (A) unspecified, (B) equal to $p = .70$, and (C) equal to $p = .001$.
[a] $P(\text{Pn}|\text{Chills present}) = a/(a+c) = 6300/6600 = .955$.
[b] $P(\text{Pn}|\text{Chills present}) = a/(a+c) = 9/1008 = .009$.

of patients in each cell and $N$ corresponds to the total number of patients in the study population.

$$\frac{P(\text{Pn}|\text{Chills})}{P(\text{No Pn}|\text{Chills})} = \frac{\frac{a}{a+b}}{\frac{c}{c+d}} \times \frac{\frac{a+b}{N}}{\frac{c+d}{N}}, \tag{2}$$

and therefore:

$$P(\text{Pn}|\text{Chills}) = \frac{a}{a+c}. \tag{3}$$

The quantity $a/(a+c)$ is the posterior probability that a patient with chills has pneumonia. This quantity is referred to in the medical literature as the predictive value of chills for identifying pneumonia. Table 16.1(B) and (C) shows the calculations for the predictive value of chills for the two prior probabilities of pneumonia given in the above examples.

Although it is important that the physician be sensitive to the base rate or prevalence of a disease to use diagnostic information correctly, recent psychological research suggests that people in general, including trained statisticians, ignore base-rate probabilities when presented with diagnostic information if they rely on intuition rather than calculation (Bar-Hillel, 1980; Hammerton, 1973; Lyon & Slovic, 1976; Tversky & Kahneman, 1974). Participants in these laboratory studies were assumed to be unable to use base-rate information because of the posterior probability estimates they made in response to pencil-and-paper word problems that presented the base-rate information in a very explicit quantitative format. This study examined physicians' ability to estimate posterior probabilities and the predictive value of information when the physicians must obtain the pneumonia base-rate information from *their experience* in a clinical setting.

This study also examined the physicians' ability to estimate the predictive value of an "absent symptom," since the absence of a symptom also can be helpful in assigning a diagnosis. Past psychological research has suggested that people do not efficiently process the "absence of cues" (Bourne & Guy, 1968; Hovland & Weiss, 1953; Nahinsky & Slaymaker, 1970). Thus we expected that physicians would not be able to use the absence of symptoms as efficiently as the presence of symptoms.

### Method

*Present and Absent Symptoms.* The 117 symptoms that were present in at least 1% of the patient population were considered to be cues that were available to the physician.

*Actual Predictive Value of the Information.* For each of the 117 symptoms a $2 \times 2$ contingency table, similar to Table 16.1(A) was constructed relating the presence of the symptom with the presence of radiographically diagnosed pneumonia. Using these contingency tables, the predictive value of the presence of each symptom (i.e., $P(\text{Pn}|\text{Symptom Present})$) was determined by calculating the ratio $a/(a+c)$. The predictive value of the absence of each symptom (i.e., $P(\text{Pn}|\text{Symptom Absent})$) was determined by calculating the ratio $b/(b+d)$.

*Physicians' Estimate of the Predictive Value of the Information.* The physician's estimate of the predictive value of the presence of a symptom was determined by calculating the mean probability of pneumonia assigned to patients with that symptom. Conversely, the physicans' estimate of the predictive value of the absence of a symptom was determined by calculating the mean probability of pneumonia assigned to patients without that symptom.

### Results

*Physicians' Sensitivity to the Predictive Value of Symptoms When Present.* For each symptom, the physicians' estimate of the predictive value of the observation of a "present" symptom was plotted against the actual predictive value of the symptom when present (see Figure 16.3). Figure 16.3 reveals the relatively poor predictive value of any single symptom at identifying pneumonia. This is largely a result of the low prior probability of pneumonia in the present clinical setting (3 cases per 100 patients). A least squared regression line of a symptom's actual predictive value on its estimated predictive value is also shown in Figure 16.3. The significantly positive slope, $s_b = .106, t(115) = 7.61, p < .001$, suggests that physicians may be sensitive to relative differences in the predictive value of symptoms when present. A slope of less than 1.0, $t(115) = 1.79, p = .08$, however, implies that this sensitivity may not be perfect. The constant in the regression equation is also significantly greater than 0, $s_c = .463, t(115) = 12.6, p < .001$.

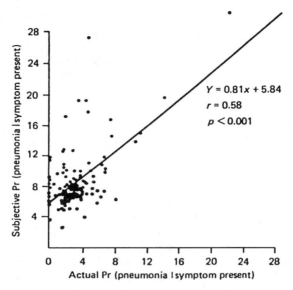

Figure 16.3. Relationship between actual predictive value (Pr) of symptoms when present and physicians' estimated predictive value.

*Physicians' Sensitivity to the Predictive Value of Symptoms When Absent.* The physicians' estimate of the predictive value of the observation of an "absent symptom" was plotted against the actual predictive value of the symptom when absent (see Figure 16.4). The results are similar to the analysis of physicians' use of the predictive value of abnormal findings: Analysis yields a regression coefficient significantly greater than 0, $s_b = .077$, $t(115) = 5.44$, $p < .001$, and less than 1.0, $t(115) = 7.57$, $p < .001$, and a constant term significantly greater than 0, $s_c = .203$, $t(115) = 25.6$, $p < .001$.

The obtained regression coefficient for the physicians' sensitivity to absent symptoms was smaller than that for present symptoms. This result agrees with the previously cited experimental research that decision makers cannot process the absence of cues as efficiently as the presence of cues. There are two reasons, however, why the difference in the obtained regression coefficients in the present study may be artificial. First, an examination of Figure 16.4 reveals that the absent symptom regression is "weighted down" by a single outlier corresponding to rhinorea (or runny nose), the presence of which may be more suggestive of a common cold than of pneumonia. If this single outlier is eliminated from the regression calculations, the resulting regression equation is $Y = .71X + 4.45$ ($r = 0.60$, $p < .001$). The new regression coefficient for the absent-symptom equation is nearly identical to that for the present-symptom equation, $s_{b_1-b_2} = .600$, $t(113) = .16$, $p > .80$. Second, even without eliminating any outliers, a t-test comparison of the two original regression coefficients fails to detect any significant difference, $s_{b_1-b_2} = .458$, $t(113) = .85$,

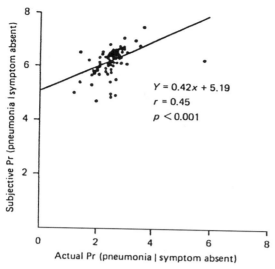

Figure 16.4. Relationship between actual predictive value (Pr) of symptoms when absent and physicians' estimated predictive value.

$p < .40$. Thus, physicians in this study appear to use the absence of a clinical finding as efficiently as the presence of a clinical finding when estimating the predictive value of the finding.

### General Discussion

This study analyzed a decision maker's ability to make judgments in a real-life setting that posed problems of genuine value for the decision maker. Decision makers in this setting might be expected to process information differently from participants in some laboratory settings because the decision makers, as experts, are more experienced with the stimuli and tasks and thus may be better able to avoid cognitive limitations (Slovic, 1969) or because more valuable, real-life problems motivate the decision maker to devote more time and energy to using more accurate problem-solving strategies (Beach & Mitchell, 1978; Christensen-Szalanski, 1978, 1980). Given this expectation, several observations of these two experiments merit further discussion.

#### Overestimation of Pneumonia Probability

The payoff matrix for various kinds of correct and incorrect diagnoses can not account for the overestimation of pneumonia probability. Although it is possible that the questionnaire did not reflect the value matrix that physicians use when estimating pneumonia probability, the estimation of probabilities theoretically should not depend upon the payoff matrix. Utility theory presupposes that the assignment of probabilities and values to the outcomes of a decision are independent processes: Only the actual decision is dependent upon the value matrix (Raiffa, 1968). Even if physicians did consider it better to assign a pneumonia diagnosis to a nonpneumonia patient than vice versa, they should not be motivated to overestimate the probability of pneumonia. Instead they should overassign a pneumonia diagnosis because the payoff matrix dictates a lower threshold probability (Swets, 1964) for the assignment of a pneumonia diagnosis.

Since the decision maker expresses the overestimation bias in a setting that should encourage the use of accurate information-processing strategies, it is unlikely that this bias is a result of the decision maker using inaccurate strategies. Interestingly, the two regression analyses of Experiment 2, with slopes less than 1.0 and constants greater than zero, imply that physicians underestimate the relative differences in the predictive values of the symptoms, but when processing the information they add a relatively large positive constant, which results in overestimation of a symptom's diagnostic value. The limited range of the results in Figures 16.3 and 16.4 makes the interpretation of these regression analyses difficult to generalize. However, perhaps in the present setting the constant that contributes to the overestimation is the physicians' perception that a person entering a clinic is sick until shown to be well.

### Use of the Absence of Information

In the present study, physicians appeared to be equally sensitive to relative changes in the predictive value of the presence and the absence of clinical findings. It is possible that physicians were using a more accurate strategy to process the absence of a cue than the usually untrained participants of psychology experiments. Another possible explanation for these results, however, is that the physicians' judgment was aided by the procedure of this study.

Hulse, Deese, and Egeth (1975, p. 269) reported that helping people to attend to the absence of cues can increase their use of the information. The procedure in this study required physicians to fill in a predefined checklist of signs and symptoms when examining patients. By using this checklist to guide their examination of the patients, physicians were required to attend to symptoms that were absent as well as to those present. Perhaps it was this increased attention that aided the physicians to use the absent-cue information. This interpretation is inconsistent with a study by de Dombal, Leaper, Horrocks, Staniland, and McCann (1974) that suggests that physicians' performance when examining patients with abdominal pain can be improved by the use of a checklist.

The design and results of the present study do not support one of these explanations over another, since the realism of the study reduced the experimenters' control of the presence of correlated symptoms. For example, if the absence of symptom $X$ always occurred with the presence of important symptom $Y$, perhaps physicians' apparent "use" of the absent symptom was simply an artifact due to this correlation. A more controlled experiment is needed to support these results before a checklist of symptoms can be recommended as an aid to the physician's judgment process.

### Use of Base-rate Information

Since base-rate information is necessary to calculate predictive value, the significant positive correlation between a symptom's actual predictive value for pneumonia and that obtained from the physician's estimate of a patient's probability of pneumonia suggests that physicians do use base-rate information. These results may not be surprising to any one who has heard his or her physician say, "You probably have ——. There's a lot of that going around now." Such a statement implies the use of base-rate information. The results of the present study, however, contradict earlier conclusions that people cannot use base-rate information.

A possible explanation for this contradiction may be that the previously reported psychology studies, which tested the participants' ability to use base-rate information when presented in quantitative word problems, did not test ability to use base-rate information obtained *from experience*. Although physicians in the present study appeared to use base-rate information, comparably trained physicians were unable to use base-rate information when it was presented quantitatively in a pencil-and-paper problem (Casscells, Schoenberger, & Graboys, 1978). The experience of a 3% base rate is more salient and thus may be easier for physicians to intuitively incorporate into their judgment processes than reading a sentence that states the base rate is 3%. Additionally, several studies have suggested that the salience of the base-rate information can mediate the participant's ability to use the information: (a) Presenting only base-rate information in the word problem (Kahneman & Tversky, 1973); (b) making the base-rate information causally related to the problem outcome (Tversky & Kahneman, 1980); and (c) repeatedly presenting to a participant copies of a specific word problem that are identical except for the base-rate (Fischhoff, Slovic, & Lichtenstein, 1979) all improved the participant's ability to use base-rate information.

## Conclusion

The present study examined physicians' decision making in a real clinical setting. Physicians overestimated the patient's probability of pneumonia but were sensitive to relative differences in the predictive value of symptoms when present and absent, and appeared to use base-rate information correctly when making clinical judgments.

The realism of the study reduced the experimenters' control over the presence of correlated symptoms and the frequency of the pneumonia base rate and therefore limits the strength of these conclusions. Nevertheless, this study also identified several unanswered research questions: (a) Do physicians underestimate the predictive value of a clinical finding but overestimate a patient's probability of pneumonia because of a perception that people entering a clinic are ill until proven well? (b) Can information processing be improved by using a checklist of symptoms when examining patients? (c) Can the experience of base-rate information enable a decision maker to use base-rate information? Although experimental settings may be needed to answer these questions, the results of the present study reaffirm the need for caution in generalizing from the laboratory setting to real-life decisions without investigating the real-life setting.

### Note

1   Christensen-Szalanski, J. J. J., & Bushyhead, J. B. *Decision analysis as a model of physician decision making* (Tech. Rep. 79–45). Department of Health Services Research, U.S. Public Health Service Hospital, Seattle, Washington, August 1979.

### References

Bar-Hillel, M. The base rate fallacy in probability judgments. *Acta Psychologica*, 1980, *44*, 211–233.

Beach, L. R., & Mitchell, T. R. A contingency model for the selection of decision strategies. *Academy Management Review*, 1978, *3*, 439–449.

Bourne, L. E., Jr., & Guy, D. E. Learning conceptual rules: II. The role of positive and negative instances. *Journal of Experimental Psychology*, 1968, *77*, 488–494.

Casscells, B. S., Schoenberger, A., & Graboys, T. B. Interpretation by physicians of clinical laboratory results. *New England Journal of Medicine*, 1978, *299*, 999–1000.

Christensen-Szalanski, J. J. J. Problem solving strategies: A selection mechanism, some implications, and some data. *Organizational Behavior and Human Performance*, 1978, *22*, 307–323.

Christensen-Szalanski, J. J. J. A further examination of the selection of problem solving strategies: The effects of deadlines and analytic aptitudes. *Organizational Behavior and Human Performance*, 1980, *25*, 107–122.

de Dombal, F. T., Leaper, D. J., Horrocks, J. C., Staniland, J. R., & McCann, A. P. Human and computer-aided diagnosis of abdominal pain: Further report with emphasis on performance of clinicians. *British Medical Journal*, 1974, *1*, 376–380.

Ebbesen, E. B. & Konečni, V. J. Decision making and information integration in the courts: The setting of bail. *Journal of Personality and Social Psychology*, 1975, *32*, 805–821.

Elstein, A. S., Shulman, L. S., & Sprafka, S. A. *Medical problem solving: An analysis of clinical reasoning*. Cambridge, Mass.: Harvard University Press, 1978.

Fischhoff, B. Hindsight ≠ foresight: The effect of outcome knowledge on judgment under uncertainty. *Journal of Experimental Psychology: Human Perception and Performance*, *1*, 288–299.

Fischhoff, B., Slovic, P., & Lichtenstein, S. Subjective sensitivity analysis. *Organizational Behavior and Human Performance*, 1979, *23*, 339–359.

Hammerton, M. A case of radical probability estimation. *Journal of Experimental Psychology*, 1973, *101*, 242–254.

Hovland, C. I., & Weiss, W. Transmission of information concerning concepts through positive and negative instances. *Journal of Experimental Psychology*, 1953, *43*, 175–182.

Hulse, S. H., Deese, J., & Egeth, H. *The psychology of learning* (4th ed.). New York: McGraw-Hill, 1975.

Kahneman, D., & Tversky, A. Subjective probability: A judgment of representativeness. *Cognitive Psychology*, 1972, *3*, 430–454.

Kahneman, D., & Tversky, A. On the psychology of prediction. *Psychology Review*, 1973, *80*, 237–251.

Lichtenstein, S., & Fischhoff, B. Do those who know more also know more about how much they know? The calibration of probability judgments. *Organizational Behavior and Human Performance*, 1977, *20*, 159–183.

Lichtenstein, S., Fischhoff, B., & Phillips, L. D. Calibration of probabilities: The state of the art. In H. Jungemann & D. deZeeuw (Eds.), *Decision making and change in human affairs*. Amsterdam: D. Reidel, 1977.

Lyon, D., & Slovic, P. Dominance of accuracy information and neglect of base rates in probability estimation. *Acta Psychologica*, 1976, *40*, 287–298.

Murphy, A. H., & Winkler, R. L. Subjective probability forecasting experiments in meteorology: Some preliminary results. *Bulletin of the American Meteorological Society*, 1974, *55*, 1206–1216.

Nahinsky, I. D., & Slaymaker, F. L. Use of negative instances in conjunctive concept identification. *Journal of Experimental Psychology*, 1970, *84*, 64–84.

Phelps, R. H., & Shanteau, J. Livestock judges: How much information can an expert use? *Organizational Behavior and Human Performance*, 1978, *21*, 209–219.

Raiffa, H. *Decision analysis: Introductory lectures on choices under uncertainty*. Reading, Mass.: Addison-Wesley, 1968.

Scheff, T. J. Decision rules and types of error, and their consequences in medical diagnosis. *Behavioral Science*, 1963, *8*, 97–107.

Slovic, P. Analyzing the expert judge: A descriptive study of a stockbroker's decision process. *Journal of Applied Psychology*, 1969, *53*, 255–263.

Swets, J. A. (Ed.). *Signal detection and recognition by human observers*. New York: Wiley, 1964.

Tversky, A., & Kahneman, D. Judgment under uncertainty: Heuristics and biases. *Science*, 1974, *185*, 1124–1131.

Tversky, A., & Kahneman, D. Causal schemata in judgment under uncertainty. In M. Fishbein (Ed.), *Progress in social psychology*. Hillsdale, N.J.: Erlbaum, 1980.

# 17    On the Elicitation of Preferences
for Alternative Therapies

*Barbara J. McNeil, Stephen G. Pauker,*
*Harold C. Sox, Jr., and Amos Tversky*

There is a growing appreciation in the general public and the medical profession of the need to incorporate patients' preferences into medical decision
making. To achieve this goal, the physician must provide the patient with
data about the possible outcomes of the available therapies, and the patient
must be able to comprehend and use these data. In this chapter we investigate how people use statistical information regarding the possible outcomes
of alternative therapies. We have focused on a particular medical problem
(operable lung cancer) and asked the participants to choose between surgery
and radiation therapy on the basis of simple descriptions of their possible
consequences. Four variables were investigated: the input data presented to
the subjects (life expectancy or cumulative probability), the characterization
or framing of the outcomes (in terms of mortality or in terms of survival),
the identification of the treatments (surgery or radiation therapy vs. unidentified treatments labeled "A" and "B"), and the population of respondents
(physicians, patients, and graduate students).

## Methods

### The Clinical Problem

Lung cancer was selected for study because it offers a clear-cut choice
between two alternative therapies – irradiation and surgery – that yield different patterns of survival probabilities. A previous study of this problem, using a formal decision-analytic approach (Raiffa, 1968; Keeney & Raiffa, 1976),
found that an appreciable number of patients preferred radiation therapy to
surgery despite the lower long-term survival associated with radiation therapy (McNeil, Weichselbaum, & Pauker, 1978), presumably because it does
not involve the risk of perioperative death.

This chapter originally appeared in the *New England Journal of Medicine*, 1982, *306*, 1259–1262.
Copyright © 1982 by the Massachusetts Medical Society. Reprinted by permission.

As in the previous study on lung cancer, we used data reported by Mountain and his colleagues on the results of surgery (Mountain, 1976; Mountain, Carr, & Anderson, 1974) and data reported by Hilton (1960) on the results of radiation therapy for operable lung cancer. These reports and others indicate that for 60-year-old patients treated with surgery the average operative mortality rate is 10%, and the average five-year survival rate is about 34%. The survival rates at one, two, three, and four years are 68, 51, 40, and 35%, respectively. For radiation therapy there is essentially no treatment mortality, and the five-year survival rate is 22%; survival rates at one, two, three, and four years are 77, 44, 28, and 23%, respectively. Other data from the National Cancer Institute on the excess risk of death from lung cancer and on age-specific annual mortality rates were used to adjust the survival data to other age groups (Axtell, Cutler, & Myers, 1972). The comparison of the two treatments shows that surgery offers better long-term prospects at the cost of a greater immediate risk.

### Input Data

Two types of data were used. The first type, called cumulative-probability data, included the probability of survival (or death) immediately after the treatment, one year after the treatment, and five years after the treatment. The one-year point was chosen because it represents the short-term range in which survival after radiation therapy is higher than survival after surgery; the five-year point was chosen because it is commonly used in medicine to evaluate and compare alternative treatments. The second type, called life-expectancy data, included the probability of survival (or death) immediately after the treatment and the life expectancy associated with each treatment – that is, the average number of years lived after the treatment.

The survival curve describing the results after surgery has a longer tail (i.e., it is more skewed to the right) than the survival curve for radiation therapy. Thus, the proportion of patients who will survive more than 10 years, for example, is greater for surgery than for radiation therapy. Consequently, the use of life expectancy, which is affected by the long tail, is expected to make surgery appear more attractive than it would with the use of one-year and five-year survival rates, which are not affected by the long tail.

### Identification of Treatment

For about half the respondents, the input data were identified as resulting from surgery or radiation therapy; for the remaining respondents, the treatments were not identified and the alternatives were labeled "A" and "B." The input data describing the results of A were identical to the results of surgery, and the data describing the results of B were identical to those of radiation therapy. This variation was introduced to assess the extent to which choices are determined by prior conceptions (or misconceptions) about surgery and radiation therapy.

### Framing of Outcome

The cumulative probabilities presented to about half the subjects referred to survival after a particular time – e.g., to a 68% chance of living for more than one year. The cumulative probabilities presented to the rest of the subjects referred to mortality – e.g., to a 32% chance of dying by the end of one year. Recent work by cognitive psychologists on the framing of decision problems indicates that the characterization of outcomes in terms of the probability of survival rather than the probability of death can have a substantial effect on people's preferences (Kahneman & Tversky, 1979; Tversky & Kahneman, 1981). More specifically, this work suggested that the impact of perioperative mortality on the comparison between the two treatments would be greater when it was framed as a difference between mortality rates of zero percent and 10%, than when it was framed as a difference between survival rates of 100% and 90%. Because the risk of perioperative death is the major disadvantage of surgery relative to radiation therapy, we hypothesized that surgery would be selected more frequently when the problem was described in terms of the probability of living than when it was described in terms of the probability of dying.

### Subject Population

Three groups of respondents were investigated: patients, physicians, and students. None of the subjects was known to have lung cancer. The patients were 238 men with chronic medical problems who were being treated as outpatients by internists at the Palo Alto Veterans Administration Medical Center. Their ages ranged from 40 to 80 years, with an average age of 58 years, which is similar to the age distribution of patients with lung cancer. The physicians were 424 radiologists whose ages ranged from 28 to 67 years, with an average age of 43 years; these subjects were taking postgraduate courses at the Harvard Medical School and the Brigham and Women's Hospital. Since physicians normally have an essential role in the choice of therapy, their own preferences are of considerable interest. The third group consisted of 491 graduate students from Stanford Business School, who had completed several courses in statistics and decision theory. Their average age was 29 years. They were included in the study so that we could examine the effects of age and analytic training.

We expected the students, who were younger than both the patients and the physicians, to choose surgery more often than the other two groups. We also expected the physicians and the students, who had more formal training than the patients, to be less affected by the variation in framing.

Table 17.1. *Numbers of Subjects Given Data in Various Ways*

| Population | Outcome Presented as Probability of Dying | | Outcome Presented as Probability of Living | |
|---|---|---|---|---|
| | Treatment Identified | Treatment Unidentified | Treatment Identified | Treatment Unidentified |
| Patients | 60 | 60 | 59 | 59 |
| Physicians | 80 | 135 | 87 | 122 |
| Students | 196 | 64 | 101 | 130 |

*Procedure*

Each subject was assigned to one of four conditions defined by the combinations of label (identified or unidentified) and frame (living or dying). The number of subjects in each group is shown in Table 17.1. All subjects received both cumulative-probability data and life-expectancy data, in that order. All subjects received the input data appropriate for their age group. Subjects who received the input data in an identified format and with outcome presented as the probability of dying were given the following instructions.

Surgery for lung cancer involves an operation on the lungs. Most patients are in the hospital for two or three weeks and have some pain around their incisions; they spend a month or so recuperating at home. After that, they generally feel fine.

Radiation therapy for lung cancer involves the use of radiation to kill the tumor and requires coming to the hospital about four times a week for six weeks. Each treatment takes a few minutes and during the treatment, patients lie on a table as if they were having an x-ray. During the course of the treatment, some patients develop nausea and vomiting, but by the end of the six weeks they also generally feel fine.

Thus, after the initial six or so weeks, patients treated with either surgery or radiation therapy feel about the same.

Next, the subjects were presented with the following cumulative probability data, which were also displayed in a table.

Of 100 people having surgery, 10 will die during treatment, 32 will have died by one year and 66 will have died by five years. Of 100 people having radiation therapy, none will die during treatment, 23 will die by one year and 78 will die by five years.

Which treatment would you prefer?

After the subjects made a choice, they were told that the above data summarized the experience of many hospitals and that they would now be asked to consider new information pertaining to a specific hospital and to make a new choice on the basis of these data.

At this single hospital, 10% of the patients who have surgery die during the perioperative period. The patients who survive treatment have a life expectancy (e.g., average number of remaining years) of 6.8 years. The life expectancy of all patients who undergo surgery (including those who die in the postoperative period) is 6.1 years. With radiation therapy, nobody dies during treatment, and the life expectancy of the patients who undergo radiation therapy is 4.7 years.

Which treatment would you prefer?

The subjects who received the data in an unidentified format were presented with different background information:

Both Treatment A and Treatment B are medications which are administered to the patient hospitalized for cancer. Both are given intravenously and neither one has significant side effects. Treatments A and B are considered equal except in their survival rates.

The input data concerning cumulative probability and life expectancy were the same as those for the identified treatments except that surgery and radiation therapy were replaced by "A" and "B," respectively. For the subjects who received the input data expressed in terms of the probability of survival, the probability of dying was replaced throughout by the probability of living. The patients were interviewed individually. The physicians and the students responded to a written questionnaire.

### Results

The percentages of respondents who chose radiation therapy rather than surgery are shown in Table 17.2 for each of the experimental conditions. The results for the cumulative-probability condition and for the life-expectancy condition were submitted to two separate 3-by-2-by-2 analyses of variance after an arcsin transformation (Snedecor & Cochran, 1967). The effects of all four independent variables were significant ($p < 0.001$). Moreover, Table 17.2 reveals a highly regular pattern: with one minor exception there are no "crossover" interactions among the major dependent variables – input data, identification of treatment, and the outcome frame. For example, all entries under "cumulative probability" exceed the corresponding entries under "life expectancy." We shall summarize the main effects in turn.

#### Input Data

As expected, subjects who had received life-expectancy data chose radiation therapy less frequently overall (27%) than did subjects who had received

Table 17.2. *Percentages of Subjects Choosing Radiation Therapy over Surgery*

| Type of Data (No. of subjects) | Outcome and Treatment Variables | | | | |
| --- | --- | --- | --- | --- | --- |
| | Dying | | Living | | |
| | Identified Treatment (336) | Unidentified Treatment (259) | Identified Treatment (247) | Unidentified Treatment (311) | Overall (1153) |
| *Cumulative probability*[a] | | | | | |
| Patients | 40 | 68 | 22 | 31 | 40 |
| Physicians | 50 | 62 | 16 | 51 | 47 |
| Students | 43 | 53 | 17 | 27 | 35 |
| Overall | 44 | 61 | 18 | 37 | 40 |
| *Life expectancy*[b] | | | | | |
| Patients | 35 | 50 | 19 | 27 | 28 |
| Physicians | 28 | 39 | 9 | 41 | 31 |
| Students | 21 | 41 | 9 | 24 | 22 |
| Overall | 25 | 42 | 11 | 31 | 27 |

[a] Immediately after treatment and at one and five years thereafter.
[b] Probability of surviving or dying from immediate treatment plus life expectancy thereafter. The dichotomy between probability of dying and probability of living in this group applies only to the data concerning the immediate treatment period.

cumulative-probability data (40%). An examination of individual choices revealed that 59% of the subjects chose surgery under both types of data and 26% chose radiation therapy under both types. Hence, 85% of the respondents made the same choice under both conditions. Fourteen percent of the respondents chose radiation therapy in the cumulative-probability condition and surgery in the life-expectancy condition; only 1% made the opposite choices.

### Identification of Treatment

Overall, radiation therapy was chosen 42% of the time when it was not identified and only 26% of the time when it was identified. Evidently, identification of the two treatments favors surgery over radiation therapy.

### Framing of Outcome

As predicted, surgery was relatively less attractive in the mortality frame (probability of dying) than in the survival frame (probability of living). On the average, radiation therapy was preferred to surgery 42% of the time in the mortality frame and 25% of the time in the survival frame.

### Subject Population

Radiation therapy was least popular among the students (28% of all responses), somewhat more popular among the patients (34%), and most popular among the physicians (39%). The general pattern of preferences, however, was very similar in all three groups despite large differences in age, income, and lifestyle.

## Discussion

We presented a large number of outpatients, physicians, and graduate students with information describing the possible outcomes of two alternative therapies for lung cancer. The respondents appeared to comprehend and use these data. An interview with the patients after the experiment indicated that they understood the data and were able to recall important items of information. However, the choices of both naive subjects (patients) and sophisticated subjects (physicians) were influenced by several variations in the nature of the data and the form in which they were presented.

The finding that data on life expectancy favored surgery whereas data on cumulative probability favored radiation therapy is not surprising in view of the fact that the survival distribution for surgery is much more skewed than the survival distribution for radiation therapy. However, this result illustrates the difficulty of selecting appropriate summary data; seemingly reasonable statistics (e.g., the mean or the median of a distribution) are likely to bias the decision maker in favor of one therapy or another.

The finding that radiation therapy was less attractive when the treatments were identified indicates that people relied more on preexisting beliefs regarding the treatments than on the statistical data presented to them. We do not know, however, whether these beliefs were based on valid evidence or reflected a widely shared bias against radiation therapy. In the former case, the input data should be expanded to include additional information that was presumably used by the subjects in the identified format only. In the latter case, subjects should be informed before the elicitation process in an attempt to reduce their biases.

Perhaps our most notable finding is the effect on people's choices of presenting the data in terms of survival or death. Surgery appeared to be much more attractive when the outcomes were framed in terms of the probability of survival rather than in terms of the probability of death. We attribute this result to the fact that the risk of perioperative death looms larger when it is presented in terms of mortality than when it is presented in terms of survival.

Unlike the preceding effects, which can be justified or at least rationalized, this effect of using different terminology to describe outcome represents a cognitive illusion. The effect observed in this study is large (25% vs. 42%) and consistent: It holds for both cumulative-probability and life-expectancy data, for both identified and unidentified treatments, and for all three populations of subjects. Much to our surprise, the effect was not generally smaller for the physicians (who had considerable experience in evaluating medical data) or for the graduate students (who had received statistical training) than for the patients (who had neither).

One might be tempted to conclude from this study that there is no point in devising methods for the explicit elicitation of patients' preferences, since they are so susceptible to the way the data are presented, and to implicit suggestions and other biases. However, it should be noted that the preferences expressed by the physicians, which are likely to play an important part in the advice they give to patients, were subject to the same biases. In addition, there is little reason to believe that more informal procedures in which the treatments are described in general terms without quantitative statistical data are less susceptible to the effects of different methods of presentation.

Variations in types of data presentation can be used to assess the sensitivity of preferences with respect to the available alternatives. If a patient prefers surgery over radiation therapy, for example, whether the data are presented as cumulative probabilities or as life expectancy and whether the probabilities are presented in terms of mortality or in terms of survival, the preference may be assumed to be reasonably certain. If, on the other hand, a change of presentation leads to a reversal of preference, then additional data, discussions, or analyses are probably needed. We suggest that an awareness of the effects of presentation among physicians and patients could help reduce bias and improve the quality of medical decision making.

### References

Axtell, L. M., Cutler, S. J., & Myers, M. H. (Eds.). (1972). *End results in cancer* (Rep. No. 4, DHEW Publication No. (NIH)73-272). Bethseda, MD: National Cancer Institute.

Hilton, G. (1960). Present position relating to cancer of the lung: Results of radiotherapy alone. *Thorax, 15*, 17–18.

Kahneman, D., & Tversky, A. (1979). Prospect theory: An analysis of decision under risk. *Econometrica, 47*, 263–291.

Keeney, R. L., & Raiffa, H. (1976). *Decisions with multiple objectives: Preference and value trade-offs.* New York: Wiley.

McNeil, B. J., Weichselbaum, R., & Pauker, S. G. (1978). Fallacy of the five-year survival in lung cancer. *New England Journal of Medicine, 299*, 1397–1401.

Mountain, C. F. (1976). The relationship of prognosis to morphology and the anatomic extent of disease: Studies of a new clinical staging system. In L. Israel & A. P. Chahinian

(Eds.), *Lung cancer: Natural history, prognosis, and therapy.* New York: Academic Press.

Mountain, C. F., Carr, D. T., & Anderson, W. A. D. (1974). A system for clinical staging of lung cancer. *American Journal of Roentgenology, Radium Therapy, and Nuclear Medicine, 120,* 130–138.

Raiffa, H. (1968). *Decision analysis: Introductory lectures on choices under uncertainty.* Reading, MA: Addison-Wesley.

Snedecor, C. W., & Cochran, W. G. (1967). *Statistical methods* (6th ed). Ames: Iowa State University Press.

Tversky, A., & Kahneman, D. (1981). The framing of decisions and the rationality of choice. *Science, 221,* 453–458.

# 18    Enhanced Interpretation
of Diagnostic Images

*David J. Getty, Ronald M. Pickett, Carl J. D'Orsi,
and John A. Swets*

Human interpretation of visual images remains a crucial part of diagnosis
and flaw detection in many fields. In clinical medicine, images on radio-
graphs, computed tomograms, sonograms, photomicrographs and so on are
viewed to reveal structure and function and to infer disease or health. In
examples from other fields, seismic patterns are studied for indication of oil
deposits; aerial photographs, for changes in ground conditions; eddy currents, for cracks in airplane wings; and polygraph recordings, for indication
of deception.

Although great effort is devoted to automation of such interpretive processes, reliance on human image readers surely will continue. Humans bring
immense intelligence and flexibility to the problem with effectiveness that,
in many instances, machines are not likely to match soon. Nonetheless, there
are some general and fundamental weaknesses in the way humans make
image-based diagnoses. The theme of this chapter is that basic human weaknesses in image interpretation can be specified, and, to a substantial extent,
overcome. One does not have to take the usual position that image readers
can only be highly trained and motivated and then left to do their work,
with an acceptance of any inadequacies that remain as natural limitations.
Various aids to the perceptual and decision processes can be constructed and
used to alleviate human limitations. This chapter demonstrates how the performance of even very sophisticated readers can be improved by such aids.

We demonstrate how the accuracy of image-based diagnoses may be increased by enhancing two main facets of the process. The first is the visual
assessment of relevant features of the image and the second is the merging
of those assessments to arrive at a diagnostic decision. We applied existing
analytical techniques to judgments made by specialists in mammography
about images of proven cases to identify the appropriate set of features for

This chapter originally appeared in *Investigative Radiology*, 1988, 23, 240–252. Copyright ©
1988 by Lippincott-Raven Publishers. Reprinted by permission.

the malignant–benign decision and their optimal weights in the merging. That information was used to construct corresponding decision aids for radiologists. The aids might be used by the mammography specialist, but in our study they were used by general radiologists.

One aid is a checklist that prompts the image reader to assess and record a scale value for each feature. The second aid is a computer program, here called a classifier, that merges those scale values in the optimal way for a diagnostic decision. For each case, the reader supplied the scale values to the computer classifier and received its estimate of the likelihood that a localized abnormality was malignant. With that estimate as guidance, the reader made a personal rating of the likelihood. The reader could place more or less weight on the classifier's estimates according to his or her judgment of how well the checklist features and their scale values captured the diagnostic information in the case at hand. The reader's likelihood estimates yield a measure of diagnostic accuracy, and we compared accuracy measures taken with and without the aids.

As mentioned, in this illustrative study we focus on the classification decision, specifically, whether an abnormality in a specified area of the image is benign or malignant. We do not consider the detection decision, that is, whether or not any focal abnormality, either benign or malignant, is present anywhere in the image. The visual features relevant to the classification decision are of an appropriate complexity to demonstrate our approach, and restricting our focus to them retains some economy and simplicity in this initial study. The clinical relevance of our specific focus is discussed in a later section.

This report is in five main sections. The first describes the development of the two aids as the basis of an enhanced reading procedure. The second describes an experimental test of the enhancements in which the performance of a group of radiologists was compared under standard and enhanced reading conditions. The third and fourth sections illustrate how one might determine the clinical significance of the enhancement effects that were achieved. The concluding section appraises the potential value of our general approach to accuracy enhancement and indicates some other ways in which it might be used.

## Development of the Enhanced Reading Procedure

Development of the enhanced procedure required three main steps. The first consisted of a survey of image features and a scaling analysis based on a perceptual-similarity study, both conducted with specialists in mammography. This step produced a comprehensive list of features and an appropriate format for recording the scale value of each feature. The second step was an exploratory reading test, with the specialists as readers, and a discriminant analysis of its results. This step produced a much smaller set of features, ones demonstrated to be effective in the diagnostic decision. These features made up the basic checklist in the later reading study. This second step also was the basis for the computer aid that merges feature data into a diagnostic probability. The final step was the specific design of the enhanced reading procedure that was to be tested in a reading study conducted with general radiologists.

### Development of a Comprehensive Feature List

Our aim was to capture the most important image features in a set that was yet small and manageable and in which features were largely independent of one another. First, individual interviews with five specialists generated several dozen features. Then, a scaling analysis of a perceptual-similarity study and group discussions with the specialists served to reduce the set to 29 features. Those procedures are described next. Then we describe how the reading test and a discriminant analysis produced the final set of 13 features.

*Interviews.* The individual interviews were aimed at identifying every image feature that the specialist deliberately considered in detecting and interpreting the significance of a localized breast abnormality. To ensure as comprehensive a consideration as possible, the specialists were asked to start at the beginning of the typical procedure and describe how cases typically presented, the overall examination procedure, and the nature of the communication back to the referring clinician or surgeon. At each step, details were pursued about what the specialists looked for in the image and how the image findings were gathered and merged into conclusions about the presence and significance of breast abnormality. We also observed and questioned some of them as they read actual cases. We then abstracted from each interview a list of all the features considered in determining whether a focal abnormality was suspect for malignancy. These features, as identified later, pertain to masses (e.g., their border characteristics) and to calcifications (e.g., their distribution) in the breast image, as the abnormalities of principal importance, or to certain secondary signs of abnormality (e.g., skin thickening). The mammograms of Figure 18.1 show features associated with clear instances of (A) a malignant mass, (B) a malignant mass containing calcifications, and (C) a benign mass.

*Scaling Analysis.* A perceptual-similarity study helps to define features that the specialist might use in the benign–malignant decision. The basic idea is to subject the specialists' ratings of the similarity of various pairs of images to a mathematical analysis that yields the features that underlie the ratings. Such a study was expected to confirm and highlight the major features identified in the interviews and could possibly reveal useful features not mentioned by the specialists. Because the analysis of a perceptual-similarity study determines

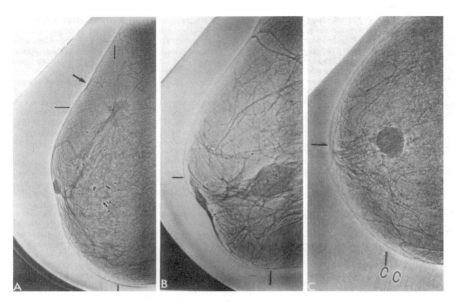

Figure 18.1. Exceptionally clear examples of malignant and benign abnormalities visible in x-ray mammograms. The locus of the main abnormality in each of these mammograms is indicated by horizontal and vertical line segments placed at the periphery of each image. (A) A malignant abnormality evidenced by a dark mass of irregular shape and with an irregular border formed of spiked projections (spiculation or stellation), all primary signs of malignancy. The arrow points to both a slight indentation in the skin (skin retraction) and thickening of the skin, the latter indicated by increased darkness of the skin; these are both secondary signs of malignancy. (B) A malignant abnormality with two other primary signs of malignancy: an indistinct or fuzzy border and a cluster of fine, sand-like particles (calcifications). Fine, clustered calcifications often appear without any visible surrounding or nearby mass. They may be contrasted with larger, more singularly isolated pieces of calcification as seen in the lower part of (A), which are not indicative of malignancy. (C) A benign abnormality, specifically a cyst, with a characteristically round or oval shape and a sharply demarcated and smooth border.

independent features, it might also show that certain features mentioned by the specialists are sufficiently correlated to be treated as one.

This study used the mammographic images of a subset of the approximately 200 cases we had obtained. Each case consisted of a cranio-caudad view and a lateral view of a single breast and a pathology report confirming by biopsy the benign or malignant status of a focal abnormality in the imaged breast. All cases were represented by Xeromammograms, as opposed to film mammograms, but our advisors believe our results to be relatively independent of that format. Our 200 cases were not obtained by random sampling but were all of the cases we could reasonably obtain. We believe, however, upon thorough examination of the set, that the cases represent reasonably well the various types of benign and malignant lesions that are seen in a referral setting, a setting in which symptomatic and screening patients are examined.

In our perceptual-similarity study, the five specialist readers rated the overall similarity of pairs of cases (given two views of each case) with respect to visual features they considered relevant to a benign–malignant decision. The ratings were made on a 10-point scale. We used 24 cases, including 12 malignant and 12 benign, so that all possible pairings of the 24 cases yielded 276 pairs to be rated. These 24 cases we judged to be representative of the total set of cases we had obtained. This procedure was then repeated in a second later session with an independent, similarly representative, set of 24 cases.

The ratings of similarity were then processed mathematically to reveal the principal independent features underlying the ratings. For this purpose, we used the analytic procedures of multidimensional scaling (MDS) and hierarchical clustering (HC). These procedures cannot be described here in any technical detail. We attempt only to characterize their purposes in general terms. A suitable introductory treatment is given elsewhere.[1]

The MDS procedure uses the similarity ratings to locate the various images in a geometric space of many dimensions in which each dimension can be interpreted as a scale for a given feature. The locations are computed under the assumption that a higher degree of rated similarity implies a smaller distance between images in the space. The pattern of rating judgments is further analyzed to reveal the set of dimensions, or axes, of the space that best accounts for the pattern. (An analogy would be to use ratings of the proximities of several cities to solve for a map of their region and to show its two dimensions.) Once the dimensions are available, the images are laid out in a row, successively in the order implied by each dimension, and studied to determine the perceptual quality that varies along that dimension. Each dimension can thus be verbally named and described as a feature that varies continuously in the amount of the particular perceptual quality.

In the HC analysis, alternatively, the mathematical processing serves only to collect into clusters groups of images judged to be highly similar, without spatial implications. Examination of the images in each cluster will often reveal the shared visual features that may be named and described. If one progressively lowers the criterion of similarity for grouping cases together, clusters are gradually merged together to form ever smaller numbers of larger clusters. The sequential pattern of these mergings can be displayed as a hierarchial tree that is useful in understanding perceptual relationships among features.

The primary result of our MDS and HC analyses was to corroborate information obtained from the specialists in the interviews. Features identified by both of these analyses as basic to the similarity judgments also were among those identified in the interviews as most important in determining malignancy. Important to us were the findings that the results of the MDS and HC analyses were consistent with one another in all instances, and the two methods yielded essentially the same feature set for each of the two independent sets of cases.

The results of the interviews and scaling analyses were compiled for presentation to the five specialists in a series of group meetings. We sought agreement on a master list of features for use in the exploratory reading test and discriminant analysis. The primary document presented to the group for consideration was a list of several dozen features and various commentaries on how individual specialists varied on their naming and interpretation. We also sought agreement on how each feature might be assessed, or scaled, by a reader. Such assessment consisted either of a subjective rating of the reader's confidence that a feature was present or the result of a physical or subjective measurement of a feature.

Differences were reconciled to produce consensus on a master list of 29 features. For the general purpose of this chapter, it should be sufficient only to note that the 29 features fall into three groups: 13 pertaining to masses, 12 pertaining to calcifications, and 4 pertaining to secondary signs. Although extensive, this list is not complete: as mentioned, it contains only features observed in single breasts and hence not features related to the symmetry of two breasts, and it does not contain certain features relevant in rare types of localized abnormality.

### Discriminant Analysis and Classifier Design

To permit reducing the 29 features to a smaller set, the five specialists participated individually in an exploratory reading test during which they recorded scale values for the 29 features for each of 100 cases with localized abnormalities (50 benign and 50 malignant). (These 100 cases included most of the cases used in the perceptual-similarity study.) The pooled data from these five tests were subjected to linear discriminant analysis to determine the smaller set of features that are effective (necessary and sufficient) in the malignant–benign decision and their optimal (relative) weights when merged into a decision. These features and weights were incorporated into the computer classifier.

For most of the cases in our sample, and we believe for mammography cases in general, the focal abnormality consisted of a mass and no clustered calcifications. Most of the remainder of the cases contained a cluster of calcifications and no mass, and a relatively small portion showed a mass and calcifications, with the calcifications either internal or external to the mass. For this reason, two computer-based classifiers were designed: one based on mass features and secondary signs that could be applied to any case with a mass and the second based on calcification features and the secondary signs that could be applied to any case with a cluster of calcifications. Thus, both classifiers could be (and were) applied to the infrequent cases having a mass and calcifications.

We developed the two different classifiers mentioned because linear-discriminant classifiers are not able to accommodate missing data; that is, a given classifier requires status values to be entered for every feature it contains. The classifier for masses was based on five mass features (four directly scaled and one derived by a simple arithmetic combination) and two secondary signs (both directly scaled). The classifier for calcifications was based on three calcification features (two directly scaled and one derived) and the same two secondary signs. Altogether, these 10 different features, used by one or the other of the two classifiers, employ values for 12 of the directly scaled features (each of the two derived features is made up of two directly scaled features that were not used directly). In most of the remainder of this chapter, the fact that two classifiers are used is of no import, and it will be convenient to speak of a computer classifier in the singular: we do so with the tacit understanding that two of them are involved.

### *Design of the Enhanced Reading Procedure*

In the specific design of the enhanced procedure, a new checklist was first formulated incorporating 13 features (the 12 features required by the computer classifiers, and one other for which we wished to collect data). Written definitions of the various items, as discussed with the general-radiologist readers, are available from the authors.

Next, data collection and computational procedures were devised to take the radiologist's feature-by-feature reports (as guided by the final checklist) and have the computer-classifier merge them, in real time, into a probability of malignancy; this probability was available for the radiologist's consideration before issuing his or her own rating of the likelihood of malignancy (both probabilities were available when both classifiers were operative). The last requirement was to create and tune a smooth and integrated procedure, with appropriate instructions for the radiologists to follow, for the reading studies that would constitute a formal test of the enhancements.

### Test of the Enhanced Reading Procedure

In the test of the enhanced reading procedure, baseline data were first obtained from six general radiologists, reading individually, and essentially in their usual way, a new set of 118 cases (58 malignant, 60 benign). After a brief training period, data were obtained on the performance of these generalists using the enhanced procedure on the same cases. Baseline data also were obtained from the five specialists who participated in developing the feature checklist, now reading the new cases individually in essentially their standard manner. We asked: What is the impact of the enhanced procedure on the performance of the generalists? How does their enhanced performance compare with the performance of the specialists?

*Readers*

The generalist readers were radiologists in community hospitals in the Boston area. Each had read an average of at least five mammograms a week for the preceding five years. Each had experience specifically in reading Xeromammograms as used in our study.

*Reading Procedure*

In the standard condition, readers examined the images in their accustomed manner with three exceptions. First, each case was represented by one breast, so that asymmetry was not at issue. Second, the focal abnormality of interest was identified for the reader, specifically, by means of cross-hairs at the edges of the image (Figure 18.1). Third, rather than giving a verbal report on the presence and significance of any abnormality, the readers rated their confidence that the localized abnormality was malignant, on a five-category scale. The five categories were: (1) definitely, or almost definitely, malignant; (2) probably malignant; (3) possibly malignant; (4) probably benign; and (5) definitely, or almost definitely, benign. This particular confidence-rating scale was used for reasons given elsewhere.[2] Responding by such a rating scale permits an analysis of accuracy in terms of the ROC described shortly.

In a training condition that followed the standard condition, the readers used the checklist on a different set of 44 cases, a subset of the cases previously used in the exploratory reading study with the specialists. Our goals in training were to familiarize the generalists with the identity, description, and appearance of each of the 13 features, and to tune their scaling of those features, through feedback, to the scaling used by the specialists and subsequently incorporated into the classifier. On a case-by-case basis, the reader recorded the scale values of the several features and simultaneously spoke them aloud so that a test administrator could enter them into a computer as data for the computer classifier. For each case, the reader received the classifier's estimate of the probability of malignancy, based on his or her own scale values for the mass and/or calcification features, before making the confidence-rating response. After giving that response, he or she received the medians of the scale values given each feature by the specialists. After groups of 15 cases, he or she received summary information about his or her average scale values for each feature relative to the specialists' averages; any relatively large discrepancies were pointed out by the test administrator as indicating a tendency to make a different assessment of a given feature than did the specialists.

In the enhanced condition, which began in the same session the training was given, the generalists examined the 118 test images under the guidance of the checklist described above and first responded with the scale values of the several features. As before, upon completing the checklist for a given case, and before making a five-category confidence-rating response, the reader was given the computer-classifier's estimate of the probability of malignancy.

*Accuracy Analysis*

The accuracy of the several reading performances is presented in terms of the relative (or receiver) operating characteristic, as described earlier.[2-6] ROC analysis is based on two quantities that fully reflect accuracy data when one considers just two alternative conditions and their corresponding diagnoses (here, benign and malignant). These quantities are the true-positive proportion, here denoted P(TP), and the false-positive proportion, here denoted P(FP). Specifically, the ROC is a plot of P(TP) against P(FP), showing their covariation (from 0 to 1) as the decision criterion for a positive response varies from strict to lenient. Thus, the ROC shows the full range of possible balances between P(TP) and P(FP). In medical terminology, P(TP) is the sensitivity of a diagnostic test and P(FP) is the complement of a test's specificity (where specificity is the true-negative proportion). An index of diagnostic accuracy drawn from an ROC has the advantage over many other indices, e.g., percentage of correct decisions, in being independent of the relative frequencies of the two alternative conditions (in the test sample or in the population), and an advantage over all other indices in being independent of the placement of the decision criterion.[7,8]

Empirical ROCs were generated in the usual manner by an analysis of each reader's confidence-rating responses. In brief, the responses of category 1 (definitely, or almost definitely, malignant) are treated as meeting the strictest criterion used (by that reader) for a positive decision; they yield low values of P(TP) and P(FP), that is, a point toward the lower left of the ROC graph. The responses of both categories 1 and 2 (including the response of probably malignant) are treated as meeting the next-strictest decision criterion used; they yield somewhat higher values of the ROC coordinates, that is, a point higher and to the right of the first one. The pattern continues until four points define an empirical ROC (the fifth point includes the responses in all categories and is thus the uninformative point at coordinate values 1.0, 1.0). Pooling the confidence-rating responses of the several readers yields a group ROC.[9] Examples are shown in figures that follow.

The resultant ROC can be read to yield the value of P(TP) corresponding to any selected value of P(FP), or vice versa, as will be illustrated. Additionally, the locus of the ROC can be measured to give a single-valued index of accuracy independent of any decision criterion, i.e., independent of any particular operating point on the ROC. Used here is the index $A_z$, which is a version of the area under the ROC. $A_z$ ranges from 0.5 for an ROC reflecting chance performance (i.e., when P[TP] = P[FP]) to 1.0 for an ROC reflecting perfect performance (i.e., when P[FP] = 0 and P[TP] = 1).[2,5]

*Curve Fits, Estimation of Parameters, and Tests
of Statistical Significance*

An objective fit was made of two empirical ROCs, one obtained in the standard mode, the other in the enhanced mode, for each reader and for the six readers as a group. In that process, maximum-likelihood estimates were made of ROC parameters (intercept and slope) and of the accuracy index $A_z$. Further, tests were made of the statistical significance ($p$-value) of the observed differences in $A_z$, and confidence limits were determined for the observed differences in P(TP) at selected values of P(FP), or vice versa.

The primary test of statistical significance used is a version of the critical-ratio (CR) test.[2] This test takes into account three sources of variance in our measurements; namely, variance across case samples, within readers, and between readers. For comparison, we also employ a $t$-test for paired data, which does not reflect case-sample variance, and hence refers strictly to generalizations to other readers of our particular sample. However, the $t$-test will apply reasonably well to a generalization to other case samples if our case sample is reasonably representative of all cases or if case-sample effects are highly correlated in the two conditions being compared, and we believe that both are good assumptions. Whenever we list two probability ($p$) values in succession, as in $p < .05; .02$, the first is that estimated by the CR-test, and the second is that estimated by the $t$-test.

*Results: $A_z$ Values*

Table 18.1 shows the results in terms of the accuracy index $A_z$. The main result (in the first two data columns) is that readings in the enhanced condition are consistently more accurate than readings in the standard condition. Five of the six readers (except Reader 2) show a gain of between .05 and .08 in $A_z$, and the mean gain is .05, from .83 to .88. In a one-tailed test, this difference has associated a $p < .02; 025$.

The five specialists read the same set of 118 cases read by the generalists. Their accuracies are shown in the far right column, with an average $A_z = .88$. Thus, the enhancement of the generalists' performance brought it to the level of the specialists. The specialists read the cases without the formal aids, and we have no data on the potential enhancement of their performance. We note the possibility, however, that their accuracies may have been increased somewhat by their intensive experience in developing the various sets of diagnostic features.

One anomaly in the data bears mention: Reader 2 showed no gain (rather, a loss of .03) from standard to enhanced mode. However, this reader performed substantially better than the other five in the standard condition (.92 rather than low .80s on the whole) and may have been performing in both readings near the effective ceiling of accuracy permitted by this set of cases. That

Table 18.1. *Accuracy ($A_z$) of the General Radiologists Under Standard and Enhanced Reading Conditions and Accuracy of the Computer Classifier and the Specialists*[a]

| General Radiologists | | | | | | |
|---|---|---|---|---|---|---|
| *Standard* | *Enhanced* | Computer Classifier | | Specialists | | |
| 1. | .83 | .90 | 1. | .87 | 1. | .83 |
| 2. | .92 | .89 | 2. | .86 | 2. | .85 |
| 3. | .80 | .85 | 3. | .82 | 3. | .89 |
| 4. | .79 | .87 | 4. | .82 | 4. | .90 |
| 5. | .83 | .90 | 5. | .90 | 5. | .91 |
| 6. | .82 | .87 | 6. | .86 | | |
| Mean | .83 | .88 | Mean | .86 | Mean | .88 |

[a] Accuracy scores are given for six general radiologists as numbered and for the computer classifier as paired with each of the six. The five specialists were not paired with either the general radiologists or the classifier performances.

possibility is strengthened by a comparison with the specialists' accuracies just mentioned, averaging .88. If this reader is omitted from the analysis, the mean gain from standard to enhanced mode is .06, rather than .05, and in a one-tailed test, $p < .006; .0005$.

The reliability of the difference between the two reading modes is further supported by the results of rereadings conducted. Specifically, three of the six readers were designated (at random, before any reading data were gathered) to read the 118 cases twice in the standard condition (about a month apart) before reading them in the enhanced condition. The other three readers read the 118 cases twice in the enhanced condition (about a month apart) after reading them once in the standard condition. In both instances, the second readings faithfully reproduced the first readings, with a mean difference of .01, and with four readers yielding a difference of no larger than that. (This difference is negligible: $p > .3$ by a two-tailed $t$-test and $p > .5$ by Hotellings' $T^2$ test). Thus, there was no improvement from one reading condition to the next resulting simply from rereading. Similarly, the improvement evidenced from standard to enhanced conditions was sustained.

To determine how the computer classifier performed relative to the readers, a ROC for the classifier (as paired with each reader) was computed by grouping its probability estimates into five rating categories of .20 in size and applying the confidence-rating analysis mentioned. It can be seen in Table 18.1 that the classifier performed slightly less well, on average, than the enhanced readers, with a mean of .86 vs. .88. Five of six readers did better than the classifier, and the sixth did equally well. In a two-tailed test, $p < .01$;

.02. We consider it likely that the readers extracted more information from the image than was represented in the scale values supplied to the classifier, as opposed to the possibility that the readers merged those values more effectively, but we have no empirical support for this conjecture.

On the other hand, with the exception of one reader (Reader 2), the computer classifier performed better than the generalist readers in the standard condition, with a mean of .86 vs. .83. In a two-tailed test, that difference has $p > .37; .25$. However, without Reader 2, the mean $A_z$ values are .81 and .85, and $p < .25; .01$. Note that we don't know how much of the overall enhancement effect was attributable to the classifier and how much to other sources (principally, the checklist), because we chose not to ask the reader for an overall rating-scale response before and after he/she received the classifier's probability estimate.

### Results: Full ROCs

The full ROCs for the first standard reading and for the first enhanced reading are portrayed as group ROCs for the six readers pooled (Figure 18.2). Note, as shown on the scales on the four sides of the graph, that the

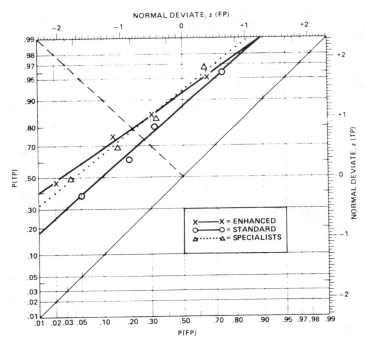

Figure 18.2. ROCs based on the six test readers for the standard and enhanced conditions and on the five specialists.

probabilities P(TP) and P(FT) are displayed on this graph so that their normal-deviate values are linearly spaced. A robust result is that empirical ROCs are straight lines on such a binormal graph.[8] This functional form of the ROC is assumed in the model mentioned earlier as underlying our curve-fitting procedures.

The two ROCs for the generalist readers are indicated by the heavy, solid lines in Figure 18.2. They are fitted to the circles for the standard condition and to the crosses for the enhanced condition. The lower ROC (standard) has an $A_z = .81$ and the upper ROC (enhanced) has an $A_z = .87$. These values differ slightly from the means of $A_z$ values of the individual readers, shown as .83 and .88 in Table 18.1.

The upper ROC is close to the ROC of the specialists, the latter as indicated in Figure 18.2 by triangles and a dotted line. The specialists' ROC has a slightly steeper slope than the generalists' enhanced ROC, but the same value of $A_z$ (.87). Note that the decision criteria used are similar for the two groups of readers. That is, the criteria used yield ROC points having nearly the same values of P(FP) at each category boundary of the rating scale, and, when the accuracies are similar, nearly the same value of P(TP).

With the full ROCs, one can observe differences between the two reading conditions at any point of interest. Thus, one can note that at the negative diagonal, where sensitivity, P(TP), and specificity, $1 - $ P(FP), are equal, there is a gain of .07 in both of these quantities in moving from standard to en-hanced modes, from .73 to .80. That is to say, in a setting similar to that of our test, and at the symmetrical decision criterion, the expectation is that, of 100 women with a malignancy, seven more would be recommended for biopsy under enhanced diagnosis, and (simultaneously), of 100 women with a be-nign localized abnormality, seven fewer would be recommended for biopsy. The section following begins with an analysis of whether or not such a sum-mary statement is a good and fair assessment of the practical significance of the present results, by examining where mammographers in the clinic ap-pear to be operating in the ROC space, and then amplifies that statement. The nature and size of the enhancement effect depends on where on the standard-reading ROC the mammographer is operating, and on how one chooses to measure the gain, in P(TP) at a constant P(FP), in P(FP) at a constant P(TP), or as a change in both probabilities.

## Clinical Relevance

To help evaluate the immediate practical significance of these results, let us briefly examine the generality of our test conditions in relation to the clinical application of mammography. One technical issue revolves about our avoid-ance of the pure detection decision. We did so in part for simplicity (there are inherent problems of definition when a particular area of the image is not specified for inspection) and in part for economy (mammographic detection is sometimes based on an observed asymmetry between a patient's breasts, which would require doubling the number of confirmed images in each of our studies). To so ignore the search process would be unacceptable for some combinations of organ and disease indicators (for example, small nodules in chest films). However, in mammography it is plausible that every significant area can be routinely scanned for features relevant to the classification of abnormalities. A second, related issue is whether the present results are more directly pertinent to instances of patient referral, in which suspected and perhaps palpable lesions are imaged, than to large-scale screening, in which the emphasis is often regarded to be on the detection of any abnormality, for which a biopsy is then done. We observe, however, that the classification decision is often made in screening and will be increasingly so: (A) as the rapid expansion of mammographic screening underway requires more conservatism in recommending further action, for example, as expanded screening outpaces the capacity for performing biopsies, and (B) as societal cost-benefit analyses lead to pressures for a higher yield of biopsy, that is, a higher ratio of malignant to benign cases among those for which a biopsy is done.

As another technical issue, we are aware that mammography often is regarded as good for detection and poor for classification but believe there may be a semantic issue here. Good for detection seems to mean "good for detection of localized (focal) abnormalities worthy of concern," which implies classification, in our terms. Thus, certain types of lesions are identified confidently with benign disease (including multiple round densities, which are usually assumed to be cysts, and diffusely spread microcalcifications). So, even in the detection role, mammographers make a classification decision. The use of mammography to classify clustered microcalcifications as malignant or benign is a subject of current interest in the literature.[13] Moreover, mammographers frequently suggest some specific degree of concern for detected lesions, a further incursion into the domain of classification. In indicating a degree of concern, mammographers often use what may be considered a third alternative, between "do a biopsy" and "do not do a biopsy," which is to recommend another mammogram after a specified period. Incidentally, this clinical option can be treated within the ROC context. Though we do not do so here, one can infer from enhanced and standard ROCs how many fewer cases would fall in that middle category under the enhanced condition, while maintaining any given values of P(TP) and P(FP) across the two conditions.[14]

### Clinical Comparison

Let us compare the present data with the results of four clinical studies of the accuracy of mammography as reviewed recently by Moskowitz.[15] They are the studies shown in that review at the top of the first table, conducted

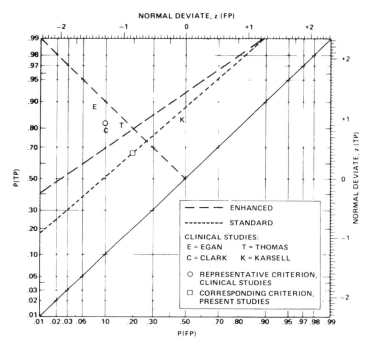

Figure 18.3. Comparison of four clinical studies (by Egan, Karsell, Clark, and Thomas) with results of the present study on a ROC graph.

in referral settings with symptomatic patients by Egan[16]; Clark, Copeland, and Egan[17]; Thomas, Fitzharris, Redding, et al[18]; and Karsell.[19] Those studies had relative frequencies or prior probabilities of cancer of .32, .33, .30, and .31, respectively, as compared with .51 in our test, close enough, we submit, to support a comparison (given further that the ROC analysis tends to neutralize differences in prior probabilities). Those studies included primarily symptomatic patients, that is, those with a palpable lump; thus, we assume that a large proportion of the cases in the four clinical studies showed rather evident, focal abnormalities in the mammogram, such that the usual decision was the classification decision of suspicious or not for malignancy.

The results of these clinical studies are shown on an ROC graph in Figure 18.3, one point from each study indicated by the initial of the investigator (E, C, T, K). For purposes of comparison, a circle is drawn at the point (.10, .82) to represent the approximate centroid of the E, C, T points, which come from the three clinical studies consistent with one another. The circle lies above the enhanced performance of the present study (represented by the large-dashed line in Figure 18.3) and the standard performance of the present study (represented by the small-dashed line). Because the large-dashed line approximates the specialists' performance in our study, as well as the enhanced performance of the generalists, we infer that our test sample contained a more difficult set of cases than did the E, C, T studies. Such a difference is consistent with the likelihood that a smaller proportion of our cases were symptomatic, i.e., with a palpable lump. Nonetheless, we submit that the results of our study are sufficiently close to those of the clinical studies to permit a reasonably valid extrapolation to the clinical setting of the comparison of enhanced and standard performances in our study.

Moreover, the E, C, T points are sufficiently clustered to infer from them a representative decision criterion, as well as a representative accuracy, for the clinical setting they represent. Consider this decision criterion to yield the operating ROC point just mentioned, at $P(FP) = .10$ and $P(TP) = .82$. We suggest that a reasonably realistic decision criterion to use in internal comparisons in the present study is one that maintains a similar balance between $P(TP)$ and $P(FP)$, that is, one that stands in about the same relationship to the negative diagonal of the ROC graph (the dashed line running to the upper left corner). As an approximation to that criterion for the standard condition, consider the operating point in Figure 18.3 denoted by the small square, at $P(FP) = .20$ and $P(TP) = .67$.

Note in relation to our assumed criterion for the standard condition (the small square in Figure 18.3) that for $P(FP)$ fixed at .20, $P(TP)$ for the enhanced condition is .80, i.e., .13 greater than for the standard condition. Reading the graph in the other direction, for $P(TP)$ fixed at .67, $P(FP)$ for the enhanced condition is .08, i.e., .12 less than for the standard condition. The indication here is that by implementing the present enhancements, one can choose between an expected gain in sensitivity and an expected gain in specificity of about .12 to .13, or elect some lesser amount of both (including .07 of each as mentioned earlier).

Those probabilities can be made more concrete by relating them to estimated numbers of additional cases correctly diagnosed. Consider $N = 1,000$ cases as the number examined and verified (by pathology exam or follow-up) and consider the prevalence of cancer in symptomatic patients in a referral setting to be .32, the mean of the prior probabilities in the four clinical studies. If one takes the observed enhancement effect entirely as a gain in sensitivity (by implementing the decision criterion that achieves that particular result), our calculations show an expectation of 42 additional malignancies found per 1,000 cases examined. Alternatively, taking the effect as a gain in specificity gives an expectation of 82 fewer false-positive decisions per 1,000 cases examined. Either is obviously a substantial improvement.

## Discussion

Let us consider briefly how the enhancement techniques demonstrated might be employed. We believe that image reading is generally a matter of identifying and scaling features and then merging the features, with varying weights, into an overall, diagnostic decision. If so, explicit attention to feature determination, definition, identification, scaling, and merging generally should repay the effort. Analytic techniques like those described here have been used by others in various contexts, including clinical medicine. They are illustrative of a general approach with possible variants.

The enhancement techniques will work in practice, we expect, because they require a reader to be systematic in assessing features and they help in, but do not take over, the difficult process of weighting and merging features. One practical possibility is that images in apparently routine cases could be interpreted without the aids and the aids could be employed only in problematic cases. Moreover, these aids should have value if used only in training. They provide a way of capturing the expertise of a specialist and of codifying it in a manner suitable for teaching others.

One seemingly appropriate general application is to an imaging modality newly introduced, for example, to magnetic resonance imaging now in medicine. If usual procedures are followed in this instance, the determination of relevant features and their relative weights will depend on many investigators working independently on parts of the task and adding pieces to the whole through conferences and journals. Neither the analysis nor the dissemination is highly organized; the results are more qualitative than quantitative, and the process is slow relative to the pace of development of the imaging equipment. The contrast in efficiency of the typical procedures to a programmatic and comprehensive approach is striking.

Another general application is to diagnostic problems for which test data show a considerable variability in accuracy across readers. A recent Air Force study, for example, showed large variability across some 120 technicians in reading eddy-current and ultrasound images for cracks in airplane wings. Substantial variability also was noted from one to another of the 16 different sites in the study. For such settings, there is great potential for analyzing the perceptual and decision-making skills of the most proficient and carrying the understanding so gained to the less proficient.

Expanding a computer classifier into an intelligent computer-based tutoring system might be an effective and acceptable way to conduct the training. Such a system would break the learning process into natural steps, focusing first on feature definition and scaling and then on feature scaling plus detection and classification. In both instances, practice cases would be presented appropriate to a student's level of competence and particular difficulties (as measured by the system), and feedback would be given of expert performance. When working in the mode of scaling plus detection and classification, feedback also could be given of the optimal weights of features in combination, and, after groups of cases, the student's patterns of scale values and weights could be displayed relative to those of the expert and the optimal classifier.

Our bottom line is that fairly simple and workable aids brought about a substantial increase in the accuracy of previously sophisticated and motivated radiologists. These aids, moreover, were based on an initial and quite rudimentary application of analytical techniques to the diagnostic problem selected. Given this encouragement, both the feature checklist and the merging algorithm can be refined through available improvements on the techniques we used and the way we used them, leading, we suppose, to greater increases in accuracy.

Our suggestion is that techniques used in psychology to study perception and decision making have potentially an important role to play in improving the processing of technical information by humans in diagnostic settings. They can help diagnostic systems take better advantage of human capabilities (for example, perceptual capabilities) that continue to resist automation, and to be less dependent on the weaker aspects of human performance (for example, in merging several kinds of information into decisions) that can be aided by automation. Though seemingly paradoxical, this role is more significant in today's computerized world. The computer makes it possible to aid human performance powerfully in critical functions that are difficult to automate.

### References

1    Shiffman SS, Reynolds ML, Young FW. Introduction to multidimensional scaling. New York: Academic Press Inc, 1981.
2    Swets JA, Pickett RM. Evaluation of diagnostic systems: methods from signal detection theory. New York: Academic Press Inc, 1982.
3    Green DM, Swets JA. Signal detection theory and psychophysics. New York: John Wiley & Sons, Inc. Reprinted Huntington, New York: Robert E. Krieger Publishing Co, 1974.
4    Swets JA. The relative operating characteristic in psychology. Science 1973;182:990–1000.
5    Swets JA. ROC analysis applied to the evaluation of medical imaging techniques. Invest Radiol 1979;14:109–121.
6    Swets JA, Pickett RM, Whitehead SF, et al. Assessment of diagnostic technologies. Science 1979;205:753–759.
7    Swets JA. Indices of discrimination or diagnostic accuracy: their ROCs and implied models. Psychol Bull 1986:100–117.
8    Swets JA. Form of empirical ROCs in discrimination and diagnostic tasks: implications for theory and measurement of performance. Psychol Bull 1986:181–198.
9    Macmillan NA, Kaplan HL. Detection theory analysis of group data: estimating sensitivity from average hit and false-alarm rates. Psychol Bull 1985;95:185–199.
10   Begg CB, Greenes RA. Assessment of diagnostic tests when disease verification is subject to selection bias. Biometrics 1983;39:207–215.
11   Greenes RA, Begg CB. Assessment of diagnostic technologies: methodologies for unbiased estimation from samples of selectively verified patients. Invest Radiol 1985;20:751–756.

12  Metz CE, Wang P-L, Kronman HB. A new approach for testing the significance of differences between ROC curves measured from correlated data. In: Deconinck F ed., Information processing in medical imaging. The Hague: Martijnus Nijhoff, 1984:431–445.

13  Sickles EA. Breast calcifications: mammographic evaluation. Radiology 1986;160: 289–293.

14  Swets JA, Swets JB. ROC approach to cost-benefit analysis. IEEE Proc Sixth Conf on Computer Applic in Radiol, Newport Beach, California. 1979;203–206. Reprinted in Ripley KL, Murray A eds. Introduction to automated arrhythmia detection. New York: IEEE Computer Society Press, 1980:57–60.

15  Moskowitz M. Screening for breast cancer: how effective are our tests? A critical review. CA 1983;33:26–27.

16  Egan RL. Present status of mammography. Ann NY Acad Sci 1964;114:794–802.

17  Clark RL, Copeland MM, Egan RL, et al. Reproducibility of the technic of mammography (Egan) for cancer of the breast. AJS 1965;109:127–133.

18  Thomas JM, Fitzharris BM, Redding WH, et al. Clinical examination xeromammography and fine-needle aspiration cytology in diagnosis of breast tumors. Br Med J 1978;2:1139–1141.

19  Karsell PR. Mammography at the Mayo Clinic: a year's experience. Mayo Clin Proc 1974;49:954–957.

# Part VI

# Experts

No matter what the field, from betting on horses to reading X-rays, from assessing a defendant's sanity to evaluating a work of art, the essence of expertise seems to involve judgments. Expertise is associated with long training and experience and is invariably expensive. We pay willingly, of course, when we believe the expert can provide us with sound judgments: which horse will win, what's our medical problem, whether the painting is authentic or not. But our faith is often shaken by the sight of two experts, apparently equally competent, in disagreement with one another. Plainly both cannot be right; perhaps neither is.

Experts offer reassurance as well as a claim to accuracy, and successful experts thus generally cultivate an appearance of high confidence. Is this confidence justified? The evidence from a large body of JDM research is very mixed. In some cases expert judges achieve impressively high agreement with one another, and with external standards. In other cases, neither sort of agreement is very evident. It is easy enough to find examples of the first sort in areas where judgment is built into a performance where excellence can be quickly and accurately evaluated: Chess players, solo musicians, race car drivers, software writers, and weather forecasters all make complex judgments, and it is easy enough to sort out the real experts from mere claimants. Examples of the second sort involve many judgments for which feedback is delayed, imperfect, or nonexistent. Many judgments about human mental states and processes are of this sort: What was the defendant's state of mind at the time of the crime? How well will this student work out if we admit her to our graduate program or hire her onto our faculty? Note, in passing, how many of these judgments inherently involve only partial feedback: We never learn how well the candidate we reject would have worked out, how our life would have been if we'd married the other person. More subtly, as Einhorn pointed out some years ago, the waiter never really finds out if his judgment about good tippers is accurate or not, since he will, sensibly, tend to give better service to the customers he judges will tip well than he does to the others, so he unknowingly makes his judgment come true. About the only safe generalization about research on expert judgment is that it is dangerous to generalize on the matter.

We have already seen a number of chapters in which expertise was involved (e.g., Swets's work on radiologists, Doyle and Shane's work on audiologists), and we will see more later (e.g., Kleinmuntz's important essay on the long-running conflict between clinical and actuarial methods for combining evidence). The three chapters included in this section place expertise at the focus of the study. Gaeth and Shanteau (Chapter 19) look at the process by which agricultural students become skilled soil judges – a skill with real economic significance, and one in which students compete on school teams. The particular interest was in how to train the students to ignore irrelevant cues such as presence or absence of excessive moisture in making their judgments. The procedures used seem to have been effective. (For another interesting applied example, see Phelps & Shanteau, 1978, in which the task for the experts was evaluating hogs – a set of stimulus materials not often seen in decision-making journals!)

Einhorn (Chapter 20) reports a study of three medical pathologists evaluating biopsy slides from patients with Hodgkin's disease, a disease that, at the time, was invariably fatal. The experts judged nine characteristics from each slide, as well as making an overall judgment of how severe the disease was. Some of the slides were presented twice. Einhorn was thus able to assess several aspects of these experts' performance: Whether they were reliable (scoring the same slide similarly on repeated presentations); whether or not they agreed with one another on how much of each characteristic was present in each slide and on their overall judgments of severity (convergent validity); whether or not they scored different characteristics differently (discriminant validity); whether or not their overall judgments were closely predictable from their ratings of the cues; and, finally, how closely they agreed on how much weight should be given to each cue in making an overall judgment. The data show surprisingly low agreement within and between these experts. The patient in this setting would be well advised to seek a second, or even a third, medical opinion before doing anything too serious.

The final chapter in this section, by Faust and Ziskin (Chapter 21), ties together our earlier interests in medical and legal issues in judgment. They are concerned with the role of psychological and psychiatric experts in the courtroom. Such experts are often called on for testimony on such matters as whether the defendant is sane enough for trial; his or her state of mind at the time of the crime; whether or not he or she is likely to behave violently in the future; and other legally important issues. The evidence the authors review paints an almost universally gloomy picture of expertise on these topics, used for these purposes. Confident or not, these experts seem not to meet the established legal tests of being "pretty likely accurate" and "able to help." Psychological and psychiatric science seems to have little to offer the courts yet in this area.

### Reference

Phelps, R. H., & Shanteau, J. (1978). Livestock judges: How much information can an expert use? *Organizational Behavior and Human Performance, 21,* 209–219.

# 19 Reducing the Influence of Irrelevant Information on Experienced Decision Makers

*Gary J. Gaeth and James Shanteau*

A fundamental and critical component of expert judgment is the ability to appropriately use available information which varies in its relevance. Ideally, experts would select and use only information which is the most relevant. There is, however, a great deal of evidence which indicates that the presence of irrelevant information can influence judgment adversely in a variety of situations. If this influence extends to experienced decision makers, then one reasonable approach to improving judgmental skill would be to train judges to reduce the use of irrelevant information. Accordingly, the four purposes of this chapter are (a) to determine whether experienced agricultural judges are influenced by irrelevant information, (b) to compare the effectiveness of two training procedures designed to reduce this influence, (c) to evaluate what impact irrelevance and training have on the accuracy of the judgments, and (d) to investigate the long-term effect of the training through a follow-up study.

## Previous Studies of Irrelevance

### Basic Research

In a recent search of the literature of Gaeth and Shanteau (1981), over 250 published reports were found from a variety of psychological areas which investigated the influence of irrelevance. We will briefly consider a few of these studies for illustrative purposes.

In a prototype study, Williams (1974) had subjects make "same–different" judgments of visual stimuli which varied on multiple dimensions. He found that reaction times were longer when the stimuli differed on irrelevant dimensions than when they were the same. Similar perceptual demonstrations of the influence of irrelevant information have been obtained in scaling tasks

This chapter originally appeared in *Organizational Behavior and Human Performance*, 1984, *33*, 263–282. Copyright © 1984 by Academic Press, Inc. Reprinted by permission.

(Besner & Coltheart, 1976; Bundesen & Larsen, 1975), reaction time analyses (Gordon, 1970; Larsen & Bundesen, 1978), and signal recognition studies (Montague, 1965).

In addition, several studies using concept formation or problem solving paradigms have concluded that the ability to ignore irrelevance is a cognitive skill (Kausler & Kleim, 1978; Rabbitt, 1965). This ability appears to depend on individual-difference factors such as age. For older adults, evidence points to an age-related decrement in the ability to separate relevant from irrelevant (Ford, Hink, Hopkins, Roth, Pfefferbaum, & Kopell, 1979; Hoyer, Rebok, & Sved, 1979). Additional research seems to indicate that very young or mentally retarded children may have greater difficulty distinguishing between relevant and irrelevant dimensions than older or normal children (Bush & Cohen, 1970; Eimas, 1966; Evans & Beedle, 1970; Low, Coste, & Kirkup, 1980; Shantz, 1967).

### Applied Research

Only a few studies have been found which dealt with the role of irrelevance in applied (i.e., nonlaboratory) settings. In one industrial study, irrelevant biodemographic information was shown to influence the evaluation of prospective teachers by school administrators (Rice, 1975). In another study on personnel selection, information on the sex, age, and physical attractiveness of hypothetical job applicants was shown to be inappropriately used by experienced business students (Nagy, 1981; also see Beach, Mitchell, Deaton, & Prothero, 1978; Griffitt & Jackson, 1970).

In the judicial setting, irrelevant information may also play a critical role. As an example, indications are that inadmissible (irrelevant) evidence has an inappropriate influence on the decisions of juries (Mitchell & Byrne, 1972; Sue, Smith, & Caldwell, 1973).

In all, irrelevant information has been found to influence psychological judgments in a variety of basic and applied research areas. The influence on experienced decision makers is especially noteworthy and will be the focus of this research.

## Soil Judgment

Soil judgment was chosen as the content area for this research for three reasons. First, the task is important, yet heavily based on psychological skills. Hand soil analysis is performed routinely as part of road and dam construction, agricultural land testing, etc. Any contribution that psychology can make to soil judgment may, in itself, have important consequences.

Second, previous experience has shown that trained agricultural students are skilled and cooperative subjects (Shanteau & Phelps, 1977). Specifically, previous work with student soil judges has confirmed both their expertise and willingness to participate (Gaeth & Shanteau, 1979; Gaeth & Shanteau, 1980). Moreover, the students were highly motivated to participate in this training research because they were attempting to qualify for the school soil judging team (a prestigious accomplishment in an agriculturally oriented program).

Finally, in contrast to many other applied areas in which irrelevance has been studied (i.e., law, personnel selection), soil judgment lends itself nicely to quantitative research. A limited description of the soil judgment task is necessary to understand this latter point.

## The Soil Judgment Task

By definition, soil texture is derived directly from the proportion of three basic constituents in the soil. These are: sand (particles between 2 and .05 mm), silt (particles between .05 and .002 mm), and clay (particles less than .002 mm). Based on the naturally occurring percentages of each of these constituents, any soil can be placed into one of 12 soil texture categories. The texture categories are specified by the USDA (United States Department of Agriculture) soil texture triangle presented in Figure 19.1. For illustration, a soil containing 40% sand, 40% silt, and 20% clay has been plotted on the soil triangle. As can be seen, it is part of the texture category "loam."

A soil analysis to determine the percent of sand, silt, and clay can be performed physically in a soils laboratory; however, the process is relatively expensive (up to $100 per sample) and time consuming (up to several months). Because of these constraints, the vast majority of field soil judgments are performed using the "feel method" (Clarke, 1936), a tactile method for determining soil composition. The laboratory analyses thus serve only as a criterion or standard. The goal for professional soil judges therefore is to produce assessments using the feel method which are equivalent to the laboratory results.

Student soil judges are indirectly trained to this standard by learning to emulate the judgments of an instructor; these instructors are usually established professional soil scientists. Therefore, the instructor both teaches the students the soil judgment process and provides the standard to which the students are typically compared.

## Irrelevant Factors in Soil Judgment

As a direct consequence of the definition of soil texture, any material in the soil other than sand, silt, and clay is irrelevant. Based on a survey of USDA soil scientists and other evidence (Gaeth & Shanteau, 1980), it was found that coarse fragments (particles in the soil which are larger than 2.0 mm) and excessive moisture (the presence of water in excess of what is used

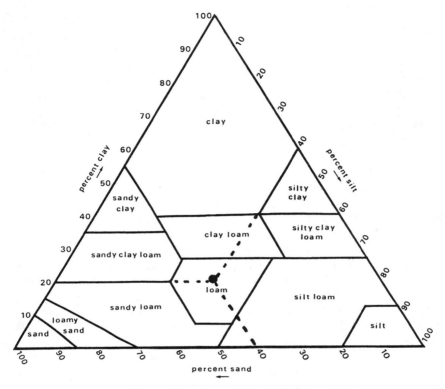

Figure 19.1. USDA Soil Classification Triangle. Soil plotted (black circle) with 40% sand, 40% silt, and 20% clay is a "loam."

when evaluating soil) were among a number of irrelevant factors which may adversely influence soil judgment. These two materials, excessive moisture and coarse fragments, were then chosen for this investigation because they occur naturally and can be controlled in specially prepared soils.

### Training Procedures

It is beyond the scope of this paper to review the previous studies on the various procedures for training decision makers (see Einhorn & Hogarth, 1981; Slovic, Fischhoff, & Lichtenstein, 1977; Slovic & Lichtenstein, 1971). Rather, we will present four general "rules" which guided the design of the two training techniques used in the research.

First, the training periods had to be fairly short, i.e., less than half an hour. We were constrained because of having skilled participants whose time was at a premium; this of course is not an uncommon limitation when working with experienced decision makers.

Second, the training programs had to be as parallel as possible to the general type of training normally given to soil judges. This was done (a) to keep our training "natural," (b) to increase the credibility of our research, and (c) to allow for its possible adoption in soil education programs.

Third, the training procedures rested on the fundamental idea that the most effective way to teach the judges to "ignore" irrelevance is to concentrate on it. This somewhat counterintuitive approach was grounded in notions from selective attention (Kahneman, 1973); you must pay at least some attention to information before you can decide not to pay attention.

Finally, the training procedures should not depend on conventional outcome feedback, i.e., the "correct" answer. Because most applied judgment problems do not have objective standards (indeed, if objective measures are readily available, expert judgment is generally unnecessary), we wanted to use a training approach with maximum generality.

Based on these four principles, two training procedures were developed: lecture training and interactive training.

*Lecture Training.* This training was designed to be roughly equivalent to the usual approach taken in the classroom. Basically the judges were warned verbally that excessive moisture and coarse fragments are irrelevant and therefore should not be allowed to influence their judgments. Thus, in accord with many other studies (e.g., Fischhoff & Slovic, 1980; Fischhoff, Slovic, & Lichtenstein, 1977; Harris, 1977), our first approach to training was to warn the soil judge about the detrimental influence of irrelevance.

*Interactive Training.* This training was designed to be similar to the experience gained from a laboratory class. Although past research has consistently shown that verbal warnings (lecture training) are not very successful (Fischhoff, 1975; Harris, 1977), there are some examples of successful training approaches from which we could build; these include the "discovery" method (Slovic & Fischhoff, 1977; Bruno & Harris, 1980) and the use of extended practice (Lichtenstein & Fischhoff, 1980). Also, an analysis of the soil judgment task demonstrates that it requires both cognitive and perceptual skill. Therefore, the interactive training, involving "hands-on" practice with soils, was intended to help the judges discover that the irrelevant factors had in fact influenced their own soil judgments.

## Method

### Participants and Stimuli

*Participants.* Twelve soil judges (two females; ten males) were recruited from an advanced soil morphology class taught at Kansas State University.[1] Coupled with this class, all judges had previous experience with soil judgment

Table 19.1. *Percentage of Sand, Silt, Clay, Coarse Fragments, and Excessive Moisture for Each Evaluation and Training Soil*

| Soil No. | Usage | % Sand | % Silt | % Clay | % C.F. Natural | % C.F. Used | % E.M. Used |
|---|---|---|---|---|---|---|---|
| 2 | Base | 5(5) | 66(70) | 29(25) | 30 | 23 | 20 |
| 4 | Base | 17(20) | 60(60) | 23(20) | 25 | 26 | 30 |
| 6 | Base[a] | 52(20) | 29(55) | 19(25) | 38 | 33 | 25 |
| 1 | Filler | 62 | 10 | 28 | — | — | — |
| 7 | Filler | 22 | 49 | 29 | — | — | — |
| 8 | Filler | 8 | 63 | 29 | — | — | — |
| 9 | Filler | 7 | 65 | 28 | — | — | — |
| 3 | Training | 23 | 61 | 16 | 44 | — | — |
| 5 | Training | 26 | 48 | 26 | 82 | — | — |

*Note:* C.F. = coarse fragments, E.M. = excessive moisture. Values in parentheses reflect the estimates made by the professional soil science instructor. The percentages are based on a mechanical analysis conducted by the Front Range Laboratory, Fort Collins, Colo.
[a] Soil 6 was also used as a training soil.

through various combinations of personal work experience, laboratory work, other classes, and prior membership on soil judging teams (college, high school, or 4H club). They were paid $12 for their participation and were each run individually through the research.

*Soil Stimuli.* Nine Kansas soil samples were used in this experiment (see Table 19.1). These nine soils included five which contained naturally occurring coarse fragments and four filler soils which did not contain coarse fragments. This collection of nine soils was separated into two sets: (a) evaluation soils and (b) interactive training soils.

For the evaluation soils, a factorial set of 12 soils was created by making 4 variations of each of 3 "base" soils; these soils all originally contained coarse fragments (2, 4, 6 in Table 19.1). The set was generated by preparing each soil according to a two levels of coarse fragments (present–not present) × two levels of moisture (present–not present) design. For the *not-present* level of coarse fragments, the sieved "base" soil was used, i.e., all coarse fragments were removed; when *present*, the level of coarse fragments was roughly equal to the amount found in the soil naturally. For the moisture factor, the *not-present* level was chosen as the dried base soil containing virtually no moisture; the *present* level was deliberately set as an amount of moisture greater than what is normally used when assessing the soil texture by hand.

Added to these 12 soils were 4 fillers yielding an evaluation set of 16. The fillers (1, 7, 8, 9) were included to disguise the factorial design. Also, the responses to several of these soils were used in the interactive training procedure as feedback.

One hundred grams of each soil were prepared and stored in 8-ounce airtight plastic containers; the containers were marked with a code number used as identification. Due to concern over the evaporation of water from the samples, the soils with moisture were prepared each day they were used.

### Procedure

Each judge attended five sessions as follows: Session 1, *preevaluation*; Session 2, *lecture training*; Session 3, *midevaluation*; Session 4, *interactive training*; and Session 5, *postevaluation*. Three different procedures were used in these sessions: one for the evaluation sessions (pre-, mid-, post-), and one for each of the two training sessions.

*Evaluation Procedure.* In each evaluation session, the judge was asked to use the "feel method" to estimate the percentage of sand, silt,[2] and clay, and to report the textural classification of each of the 16 evaluation soils. The experimenter repeated the judge's responses aloud in order to guarantee accurate recording. In addition, the time required for the soil judgments was recorded with a stopwatch; however, this dependent measure will not be considered here.[3] Finally, the judge was asked to indicate the likelihood that the texture judgment was correct; these likelihood ratings do not pertain to the issue of training efficacy and so will not be considered further here. Once the judge was satisfied with the responses, he/she was not allowed to change them. This same procedure was repeated in the mid- and postevaluation session for each of the 16 soils.

*Training Procedures.* The lecture training was given first followed within a period of 7 days by the midevaluation and interactive training. For half of the judges, the content of both training procedures dealt with the influence of coarse fragments; for the other half, the content dealt with excessive moisture. Although the training content was different, the training procedures were parallel in structure. The results indicated that the training generalized from one irrelevant factor to the other. Therefore, the two groups were combined in the analyses.

*Lecture Training.* A 30-min lecture training session consisted of verbal instructions recited to the judge by the experimenter. A set of concealed cue cards was used to produce uniformity.

In the first section of the lecture training procedure, evidence was presented that the irrelevant factor involved could cause erroneous judgments. Second, a formal definition of what constitutes the irrelevant factor was given. In the last section, seven suggestions were presented, each designed to help the soil judge deal with problems caused by the irrelevant factor. These were both physical ("remove as much water as possible") and cognitive ("make a judgment as to how much clay has been lost"). After completion of the three sections, the judge was asked to summarize the essentials of the training instructions in his/her own words. Any deletions or misunderstandings were corrected to ensure that the desired information had been communicated.

*Interactive Training.* A 30-min interactive training session was divided into four sections. In the first section, the judge was shown an outline of the seven suggestions from the prior lecture training and asked to paraphrase them. Training suggestions which were forgotten or mistakenly recalled were corrected.

The next part of the interactive training required the judge to assess a soil containing added irrelevant materials (either excessive moisture or coarse fragments). This soil had been shown earlier as a filler with the irrelevant material removed. Then the judge's current response was compared to the earlier response in an unfavorable light.[4] The point was made that any difference in the responses could only be due to the presence of the irrelevant factor; the differences were frequently quite large.

The third section of the interactive training involved the presentation of a set of three soils, two of which had never been analyzed by the judge (3 and 5); a third soil (6) was included to determine whether familiarity with specific evaluation soils influenced training effectiveness. The basic training strategy was based on the concept of successive approximations. To implement this strategy, each soil was initially assessed without any of the irrelevant factors present. Then, in successive stages, increasing amounts of irrelevant material were added and the soil was assessed again. The judge was reminded that the percentage judgments should not change as the irrelevant material increased. At each stage in order to focus attention on the irrelevance, the judge was also asked to estimate the amount of the irrelevant factor present in the soil sample.

In the last section, the judge reassessed a soil which had been seen in the first session as a filler. Then, however, the soil did not contain any irrelevant factors. In the training session, it contained a relatively large amount of irrelevant material. The training response was then compared to the one made earlier in as favorable a light as possible (see note 4). This was done to provide encouragement and to help the judge leave the training with a feeling of accomplishment. The interactive training procedure was followed by the postevaluation session and debriefing.

### Derivation of Dependent Measure

To evaluate both the influence of the irrelevant factors and the impact of the training procedures, analyses based on response differences were used.

The use of a derived dependent measure is necessary because individual differences in the judges' raw responses can bias the analyses at the group level. Derived scores were computed on an individual soil/judge basis: the response to the "irrelevance-absent" for each base soil was used as a standard, and the absolute difference between it and each of the three "irrelevance-present" instances to the soil was then obtained. Thus, the derived scores reflected the discrepancies between the base, or irrelevance-absent response, and irrelevance-present responses (calculated for each soil and judge).

## Results

The results relate directly to the first three issues raised in the introduction. First, do the irrelevant factors influence the judges' soil estimates? Second, do either of the training procedures reduce the influence of the irrelevant factors? Third, what influence does irrelevance and the subsequent training have on the accuracy of the judgments? (The fourth issue, related to long-term impact, will be taken up at the end of the section.) After presenting the results pertaining to these three main questions, some additional findings will be considered. All reported efforts were significant at $p < .05$.

### Influence of Irrelevant Factors

The initial influence of the irrelevant factors was reflected in the size of the preevaluation derived scores. The mean values for the three irrelevance conditions (coarse fragments, no moisture; no coarse fragments, excessive moisture; and coarse fragments, excessive moisture) were 12.1, 12.2, and 13.5 for sand, and 7.1, 10.2, and 7.1 for clay, respectively. For each of these conditions, a one-tail $t$-test against zero difference was significant. When present, therefore, the irrelevant materials caused both the sand and clay estimates to be different than those given for the otherwise identical base soil.

### Impact of Training

The training efficacy was examined by looking at changes in the derived scores across the evaluation sessions for both sand and clay. The resulting means are shown in Figure 19.2.

For both sand and clay, the means of the scores decreased ($F(2, 20) = 4.41$ and $F(2, 20) = 3.92$, respectively). A Newman–Keuls comparison of the means showed that for both scores, the decrease was significant only in the third evaluation session, i.e., following interactive training.

### Accuracy

The soil laboratory analysis (see Table 19.1) was used to compute an accuracy score based on the absolute difference between the judges' estimates

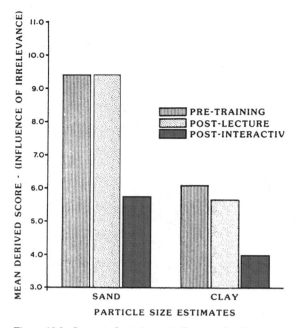

Figure 19.2.   Impact of training on influence of irrelevance as reflected in magnitude of derived scores.

for each soil and the corresponding laboratory analysis. It should be pointed out that examination of accuracy is quite important since it is possible for the training to reduce the influence of irrelevance, but not to improve accuracy.

Figure 19.3 shows the assessment errors for each of the three base soils for sand. The sand means for soils 2 and 4 became more accurate, while the estimates for soil 6 became less accurate. A significant session × soils interaction was obtained, $F(4, 40) = 5.20$ for sand; there was no significant change in the accuracy for clay.

### Additional Accuracy Results

Although the laboratory analyses remain the accepted standard for soil judgments, student judges are seldom able to compare their responses against this standard. Instead, the criterion to which they are routinely trained is their soil instructor's judgments. The estimates from the students' instructor appear in parenthesis in Table 19.1 for each soil. In the case of soils 2 and 4, his estimates are quite close to the laboratory analyses. However, his values for soil 6 are noticeably different from the laboratory standard.[5]

A set of accuracy analyses parallel to those presented earlier, but using the instructor as the standard, was conducted. The mean assessment errors

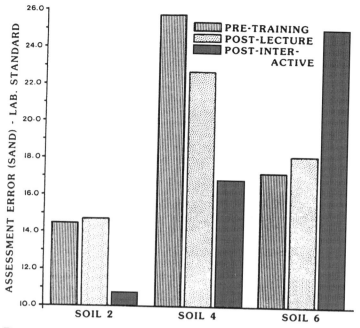

Figure 19.3. Change in assessment errors across evaluation sessions when laboratory analysis is used as standard.

for this analysis are given in Figure 19.4 for sand. In this case, the "instructor-based" accuracy increased significantly across sessions ($F(2, 20) = 4.85$) and was greatest following interactive training. Moreover, the convergence toward increased agreement occurred for all soils, including soil 6. As with the analysis based on the laboratory criterion, there was no significant change for clay.

*Follow-up*

In order to evaluate the long-term effects of training, an effort was made to recontact the judges at a later time. Five of the original 12 soil judges agreed to participate in the follow-up. They were contacted from 12 to 21 months after the completion of the original training study and were asked to judge the same set of soils used in the initial evaluations; however, they believed it was a different set. Two of the five judges were not available in person and so were sent the soils through the mail. This seemed to pose no problem because they were still familiar with the procedure and simply filled out their responses in a booklet rather than responding verbally.

The results showed that the influence of the irrelevant materials was consistently less than it was prior to the training. Figure 19.5 gives the difference

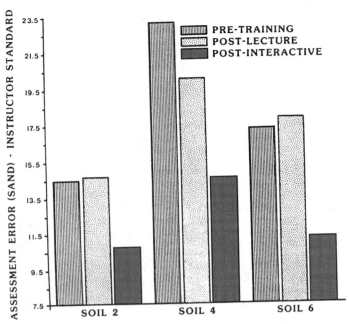

Figure 19.4. Change in assessment errors across evaluation sessions when soil instructor's responses are used as standard.

scores in the four evaluation sessions for these five judges. A $t$-test comparing the pretest influence of irrelevance with the follow-up showed a significant decrease for sand and a large, but nonsignificant, decrease for the clay percentages (5.08 versus 3.35). The issue of accuracy was again considered in the follow-up. In the case of these five soil judges the size of the errors decreased significantly for the sand estimates (18.42 versus 12.72) while there was no significant change for the clay errors (6.50 versus 7.45). In summary, at least for these soil judges, the training seemed to have had a lasting impact, both in terms of reducing the influence of irrelevance and in increasing accuracy for the sand estimates.

## Discussion

The results indicated that (a) the soil judges were adversely influenced by irrelevant factors, (b) the training procedures were effective in reducing this influence, (c) the training also increased accuracy, and (d) the training shows evidence of long-term effectiveness. Several implications of these results are discussed below.

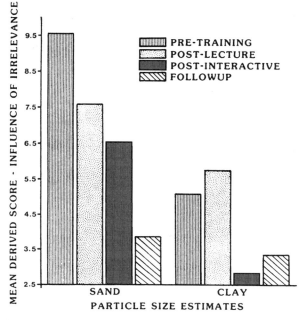

Figure 19.5.   Impact of training on influence of irrelevance as reflected in magnitude of derived scores for subjects in follow-up session.

### Impact of Irrelevance

Our results show that both irrelevant factors (coarse fragments and excessive moisture) produced changes in the judges' estimates. Two aspects of this finding are especially noteworthy. First, unlike the vast majority of previous studies of irrelevance, experienced judges were used here as subjects; moreover, they were motivated and cared about what they were doing. Second, the judges were asked to make judgments that were natural for them. In contrast, many studies using experts require that they work on unfamiliar tasks. This lends credence to the notion that the adverse influence of irrelevance, although typically demonstrated in laboratory studies, extends to at least some applied tasks.

### Efficacy of Training

As shown here, the training was successful in reducing the influence of irrelevant information both in the initial experiment and in the follow-up. Moreover, the evidence at the group level suggests that the interactive training played a critical role. A similar pattern of results was also seen for individual soil judges; for seven of the nine judges who were influenced by training, the improvement occurred following interactive training. In addition, the judges' verbal statements after the experiment revealed that the interactive training was more memorable than the lecture training. However, these results do not allow the conclusion that interactive training is entirely responsible for the impact of training; there are at least three alternatives.

One potential explanation is that the training impact was simply due to practice. If practice were responsible, then it follows that the responses to filler soils should have increased in accuracy across evaluation sessions. The judgments for the fillers, however, did not change across sessions ($F(2, 22) = .43$ for sand, and $F(2, 22) = 1.82$ for clay). Therefore, this explanation can be dismissed since practice alone is apparently not sufficient to account for the training efficacy.

A second possible explanation is that interactive training may have an effect because of the repetition of the lecture training suggestions; the basic ideas in lecture training were summarized as a part of interactive training. This explanation cannot be immediately dismissed; indeed, there is research which shows that repeated lecture training can be successful (Bruno & Harris, 1980; Lichtenstein & Fischhoff, 1980).

A final possibility is that training works because of a combination of the lecture and interactive approaches. The lecture may have supplied necessary cognitive knowledge, while the interactive training provided the perceptual skill needed to use this knowledge. This possibility also deserves some consideration. Thus additional research is needed to establish the locus of the training effect.

Nonetheless, there was both a substantial reduction in the influence of irrelevance and an increase in accuracy following the interactive training in this study. Given the ineffectiveness of prior training procedures, this result is quite encouraging and, in itself, represents a major accomplishment. It would be interesting to determine whether the success of the present approach to training expert judges generalizes to other decision tasks.

### Effects on Accuracy

The answer to the question, does the training improve accuracy, leads to a qualified "yes" for the sand estimates; training did not effect the clay estimates. The reason for the qualification stems from the choice of an accuracy standard. For the laboratory-derived standard, the accuracy increased for soil 2 and 4, and decreased for soil 6. However, for the instructor-derived standard, accuracy increased for all three soils. The situation which occurred with soil 6 is interesting in its own right and reveals the critical importance of selecting an appropriate accuracy standard in applied research studies.

## Long-term Effects

The finding of a long-lasting impact of training is especially encouraging. Since previous efforts at training decision makers have frequently failed, the finding of continued impact up to a year and a half later is certainly noteworthy.

Of course, it might be argued that the judges may have simply recalled their prior training session when they were recontacted; in practice, however, this training may have otherwise been forgotten. Although such partial forgetting is certainly possible, what is nonetheless significant is that judges could still recall their training experience. Indeed, several follow-up judges reported having clear memories of the interactive phase a year or more after training. Therefore, the training apparently had a considerable impact on the judge's memory.

## Implications of Training

*Focus on Irrelevance.* Taking an extreme position, there are two diametrically opposed approaches to training to reduce the influence of irrelevance. The commonsense approach dictates that concentration on the relevant dimensions will, by default, result in a decreased influence in irrelevant dimensions. Without question this position has logical merit. For example, the physician concerned with a diagnosis is unlikely to be influenced by the weather. Clearly, exclusive concentration on relevant dimensions successfully diminishes the use of irrelevant dimensions which are not related to the judgment at hand.

When the relevant and irrelevant dimensions are perceptually similar, however, the problem is different. For example, in a concept formation task, the subject may know that one dimension, e.g., texture, is irrelevant to the concept of, e.g., shape. Nevertheless, reaction time analyses show that subjects cannot simply ignore the irrelevant dimension through concentration on the relevant dimension (Williams, 1974). In the present case, distinguishing coarse fragments from sand is often quite difficult. Simply telling subjects to concentrate on the relevant information does not suffice as training.

The alternative approach which we adopted suggests that the training is more effective when the judges pay active attention to misleading irrelevant information. They are then told how to compensate for the effects of irrelevance. In addition, the suggestions which presumably helped them do this also increased accuracy.

*Generality.* The training procedures used in this study were designed to be useful in other applied judgment problems; most critically, the procedures do not depend on outcome (accuracy) feedback. A brief distillation of the interactive session may provide some additional insights into the training strategy.

The interactive training used a set of test stimuli which varied on only the irrelevant dimensions. In this case, a factorial design was used which contained stimuli with the irrelevant information both present and not present. However, a formal design is not necessary; if two stimuli differ by only irrelevant information, and the judge responds differently to them, then an influence of irrelevance has been established. This comparison can then be shown directly to the judge. In the case of the soil judges, we found this demonstration to have a considerable impact. Indeed, some of the follow-up judges commented that even after more than a year, this part of the personalized feedback was quite memorable.

The next phase of the interactive training involved practicing the lecture suggestions with real stimuli. A test set was used which contained stimuli varying only on the degree to which the irrelevant information is present. The judges then practiced responding to this stimulus set with the goal of learning to make exactly the same response even when the irrelevant material varied.

Finally, the judge looked at a new set of stimuli to determine if the influence of irrelevance had been reduced. Assessing the effectiveness of the training and recycling through it again may be necessary if the desired goals have not been met or if a refresher is needed.

Several other aspects of the training may also influence its potential for generality. First, outcome feedback was not used as part of the training procedures. When available, however, this may provide a useful addition. The judges could then be shown that the irrelevant information not only changed their judgments, but made them less accurate.

Second, our training relied heavily on the prior training and the previous experience of the judges. Because of that, we did not assume that any single suggestion would work for all the judges; rather we depended on the judges' skill to help them discover which one of the suggestions worked best. Hence, it may be very important to construct a set of suggestions from which the trainees can choose. Most likely, this contributed to the long-term success of this training.

*Extensions.* Without question the success of the training procedures used in this study depended heavily on specific tailoring to the soil judgment task. In fact, because soil judgment is largely "perceptual" in nature, the training (especially the interactive procedure) reflected a perceptual emphasis.

This may create some concern over the generalizability of the training to other less perceptually based judgment problems. However, we have recently been successful in adapting these training procedures to the problem of bias in personnel selection; sex, age, race may be considered as irrelevant, but influencing, factors. Similar training was useful in reducing the influence of these factors (Gaeth & Shanteau, 1982). Interestingly, it appears that in this more cognitively oriented task the lecture training may be nearly as effective as the interactive training.

Therefore, the training approach outlined in this study is apparently not restricted to perceptually based tasks. Instead, the approach seems to be generalizable to other types of judgment situations which involve various types of irrelevant information.

### Notes

1  All but one of the class members agreed to participate. One judge who participated was dropped from the analysis because of his inadequate familiarity with the USDA soil texture classification system. This judge had recently come from Europe and was taking the course as an introduction to the USDA soil judgment system.

2  The judges generally determine the amount of silt in a soil by first calculating the percent of sand and clay, and then subtracting from 100% to get the silt percentage. Thus, the silt values are both psychologically and statistically dependent on the sand and clay values. Because of this dependency, none of the analyses for the silt estimates will be reported.

3  Timings were taken of all soil assessments. It was hoped that these could be used as a measure of cognitive effort spent on each soil judgment. Unfortunately, because the judges were each run individually, some had a tendency to discuss what they were doing with the experimenter. It was decided that it was more important to maintain a cooperative environment and allow them to verbalize in a natural fashion than to demand silence.

4  There were two possible comparison responses available from the preevaluation session which could be used. In the initial stages of the interactive training, the preevaluation response which was the most distant from the training response was selected to impress upon the judge that the irrelevant information had a major influence. At the end of the interactive training, the preevaluation response which was closest to the training response was used in order to provide encouragement.

5  At a later time, the soil instructor was given an opportunity to reevaluate soil 6. At this time he reported that he may have initially misinterpreted the fine sand as silt. Consideration of the detailed laboratory results (which he was not aware of) showed that a large portion of sand was indeed very fine, i.e., the physical size difference in these particle classes is very small. This gives some idea of the highly developed perceptual skills needed for the soil judgment task. Almost all the soil judges were "fooled" by the fine sand present in soil 6 and interpreted it as silt. However, when the soils instructor estimates were used as a standard, the accuracy increased across the evaluation session for all soils, including soil 6. Thus, the soil judges were converging to what, to them, may be considered to be the more appropriate standard. This relationship between the instructor and the students bears an interesting resemblance to previous work in animal science by Phelps (1977). She found that the judgment strategies of student livestock judges were quite similar to those of the instructor they were currently training with. In some cases, this was to the detriment of the accuracy of their judgments. Thus, the students were making their judgments in a fashion consistent with their current instructor, regardless of the absolute accuracy standard.

## References

Beach, L. R., Mitchell, T. R., Deaton, M. D., & Prothero, J. Information relevance, content, and source credibility in the revision of opinions. *Organizational Behavior and Human Performance*, 1978, *21*, 1–16.

Besner, D., & Coltheart, M. Mental size scaling examined. *Memory & Cognition*, 1976, *4*, 525–531.

Bruno, K. J., & Harris, R. J. The effect of repetition on the discrimination of asserted and implied claims in advertising. *Applied Psycholinguistics*, 1980, *1*, 307–321.

Bundesen, C., & Larsen, A. Visual transformation of size. *Journal of Experimental Psychology: Human Perception and Performance*, 1975, *1*, 214–220.

Bush, E. S., & Cohen, L. B. Effects of relevant and irrelevant labels on short-term memory in nursery-school children. *Psychonomic Science*, 1970, *18*, 228–229.

Clarke, G. R. *The study of soil in the field*. Oxford: Claredon Press, 1936.

Eimas, P. D. Effects of overtraining on irrelevant stimuli and training task reversal on reversal discrimination learning in children. *Journal of Experimental Child Psychology*, 1966, *3*, 315–323.

Einhorn, H. J., & Hograth, R. M. Behavioral decision theory: Processes of judgment and choice. *Annual Review of Psychology*, 1981, *21*, 53–88.

Evans, R. A., & Beedle, R. K. Discrimination learning in mentally-retarded children as a function of irrelevant dimension variability. *American Journal of Mental Deficiency*, 1970, *74*, 568–573.

Fischhoff, B. Hindsight ≠ Foresight. The effect of outcome knowledge on judgment under uncertainty. *Journal of Experimental Psychology: Human Perception and Performance*. 1975, *1*, 288–299.

Fischhoff, B., & Slovic, P. A little learning . . . . : Confidence in multicue judgment. In R. Nickerson (Ed.), *Attention and performance, VIII*. Hillsdale, N.J.: Erlbaum, 1980.

Fischhoff, B., Slovic, P., & Lichtenstein, S. Knowing with certainty: The appropriateness of extreme confidence. *Journal of Experimental Psychology: Human Perception and Performance*, 1977, *3*, 552–564.

Ford, J. M., Hink, R. F., Hopkins, W. F., Roth, W. T., Pfefferbaum. A., & Kopell. B. S. Age effects on event-related potentials in a selective attention task. *Journal of Gerontology*, 1979, *34*, 388–395.

Gaeth, G. J., & Shanteau, J. *Psychological analysis of the 1978 national soil judging contest.* (Applied Psychology Report No. 79-10.) Manhattan, Kan.: Kansas State University, 1979.

Gaeth, G. J., & Shanteau, J. *Hand method of soil texture assessment: A psychological analysis of accuracy.* Paper presented at the SCSS Conference, Fort Collins, Colorado, 1980.

Gaeth, G. J., & Shanteau, J. *A bibliography of research on the effects of irrelevance in psychology.* (Applied Psychology Report No. 81-13.) Manhattan Kan.: Kansas State University, 1981.

Gaeth, G. J., & Shanteau, J. Reducing bias in personnel selection by cognitive training. *Bulletin of Psychonomic Society*, 1982 (abstact).

Gordon, I. E. Donders' c-reactions and irrelevant stimulus variety. *British Journal of Psychology*, 1970, *61*, 359–363.

Griffitt, W., & Jackson, T. Influence of information about ability and nonability on personnel selection decisions. *Psychological Reports*, 1970, *27*, 959–962.

Harris, R. J. The comprehension of pragmatic implications in advertising. *Journal of Applied Psychology*, 1977, *62*, 603–608.

Hoyer, W. J., Rebok, G. W., & Sved, S. M. Effects of varying irrelevant information on adult age differences in problem solving. *Journal of Gerontology*, 1979, *34*, 553–560.

Kahneman, A. *Attention and effort.* Englewood Cliffs, N.J.: Prentice-Hall, 1973.

Kausler, D. H., & Kleim, D. M. Age differences in processing relevant versus irrelevant stimuli in multiple-item recognition learning. *Journal of Gerontology,* 1978, *33,* 87–93.

Larsen, A., & Bundesen, C. Size scaling in visual pattern recognition. *Journal of Experimental Psychology: Human Perception and Performance.* 1978, *4,* 1–20.

Lichtenstein, S., & Fischhoff, B. Training for calibration. *Organizational Behavior and Human Performance,* 1980, *26,* 149–171.

Low, L. A., Coste, E., & Kirkup, C. Developmental differences in concept transfer as a function of variability of irrelevant features during acquisition. *Bulletin of Psychonomic Society,* 1980, *16,* 19–22.

Mitchell, H. E., & Byrne, D. *Minimizing the influence of irrelevant factors in the courtroom: The defendant's character, judge's instructions, and authoritarianism.* Paper presented at the Annual Meeting of the Midwestern Psychological Association, Cleveland, May 1972.

Montague, W. E. Effect of irrelevant information on a complex auditory-discrimination task. *Journal of Experimental Psychology,* 1965, *69,* 230–236.

Nagy, C. *How are personnel selection decisions made? An analysis of decision strategies in a simulated personnel selection task.* Unpublished doctoral dissertation, Kansas State University, 1981.

Phelps, R. H. *Expert livestock judgment: A descriptive analysis of the development of expertise.* Unpublished doctoral dissertation, Kansas State University, 1977.

Rabbitt, P. An age decrement in the ability to ignore irrelevant information. *Journal of Gerontology,* 1965, *20,* 233–238.

Rice, M. F. Influence of irrelevant biographical information in teacher evaluation. *Journal of Educational Psychology,* 1975, *67,* 658–662.

Shanteau, J., & Phelps, R. H. Judgment and swine: Approaches and issues in applied judgment analysis. In M. F. Kaplan & S. Schwartz (Eds.), *Human judgment and decision processes in applied settings.* New York: Academic Press, 1977.

Shantz, C. U. Effects of redundant and irrelevant information on children's seriation ability. *Journal of Experimental Child Psychology,* 1967, *5,* 208–222.

Slovic, P., & Fischhoff, B. On the psychology of experimental surprises. *Journal of Experimental Psychology: Human Perception and Performance,* 1977, *3,* 544–551.

Slovic, P., Fischhoff, B., & Lichtenstein, S. Behavior decision theory. *Annual Review of Psychology,* 1977, *28,* 1–39.

Slovic, P., & Lichtenstein, S. Comparison of Bayesian and regression approaches to the study of information processing in judgment. *Organizational Behavior and Human Performance,* 1971, *6,* 649–744.

Sue, S., Smith, R. E., & Caldwell, C. Effects of admissible evidence on the decisions of simulated jurors: A moral dilemma. *Journal of Applied Social Psychology,* 1973, *3,* 345–353.

Williams, C. The effect of an irrelevant dimension on "same–different" judgments of multi-dimensional stimuli. *Quarterly Journal of Experimental Psychology,* 1974, *26,* 26–31.

# 20 Expert Judgment: Some Necessary Conditions and an Example

*Hillel J. Einhorn*

In an age of increasing specialization, it is quite likely that greater numbers of people will have to rely on expert judgment. It is therefore an important matter to discuss some of the conditions that produce "expertise." Is an expert simply one who is very skillful with training and knowledge in some specialized field or are there perhaps more objective criteria that can be used? The purpose of this study is to discuss and illustrate some necessary, if not sufficient, conditions for defining expertise within a given situation. The type of situation to be considered is one in which several judges have to deal with multidimensional information. This information has to be measured and combined into a decision or global judgment. This is a very general task, specific examples of which might include: (a) radiologists viewing an X ray and coming to a diagnosis; (b) businessmen making a sales forecast for a new product; (c) art critics viewing a painting and judging its quality, etc.

The expert must *identify* information or cues from the multidimensional stimulus he encounters. These cues are diagnostic (i.e., contain information) about the final decision or judgment. The expert's ability to identify cues can be seen as a problem of extracting weak signals from a background of noise (e.g., Green & Swets, 1966). While each cue is related to the final categorization, it also serves the function of leading the expert to other cues that will also be of importance in the determination of the final categorization. For example, consider the cue of "product safety." While this cue can be related to how much sales we can expect, it is also indicative of other cues in the product (its price may be higher due to safety features). When one considers that the expert may deal with many cases in the course of time,

This chapter is an abbreviated version of an article that originally appeared in the *Journal of Applied Psychology*, 1974, 59(5), 562–571. Copyright © 1974 by the American Psychological Association.

it is not unreasonable to assume that he builds up expectations regarding both what variables typically covary together and the strength of this co-variation.

Consider that the expert must measure two cues that he considers to be highly related, for example, the degree of workmanship and the quality of material in a particular product. If he believes that these cues covary together, it is quite likely that his measurement of one cue will affect his measurement of the other. This is similar to what has been termed a *logical error* (Guilford, 1954); that is, traits that logically go together are rated in similar ways. The relationship different experts expect between cues may vary due to their different experience and training. Furthermore, this is not an error but reflects each expert's way of *organizing information into clusters or dimensions*.[1] From a psychological point of view, this clustering of information serves to reduce the dimensionality of the information one has to process; that is, instead of having to process many cues, one only has to deal with a smaller number of general factors.

While cues are being identified and clustered together, the expert is *measuring the amount* of the cue. The businessman may say that a product is "tasty," but *how* "tasty"? In many types of situations the expert will have to serve as a measuring instrument for cues that cannot be measured in more objective ways (cf. Sawyer, 1966).

There are three issues that are important in discussing the measurement of cues: (a) intrajudge reliability, (b) construct validity (Cronbach & Meehl, 1955), and (c) judgmental bias. With regard to intrajudge reliability, it should be obvious that unless the expert can reproduce his measurements of the cues, there is little more that can be said in defense of his expertise. Therefore, high intrajudge reliability is a necessity for expertise. With regard to construct validity, it should be the case that the cues being measured should have status as explanatory concepts. Operationally, we would expect that the cues show both convergent and discriminant validity when they are considered as traits (judges are considered methods) in a multitrait–multimethod matrix (Campbell & Fiske, 1959). Finally, with regard to judgmental bias, we should expect that expert judges will not show such well-known biases as *leniency*, *halo*, etc. (Guilford, 1954; Ghiselli & Brown, 1955). All three of the above criteria should be considered in evaluating expertise.

After cues are identified, measured, and clustered, the important cognitive work of *weighting and combining* to form a global evaluation follows. This part of the judgment task has received the greatest amount of attention (Slovic & Lichtenstein, 1971). The results of a large number of studies have shown that judges are quite poor at weighting and combining information accurately, that is, in accord with the objective validity of the information. However, objective validity implies that the criteria used as the basis for comparing the global evaluation were themselves relevant to the ultimate criteria in question (Thorndike, 1949). In many cases, availability of criteria, not relevance, was used to define the objective measure. It is therefore possible that global judgments have more validity than it has been possible to demonstrate thus far.

Since questions of criterion relevance cannot be fully answered, and since some situations contain no criteria, is there some other way of evaluating global judgments? Let us take the same line of inquiry that was used in the measurement of traits; that is: Is the global evaluation an operational concept in the sense of possessing convergent validity? While it would seem important that experts agree on their evaluations (as a condition for expertise), the issue is considerably more complicated. The concept of agreement can itself be thought of in two ways: (a) agreement "in fact" and (b) agreement "in principle." The former refers to actual agreement of evaluation, whereas the latter refers to agreement with respect to weighting and combining policy, that is, *how* the global evaluation is to be formed once the inputs are specified. Although one may have agreement in principle, there may be disagreement with respect to the coding of input (note that coding of input is also dependent on the perceived covariation of the cues). Therefore, agreement in fact will be a function of weighting and combining similarity *and* similarity in coding cues. On the other hand, it should not be assumed that agreement in principle is easy to achieve. This is due to the fact that learning probabilistic relationships in the natural environment may be quite difficult. This implies that there is great room for individual differences in the evaluation of the diagnosticity of cues and subsequently, large differences in the weights assigned to those cues. Furthermore, even when training is rigorous and the conditions for learning optimal, similar weighting policies may reflect training in a particular school of thought. It seems that policies would be very similar within but not between competing schools (a practical application of this is Naylor & Wherry's, 1965, technique for grouping judges on the basis of similarity of their weighting policies).

Although the difficulty of achieving either type of agreement is great, it should be the case that there is at least a common core of knowledge which is germane to a particular area of inquiry. Furthermore, expertise consists, to some extent, of knowing that common core. Therefore, as a practical guide it is proposed that there be at least some agreement, both in fact and in principle, for the global evaluation.[2]

With the discussion of the factors involved in expert judgment, there is a need to illustrate, in a concrete manner, how the various criteria discussed in this study can be used in evaluation of real experts. The purpose of the present study is to make explicit the processes assumed to be present in the preceding discussion. The details of the study to be described appear in Coppleson, Factor, Strum, Graff, and Rappaport (1970) and Einhorn (1972).

## Method

*Subjects*

The judges we considered were three medical pathologists. This specialty requires considerable training and is of special importance since the pathologist's report is often the ultimate criterion that is used for the diagnosis of various diseases.

*Procedure*

The three pathologists independently viewed 193 biopsy slides taken from patients having Hodgkin's disease, a cancer of the lymph system. The biopsies were taken when the patient first entered the hospital. The only information given to the pathologists was the biopsy slide. All the slides used in this study were taken from patients who had died and from whom complete data were available with respect to the ratings to be described.

For each slide, the pathologist had to give his judgment of the amount of nine histological characteristics that were chosen, a priori, to be important. The histological signs were as follows: benign histiocytes, malignant histiocytes, eosinophils, necrosis, plasma cells, neutrophils, lymphocytes, Sternberg-Reed distribution, and Sternberg-Reed cells. For each of these signs, with the exception of Sternberg-Reed distribution (which was measured on a 2-point scale), a 6-point scale was used, which was developed by the pathologists.

In addition to the judgments of the amounts of the histological characteristics, a global judgment concerning the classification of the disease in terms of severity was also made. This judgment was measured on a 9-point scale (higher values representing greater severity). The global judgment was made after the judgments of the histological signs. Finally, 26 of the slides were repeated twice each so that estimates of test–retest reliability (the ability to reproduce the judgments) could be obtained.

Although the judges picked out the signs they expected to measure, one would expect that experts with experience in this task would have little difficulty in recognition of attributes, whereas the judgment of amount would be of most concern. However, definitions of each sign were not given so that any differences the judges had in this regard would be revealed in the later analyses. Of special importance is the fact that the multidimensional stimulus was viewed intact, so that interactions, context effects, etc. could play whatever role they normally did in the task.

## Results

The first question addressed was whether the ratings or cue measurements were reliable; that is: Could the expert, when viewing exactly the same slide on two occasions, give the same response? Mean intrajudge reliability for the signs ranged from .19 to .93 (over the three judges), while the mean global judgment reliability was .63 (over the three judges). The mean reliability for the three judges (over signs) ranged from .64 to .74. Judge 2 had a slightly higher reliability for the signs, but his reliability on the global judgment (.46) was considerably lower than that of the other judges (.69, .71). The average reliability over both judges, signs, and global judgments was .69.

Convergent and discriminant validity were examined for evidence of construct validity. Convergent validity refers to the fact that different methods (judges) should converge in measuring the same trait (sign); the correlation between judges for the same sign should be greater than zero. Discriminant validity, on the other hand, is defined by three conditions: (a) The correlation between the same traits (signs) for different judges should be higher than the correlation between different traits as measured by different judges. (b) The correlation between the same signs as measured by different judges should be higher than the correlations between different signs as measured by the same judge. (c) The pattern of correlations should be the same in the submatrices of the multitrait–multimethod matrix. This refers to the ordering in both sign and magnitude of the correlations in the heterotrait–heteromethod matrices.[3]

The multitrait–multimethod (multisign–multijudge) matrix is shown in Table 20.1.

Looking first at convergent validity, 29 of the 30 correlations between judges' measures of signs were significant at $p < .01$. Furthermore, the average of these correlations was .56 – evidence of convergent validity. It should be noted that convergent validity, in situations where a single judge is defined as a method, is the same as *inter*judge reliability, or agreement. The amount of agreement was considerably different for the various signs (.33 to .80). Notice should be given to the fact that the greatest amount of disagreement was with respect to the global judgment (.27). This finding is in accord with earlier remarks about the global judgment being a composite variable. As far as the mean agreement for the three pairs of judges, over all signs, Judges 1 and 2 agreed with each other most (.64), with Judges 1 and 3 next (.52), and Judges 2 and 3 agreeing least (.50).

In analyzing discriminant validity of 540 comparisons, there were only 20 violations (or 4%) of the requirement that the correlation between the same signs for different judges be higher than the correlation between different signs as measured by different judges. Additionally, there were only 32 violations of the 540 comparisons (or 6%) of the requirement of discriminant validity that correlations between the same signs as measured by different judges be higher than the correlations between different signs as measured by the same judge. Given that this requirement is quite stringent and the percentage of violations small, it seems fair to conclude that this condition was also met. Examination of the submatrices further showed that the pattern of correlations was the same in the submatrices, indicating that the third condition for discriminant validity had been met. Therefore, it seems fair to conclude that these data showed both convergent and discriminant validity.

Guilford (1954) presented an analysis of variance approach for dealing with judgmental biases found in the use of rating scales. While the situation that this approach was originally developed for involved raters rating employees on various traits, the general idea is applicable to any situation where judges rate objects on a number of dimensions (Stanley, 1961, also discusses this basic design). Although Guilford's procedure is applicable to the present data, there is a slight difference. In Guilford's example (pp. 280–288), each rater rates each ratee on each attribute only once. In the present study, using the 26 repeat slides, we have a Judges × Slides × Signs design with two replications. The last two factors are repeated and therefore an appropriate way to analyze these data is given by Winer (1962, pp. 319–337). This analysis of variance is presented in Table 20.2.

Note first that the main effect for judges is not significant. Since this effect represents the judges' overall tendency to rate the amount of the signs, this indicates a lack of a *leniency* error. (Leniency in this case refers to a tendency to overvalue or undervalue the slides in general). The lack of an effect in the present context is more in accord with what one would expect from expert judges. The two other main effects simply indicate that different slides and different signs have varying means. What is of major concern are the interactions involving the judges' factor. These involve the differential effect of judges on slides (A × B), on signs (A × C) and on Slides × Signs (A × B × C). These interactions should be nonsignificant; that is, differential effects due to judges are not consistent with the fact that the shared core of expertise is influencing their measurement. Consider the Judges × Slides (A × B) interaction. This interaction involves the particular judge's tendency to overvalue or undervalue particular slides. This can be conceptualized as a *halo* effect; that is, a general tendency dominates the ratings of the particular attributes. In this situation, a halo effect would mean that the pathologists first get a general impression of severity and then work at rating the signs in accord with this general impression. However, this interaction is not significant indicating the absence of any halo. Both the Judges × Signs (A × C) and the Judges × Signs × Slides (A × B × C) are significant, although the magnitude of these interactions is quite small. The former interaction indicates that the judges differentially rate the signs; that is, some judges *see* more or less of some signs than others. The three-way interaction indicates that judges differentially rate signs depending on what slide the sign appears in. This is a type of context effect that is specific to the judges. However, it should be stressed that the significant interactions are all quite small. For these particular experts then, there seems to be only slight bias in their judgmental ratings.

Table 20.1. *Multitrait (Signs)–Multimethod (Judges) Matrix*

| | Lukes | BH | MH | Eos. | Nec. | PC | Neut. | Lymph. | S-R D. | S-R C. |
|---|---|---|---|---|---|---|---|---|---|---|
| **Judge 1** | | | | | | | | | | |
| Lukes | (690) | | | | | | | | | |
| BH | −044 | (430) | | | | | | | | |
| MH | 302 | −061 | (820) | | | | | | | |
| Eos. | 217 | −116 | 138 | (860) | | | | | | |
| Nec. | 058 | 100 | 370 | 134 | (840) | | | | | |
| PC | 126 | −035 | 061 | 104 | 105 | (470) | | | | |
| Neut. | 212 | 114 | 193 | 294 | 302 | 189 | (490) | | | |
| Lymph. | −310 | −212 | −447 | −420 | −288 | −159 | −422 | (850) | | |
| S-R D. | 280 | −094 | 539 | 172 | 160 | 007 | 184 | −339 | (220) | |
| S-R C. | 306 | −131 | 449 | 027 | 191 | 029 | 129 | −139 | 461 | (590) |
| **Judge 2** | | | | | | | | | | |
| Lukes | **400** | 016 | 135 | −091 | 116 | 038 | −086 | −021 | 160 | 275 |
| BH | −041 | **446** | 049 | −108 | 190 | −012 | 027 | −231 | −017 | −083 |
| MH | 241 | −096 | **634** | 071 | 144 | 060 | 082 | −318 | 484 | 402 |
| Eos. | 109 | −037 | 114 | **824** | 099 | 069 | 266 | −387 | 119 | −048 |
| Nec. | 121 | 128 | 382 | 142 | **858** | 069 | 301 | −320 | 230 | 195 |
| PC | 013 | −098 | −047 | 132 | 069 | **600** | 161 | −157 | −115 | −100 |
| Neut. | 239 | −007 | 235 | 294 | 368 | 217 | **655** | −471 | 270 | 153 |
| Lymph. | −217 | −133 | −356 | −348 | −316 | −088 | −424 | **686** | −264 | −120 |
| S-R D. | 160 | −078 | 285 | −037 | 056 | 072 | 056 | −118 | **489** | 266 |
| S-R C. | 156 | −093 | 315 | −018 | 080 | 044 | 031 | −115 | 332 | **596** |
| **Judge 3** | | | | | | | | | | |
| Lukes | **209** | 069 | 233 | 090 | 170 | 093 | 101 | −225 | 141 | 229 |
| BH | −037 | **305** | −093 | −072 | −129 | 020 | −103 | −104 | 072 | −042 |
| MH | 222 | 053 | **500** | 084 | 354 | 111 | 214 | −351 | 365 | 412 |
| Eos. | 190 | −058 | 075 | **776** | 094 | 050 | 322 | −409 | 169 | 049 |
| Nec. | 118 | 031 | 282 | 188 | **572** | 154 | 479 | −442 | 194 | 140 |
| PC | 139 | −008 | −004 | 086 | 094 | **420** | 189 | −180 | −061 | 011 |
| Neut. | 265 | 004 | 195 | 277 | 362 | 159 | **674** | −516 | 206 | 100 |
| Lymph. | −188 | −239 | −324 | −245 | −318 | −115 | −393 | **614** | −215 | −131 |
| S-R D. | 255 | −080 | 252 | 319 | 162 | 086 | 272 | −260 | **365** | 295 |
| S-R C. | 275 | −087 | 298 | 120 | 221 | 049 | 215 | −173 | 386 | **558** |

Table 20.1. *(continued)*

| | | | | | Judge 2 | | | | | |
|---|---|---|---|---|---|---|---|---|---|---|
| | *Lukes* | *BH* | *MH* | *Eos.* | *Nec.* | *PC* | *Neut.* | *Lymph.* | *S-R D.* | *S-R C.* |
| Lukes | (460) | | | | | | | | | |
| BH | 051 | (710) | | | | | | | | |
| MH | 179 | −036 | (860) | | | | | | | |
| Eos. | −113 | −021 | 015 | (900) | | | | | | |
| Nec. | 108 | 102 | 180 | 129 | (840) | | | | | |
| PC | −051 | 031 | −086 | 131 | 053 | (530) | | | | |
| Neut. | 033 | 095 | 139 | 339 | 374 | 191 | (640) | | | |
| Lymph. | −062 | −237 | −282 | −407 | −305 | −127 | −536 | (760) | | |
| S-R D. | 169 | −031 | 451 | −033 | 100 | −109 | 076 | −088 | (170) | |
| S-R C. | 169 | −113 | 511 | −074 | 043 | −065 | 045 | −072 | 386 | (830) |
| *Judge 3* | | | | | | | | | | |
| Lukes | **199** | −022 | 232 | 054 | 168 | 049 | 054 | −197 | 049 | 193 |
| BH | −040 | **327** | −047 | −020 | −137 | 032 | −126 | −031 | 130 | 056 |
| MH | 184 | 042 | **503** | −005 | 367 | −009 | 224 | −279 | 291 | 323 |
| Eos. | −035 | −017 | 027 | **783** | 094 | 082 | 315 | −406 | 017 | 009 |
| Nec. | 029 | 076 | 097 | 158 | **561** | 106 | 510 | −393 | 115 | 142 |
| PC | −015 | 122 | −019 | 057 | 032 | **527** | 191 | −170 | −071 | 048 |
| Neut. | 016 | 076 | 080 | 261 | 341 | 102 | **652** | −446 | 136 | 105 |
| Lymph. | −052 | −182 | −195 | −220 | −331 | −046 | −386 | **629** | −126 | −102 |
| S-R D. | 075 | −043 | 179 | 251 | 141 | 045 | 327 | −231 | **124** | 201 |
| S-R C. | 267 | −151 | 275 | 022 | 245 | −129 | 207 | −169 | 278 | **423** |

| | | | | | Judge 3 | | | | | |
|---|---|---|---|---|---|---|---|---|---|---|
| | *Lukes* | *BH* | *MH* | *Eos.* | *Nec.* | *PC* | *Neut.* | *Lymph.* | *S-R D.* | *S-R C.* |
| *Judge 3* | | | | | | | | | | |
| Lukes | (710) | | | | | | | | | |
| BH | −159 | (400) | | | | | | | | |
| MH | 335 | −119 | (720) | | | | | | | |
| Eos. | 119 | −006 | 072 | (950) | | | | | | |
| Nec. | 086 | −060 | 309 | 191 | (550) | | | | | |
| PC | 175 | 100 | 028 | 136 | 165 | (570) | | | | |
| Neut. | 113 | −016 | 186 | 343 | 672 | 162 | (550) | | | |
| Lymph. | −229 | −089 | −436 | −331 | −443 | −158 | −455 | (730) | | |
| S-R D. | 056 | 011 | 250 | 306 | 351 | 002 | 345 | −164 | (160) | |
| S-R C. | 343 | 080 | −427 | 133 | 258 | −043 | 276 | −302 | 407 | (590) |

*Note*: Correlations are based on $n = 193$. Validity diagonals are in boldface. Correlations in parentheses are intrajudge reliabilities ($n = 26$). Lukes = judgment of severity; BH = benign histiocytes; MH = malignant histiocytes; Eos. = eosinophils; Nec. = necrosis; PC = plasma cells; Neut. = neutrophils; Lymph. = lymphocytes; S-R D. = Sternberg-Reed distribution; S-R C. = Sternberg-Reed cells.

Table 20.2. *Analysis of Variance for Judges × Slides × Signs*

| Source | SS | df | MS | F |
|---|---|---|---|---|
| Judges (A) | 2.38 | 2 | 1.19 | <1 |
| Subjects × within | 3.88 | 3 | 1.29 | |
| Slides (B) | 160.70 | 25 | 6.43 | 14.61** |
| A × B | 21.10 | 50 | .44 | 1.47 |
| B × subjects within | 22.75 | 75 | .30 | |
| Signs (C) | 975.63 | 8 | 187.80 | 257.26** |
| A × C | 26.37 | 16 | 1.65 | 2.26* |
| C × subjects within | 17.62 | 24 | .73 | |
| B × C | 976.08 | 200 | 4.88 | 13.94** |
| A × B × C | 159.15 | 400 | .40 | 1.14* |
| B × C × subjects within | 208.93 | 600 | .35 | |

*Note:* All factors are assumed fixed.
\* $p < .05$.
\*\* $p < .001$.

One final analysis is necessary to complete the results on bias. Because of the qualitative difference between the global judgment and the individual cues, a separate one-way analysis of variance (repeated measures on each slide for the three judges) was performed on the global judgments. The results showed a significant effect with Judges 1 and 2 being most different ($\bar{Y}_1 = 2.98$, $\bar{Y}_2 = 4.61$). Therefore, Judge 2 saw more severity generally than did Judge 1, although both judges did *not* see different amounts of the signs. As has been pointed out before, this is consistent with the remarks made concerning the difficulty of achieving agreement on global variables. . . .

In order to examine the weighting process, the combining function was assumed to be additive (Dawes & Corrigan, 1974). The weights given to the cues were determined by regressing the global judgment on the nine cues, for each judge. . . . The results of this analysis are shown in Table 20.3.

It can be seen that the ability to model the judge varies among these three judges. The multiple correlation for Judge 2 is low, as compared to the other two judges. What is most important is the fact that the weights for the cues vary greatly across the three judges. Consider Experts 1 and 2. As we have previously seen, these two experts have very similar factor structures, yet they weight the cues quite differently in coming to their global judgment. As a matter of fact, the cue that is weighted most heavily by Judge 1, Sternberg-Reed cells, is not weighted significantly by Judge 2. Consider the weighting policies of Judges 1 and 3. They do agree that Sternberg-Reed cells should be weighted most highly, yet Judge 3 weights three other cues as being important (benign histiocytes, malignant histiocytes, and plasma cells), while Judge 1 does not. Clearly then, in addition to there being low agreement in

Table 20.3. *Beta Weights for Cues in Predicting Global Judgment*

| | | | | | | | | | | |
|---|---|---|---|---|---|---|---|---|---|---|
| | | | | | Cues | | | | | |
| Judges | BH | MH | Eos. | Nec. | PC | Neut. | Lymph | S-R D. | S-R C. | Multiple R |
| 1 | .00 | .12 | .11 | −.13* | .08 | .08 | −.16* | .05 | .22*** | .46*** |
| 2 | .04 | .07 | −.13* | .08 | −.03 | .00 | −.05 | .09 | .09 | .27* |
| 3 | −.14** | .22*** | .07 | −.11 | .19*** | .02 | −.07 | −.11 | .29*** | .49*** |

*Note:* Results are based on regressions with $n = 193$. BH = benign histiocytes; MH = malignant histi-ocytes; Eos. = eosinophils; Nec. = necrosis; PC = plasma cells; Neut. = neutrophils; Lymph. = lym-phocytes; S-R D. = Sternberg-Reed distribution; S-R C. = Sternberg-Reed cells.
* $p < .10$.
** $p < .05$.
*** $p < .01$.

fact, there is also low agreement in principle. From our previous results we can say that disagreement in fact is mostly accounted for by disagreement in principle, since the judges seem to code the data in very similar ways.

## Discussion

The implications of the results on information weighting for defining ex-pertise are problematic. If one requires that experts have similar weighting policies, the problem of adequately defining *similarity* is immediately raised. For example, Judges 1 and 3 do agree on the importance of Sternberg-Reed cells, yet they do not agree on the weighting of the other cues. On the other hand, Judge 2 is clearly different from either Judges 1 or 3. It should be men-tioned that Judge 2 was a resident of Judge 1 and was learning this task to some extent. His low correlation suggests another possible criterion for ex-pertise – experts should have at least one significant cue weight. The reason for this is that at least some information in the cues should be used in forming the global judgment.

Although requiring experts to have similar weighting policies would be a very stringent requirement, it would seem that the combining of information lies at the core of expertise. Learning the important relationships between cues and criteria should be one of the most important kinds of learning that is involved in mastering a particular area. Therefore, it is tentatively suggested that experts should exhibit similar weighting policies.

It was stated at the outset that the conditions discussed in the present study were necessary but not sufficient. This clearly implies that other factors are indicative of expertise. Consider our example of businessmen making a forecast of sales for a new product. Whereas they may agree on what some of the relevant attributes of the product are, the real expert may discern/form cues that no one has ever seen before. Similarly, the expert may be the one who can discern and use contingent relationships between cues, that is, complex interactions among cues. These aspects of cue formation and utilization may be an important aspect of expertise.

A second consideration not discussed in this study is how alternatives are first formed in the decision/judgment process. For example, although there may be several ways to market a new product, the expert may be able to elucidate alternatives that have not been thought of before. Again, this is a creative process that we know little about.

A third consideration, somewhat related to the first two, is how the task is *structured*. By this is meant how the problem is defined and the manner in which a solution will be attempted. For example, the process of information search will greatly structure the task. Kleinmuntz (1968) suggests that the expert searches his environment for those cues that yield the greatest amount of information, and this leads to a shortening of the "decision tree" used to reach a judgment. These types of problems have not been discussed in this study since the experiment served to structure the task. However, in nonexperimental settings, this structuring will undoubtedly be of great importance.

A major criticism of the conditions for expertise stated in the present context may be that too much stress has been put on agreement. This agreement has been with respect to clustering, measuring, and weighting cues. As is well known, the history of science is replete with oddballs who did not agree with anyone, yet were proved to be correct by subsequent events. This criticism has value, yet it conceals the fact that eventually some relevant criterion other than agreement became available (possibly due to new instrumentation or unusual events). However, from a practical point of view, we cannot afford to wait long periods of time to see who may be correct. Actions and decisions have to be taken within a limited time perspective. Therefore, although agreement is by no means the only criterion, it is one that seems relevant to the discussion of expertise.

Where a relevant, or partially relevant criterion can be known within a reasonable time period, expertise can be determined by one's track record. If it is found that two experts do equally well in terms of matching a criterion (and this is significantly higher than some base rate value), yet they do not meet the requirements discussed in the present study (especially that of similar weighting), what are we to say? We can only say that in a highly probabilistic world, there may be many routes to the same goal (cf. Hammond, 1955) and that there may be more than one way to perform the cognitive tasks involved in judgment.

### Notes

1  It has been noted that in situations where an objective measure of the relationship between cues is given, subjects find it very difficult to learn them if they

are different from their preconceived ideas of what "go together" (Chapman & Chapman, 1969).

2 In cases where experts are from competing schools, we might expect high negative correlations.

3 These conditions can be expressed formally. Let, $x_{ijs}$ = rating on $i$th slide by $i$th judge for $s$th sign. Let $i \neq i'$, $j \neq j'$, $s \neq s'$. Convergent validity then refers to $\rho_{x_{.js'}x_{.j's}} > 0$ (correlating over $i$). The two conditions for discriminant validity are:

$$\text{(a)} \quad \rho_{x_{.js'}x_{.j's}} > |\rho_{x_{.js'}x_{.j's'}}|; \qquad \text{(b)} \quad \rho_{x_{.js'}x_{.j's}} > |\rho_{x_{.js'}x_{.js'}}|.$$

Absolute value operators are used, since it is the magnitude rather than the sign of the correlation that is important.

### References

Campbell, D. T., & Fiske, D. W. (1959). Convergent and discriminant validity by the multitrait–multimethod matrix. *Psychological Bulletin, 56,* 81–105.

Chapman, L. J., & Chapman, J. P. (1969). Illusory correlation as an obstacle to the use of valid psychodiagnostic signs. *Journal of Abnormal Psychology, 74,* 271–280.

Coppleson, L. W., Factor, R. M., Strum, S. B., Graff, P. W., & Rappaport, H. (1970). Observer disagreement in the classification and histology of Hodgkin's disease. *Journal of the National Cancer Institute, 45,* 731–740.

Cronbach, L. J., & Meehl, P. E. (1955). Construct validity in psychological tests. *Psychological Bulletin, 52,* 281–302.

Dawes, R. M., & Corrigan, B. (1974). Linear models in decision making. *Psychological Bulletin, 81,* 95–106.

Einhorn, H. J. (1972). Expert measurement and mechanical combination. *Organizational Behavior and Human Performance, 7,* 86–106.

Ghiselli, E. E., & Brown, C. W. (1955). *Personnel and industrial psychology.* New York: McGraw-Hill.

Green, D. M., & Swets, J. A. (1966). *Signal detection theory and psychophysics.* New York: Wiley.

Guilford, J. P. (1954). *Psychometric methods.* New York: McGraw-Hill.

Hammond, K. R. (1955). Probabilistic functioning and the clinical method. *Psychological Review, 62*(4), 255–262.

Kleinmuntz, B. (1968). The processing of clinical information by man and machine. In B. Kleinmuntz (Ed.), *Formal representation of human judgment* (pp. 149–186). New York: Wiley.

Naylor, J. C., & Wherry, R. J., Sr. (1965). The use of simulated stimuli and the "JAN" technique to capture and cluster the policies of raters. *Educational and Psychological Measurement, 25,* 969–986.

Sawyer, J. (1966). Measurement *and* prediction, clinical *and* statistical. *Psychological Bulletin, 66,* 178–200.

Slovic, P., & Lichtenstein, S. (1971). Comparison of Bayesian and regression approaches to the study of information processing in judgment. *Organizational Behavior and Human Performance, 6,* 649–744.

Stanley, J. C. (1961). Analysis of unreplicated three-way classifications with applications to rater bias and trait independence. *Psychometrika, 26,* 205–219.

Thorndike, R. L. (1949). *Personnel selection.* New York: Wiley.

Winer, B. J. (1962). *Statistical principles in experimental design.* New York: McGraw-Hill.

# 21    The Expert Witness in Psychology and Psychiatry

*David Faust and Jay Ziskin*

The expert testimony of psychologists and psychiatrists at hearings and trials alters many lives (1). Clinicians participate in up to 1 million legal cases annually (2). Depending on the expert's opinion, an individual may be confined to a mental institution, receive huge monetary awards, obtain custody of a child, or lose his or her life.

Do psychiatrists and psychologists promote or obstruct courtroom justice? Passionate debate on a matter of such great practical and moral import may be inevitable but cannot resolve the issues. However, there is sufficient scientific evidence on the diagnostic and predictive accuracy of clinicians to permit dispassionate evaluation (3). We review the scientific evidence and its application to legal standards for expertise.

## Standards for According Expert Status

The interpretation of research on the performance of clinicians requires familiarity with legal standards for expert status. The standards are somewhat complicated, broadly interpreted, and continually evolving, but they can be reduced to two essentials (4). First, in branches of medicine, an expert must be able to state opinions with "reasonable medical certainty." This phrase itself is somewhat ambiguous but "pretty likely accurate" is as close a translation as any. An expert should be reasonably certain about the issues or questions pertinent to the case at hand, not merely about his field in general or other specific issues. The physician who is reasonably certain about diagnosis but not etiology may be allowed to testify on the former but not the latter. Second, an expert should be able to help the judge or jury reach a more valid conclusion than would be possible without the expert's testimony. If laypersons are as accurate as the expert or equally accurate with or without the expert's help, the expert is not needed.

These standards are easily framed as empirical questions that we will examine in order. (i) Can expert witnesses in psychology and psychiatry answer forensic questions with reasonable accuracy? (ii) Can experts help the judge and jury reach more accurate conclusions than would otherwise be possible?

### Reasonable Certainty

*Reliability and Validity of Clinical Judgment.* The expert witness may attempt to determine the current, prior, or future state of the person under examination. Can the person comprehend the charges against him? Could an individual appreciate the consequences of his actions at the time of the crime? Will an injury preclude future employment? These questions vary in difficulty. We will first review clinicians' successes in answering the simpler and more practiced questions common to everyday clinical work – those that form the basis for addressing the more complex and less familiar questions common to the courtroom.

There is perhaps nothing more fundamental or basic to the science of psychiatry than the classification or diagnosis of patients, and no more fundamental a hurdle than reliability, or cross-clinician consistency in the diagnoses rendered. If clinicians assign widely varying diagnoses, classification will be as much a product of extraneous factors or the diagnostician's idiosyncrasies as it is the examinee's actual status.

Psychiatry has been continuously plagued by difficulties in achieving reliable classification. The American Psychiatric Association has revised the official diagnostic manual at a quickening pace: The first *Diagnostic and Statistical Manual of Mental Disorders* (DSM-I) was published in 1952, DSM-II in 1968, DSM-III in 1980, and DSM-III-Revised in 1987. The next revision, DSM-IV, is slated for publication in the early 1990s. This process of revision little resembles the refinement of categories or cumulative gains common to advanced scientific fields. DSM-I and -II often produced poor interrater agreement (5), and the diagnostic system was radically altered with the publication of DSM-III. DSM-III introduced more specific classification procedures, changed hundreds of diagnostic criteria, and added or eliminated numerous categories of disorder. DSM-III-R introduced about 200 additional changes in diagnostic guidelines and criteria.

The initial DSM-III field trials appeared to demonstrate improved diagnostic reliability, but serious methodological shortcomings raised doubts about the results (6). A number of subsequent studies showed that rate of disagreement for specific diagnostic categories often equals or exceeds rate of agreement (7–9). The reliability of DSM-III-R awaits testing because many of the changes were intended to improve agreement but were made in the absence of formal checks on reliability.

Problems with diagnostic reliability illustrate more general difficulties in achieving interclinician agreement on descriptions of current status. For example, Stoller and Geertsma (10) found that highly experienced psychiatrists who viewed the same psychiatric interview could not agree on the patient's diagnosis, intrapsychic motivations and conflicts, or conscious and unconscious feelings. Problems achieving reliable, much less valid, descriptions of current states help anticipate the results of studies examining the more difficult judgments involved in the determination of prior and future states.

Studies that compare clinician's predictions against objectively determinable, hard data commonly show that error rate exceeds accuracy rate (3). In one study, for example, a series of military recruits was retained in service despite psychiatrists' recommendations that they be discharged for severe psychiatric liabilities (11). After 2 years, most of these individuals had remained on active duty and their overall rate of success and adjustment was not substantially different from that of matched controls initially judged to be free of pathology.

*Reliability and Validity of Forensic Judgments.* The research on reliability and validity cited above mainly examines clinical questions, not forensic questions, and the two can differ substantially. A clinical diagnosis, for example, may relate minimally to the issues of forensic interest. The clinical criteria for "insanity" or psychosis do not include such tests of legal insanity as the capacity to appreciate the consequences of one's action or to resist an impulse. A determination that the clinical criteria have been met does not establish satisfaction of the legal criteria. The considerable heterogeneity among individuals who fall within the same diagnostic category further limits forensic value. When a jury considers a criminal defense of diminished mental capacity, a diagnosis such as "posttraumatic stress disorder" offers little guidance. According to the diagnostic manual, individuals with this disorder can show either substantial or minimal impairment in judgment. Additionally, most available research addresses clinical distinctions, and there may be little or no research that pertains to forensic distinctions.

Clinicians who enter the forensic arena also shift from their more familiar role as the patient's helping agent and instead seek to uncover truth, whatever its implications for the person under examination (3, 12). The clinician thus becomes a potential adversary. The forensic role is often less familiar or practiced, the clinician's engrained tendency to support or empathize may cloud objectivity, and the person being examined may be less inclined to disclose information openly and honestly. Clinicians, who usually focus primarily on the patient's subjective reality, must now attempt to determine objective reality, a task for which they may be minimally trained.

The expert witness thus becomes engaged in less familiar questions and activities, often with minimal research backing. Not surprisingly, studies examining the accuracy of judgments directly pertinent to forensic assessment, such as the ability to detect the simulation of disorder (that is, malingering) or to predict violence, have shown particularly high rates of error among clinicians.

A determination of a subject's credibility is often essential in forensic assessment. The potential benefits of a favorable courtroom decision, such as relief from serious criminal charges or large financial gains, can lead individuals to feign disorder. Studies show, however, that clinicians often cannot distinguish the psychological test results of normal subjects asked to feign psychosis (or to simulate brain damage) and actual diagnosed cases (13–15). Faust et al. (16) asked children to lower their performance on tests used to assess brain dysfunction but provided no specific instructions to the children on how to achieve this end. Most practitioners who subsequently reviewed the cases considered the test results abnormal and identified brain damage as the underlying cause. Although the researchers had listed malingering as one of three possible explanations for the test findings, not one practitioner made the correct identification.

Forensic experts frequently appraise the potential for violent behavior. Their opinions may influence decisions involving criminal sentencing or involuntary commitment. Studies on the prediction of violence are consistent: clinicians are wrong at least twice as often as they are correct (17). Steadman (18) followed 967 individuals who were originally placed in maximum security hospitals on the basis of a psychiatric determination of dangerousness but later released by court order into ordinary mental hospitals. Four years latter about half the sample was still in ordinary mental hospitals where violence should have been easily detected, but only 26 subjects in the sample were known to have committed violent acts. These results may overestimate clinical error, for one cannot determine how many individuals discharged into the community committed undetected violent acts. Studies on short-term prediction that are limited to patients within controlled settings provide more reliable measurement of violent episodes. Clinicians' accuracy may not be as low as some of the long-term studies suggest, or short-term prediction may not be as difficult, but error still predominates (19).

## Assistance to the Judge and Jury

Studies show that professional clinicians do not in fact make more accurate clinical judgments than laypersons (3). Some studies show a slight professional advantage and some a slight lay advantage, but most often the groups perform similarly. An early study examined success in distinguishing the visual-motor productions of normal versus brain-damaged individuals on a commonly employed screening test (20). Professional psychologists performed no better than office secretaries. In another study, lay interviewers using standardized questions produced information of equal or greater validity than psychiatrists conducting interviews in their preferred manner (21). Leirer et al. found that high school students and professionals working from a common data base experienced comparable difficulty predicting violent behavior and weighted data similarly (22). The similarity in data interpretation suggests that both groups relied on common assumptions about potentially violent individuals, or shared cultural stereotypes. Other studies have shown similarities in cue use among professionals and laypersons, which may help explain the outcome of comparative studies (23). When judgment rests on conventional beliefs or stereotypes rather than empirical knowledge, professionals are unlikely to surpass laypersons.

Furthermore, there is almost no evidence that a select group of professionals with extensive experience or special qualifications performs better than other professionals. Virtually every available study shows that amount of clinical training and experience are unrelated to judgmental accuracy (24). A recent study included a representative national sample of U.S. neuropsychologists, practitioners who specialize in the assessment of brain–behavior relations (25). The practitioners reviewed neuropsychologic test results in a series of cases in order to determine the presence, location, and cause of brain damage. No significant relations were obtained between judgmental accuracy and education or experience, even when analysis was limited to extreme groups, for example, when level of clinical experience was almost 25 times as great in one group as another.

We have focused on the accuracy of clinical judgment. In contrast, actuarial methods, which eliminate the human judge and base conclusions solely on empirically established frequencies, consistently equal or outperform professionals and laypersons (26). If expertise is defined solely by accuracy, the actuarial method is the "expert." Nevertheless, actuarial procedures typically yield modest levels of accuracy and few procedures, as yet, directly address forensic questions. A notable exception is the set of indices on the Minnesota Multiphasic Personality Inventory (MMPI), which are sensitive to the exaggeration or simulation of disorder (27).

Although experts develop actuarial procedures, actuarial output is often readily understood by laypersons. An output statement may read, for example, "Individuals who obtain similar test results engage in violent behavior in about 20% of cases." Although more than 100 studies demonstrate the superiority of actuarial data combination over clinical judgment, few experts rely strictly on actuarial procedures; indeed, many do not even know that such methods exist. Other experts modify actuarial conclusions at their discretion, although research suggests that this decision strategy results in fewer corrected errors than correct conclusions overturned (26). When actuarial procedures are applicable and intelligible to laypersons, the expert's involvement in the interpretive process is unnecessary. In fact, the expert will most likely move the jury further from the truth, not closer to it, given the common tendency to countervail actuarial conclusions and thereby decrease overall judgmental accuracy.

### Factors Limiting Clinical Judgment

An understanding of the factors that underlie research findings and that foster clinicians' misappraisal of their judgmental accuracy may help assuage unfounded inferences about experts' mental power or honesty. A more productive social science–law relation also ultimately depends on a better understanding of the factors underlying judgment error and the development of corrective procedures.

*Limits in Scientific Knowledge.* Practitioners are limited by the state of their science. The inadequacies of classification have been described. In addition, psychology lacks a formalized, general theory of human behavior that permits accurate prediction. Most personality theories are verbal summaries of loosely bound conjectures. The subject matter of the field itself – human thought and behavior – resists objective, direct, or reliable observation and measurement.

One manifestation of the fledgling state of scientific psychology is the tremendous diversity within the field, a situation that is incongruous with the law's preference for standard procedures and authoritativeness. There are dozens of personality theories and hundreds of approaches to psychotherapy (28). Two neuropsychologists may administer entirely different test batteries to the same examinee. This diversity in theory and practice breeds the divergence in opinion that makes the "battle of the experts" a regular courtroom occurrence.

Furthermore, the instability of theory and method hinders the accumulation of scientific knowledge. What is new may not be better, but only a fresh attempt to solve a recalcitrant problem. Each time the official diagnostic manual changes one must discard hundreds of investigations relating scores on psychological tests to what are now obsolete categories of disorder. The MMPI, perhaps the best researched psychological test, is itself undergoing revision; thus, investigators must reevaluate the relation of MMPI scores to a recently revised diagnostic manual that will be re-revised within a few years.

*Limits in Clinical Judgment.* The clinician, who is limited by the state of his scientific field and likely disregards or undervalues actuarial data combination, depends mainly on subjective methods of data interpretation. Without the safeguards of the scientific method, clinicians are highly vulnerable to the problematic judgment practices and cognitive limitations common to human beings (29, 30).

For example, clinicians disregard or underuse information about the frequency of occurrence, or base rates (31). Many diagnostic signs within psychology show associations of modest strength, at best, with the condition or event of interest. For example, a test indicator of suicidal intent may occur in 80% of true cases but also in 10% of negative cases. As such, the value of this and other diagnostic indicators is never constant but relative to the frequency of events. If suicidal intent is present in one per 1,000 patients, this one patient will likely be identified correctly. However, 10% of the remaining 999 patients, or about 99, will be misidentified as suicidal, resulting in almost 100 times more errors than correct identifications. If the frequencies shift, the sign's value shifts also. Given typical limitations in the strength of signs and the low frequency of most psychiatric disorders, numerous diagnostic signs produce more errors than correct identifications. Many faulty signs remain popular because disregard of base rates and associated principles of probability preclude an accurate determination of their worth.

Clinicians also overvalue supportive evidence and undervalue counterevidence (32). In psychology, the selective pursuit of supportive evidence is especially pernicious. Individual behavior is highly variable across time and situation, and tremendous overlap exists across criteria for various psychiatric disturbances and between the characteristics of aberrant and normal individuals. The lives of normal individuals commonly contain the full range of trauma, stress, and turmoil found among the disordered (33). Clinicians typically expect to find abnormality, and a search for supportive evidence will almost always "succeed" regardless of the examinee's mental health. In one study that enhanced the expectancy to find abnormality, every psychiatrist who heard a script portraying a well-adjusted individual nevertheless diagnosed mental disorder (34). This tendency to assume the presence of abnormality and then seek supportive evidence fosters "overpathologizing," that is, the frequent misidentification of individuals as abnormal.

Selective attention to supportive evidence also fosters "illusory correlations," or the belief in relations that appear to be, but are not, valid (23). Suppose that a diagnostic "sign" and a disorder are actually unrelated but sometimes co-occur by chance alone. The clinician who neglects instances in which the sign or disorder appears independently, and rather focuses on co-occurrences, comes to believe that the two are related. For example, some clinicians believe that individuals who produce human figure drawings with accentuated eyes have "paranoid" traits. The repeated "discovery" of "confirming" instances, embedded in the context of salient personal experience, creates a compelling illusion that overpowers any awareness of contrary instances or scientific research. Clinicians continue to use human figure drawings despite scientific evidence that disconfirms the perceived association between accentuated eyes and paranoia, and other assumed relations between drawing characteristics and personality traits.

Studies on experience and accuracy show that the conditions under which clinicians practice do not promote experiential learning, a finding that confirmatory bias and illusory correlation help to explain. Clinicians often receive little or no outcome information or feedback about their judgments, which precludes self-correction. The feedback clinicians do receive is often garbled and prone to the same problematic judgment practices that hinder original case appraisals.

Most clinical feedback occurs in the context of therapy. This feedback is skewed and confounded with outcome. To illustrate – clientele particularly pleased with services may be most likely to make follow-up contacts with the therapist, in which they further express praise and thanks. The therapist obtains a select, rather than a representative sample of the varying pieces that comprise outcome as a whole. Further, therapists' initial appraisals produce actions that can lead to self-fulfilling prophesies. The therapist who decides he would not work well with a patient and transfers the case will never find his judgment disconfirmed. Additionally, clients may purposely or inadvertently provide misleading feedback. Clinicians often evaluate their own judgmental accuracy by observing patients' agreement with their interpretations or descriptions. However, research shows that individuals believe in overly general personality descriptors of dubious validity, a form of suggestibility that provides a livelihood for astrologers and palm readers and misguides clinicians (35).

Selective attention to supportive evidence similarly affects clinicians' appraisals of their own judgmental accuracy (36). A clinician will inevitably receive some outcome information that appears to support his conclusions. The clinician who tells patients that they appear depressed will often obtain affirmation regardless of accuracy, either because patients mistakenly accept the clinicians' opinion or are hesitant to disagree with a person upon whom they depend. The number of instances that appear to provide confirmation exceeds its actual frequency, a problem compounded by the underweighting of conflicting evidence. Given the ambiguity of feedback and the clinician's reliance on theories that allow contradictory interpretations of identical outcomes, counterevidence is easily incorporated into prior beliefs. The patient who challenges a conclusion is viewed as "resisting" the truth or "repressing" it from conscious awareness. The result of these clinical practices and mental habits is overconfidence in judgmental abilities (37). In a study on the detection of malingering, most clinicians expressed extreme confidence on a diagnostic task in which error rate ranged from 90 to 100% (15).

*Self-appraisal of Clinical Judgment.* Overconfidence is one facet of a more general problem appraising one's own judgmental success and decision processes. Research methods that compare subjective impressions to objective measures of data utilization have revealed substantial discrepancies (30). Clinicians may believe that certain variables that actually exerted minimal influence on their conclusions played a key role, and vice versa (38). For example, a clinician's conclusion may be largely determined by potentially biasing information (for example, a prior opinion) which is sincerely thought to have had no influence.

Clinicians commonly propose that their conclusions rest on a careful weighting of many variables, whereas objective analysis typically shows that only a few variables, perhaps two or three, exert a significant impact (39–40). Clinicians also assert that complex configural analysis or data integration is necessary to reach accurate conclusions – that one never considers a datum in isolation but rather the "whole" or overall pattern of results. However, numerous studies suggest that no clinician, or human being for that matter, can begin to manage such complex cognitive operations (41–43). The attempt to grasp interactions among even two or three variables can outstrip human cognitive capacities. Further, clinicians' judgments can usually be reproduced or duplicated by mathematical formulas that simply add variables together and disregard interactions (24, 44).

The expert's misappraisals of his judgmental accuracy and processes create special complications in the courtroom. Courtroom opinions often defy the type of objective verification possible in the sciences. How does one verify a statement like the following: "I know just what she was thinking when she committed suicide." The judge or jury, lacking both objective data on the particular expert's judgmental success and familiarity with the relevant research, often must rely on indirect, intuitively plausible markers of accuracy: the expert's stated confidence and description of his judgmental processes and powers, and his background training, experience, and credentials. These supposed markers of accuracy are potentially prejudicial. Clinicians miscalibrate confidence and misappraise their own judgmental processes and success. Training and experience are unrelated to accuracy. The expert, misled by subjective self-appraisal and illusory beliefs, and unshaken by massive negative scientific evidence, attempts to persuade jurors to share the same misplaced faith in false markers. The expert's persuasive effort may well succeed because it aligns so closely with common belief.

### Conclusions and Implications

We began by asking whether expert witnesses achieve reasonable certainty and aid the trier of fact. The scientific evidence clearly suggests that clinicians fail to satisfy either legal standard for expertise. Clinicians frequently cannot agree on psychiatric diagnoses of current states, much less provide trustworthy answers to less familiar and more difficult forensic questions, which often demand projections backward or forward in time. Considerable research also shows that clinicians' judgmental accuracy does not surpass that of laypersons. However, actuarial methods may satisfy one of the standards. Although actuarial procedures rarely address questions of direct forensic interest and usually achieve modest results, rather than reasonable certainty, their accuracy does surpass both professionals and laypersons. It is for the courts to decide whether clinicians' failure to meet both standards should exclude them as expert witnesses, and whether satisfaction of the second standard alone is sufficient to admit actuarial conclusions as courtroom evidence.

Should the courts admit actuarial methods, research suggests a limited role for experts. A knowledgeable expert can inform the court whether an actuarial procedure is applicable to the particular examinee and question of interest. For example, MMPI indices for malingering may sometimes aid the court, but the MMPI should not be used with individuals of limited intellectual endowment. The expert may also help as needed to explain output statements, which may contain psychological jargon, and can review relevant research on the accuracy of the particular actuarial technique. However, according to available research, the expert's involvement should end in the explanation of the actuarial procedure. The expert's involvement in the interpretation of the clinical data, or attempts to "refine" or modify actuarial conclusions, produce inferior overall results.

Experts who are aware of the negative scientific evidence may assert that the research does not apply to them. Many of the psychologists and psychiatrists who participated in judgment studies probably held the same prior belief, although the research showed otherwise. Clinicians who claim exemption almost always lack objective data on their judgmental accuracy. Given the many studies that raise serious doubt about clinical judgment and the obstacles to valid self-appraisal of judgmental success, the clinician who makes a counterclaim should bear the burden of proof. The validity of counterclaims could be appraised directly. Certifying bodies could conduct objective evaluation of the clinician's performance on a representative sample of cases that can be verified against objective data. There are no definitive means for verifying certain types of clinical judgments, including most diagnoses, but research methods permit objective evaluation of performance on many judgment tasks. For example, clinicians can be asked to predict occupational success and their judgments compared to known outcomes in actual cases.

What of the possible conclusion that the involvement of expert witnesses is not helpful but does no harm? As discussed, expert testimony may exert a prejudicial affect on juries. Confidence and accuracy can be inversely related, and yet the jury may well accept the opinion of an expert who exudes confidence over that of an opposing expert who expresses appropriate caution. Expert evidence is readily subject to abuse due to its highly subjective nature and vulnerability to biases. The involvement of experts wastes many hours of already too scarce court time and costs taxpayers millions of dollars. Experts also create malpractice risks for colleagues. Each time an expert witness claims he can predict violent behavior with reasonable

346 FAUST AND ZISKIN

certainty, he endorses a falsehood. A competent clinician who could not have anticipated his patient's violent episode may thus be held legally accountable.

As the courts and the public come to realize the immense gap between experts' claims about their judgmental powers and the scientific findings, the credibility of psychology and psychiatry will suffer accordingly. Psychological research should eventually yield more certain knowledge and methods that provide meaningful assistance to the trier of fact. Ironically, unlike the current situation in which expert testimony is often admitted despite the negative research on its value, the erosion of credibility may reverse this trend. The courts, having learned to distrust clinicians' claims, may refuse to admit testimony based on truly useful knowledge and methods despite more than adequate supportive studies.

### References and Notes

1   This chapter addresses clinical evaluation and does not necessarily pertain to courtroom experts who do not assess individuals but rather limit their testimony to research findings, such as studies on the reliability of eyewitnesses. In the subsequent text, "clinician" is used to refer to both psychologists and psychiatrists.

2   S. Pollack, in *The Psychiatric Consultation*, P. Soloman, Ed. (Grune & Stratton, New York, 1968).

3   J. Ziskin and D. Faust, *Coping with Psychiatric and Psychological Testimony* (Law and Psychology Press, Venice, CA, 1988), vols. 1 to 3.

4   *Frye* vs. *U.S.*, 293 Fed. 1013, 1014 (D.C. Cir. 1923).

5   R. L. Spitzer, J. Endicott, E. Robins, *Am. J. Psychiatr. 132*, 1187 (1975).

6   H. Kutchins and S. A. Kirk, *Social Work Res. Abstr. 3* (1986).

7   R. E. Drake and G. E. Vaillant, *Am. J. Psychiatr. 142*, 553 (1985).

8   P. Lieberman and F. Baker, *Hosp. Commun. Psychiatr. 36*, 291 (1985).

9   G. Mellsop, F. Varghese, S. Joshua, A. Hicks, *Am. J. Psychiatr. 139*, 1360 (1982).

10   R. J. Stoller and H. Geertsma, *J. Nerv. Ment. Disord. 151*, 58 (1963).

11   J. A. Plag and R. J. Arthur, *Am. J. Psychiatr. 131*, 534 (1965).

12   R. Roesch, *J. Consult. Clin. Psychol. 47*, 542 (1979); R. Rogers and W. Seman, *Behav. Sci. Law 1*, 89 (1983).

13   S. Albert, H. M. Fox, M. W. Kahn, *J. Person. Assess. 44*, 115 (1980).

14   R. K. Heaton, H. H. Smith, Jr., R. A. W. Lehman, A. T. Vogt, *J. Consul. Clin. Psychol. 46*, 892 (1978).

15   K. Hart, "The capacity of adolescents to fake believable defects on neuropsychological testing," paper presented at the Annual Convention of the American Psychological Association, New York, September 1987.

16   D. Faust, K. Hart, T. J. Guilmette, *J. Consult. Clin. Psychol.*, in press.

17   J. Monahan, *Am. J. Psychiatr. 141*, 10 (1984); P. D. Werner, T. L. Rose, J. A. Yesavage, *J. Consult. Clin. Psychol. 51*, 815 (1983).

18   H. J. Steadman, *Am. J. Psychiatr. 130*, 317 (1973).

19   P. D. Werner, T. L. Rose, J. A. Yesavage, K. Seeman, ibid. *142*, 263 (1984).

20   L. R. Goldberg, *J. Consult. Psychol. 23*, 25 (1959).

21   L. N. Robins, *Arch. Gen. Psychiatr. 42*, 918 (1985).

22  Y. O. Leirer, P. D. Warner, T. L. Rose, J. A. Yesavage, "Predictions of violence by high school students and clinicians," paper presented at the Annual Convention of the Oregon Psychological Association, Newport, Oregon, Spring 1984.

23  L. J. Chapman and J. P. Chapman, *J. Abnorm. Psychol.* 72, 193 (1967); ibid. *74*, 271 (1969).

24  L. R. Goldberg, *Am. Psychol.* 23, 483 (1968); J. S. Wiggins, *Clin. Psychol. Rev. 1*, 3 (1981).

25  D. Faust et al., *Arch. Clin. Neuropsychol.* 3, 145 (1988).

26  P. E. Meehl, *Clinical Versus Statistical Prediction.* (Univ. of Minnesota Press, Minneapolis, 1954); *J. Person. Assess.* 50, 370 (1986); J. Sawyer, *Psychol. Bull. 66*, 178 (1966).

27  R. Rogers, *Behav. Sci. Law 2*, 93 (1984).

28  A. E. Kazdin, in *Handbook of Psychotherapy and Behavior Change*, S. L. Garfield and A. E. Bergin, Eds. (Wiley, New York, ed. 3, 1986), pp. 23–68.

29  A. Tversky and D. Kahneman, *Science 185*, 1124 (1974).

30  D. Faust, *Prof. Psychol.* 17, 420 (1986).

31  P. E. Meehl and A. Rosen, *Psychol. Bull. 52*, 194 (1955); A. Tversky and D. Kahneman, in *Progress in Social Psychology*, M. Fishbein, Ed. (Erlbaum, Hillsdale, NJ, 1978), pp. 49–72.

32  D. C. Turk and P. Salovey, *Cogn. Therapy Res. 9*, 19 (1985).

33  H. Renaud and F. Estess, *Am. J. Orthopsychiatr.* 31, 786 (1961).

34  M. K. Temerlin and W. W. Trousdale, *Psychother. Theory Res. Practice. 6*, 24 (1969).

35  C. R. Snyder, *J. Clin. Psychol.* 30, 577 (1974); C. R. Snyder, R. J. Shenkel, C. R. Lowery, *J. Consult. Clin. Psychol.* 45, 104 (1977).

36  R. M. Dawes, *Clin. Psychol. Rev. 6*, 425 (1986).

37  B. Fischhoff, in *Judgment Under Uncertainty*, D. Kahneman, P. Slovic, A. Tversky, Eds. (Cambridge Univ. Press, Cambridge, 1982), pp. 422–444.

38  S. Oskamp, *Clin. Psychol.* 23, 411 (1967).

39  H. U. Fisch, K. R. Hammond, C. R. B. Joyce, *Br. J. Psychiatr. 140*, 378 (1982).

40  J. S. Gillis and T. J. Moran, *J. Clin. Psychol.* 37, 32 (1981).

41  P. Slovic and S. C. Lichtenstein, *Organ. Behav. Human Perform. 6*, 649 (1971).

42  D. Faust, *The Limits of Scientific Reasoning* (Univ. of Minnesota Press, Minneapolis, 1984).

43  A. Newell and H. A. Simon, *Human Problem Solving* (Prentice-Hall, Englewood Cliffs, NJ, 1972).

44  R. M. Dawes, *Am. Psychol.* 34, 571 (1979).

# Part VII

# Forecasting and Prediction

To make a sensible decision one needs to make two sorts of predictions: What will happen if I do $X$? And will I like it? The first prediction is about the external world: What will my life be like if I marry this person, move to that city, change to this other career? The second prediction is about one-self: How will I react to these external facts? Will I enjoy being in a marriage like this, living in a city like that, working at a career like this? This duality is visible even in the stark SEU model, where expectations reflect our predictions about the outside world and utilities reflect those about our inner responses. Clearly, one needs to make both predictions well to be a good decision maker. There is evidence (e.g., Kahneman & Snell, 1992) that the prediction of one's utility may be less straightforward than one would think: It may be hard to predict what we will enjoy and what we will not.

The chapters in this section are mainly concerned with the first sort of prediction: What is likely to happen? The first, by Fischhoff (Chapter 22), takes up the most basic issue: Just what does it mean to make a forecast or prediction, and how well do people understand one another when they share predictions? Many professions make their livings by producing forecasts, for the weather, business conditions, crime rates, university applicants, and so on. Often, though, they do not seem to have a clear picture of the information needs of their audience. A JDM perspective can help to make a forecast more useful, by shaping what is said and how it is reported.

A forecast, to Fischhoff, is simply the attachment of a set of probabilities to a set of future events. Forecasts can be misunderstood when either the events or the probabilities associated with them are not stated clearly; when they don't match what the audience needs to know; when the probability is stated overconfidently or the relevance or clarity of the event being forecast is exaggerated; or when the event–probability pairs are detached from the background of knowledge from which they were generated or the context to which they will be applied. He illustrates his framework with an example of what it would take for a forecast of a severe storm by television weather forecasting service to be maximally useful to its audience.

We noted earlier the astonishing and much-replicated finding that a whole range of interesting and important predictions are done better by simple weighted averages of the known predictors than they are by experts working from the same sets of predictors. Dawes, in Chapter 23 in this section, summarizes much of the relevant literature and speculates as to why this unexpected result should occur. His examples come from an amazing range of topics: predicting students' success in graduate school; survival time for Hodgkin's disease patients; bankruptcy rates for firms; and the drinking rates of alcoholic and nonalcoholic experimental subjects. Dawes, as always, offers trenchant practical advice and homely examples, as well as a careful reading of the scientific literature.

The last selection in this section, by Stewart and Lusk (Chapter 24), is somewhat more technical, in the sense of calling for some high school algebra and elementary statistical theory. Even if you skip the technical details, however, a few of the basic ideas are worth considering. First, what is "skill" in making a prediction? If, for example, you wanted to predict the daily temperature in your home town with zero average error, all you need to do is to find the long-run average temperature and predict that every day. Some days will be over, some under, and your average error will be zero. No one would pay you for such an unskilled forecast, of course, so zero average error can't be what we value. Mean squared error (MSE) is a much better measure of forecast skill: more precisely, your MSE compared to the MSE of a dumb prediction like predicting the average.

The second key point is that you can break up the resulting skill score (known as the Brier score, after its inventor) into three independent terms. The first reflects how well the prediction correlates with what it is you're trying to predict – the temperature, the Dow Jones Average, the Bulls' total score. The second term reflects whether or not you are being properly "regressive," predicting closer to the average when your information is poor. The third terms reflects whether your average prediction matches the mean of what you are trying to predict, not biased toward optimism or pessimism. This breakdown of the overall skill score is very helpful in identifying the source of prediction errors.

The third key part of Stewart and Lusk's chapter is to tie the skill score to an expanded treatment of the Lens Model we discussed earlier in the book. Here they consider two further sources of error in making predictions: slippage between what the cues measure and what is really true (e.g., reported unemployment rate vs. actual unemployment rate); and, second, slippage between the cue value and what the judge actually uses (e.g., misreading the published report of unemployment). This expanded treatment allows the authors to specify five further elements of good prediction performance. The rest of their chapter looks at what is known about each, and what might be done to help. The chapter thus provides a valuable introduction to research on prediction skills and an orderly approach to the literature, even for those who do not want to dig into the mathematics.

### Reference

Kahneman, D., & Snell, J. (1992). Predicting a changing taste: Do people know what they will like? *Journal of Behavioral Decision Making, 5,* 187–200.

# 22    What Forecasts (Seem to) Mean

*Baruch Fischhoff*

## 1. Introduction

Several months ago, I was approached by a producer from the Weather Channel, a 24-hour-a-day cable television station devoted to weather forecasting, for help with a forthcoming special (Superstorm, 1993). The Weather Channel's staff had been shaken by the high death toll from the massive winter storm that hit the Eastern Seaboard of the United States in March 1993. From the Channel's perspective, its experts had seldom had such clear indicators of a major weather event, nor expressed themselves with such confidence. Nonetheless, hundreds of people still died, from exposure, heart attacks, falling tree limbs, road accidents, and the like. No one has counted the number of injuries, illnesses, and close calls. The special was intended to encourage surviving viewers to take future forecasts more seriously. The production process seemed designed to help the Channel itself figure out where it had failed.

Obviously, the value of forecasts comes from providing needed answers in a usable form. Somehow or other, the Weather Channel's "superstorm" forecasts either were not answering the questions that viewers were asking or were not being understood as intended (assuming, of course, that the people who became casualties had heard the Channel's warnings or the relayed messages of others who had). Although the failures of these forecasts were particularly dramatic and tragic, I suspect that most forecasters believe that they have seen clients suffer when their forecasts were ignored or misinterpreted.

Working with the Weather Channel got me to thinking about the general conditions under which the message of a forecast can get lost in the transmission. At first glance, the communication task seems straightforward.

All that needs to be explained is the probability attached to some future event. That same basic challenge arises whether one is predicting weather, economic events, nuclear power plant performance, surgery outcomes, or market penetration.

There seem to be four basic ways in which one could fail to communicate either the probability or the event portion of a forecast. In each case, the problem may be either that we have nothing to say about that aspect of the forecast, because we have not done the needed research, or that we are not saying it well enough to be understood by our audience.

1. Ambiguity: not saying clearly what events we are forecasting or how likely we think that they are.
2. Irrelevance: not offering forecasts that address our clients' informational needs.
3. Immodesty: not admitting the limits to our knowledge.
4. Impoverishment: not addressing the broader context within which forecasts (and contingent decisions) are made.

The following sections examine each of these possibilities in turn, drawing on research and anecdotes concerning a variety of forecasting tasks. Each section looks separately at interpreting probabilities and events. The concluding section considers the risks and benefits of both ignoring and acknowledging these issues.

## 2. Ambiguity

It is hard to follow any news medium for very long without encountering a health or safety warning, such as "don't drink and drive," "practice safe sex," "don't do drugs," or "avoid apples treated with Alar." Each such warning carries an implicit forecast regarding the occurrence of some misfortune, should the ill-advised course of action be pursued. Unfortunately, these are typically not very precise forecasts. They fail to say exactly which actions should be avoided, which consequences can follow, or how likely that connection is. Recipients who hoped to act on these warning would have to guess what exact message was intended. Their guess could be wrong, if, for example, those who issued the warning had different linguistic norms or thresholds of concern (reflecting their aversion to particular outcomes and the costs of avoidance).

### 2.1. Probabilities

The ambiguity in qualitative expressions of probability is well documented, in this journal (Beyth-Marom, 1982) and elsewhere (Lichtenstein and Newman, 1967, and Wallsten et al., 1986). A given term such as "likely"

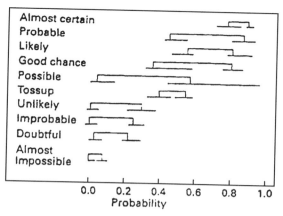

Figure 22.1. Upper and lower probability limits for probability expressions. (Upper bars show mean lower and upper probability limits provided by subjects for each verbal expression. Lower left- and right-hand bars show the interquartile ranges provided for the lower and upper limits, respectively.) (*Source:* Wallsten et al., 1986.)

or "rarely" can be interpreted as implying different probabilities to different people in a single context and different probabilities to the same person in different contexts. Such ambiguity has been found even within communities of professionals, such as physicians and intelligence officers (e.g., Beyth-Marom, 1982, and Merz et al., 1991). Figure 22.1 shows typical results.

The criticality of such ambiguity depends, of course, on how the forecast is used. Sometimes, an inferred probability of 1% and 10% will lead to the same choice; sometimes not. The risk of letting consumers make their own interpretations presumably increases with the diversity of potential users and contingent decisions – in the sense of there being a greater chance of people making wrong guesses and then, as a result, making wrong choices.

There are some interesting studies examining the variability in people's interpretation of different verbal labels in different circumstances (e.g., Cohen et al., 1958, Hamm, 1991, Holyoak and Glass, 1978, Poulton, 1989, and Zimmer, 1984). In theoretical terms, these studies have improved our understanding of how people extract meaning from context (psycholinguistics) and how they use numeric scales (psychophysics). In practical terms, these studies can show how to use the least ambiguous terms, making clear which risks are posed by the residual ambiguities. However, the sensible solution is just to be explicit. If one has, in fact, done the work needed to determine a probability, then give it. If recipients are uncomfortable with numbers, then let them substitute the verbal label that works for them.

## 2.2 Events

Much less research attention has been given to potential ambiguity in the events to which these probabilities (or verbal likelihood labels) are attached. Imagine, for example, a public service announcement saying, "If you drink and drive, you will have a 5% chance of getting into an accident." The number provides some information. However, its practical implications would be very different if it was referring to the risk from driving home following a single beer rather than that from a lifetime of trips made by a heavy drinker.

Some years ago, Allan Murphy, who has worked hard to institutionalize the use of explicit probabilities in weather forecasting (e.g., Murphy and Winkler, 1984), found his accomplishments threatened by the claim that such forecasts confused lay people. Collecting behavioral data to discipline these speculations, Murphy et al. (1980; also Murphy and Brown, 1984) found that the confusion concerned the event and not the probability. Thus, participants in the initial study were divided fairly evenly over whether 70% referred to the area that would experience rain, the time that it would rain, or the chance of at least some rain somewhere.

The converse of this ambiguity emerges in surveys that ask respondents to estimate the likelihood of some event, whose exact identity they must guess. For example, the National Health Information Survey (1987) is a well-funded effort which is used, among other things, to assess the effectiveness of the AIDS information programs of the Centers for Disease Control. It asks questions such as, "How likely is it that you can get AIDS from sharing plates and other eating utensils?" We presented this question to a class at an Ivy League college. After answering, they were asked what they thought had been meant by "sharing plates and other eating utensils." Table 22.1 shows the distribution of their choices among the options that we offered for this and a second question from the survey. Even within this fairly homogeneous sample, there was considerable disagreement over what event was meant (Fischhoff, 1989, and Linville et al., 1993).

Moreover, even if all respondents agreed about the interpretation of an event, one would still have to guess what that was. In Table 22.1, that guessing requires an understanding of the culinary habits of a population of young adults. Other bits of cross-cultural knowledge would be needed for other questions. Presumably, the problems that we face in interpreting others' forecasts have their counterparts in their attempts to interpret ours. Thus, similar research would be needed to anticipate what people would infer from the forecast that, "according to the best available technical knowledge, the probability of HIV transmission is $3 \times 10^{-11}$ for sharing plates and other eating utensils."

Quadrel (1990) found even greater disagreement, using an open-ended approach to investigate the same issue. She asked adolescents to think aloud as they assessed the probability of deliberately ambiguous events like "getting

Table 22.1. *Interpretations of AIDS Risk Questions*

How did you interpret "sharing plates, forks, or glasses with someone who has AIDS"?
–    Sharing utensils during a meal (E.g., passing them around, eating off one
      another's plates) (81.8%)
–    Using the same utensils after they have been washed (10.9%)
–    I was uncertain about the interpretation (5.8%)
–    Multiple interpretations (1.5%)

Did you interpret "sharing plates, forks, or glasses with someone who has AIDS" as
–    Occurring on a single occasion? (39.1%)
–    Occurring on several occasions? (19.6%)
–    Occurring routinely? (27.5%)
–    I was uncertain about the interpretation (12.3%)
–    Multiple interpretations (1.4%)

How did you interpret "having sex with a person who has AIDS"?
–    Having vaginal intercourse without a condom (72.5%)
–    Having vaginal intercourse with a condom (4.3%)
–    Having other kinds of sex (6.5%)
–    I was uncertain about the interpretation (6.7%)
–    Multiple interpretations (8.0%)

Did you interpret "having sex with a person who has AIDS" as
–    Occurring on a single occasion? (61.6%)
–    Occurring on several occasions? (22.5%)
–    Occurring on many occasions? (7.2%)
–    I was uncertain about the interpretation (5.1%)
–    Multiple interpretations (3.6%)

Entries are the percentage of subjects (in a sample of 135 students at an Ivy League College)
who reported having inferred each definition of the phrase when they had answered a question about the degree of risk that it entailed.

into an accident after drinking and driving" or "getting AIDS as the result of
sex." She found that they raised a wide variety of concerns, most of which
are arguably relevant to an objective determination of risk. Each column in
Table 22.2 shows the number of her subjects who thought that each of three
aspects of the "dose" of a risky event were relevant to the probability of a
risky outcome. For seven of these nine events, they felt the need to make
some assumption about the amount of exposure.[1] In a sense, these teens
(many of whom came from treatment homes) were more sophisticated than
the investigators who designed the surveys from which these ambiguous
questions were taken or adopted. Presumably, such teens are similarly confused about the meanings of the ambiguous risk forecasts communicated to
them in health classes and public service announcements.[2]

    Competent professionals know exactly what they are talking about when
they issue forecasts. However, they have an obligation to determine what

Table 22.2. *Intuitive Interpretations of Ambiguous Event Descriptions*

| Dose | Drink and Drive | Smoke and Cancer | Cocaine and Addiction | AIDS | Smoke and Addiction | Cocaine and Health | Marijuana | Alcohol and Addiction | Pregnancy |
|---|---|---|---|---|---|---|---|---|---|
| Amount | 49 | 52 | 39 | 2 | 40 | 31 | 32 | 41 | 5 |
| Potency | 15 | 13 | 1 | 0 | 12 | 5 | 7 | 8 | 0 |
| Method | 4 | 3 | 7 | 4 | 1 | 10 | 10 | 1 | 4 |

*Source:* Quadrel (1990); Quadrel et al. (1994).
Entries are the number of subjects (in a sample of 61 adolescents) who spontaneously referred to each aspect of the dose involved in nine incompletely described risk events. For example, 49 raised the issue of how much "drinking" or "driving" was implied in a vague statement about that risk.

their clients think they are talking about. Problems can arise even with commonly issued forecasts. There may be no natural way for recipients to realize that they have consistently misinterpreted a term like unemployment, bankruptcy, viewer, room, GNP, or race. Survey researchers sometimes call such ostensibly objective and common terms, *quasi-facts* (Turner and Martin, 1984). They have created some useful worked examples of how to improve the understanding of technical terms, and to assess their residual ambiguity (Bailar and Rothwell, 1984, and Turner et al., 1992). Other help can be found in the psychological literature on categorization (Murphy and Medin, 1985) and its applications to tasks like improving the accessibility of information in places like the Yellow Pages or computerized databases (Fischhoff et al., 1987, and Furnas et al., 1983). One design consideration is to decide when one might sacrifice clarity in order to use terms whose ambiguities are more readily apparent (Fischhoff and MacGregor, 1986, Fischhoff et al., 1987).

An exogenous barrier to communication arises when the technical community changes its definitions to reflect changes in law, theory, or methodology. As a result, it is now asking about or telling about a different event, even though the wording remains the same. For example, over time, there may be shifts in the meaning of terms like "risk," "unemployed," "privacy," "electronics," "child abuse," or "electorate." Those changes may proceed in different directions and at different paces for different groups. A subsequent section deals with the false immodesty in a forecast that fails to reveal that it reflects a best guess at both how an event should be defined and how likely it is to happen.

### 3. Irrelevance

Even if it is well understood, a forecast is of little use unless it provides information that potential consumers need. Indeed, it is the desire to be more relevant that motivates most revisions in the terms, models, and analytical procedures of forecasts. For example, serious attempts are now being made to include environmental effects in national accounts and, hence, in forecasts of the effects of various public policies and natural processes. The results should be more relevant to those concerned with the health of nations, even if they will need to be educated about the nuances of a new set of measures (Costanza, 1991).

### 3.1. Probabilities

Whatever the event, users need not only a best guess at how it will turn out, but also some indication of the confidence that can be placed in that estimate. Having more confidence in a forecast allows one to take more decisive action, to curtail information collection, to plan for a narrower range of possible contingencies, and to invest less in vigilance for surprises.

When forecasters fail to express their uncertainty, then their clients must guess. If clients guess wrongly, then they risk unduly aggressive or cautious action. The former might happen if they assumed that estimates lacking any qualification needed no qualification. The latter might happen if clients refused to trust experts who gave unqualified predictions. In either case, the errors would reflect a failure to provide the kind of estimate most relevant to the client's purposes (Fischhoff et al., 1978, Krysztofowicz, 1983, and Morgan and Henrion, 1990).

When forecasting continuous events (e.g., interest rates, market share), a familiar convention is to offer a probability distribution over possible values (and not just the mean, median, or mode). A less ambitious expression of uncertainty is that of confidence intervals, bounding the set of possible values with some degree of certainty. With discrete events (will/will not happen), the associated probability is sometimes held to incorporate all relevant beliefs. The less the uncertainty, the closer the probability will be to 0 or 1. Others argue that intermediate probabilities can be held with different degrees of confidence, the knowledge of which can improve contingent decisions. Whatever the logical status of such "second-order probabilities," analysts may owe clients whatever insight they have about the stability of their knowledge (Gärdenfors and Sahlin, 1982 and 1989, Morgan and Henrion, 1990, Shafer, 1975, and von Winterfeldt and Edwards, 1986).

The definitiveness of an estimate depends on the extent of the knowledge upon which it is based. An estimate could, for example, reflect the data in a single study, the data from all similar studies, or the data and observations from all sources available to the forecaster. Such summaries might be based on classical statistics, meta-analysis, and Bayesian statistics, respectively. Each strategy can be followed competently. However, users will be misled if they assume greater or less comprehensiveness than is warranted.

For example, Fortney (1988) reported the results of a meta-analysis on all available studies of the health effects of oral contraceptives. She concluded, with great confidence, that a non-smoking woman who used the Pill throughout her reproductive career would do something between increasing her life expectancy by 4 days and decreasing it by 80 days. In addition, she was able to say that it was highly unlikely that this forecast would change because the existing data base was so great that no conceivable study could materially change the conclusions. The value of such an explicit expression of uncertainty can be compared to the implicit claims of definitiveness accompanying the typical newspaper account of the hot new medical study.

## 3.2. Events

It is a conversational norm to tell people things that they need to know (Grice, 1975). As a result, the issuing of forecasts carries an implication of relevance. Nonetheless, it is easy enough to think of processes leading to forecasts that violate this expectation. For example, government agencies may routinely issue forecasts of economic variables having great relevance to some members of its audience, but none to others (depending on the decisions that each faces). Sometimes, maintaining continuity in a time series may mean staying committed to questions and forecasts of decreasing relevance. Authorities may present laundry lists of potential side effects, predicting what might happen as the result of medical procedures, with little guidance as to what really matters. Disproportionate effort may go into refining estimates of the readily calculable part of a problem, even when those constitute a relatively small portion of it. Forceful analysts may seize center stage for the results of whatever it is that they compute.

The work can be competently executed, qualified, and communicated, yet still miss the mark if it fails to address recipients' concerns. If this irrelevance, or marginal relevance, is recognized, then recipients may resent the misappropriation of their time and resources. If it is not recognized, then recipients may misidentify the nature of their concerns, assuming that a result must be important if an apparent expert brings it to their attention.

Relevance is defined most clearly within the context of specific decisions. One can then use techniques like value-of-information analysis to determine how much of a practical difference knowing a forecast makes. Even posing the question can be informative. For example, public health officials in several countries have tried to promote testing for radon by showing forecasts of the risks that it poses to individuals and to society as a whole. A little thought shows that the homeowners also need an estimate of the probability that they can reduce the risk for an investment within their budget (Evans et al., 1988, and Svenson and Fischhoff, 1985). However, institutional priorities and inertia have led to much less being spend on improving estimates of remediation efficacy.

Merz (1991) and Merz et al. (1993) performed a formal analysis of the relevance of risk estimates for a dozen side effects of carotid endarterechtomy, a surgical procedure that reduces the risk of a stroke by scraping plaque from the major artery leading to the brain. Unfortunately, things can go wrong, including the general risks of surgery. Merz simulated the impact of learning about the probabilities of these side effects for a population of hypothetical patients (differing in their physical states and preferences). He found that knowing about a few of these side effects would change the decisions of a significant fraction of patients. Most of the side effects, however, were relevant to only a minute portion of patients. He argued that, while nothing should be hidden from patients, physicians should concentrate on communicating the few critical forecasts. Between the time that Merz submitted his dissertation and its defense, the results of a major clinical trial were released. Incorporating them in his model made little difference to its conclusions. That is, from this perspective, the trial had little practical importance, whatever it might have contributed to the understanding of fundamental physiological processes. It would take a separate analysis to determine whether, with foresight, the trial had any reasonable chance of producing decision-relevant information.

In other cases, it may take a major intellectual effort to discern the logical structure of the decisions that forecasts might serve. At present, the United States spends something of the order of $1–2 billion dollars annually to forecast the effects of the build-up of greenhouse gases (Office of Technology Assessment, 1993). Much more of that research is focused on predicting climate, through large-scale atmospheric and oceanographic models, than on predicting social and economic effects (or on the impacts of possible remedial strategies). It is hard to find any reasoned basis for this allocation, beyond institutional politics. The observer of this research might reasonably conclude that we need to understand climate before we can start to think seriously about related actions. The counterargument is that, without some serious analysis of the relevance of forecasts, it is hard to know if forecasting resources are being invested wisely and if their conclusions are being given the proper weight (Dowlatabadi and Morgan, 1993, and Rubin et al., 1992). Waiting for excellent information can mean paralysis, in effect denying the need to face the kinds of gambles being taken. Figuring out what events to forecast may be as interesting and important as actually doing the forecasting.[3]

## 4. Immodesty

Unless forecasters say how confident they are in forecasts, recipients are left to guess. However, even when confidence or lack of it is stated, recipients may still be left guessing whether the forecasters have overstated or understated how much they know. Like other possible biases, these, too, can have both motivational and cognitive roots. On the motivational side, the dominant incentive sometimes leads one to exaggerate one's confidence, for example, when business or attention goes to those who appear most knowledgeable. At other times, it pays to hedge aggressively, so as to avoid public commitment and accountability. The research literature suggests cognitive processes hampering people's ability to evaluate themselves.

### 4.1. Probabilities

As mentioned, uncertainty about forecasts is typically expressed in terms of the probabilities of discrete events occurring or subjective probability distributions over possible values of continuous quantities. Many studies have shown similar patterns: individuals have some, imperfect, understanding of

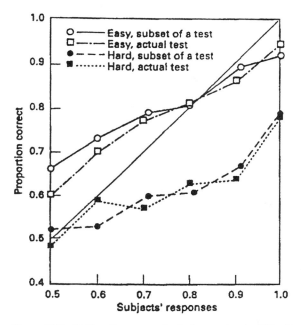

Figure 22.2. Calibration curves for tasks varying in difficulty level. Statements assigned each probability of being correct (0.5, 0.6, . . . ,1.0) are grouped. Each point on each curve represents the proportion of statements assigned the indicated probability that were, in fact, correct. (*Source:* Lichtenstein & Fischhoff, 1977.)

how much they know. The most commonly observed overall tendency has been overconfidence, which increases as people's knowledge decreases and shifts to underconfidence when they know a lot (Lichtenstein and Fischhoff, 1977, Lichtenstein et al., 1982, and Yates, 1989).

Figure 22.2 shows an early representation of this pattern. It shows the proportion of correct predictions among those statements assigned each probability of being correct. Overconfidence is reflected in points below the diagonal. One interpretation of the overall trend is that people enter a task expecting some intermediate level of difficulty and adjust insufficiently when tasks prove harder or easier. One interpretation of the flatness of each curve is that people feel that they can (and, perhaps, should) use the entire response scale, but are unable to make the necessary distinctions between different levels of knowledge.[4]

The critical question for the consumers of forecasts is whether similar patterns of behavior will be observed in the kinds of experts who produce them. Ayton (1992) provides a recent critical review of this topic, finding, it would seem, enough evidence of inappropriate expert confidence (mainly overconfidence) to justify caution. For practical purposes, as long as there is some significant and unpredictable tendency for expert miscalibration, users are left guessing about how much trust to place in forecasts.

After a review conducted 10 years earlier (Fischhoff, 1982), I concluded that confidence assessment could be viewed as a complex skill, whose acquisition requires the proper conditions for learning: prompt, unambiguous feedback with rewards for performance (and not, say, for bragging or hedging). The excellent performance of weather forecasters assessing the probability of precipitation (Murphy and Winkler, 1984) fits this pattern, as does that of expert bridge players predicting whether they will make a contract (Keren, 1987).

Figures 22.3–22.5 present several expressions of these potential problems. Figure 22.3 shows (something akin to) subjective confidence intervals, used by particle physicists to express confidence in estimates of physical constants

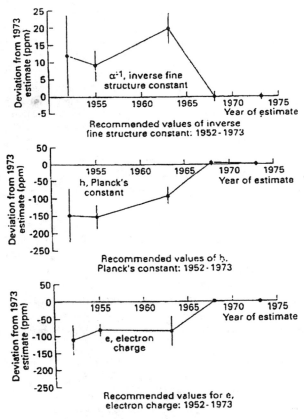

Figure 22.3. Confidence intervals surrounding estimated values of physical constants. (*Source:* Henrion & Fischhoff, 1986.)

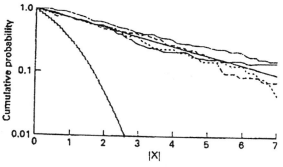

Figure 22.4. Annual energy outlook forecasts. The plots depict the cumulative probability that new measurements, $a$, will be at least $|x|$ standard deviations $d$ away from the old results $A$; $x = (a - A)/d$. 1983 to 1990 (heavy dotted line); 1985 to 1990 (dashed line); 1987 to 1990 (solid line), aggregated forecasts for all three forecast years (heavy dashed line); exponential distribution, $e^{-|x|/3}$, corresponding to $u = 3.4$ (heavy solid line); gaussian (thin solid line with vertical bars). (*Source:* Shlyakhter et al., 1994.)

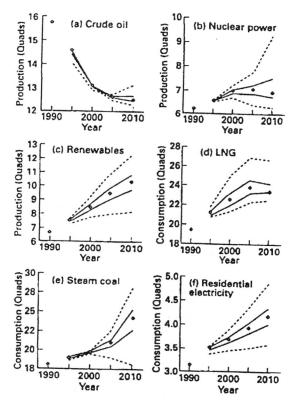

Figure 22.5. Confidence intervals for six production and consumption sectors. In each, the diamonds and solid confidence limits are from the Annual Energy Outlook of the U.S. Department of Energy (1992). Dashed confidence intervals are adjusted to reflect overconfidence in historical projections. (*Source:* Shlyakhter et al., 1994.)

(Henrion and Fischhoff, 1986). These intervals narrow over time, as scientific knowledge improves. However, current best guesses (and the ranges of those guesses) are typically outside the previous ranges of reasonable possibilities. Kammen, Shlyakhter, and their co-workers (Kammen and Marino, 1993, Shlyakhter and Kammen, 1992 and 1993; Shlyakhter et al., 1993, 1994) have demonstrated similar patterns in a reanalysis of these data, as well as in analyses of other estimates and forecasts, drawn from physics, climatology, demographics, and energy policy. Figure 22.4 shows their evaluation of U.S. government Annual Energy Outlook forecasts. In it, forecasts are characterized in terms of the absolute value of the difference between the forecast value and a subsequently determined "exact value," divided by the standard deviation of the forecasts. If estimates were drawn from a gaussian distribution, then one would expect these scores to fall along the leftmost curve in the figure. In three sets of particle data, these authors found a much higher rate of large deviations. Figure 22.5 translates these results into revised confidence intervals (dashed lines) around best-guess forecasts (squares) for several major sets of data, by adjusting forecaster-provided forecasts (solid lines) in keeping with the overconfidence demonstrated in analyses like that in Figure 22.4.

### 4.2. Events

As noted above, one practical challenge to the communication of forecasts, or even descriptions of current and historical situations, is change in the definition of terms. Because these issues can apply to analyses of current, historical, or future states, I will use the term "analyst" rather than "forecaster." As mentioned, for theoretical, political,[5] or methodological reasons, the consumers of analyses may suddenly find themselves facing a new definition of "money supply" "unemployment," "gross domestic product," "health effect," or "manslaughter," etc. In addition to the technical problems of ensuring that recipients understand what the experts are currently talking about, there is the conceptual problem of whether the experts know what they are talking about. Even if a definition is revised because of indisputable scientific advances in theory or measurement, the change is an admission that the preceding definition was flawed. If recipients of a previous analysis were unaware of that conceptual instability, then they would have placed undue confidence in it. They should also be asking about the stability of the current definition.

In attempting to assess the confidence that definitions deserve, it may be useful to distinguish between situations in which the analysts are working with the best definition they can manage and situations in which the analysts have chosen one out of a set of competing definitions. In the former situation, one needs an epistemological appraisal of the state of the science, a topic pursued in the following section. In the latter situation, if the full definition is given and one has precise informational needs, then one can assess the relevance of the definition that was used (the topic of the previous section). Without that precision, one must guess at how much confidence to place in analysts' implicit or explicit claims of being on the right topic.

One part of that assessment is an examination of the analysts' incentive structure. Namely, are they motivated to exaggerate the pertinence of their focal variable? Does the nature of their business require them to sell the same analysis to multiple users? Do they have a reasoned basis for defending their chosen definitions (beyond, say, analytical convenience or convention)? Are they afraid of challenging their clients to be more precise about their needs?

For example, there are many ways to define "risk," such as that arising from a new technology. Some analysts compute expected change in life expectancy, while others compute expected rate of premature deaths. In addition to the technical differences in the computations, there are ethical differences as well (Crouch and Wilson, 1981, and Fischhoff et al., 1984). The latter measure treats a death as a death, regardless of who experiences it, whereas the former measure places extra value on deaths among the young (because more days will be lost with each death). Unless these issues are explained, the recipient is confidently being led off target.

Another form of possibly unwitting overconfidence in event definitions occurs when the analyst is free to try alternative model specifications until some seemingly reasonable results arise. For example, regression techniques are often used to value particular features of goods, as a function of the preferences "revealed" in market actions. Analysts often have considerable freedom to try different models, including different versions of the dependent variable, each of which has enough intuitive appeal to allow it to be justified, should it produce acceptable results (Bentkover et al., 1985, and Fischhoff and Furby, 1988). Under those circumstances, the recipient of the analysis does not know how many degrees of freedom have been "used up," prior to settling on the version that was delivered.

Finally, predicted events may be so complex that it is hard to know which parts of them to take seriously. After the accident at Three Mile Island, there was some debate over whether that event sequence had been included in the elaborate probabilistic analyses conducted in the preceding decade. Under those circumstances, it is unclear whether the analysts are predicting anything at all.

## 5. Impoverishment

Many of these issues arise, in part, because of the attempt to present (and use) forecasts in isolation. At times, that is a workable arrangement. At other times, though, one needs to understand the nature of the enterprise that produced the forecasts. Without such an epistemological background, even explicit statements of uncertainty may represent misplaced imprecision.

### 5.1. Probabilities

One fundamental question concerns the kind of evidence that is allowed. At one extreme, probabilities are restricted to estimates of the relative frequency of an event with recurring opportunities to occur. At the other extreme, probabilities can summarize evidence from whatever (potentially diverse) sources seem relevant. Many forecasts lie somewhere along this frequentist–subjectivist continuum. Even if restricted to historical data, they incorporate an element of judgment, at least in the selection and application of statistical models. There are (long-standing) arguments for these different positions. Recipients need to know which view prevailed. Knowing what kind of probability they are facing is essential for judging how inclusive and reliable the analytical process has been (Gärdenfors and Sahlin, 1989, and Shafer and Tversky, 1985).

Providing such a description is far from trivial, requiring a thicker description than even second-order probabilities. In order to meet such needs, Funtowicz and Ravetz (1990) have developed an alternative notation, describing what they call the "pedigree" of numerical estimates. Table 22.3 shows the three components of pedigree: the quality of the theoretical model generating the estimate, the quality of the data used, and the degree of social acceptance for the procedure. Funtowicz and Ravetz are philosophers of science, who derived the scheme from normative considerations, regarding what people ought to know about expert-generated estimates. Although the scheme has been applied to a variety of analyses, its interpretation by lay recipients has yet to be explored.

### 5.2. Events

Analysts work with abstractions of real-world situations. They should not be held responsible for the intrusion of issues outside their domain – providing they have circumscribed the limits to analysis. Thus, the consumers of probabilistic risk analyses need to know if the failure rates are being predicted on the basis of models that neglect human sources of error (such as operator, maintenance, or designer oversight), or treat these sources of error with procedures derived from hard-surface engineering. The consumers of flood forecasts need to know whether an attempt has been made to consider the cumulative effects of changes in land use (e.g., paving, flood control). The consumers of economic forecasts need to know whether the possibilities of major disruptions (e.g., wars) have been considered, as well as whether the model distinguishes between good and bad expenditures (e.g., waste disposal).

Table 22.3. *The Pedigree of Numerical Estimates*

| | | Source of Uncertainty | |
| --- | --- | --- | --- |
| Score | *Theoretical* *(Quality of Model)* | *Empirical* *(Quality of Data)* | *Social* *(Degree of Acceptance)* |
| 4 | Established theory • many validation tests • causal mechanisms understood | Experimental data • statistically valid samples • controlled experiments | Total • all but cranks |
| 3 | Theoretical model • few validation tests • causal mechanisms hypothesized | Historical/field data • some direct measurements • uncontrolled experiments | High • all but rebels |
| 2 | Computational model • engineering approximations • causal mechanisms approximated | Calculated data • indirect measurements • handbook estimates | Medium • competing schools |
| 1 | Statistical processing • simple correlations • no causal mechanisms | Educated guesses • very indirect approximations • "rule of thumb" estimates | Low • embryonic field |
| 0 | Definitions/assertions | Pure guesses | None |

*Source:* Funtowicz and Ravetz (1990).

Circumscribing a model in this way requires self-reflection and candor on the analyst's part. It may mean overcoming the cognitive tendency to view what is customarily modeled as being what really matters, as well as the motivational tendency to deny the poverty of one's reach. However, it is only by knowing these facts that consumers can create their own assessment of pedigree, anticipate the direction of systematic biases, predict the rate of forecasting progress, judge the meaning of agreement among forecasters, and know where else to go for help. At this level, we know very little about what people take away from forecasts. Wagenaar et al. (1985) and others (Berry, 1986, Hyatt et al., 1978, and cited in Ayton, 1988) found that people remember rather little of broadcast weather forecasts, even when unusual steps are taken to ensure comprehensibility. Perhaps people's attention and commitment wander when they have deep questions regarding the nature of forecasts, but do not know where to begin asking questions or getting answers.

## 6. (Where) Did the Weather Channel Go Wrong?

To be useful, a conceptual scheme should at least be able to shed some light on past experience. Table 22.4 applies one such scheme heuristically to the experience of the Weather Channel with the storm of March 1993, although a more detailed review of the tapes and assessment of viewers' interpretations would be needed to confirm these speculations.

Ambiguity does not seem to have been the problem. Both the probability and the event were clearly stated: a very large storm, with unusual winds and precipitation, was certain to occur over a large (and specified) area of the eastern United States. The probability side of the forecasts holds up fairly well on the remaining criteria. The Channel said explicitly how much confidence could be placed in them (total), as well as giving an indication of whether those assertions could be trusted. There were even some efforts to explain the sources of their confidence, by showing the quality of their observational data, the strength of the underlying theory, and the convergence of unstoppable weather phenomena. If this aspect of the forecast is to be faulted, it might be for failing to reconcile the proclaimed trustworthiness of this forecast with failures in the past. Thus, the Weather Channel's ability to make the case for this forecast may have been limited by the absence of a context for understanding the successes and failures of previous forecasts. Even if the Weather Channel changed its practices, it would still have to face the confusion created by the less enlightened practices of other weather forecasters.

It is on the event side of the ledger than things seem to unravel. The Channel predicted aggregate weather, with considerable accuracy. However, the fate of individuals is determined by much finer phenomena, such as the weight of snow on electric lines, the traction on icy roads, and the melt rate

Table 22.4. *Where Did the Weather Channel Go Wrong?*

| Threats to Communicating Forecasts | Description of | |
|---|---|---|
| | *Probabilities* | *Events* |
| Ambiguity | Certain to happen | Clear on weather |
| Irrelevance | Certain | Just weather |
| Immodesty | You can really trust us this time | Ignored resolution (time, space) |
| Impoverishment | Gave sources of confidence, ignored historical record | Ignored ties of weather to life |

on the sidewalks that they might be tempted to shovel. Thus, the Weather Channel was not predicting the event that really mattered to recipients. Of course, it would be impossible for a general service forecaster to make (or deliver) driveway-by-driveway predictions. Indeed, there is money to be made customizing weather forecasts for specific clients. Nonetheless, ordinary recipients may need extra help to understand the limits to a general forecast's resolution.

As a matter of enrichment, one could explain why the details matter, thereby creating the potential links between weather and life. These connections would, in effect, be classes of miniforecasts, of much greater specificity and much less confidence than the synoptic forecasts. For example, one might say, "Such storms can produce uncommonly heavy snow. Shovelling such snow can, in turn, produce cardiac arrest among individuals with previously undiagnosed heart problems." or "Such storms typically produce scattered collapses of transportation systems, leaving people stranded for extended periods of time, possibly without proper protection against exposure." The deliberate tentativeness of such mini-forecasts may help to convince recipients of the uncertainties that they face. The critical general messages may be that "storms like this are so far outside everyday experience that intuitions cannot be trusted," and "this means you."

For such messages to work, recipients need an understanding not just of the weather, but of its role in their lives. For example, recipients might just not be able to imagine how one's heart could fail from a little shovelling. Improving people's mental model of their own physiology has increased adherence to medical regimes (Leventhal and Cameron, 1987). Perhaps the Weather Channel should team up with the Medicine Channel, in order to fulfil their mutual commitments to listeners.

## Conclusion

### An Error Matrix

Ideally, all forecasts would be entirely transparent, so that they mean (to the forecaster) what they seem to mean (to the recipient). When problems remain, the critical question is whether they are recognized or ignored. Table 22.5 suggests the consequences of pitfalls being acknowledged or ignored by the forecaster, as a function of whether the recipient is aware or ignorant of the possibility.

If both are aware of a problem (Cell A), then they can form a partnership, trying to improve communication and sharing frustration with a reality that poses complexity, ambiguity, and uncertainty. If forecasters are aware of problems that escape the attention of clients (Cell C), then there is, in principle, an opportunity for education – assuming that clients are willing to deal with those problems. If clients are unwilling, then they may find

Table 22.5. *Risks of (Mis)communication*

| Client | Forecaster | |
|---|---|---|
| | *Addresses Pitfall* | *Ignores Pitfall* |
| Recognizes pitfall | *A*<br>Partnership;<br>mutual frustration<br>with reality (for<br>making forecasting<br>hard) | *B*<br>Lost business;<br>frustration with forecasters<br>(for avoiding obvious<br>problems) |
| Ignorant of pitfall | *C*<br>Education of client;<br>frustration<br>with forecasts<br>(for failing to meet<br>needs) | *D*<br>Folie à deux<br>frustration with future<br>(for which one is<br>unprepared) |

the forecasts quite frustrating, full of qualifications and explanations without clear justification. The resulting confusion might, however, at least keep them from relying too heavily on the forecasts, which they realize that they do not really understand.

If forecasters fail to deal with problems which potential clients recognize (Cell B), then they may lose respect and even business for failing to level with those clients. The frequency of such client sophistication might determine how willing forecasters are to take such gambles.[6] If no one recognizes the potential pitfalls (Cell D), then there is joint folly (or what psychoanalysts sometimes call a folie à deux). When both forecaster and client exaggerate the quality of forecasts, the client will often win the race to the poorhouse, discovering empirically the price of undue faith in forecasts.

### A Cautionary Anecdote

Some years ago, I was invited to a meeting of academics and senior U.S. military officers, primarily from the Navy. I was eager for the opportunity to try out a conceptualization of command and control that I had been developing with some colleagues (Fischhoff and Johnson, 1990, Lanir et al., 1988). Briefly, it asked how the strengths and weaknesses of individual decision making are enhanced or complicated by being embedded in organizations of increasing complexity.

The following speaker, a rear admiral, paid me the great honor of throwing away his prepared talk to see what he could make of our theory. I was immediately eager to see what he made of our attempt to integrate individual and organizational perspectives. He began, "Professor Fischhoff has said that decisions have three components: options, outcomes, and uncertainties. Let me see if that fits any of the decisions that I have made." At one level, he proceeded to show the opaqueness of some terms that are at the center of our enterprise. At another level, he showed the magnitude of the potential gaps between the conceptualizations of practitioners and those who have adopted the analytical turn of mind. Although he was able to make some sense out of our basic conceptual scheme, the particular elaboration that I had presented required an unrealistic degree of fluency.

### A Sketchy Workplan

Unless we have the chance to interact directly with the recipients of our messages, it is hard to know what they make of what we say. If this seems like a worthy topic for systematic study, then we are fortunate in having some seemingly useful procedures for beginning the work. Some could be applied almost immediately by practitioners. For example, there is no good reason (other than the effort and resources demanded) why performance records should not be created and publicized, thereby calibrating the confidence placed in forecasts, or why think-aloud protocols should not be used to anticipate recipients' interpretations of forecasts. A modest investment in transfer of technology should be able to make these research techniques available for many applications. If not, then there is something to be learned about the technique by figuring out how to make this step.

In other cases, though, the work has hardly begun. As one goes down and to the right in tables like Table 22.4, the communication task involves communicating the forecaster's worldview to the consumer. That requires both empirical work regarding lay epistemology and theoretical work regarding the nature of forecasting. It would not be the first time that taking teaching seriously helped to clarify one's thinking.

#### Notes

1 The two exceptions were troubling for quite a different reason. Her subjects did not see the relevance of the amount of sex to the probability of AIDS and pregnancy (see also Linville et al., 1993).

2 A minister doing pastoral work with AIDS sufferers recently told me about a patient who said, "I thought that the risks to intravenous drug users didn't include me, since I only skin popped." There is, of course, always some chance of willful misinterpretation, as people construe evidence to fit the actions that they intended to take anyway. However, part of the expert's job is to be explicit enough to close such loopholes.

3 A problem with analogous complexity is prioritizing the testing of chemicals for toxicity from the very large matrix of possibilities: 50,000 or so chemicals, various

toxic endpoints and several tests for each, which could be conducted some number of times (National Research Council, 1983).

4 Yates (1989) offers an insightful summary of the research results and methods. One topic attracting some attention currently is an apparent discrepancy between the confidence expressed in a set of forecasts and in the individual members of a set (Sniezek and Buckley, 1991, Sniezek et al., 1990). As this topic evolves, the critical question for forecasters is which task is more pertinent. That is, are decisions made on the basis of confidence in individual forecasts or in sets of forecasts?

5 An example of a politically motivated change would be tightening the definition of "actively seeking employment" in order to reduce the apparent unemployment rate.

6 The legendary, and unacknowledged, ambiguity and immodesty of the annual forecasts that appear in supermarket tabloids suggests a perception of clients who are either very unsophisticated or very forgiving.

### Reference

Ayton, P., 1992, On the competence and incompetence of experts, in: G. Wright and F. Bolger, eds., *Expertise and Decision Support* (Plenum, New York), 77–105.

Ayton, P., 1988, Perceptions of broadcast weather forecasts, *Weather*, 43, 193–197.

Bailar, B. A. and N. D. Rothwell, 1984, Measuring employment and unemployment. in: C. F. Turner and E. Martin, eds., *Surveying Subjective Phenomena* (Russell Sage Foundation, New York), 129–142.

Bentkover, J. D., V. T. Covello and J. Mumpower, eds., 1985, *Benefits Assessment: The State of the Art* (D. Reidel, Dordrecht).

Berry, C., 1986, What's wrong with the weather? *European Broadcasting Union Review*, 37, 34–37.

Beyth-Marom, R., 1982, How probable is probable? Numerical translation of verbal probability expressions, *Journal of Forecasting*, 1, 257–269.

Cohen, J., E. S. Dearnley and C. E. M. Hansel, 1958, A quantitative study of meaning, *British Journal of Educational Psychology*, 28, 141–148.

Costanza, R., ed., 1991, *Ecological Economics* (Columbia University Press, New York).

Crouch, E. A. C. and R. Wilson, 1981, *Risk/Benefit Analysis* (Ballinger, Cambridge, MA).

Dowlatabadi, H. and G. Morgan, 1993, A model framework for integrated studies of climate change, *Energy Policy*, 21, 209–221.

Evans, J. S., N. C. Hawkins and J. D. Graham, 1988, The value of monitoring for radon in the home, *Journal of the Air Pollution Control Association*, 38, 138–145.

Fischhoff, B., 1982, Debiasing, in: D. Kahneman, P. Slovic and A. Tversky, eds., *Judgment under Uncertainty: Heuristics and Biases* (Cambridge University Press, New York) 422–444.

Fischhoff, B., 1989, Making decisions about AIDS, in: V. Mays, G. Albec and S. Schneider, eds., *Primary Prevention of AIDS* (Sage, Newbury Park, CA), 168–205.

Fischhoff, B. and L. Furby, 1988, Measuring values: A conceptual framework for interpreting transactions, *Journal of Risk and Uncertainty*, 1, 147–184.

Fischhoff, B. and S. Johnson, 1990, The possibility of distributed decision making: Appendix to Distributed Decision Making: Workshop Report (National Academy Press, Washington, DC), pp. 25–58.

Fischhoff, B. and D. MacGregor, 1986, Calibrating databases, *Journal of American Society for Information Sciences*, 37, 222–233.

Fischhoff, B., D. MacGregor and L. Blackshaw, 1987, Creating categories for databases, *International Journal of Man-Machine Systems*, 27, 33–63.

Fischhoff, B., P. Slovic and S. Lichtenstein, 1978, Fault trees: Sensitivity of assessed failure probabilities to problem representation. *Journal of Experimental Psychology: Human Perception and Performance*, 4, 330–344.

Fischhoff, B., S. Watson and C. Hope, 1984, Defining risk, *Policy Sciences*, 17, 123–139.

Fortney, J., 1988, Contraception: A life long perspective, in: *Dying for love* (National Council for International Health, Washington, DC).

Funtowicz, S. O. and J. R. Ravetz, 1990, *Uncertainty and Quality in Science for Policy* (Kluwer, Boston).

Furnas, G. W., T. K. Landauer, L. M. Gomez, and S. T. Dumais, 1983, Statistical semantics: Analysis of the potential performance of key-word information systems, *Bell System Technical Journal*, 62, 1753–1806.

Gärdenfors, P. and N. E. Sahlin, 1982, Unreliable probabilities, risk taking and decision making, *Synthese*, 53, 361–386.

Gärdenfors, P. and N. E. Sahlin, eds., 1989, *Decision, probability, and utility* (Cambridge University Press, Cambridge).

Grice, H. P., 1975, Logic and conversation, in: P. Cole and J. L. Morgan, eds., Syntax and Semantics, *Vol. 3, Speech acts* (Academic Press, New York), 41–48.

Hamm, R. M., 1991, Selection of verbal probabilities, *Organizational Behavior and Human Decision Processes*, 48, 193, 223.

Henrion, M. and B. Fischhoff, 1986, Assessing uncertainty in physical constants, *American Journal of Physics*, 54, 791–798.

Holyoak, K. J. and A. L. Glass, 1978, Recognition confusion among quantifiers, *Journal of Verbal Learning and Verbal Behavior*, 17, 249–264.

Hyatt, D., K. Riley and N. Sederstrom, 1978, Recall of television weather reports, *Journalism Quarterly*, 55, 306–310.

Kammen, D. M. and B. D. Marino, 1993, On the origin and magnitude of pre-industrial anthropogenic $CO_2$ and $CH_4$ emissions, *Chemosphere*, 26, 69–85.

Keren, G., 1987, Facing uncertainty in the game of bridge: A calibration study, *Organizational Behavior and Human Decision Processes*, 39, 98–114.

Krysztofowicz, R., 1983, Why should a forecaster and a decision maker use Bayes' Theorem, *Water Resources Research*, 19, 327–336.

Lanir, Z., B. Fischhoff and S. Johnson, 1988, Military risk taking: $C^3I$ and the cognitive functions of boldness in war, *Journal of Strategic Studies*, 11, 96–114.

Leventhal, H. and L. Cameron, 1987, Behavioral theories and the problem of compliance, *Patient Education and Counseling*, 10, 117–138.

Lichtenstein, S. and B. Fischhoff, 1977, Do those who know more also know more about how much they know? The calibration of probability judgments, *Organizational Behavior and Human Performance*, 20, 159–183.

Lichtenstein, S., B. Fischhoff and L. D. Phillips, 1982, Calibration of probabilities: State of the art to 1980, in: D. Kahneman, P. Slovic and A. Tversky, eds., *Judgment under uncertainty: Heuristics and biases* (Cambridge University Press, New York), 306–334.

Lichtenstein, S. and J. R. Newman, 1967, Empirical scaling of common verbal phrases associated with numerical probabilities, *Psychonomic Science*, 9, 563–564.

Linville, P. W., G. W. Fischer and B. Fischhoff, 1993, Perceived risk and decision making involving AIDS, in: J. B. Pryor and G. D. Reeder, eds., *The social psychology of HIV infection* (Erlbaum, Hillsdale, NJ), 5–38.

Merz, J. F., 1991, Toward a standard of disclosure for medical informed consent:

Development and demonstration of a decision-analytic methodology. Ph.D. dissertation, Carnegie Mellon University.

Merz, J., M. Druzdzel and D. J. Mazur, 1991, Verbal expressions of probability in informed consent litigation, *Medical Decision Making*, 11, 273–281.

Merz, J., B. Fischhoff, D. J. Mazur and P. S. Fischbeck, 1993, Decision-analytic approach to developing standards of disclosure for medical informed consent, *Journal of Toxics and Liability*, 15, 191–215.

Morgan, M. G. and M. Henrion, 1990, *Uncertainty* (Cambridge University Press, New York).

Murphy, A. H., S. Lichtenstein, B. Fischhoff and R. L. Winkler, 1980, Misinterpretations of precipitation probability forecasts, *Bulletin of the American Meteorological Society*, 61, 695–701.

Murphy, A. and B. Brown, 1984, Comparable evaluation of subjective weather forecasts in the United States, *Journal of Forecasting*, 3, 369–393.

Murphy, A. and R. Winkler, 1984, Probability of precipitation forecasts, *Journal of the American Statistical Association*, 79, 391–400.

Murphy, G. L. and D. L. Medin, 1985, The role of theories in conceptual coherence, *Psychological Review*, 92, 289–316.

National Health Information Survey, 1987, Knowledge and attitudes about AIDS: Data, National Center for Health Statistics, Advance Data, No. 146.

National Research Council, 1983, *Priorities for chemical toxicity testing* (National Research Council, Washington, DC).

Office of Technology Assessment, 1993, Preparing for an uncertain climate (2 *vols.*) (Office of Technology Assessment, Washington, DC).

Poulton, E. C., 1989, *Bias in quantifying judgment* (Lawrence Erlbaum, Hillsdale, NJ).

Quadrel, M. J., 1990, Elicitation of adolescents' risk perceptions: Qualitative and quantitative dimensions, Ph.D. dissertation, Carnegie Mellon University.

Quadrel, M. J., B. Fischhoff and C. Palmgren, 1994, Adolescents' definitions of risk behaviors, Unpublished work.

Rubin, E. S., L. B. Lave and M. G. Morgan, 1992, Keeping climate change relevant, *Issues in Science and Technology*, (Winter) 47–55.

Shafer, G., 1975, *A mathematical theory of evidence* (Princeton University Press, Princeton, NJ).

Shafer, G. and A. Tversky, 1985, Languages and designs for probability judgment, *Cognitive Science*, 9, 309–339.

Shlyakhter, A. I. and D. M. Kammen, 1992, Sea-level rise or fall? *Nature*, 357, 25.

Shlyakhter, A. I. and D. M. Kammen, 1993, Uncertainties in modeling low probability/high consequence events: Application to population projections and models of sea-level rise, *Second International Symposium on Uncertainty Modeling and Analysis* (IEEE Computer Society Press, Washington, DC), 246–253.

Shlyakhter, A. I., D. M. Kammen, C. L. Broido and R. Wilson, 1994, Quantifying the credibility of energy projections from trends in past data: The US energy sector, *Energy Policy*, 22, 119–131.

Shlyakhter, A. I., I. A. Shlyakhter, C. L. Broido and R. Wilson, 1993, Estimating uncertainty in physical measurements. Observational and environmental studies: Lessons from trends in nuclear data, *Second International Symposium on Uncertainty Modeling and Analysis* (IEEE Computer Society Press, Washington, DC), 310–317.

Sniezek, J. A. and T. Buckley, 1991, Confidence depends on level of aggregation, *Journal of Behavioral Decision Making*, 4, 263–272.

Sniezek, J. A., P. W. Paese and F. S. Switzer, 1990, The effect of choosing on confidence in choice, *Organizational Behavior and Human Decision Processes*, 46, 264–282.

Superstorm, 1993 (1993). Atlanta, GA: The Weather Channel.

Svenson, O. and B. Fischhoff, 1985, Levels of environmental decisions, *Journal of Environmental Psychology*, 5, 55–68.

Turner, C., J. T. Lesser, and J. C. Gfroerer, 1992, *Survey Measurement of Drug Use* (National Institute of Drug Abuse: Research Triangle Park, NC).

Turner, C. F. and E. Martin, eds., 1984, *Surveying Subjective Phenomena* (Russell Sage Foundation, New York).

US Department of Energy, 1992, *Annual Energy Outlook, with Projections to 2010* (DOE/EIA-0383(92)). Washington, DC, The Department.

Wagenaar, W. A., R. Schreuder and A. H. C. van der Heijden, 1985, Do TV pictures help people to remember the weather? *Ergonomics*, 28, 765–772.

Wallsten, T., D. V. Budescu, A. Rapoport, R. Zwick and B. Forsyth, 1986, Measuring the vague meanings of probability terms, *Journal of Experimental Psychology: General*, 115, 348–365.

von Winterfeldt, D. and W. Edwards, 1986, *Decision Analysis and Behavioral Research* (Cambridge University Press, New York).

Yates, J. F., 1989, *Judgment and decision making* (Wiley, Chichester).

Zimmer, A. C., 1984. A model for the interpretation of verbal predictions, *International Journal of Man-Machine Systems*, 20, 121–134.

# 23 Proper and Improper Linear Models

*Robyn M. Dawes*

### Ben Franklin

Ben Franklin suggested in a letter to his friend Joseph Priestley in 1772.[1]

I cannot, for want of sufficient premises, advise you *what* to determine, but if you please I will tell you *how* . . . . My way is to divide half a sheet of paper by a line into two columns; writing over the one *Pro*, and over the other *Con*. Then, during three or four days' consideration, I put down under the different heads short hints of the different motives, that at different times occur to me *for* or *against* the measure. When I have thus got them all together in one view, I endeavor to estimate the respective weights . . . . [to] find at length where the balance lies . . . . And, though the weight of reasons cannot be taken with the precision of algebraic quantities, yet, when each is thus considered, separately and comparatively, and the whole matter lies before me, I think I can judge better, and am less liable to make a rash step; and in fact I have found great advantage for this kind of equation, in what may be called *moral* or *prudential algebra*.

Franklin's "prudential algebra" involves nothing more than a *weighted average* of reasons for and against a particular course of action. Each positive reason is assigned a score of $+1$, each negative one a score of $-1$. The scores are then given intuitive *importance weights*. The course of action with the higher resulting sum is judged to be the more desirable one.

Why should this procedure lead to better decisions than making an intuitive judgment at the outset? After all, the weights are intuitive. Doesn't Franklin's method simply substitute one type of intuition for another? Yes, it does, but his method is based on a superior type of intuition. Reasons for adopting a course of action are often *psychologically incomparable*, and research has indicated that people make poor intuitive global judgments when the factors are incomparable. By *poor* I mean they are inferior to those based on

Reprinted from *International Journal of Forecasting*, 2, R. M. Dawes, "Proper and Improper Linear Models," 5–14, copyright © 1986, with kind permission from Elsevier Science – NL, Sara Burgerhartstraat 25, 1055 KV Amsterdam, The Netherlands.

intuitive weighting – and nowhere near as good as the judges believe them to be. People tend to have misplaced faith in their global intuitive judgments. We are grossly overconfident when we make such judgments, and selective memory for our successes (perhaps a mentally healthy trait) feeds our overconfidence.

What leads me to conclude that intuitive weighting schemes are superior to global intuitive judgment and that people are overconfident? These conclusions are supported by studies in which there are "correct" answers (e.g., medical diagnoses determined after extensive tests or autopsies). When judgment can be compared with such external standards of accuracy, weighting schemes *consistently* are found to be superior to intuitive global judgment, and judges consistently are found to be overconfident in their global judgments. Of course, such studies are relevant only to situations in which a complex (multivariate) strategy or stimulus can be broken down (decomposed) into simpler components – as, in Franklin's example, the probable value of a course of action can be broken down into reasons for pursuing or avoiding it.

Before reviewing this evidence, however, let us consider an example. Imagine that you must select a spy to infiltrate a Spanish-speaking terrorist organization. There are two candidates:

A is a native Spanish speaker, is moderately intelligent, shows no evidence in his past of being particularly trusted or liked by people who know him, and is highly committed to your cause. B speaks fluent Spanish but is not a native speaker (although none of five experts was able to detect an accent), is highly intelligent, and shows evidence in his past of being trusted and liked by people who know him, but you have doubts about the depth of his commitment to your cause.

Now try to make a global judgment. Does A or B "strike" you as more appropriate? Why? A hunch; an intuition? Perhaps A or B reminds you of some *particular* individual who has succeeded or failed at this type of mission in the past or who is stereotypic ("representative") of a class of people who have succeeded or failed. Perhaps it is easier to *imagine* A's or B's succeeding or failing. Perhaps memory, representativeness, and ease of imagination are all factors – conscious or unconscious – influencing your hunch or intuition. But these factors are *poor* predictors. Recall that the ease with which you can imagine events is determined by many variables other than their likelihood.

Instead, consider applying Franklin's prudential algebra – that is, developing a linear model with intuitive weights. If you do that, you will be *forced* to consider the relative importance of the four characteristics: native speech, intelligence, ability to inspire trust, and commitment to cause. There are many ways to construct such a model. Two good ways are (1) to analyze what the mission requires and weight the four characteristics accordingly, and (2) to determine weights by how the four characteristics have correlated with success or failure on similar missions in the past. (This is quite different from "matching" A and B to selected people in the past who happen to come to mind.)

Too many people prefer to make global intuitive judgments based on hunch "hit" or ad hoc choice of variables. Many such "snap" judgments are based on some *plausible* explanation that may or may *not* be valid. For example, J. C. Penney took potential executives to lunch. If they salted their food before tasting it, he concluded that they lacked an "inquiring frame of mind" and rejected them.[2] (Penney did well, but we have no evidence he wouldn't have done equally well had he selected executives at random from among the applicants.) Other snap judgments are based on hunch. But unless the person making such a judgment has some evidence (empirical or theoretical, not just intuitive plausibility) that the hunch is valid, it is in my view arbitrary, stupid, and unethical.

Moreover, intuitive global judgments engender overconfidence. Consider, for example, a letter to "Dear Abby" published in 1975:

DEAR ABBY: While standing in a checkout line in a high-grade grocery store, I saw a woman directly in front of me frantically rummaging around in her purse, looking embarrassed. It seems her groceries had already been checked, and she was a dollar short. I felt sorry for her, so I handed her a dollar. She was very grateful, and insisted on writing my name and address on a loose piece of paper. She stuck it in her purse and said, "I promise I'll mail you a dollar tomorrow." Well, that was three weeks ago, and I still haven't heard from her! Abby, I think I'm a fairly good judge of character, and I just didn't peg her as the kind that would beat me out of a dollar. The small amount of money isn't important, but what it did to my faith in people is. I'd like your opinion.

SHY ONE BUCK

Note that Shy One Buck did not lose faith in her ability to "peg" people on the basis of almost no information whatsoever; she lost her faith in people. Shy One Buck still believes she is a good "judge of character" based on a single instant's interaction. It is other people who are no damn good. (Note also the gradiosity of this loss of faith – in people in general, not in people's memory or their ability to avoid losing loose pieces of paper.)

I cannot guarantee that a choice based on intuitive weighting will necessarily work better than one based on global intuition – just that it *usually* will. This generalization is not a global intuitive judgment of my own; it is based on a large body of research findings.

### The Research

The research began by addressing the question of whether trained experts' intuitive global predictions were better than statistically derived weighted averages of the relevant predictors.[3] Such weighted averages are termed *linear models*. This question has been studied extensively by psychologists, educators, and others interested in predicting such outcomes as college success, parole violation, psychiatric diagnosis, physical diagnosis and prognosis, and business success and failure. In all of these studies, the information on which clinical experts based their predictions was the same as that used to construct linear models. Typically, this information consisted of test scores or biographical facts, but some studies included observer ratings of specific attributes as well. All of these variables could easily be represented by (coded as) numbers having positive or negative relationships to the outcome to be predicted. (For example, higher test scores and grade point averages predict better performance in subsequent academic work; higher leucocyte count predicts greater severity of Hodgkin's disease.)

In 1954 Paul Meehl published a highly influential book in which he summarized approximately 20 such studies comparing the clinical judgment method with the statistical one.[4] *In all studies, the statistical method provided more accurate predictions, or the two methods tied.* Approximately 10 years later, Jack Sawyer reviewed 45 studies comparing clinical and statistical prediction.[5] Again, there was *not a single study* in which clinical global judgment was superior to the statistical prediction (termed *mechanical combination* by Sawyer). Unlike Meehl, Sawyer did not limit his review to studies in which the clinical judge's information was identical to that on which the statistical prediction was based; he even included two studies in which the clinical judge had access to *more* information (an interview) but did *worse.* (In one of these, the performance of 37,500 sailors in World War II in navy "elementary" school was better predicted from test scores alone than from the ratings of judges who both interviewed the sailors and had access to the scores.[6])

(The near-total lack of validity of the *unstructured* interview as a predictive technique had been documented and discussed by E. Lowell Kelly in 1953.[7] There is no evidence that such interviews yield important information beyond that of past behavior – except whether the interviewer likes the interviewee, which *is* important in some contexts. Some of my students maintain it is necessary to interview people to avoid choosing "nerds," but they cannot explain how they would spot one, or even what they mean by the term.)

A particularly striking example of clinical versus statistical prediction was conducted by Hillel Einhorn.[8] He studied the longevity of patients with Hodgkin's disease during an era when the disease was invariably fatal (prior to the late 1960s). This world expert on Hodgkin's disease and two assistants rated nine characteristics of biopsies taken from patients and then made a global rating of the "overall severity" of the disease process for each patient. Upon the patients' deaths, Einhorn correlated the global ratings with their longevity. While a rating of "overall severity" is not precisely the same as a prediction of time until death, it should predict that. (At least, the world's expert thought it would.) Einhorn found that it does not. (In fact, the slight trend was in the *wrong* direction; higher severity ratings were associated with longer survival time.) In contrast, a multiple regression analysis of the biopsy characteristics scaled by the doctors succeeded in predicting how long the patients lived. The prediction was not strong, but statistically reliable.

Another striking example is a study by Robert Libby. He asked 43 bank loan officers (some senior – in banks with assets up to four billion dollars) to predict which 30 of 60 firms would go bankrupt within three years of a financial report. The loan officers requested, and were provided with, various financial ratios – for example, the ratio of liquid assets to total assets – in order to make their predictions. Their individual judgments were 75% correct, but a regression analysis of the ratios themselves was 82% accurate.[9] In fact, the ratio of assets to liabilities *alone* predicted 80% correctly. Both these studies indicate that experts correctly select the variables that are important in making predictions, but that a linear model that combines these variables in an optimal way is superior to the global judgment of these very same experts.

The finding that linear combination is superior to global judgment is strong; it has been replicated in diverse contexts, and *no* exception has been discovered. (A recent study on lie detection alleged that "trained" use of polygraph techniques is superior to linear models, but it turned out that the statistics had been miscomputed.[10]) As Meehl was able to state 30 years after his seminal book was published, *"There is no controversy in social science which shows such a large body of qualitatively diverse studies coming out so uniformly in the same direction as this one"* (italics added).[11]

What effect have these findings had on the *practice* of expert judgment? Almost zilch. Meehl was elected president of the American Psychological Association at a strikingly young age, and the implications of his work were ignored by his fellow psychologists. States license psychologists, physicians, and psychiatrists to make (lucrative) global judgments of the form "It is my opinion that . . . ," in other words, to make judgments inferior to those that could be made by a juror with a programmable calculator. For reasons outlined later in this chapter – and interspersed throughout the book – people have great misplaced confidence in their global judgments, a confidence that is strong enough to dismiss an impressive body of research findings and to find its way into the legal system.

My own role in this work was to question whether it is necessary to use statistically optimal weights in linear models for them to outperform experts. I have found that it is not. For years the nagging thought kept coming back to me: maybe *any* linear model outperforms the experts. The possibility seemed absurd, but when a research assistant had some free time I asked him to go to several data sources we had stored in computers and to construct linear models with weights "determined randomly except for sign." (It seemed reasonable that in any prediction context of interest, we would know the direction in which each variable predicted the outcome.) After the first 100 such models outperformed our clinical judges, we constructed 20,000 such "random linear models" – 10,000 by choosing coefficients at random from a normal distribution, and 10,000 by choosing coefficients at random from a rectangular distribution. We had three data sets: (1) final diagnoses of neurosis versus psychosis of roughly 860 psychiatric inpatients, predicted from scores on the Minnesota Multiphasic Personality Inventory (MMPI),[12] (2) first-year graduate-school grade point averages (GPAs) of psychology students at the University of Illinois, predicted from 10 variables assessing academic aptitude prior to admissions and personality characteristics assessed shortly thereafter,[13] and (3) faculty ratings of performance of graduate students who had been at the University of Oregon two to five years, predicted from undergraduate GPAs, Graduate Record Examination scores (GREs), and a measure of the selectivity of their undergraduate institutions. All three predictions had been made both by linear models and by "experts" ranging from graduate students to eminent clinical psychologists. On the average, the random linear models accounted for 150% more variance between criteria and predictions than did the holistic clinical evaluations of the trained judges.[14] For mathematical reasons, *unit weighting* (that is, each variable is standardized[15] and weighted +1 or −1 depending on direction) provided even better accountability, averaging 261% more variance.[16,17] Unit or random linear models are termed *improper* because their coefficients (weights) are not based on statistical techniques that optimize prediction. The research indicates that such improper models are almost as good as proper ones.

The inference is simple. Since random and unit weights predict actual outcomes much better than global judgment, intuitive weighting should also. It is then reasonable to conclude that such weights should also outperform global judgment in situations where there is no outcome to predict. That is, the results in the prediction situations can be used as a guide for preference – assuming that methods that consistently predict better than others when there is an outcome to be predicted will also work better when there is not. Of course, there is no way to check this assumption, because there is no outcome in preference situations. But human intuition would have to have almost magical properties were it to be superior to intuitive weighting when we are making choices of what to do, while simultaneously being consistently inferior when we are trying to predict what will happen. Ben Franklin's advice was wise.

Let us apply my conclusion to an example – to the "desirability" of bullets to be used by police officers in Denver, Colorado – as presented by K. R. Hammond and L. Adelman:[18]

In 1974, the Denver Police Department (DPD), as well as other police departments throughout the country, decided to change its handgun ammunition. The principal reason offered by the police was that the conventional round-nose bullet provided insufficient "stopping effectiveness" (that is, that ability to incapacitate and thus to prevent the person shot from firing back at a police officer or others). The DPD chief recommended (as did other police chiefs) the conventional bullet be replaced by a hollow-point bullet. Such bullets, it was contended, flattened on impact, thus decreasing ricochet potential. The suggested change was challenged by the American Civil Liberties Union, minority groups, and others. Opponents of the change claimed that the new bullets were nothing more than outlawed "dum-dum" bullets, that they created far more injury than the round-nosed bullets, and should, therefore, be barred from use. As is customary, judgments on this matter were formed privately and then defended publicly with enthusiasm and tenacity, and the usual public hearings were held. Both sides turned to ballistics experts for scientific information and support.

The disputants focused on evaluating the merits of specific bullets – confounding the physical effect of the bullets with the implications of social policy. Rather than distinguish questions of what each kind of bullet would accomplish (the social policy issue) from questions concerning ballistic characteristics of specific bullets, advocates merely argued for one bullet or the other as a totality. Thus, as Hammond and Adelman pointed out, social policymakers inadvertently adopted the role of (poor) ballistics experts, and vice versa. What Hammond and Adelman did was ascertain the important policy dimensions from the policymakers, and then get professional ratings for each kind of bullet with respect to those dimensions from the ballistics experts. The dimensions identified by the social policymakers were stopping effectiveness (the probability that someone hit in the torso could not return fire), probability of serious injury, and probability of harm to bystanders. The ballistics experts' ratings of the bullets with respect to these dimensions indicated that the last two dimensions were almost perfectly confounded with each other though not perfectly confounded with the first. Bullets do not vary along a single dimension that confounds effectiveness with lethalness. The probability of serious injury *and* harm to bystanders is highly related to the penetration of the bullet, whereas the probability of a bullet's effectively stopping someone from returning fire is highly related to the width of the entry wound. Because policymakers could not agree about the weights to be given to the three dimensions, Hammond and Adelman suggested that they be weighted equally. Combining the equal weights with the (independent) judgments of the ballistic experts, Hammond and Adelman discovered that a bullet not even considered by the disputants "has greater stopping effectiveness and is less apt to cause injury (and is less apt to threaten bystanders) than the standard bullet then in use by the DPD."

It is also possible to modify conclusions, as was done, for example, by David Osborn in choosing Fulbright Professors in the mid 1960's. His method is described as follows:

One of the most imaginative attempts to evaluate the effectiveness of programs with hard-to-assess objectives is a method devised by David Osborn, Deputy Assistant Secretary of State for Educational and Cultural Affairs.... Osborn recommends a scheme of cross-multiplying the costs of the activities with a number representing the rank of its objectives on a scale. For instance, the exchange of Fulbright professors may contribute to "cultural prestige and mutual respect," "educational development," and gaining "entry," which might be given scale numbers such as 8, 6, and 5, respectively. These numbers are then multiplied with the costs of the program, and the resulting figure is in turn multiplied with an ingenious figure called a "country number." The latter is an attempt to get a rough measure of the importance to the U.S. of the countries with which we have cultural relations. It is arrived at by putting together in complicated ways certain key data, weighted to reflect cultural and educational matters, such as the country's population, gross national product, number of college students, rate of illiteracy, and so forth. The resulting numbers are then revised in the light of working experience, as when, because of its high per capita income, a certain tiny Middle Eastern country turns out to be more important to the U.S. than a large Eastern European one. At this point, country numbers are revised on the basis of judgment and experience, as are other numbers at other points. But those who make such revisions have a basic framework to start with, a set of numbers arranged on the basis of many factors, rather than single arbitrary guesses.[19]

The problem with this procedure is revising "on the basis of judgment." The small amount of research available indicates that linear models modified by reflexive judgment in fact predict more poorly than these same models without modification.[20]

### Explanations for the Research Findings

Why is it that linear models – even random ones – predict better than clinical experts? We can possibly explain this finding by hypothesizing a mathematical principle, a principle of "nature," and a psychological principle.

The mathematical principle is that monotone ("ordinal") interactions are well approximated by linear models. Such interactions are illustrated in Figure 23.1b. Two factors "interact" in that their combined import is much greater than the sum of their separate imports, but they do not interact in the sense that the *direction* in which one variable is related to the outcome is dependent upon the magnitude of the other variable. It is not, for example, true of monotone interactions that high-highs are similar to low-lows, but that high-highs (or low-lows) are much higher (or lower) than would be predicted by a separate analysis of each variable. If high-highs are similar to low-lows, the interaction is termed *crossed*, illustrated in Figure 23.1a.

For example, a doctoral student subjected identified alcoholic and non-alcoholic prisoners to a benign or stressful experience.[21] He then had them spend 20 minutes in a waiting room before being interviewed by a psychologist about their experience. A nonalcoholic punch was available in the waiting room, and the variable of interest was how much punch the prisoners consumed. The alcoholic and nonalcoholic prisoners drank virtually

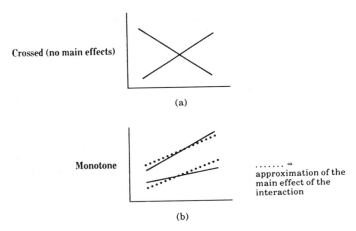

Figure 23.1.  Crossed (a) versus monotone (b) interactions

identical amounts after experiencing the benign situation. After the stressful situation, however, the alcoholic prisoners drank twice as much punch as the nonalcoholics did. Thus, a true interaction was found between stress and drinking behavior of diagnosed alcoholics, but the data analysis indicated that this interaction could *be well approximated* by the two simple main effects: that is, alcoholics drank more punch, and all prisoners drank more punch after being stressed.[22] Another mathematical principle is that coefficients are not as important in linear models as their signs.[23] Thus arbitrary (random) linear models can approximate monotone interaction effects. And, of course, they approximate main effects.

The principle of nature that might explain the finding is that most interactions that exist are, in fact, monotone. It is easy to hypothesize crossed interactions, but extraordinarily difficult to find them, especially in the areas of psychology and social interactions. Because the optimal amount of any variable does not depend upon the value of the others, what interactions there are tend to be monotone. And while a number of crossed interactions have been hypothesized in social interactions (e.g., authoritarian leadership is more effective in some types of situations while "cool" leadership works better in others), they tend to be supported only by verbal plausibility and selective post hoc data analysis. In fact, interactions of *any* sort tend to be ephemeral, as was discovered by Goldberg in his analysis of how the "match" between teaching style and student characteristics predicts student success.[24] Of 38 interactions he thought he had discovered in the first half of an extensive data set, only 24 "cross-validated" *in the right direction* in the second half (not significantly different from chance expectation of 19).

The psychological principle that might explain the predictive success of linear models is that people have a great deal of difficulty in attending to two or more noncomparable ("analyzable") aspects of a stimulus or situation at once. Attention shifts from one to the other and back again. For example, when Roger Shepard asked subjects to make similarity judgments about circles of various sizes containing "spokes" (radii) at various angles, the subjects tended to attend to size *or* angle, but not both.[25] The experience of people evaluating academic applicants is similar. Often they anchor their judgment on a particularly high or low grade point average or test score and then attempt to adjust in light of less vivid information in the applicant's folder. In fact, how *could* an admissions committee member integrate test information and GPA information without knowing something about the distribution and predictability of each within the applicant pool? (Thus, a purely statistical integration will be superior to a global judgment.)

Given that monotone interactions can be well approximated by linear models (a statistical *fact*), it follows that because most interactions that do exist in nature are monotone and because people have difficulty integrating information from noncomparable dimensions, linear models will outperform clinical judgment. The only way to avoid this broad conclusion is to claim that training makes experts superior to other people at integrating information (as opposed, for example, to knowing what information to look for), and there is no evidence for that. There is no evidence that experts *think differently* from others.

### Objections

The conclusion that random or unit weights outperform global judgments of trained experts is not a popular one with experts, or with people relying on them. First of all, it is an affront to the narcissism of many of them. One common response is to challenge the expertise of the research experts making the global predictions. "Minnesota clinicians!" snorted a professor of psychology at the University of Michigan. Little did he know that most of the Minnesota clinicians had obtained their Ph.D.s at Michigan. "Had you used Dr. X," the dean of a prestigious medical school informed me, "his judgments would have correlated with longevity." In fact, Dr. X was the subject of the study.

Another objection is to maintain that the outcomes better predicted by linear models are all short-term and trivial (like ending up back in jail or flunking out of graduate school). The claim is made that "truly important long-term outcomes" can be predicted better by global judgments. But as Jay Russo points out, this objection implies that the long-term future can be predicted better than the short-term future. Such prediction is possible for variables like death (100 years from now) and rabies (after the incubation period), but those variables, which are very rare, are *not* of the type predicted in these studies. Moreover, as we come to understand processes (e.g., the existence of the rabies or AIDS virus in the blood), "incubation period" becomes nothing more than a manner of speech, and aging is more readily predicted than is death.

A final objection is the "10,000 Frenchmen can't be wrong" one. Experts have been revered – and well paid – for years for their "it is my opinion that" judgments. As James March points out, however, such reverence may serve a *purely social function*. People and organizations have to make decisions, often between alternatives that appear equally good or bad. What better way to justify such decisions than to consult any intuitive expert, and the more money she or he charges, the better. "We paid for the best possible medical advice" can be a palliative for a fatal operation, just as "throwing" the I Ching can relieve someone of regretting a bad marriage. An expert who constructs a linear model is not as impressive as one who gives advice on a "burst" of intuition derived from "years of experience." (One highly paid business expert I know constructs linear models in secret, "bootlegging" computer time from another branch of his company.) So we value global judgment of experts independently of its validity.

But there is also a structural reason for doubting the inferiority of global judgment. It has to do with the bias of available feedback. When we construct a linear model in a prediction situation, we know exactly how poorly it predicts. In contrast, our feedback about our global judgments is flawed. Not only do we selectively remember our successes, we often have *no knowledge* of our failures – and any knowledge we do have may serve to "explain" them (away). Who knows what happens to rejected graduate school applicants? Professors have access only to accepted ones, and if the professors are doing a good job, the accepted ones will likewise do well – exonerating the professors' judgment. What happens to people misdiagnosed as "psychotic"? If they are lucky, they will disappear from the sight of the authorities diagnosing them; if not, they are likely to be placed in an environment where they may soon become psychotic. Finally, therapy patients who commit suicide were too sick to begin with – as is easily established from perusal of their files.

The feedback problem is well illustrated by an article in praise of "intuition" by Nancy Hathaway that appeared in the October 31, 1984, issue of the *San Francisco Chronicle*. She writes, "Most people rarely receive intuitions so major that they change their lives. From time to time, however, it does happen. There are even legends of people following their intuitions in business decisions: the late Ray Kroc, who bought MacDonald's despite evidence offered by his advisors that it would be a bad investment, did it because 'I felt in my funny bone that it was a sure thing.' " So we know about Ray Kroc. How many investors had "funny bone" feelings that led to ruin? We don't know (absent the type of *prospective* study – similar to those done of linear models). If 36 people have an intuitive feeling that the next role of the dice will be snake-eyes and are willing to bet even odds on that hunch, on the average one will win. That person is the one most likely to come to our attention; for one thing, the others probably won't talk about it much.

Hillel Einhorn and Robin Hogarth have examined availability of feedback sources, and demonstrated how they *systematically* operate to make intuitive judgment appear valid.[26] Their prototype is of the waiter who decides he can judge whether people tip well from way they dress. A judgment that some people are poor tippers leads to inferior service, which in turn leads to poor tips – thereby "validating" the waiter's judgment. (Again, not all prophecies are self-fulfilling; there must be a mechanism; intuitive judgment provides one.)

In contrast, the systematic predictions of linear models yield data on just how poorly they predict. For example, in Einhorn's study only 18% of the variance in longevity of Hodgkin's disease patients is predicted by the best linear model, but that is opposed to zero percent for the world's foremost authority. Such results bring us abruptly to an unpleasant conclusion: a lot of outcomes about which we care deeply are not very predictable. For example, it is not comforting to members of a graduate school admissions committee to know that only 23% of the variance in later faculty ratings of a student can be predicted by a unit weighting of the student's undergraduate GPA, his or her GRE score, and a measure of the student's undergraduate institution selectivity – but that is opposed to 4% based on judges' global ratings of the applicant. We *want* to predict outcomes important to us. It is only rational to conclude that if one method (a linear model) does not predict well, something else may do better. What is not rational – in fact, irrational – is to conclude that this "something else" is intuitive global judgment.

The point is that many outcomes are not all that predictable. Academic success, for example, is influenced by whom one shares an office with as a graduate student, by which professors happen to have positions available for research assistants, by the person or people with whom one has libidinal involvement (often met on a "chance" basis), by the relative strengths of those with whom one competes for the first job (as judged by the professors who happen to be appointed to the "search committee"), and so on. Moreover, there are clearly self-exacerbating features to an academic career. A "little bit of luck" may lead a new Ph.D. to obtain a position in an outstanding university (or an M.D. in an outstanding hospital or a J.D. in an outstanding law firm), and the consequent quality of colleagues may then significantly reinforce whatever talents the individual brings to the job. (Conversely, a little bit of ill luck may saddle the new Ph.D. with a nine-course per year teaching load, inadequate institutional resources for scholarly or research productivity, and "burnt-out" colleagues. Not many people move from a patent office to a full professorship after publishing a three-page paper, as Einstein did.)

One field in which people find linear models of judgment particularly distasteful is that of *assessing other people*. Is it not important, for example, to *interview* students applying for graduate school? In a word, no. What can an interviewer learn in a half-hour to an hour that is not present in the applicant's record? As Len Rorer points out, belief that one's own interviewing skills provide a pipeline to such information is self-confidence bordering on *hubris*.[27] Moreover, even if the interviewer *thinks* he or she has picked up some highly positive or negative quality in the interview, is it really fair to judge applicants *on the impression they make in a single interview conducted by a single interviewer,* as opposed to a record of actual accomplishment (or failure) over a college career? A GPA is a "mere number," but it represents the combined opinion of some 50 or so professors over several years; some professors may be biased for or against particular students, but surely a combined impression based on actual work over time is fairer than one based on a brief interaction with a single person. Furthermore, GPAs predict better than interviews; is it fair to judge someone on the basis of something that does not work? (In contrast, an interview can be used as a recruiting device – for selling the applicant on the school. Again, however, the interviewee would be wiser to make her or his choice on other grounds.)

A colleague of mine in medical decision making tells of an investigation he was asked to make by the dean of a large and prestigious medical school to try to determine why it was unsuccessful in recruiting female students. My colleague studied the problem statistically "from the outside" and identified a major source of the problem. One of the older professors had cut back on his practice to devote time to interviewing applicants to the school. He assessed such characteristics as "emotional maturity," "seriousness of interest in medicine," and "neuroticism." Whenever he interviewed an unmarried female applicant, he concluded she was "immature." When he interviewed a married one, he concluded she was "not sufficiently interested in medicine," and when he interviewed a divorced one, he concluded she was "neurotic." Not many women were positively evaluated on these dimensions, which of course had nothing to do with gender.

### Implications for Choice

Back to Ben Franklin. The implications of all this research is that if we wish to make choices involving multiple factors we would do well to construct *our own* (improper) linear models. That is in essence what Franklin advised, and the advice is echoed in popular books on decision making that recommend the listing of possible consequences of choices and of our own values (although few such books cite research support for their recommendation). Decision involves predicting our future "states of mind." Given that linear models predict better than intuitive judgment in situations where the accuracy of prediction can be checked, why not this one as well?[28] Of course, there are problems. How do we determine and define the variables? Might not many of them be related? For example, in assessing a possible job, should we list "money," "status," and "autonomy" as separate characteristics? First, how do we know they are important to us? Secondly, aren't they related?

Isn't it true that "high-level" jobs tend to be high on all three while "low-level" jobs are low on all? If so, shouldn't we just list "job level" rather than its separate components?

The answer to the question of importance is rather easy. It is *our* decision. In constructing a weighting scheme, we will list the variables that are important to *us*. If, for example, we think of "job level" in a global and amorphous way, then we should list it. If, on the other hand, money, status, and autonomy each strikes us as psychologically salient, distinct, and important, then we should list them separately. Franklin advised his friend not *what* to decide but *how* to decide it. When suggesting a list he was not advising what should be on it, but rather how to become explicit about what is important to the decision maker. Research indicates that when specific variables are known, a linear model predicts better than global judgment. (Often, in fact, simply determining the variables makes the choice obvious.) Moreover, the weights assigned to the variables are those of the individual making the choice. If, for example, sexual compatibility is more important to a person choosing a mate than is character, altruism, or sanity, then there is no reason the person should not choose on that basis – and live with the consequences. (Some of my colleagues would disagree.) Again, the point of this chapter is not what, but how. Thus, the answer to the related variables question may be found in a distinction made by Wendell Garner.[29] The fact that two dimensions are correlated in nature (such as height and weight) does not imply that they are not psychologically independent and distinct for the perceiver or judge. If they are distinct, specify them as such.

Once we have determined the variables, we face the problem of evaluating and weighting them. To do so, we must assume that we have *some* insight into our values and "value systems" – and in particular into how we compare conflicting values. My own work has demonstrated that this insight need not be total or profound; evaluations and weights that are "reasonable" provide outcomes very close to those based on optimal ones. Granted these assumptions, the decision is then *decomposed* so that each variable can be considered separately, and the results are combined according to a linear weighting scheme. The reason – once again – for believing that such decomposition can work well in a choice situation that lacks a criterion for evaluating the outcome is that it works in situations where one is present.

Of course, it is not always a simple matter to determine values, and the applied decision experts may be helpful. In fact, there are systematic cognitive biases in achieving valid decomposition, just as there are governing automatic choice. Thus, Tversky has shown that when matching procedures are used to determine the relative importance of identified variables, the result is that a systematic underestimation of the degree of discrepancy is inferred from choice situations.[30] For example, most baseball experts consider batting average to be more important than home run hitting. Their implicit weighting of the two variables can be determined by asking them to match two players by assigning a value to one of the two variables so that the two players have equal value in their judgment. This could be done, for example, by deciding on the number of home runs a player with a batting average of .310 would have to hit per year to be of the same value as a player who has a .334 batting average and hits 15 home runs per year. Such matching judgments *systematically underestimate* the importance these judges ascribe to batting average relative to home runs when they are asked to choose the more valuable player among pairs.

Which procedure is better for determining "true" value? For that matter, what *is* such value? This chapter – and indeed this book – is not addressed to those very difficult questions. What *can* be concluded is that the procedure of looking first *within* each variable and then comparing across by some weighting system is superior to that of making global intuitive judgments *across* variables regarding each choice in isolation....

### Mere Numbers

The philosophy presented in this chapter is based on the premise that "mere numbers" are in fact *mere* – neither good nor bad. Just as numbers can be used to achieve either constructive or destructive goals in other contexts, they can be used for good or ill in decision making. *Research* indicates that numbers in a linear model can be well used in making predictions. The implication that they can serve well also in choice and preference contexts is immediate. Using them, however, requires us to overcome a view (*not* supported by the research) that the "mysteries of the human mind" allow us to reach superior conclusions without their aid. The mysteries are there, but not in this context. To do well by ourselves and to treat other persons fairly, we must overcome the hubris that leads us to reject adding numbers to evaluate them, and to experience no more shame when we do so than when we use numbers in determining how to construct a bridge that will not collapse.

### References and Notes

1   In Bigelow, J. (ed.) (1887). *The Complete Works of Benjamin Franklin.* New York: Putnam, p. 522.
2   Referenced in Webb, E. J.; Campbell, D. T.; Schwartz, R. D.; and Sechrest, L. (1966). *Unobtrusive Measures: Non-reactive Research in the Social Sciences.* Chicago: Rand McNally.
3   The criteria for evaluating the success of prediction was the *product moment correlation coefficient* between prediction and outcome; the weights that optimize this coefficient were determined by *multiple regression.*
4   Meehl, P. E. (1954). *Clinical versus Statistical Predictions: A Theoretical Analysis and Revision of the Literature.* Minneapolis: University of Minnesota Press.
5   Sawyer, J. (1966). Measurement *and* prediction, clinical *and* statistical. *Psychological Bulletin, 66,* 178–200.

6   Bloom, R. F., and Brundage, E. G. Predictions of success in elementary schools for enlisted personnel. In Stuit, D. B. (ed.). *Personnel Research and Test Development In the Bureau of Naval Personnel*. Princeton, N.J.: Princeton University Press.

7   Kelly, E. L. (1954). Evaluation of the interview as a selection technique. In *Proceedings of the 1953 Invitational Conference on Testing Problems*. Princeton, N.J.: Educational Testing Service.

8   Einhorn, H. J. (1972). Expert measurement and mechanical combination. *Organizational Behavior and Human Performance, 13*, 171–192.

9   See Beaver, W. H. (1966). Financial ratios as predictors of failure. In *Empirical Research in Accounting: Selected Studies*. Chicago: University of Chicago, Graduate School of Business Institute of Professional Accounting. Duncan, E. R. (1972). A discriminant analysis of predictors of business failure. *Journal of Accounting Research, 10*, 167–179. Libby, R. (1976). Man versus model of man: Some conflicting evidence. *Organizational Behavior and Human Performance, 16*, 1–12.

10  I admit that I might not have discovered this error as the result of close scrutiny had the outcome been different. Others discovered it as well, and the author subsequently retracted – and has since become an outspoken critic of polygraph testing.

11  Meehl, P. E. (1986). Causes and effects of my disturbing little book. *Journal of Personality Assessment, 50*, 370–375.

12  I am indebted to Professor Lewis R. Goldberg of the University of Oregon for sharing this data set.

13  I am indebted to the late Professor Nancy Hershberg of the University of Illinois for sharing this data set.

14  I hope that the reader not familiar with the concepts of "normal distribution," "rectangular distribution," and "amount of variance accounted for" will nevertheless appreciate the general conclusion.

15  All variables are transformed to have an average of zero and a standard deviation of one; this transformation is accomplished by subtracting the average from each untransformed score and dividing by the standard deviation.

16  The results when published engendered two responses. First, many people didn't believe them – until they tested out random and unit models on their own data sets. Then, other people showed that the results were trivial, because random and unit linear models will yield predictions highly correlated with those of linear models with optimal weights, and it had already been shown that optimal linear models outperform global judgments. I concur with those proclaiming the results trivial, but not realizing their triviality at the time, I luckily produced a "citation classic" – and without being illustrated with real data sets, the trivial result might never have been so widely known.

17  My own work is summarized in Dawes, R. M. (1979). The robust beauty of improper linear models. *American Psychologist, 34*, 571–582.

18  Hammond, K. R., and Adelman, L. (1976). Science, values, and human judgment. *Science, 194*, 389–396.

19  Held, V. (summer 1966). PPBS comes to Washington. *The Public Interest*, no. 4, 102–115; quotation from pp. 112–113. As cited in Etzioni, Amitai (December 1967). Mixed scanning: A "third" approach to decision making. *Public Administration Review*, 390.

20  See Arkes, H. R.; Dawes, R. M.; and Christensen, C. (1986). Factors influencing the use of a decision rule in a probabilistic task. *Organizational Behavior and Human Decision Processes, 37*, 93–110. Also, Goldberg, L. R. (1968). Simple models or simple processes? Some research on clinical judgment. *American Psychologist, 23*, 483–496.

21  Glass, L. B. (1967). The generality of oral consummatory behavior of alcoholics under stress. Unpublished doctoral dissertation, University of Michigan.

22  Statistically, the "amount of variance" accounted for by a monotone interaction is one-ninth that accounted for in a comparable crossed interaction situation.

23  Wainer, H. (1976). Estimating coefficients in linear models: It don't make no nevermind. Psychological Bulletin, 83, 312–317.

24  Goldberg, L. R. (1972). Student personality, characteristics and optimal college learning conditions: An extensive search for trait-by-treatment interaction effects. Instructional Science, 1, 153–210.

25  Shepard, R. N. (1964). Attention and the metric structure of the stimulus. Journal of Mathematical Psychology, 1, 54–87.

26  Einhorn, H. J., and Hogarth, R. M. (1978). Confidence in judgment: Persistence of the illusion of validity. Psychological Review, 85, 395–416.

27  Rorer, L. G. A circuitous route to bootstrapping selection procedures. ORI Research Bulletin, 12, no. 9.

28  A colleague has suggested that our intuitive judgments may be valid because we have feedback from our satisfaction or regret after making various choices. This explanation presents a number of problems: (1) We don't know how satisfied we would feel if we had chosen something else. (2) Aside from the "choices" we make habitually in everyday life, few of our "choices"/judgments are repeated without change – and we are least apt to modify habitual choices. (3) We have difficulty assessing the role of factors over which our choice had no effect in determining the outcome. (4) In fact, all the objections to "learning from experience" apply to intuitive learning as well as explicit learning. (5) What I suspect we regret in such cases is not the choice itself given the information we had available, but the "failure to put forth the effort" to gather more information or to consider the problem more carefully.

29  Garner, W. R. (1970). The stimulus in information processing. American Psychologist, 25, 350–358.

30  Tversky, A. N. (1986). Paper presented at the 1986 convention of the American Psychological Association, Washington, D.C.

# 24 Seven Components of Judgmental Forecasting Skill: Implications for Research and the Improvement of Forecasts

*Thomas R. Stewart and Cynthia M. Lusk*

In any field requiring judgmental forecasts, the performance of professional forecasters depends jointly on (1) the environment about which forecasts are made, (2) the information system that brings data about the environment to the forecaster, and (3) the cognitive system of the forecaster. For example, in weather forecasting the environment includes the atmosphere and the land, ocean, and solar features that affect weather. The information system includes the instruments, observations, and algorithms that produce information about past and current weather and the communication and display systems that bring that information to the forecaster. The cognitive system consists of the perceptual and judgmental processes that the forecaster uses to acquire information, aggregate it, and produce the forecast.

This chapter describes how certain properties of these three systems combine to determine forecasting performance. A commonly used measure of skill (the "skill score" based on the mean-square-error) is analyzed into seven components. Since each component describes a different aspect of forecast performance, the decomposition suggests a framework for research on judgmental forecasting.

The next section describes the basic measure of forecasting skill adopted in this chapter. Then a decomposition of that measure recently developed by Allan Murphy is described. In the following sections, a further decomposition into seven components based on the "lens model equation" is developed. Finally, selected research on each of the seven components and implications for improving forecasting skill is reviewed.

Although this chapter focuses on judgmental forecasting, much of the material discussed is equally applicable to other types of professional judgment (e.g., diagnostic judgments made by physicians). Furthermore, the decomposition we propose can be applied to either probabilistic or deterministic

This chapter originally appeared in *Journal of Forecasting*, 1994, 13, 579–599. Copyright © 1994 by John Wiley & Sons, Inc. Reproduced by permission of John Wiley & Sons Limited.

judgments, and we have relied on the literature describing both types of judgment where appropriate.

## Measurement of Forecasting Performance

The most commonly used measures of forecasting performance can be roughly classified into three main groups: (1) those based on mean-square-error, (2) those based on correlation, and (3) those based on signal detection theory (SDT). The decomposition used in this chapter combines measures from the first two groups. Although SDT is a powerful and elegant technique (Harvey et al., 1992), we did not find it suitable for our analysis because no decomposition comparable in analytic power to the lens model equation (described below) is available in the SDT framework. Furthermore, the measures provided by SDT are independent of biases in the means or standard deviations of forecasts. Since those biases have been the focus of a substantial body of research and they can be important to the users of forecasts, it is important to include them in any formulation that purports to describe forecasting performance. It should also be noted that there is a strong conceptual similarity between the SDT model and the other two types of measures (Yates and Curley, 1985, p. 69).

The mean-square-error (MSE) is defined as:

$$MSE_Y = \left(\frac{1}{n}\right) \Sigma (Y_i - O_i)^2$$

where $n$ is the number of forecasts, $Y_i$ is the $i$th forecast, and $O_i$ is the observed value corresponding to that forecast.

The skill of a forecast is measured by comparing its MSE with that of a reference forecast. One possible reference is a constant forecast of the mean of the variable being forecast. The MSE for such a reference forecast would be:

$$MSE_B = \left(\frac{1}{n}\right) \Sigma (\bar{O} - O_i)^2$$

where $\bar{O}$ is the mean of the observed events in the sample. A skill score is then defined by:

$$SS = 1 - \left(\frac{MSE_Y}{MSE_B}\right).$$

For both probabilistic and deterministic forecasts, this skill score is 1.0 for perfect forecasts, 0.0 if the forecast is only as accurate as the reference forecast, and negative if the forecast is less accurate than the reference forecast. Although not the only possible choice of a reference forecast (Murphy, 1988), the sample mean permits a decomposition of skill that is simple, elegant, and useful for understanding the components of skill.

## Decomposition of Skill

This section describes in three steps the logic for decomposing the skill score into seven components.

### Step 1: Murphy's Decomposition

A variety of decompositions of MSE and skill scores have been developed (Cronbach, 1955; Sanders, 1963; Murphy, 1972a,b, 1973, 1988; Theil, 1966; Yates, 1982; Lee and Yates, 1992). We have used a decomposition developed by Murphy (1988) because it most clearly shows the relation between the correlation coefficient and the skill score. Murphy showed that the skill score can be decomposed as follows:

$$SS = (r_{YO})^2 - \left[r_{YO} - \left(\frac{s_Y}{s_O}\right)\right]^2 - \left[\frac{(\bar{Y} - \bar{O})}{s_O}\right]^2$$

where $r_{YO}$ is the correlation between the forecast and the observed event; $s_Y$ and $s_O$ are the standard deviations of the forecast and the observed event, respectively; and $\bar{Y}$ and $\bar{O}$ are the means of the forecast and the observed event.

The first term in Murphy's decomposition is the squared correlation coefficient. For probability forecasts, the correlation is closely related to the "resolution" of forecasts (Sanders, 1963; Murphy, 1973). Resolution reflects "the ability to discriminate occasions when event A will and will not take place" (Yates, 1982, p. 136). The correlation is equal to the skill score only when the second and third terms, which measure forecast bias, are zero. Murphy (1988) stated that the correlation can be considered a measure of "potential" skill in the forecast; that is, the skill that the forecaster could obtain by eliminating bias from the forecasts.

Murphy called the second term "conditional bias." It is zero when the slope of the regression line for predicting observed events from forecasts is 1.0. This term could also be called "regression bias" because it indicates whether the standard deviations of the forecasts are appropriately reduced to account for a less than perfect correlation. When the correlation is low, the variability of the forecasts, as measured by their standard deviation, must be reduced in order to maintain a slope of 1.0. If regression analysis were used to make forecasts, this reduction would occur automatically (Stewart and Reagan-Cirincione, 1991) and conditional bias would be zero.

Murphy called the third term "unconditional bias." It reflects the match between the mean of the forecasts and the mean of the observations. As the difference between these means increases, the intercept of the regression line departs from zero. For probability forecasts, this term of Murphy's decomposition could be called "base rate bias" because it measures how well the mean forecast matches the base rate of event occurrence in the sample.

### Step 2: Decomposition of the Correlation – The Lens Model Equation

The lens model equation (LME) for decomposing the correlation coefficient was developed by Hursch et al. (1964) and has been revised and extended by Tucker (1964), Castellan (1973), Stewart (1976), and Cooksey and Freebody (1985). The LME shows that the correlation is determined by properties of the environmental system, the cognitive system, and the relations between them. Stewart (1990) and Lee and Yates (1992) have shown that combining the lens model decomposition with a skill score or MSE decomposition can provide a useful tool for analyzing forecasting skill. In this chapter, we expand upon this idea and extend the formulation described by Stewart (1990).

The lens model equation is based on Brunswik's (1956) lens model (Figure 24.1). On the left is the observed event, that is, what actually occurred after the forecast was made. On the right is the forecast itself. Intervening between the forecast and the event are the items of information, or "cues," used to make the forecast.

In this schematic representation of the lens model, the lines connecting the cues and the observed event represent relations between the cues and the observed event in the environmental system. Lines connecting the cues and the forecast represent relations between the cues and the forecast in the cognitive system, that is, how the forecaster uses cues. Lines connecting cues indicate that there are relations among the cues themselves; that is, they are not independent (only a few representative lines have been drawn).

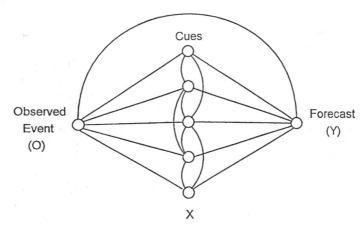

Figure 24.1. Brunswik's lens model.

Since the forecast event is not fully determined by the cues, it cannot be predicted with certainty. Similarly, because some inconsistency is pervasive in human judgment, forecasts also are not perfectly related to the cues. Therefore, the relations on both sides of the lens model are probabilistic; that is, there is an element of uncertainty in the relation between the cues and both the observed event and the forecast. This is an example of the parallelism between properties of the environmental and cognitive sides of the lens model that is central to Brunswik's theory (Hammond et al., 1975).

These probabilistic relations can be expressed formally by partitioning variables representing the observed event and the forecast into two components – one that is a function of the cues and another that is unrelated to them. This partitioning can be written as:

$$O = M_{O.X}(X_1, X_2, \ldots, X_n) + E_{O.X}$$
$$Y = M_{Y.X}(X_1, X_2, \ldots, X_n) + E_{Y.X}$$

where the $X_i$ are the cues; $M_{O.X}$ and $M_{Y.X}$ represent models that describe the relations between the cues and the event and the cues and the forecast, respectively; and the $E$'s, which represent the residuals or "errors" of the models, are not related to the $M$'s.

This partitioning of the forecast and the observed event can be used to derive a partitioning of the correlation between them (Stewart, 1976). Based on that partitioning, Tucker (1964) developed the following form of the lens model equation:

$$r_{YO} = R_{O.X}G R_{Y.X} + C\sqrt{1 - R_{O.X}^2}\sqrt{1 - R_{Y.X}^2}$$

where

> $R_{O.X}$ is the correlation between $O$ and $M_{O.X}$,
> $G$ is the correlation between $M_{O.X}$ and $M_{Y.X}$,
> $R_{Y.X}$ is the correlation between $Y$ and $M_{Y.X}$, and
> $C$ is the correlation between $E_{Y.X}$ and $E_{O.X}$.

If $M_{Y.X}$ captures all the systematic relations between the cues and the forecast, then $E_{Y.X}$ will be unrelated to the outcome event and $C$ will be small.[1] The following approximation then holds:

$$r_{YO} \cong R_{O.X}G R_{Y.X}$$

This formulation expresses the correlation as the product of three components:

- $R_{O.X}$: *The strength of the relation between the observed event and the cues.* If $M_{O.X}$ is the optimal model of the observed event (that is, it exhausts all the systematic relations between the cues and the observed event), then this component measures the maximum *predicability* of the observed event for the given set of cues.

- G: *The match between the environmental model and the forecast model.* This is correlation between (1) the model of the systematic relations between the observed event and the cues, and (2) the model of the forecaster's cue utilization.[2] In other words, it is a measure of how well the model of the forecast matches the environmental model.
- $R_{Y.X}$: *The strength of the relation between the forecast and the cues.* If $M_{Y.X}$ exhausts all the systematic relations between the cues and the forecast, then this component could be considered a measure of the *reliability* of the forecast.[3]

### Step 3: Further Decomposition Based on Expanded Lens Model

For a given set of cues, environmental predictability could be limited by (1) errors in the cues or (2) imperfect relations between the cues and the observed event. Similarly, forecaster unreliability could be due to (1) unreliability in acquiring cue information or (2) unreliability in organizing that information into a forecast. These concepts form the basis for a further decomposition of environmental predictability and forecast reliability.

Figure 24.2 presents a version of the lens model that has been expanded by inserting two additional sets of variables. One set, labeled "true descriptors," is interposed between the cues and the observed event. These variables represent the "true" environmental conditions that the observed cues are intended to capture. For example, the windspeed at a ground station might be 24 m/s, but, due to instrument error or time delays, the reading transmitted to the weather forecaster as a cue might be 22 m/s. In the case of economic forecasting, an example of a true descriptor would be actual unemployment, while the cue available to the forecaster is an estimate based on a survey.

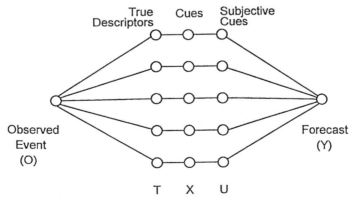

Figure 24.2.  An expanded lens model.

The expanded lens model acknowledges that the cues available to the forecaster often provide an imperfect representation of the true conditions in the environment.

A second set of variables, labeled "subjective cues," is interposed between the cues and the forecast. These variables represent the subjective data that the forecaster integrates into a forecast. For example, colored images on a radar display might indicate that windspeed in a storm is 24 m/s, but the weather forecaster might interpret it as 28 m/s. The forecaster would then base the forecast on the subjective value of 28 m/s, rather than on the objective data of 24 m/s. An example of a subjective cue in economic forecasting would be the forecaster's inspection of a time series to detect patterns or cycles. Different forecasters could arrive at differing subjective interpretations of the graph because they use different conceptual models to interpret the data.

### Decomposition of Environmental Predictability

The expanded lens model indicates that there are two factors that limit predictability of the environment ($R_{O.X}$): (1) imperfect relations between the cues and the true descriptors and (2) imperfect relations between the true descriptors and the observed event. These two components can be formally separated by defining a function, $M_{O.T}$, to represent the systematic functional relations between the event and the true descriptors ($T_i$):

$$O = M_{O.T}(T_1, T_2, \ldots, T_n) + E_{O.T}$$

It is assumed that $M_{O.T}$ is not correlated with $E_{O.T}$.

$R_{O.T}$ is defined as the correlation between $O$ and $M_{O.T}$. It is a measure of the predictability of the environment, given true descriptors. Since true descriptors are, by definition, not readily available to the forecaster, it will usually be difficult to measure them. Because of the difficulty of measuring the true descriptors, and because the optimal environmental model relating those descriptors to the observed event is generally unknown, it will generally be impossible to obtain a good estimate of $R_{O.T}$.[4] Therefore, the decomposition of environmental predictability based on the expanded lens model is more useful conceptually than analytically.

The ratio of $R_{O.X}$ to $R_{O.T}$ theoretically lies between 0.0 and 1.0 and represents the effect of measurement error, or lack of fidelity in the information system, on forecast skill. Let $V_{T.X}$ denote that ratio. Then,

$$R_{O.X} = R_{O.T}\left(\frac{R_{O.X}}{R_{O.T}}\right) = R_{O.T}V_{T.X}$$

thus decomposing the previous measure of environmental predictability into the product of "environmental predictability" given true predictors ($R_{O.T}$) and "fidelity of the information system" ($V_{T.X}$).

$V_{T.X}^2$ is the proportion of valid variance (with respect to $O$) in the true descriptors that is maintained in the observed cues, $X_i$. Expressions for $V_{T.X}$ depend on the form of $M_{O.T}$ and on the relation between the $T_i$ and the $X_i$. For example, if $M_{O.T}$ is linear and the $X_i$ are obtained by adding random error ($E_i$) to the $T_i$, i.e., $X_i = T_i + E_i$, then it can be shown that[5]

$$V_{T.X}^2 = \frac{s_{\hat{O}_T}^2}{s_{\hat{O}_T}^2 + s_{E_x}^2} \qquad \text{where} \qquad \hat{O}_T = \sum_{i=1}^{n} b_i T_i + k \qquad \text{and} \qquad s_{E_x}^2 = \sum_{i=1}^{n} b_i^2 s_{Ei}^2$$

($b_i$ are least squares regression weights)

Unsurprisingly, the fidelity of the information system decreases as the total error variance in the cues increases relative to the variance of the true-descriptor regression model.

### Decomposition of Forecast Reliability

The expanded lens model indicates that forecaster reliability is reduced by two factors – imperfect relations between objective cues and subjective cues (unreliability of subjective interpretation of cues[6]), and imperfect relations between the subjective cues and the forecast (unreliability of information processing). These two components can be formally separated by defining a function, $M_{Y.U}$, that captures the systematic relations between the subjective cues ($U_i$) and the forecast:

$$Y = M_{Y.U}(U_1, U_2, \ldots, U_n) + E_{Y.U}$$

$M_{Y.U}$ is assumed to be uncorrelated with $E_{Y.U}$.

$R_{Y.U}$ is defined as the correlation between $Y$ and $M_{Y.U}$. Assuming that $M_{Y.U}$ captures all the systematic variance in the forecast, $R_{Y.U}$ is a measure of the forecaster's information-processing reliability.

If the true values of the subjective cues ($U_i$) were known, then they would, in general, be better predictors of the forecast than the objective cues ($X_i$) because the objective data are imperfectly related to the subjective cues that are integrated into the forecast. As a result, $R_{Y.X}$ will be less than $R_{Y.U}$, and ($R_{Y.X}/R_{Y.U}$) represents the effect of unreliability of information acquisition on forecast skill. Let $V_{U.X}$ denote that ratio. Then,

$$R_{Y.X} = R_{Y.U}\left(\frac{R_{Y.X}}{R_{Y.U}}\right) = R_{Y.U} V_{U.X}$$

thus decomposing forecast reliability into the product of reliability of information processing ($R_{Y.U}$) and the reliability of information acquisition ($V_{U.X}$).

As was shown for $V_{T.X}$, expressions for $V_{U.X}$ can be derived if assumptions are made about the form of the model relating subjective cues to the forecast and about the nature of the relation between the objective cues and the subjective cues. Assuming a linear $M_{Y.U}$ and $U_i$ resulting from adding random error to the $X_i$, it can be shown that the reliability of information acquisition decreases as the error variance in the subjective cues increases, relative to the variance in the subjective-cue regression model.

## Summary

In three stages, the skill score has been decomposed into seven components. First, Murphy's decomposition separates bias from the correlation. Second, the lens model equation (with some assumptions) separates the effects of environmental predictability and forecast reliability from the match between cue-event relations and cue-forecast relations. Third, an extension of the lens model equation decomposes both environmental predictability and forecast reliability into two components each. The steps in the decomposition are illustrated in Figure 24.3.

The first two decompositions are useful for empirical analysis of forecast performance (Stewart, 1990), but the data necessary to estimate all the parameters of the full decomposition will rarely be available. In particular, obtaining the data necessary to measure fidelity of the information system will be impossible in most field studies. Although it is possible (and, we would argue, desirable) to obtain the measures of subjective cue values necessary to estimate reliability of information acquisition, they rarely are available in studies conducted outside the laboratory. For purposes of this chapter, therefore, we emphasize the conceptual and theoretical value of the full decomposition.

## Implications for Improving Performance

Since the full decomposition is presented for the first time here, no individual study addresses all its elements. Representative research on factors that affect components of skill and methods for improving forecast skill is reviewed in this section. Table 24.1 summarizes the second topic – implications of research for improving forecasts.

There is a column in Table 24.1 for each component of skill. The rows include both methods for improving skill that have been evaluated in the literature reviewed here and other methods that have not been studied but are included because research and theory suggest that they are worthy of study. Marked cells indicate a close theoretical or empirical match between skill component and method. The greater number of rows in the table associated with columns 3–7 reflects the emphasis in this chapter on the components of skill that are fully or partially within the forecaster's control.

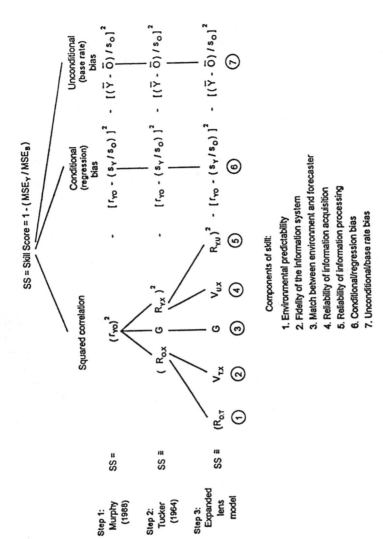

Figure 24.3. Summary of decomposition equations.

Table 24.1. *Components of Skill Addressed by Selected Methods for Improving Forecasts*

| | Method for Improving Forecasts | Component of Skill[a] | | | | | | |
|---|---|---|---|---|---|---|---|---|
| | | 1 | 2 | 3 | 4 | 5 | 6 | 7 |
| A | Identify new descriptors through research | X | | | | | | |
| B | Develop better measures of true descriptors | | X | | | | | |
| C | Train forecaster about environmental system | | | X | | | | |
| D | Experience with forecasting problem | | | X | | | X | X |
| E | Cognitive feedback | | | X | | | | |
| F | Train forecaster to ignore nonpredictive cues | | | X | | | | |
| G | Develop clear definitions of cues | | | | X | | | |
| H | Training to improve cue judgments | | | | X | | | |
| I | Improve information displays | | | | X | | | |
| J | Bootstrapping – replace forecaster with model | | | | | X | | |
| K | Combine several forecasts | | | | | X | | |
| L | Require justification of forecasts | | | | | X | X | |
| M | Decompose forecasting task | | | | | X | | |
| N | Mechanical combination of cues | | | | | X | | |
| O | Statistical training | | | | | | X | X |
| P | Feedback about nature of biases in forecast | | | | | | X | X |
| Q | Search for discrepant information | | | | | | X | |
| R | Statistical correction for bias | | | | | | X | X |

[a] 1 Environmental predictability
2 Fidelity of the information system
3 Match between environment and forecaster
4 Reliability of information acquisition
5 Reliability of information processing
6 Conditional/regression bias
7 Unconditional/base rate bias

Where marked cells in Table 24.1 are referred to in the following text, cell references are included in parentheses.

### Environmental Predictability

Environmental predictability determines an upper bound on forecast performance and therefore indicates how much improvement is possible through attention to other components. In laboratory studies, tasks with known environmental predictability have been studied (e.g., Armelius, 1979; Hagafors and Brehmer, 1983). Brehmer (1976) found that a decrease in environmental predictability for a laboratory task was associated with a decrease in judgmental consistency.

In field studies, environmental predictability often cannot be estimated with any accuracy. Furthermore, for a given set of information, environmental predictability is fixed and not under the control of the forecaster. It may be possible to improve predictability by identifying valid new descriptors that can be used in forecasting (A1). Since our interest here is in the more subjective aspects of forecasting skill, we will not discuss environmental predictability further.

## Fidelity of the Information System

Forecasting skill may be degraded if the information system that brings data to the forecaster does not accurately represent actual conditions, i.e., if the cues do not accurately measure the true descriptors. Fidelity of the information system refers to the quality, not the quantity, of information about the cues that are currently being used.

The available research indicates, surprisingly, that for some tasks, measurement error in cues may not be a major determinant of performance. In a review of forecasting methods for marketing, Armstrong et al. (1987) report that measurement error in the environmental inputs to a market forecasting model had little impact on the accuracy of environmental forecasts. York et al. (1987) investigated the effect of cue unreliability in a multiple cue probability learning (MCPL) task. They compared a group that received "true scores" to groups that received cue values with random error added to the true score values and concluded that measurement error in the predictor does not affect performance. However, their task was structured so that the five values presented for each cue could be averaged for optimal performance.

The generality of these findings and the reasons for them require further investigation. If the cues available to judges are poor predictors, then more accurate measurement of them might not improve judgment. A more likely explanation is that redundancy in the cues, or multiple measurement of the same cue, cancels out the effect of measurement error. In the case of redundant information, error in measurement of a single cue might have little effect on the predictability of the entire set because fidelity of the information system depends on the ability of *all* the cues available to the forecaster to recover the valid variation in the true predictors. Therefore, errors in individual cues might not have much effect on overall system fidelity.

Problems with the fidelity of the information system need not be limited to the traditional concept of measurement error. Another kind of error, called system failure error (O'Connor et al., 1989) could be more devastating. In this case, all valid information is lost due to, for example, instrument failure. If the forecaster were unaware of system failure, he or she could be seriously misled by the information provided. The urgency of correcting system failure would override all other components of skill until the failed system were repaired or replaced.

Measurement error and accuracy of information is a major concern to forecasters in any domain. Designers of information systems for forecasting will naturally seek to maximize the fidelity of the system by obtaining the best possible measures (B2). The problems involved in doing so are domain-specific, and it is likely that they will have been addressed, with varying degrees of success, in situations where important forecasts are made. For example, in the weather domain, Bader et al. (1988) acknowledge that quality control is becoming increasingly important and provide examples of how meteorological data can be cross-checked.

Environmental predictability and fidelity of the information system are components of skill that are determined by the forecast domain, the available information relevant to the forecast, and the information system. They are beyond the control of the forecaster, at least in the short run. We now turn to elements of the decomposition that are directly influenced by the forecaster's behavior.

### Match between Environment and Forecaster

The match between the model of the forecaster and the environmental model is measured by the correlation ($G$), over a set of forecasts, between the forecaster model ($M_{Y.X}$) and the environmental model ($M_{O.X}$). It is an estimate of the potential skill that the forecaster's current strategy could achieve if the environment were perfectly predictable (given the cues) and the forecasts were unbiased and perfectly reliable.

In some applications of the lens model equation, the $G$ parameter has been called "knowledge" (Hammond et al., 1973; Beal et al., 1978). As Beal et al. (1978) point out, however, $G$ does not represent knowledge in the traditional sense of mastery of a subject area or an intellectual field. Rather, $G$ measures the individual's knowledge of the requirements of the prediction task and the ability to apply that knowledge to forecasting. See Castellan (1992) for an important discussion of $G$ and cautions regarding its use.

An obvious way to improve the environment/forecaster match is to have the forecaster learn more about the nature of the environmental system (C3). Thus, a weather forecaster's performance might be improved by learning more about atmospheric science (a basic premise of National Weather Service training programs), or economic forecasts might be improved by learning more economics. Such learning does not guarantee improved performance, however, because forecasters who are extremely knowledgeable about the environmental system might still have low $G$'s if they are unable to apply that knowledge to the forecasting task (Gedzelman, 1979).

Increasing the forecaster's experience with the task (D3) is another obvious way to improve $G$. As Brehmer (1980) has argued, the nature of experience and human information-processing biases are such that it is very difficult to learn a complex task from experience alone. If Brehmer's arguments apply to a forecasting problem, then the improvement in $G$ with experience alone could be very slow.

A study conducted by Stael von Holstein (1971) suggested that if experience were accompanied by extensive feedback and discussion of the results, the forecaster–environment match could improve. He conducted a study of probabilistic forecasts of temperature and precipitation, providing feedback regarding accuracy (using a quadratic scoring rule) and the probability distributions, as well as outcome feedback. He did not find a change in accuracy over time. However, he found that research assistants performed better than meteorologists. He argued this was because the research assistants had opportunities to discuss their feedback, whereas the meteorologists received feedback in written form with no discussion. He further suggests that the meterologists would have benefited from more extensive feedback.

A method that has been found useful in accelerating the rate of learning complex judgment tasks is "cognitive feedback" (E3) (Hammond, 1971). A review by Balzer et al. (1989) distinguishes among three types of cognitive feedback: task information, cognitive information, and functional validity information. Task information includes feedback regarding the task uncertainty, relation between cues and the observed event, and cue intercorrelations. Cognitive information mirrors the task information in terms of how the judge weighs cue information and reliability. Functional validity information includes achievement (i.e., the correlation coefficient), $G$, and $C$. The authors suggest that task information is the most important feedback component and suggest that, if available, it should be used to train judges. Information about the level and variability of the criterion may also be useful task information. They further suggest that cognitive information is of little value. Functional validity information has not been extensively studied.

Wigton et al. (1990) investigated diagnostic judgments of pharyngitis for physicians and medical students. During a six-month intervention they provided cognitive feedback which included learner's weights and the optimal weights, as well as "probability feedback" (the probability of a positive culture calculated from the optimal cue weights). They found that judgments became better calibrated and more accurate (as measured by the correlation). Matching ($G$) also increased, but consistency did not. They suggested that increased performance was due to better conformity with the models rather than increased consistency. They also found that students improved more than physicians. The physicians were reluctant to adopt the model's weights.

In contrast to most studies, Tape et al. (1992) found that $G$ increased with outcome feedback (the correct judgment for each case), but not with cognitive feedback. They suggest that the value of cognitive feedback depends upon the task and that it may be more useful when the cue-event relationships "are complex and the combining rule is not known" (p. 213).

Gaeth and Shanteau (1984) were successful in helping soil judges reduce the influence of irrelevant facts and increase accuracy (F3). They attribute the most success to "interactive training." Such training included not only verbal suggestions for reducing the effect of irrelevant information but also experience (with feedback) with soils containing irrelevant factors. In the medical domain, Wigton (1988) has also suggested that training should include materials designed to discourage reliance on nonpredictive cues currently in use.

In summary, the available research suggests that when the environmental model relating cues to observed events is known, information about the model should be provided to forecasters as part of their training. In most cases, the environmental model will not be known, and that is precisely why judgmental forecasting is used. In such cases, it may be possible to estimate a model, or at least distinguish between relevant and irrelevant cues, by analyzing historical data or analyzing the forecasts of established experts. Training and practice with the task might be used to reduce reliance on irrelevant cues. When the environmental model is not known and cannot be estimated, feedback to the judges on the attributes of their judgments, along with a discussion of the results, may enhance performance.

### Reliability of Information Acquisition

Reliability of information acquisition is the extent to which the forecaster can reliably interpret the objective cues. The evidence suggests that unreliability of information acquisition is pervasive. In a review of research on reliability of clinical judgments in medicine, Koran (1975) found a wide range of intra- and interobserver reliability in extracting cardiovascular, gastrointestinal, and respiratory cues from physical examination. He further reports a range of reliabilities for interpreting diagnostic procedures (e.g., electrocardiography). Einhorn (1974) studied pathologists viewing biopsy slides of cancer patients and reports a wide range of mean intrajudge reliabilities for cues. He also demonstrated a procedure for identifying three cue judgment biases: (1) under- or overvaluing signs in general ("leniency error"), (2) the tendency to over- or undervalue particular cases (halo effect), and (3) under- or overvaluing particular signs.

Results of an experiment conducted by Brehmer (1970) indicated that unreliability in judging cues made learning more difficult and had an effect similar to that of unpredictability in the environment. This suggests that unreliability in information acquisition may affect not only the quality of the forecasts, but also forecasters' ability to learn from experience.

Lusk and Hammond (1991) distinguish between "primary" cues that are directly observable from the presented information and "secondary" cues that must be extracted from a combination of the primary cue values. In studies comparing presentation of primary and secondary cues, they found more disagreement among weather forecasters' probability judgments in the primary cue condition than in the secondary cue condition, which they suggest was due to differential integration of the primary cue information into secondary cue values. They also found that the degree of disagreement on secondary cue values varied considerably by cue. They suggest that this may have been related to differences in proximity of secondary cues to the primary cues. That is, the differences may be due to the varying degrees of subjectivity involved in making the secondary cue judgments.

A special case of secondary cues are cues that describe future, rather than current, conditions and therefore must themselves be forecasted. The evidence reviewed by Armstrong et al. (1987) indicates that unreliability introduced by integrating information to forecast a cue may not be a serious problem. They reviewed 18 studies comparing conditional econometric forecasts (actual data on the causal variables) and unconditional forecasts (causal variables must be forecasted) and found that 10 studies showed that conditional forecasts were less accurate than unconditional forecasts, 5 showed no difference, and only 3 studies found greater accuracy for conditional forecasts.

Although the research on reliability of information acquisition has not been extensive, the available studies suggest that it is more likely to be a problem in tasks, such as weather forecasting or medical diagnosis, that require interpretation of images or recognition of complex patterns in data that are distributed over time and/or space. For example, Kerr (1991) reported that, in a recent workshop on frontal analysis, different meteorologists placed the same cold front in a variety of geographic positions. The studies reviewed in this and the previous section suggest that in these kinds of tasks, reliability may be more important than fidelity of the information system in limiting forecasting skill, as well as less costly to correct.

Empirical estimates of unreliability in information acquisition could be obtained by having forecasters make repeated cue judgments from the same data or by having different forecasters judge cues based on the same data. Lusk and Hammond (1991) suggested that identification of specific cues demonstrating high levels of disagreement among forecasters makes it possible to focus on variables with the greatest potential for improving judgment.

Despite its importance to forecasting, we have not found any studies that specifically evaluate methods for improving reliability of information acquisition. There are several general suggestions that deserve study and are included in Table 24.1. Lusk et al. (1990) recommend that clear operational definitions be developed for each cue (G4). Reliability might also be improved through forecaster training focused on troublesome cues (H4) or by designing improved displays, taking into account factors that affect reliability (I4).

### Reliability of Information Processing

Unreliability in processing subjective information is pervasive in human judgment, and some studies have found that it increases as the predictability of the environment decreases (Brehmer and Brehmer, 1988; Camerer, 1981). Unreliability may also increase as the amount of information available for forecasting increases (Stewart et al., 1992; Lee and Yates, 1992). Although additional information could serve to improve the forecaster's understanding of the environmental conditions at the time of the forecast, it also increases the complexity of the forecasting task and may impose a cognitive burden on the forecaster that exceeds human information-processing capacity. It is not surprising, therefore, that a number of studies have found that people use only a subset of available information (Brehmer and Brehmer, 1988) and that the accuracy of forecasts does not increase with increasing information (Armstrong, 1985; Brockhoff, 1984; Lusk and Hammond, 1991).

Indirect evidence that information-processing reliability affects the accuracy of judgments comes from studies showing that simple techniques for increasing reliability result in improved accuracy. One such technique, "bootstrapping," substitutes the regression model of the forecasts for the original forecasts (J5). Often forecasts based on the perfectly reliable regression model perform better than the original forecasts produced by the less than perfectly reliable human (Armstrong, 1985; Camerer, 1981). Another simple technique for increasing reliability is averaging the forecasts that were made independently by several individuals (K5) (Kelley, 1925; Stroop, 1932). Greater reliability is one of the reasons that group average forecasts generally outperform members of the group (Armstrong, 1985; Stael von Holstein, 1971).

A study by Hagafors and Brehmer (1983) suggests that reliability might increase if the forecaster were asked to verbally justify forecasts (L5). They found that having to justify one's opinion led to higher consistency when no outcome feedback is provided. It is interesting that the effect of justification was higher in low predictability than in high predictability conditions, suggesting an interaction between the benefits of justification and environmental predictability. They also found that outcome feedback reduced consistency. They suggest that subjects use feedback to test hypotheses, and the hypotheses keep changing, resulting in decreased reliability. Without feedback, hypothesis testing cannot occur and reliability increases. York et al. (1987), however, found that outcome feedback does not always reduce reliability. It may be that outcome feedback can provide increased motivation that increases reliability.[7]

Some decision aids have been designed to reduce the cognitive burden on the forecaster and increase reliability. Generally, they involve decomposition of the task into manageable units and the use of computers or an algorithm to assist in processing information (M5, N5) (Dawes, 1979; Einhorn, 1972; Dawes and Corrigan, 1974; Hammond et al., 1977; Brehmer and Joyce, 1988). For example, MacGregor et al. (1988) investigated varying degrees of problem decomposition ranging from no structure to a full algorithm condition where subjects were asked to provide estimates of intermediate quantities and were provided with combination rules. They found, in general, that increased accuracy and reliability across subjects was associated with greater decomposition of the task.

### Bias – Conditional (Regression Bias) and Unconditional (Base Rate Bias)

Together, the two bias terms in the decomposition measure forecast "calibration." Almost all the research on calibration has addressed probabilistic judgments. We do not know whether these results will generalize to deterministic forecasts.

One of the common findings in research on calibration is overconfidence; that is, people make probability judgments that are more extreme than they should be, given the evidence and their knowledge. Overconfidence (or underconfidence) would increase conditional bias. Lichtenstein et al. (1982) report that overconfidence is pervasive and is most extreme with tasks of greater difficulty. They also report that calibration varies with the type of forecast. For example, the calibration of weather forecasters has improved over the years and is continuing to improve, but physicians are not well calibrated. They suggest that some weather forecasters may be well calibrated because, unlike physicians, meteorologists have a lot of practice with probability judgments, the task is always the same, and they receive outcome feedback. This suggests that, for some tasks, experience with the forecasting problem may improve calibration (D6, D7).

Fischhoff (1982) identifies three assumed sources of biases that have been addressed by researchers: faulty tasks, faulty judges, and the mismatch between judges and tasks. He reviewed the literature on overconfidence to determine the extent to which manipulations of each source were successful. He concluded that studies attempting to address faulty tasks (e.g., clarifying instructions and using better response modes) have been generally unsuccessful. Research on faulty judges has been more successful. Fryback (1985) argues that to improve subjective probability assessments, clinicians should keep records of their judgments and receive statistical training (O6, O7), but he provides no data on the success of this method. Lichtenstein and Fischhoff (1980) provided subjects with feedback regarding their judgments, including calibration curves and measures of overconfidence, calibration, knowledge, and resolution (P6, P7); and they found improvement in calibration without affecting resolution. Murphy and Daan (1984) provided detailed feedback including reliability diagrams and quantitative scores describing calibration, resolution, and skill (P6, P7). The nature and implications of this feedback were discussed, emphasizing the need to separate the forecast formulation process from the process of using the forecast as a means of reducing the preference for false alarms over misses. They found improvement in skill due primarily to increases in calibration, with little improvement in resolution. They assert that the lack of improvement in resolution is not surprising since it is limited by the state of the art of weather forecasting.

Regarding the mismatch between judges and the task, encouraging judges to search for discrepant information has resulted in improved calibration (Q6; Q7 is blank because evidence suggests that the search for discrepant information acts mainly on overconfidence). Koriat et al. (1980) had subjects list reasons supporting and/or contradicting responses. They found that listing contradictory reasons improved confidence judgments. They suggest that such judgments are made in two stages, both of which involved bias: (1) knowledge search, which favors positive evidence, and (2) evidence review, during which negative evidence is disregarded and confidence assigned. Arkes et al. (1987) found that subjects who anticipated having to justify their answers to a group demonstrated a drop in confidence and improvement in calibration (L6). Fischhoff and MacGregor (1982) discovered that asking subjects to list reasons that their answers might be correct and/or incorrect had a small, but consistent effect on reducing overconfidence (L6). They suggested that other desirable features of the thought listing procedure might be: (1) providing a record of reasons for one's forecasts in order to avoid hindsight bias once the outcome is known (Fischhoff, 1975), (2) allowing for external review of one's reasoning, which might lead to correction of misconceptions (Hogarth and Makridakis, 1981), and (3) helping raise one's alertness to new evidence that should prompt revisions of a forecast.

Another approach to improving calibration is to apply a correction formula to the forecasts when the judge's biases are known (R6, R7). Ahlburg (1984) used Theil's (1966) decomposition to identify sources of error in price expectations and forecasts of new housing starts. He identified bias and regression components of forecast error and applied a correction to the forecasts based on a model of the environment and improved accuracy. Theil (1966) and Stewart and Reagan-Cirincione (1991) have provided formulas for debiasing forecasts. Application of such formulas assumes that the forecaster's biases are stable over time and that the knowledge that forecasts are being adjusted does not, itself, cause the forecaster to change.

The previous research indicates that biases are pervasive and sometimes difficult to overcome. Some evidence suggests that experience with probabilistic judgments reduces bias. Extensive individual feedback on the nature of the biases can decrease biases. Procedures requiring judges' justification of responses and/or consideration of contradictory reasoning can also decrease bias. In addition, it may be possible in some cases to adjust the forecasts to remove bias.

### Discussion

The decomposition we have proposed provides a framework for research on judgmental forecasting and for diagnosing forecasting problems and prescribing methods for improving forecasts. Table 24.1 summarizes, with appropriate caveats regarding the lack of adequate research on judgmental forecasting, a number of suggestions for improving forecasts, beginning with the identification of new cues through research. Since poor performance may be due to a ceiling on environmental predictability, rather than to subjective aspects of the forecasting process, attempts to increase the ceiling through research and development are fundamental to the forecasting process. Likewise, sources of error in the information system will limit even the best forecaster's performance. Since the first five components of skill combine multiplicatively, efforts to increase the ceiling on environmental predictability and improve the fidelity of the information system will increase the potential improvement to be gained by attention to the subjective components of the forecast. Unfortunately, in many domains, efforts to improve forecasts are entirely devoted to research and development and to improving the information system because it is assumed that increasing the amount and quality of information is all that is necessary to improve forecasts.

There is probably a point in any forecasting domain where addressing the subjective components becomes more cost effective than further technical research and development. Reliability of information acquisition appears to be an important source of problems, and potential improvement, for those forecasting tasks that rely on judgment processes to acquire information. Surprisingly little research is available on this component. The few available studies provide examples of how to identify cues that are adversely affected by unreliability.

Although the other judgmental components of forecasts have been more thoroughly investigated and several methods for improvement have been suggested, more research is needed to identify which are most likely to cause difficulties in particular forecasting contexts and which can be most effectively improved. Most previous studies of judgmental skill have investigated overall skill or perhaps only one or two of its components. It is quite possible, however, that methods designed to address one component have unintended effects on others. For example, bootstrapping (row J) directly affects reliability of information processing, but it will also decrease the standard deviation of forecasts, possibly influencing conditional bias. Identification of new descriptors (row A) to increase environmental predictability may also decrease reliability of information processing by forcing the forecaster to cope with increasing amounts of information. Because of the possibility of indirect and unanticipated effects of methods on skill components, a thorough understanding of forecasting skill requires studies designed to collect data about all relevant components.

### Notes

1   Although C is usually found to be low in practice, high values are possible. High values of C indicate either that the relation between the cues and the forecast have not

been adequately modeled or that one or more cues that are available to the forecaster are not included in the model. In either case, revision of the model is indicated. For discussion of the implications of various values of $C$, see Stewart (1988).

2   For brevity, we use "correlations between models" to refer to "correlations between the outputs of models." There is no loss of clarity.

3   Reliability refers to the ability of a measurement procedure to produce the same results if the same objects are measured on repeated occasions. Unreliability is due to random or error variance which may reflect a number of sources of measurement error (Kerlinger, 1973). When the term "reliability" is used in connection with human judgment, it refers to the extent to which identical information leads to identical judgments, that is, the proportion of systematic or repeatable variance in the judgments. The term "consistency" is used to refer to the fit of a specific model to a set of judgments. If the model captures all of the systematic variance in the judgments, then consistency with respect to that model is identical to reliability.

4   In the case of weather forecasting, there have been attempts to estimate true environmental unpredictability (Barnett and Preisendorfer, 1978; Chu and Katz, 1987).

5   The derivation of this formulation is available from the authors.

6   Systematic errors in the transformation from objective to subjective cues are also possible. For example, a forecaster could consistently interpret a cue as too high or too low. This type of systematic error could result in an increase in unconditional bias or, if it affected the cue weight, could reduce the match between the forecaster and the environment. We thank Michael Doherty for pointing out this possibility.

7   Michael Doherty, personal communication, 1993.

## References

Ahlburg, D. A. 'Forecast evaluation and improvement using Thiel's decomposition,' *Journal of Forecasting*, 3 (1984), 345–51.

Arkes, H. R., Christensen, C., Lai, C. and Blumer, C., 'Two methods of reducing overconfidence,' *Organizational Behavior and Human Decision Processes, 39* (1987), 133–44.

Armelius, K. 'Task predictability and performance as determinants of confidence in multiple-cue judgments,' *Scandinavian Journal of Psychology, 20* (1979), 19–25.

Armstrong, J. S. *Long Range Forecasting*, 2nd edition, New York: Wiley, 1985.

Armstrong, J. S., Brodie, R. J. and McIntyre, S. H. 'Forecasting methods for marketing: Review of empirical research,' *International Journal of Forecasting, 3* (1987), 355–76.

Bader, M. J., Browning, K. A., Forbes, G. S., Oliver, V. J. and Schlatter, T. W., 'Towards improved subjective interpretation of satellite and radar imagery in weather forecasting: Results of a workshop,' *Bulletin of the American Meteorological Society, 69* (1988), 764–9.

Balzer, W. K., Doherty, M. E. and O'Connor, R., Jr., 'Effects of cognitive feedback on performance,' *Psychological Bulletin, 106* (1989), 410–33.

Barnett, T. P. and Preisendorfer, R. W. 'Multifield analogy prediction of short-term climate fluctuations using a climate state vector,' *Journal of Atmospheric Science, 35* (1978), 1771–87.

Beal, D., Gillis, J. S. and Stewart, T. R., 'The lens model: Computational procedures and applications,' *Perceptual and Motor Skills*, Monograph Supplement 1, *46* (1978), 3–28.

Brehmer, A. and Brehmer, B., 'What have we learned about human judgment from thirty years of policy capturing?' in Brehmer, B. and Joyce, C. R. B. (eds), *Human Judgment: The Social Judgment Theory View*, Amsterdam: North-Holland, 1988.

Brehmer, B., 'Inference behavior in a situation where the cues are not reliably perceived,' *Organizational Behavior and Human Decision Processes, 5* (1970), 330–47.

Brehmer, B., 'Note on the relation between clinical judgment and the formal characteristics of clinical tasks,' *Psychological Bulletin, 83* (1976), 778–82.

Brehmer, B., 'In one word: Not from experience,' *Acta Psychologica, 45* (1980), 223–41.

Brehmer, B. and Joyce, C. R. B. (eds), *Human Judgment: The Social Judgment Theory View*, Amsterdam: North-Holland, 1988.

Brockhoff, K. 'Forecasting quality and information,' *Journal of Forecasting, 3*(1984), 417–28.

Brunswik, E. *Perception and the Representative Design of Psychological Experiments*, 2nd edition, Berkeley: University of California Press, 1956.

Camerer, C., 'General conditions for the success of bootstrapping models,' *Organizational Behavior and Human Decision Processes, 27* (1981), 411–22.

Castellan, N. J., 'Comments on the "lens model" equation and the analysis of multiple cue judgment tasks,' *Psychometrika, 38* (1973), 87–100.

Castellan, N. J., Jr., 'Relations between linear models: Implications for the lens models,' *Organizational Behavior and Human Decision Processes, 51* (1992), 364–81.

Chu, P.-S. and Katz, R. W. 'Measures of predictability with applications to the Southern Oscillation,' *Monthly Weather Review, 115* (1987), 1542–49.

Cooksey, R. W. and Freebody, P., 'Generalized multivariate lens model analysis for complex human inference tasks,' *Organizational Behavior and Human Decision Processes, 35* (1985), 46–72.

Cronbach, L. J., 'Processes affecting scores on "understanding of others" and "assumed similarity,"' *Psychological Bullein, 52* (1955), 177–93.

Dawes, R. M. 'The robust beauty of improper linear models in decision making,' *American Psychologist, 7* (1979), 571–82.

Dawes, R. M. and Corrigan, B., 'Linear models in decision making,' *Psychological Bulletin, 81* (1974), 95–106.

Einhorn, H. J., 'Expert measurement and mechanical combination,' *Organizational Behavior and Human Decision Processes, 7* (1972), 86–106.

Einhorn, H. J., 'Expert judgment: Some necessary conditions and an examples,' *Journal of Applied Psychology, 59* (1974), 562–71.

Fischhoff, B. 'Hindsight ≠ foresight: The effect of outcome knowledge on judgment under uncertainty,' *Journal of Experimental Psychology: Human Perception and Decision Processes, 1* (1975), 288–99.

Fischhoff, B., 'Debiasing,' Kahneman, D., Slovic, P. and Tversky, A. (eds), *Judgment under Uncertainty: Heuristics and Biases*, New York: Cambridge University Press, 1982.

Fischhoff, B. and MacGregor, D. 'Subjective confidence in forecasts,' *Journal of Forecasting, 1* (1982), 155–72.

Fryback, D. B., 'Decision maker, quantify thyself!' *Medical Decision Making, 5* (1985), 51–60.

Gaeth, G. J. and Shanteau, J. 'Reducing the influence of irrelevant information on experienced decision makers,' *Organizational Behavior and Human Decision Processes, 33* (1984), 263–82.

Gedzelman, S. D., 'Reply to "Comment on forecasting skill of beginners" and "Rebuttal to forecasting skill of beginners,"' *Bulletin of the American Meteorological Society, 60* (1979), 1208–9.

Hagafors, R. and Brehmer, B., 'Does having to justify one's judgments change the nature of the judgment process?' *Organizational Behavior and Human Decision Processes, 31* (1983), 223–32.

Hammond, K. R., 'Computer graphics as an aid to learning,' *Science, 172* (1971), 903–8.

Hammond, K. R., Summers, D. A. and Deane, D. H. 'Negative effects of outcome-feedback in multiple-cue probability learning,' *Organizational Behavior and Human Decision Processes, 9* (1973), 30–34.

Hammond, K. R., Stewart, T. R., Brehmer, B. and Steinman, D. O., 'Social judgment theory,' in Kaplan, M. F. and Schwartz, S. (eds), *Human Judgment and Decision Processes,* New York: Academic Press, 1975.

Hammond, K. R., Rohrbaugh, J., Mumpower, J. and Adelman, L., 'Social judgment theory: Applications in policy formation,' in Kaplan, M. F. and Schwartz, S. (eds), *Human Judgment and Decision Processes in Applied Settings,* New York: Acaemic Press, 1977.

Harvey, L. O., Jr., Hammond, K. R., Lusk, C. M. and Mross, E. F., 'The application of signal detection theory to weather forecasting behavior,' *Monthly Weather Review, 120* (1992), 863–83.

Hogarth, R. M. and Makridakis, S., 'Forecasting and planning: An evaluation,' *Management Science, 27* (1981), 115–38.

Hursch, C. J., Hammond, K. R. and Hursch, J. L., 'Some methodological considerations in multiple-cue probability studies,' *Psychological Review, 71* (1964), 42–60.

Kelley, T. L., 'The applicability of the Spearman–Brown formula for the measurement of reliability,' *Journal of Educational Psychology, 16* (1925), 300–3.

Kerlinger, F. N., *Foundations of Behavioral Research,* 2nd edition, New York: Holt, Rinehart and Winston, 1973.

Kerr, R. A., 'A frontal attack on a paradigm of meteorology,' *Science, 254*(1991), 1591–2.

Koran, L. M., 'The reliability of clinical methods, data, and judgments,' *New England Journal of Medicine, 293* (1975), 642–6, 695–701.

Koriat, A., Lichtenstein, S. and Fischhoff, B. 'Reasons for confidence,' *Journal of Experimental Psychology: Human Learning and Memory, 6* (1980), 107–18.

Lee, J.-W. and Yates, J. F. 'How quantity judgment changes as the number of cues increases: An analytical framework and review,' *Psychological Bulletin, 112*(1992), 363–77.

Lichtenstein, S. and Fischhoff, B., 'Training for calibration,' *Organizational Behavior and Human Decision Processes, 26* (1980), 149–71.

Lichtenstein, S., Fischhoff, B. and Phillips, L. D., 'Calibration of probabilities: The state of the art to 1980,' in Kahneman, D., Slovic, P. and Tversky, A. (eds), *Judgment under Uncertainty: Heuristics and Biases,* New York: Cambridge University Press, 1982.

Lusk, C. M. and Hammond, K. R. 'Judgment in a dynamic task: Microburst forecasting,' *Journal of Behavioral Decision Making, 4* (1991), 55–73.

Lusk, C. M., Stewart, T. R., Hammond, K. R. and Potts, R. J., 'Judgment and decision making in dynamic tasks: The case of forecasting the microburst,' *Weather and Forecasting, 5* (1990), 627–39.

MacGregor, D., Lichtenstein, S. and Slovic, P. 'Structuring knowledge retrieval: An analysis of decomposed quantitative judgments,' *Organizational Behavior and Human Decision Processes, 42* (1988), 303–23.

Murphy, A. H., 'Scalar and vector partitions of the probability score: part I. The two-state situation,' *Journal of Applied Meteorology, 11* (1972a), 273–82.

Murphy, A. H., 'Scalar and vector partitions of the probability score: part II. The N-state situation,' *Journal of Applied Meteorology, 11* (1972b), 1183–92.

Murphy, A. H., 'A new vector partition of the probability score,' *Journal of Applied Meteorology, 12* (1973), 595–600.

Murphy, A. H., 'Skill scores based on the mean square error and their relationships to the correlation coefficient,' *Monthly Weather Review, 116* (1988), 2417–24.

Murphy, A. H. and Daan, H., 'Impacts of feedback and experience on the quality of subjective probability forecasts: Comparison of results from the first and second years of the Zerikzee experiment,' *Monthly Weather Review, 112* (1984), 413–23.

O'Connor, R., Doherty, M. E. and Tweney, R. D., 'The effects of system failure error on predictions,' *Organizational Behavior and Human Decision Processes, 44* (1989), 1–11.

Sanders, F., 'On subjective probability forecasting,' *Journal of Applied Meteorology, 2* (1963), 191–201.

Stael von Holstein, C.-A., 'An experiment in probabilistic weather forecasting,' *Journal of Applied Meteorology, 10*(1971), 635–45.

Stewart, T. R., 'Components of correlations and extensions of the lens model equation,' *Psychometrika, 41* (1976), 101–20.

Stewart, T. R., 'Judgment analysis: Procedures,' in Brehmer, B. and Joyce, C. R. B. (eds), *Human Judgment: The Social Judgment Theory View*, Amsterdam: North-Holland, 1988.

Stewart, T. R., 'A decomposition of the correlation coefficient and its use in analyzing forecasting skill,' *Weather and Forecasting, 5* (1990), 661–6.

Stewart, T. R. and Reagan-Cirincione, P. 'Coefficients for debasing forecasts,' *Monthly Weather Review, 119* (1991), 2047–51.

Stewart, T. R., Moninger, W. R., Heideman, K. F. and Reagan-Cirincione, P., 'Effects of improved information on the components of skill in weather forecasting,' *Organizational Behavior and Human Decision Processes, 53* (1992), 107–4.

Stroop, J. R. 'Is the judgment of the group better than that of the average member of the group?' *Journal of Experimental Psychology, 15* (1932), 550–62.

Tape, T. G., Kripal, J. and Wigton, R. S., 'Comparing methods of learning clinical prediction from case simulations,' *Medical Decision Making, 12* (1992), 213–21.

Theil, H., *Applied Economic Forecasing*, Amsterdam: North-Holland, 1966.

Tucker, L. R., 'A suggested alternative formulation in the developments by Hursch, Hammond, and Hursch, and by Hammond, Hursch, and Todd,' *Psychological Review, 71* (1964), 528–30.

Wigton, R. S., 'Applications of judgment analysis and cognitive feedback to medicine,' in Brehmer, B. and Joyce, C. R. B. (eds), *Human Judgment: The Social Judgment Theory View*, Amsterdam: North-Holland, 1988.

Wigton, R. S., Poses, R. M., Collins, M. and Cebul, R. D., 'Teaching old dogs new tricks: Using cognitive feedback to improve physicians' diagnostic judgments on simulated cases,' *Academic Medicine, 65* (1990), S5–S6.

Yates, J. F., 'External correspondence: Decompositions of the mean probability score,' *Organizational Behavior and Human Decision Processes, 30* (1982), 132–56.

Yates, J. F. and Curley, S., 'Conditional distribution analyses of probabilistic forecasts,' *Journal of Forecasting, 4* (1985), 61–73.

York, K. M., Doherty, M. E. and Kamouri, J., 'The influence of cue unreliability on judgment in a multiple-cue probability learning task,' *Organizational Behavior and Human Decision Processes, 39* (1987), 303–17.

# Part VIII

# Bargaining and Negotiation

Situations in which two or more people who want different things try to make a deal they can all agree on are commonplace: buying a house, setting terms of an employment contract, negotiating a treaty to stop a war or reduce pollution, or deciding how to spend an evening out with a friend. Various disciplines have contributed to the study of such issues, both normatively and descriptively. There has been a surge of interest recently driven by efforts to connect JDM research to the work of more traditional negotiation studies. This new approach treats the negotiating parties as human decision makers facing complex judgment tasks, trying to settle on a course of action after thinking about both the external world of partners and deals and their internal world of priorities and preferences.

Some of the terminology of earlier work has carried over into these newer studies. A "two-party, single-issue" negotiation considers two individuals bargaining over one issue such as the price at which they will trade something. The higher the price the happier one person, the less happy the other: the situation is "zero-sum" or "fixed pie," in that whatever one side wins the other loses. Each is assumed to have a "reservation price" at which he or she will walk away from the deal. For the buyer, it's the maximum he or she is prepared to pay, for the seller the least he or she is prepared to accept. If the buyer's maximum is higher than the seller's minimum, there is a "bargaining zone" in which deals acceptable to both parties can be struck. (This model generally doesn't have much to say about the pleasure or pain each party derives from the process of bargaining itself. Judging from the way many people react to buying cars, it seems that bargaining is commonly highly aversive).

More complex concerns emerge when the deal involves multiple issues. The idea of a reservation price generalizes to a BATNA (Best Alternative to a Negotiated Agreement). Of all the possible agreements, only a relatively few fall on what is called the "efficient frontier," a set of agreements in which one party's deal can be improved only by reducing the payoff to the other. (This sounds trivial, but isn't. In complex deals, it is easy to end up with deals that could be improved for one party without hurting the other, or even improved for both!) A simple example is the "integrative solution" where both parties are better off than they would be by simply splitting the difference. The folksy example, often cited, is of two sisters splitting an orange. If one wants juice to drink, the other wants peel for cooking, both can be completely satisfied (an "integrative solution"), but not by simply cutting the orange in half.

With this terminology in hand, we turn to the chapters. Chapter 25, by Mumpower, takes an in-depth look at the way negotiating behavior is shaped by the nonobvious "structure" of the problem – centrally, the way the players' payoffs fit with one another. In the simplest case (two players, one issue, linear payoffs) one player's gain is the other's loss, and the structure is that of the simple bargaining zone model sketched above. With just a little more complexity, however (e.g., two issues, with different issues important to each player), the range of possible solutions opens up, to include both "integrative solutions" of the orange-splitting sort and jointly damaging solutions far from the efficient frontier. The effectiveness of different negotiation strategies such as compromising or horsetrading is highly dependent on the structure of these solution spaces. As Mumpower notes, figuring them out is very difficult, especially when one is unclear about one's own preference structures, let alone about those of one's opponent. Dozens of Lens Model studies suggest that we are often unclear in exactly this way, and that serious negotiation problems can result (see also Balke, Hammond, & Meyer, 1973, for an early example of the problem and a promising solution). Mumpower thus follows the Brunswikian tradition of giving serious attention to the structure of the judgment task.

A similar agenda-setting purpose is clear in Chapter 26, by Bazerman, Neale, Valley, Zajac, and Kim. Bazerman and his colleagues were influential figures in bringing JDM ideas to negotiation research in the 1980s and 1990s. The chapter reprinted here tries to open up further territory by considering the role of third parties (mediators and agents) in helping or hindering the basic two-party process. Prior work (e.g., Notz & Starke, 1978) has looked at different arbitration rules, such as "final offer," where the arbitrator can break an impasse only by picking one or other of the parties' last offers. (Note how this sets up an incentive for each side to try to be more reasonable than the other, and thus tends to head off an impasse). Bazerman et al. try to extend this work to lab studies of agents (like real estate agents, who collect a percentage of the selling price if the deal goes through); mediators (whose interest is in the deal per se); or simple observers. The interest here is mainly conceptual and methodological – how to think about the issues, and how you might run experiments on them. The data are somewhat disappointing, with relatively small or insignificant results. Note, however, that in a big-money context like a real estate transaction, even a small percentage difference can be a lot of money.

### References

Balke, W. M., Hammond, K. R., & Meyer, G. D. (1973). An alternative approach to labor–management negotiations. *Administrative Science Quarterly, 18*, 311–327.

Notz, W. W., & Starke, F. A. (1978). The impact of final offer vs. conventional arbitration on the aspirations and behaviors of bargainers. *Administrative Science Quarterly, 23*, 189–203.

# 25 The Judgment Policies of Negotiators and the Structure of Negotiation Problems

*Jeryl L. Mumpower*

## Introduction

Negotiations frequently result in suboptimal agreements. As Raiffa (1982) has observed, "Often, disputants fail to reach an agreement when, in fact, a compromise does exist that could be to the advantage of all concerned. And the agreements they do make are frequently inefficient: they could have made others that they all would have preferred" (p. 358).

Negotiation processes and outcomes, especially the type of suboptimal ones cited by Raiffa, have attracted the attention of scholars from a variety of fields, both descriptive and prescriptive, including psychology, decision theory, labor relations, and game theory (e.g., Axelrod 1985; Bazerman and Lewicki 1983; Druckman 1977; Fisher and Ury 1981; Kressel and Pruitt 1985; Lax and Sibenius 1986; Luce and Raiffa 1957; Raiffa 1982; Rubin and Brown 1975; von Neumann and Morgenstern 1947; Walton and McKersie 1965). In an influential series of recent studies, Bazerman, Neale, and their colleagues have drawn attention to the frequently dysfunctional effects of cognitive heuristics and biases in negotiation (e.g., Bazerman 1983; Bazerman and Carroll 1987; Bazerman and Neale 1983; Neale and Bazerman 1983, 1985). Also, there have been a number of recent efforts to develop Negotiation Support Systems (NSS), a type of Group Decision Support System intended to support negotiators or mediators (for a review, see Foroughi and Jelassi 1990).

This chapter presents a scheme for describing negotiation problems in terms of negotiators' judgment policies concerning the utility of potential settlements. It describes how negotiators' judgment policies jointly determine the *structure* of the negotiation problem; that is, the joint distribution

Reprinted by permission, Jeryl L. Mumpower, "The Judgment Policies of Negotiators and the Structure of Negotiation Problems," *Management Science*, 37, 10, October 1991. Copyright ©1991 by The Institute for Management Sciences (currently INFORMS), 2 Charles Street, Suite 300, Providence, RI 02904 USA.

of negotiators' utilities across all possible settlements. It is shown that some negotiation problem structures permit settlements that are simultaneously efficient, maximize joint utility, and minimize inequality, while others do not. Several different strategies for achieving settlement with the other party are described; these strategies may lead to quite different outcomes, depending on characteristics of the problem structure. It is shown how both the negotiation problem structure and the negotiators' strategies for reaching settlement influence the negotiation "dance," or sequence of offers and counteroffers that typifies negotiation processes. An approach for characterizing the degree of conflict inherent in different negotiation problem structures is proposed. Finally, the implications of the present analysis and directions for future theoretical and empirical research are reviewed.

### Judgment Policies of Negotiators

Negotiations arise from a variety of different types of disputes. This chapter focuses on a common form of negotiations in which individuals are in conflict because they want different things, but must settle for the same thing (see Coombs 1987). The most commonly cited example of this type of negotiations is the situation where labor and management must reach a contract.

The present analysis is grounded in Social Judgment Theory (SJT), which emphasizes the role of judgmental factors in interpersonal conflict and conflict resolution (e.g., Brehmer 1976, 1984; Brehmer and Hammond 1973, 1977; Hammond 1965; Hammond and Brehmer 1973; Hammond and Grassia 1985; Hammond et al. 1966). It represents an extension of previous SJT research on negotiation, mediation, and negotiation support (e.g., Balke et al. 1973; Darling and Mumpower 1990; Holzworth 1983; Mumpower 1988; Mumpower et al. 1988), but addresses general issues of broad relevance for both theory and practice.

The resolution of negotiations requires parties to reach a joint decision about a settlement. In the SJT view, many negotiations can be conceptualized as hierarchical, $n$-party judgment problems. For an extended discussion of such a conceptual framework, see Mumpower (1988). A simplified version is adequate for the present analysis.

Potential settlements consist of different combinations of values for the issues explicitly or implicitly under negotiation. Relevant issues may include both those formally or by common consent "on the table," as well as factors such as the estimated desirability of the settlement for the other negotiator; the perceived equity of the settlement; and additional factors not subject to direct bargaining (e.g., the desirability of potential settlements to third parties).

In a simple two-party, two-issue negotiation problem, each negotiator judges the utility of potential settlements. Let $U_{i[a,b]}$ represent judgments by the $i$ negotiators, $i = 1, 2$, of the utility of any or all potential settlements defined in terms of a pair of values $[a, b]$ for Issue A and Issue B, respectively.

Judgments of utility are assumed to be a function of the values of the issues. Typically, in the SJT approach, regression-based *judgment policies* are constructed that describe the relationships between values of the issues, $[a, b]$, and judgments of utility, $U_{i[a, b]}$ in terms of three key components: (1) *weights*, or the relative importance placed on each issue; (2) *function forms*, or the functional relationships between each issue and judgments of utility (for present purposes, function forms can be considered identical to *value* or *utility curves*); and (3) the *organizing principle*, or the way judgments regarding individual issues are combined into an evaluation of overall utility.

### How the Judgment Policies of Negotiators Define the Structure of the Negotiation Problem

Negotiators' judgment policies, in combination with one another, determine the structure of negotiation problems. This point can be illustrated in the context of a 2-party, 2-issue negotiation situation, in which one negotiator wants both issues settled at the highest possible level and the other wants both issues settled at the lowest possible level.

Six different variations of this basic situation are summarized in Figure 25.1. These six cases involve different combinations of linear, concave, and convex function forms. Linear function forms signify a constant marginal rate of change in utility. Concave function forms reflect decreasing marginal utility as settlements on an issue approach the negotiator's ideal; for purposes of the present analysis they are defined as proportional to the square roots of the issue values. Convex function forms reflect increasing marginal utility; they are here defined as proportional to the squares of issue values. In the present examples, Negotiator 1 and Negotiator 2 are mirror images of one another.

No claim is made for the representativeness of these six cases. Indeed, they surely are not equally likely, but each case represents a plausible variant of the circumstance in which both function forms are positive monotonic for one negotiator and both are negative monotonic for the other. (For the examples in this chapter, each issue may range in value from 0 to 100. Single-attribute and overall utilities also range from 0 for the least preferred outcome, to 100 for the most preferred.)

Consider several variants of the circumstance in which each negotiator gives nontrivial weight to each issue. Three different relative weight conditions are considered: (1) *equal weights* (each negotiator assigns a weight of 0.5 to each issue); (2) *same issue more important* (each negotiator assigns a weight of 0.3 to Issue A and a weight of 0.7 to Issue B); and (3) *different issues more important* (Negotiator 1 assigns a weight of 0.3 to Issue A and a weight of 0.7 to Issue B; for Negotiator 2, the weights on issues are reversed). For present purposes, it will be assumed that negotiators' judgment policies are adequately represented by a simple weighted average model.

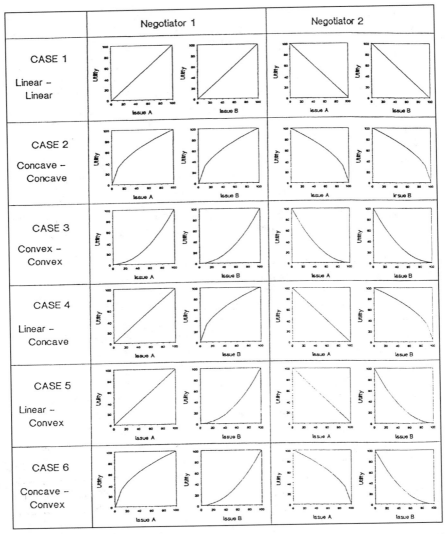

Figure 25.1.  Six different cases of function forms. Each graph shows the negotiators' utilities as a function of where they settle on Issue A and Issue B.

Figure 25.2 presents the feasible settlement spaces (i.e., the joint distribution of utilities across all possible settlements) and efficient frontiers for the 18 different negotiation problem structures that result from crossing the six function form cases with the three relative weight conditions. As simple visual inspection readily reveals, the feasible settlement spaces and efficient frontiers vary markedly in shape and contour. Variations in how negotiators evaluate the utility of potential settlements may result in distinctly different

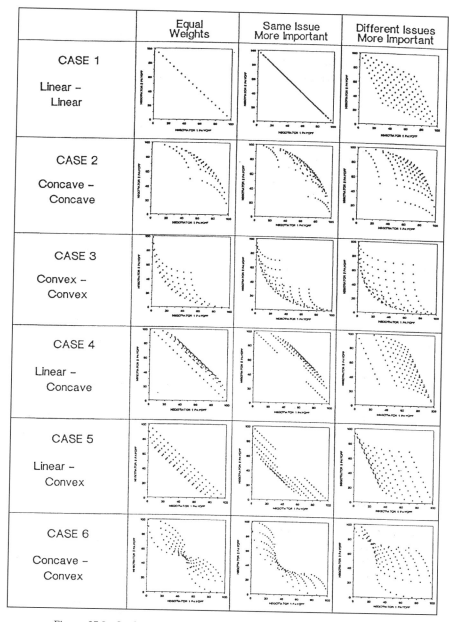

Figure 25.2. Settlement spaces and efficient frontiers given various negotiators' judgment policies. Each graph shows the possible settlement points in terms of the payoffs each gives to Negotiator 1 and Negotiator 2.

feasible settlement spaces and efficient frontiers. Quite different negotiation problem structures may occur even within the limited set of problems for which each negotiator associates nontrivial weights with both issues and function forms are monotonic.

Note that boundaries bowing toward the northeast – those typically employed in depictions of efficient frontiers – are not universal. As will be demonstrated below, different shapes and configurations of feasible settlement spaces and efficient frontiers are likely to have significant implications for the process and outcome of negotiations. Nonconvex settlement spaces (those where the efficient frontier "bows-in") are likely to prove particularly troublesome. In the von Neumann and Morgenstern (1947) tradition, the problem is typically avoided by assuming that negotiators may enter into probabilistic gambles involving pairs of feasible settlement points. Such gambles permit the feasible settlement space to be "filled-in" so that it becomes a convex set. Luce and Raiffa (1957) propose that equivalent results can be obtained by having negotiators "take turns" across repeated negotiations or by relying on the issuance of chit-like devices. The present analysis takes the position that probabilistic gambles are not always realistic options, and that many significant negotiations involve neither repeated plays nor high levels of trust between negotiators.

Even simple negotiation problems may pose difficult cognitive challenges for negotiators. Since the structure of negotiation problems is determined by the interaction between negotiators' value structures, the negotiators themselves – who may be uncertain about their own values and preferences (Brehmer and Brehmer 1988) and are even more likely to be unclear about those of their antagonist (Balke et al. 1973; Brehmer 1976) – will frequently find it difficult to recognize the precise nature of the problem structure they face. Indeed, if the negotiators do not have well-defined utility functions, the structure of the negotiation problem itself may be ill-defined, ambiguous, and evolving.

## Three Criteria for Describing Negotiated Settlements

Although graphic depictions make clear that negotiation problem structures may take a variety of forms, a more systematic basis for distinguishing among feasible negotiated settlements is desirable. The present analysis employs three widely used criteria:

*Efficiency.* Although it is commonly subject to systematic behavioral violation (McClelland and Rohrbaugh 1978; Rohrbaugh et al. 1980), efficiency is the only measure that enjoys widespread (but still not universal) support as a criterion for distinguishing optimal from suboptimal negotiated settlements (e.g., Harsanyi 1976; Keeney and Kirkwood 1975; Rawls 1971; Sen 1973). Settlements are described as inefficient if they do not lie on the efficient frontier and, thus, one or both parties could increase their utility without loss to the other.

*Joint Utility.* There are substantial differences of opinion concerning appropriate definition and measurement of social welfare, which gives weight to the interests of all relevant parties. One or more potential agreements, however, will maximize the simple sum of the joint utilities for negotiators, an operational definition that has commonly been used in previous research (e.g., see MacCrimmon and Messick, 1976; McClelland and Rohrbaugh 1978; Rohrbaugh et al. 1980). Such settlements will necessarily lie on the efficient frontier, but not all points on the efficient frontier will satisfy this criterion.

*Equality.* Settlements may be more desirable for one negotiator than the other. Definitions of equity or fairness are highly problematic. For present purposes, it will be useful to distinguish between those settlements that yield equal levels of utility to each negotiator and those that do not. At least one equal-valued agreement will lie on the efficient frontier.

Although all the above three criteria have been proposed as potential measures of the optimality of negotiated settlements, the present analysis makes no assumptions in this regard. Neither is it assumed that negotiators themselves attempt to reach settlements that are efficient, maximize joint utility, or minimize inequality. (The motives and objectives of negotiators in bargaining situations have been the subject of extensive theoretical analysis and empirical study; e.g., Liebrand 1988; Liebrand and van Run 1985; MacCrimmon and Messick 1976.) The three criteria are simply helpful in distinguishing among structures that differ with respect to the opportunities the negotiation problem affords and the constraints it imposes on negotiators, task characteristics that may have significant behavioral implications.

## Strategies for Reaching Negotiated Settlements

The resolution of negotiations ordinarily requires settlement of differences by mutual concessions. For disputes involving multiple issues, two fundamental strategies of concession can be identified. The first consists of *compromise* – agreeing to a value intermediate between each negotiator's initial bargaining positions for each issue under dispute. The second can be described as *horsetrading* – the parties agree to trade-offs such that each obtains what he or she bargains for on certain issues, in exchange for granting the other what he or she wants on other issues. (This strategy is also commonly identified as *logrolling*; e.g., Froman and Cohen 1970.) Although the two strategies constitute a useful distinction, clearly they represent ends of a continuum, not a pure dichotomy.

Neither strategy leads always to efficient agreements. Depending on the problem structure, only one, neither, or both strategies may lead to agreements that are efficient. Similarly, no strategy always leads to settlements that maximize joint utility or minimize inequality. These points may be illustrated by examining in greater detail five types of negotiation problem structures:

1. *Multiple Strategies Lead to Settlements That Simultaneously Satisfy All Three Criteria.* Efficient agreements can sometimes be reached through multiple strategies, including both compromise and horsetrading. Consider the situation in which function forms for both issues are positive linear for Negotiator 1 and negative linear for Negotiator 2. Equal-valued changes in the issues thus yield a constant marginal rate of change in utility. When weights on the two issues are equal, the feasible settlement space and its efficient frontier (Figure 25.3) consist of a straight line.

In this case, all potential settlements lie on the efficient frontier and also yield the same joint utility. Equal-valued utilities for the two negotiators result from: (a) compromising; (b) horsetrading; or (c) agreeing to values for Issue A and Issue B that are equally distant from their midpoints, in opposite directions; e.g., [60, 40], [20, 80], etc.

2. *Compromise, but not Horsetrading, Leads to Agreements That Simultaneously Satisfy All Three Criteria.* Efficient agreements can sometimes be reached through compromise, but not through horsetrading. Consider the situation in which function forms for both issues are positive concave for Negotiator 1 and negative concave for Negotiator 2. When weights on the two issues are equal, the efficient frontier curves out toward the northeast (Figure 25.4). Compromising on midpoint values for Issues A and B not only lies on the efficient frontier, but also maximizes the sum of utilities and yields equal utility for both negotiators. Whereas a compromise strategy yields an efficient outcome, a horsetrading strategy lies far off the efficient frontier.

In general, if function forms are concave, compromise strategies tend to lead to settlements that lie on or near the efficient frontier. Quite commonly, negotiators adopt bargaining positions in which they ask for more than they would be willing to settle for (i.e., they exaggerate their reservation prices). The marginal rate of change in utility thus decreases as the value of an issue nears the negotiator's initial bargaining position. In other words, the function forms are concave. This may well account for the frequency with which compromise strategies have been observed in studies of negotiation behavior; when function forms are concave, compromise tends to lead to relatively attractive settlements for both parties.

3. *Horsetrading, but not Compromise, Leads to Agreements That Simultaneously Satisfy All Three Criteria.* Efficient agreements can sometimes be reached through horsetrading, but not through compromise. Consider the situation in which function forms for both issues are positive convex for Negotiator 1 and negative convex for Negotiator 2. Equal-valued changes in the issues thus result in an increasing marginal rate of change in utility. Figure 25.5

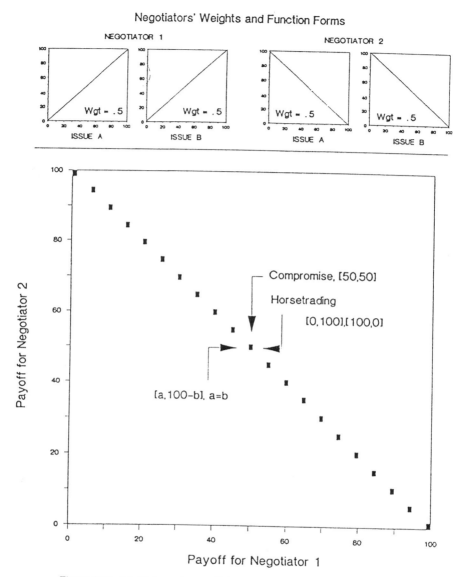

Figure 25.3.  Multiple routes to efficient settlements.

presents the efficient frontier and settlement space when the negotiators regard the two issues as equally important. Horsetrading results in a settlement that not only lies on the efficient frontier, but also maximizes the sum of utilities and yields equal utilities for both negotiators. Whereas a horsetrading strategy produces an efficient outcome, a compromise strategy

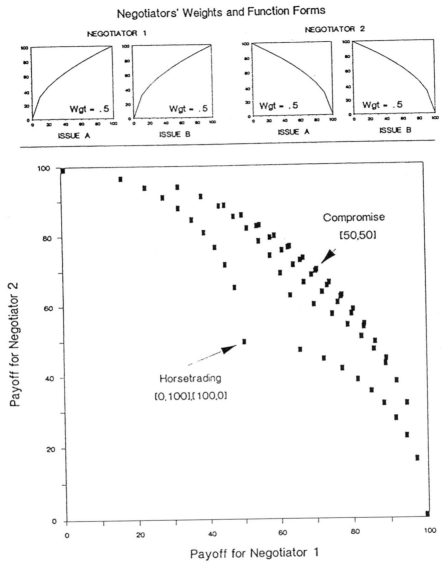

Figure 25.4. Compromise leads to efficient settlements.

yields the lowest possible joint utility and the lowest-valued equitable settlement.

Horsetrading strategies usually lead to settlements on or near the efficient frontier whenever the parties place greater weight on different issues, so that each negotiator can win on the issue more important to him or her.

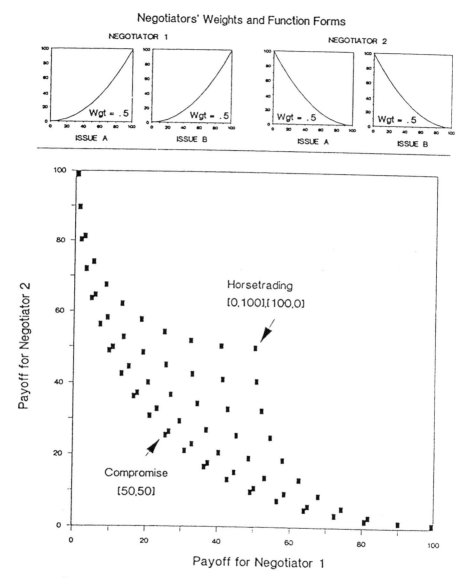

Figure 25.5. Horsetrading leads to efficient settlements.

As the present example illustrates, horsetrading may also lead to efficient agreements when function forms are convex and, thus, when intermediate values on the issues are distinctly unsatisfactory to both parties.

4. *Proportional Compromise Leads to Agreements That Simultaneously Satisfy All Three Criteria.* Efficient agreements can sometimes be reached neither

through compromise nor horsetrading, but only through a strategy that may be described as proportional compromise, in which the extent of each negotiator's concessions reflect the relative weight associated with the issue.

As an example, consider the situation in which function forms for both issues are positive concave for Negotiator 1 and negative concave for Negotiator 2. Figure 25.6 depicts the efficient frontier when negotiators regard different issues as more important. In this situation, an efficient agreement that also maximizes joint utility and minimizes inequality can be reached only by setting each issue at a value that approaches, but does not reach, the initial bargaining position of the negotiator who regards it as more important.

Negotiators may sometimes settle disputes in such a manner, compromising on issues under dispute, but not splitting their differences "down the middle." Instead, each issue is settled at a value that favors the negotiator who regards it as more important, but falls short of that party's bargaining position. Such a heuristic may lead to efficient settlements, given two common conditions. First, the negotiators must rate different issues as more important. Second, their function forms must be concave.

5. *No Strategy Leads to Agreements That Simultaneously Satisfy All Three Criteria.* Sometimes it is impossible to reach an agreement that is simultaneously optimal in terms of all three criteria. As an example, consider the situation in which Negotiator 1 associates a positive convex function form with both issues, and Negotiator 2 associates a negative convex function form with both issues.

When both negotiators regard the same issue as more important, the efficient frontier (Figure 25.7) consists of a scallop-like shape, bowed inward. No settlement will simultaneously satisfy all three criteria. Settlements that maximize joint utility will not yield equal utilities; agreements that yield equal utilities will not maximize joint utility. Horsetrading maximizes joint utility, but one party fares much better than the other in terms of utility. Compromise leads to a settlement far off the efficient frontier. An equally valued settlement on the efficient frontier can be reached only through a relatively nonintuitive strategy, i.e., one party wins completely on the less important issue, while the other gets most but not everything on the more important issue.

### Distributive Versus Integrative Settlements

Walton and McKersie (1965) introduced an influential, widely cited distinction between distributive and integrative bargaining. Distributive bargaining is commonly identified as involving the division of resources; it refers to situations in which there is a fixed supply of some resource, and one's gain is the other's loss. These constitute zero-sum bargaining situations. Integrative bargaining refers to situations in which the negotiators cooperatively face a common problem or in which the parties' interests are not diametrically opposed. These constitute variable-sum bargaining situations.

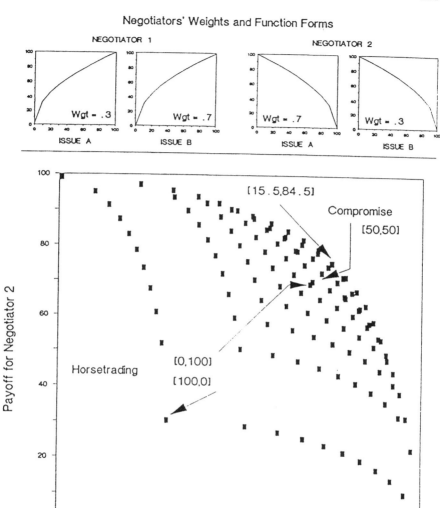

Figure 25.6. Proportional compromise leads to efficient settlements.

Negotiators often treat negotiations as distributive situations, even when they hold integrative potential. Bazerman (1983) has attributed this tendency to the "mythical fixed-pie of negotiations," noting that negotiators tend to assume that their interests are in direct conflict with the other negotiator's. According to Bazerman, this belief leads disputants to view negotiations as

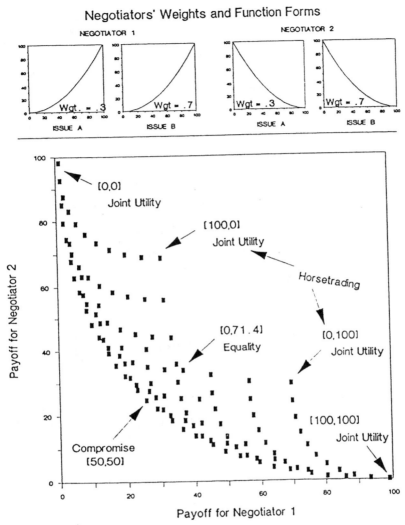

Figure 25.7. No strategy leads to efficient settlements that maximize joint utility and yield equal utilities.

a competitive process, resulting in a win-lose orientation and a distributive, rather than integrative, approach to bargaining.

In the contemporary literature, compromise strategies are sometimes implicitly defined as synonymous with distributive tactics, while horsetrading strategies are seen as integrative. This characterization is not altogether correct. It is motivated by the observation that joint gains can often be maximized through trade-offs. As the preceding analyses demonstrate, however, this observation does not apply across all situations. Horsetrading is sometimes integrative, sometimes not. The same goes for compromise. The structure of the negotiation problem determines which strategy, if either, will take advantage of the problem's integrative potential. For problems characterized by linear function forms and unequal weights on issues across negotiators (a common form of problem used in empirical research on negotiation), horsetrading will indeed be integrative, but it will not necessarily be so for other sorts of problems; e.g., those involving concave function forms.

Can negotiators reasonably be expected to discriminate those situations in which horsetrading is more integrative from those in which compromise is more integrative? Probably not. The differences between the conditions that make one strategy preferable to the other may be subtle, consisting of apparently slight differences in the shapes of function forms or relative weights associated with issues. Under the most cooperative of circumstances, it may be hard for negotiators to ascertain which strategy is better, and such difficulties are likely to be compounded in adversarial situations in which the parties are not fully forthcoming with one another.
. . .

## Conclusion

The present analysis demonstrates that (a) the structure of negotiation problems (i.e., the joint distribution of utilities across all feasible settlements) is a function of negotiators' judgment policies; (b) variations in how negotiators evaluate the utility of potential settlements may result in distinctly different feasible settlement spaces and efficient frontiers; and (c) the structure of negotiation problems may have important implications for both process and outcome of negotiations. Although the analysis was developed within the context of Social Judgment Theory, the conclusions are generally applicable to any approach that makes use of utility-like concepts to describe negotiators' preferences.

Future empirical research should clarify the impacts of negotiation problem structure on variables such as (a) negotiators' perceived difficulty in reaching settlement; (b) the amount of time required to reach agreement; (c) the number of offers and counteroffers exchanged; (d) negotiators' satisfaction with process and outcome; (e) attitudes and affect toward other negotiators; and (f) the pattern of the negotiation dance. Empirical studies also should be conducted to ascertain for which specific problem structures negotiators are relatively more or less likely to reach settlements that are efficient, maximize joint utility, and minimize inequality.

A promising direction for future research is investigation of the tendency for negotiators to reach compromises on issues in a stepwise fashion instead of integrating multiple issues into potentially beneficial packages of trade-offs (Bazerman 1983; Foroughi and Jelassi 1990). A potential explanation for this "compromise bias" is simply that, for the most frequently encountered negotiation problem structures, issue-by-issue compromise constitutes a good approach for reaching satisfactory agreements. The heuristics that people bring to negotiations are likely to be habits precisely because they work well for commonly encountered problem environments. Because negotiators typically find it difficult to detect the precise nature of the negotiation problem structure, they are likely to try first whatever strategy has in the past most frequently proved appropriate, abandoning it only after interactions with the other negotiator indicate that the strategy will not work well in this particular circumstance. If their default strategies lead to passably satisfactory settlements, the negotiators may never discover that more efficient ones exist. The key to better understanding of dysfunctional phenomena such as the compromise bias is a focus on (a) the judgment policies of negotiators, (b) the characteristics of the negotiation problem structure, and, most important, (c) the interaction between the two.

A second promising avenue for future research is extension to negotiation problems involving more than two issues. In multi-issue problems, when negotiators address and resolve issues sequentially, they transform the negotiation problem structure. Empirical research should be conducted to determine whether negotiators sometimes incrementally transform relatively benign negotiation problem structures into more problematic ones. This might occur, for example, if negotiators tended to reach a settlement on easier, less important issues first, leaving for later more important issues where their conflict of interest is much greater.

Finally, the present research is motivated by practical concerns regarding the development and application of NSS (e.g., Darling and Mumpower 1990; Mumpower 1988; Mumpower et al. 1988). NSS design needs to take into account the underlying structure of the negotiation problem. Certain problem structures make it more difficult for negotiators to reach efficient (or otherwise satisfactory) solutions, and NSS design should take into account the opportunities and constraints inherent in various structures.

Regardless of the intended purpose of an NSS, accurate specification of negotiation problem structure will prove a key element in successful design and implementation. Developing valid and reliable judgment models is critically important, because, as the present analysis has shown, even seemingly minor differences in such models may imply substantial differences in the underlying problem structure. Because concealment and misrepresentation are often norms in negotiations, developing accurate judgment models may constitute a major stumbling block to successful implementation of NSS; parties may be reluctant to articulate clearly and publicly their preferences and values. For this reason, perhaps NSS development should initially focus on supporting only one negotiator or supporting a neutral facilitator. For an NSS supporting a single negotiator, judgment models could be developed for that one party and pitted against hypothetical models of the other negotiator. For an NSS supporting a neutral facilitator, negotiators might more readily be persuaded to divulge information about their preferences and values if it were intended solely for use by the mediator in attempting to facilitate an agreement in the joint interests of both parties.

### References

Axelrod, R. M., *The Evolution of Cooperation*, Basic Books, New York, 1985.

Balke, W. M., K. R. Hammond and G. D. Meyer, "An Alternative Approach to Labor-Management Relations," *Admin. Sci. Quart.*, *18* (1973), 311–327.

Bazerman, M. H., "Negotiator Judgment: A Critical Look at the Rationality Assumption," *Amer. Behavioral Scientist*, *27* (1983), 211–228.

—— and J. S. Carroll, "Negotiator Cognition," *Res. Organizational Behavior*, *9* (1987).

—— and R. J. Lewicki, *Negotiating in Organizations*, Sage, Beverly Hills, CA, 1983.

—— and M. A. Neale, "Heuristics in Negotiation: Limitations to Dispute Resolution Effectiveness," in *Negotiating in Organizations*, M. H. Bazerman and R. J. Lewicki (Eds.), Sage, Beverly Hills, CA, 1983.

Brehmer, B., "The Role of Judgment in Small-Group Conflict and Decision Making," in *Progress in Applied Social Psychology*, G. M. Stephenson and J. H. Davis (Eds.), Wiley, New York, 1984.

——, "Social Judgment Theory and the Analysis of Interpersonal Conflict," *Psychological Bulletin*, *83* (1976), 985–1003.

—— and A. Brehmer, "What Have We Learned about Human Judgment from Thirty Years of Policy Capturing?," in *Human Judgment: The SJT Approach*, B. Brehmer and C. R. B. Joyce (Eds.), North-Holland, Amsterdam, 1988, 75–114.

—— and K. R. Hammond, "Cognitive Sources of Interpersonal Conflict: Analysis of Interactions between Linear and Nonlinear Cognitive Systems," *Organizational Behavior and Human Performance*, *10* (1973), 290–313.

Coombs, C. H., "The Structure of Conflict," *Amer. Psychologist*, *42* (1987), 355–363.

Darling, T. A. and J. L. Mumpower, "Modeling the Cognitive Influences on the Dynamics of Negotiation," in *Proc. 23rd Hawaii Internat. Conf. System Sciences. Vol. IV*, R. H. Sprague (Ed.), IEEE Computer Society Press, Washington, 1990, 22–30.

Druckman, D., *Negotiation: Social-Psychological Perspectives*, Sage, Beverly Hills, CA, 1977.

Fisher, R. and W. Ury, *Getting to YES: Negotiating Agreement without Giving in*, Houghton Mifflin, Boston, 1981.

Foroughi, A. and M. T. Jelassi, "NSS Solutions to Major Negotiation Stumbling Blocks," in *Proc. 23rd Hawaii Internat. Conf. System Sciences. Vol. IV*, R. H. Sprague (Ed.), IEEE Computer Society Press, Washington, 1990, 2–11.

Froman, L. A. and M. D. Cohen, "Compromise and Logroll: Comparing the Efficiency of Two Bargaining Processes," *Behavioral Sci.*, *15* (1970), 180–183.

Hammond, K. R., "New Directions in Research on Conflict Resolution," *J. Social Issues*, *21* (1965), 44–66.

—— and B. Brehmer, "Quasi-Rationality and Distrust: Implications for International

Conflict," in *Human Judgment and Social Interaction*, L. Rappoport and D. Summers (Eds.), Holt, Rinehart, & Winston. New York, 1973, 338–391.

—— and J. Grassia, "The Cognitive Side of Conflict: From Theory to Resolution of Policy Disputes," in *Applied Social Psychology Annual*, Vol. 6, S. Oskamp (Ed.), Sage, Beverly Hills, CA, 1985, 233–254.

——, F. Todd, M. M. Wilkins and T. O. Mitchell, "Cognitive Conflict between Persons: Application of the Lens Model Paradigm," *J. Experimental Social Psychology*, 2 (1966), 343–360.

Harsanyi, J. C., *Essays on Ethics, Social Behavior, and Scientific Explanation*, Reidel, Boston, 1976.

Holzworth, J., "Intervention in a Cognitive Conflict," *Organizational Behavior and Human Performance*, 32 (1983), 216–231.

Keeney, R. L. and C. W. Kirkwood, "Group Decision Making Using Cardinal Social Welfare Functions," *Management Sci.*, 22 (1975), 430–437.

Kressel, K. and D. Pruitt, "Themes in the Mediation of Social Conflict," *J. Social Issues*, 41 (1985), 179–198.

Lax, D. A. and J. K. Sebenius, *The Manager as Negotiator: Bargaining for Cooperation and Competitive Gain*, Free Press, New York, 1986.

Liebrand, W. B. G., "The Ring Measure of Social Values: A Computerized Procedure for Assessing Individual Differences in Information Processing and Social Value Orientation," *European J. Personality*, 2 (1988), 217–230.

—— and G. J. van Run, "The Effects of Social Motives on Behavior in Social Dilemmas in Two Cultures." *J. Experimental Social Psychology*, 21 (1985), 86–102.

Luce, R. D. and H. Raiffa, *Games and Decisions: Introduction and Critical Survey*, Wiley, New York, 1957.

MacCrimmon, K. R. and D. M. Messick, "A Framework for Social Motives," *Behavioral Sci.*, 25 (1976), 86–100.

McClelland, G. and J. Rohrbaugh, "Who Accepts the Pareto Axiom? The Role of Utility and Equity in Arbitration Decisions," *Behavioral Sci.*, 23 (1978), 446–456.

Mumpower, J. L., "An Analysis of the Judgmental Components of Negotiation and a Proposed Judgmentally-Oriented Approach to Mediation," in *Human Judgment: The SJT Approach*, B. Brehmer and C. R. B. Joyce (Eds.), North-Holland, Amsterdam, 1988, 465–502.

——, S. Schuman and A. Zumbolo, "Analytical Mediation: An Application in Collective Bargaining," in *Organizational Decision Support Systems*, R. Lee et al. (Eds.), North-Holland, Amsterdam, 1988.

Neale, M. A. and M. H. Bazerman, "Perspectives for Understanding Negotiation: Viewing Negotiation as a Judgment Process," *J. Conflict Resolution*, 29 (1985), 33–55.

—— and ——, "The Effect of Perspective Taking Ability on the Negotiation Process under Different Forms of Arbitration," *Industrial and Labor Relations Rev.*, 36 (1983), 378–388.

Raiffa, H., *The Art and Science of Negotiation*, Belknap/Harvard University Press, Cambridge, MA, 1982.

Rawls, J., *A Theory of Justice*, Harvard University Press, Cambridge, MA, 1971.

Rohrbaugh, J., G. McClelland and R. Quinn, "Measuring the Relative Importance of Utilitarian and Egalitarian Values: A Study of Individual Differences about Fair Distribution," *J. Appl. Psychology*, 65 (1980), 34–49.

Rubin, J. Z. and B. R. Brown, *The Social Psychology of Bargaining and Negotiation*, Academic, New York, 1975.

Sen, A., *On Economic Inequality*, Norton, New York, 1973.

von Neumann, J. and O. Morgenstern, *Theory of Games and Economic Behavior* (2nd ed.), Princeton University Press, Princeton, NJ, 1947.

Walton, R. E. and R. B. McKersie, *A Behavioral Theory of Labor Negotiation*, McGraw-Hill, New York, 1965.

# 26 The Effect of Agents and Mediators on Negotiation Outcomes

*Max H. Bazerman, Margaret A. Neale, Kathleen L. Valley, Edward J. Zajac, and Yong Min Kim*

The field of negotiation research has been a major area of growth in recent years. Most of this research has focused on two-party negotiation, often within a mixed-motive context (Walton & McKersie, 1965), which emphasizes the integrative potential that exists (Fisher & Ury, 1981; Raiffa, 1982; Bazerman, Lewicki, & Sheppard, 1991; Neale & Bazerman, 1991). Some extensions of this perspective have focused on multiparty negotiations (Mannix, Thompson, & Bazerman, 1989; Brett & Rognes, 1986). While this research has moved beyond dyadic negotiation, it typically studies actors negotiating their own outcomes. Participants are led to believe that their objective is to maximize their individual benefit. In contrast, many negotiations occur through third parties such as agents or mediators, where these additional parties may operate under competing motives: to optimize the outcome in favor of the principals; to maximize their own personal gain; or to simply gain an agreement.

While the theoretical and empirical literature on principal–agent relationships has also grown dramatically in recent years (Eisenhardt, 1989; Jensen & Meckling, 1976; Ross, 1973; Zajac, 1990), there is virtually no empirical research on the impact of self-interested agents on the negotiation process. A considerable amount of research within the industrial relations literature examines the impact of institutional third parties (mediators, arbitrators, etc.). As a result of its industrial relations heritage, the empirical literature on intermediaries has focused on the impact of formally assigned third-party neutrals on negotiator behavior (Johnson & Pruitt, 1972; Neale & Bazerman, 1983). For example, research has focused on the impact of mediation versus arbitration, and the differential effects of alternate forms of arbitration (McGillicuddy, Welton & Pruitt, 1987). With some notable exceptions (Bartunek, Benton, & Keys, 1975, for example), past research has often focused on the impact of the threat of third-party intervention and its effect on

This chapter originally appeared in *Organizational Behavior and Human Decision Processes*, 1992, 53, 55–73. Copyright © 1992 by Academic Press, Inc. Reprinted by permission.

negotiator behavior *prior* to using the third party, rather than on the direct impact of *using* third-party procedures per se (Grigsby & Bigoness, 1982; Neale & Bazerman, 1983; Notz & Starke, 1978). This industrial relations perspective does not capture the essence of the third-party roles negotiators face. They may often use third parties who have an incentive to get an agreement and/or have their own incentive structure separate from that of the disputing parties.

A special case of the agency problem (Arrow, 1985; Ross, 1973) involves the use of agents as third parties who act for, on behalf of, or as the representatives of the principals. Agents are called for in many situations because of their specialized knowledge and their skill at matching buyers and sellers. The agents may transmit information for the principals or act as deal makers if the principals delegate such responsibility to them. While we acknowledge their benefits, using agents incurs costs. One obvious cost is that whatever compensation an agent receives from the transaction must come from one or both of the parties. The principal may assume that the agent will negotiate a settlement that covers the additional costs incurred. However, a critical issue in the agency literature is that the agent's incentive structure may not match the incentive structure of the buyer or the seller, despite the implicit representation in the process (Rubin & Sander, 1988). Common organizational examples of this mixed-incentive structure include union negotiators in a contract dispute, who may have political concerns, or leasing agents, who have personal profit concerns.

This chapter examines how agent and mediator interventions affect the behavior of negotiators. The first study explores the impact of alternative third-party roles (agents and mediators) on the outcomes of negotiation. Specifically, we examine the impact of these forms of third-party intervention on the likelihood of impasse and the negotiated price if an agreement is obtained. In the second study, we explore the nature of the negotiated relationship between principals and an agent.

## Study 1

Study 1 examines how informal third-party roles affect the *outcomes* of negotiation *through the direct use of the third-party structure*. Thus, this study focuses on the impact of negotiating with neutral third parties (mediators) and nonneutral third parties (agents) in comparison to negotiating without the use of third parties. We outline the roles of agent and mediator, create a set of predictions concerning how these roles are expected to affect negotiation outcomes, and provide an empirical test of these predictions in real estate negotiation simulations.

In the real estate setting, the potential buyer and seller often depend on the real estate agent(s). In a typical sale, the agent is legally working for the seller, and the seller formally pays the commission – normally 6%. Since the agent receives a commission based on the selling price, the agent has some incentive to be biased toward the interests of the seller. The incentive structure of this self-interested agent may affect the information transmitted in the negotiation process.

In contrast to an agent's incentive, the mediator's role is to help disputing parties reach agreement (Kolb & Rubin, 1991; Sheppard, 1983, 1984). Typically, any fee the mediator receives is independent of the nature of the negotiation outcome. When the parties are unable to reach a settlement, the mediator can take an active role of applying pressure, channeling communications, allowing the parties to save face, persuading and leading the group in its task accomplishment and social relationship (Kolb, 1983). A mediator can also try to help the parties to see the negotiation from a more rational perspective (Neale & Bazerman, 1991). That is, the mediator can help the parties to make decisions that maximize their own utility. However, a mediator, by definition, cannot impose a settlement. Mediators have an incentive to help the parties reach an agreement – their reputations depend on their success at reaching agreements (Goldberg, Green, & Sander, 1985). Whether mediators should be concerned with the specific nature of the agreement is an ongoing dispute in the mediation literature (Susskind & Cruikshank, 1987; Goldberg et al., 1985; Kolb & Rubin, 1991).

On the basis of this preliminary overview of the roles of agents and mediators, one finds that while both types of third parties try to achieve the goal of encouraging agreement, the means they use to achieve this objective can have an important influence on the negotiated outcomes. Two critical questions arise. What impact do these third-party roles have on the likelihood of agreement? What will be the nature of the resulting agreements?

The way in which a third party influences the likelihood of agreement differs with the type of third party used. The use of an agent is likely to make it more difficult to reach agreement for at least two reasons. First, the more nodes in a communication channel, the greater is the probability of omissions or distortions in the message after it leaves its source (Hopper, 1976). Negotiating through an agent may be less efficient than direct bargaining because of the increased noise in the communication channel. In addition, the commission an agent receives must come out of the surplus otherwise available to the parties. The difference between the amount the buyer is willing to pay for a given property and the amount the seller is willing to accept determines the bargaining zone for the negotiation. An agent's commission is paid out of the seller's surplus, effectively reducing the size of the bargaining zone. Although a skilled agent may provide many of the benefits that have been associated with mediators in the literature, we argue that the communication complexity and the reduced bargaining zone will overwhelm any problem-solving skills the agent brings to the negotiation. Thus, the presence of an agent in a negotiation is expected to decrease the likelihood of settlement.

In contrast to the use of an agent, using a mediator may increase the likelihood of an agreement. The mediator's role is to provide unbiased conciliatory efforts toward resolving a dispute. In essence, the mediator provides the negotiation with an extra mind to help the parties think through the problem in a less partisan manner. The mediation process puts a great deal of pressure on the parties to appear reasonable. As a result, we predict that mediation will increase the likelihood of agreement in comparison to negotiating without a third party or negotiating through an agent.

Similar to the impact on settlement rates, the effect a third party has on the nature of the agreement will differ between agents and mediators. The use of an agent is expected to increase the sales price of the housing unit, since the seller will have to pay the agent's fee out of his/her surplus. However, the amount of the increase is unclear. One extreme prediction is that the sales price will increase by the amount of the agent's fee, for it is the seller who formally pays the commission. In addition, the agent has the incentive to increase the sales price, which pushes the price toward the point where the seller gets the additional amount in the sales price to cover the commission. This is a typical argument provided by realtors for why the seller should hire an agent rather than selling a house without an agent. In contrast, when individuals or professional appraisers evaluate the market value of a home, they do not provide one figure with an agent and one without. Rather, market value implies a set figure specifying the value of the home regardless of whether an agent is involved. This suggests that the price of the house will not change as a result of agent intervention. Note the initial logic implies that the buyer implicitly pays the agent fee, while the latter logic implies that the seller pays the agent fee. In one study of actual real estate negotiations (in which comparability was controlled for based on characteristics of transferred property), Jud and Frew (1986) found sellers and buyers roughly shared the cost of the realtor commission. While we clearly expect a result between the two, resulting in an increase in the sales price, we offer no clear prediction concerning the degree to which the buyer versus the seller can be expected to pay for the agent.

The mediator, in contrast to the agent, is unlikely to have the incentive to increase the negotiated price. The mediator is in a position of trying to resolve the conflict between buyer and seller impartially. The mediation process has been criticized for coopting the less powerful parties in negotiations, because of the implicit value mediation places on getting an agreement (Roehl & Cook, 1989). Alternatively, mediators have been accused of putting pressure on *both* sides, even when one side's position may be justified based on market forces, etc. (Carnevale & Conlon, 1987). This behavior increases the likelihood that the mediator will obtain bilateral concessions. In the study presented in this chapter, information on market values of comparable properties was provided for principals and agents. The market value of a property is expected to form an anchor from which the buyer and seller will adjust their offers. As a result of the anchoring and adjustment bias (Bazerman, 1990; Slovic & Lichtenstein, 1971; Tversky & Kahneman, 1974), parties are expected to keep their offers centered around the market anchors, unless some external pressure is exerted to move them away from this point. We predict that mediators will push the parties toward an agreement in the middle of the bargaining zone, regardless of whether the anchor provided favors the buyer or the seller.

The arguments provided above lead to the following formal hypotheses to be tested in Study 1:

H1: The use of an agent will increase the selling price of a house in comparison to negotiating with no intermediary.

H2: The use of a mediator will lead parties to reach agreements closer to the midpoint of the bargaining zone than if they negotiated with no intermediary.

H3: The use of an agent will increase the impasse rate in comparison to negotiating with no intermediary.

H4: The use of a mediator will decrease the impasse rate in comparison to negotiating with no intermediary.

## Methods

*Subjects.* All 294 subjects were MBA students at a large midwestern university. Their average age was 26 and they averaged 3.6 years of work experience. Subjects participated in the experiment as part of course activities.

*Design.* The design simulated three different property transactions (house, townhouse, and condo) across three third-party conditions (no-agent, agent, mediator), crossed with two sets of market anchors (high or low market anchors) describing the value of the properties. These factors were fully crossed in a $3 \times 3 \times 2$ design, creating 18 different negotiation contexts. Property and third-party condition were varied within subject, while the market anchor was varied between subject.

*Description of Negotiation Simulations.* Three different simulations were used, to allow for multiple use of the same subjects in a within-subjects design. All three were structurally similar, but varied on surface characteristics. One case, "house," had an asking price of $235,900, with the buyer's reservation price set at $230,000, and the seller's reservation price set at $210,000. The second case, "townhouse," had an asking price of $195,000, with the buyer's reservation price set at $190,000, and the seller's reservation price set at $175,000. The third case, "condo," had an asking price of $139,500, with the buyer's reservation price set at $138,000, and the seller's reservation price set at $128,000. For each property, a brief description of the real estate was given, and several features of the property such as inside and outside amenities were depicted in the description. In addition, comparison data on similar properties recently sold in the neighborhood were given as a reference.

To test the impact of the tendency of mediators to push the agreement toward the middle of the bargaining zone, we created two versions of each of the three housing simulations. In one form, the comparison data implied that a figure around the seller's reservation price was the fair market price on the unit (low anchor). In the other form, the comparison data implied that a figure around the buyer's reservation price was the fair market price on the unit (high anchor). All members of the same class participated under three "high" anchor simulations or under three "low" anchor simulations, making "anchor" a between-subjects variable.

*Assignment of Participants to Roles.* Each subject participated in each of the three simulations of the experiment in a different role – buyer, seller, or third party. Since the third-party role is one of the manipulations, they were assigned to one of three possible third-party conditions. They were involved in simulations under the other two third-party roles in their other two simulations. Thus, all subjects participated in each of the three different housing simulations, and under each of the three third-party roles.

To create the three third-party conditions (no-agent, agent, mediator), three intermediary roles were created. In the "no-agent" condition there was an "observer," who was simply required to verify the agreement with the buyer and the seller after the close of the agreement and return the signed agreement to the instructor. The "agent" was assigned the role of helping the parties reach agreement. In this condition, the buyer and seller could communicate to one another only through the agent. Participants were told the buyer and the seller were not to meet directly with one another at any point in the negotiation – they were allowed to meet only with the agent. The agent version informed all parties that it is normal for the seller to pay the agent a commission of 6% of the transaction price upon sale of the property. However, the subjects were also told that the rate of 6% was not legally binding and was negotiable. If no sale was consummated, the agent received no commission. In the "mediator" condition, the mediator was told (consistent with the understanding of the other parties) that "Buyers and sellers pay a flat fee to your organization to obtain access to your services. However, you are paid your service fee only if you get an agreement between a buyer and a seller. Thus, your pay is dependent on getting buyers and sellers to agree to sign a final agreement." The parties were able to use the mediator in any way that they chose. However, the parties were required to include the mediator in any face-to-face meeting.

Participants were told how each party would be evaluated. In the "no-agent" version, net surplus to the buyer (seller) was the amount under (over) the reservation price. In the "agent" version, the buyer's net surplus was again the amount under his/her reservation price. The seller's net surplus was the amount over the reservation price minus the realtor commission. As such, the agent's commission reduces the size of the effective bargaining zone. Obviously, the agent's net surplus was the commission received. Buyer and seller surplus was calculated exactly the same in the mediator condition as in the no-agent condition. The mediator was told that "You will be evaluated on whether or not you get the two parties to agree to a settlement. If they agree, you are a success. If they do not agree, you have failed in this exercise."

*Procedure.* Explanation of the simulation to each class of 27, 30, or 33 subjects took about 15 min. No participants interacted with the same party more than once in their three simulations. Since all subjects participated in all three cases, there were three unique negotiating groups to which each subject belonged. Subjects were allowed to negotiate the three cases in any order and were not required to conclude one negotiation before initiating others. Participants were told they had 6 days outside of class to conduct the three negotiations. Failure to reach agreement within the designated time period was defined as an impasse. Subjects were required to submit the results of their negotiations 1 day prior to the next class meeting. Subjects informally reported spending between 4 and 10 h to conduct the three negotiations.

Each participant received three packets of materials which included: (1) instructions for each role; (2) description of the real estate; (3) information about sales prices of real properties recently sold in the neighborhood; (4) payoff table of the costs or savings surrounding the extra two issues besides price; (5) note on how each party would be evaluated; and (6) agreement form to be signed by all concerned parties in the negotiation. (A complete set of materials is available from the authors.)

An Agreement Form, to be signed by all concerned parties in the negotiation, was used to record the contract to which a buyer, seller, and third party agreed. The third party was responsible for returning the form by the deadline. Instructions indicated that each party should maximize his/her profit in the negotiation. Results would be posted in the next class period. Use of the telephone was allowed, but any agreement had to be confirmed in writing on the Agreement Form.

### Results

The data tend to support the hypothesis that the use of an agent will increase the selling price in comparison to negotiating with no intermediary. The means for each condition are presented in Table 26.1. For all properties, the selling price of the property was higher when an agent was used than when no intermediary was involved in the negotiation ($p < .05$). In addition, in a full regression that includes controls for the type of property sold, the

Table 26.1. *Mean Sales Price by Condition*

|  | No Intermediary | Agent | Mediator |
|---|---|---|---|
| House (BZ: $210,000–230,000) | | | |
| High anchor | $221,862 | $224,484 | $222,167 |
| Low anchor | 219,132 | 221,621 | 219,339 |
| Townhouse (BZ: $175,000–190,000) | | | |
| High anchor | $183,383 | $186,500 | $184,800 |
| Low anchor | 180,448 | 182,610 | 181,153 |
| Condo (BZ: $128,000–138,000) | | | |
| High anchor | $133,478 | $132,012 | $133,745 |
| Low anchor | 132,492 | 133,373 | 132,403 |

selling price is significantly higher when an agent is used than under either of the other two conditions ($p < .05$). Two dummy variables were used to represent the properties.

Given that price increases when an agent is used, a question arises whether the increase covers the commission the seller pays the agent. To what extent is the agent commission being paid by the seller versus the buyer? One way to gain insight into this question is to determine the percentage of the commission coming out of seller surplus versus buyer surplus. If we define $P_a$ to be the average selling price with an agent, $P_{na}$ to be the average selling price with no intermediary, and $P_{a-c}$ to be the average selling price with an agent less the commission, then $[(P_a - P_{na})/(P_a - P_{a-c})]$ is equal to the percentage of the commission coming from the buyer's surplus. $\{1-[(P_a - P_{na})/(P_a - P_{a-c})]\}$ is equal to the percentage of the commission coming from the seller's surplus. Using this equation, we find that the buyer pays 28.1% of the commission in the house case, 39.4% of the commission in the townhouse case, and 23.1% of the commission in the condo case.

The second hypothesis, that when using a mediator the selling price will be closer to the midpoint of the bargaining zone than when no intermediary was used, was not supported. Our design assumed that large differences would exist between high and low anchor conditions for each of the three properties, and that this hypothesis would be tested by looking for movement toward the middle of the range, away from the high and low anchors, when mediation was used. Surprisingly, the differences between high and low anchor conditions were quite small, eliminating the potential of providing evidence for Hypothesis 2.

The incidence of impasse relative to settlement is shown in Table 26.2. The data show support for Hypothesis 3, that the use of an agent would increase the impasse rate in comparison to negotiating with no intermediary (11 impasses of 99 negotiations with an agent; 5 impasses of 98 negotiations

Table 26.2. *Impasses/Settlements by Property and Third-Party Role*

|              | No Intermediary | Agent | Mediator | Total  |
|--------------|-----------------|-------|----------|--------|
| House        | 1/31            | 5/29  | 0/32     | 6/92   |
| Townhouse    | 2/31            | 3/30  | 1/31     | 6/92   |
| Condo        | 2/31            | 3/29  | 1/32     | 6/92   |
| Column total | 5/93            | 11/88 | 2/95     | 18/276 |

*Note:* $\chi^2$ significant at .05.

with no intermediary, $p < .05$). The data do not support Hypothesis 4, that the mediator would decrease the impasse rate in comparison to negotiating with no intermediary (2 impasses of 97 negotiations with a mediator; 5 impasses of 98 negotiations with no intermediary, $p = $ ns). Obviously, the limited number of impasses make the testing of impasse predictions more difficult. It is interesting to note, however, that the direction of impasse results (agent > no intermediary > mediator) held up under each of the three property simulations.

### Discussion

The results generally support our predictions concerning the impact of mediators and agents on impasse rates: agents hurt and mediators help. Buyers and sellers acting solely through an agent cannot speak directly to one another. The information they pass to one another through the agent may be insufficient, misunderstood, or simply misrepresented. There were several incidents where the participants playing the role of agent in this study clearly misrepresented one or both of the parties, by withholding information or providing false information. In debriefing, the agents claimed to be trying to ensure that the sales price was as high as possible, but the potential result was impasse where settlement was clearly in all three parties' interests.

Unfortunately, the small number of impasses in this study hinders our ability to reach conclusions concerning the impact of mediators on impasse rates. While the predicted pattern was observed across all three property simulations, the statistical test comparing impasse rates of mediation to the no-intermediary condition was not significant. Another explanation of why the effect for mediation was not significant is that the participants in this study were not trained in mediation techniques. Their marginal effectiveness at bringing about settlement may reflect the benefits of the mediation process, mitigated by the inexperience of the mediators. A third explanation is that while mediators may facilitate settlement, the presence of an extra party in the communication network makes interaction more complicated. Thus, some of the positive effects of the mediator are counteracted.

This study highlights a more general problem with using laboratory studies to understand negotiation. The negotiation literature is lacking in controlled studies that look at settlement as the dependent variable. Why? It may be that the demands for agreement in a laboratory are so high that subjects will go to extremes to reach agreement. This raises an important question concerning how we can study this important dependent variable in controlled contexts.

The results also show that agents raise the sales price of the property, and both the buyer and seller contribute to the payment that the agent receives. While the seller pays a greater proportion of the commission, the amount paid by the buyer is still quite significant. This is consistent with field data by Jud and Frew (1986). This counteracts the impression many people have, based on the fact that the seller formally pays the commission. Thus, a "for-sale-by-owner" situation does imply savings to both parties in the negotiation.

While this study provides evidence for the self-serving behavior of agents, it raises many questions regarding how this affects the principals in a negotiation. To what extent do negotiators realize that the agent is a self-interested, not a neutral, third party? Do negotiators adjust their behavior toward the agent to take this into account? These are questions addressed in the second study.

### Study 2

An often overlooked issue existing in negotiations through agents is the implicit or explicit negotiation between the principals and the agent(s). The terms we use to describe a negotiation process often lead us to conceptualize the negotiation in a way that includes putting buyer and seller on different sides and viewing the agent as a neutral or as a representative of one side. In contrast, an economic analysis would suggest that if the buyer has a reservation price, and the seller has a reservation price (net of paying the agent), then payment to the agent must come out of the surplus. Thus, the parties are in a negotiation not only with each other, but also with the agent. This study initiates the empirical examination of the negotiated relationship between the principals and their agent.

To start the investigation of the negotiation relationship between the principal and the agent, it is necessary to confront the counterrational fact that realtors most commonly receive 6% of the sales price of residential real estate. In the large majority of residential transactions, the real estate commission is not negotiated (Jud & Frew, 1986). This outcome is very different from what would be expected given an economic analysis of a three-party negotiation game in which a fixed amount of surplus is available to be divided. While such an analysis yields no equilibrium solution, Nash (1950) would predict that the settlement would maximize the product of the surpluses of the three parties. This occurs when the total surplus is equally divided among the parties. Thus, holding sales price constant, it is reasonable to expect agent commission rate to decrease with a decrease in the size of the bargaining zone. Why is actual behavior so different from this expectation?

One powerful explanation of the stability of the 6% commission is the institutionalized nature of this commission rate. Institutionalization theory (DiMaggio & Powell, 1983; Zucker, 1977) argues that action can be perpetuated because acts take on a "taken-for-granted" nature. According to Meyer and Rowan (1977), institutionalization involves the processes by which social roles, obligations, or actualities come to take on a rule-like status in social thought and action. For highly institutionalized acts, it is sufficient for one person simply to tell another this is the way things are done (Zucker, 1977). The institutionalized nature of the 6% fee or "the standard 6," as it is referred to by real estate agents, is a carryover from the days when fees were set by local real estate boards (Allen, 1990). It is now illegal for these fees to be fixed, but the norm continues to guide agent behavior. "While boards no longer published a fee schedule that could be enforced, members [of real estate boards] continued to act as if a schedule were fixed" (Allen, 1990). Economic theory argues that behavior will only continue to the extent it is in the interest of the parties involved. Agents are expected to provide specific facts and advice to the buyers and sellers to aid them in their decision making. How much is this assistance worth? The only parties with a continuing interest in answering this question are the agents, and it is in their interest to keep the answer at 6%.

Another possible explanation for the rigidity of the 6% commission comes from the psychological literature on anchoring and adjustment (Slovic & Lichtenstein, 1971; Tversky & Kahneman, 1974). Given that the 6% fee has been at least partially institutionalized, an interesting question becomes what adjustment would be made if the parties recognized the 6% as a high figure in a specific transaction and negotiated an adjustment to the commission rate. Slovic and Lichtenstein (1971) have shown that if people use an anchor (e.g., 6%), and make an adjustment from that anchor, the adjustment will be insufficient in comparison to the decision that would have been made without the anchor, even if the party(s) knows the anchor was (completely) irrelevant (Bazerman, 1990). Thus, to the extent the parties anchor on 6% they will end up closer to that figure than they would have had they started with a blank slate.

Finally, Staw, Sandelands, and Dutton (1981) argue that under scarcity (e.g., insufficient joint surplus for the deal to be completed), individuals within a system are likely to become more rigid in their behavior, and less open to novel alternatives. To the extent that reducing the agent's commission is thought of as something out of the ordinary, Staw et al. (1981) would suggest that scarcity provides a barrier to creativity that may prevent the flexibility of adjusting the commission.

Despite the relevance of these behavioral explanations for the rigidity of the 6% commission, there are stories of real estate agents cutting their commissions. The most common reason given for this behavior is to "close the deal" – the buyer and seller are a couple thousand off, and the agent feels that if he/she does not yield on commission, the deal will fall through. Thus, the pressure of a reduced bargaining zone may lead one of the three parties involved – the buyer whose budget is restricted, the seller whose alternative is slightly less desirable, or the agent who is paid only if a sale is made – to initiate discussion of a reduced commission. This argues that the 6% commission rate is most likely to be adjusted when it is economically necessary in order for an agreement to be reached. Yet, even under these conditions, we expect the adjustment will be less than suggested by a Nash (1950) solution. Thus, as the size of the bargaining zone decreases, the size of the commission is expected to decrease, but not to the same degree as the surplus of the parties decreases.

Based upon the arguments provided above, the following hypotheses are proposed:

H1: The percentage of the sales price that the agent receives will be lower when the bargaining zone is smaller.

H2: The percentage of the total surplus that the agent receives will be higher when the bargaining zone is smaller.

### Methods

*Subjects.* All 93 subjects were MBA students at a large midwestern university. Their average age was 26. The subjects had an average of 3.6 years of work experience. The exercise was part of the course requirements.

*Design.* The design simulated three different property transactions (house, townhouse, and condo) crossed with two different size bargaining zones ($20,000 or $10,000). These two factors were fully crossed in a $3 \times 2$ design, creating six different negotiation contexts.

*Description of Negotiation Simulations.* Three different simulations were used, to allow for multiple use of the same subjects. The three were similar to the cases used in Study 1, with the modifications listed below. While the anchor was a manipulation in Study 1, in this study the anchor was a constant and always set equal to the middle of the bargaining zone. One case, "house," had an asking price of $235,900, with the midpoint of the bargaining zone equal to $220,000 (also the imputed value of the comparison houses). In the $20,000 zone condition, the buyer's reservation price was set at $230,000, and the seller's reservation price set at $210,000. In the $10,000 zone condition, the buyer's reservation price was set at $225,000, and the seller's reservation price set at $215,000.

The second case, "townhouse," had an asking price of $195,000, with the midpoint of the bargaining zone equal to $180,000 (also the imputed value of the comparison houses). In the $20,000 zone condition, the buyer's reservation price was set at $190,000, and the seller's reservation price set at $170,000. In the $10,000 zone condition, the buyer's reservation price was set at $185,000, and the seller's reservation price set at $175,000. The third case, "condo," had an asking price of $139,500, with the midpoint of the bargaining zone equal to $128,000 (also the imputed value of the comparison houses). In the $20,000 zone condition, the buyer's reservation price was set at $138,000, and the seller's reservation price set at $118,000. In the $10,000 zone condition, the buyer's reservation price was set at $133,000, and the seller's reservation price set at $123,000.

*Assignment of Participants to Roles.* Assignment was made in the same manner as in Study 1, except that Agent was the only third-party role assigned. The "agent" was assigned the role of helping the parties reach agreement, and was the only means by which the buyer and seller could communicate. Participants were told that the buyer and the seller were not to meet directly with each other at any point in the negotiation – they were allowed to meet only with the agent. All parties were told that when a sale is made, it is normal for the seller to pay the agent 6% of the transaction price of the property as commission. However, the subjects were also told the rate of 6% was not legally binding and was negotiable. If no sale were consummated, the agents received no commission.

The participants were told how each party would be evaluated. The *buyer's net surplus* was the amount of the purchase price under his/her reservation price. The *seller's net surplus* was the amount over his/her reservation price, minus the realtor commission. The agent's commission thus reduces the size of the bargaining zone. The *agent's net surplus* was the commission received.

*Procedure.* Explanation of the simulation to each class of 30 or 33 subjects took about 15 min. Participants were told they had 7 days outside of class to conduct their three negotiations. Failure to reach agreement within the designated time period was defined as an impasse. All other procedures were the same as in Study 1. (A complete set of materials is available from the authors.)

### Results

The means for the commission rate and the percentage of the surplus received by the agent in each of the six conditions are shown in Table 26.3. The hypotheses were analyzed formally using two regression equations ($n = 93$)

Table 26.3. *Mean Commission Percentages (Standard Deviations) by Condition*

| | Agent Commission as Percentage of Sales Price | | |
| --- | --- | --- | --- |
| | *House** | *Townhouse** | *Condo** |
| $10,000 bargaining zone | 1.8838 (.929) | 2.2947 (.589) | 3.1650 (1.255) |
| $20,000 bargaining zone | 3.7279 (1.604) | 4.3000 (1.198) | 4.6980 (1.719) |
| | Agent Commission as Percentage of Total Surplus | | |
| | *House* | *Townhouse* | *Condo* |
| $10,000 bargaining zone | .4017 (.180) | .4175 (.109) | .4092 (.164) |
| $20,000 bargaining zone | .3938 (.169) | .3950 (.112) | .3191 (.104) |

* $p < .01$.

which tested for the impact of bargaining zone, while controlling for type of property sold. Two dummy variables were used to represent the three different properties. The results of this regression equation support the hypothesis that agent commission, when measured as a percentage of the sales price of the property, will be lower when the bargaining zone is smaller ($t = 6.797, p < .001$). This effect was also significant for each of the three properties when analyzed separately (see Table 26.3).

The second hypothesis, that agent commission, when expressed as a percentage of total surplus available to the three parties, will be higher when the bargaining zone is smaller, was not supported. While effects were in the predicted direction, they were not significant.

### Discussion

Our second study examined the nature of the negotiated relationship between an agent and the parties. We found reducing the size of the bargaining zone led to a reduced commission, when commission was expressed as percentage of transaction price. But, as the bargaining zone shrinks, agent commission is not reduced proportionately. Thus, commission expressed as percentage of total surplus actually increased as the zone decreased, though not significantly.

The effects of institutionalization may not have been strong enough to keep the agent's commission as high as possible. As the zone shrinks, agents are forced to reduce their commissions, but strong norms pulling agent fees to 6% serve as an anchor when the agent is forced to negotiate his/her commission. These norms operate in the real estate market, but are not so influential in a simulated setting.

Another explanation of why the agents were willing to negotiate away more of their commission than we expected may result from the lack of extra information brought to the negotiation solely by the agent. In a real estate transaction, the agent often has access to information that is difficult for the buyer or seller to obtain. While in many markets this information is available to the public, buyers and sellers may not be aware of this or may be unwilling to invest the time required to collect it. Thus, agents provide a resource, information, for which buyers and sellers are willing to pay. In this study, all information was provided to all parties. The differential knowledge of the agent was taken out of the negotiation and the justification for retaining a 6% commission was reduced.

### General Discussion

This study has several objectives: to open up a new agenda for empirical research in negotiation; to begin to understand the unique nature of the *negotiated* relationship between third parties and their respective principals; to assess one form of agency costs in buyer–seller relationships; and to consider the impact of third parties, such as agents and mediators, on the outcomes of negotiation. While these initial studies are far from conclusive, they do offer a number of suggestions for future research attention. First, it is important to realize that any surplus received by an agent must come from somewhere, i.e., from the parties. The specific structure of a third party's incentive contract can make it more, rather than less, difficult for buyers and sellers to reach an agreement. Second, the results suggest that the payment to a third party is made by all the parties in the negotiation (i.e., the buyer and the seller), not just by the party making the formal payment (the seller). Third, there is some indication that mediators do reduce the likelihood of impasse, although this result was not significant. Finally, the results from the second study support the notion that the agent should be thought of as a negotiator with his/her own self-interest. While these results support the view of the principal–agent relationship as discussed in the agency theory literature (Ross, 1973), we believe they are contrary to conventional wisdom concerning the role of the agent, where he/she is perceived as a member of one negotiation side.

This line of research also has theoretical and empirical implications for both the agency and transaction cost literatures (Williamson, 1975), which are part of what is increasingly referred to as the field of "organizational economics" (Barney & Ouchi, 1986). Theoretically, the agency literature typically studies the divergence of interests between principals and agents, but not the role of agents as third parties in buyer–seller relationships. Transaction cost theory, on the other hand, is centrally concerned with the structure of buyer–seller relationships, but not with the possibility that the third parties entrusted to govern such relationships may themselves be self-interested. This study examines buyer–seller relationships with self-interested third parties, a "hybrid" situation relevant to agency and transaction cost theory.

Empirically, the agency and transaction cost literatures are heavily reliant on the notion of agency and transaction costs, respectively, but these costs have typically been difficult to measure directly using field and archival data. This study shows how an experimental design enables the direct observation and measurement of one type of agency or transaction costs in buyer–seller relationships.

Future research should also examine the impact of agents in a world where the commission rate has a higher level of institutionalized acceptance. Other important questions to be addressed include the impact of third parties on the integrativeness of agreements, and the impact of giving information to a third party on the nature of the resulting agreement. We also need to examine contexts in which more than one agent is involved. Finally, we need to learn more about the process involved in negotiations through agents.

This chapter fits into a more general research theme of extending the boundaries of the nature of negotiation research. The vast majority of existing negotiation research focuses on two-party negotiation. Only recently have groups been conceptualized as negotiations (Brett & Rognes, 1986; Bazerman, Mannix, & Thompson, 1988). We believe a negotiation perspective is likely to have a significantly greater impact if we expand our focus to include group behavior, third parties, negotiation in markets, and a variety of other more complex social contexts.

### References

Allen, J. L. (1990). "There was some carryover" of a set fee schedule. *Chicago Tribune.* March 18, 1990, Section 16, 2H.

Arrow, K. J. A. (1985). Agency costs versus fiduciary duties. In J. W. Pratt & R. J. Zeckhauser (Eds.), *Principals and agents: The structure of business.* Boston, MA: Harvard Business School Press.

Barney, J. B., & Ouchi, W. G. (1986). *Organizational economics.* San Francisco: Jossey-Bass.

Bartunek, J. M., Benton, A. A., & Keys, C. B. (1975). Third party intervention and the bargaining behavior of group representatives. *Journal of Conflict Resolution*, 19, 532–557.

Bazerman, M. H. (1990). *Judgement in managerial decision making* (2nd ed.). New York: Wiley.

Bazerman, M. H., Lewicki, J. J., & Sheppard, B. H. (1991). *Research on negotiation in organizations.* Greenwich, CT: JAI Press.

Bazerman, M., Mannix, H. E., & Thompson, L. (1988). Groups as mixed-motive negotiations. In E. J. Lawler and B. Markovsky (Eds.), *Advances in group processes: Theory and Research*, 5. Greenwich, CT: JAI Press.

Brett, J., & Rognes, J. (1986). Intergroup relations in organizations: A negotiations perspective. In P. S. Goodman (Ed.), *Designing effective work groups.* San Francisco: Jossey-Bass.

Carnevale, P. J., & Conlon, D. (1987). Time pressure and mediator strategy in a simulated organizational dispute. *Organizational Behavior and Human Decision Processes*, 40, 111–133.

Carnevale, P. J., Lim, R. G., & McLaughlin, M. E. (1989). Contingent mediator behavior and its effectiveness. In K. Kressel & D. G. Pruitt (Eds.), *Mediation research: The process and effectiveness of third party intervention*. San Francisco: Jossey-Bass.

DiMaggio, P. J., & Powell, W. W. (1983). The iron cage revisited: Institutional isomorphism and collective rationality in organizational fields. *American Sociological Review*, 48, 147–160.

Eisenhardt, K. (1989). Agency theory: An assessment and review. *Academy of Management Review*, 14, 57–74.

Fisher, R., & Ury, W. (1981). *Getting to yes*. Boston: Houghton-Mifflin.

Goldberg, S. B., Green, E. D., & Sander, F. A. E. (1985). *Dispute resolution*. Boston: Little, Brown.

Grigsby, D. W., & Bigoness, W. J. (1982). Effects of mediation and alternative forms of arbitration on bargaining behavior: A laboratory study. *Journal of Applied Psychology*, 67, 549–554.

Hopper, R. (1976). *Human message systems*. New York: Harper & Row.

Jensen, M. C., & Meckling, W. H. (1976). Theory of the firm: Managerial behavior, agency costs, and ownership structure. *Journal of Financial Economics*, 3, 305–350.

Johnson, D. F., & Pruitt, D. G. (1972). Preintervention effects of mediation versus arbitration. *Journal of Applied Psychology*, 56, 1–10.

Jud, D. G., & Frew, J. (1986). Real estate brokers, housing prices and the demand for housing. *Urban Studies*, 23, 21–31.

Kolb, D. M. (1983). *The mediators*. Cambridge, MA: MIT Press.

Kolb, D. M., & Rubin, J. Z. (1991). In M. H. Bazerman, R. J. Lewicki, & B. H. Sheppard (Eds.), *Research in negotiation in organizations*. Greenwich, CT: JAI Press.

Mannix, E. A., Thompson, L. L., & Bazerman, M. H. (1989). Small group negotiation. *Journal of Applied Psychology*, 74, 508–517.

McGillicuddy, N. B., Welton, G. L., & Pruitt, D. G. (1987). Third party intervention: A field experiment comparing three different models. *Journal of Personality and Social Psychology*, 53, 104–112.

Meyer, J. W., & Rowan, B. (1977). Institutionalized organizations: Formal structure as myth and ceremony. *American Journal of Sociology*, 83, 340–363.

Nash, J. F. (1950). The bargaining problem. *Econometrica*, 18, 155–162.

Neale, M. A., & Bazerman, M. H. (1983). The role of perspective-taking ability in negotiating under different forms of arbitration. *Industrial and Labor Relations Review*, 36, 378–388.

Neale, M. A., & Bazerman, M. H. (1991). *Negotiator cognition and rationality*. In press.

Notz, W. W., & Starke, F. A. (1978). The impact of final offer vs. conventional arbitration on the aspirations and behaviors of bargainers. *Administrative Science Quarterly*, 23, 189–203.

Raiffa, H. (1982). *The art and science of negotiation*. Cambridge, MA: Harvard Univ. Press.

Roehl, J. A., & Cook, R. F. (1989). Mediation in interpersonal disputes: Effectiveness and limitations. In K. Kressel & D. G. Pruitt (Eds.), *Mediation research: The process and effectiveness of third party intervention*. San Francisco: Jossey-Bass.

Ross, S. (1973). The economic theory of agency: The principal's problem. *American Economic Review*, 63, 134–139.

Rubin, J. Z., & Sander, F. E. A. (1988). When should we use agents: Direct vs. representative negotiation. *Negotiation Journal*, 4, 395–401.

Sheppard, B. H. (1983). Managers as inquisitors: Some lessons from the law. In M. H.

Bazerman, R. J. Lewicki, & B. H. Sheppard (Eds.), *Research in negotiation in organizations*. Greenwich, CT: JAI Press.

Sheppard, B. H. (1984). Third party conflict intervention: A procedural framework. *Research in Organizational Behavior, 6*, 141–190.

Slovic, P., & Lichtenstein, S. (1971). Comparison of Bayesian and regression approaches to the study of information processing in judgment. *Organization Behavior and Human Performance, 6*, 649–744.

Staw, B. M., Sandelands, L., & Dutton, J. (1981). Threat rigidity effects in organization behavior. *Administrative Science Quarterly, 26*, 501–524.

Susskind, L., & Cruikshank, J. (1987). *Breaking the impasse: Consensual approaches to resolving public disputes*. New York: Basic Books.

Tversky, A., & Kahneman, D. (1974). Judgement under uncertainty: Heuristics and biases. *Science, 185*, 1124–1131.

Walton, R. E., & McKersie, R. B. (1965). *A behavioral theory of labor negotiations: An analysis of social interaction system*. New York: McGraw-Hill.

Williamson, O. E. (1975). *Markets and hierarchies: Analysis and antitrust implications*. New York: The Free Press.

Zajac, E. J. (1990). CEO selection, succession, compensation and firm performance: A theoretical integration and empirical analysis. *Strategic Management Journal, 11*, 217–230.

Zucker, L. G. (1977). The role of institutionalization in cultural persistence. *American Sociological Review, 42*, 726–743.

# Part IX

# Risk

Ideas of risk, in both the everyday and technical senses, pervade efforts to apply decision thinking to practical problems. A certain group is "at risk" for some disease; nuclear power involves "risk" of catastrophic accident; drivers who use seat belts or bikers who wear helmets reduce their "risks" of serious injury. There is an active professional speciality of "risk assessment," researchers study people's "risk perception" of the dangers associated with radon or smoking, and "risk communication" specialists work on methods for informing them more accurately.

The term *risk* is used in several different ways in these literatures, and it may be helpful to clarify some of the different usages. The general idea is the lay or dictionary definition: a situation of risk presents some chance of injury, damage or loss, a hazard or dangerous chance. There are thus two elements: uncertainty of outcome, and loss. (No one speaks of the "risk" of winning the lottery.) To an investment analyst, one stock is "riskier" than another if its price varies more from day to day (which may or may not correspond to the layperson's concern with "risk of losing one's money"). One technical usage can be set aside right away. Decision theorists commonly distinguish three sorts of decision situations, based on how predictable beforehand the results of one's actions are. If the results can be predicted for sure, the situation is called "decision under certainty"; some consumer choices might approximate this. If the outcomes are unsure but one knows their probability, as in a lottery, the situation is referred to as one of "risk." If one knows only the possible outcomes, with no knowledge of their probabilities, the situation is referred to as "decision under uncertainty." Different decision strategies are appropriate for each. For example, expectation rules such as SEU may be appropriate under risk, while possibility rules such as minimax might be better under uncertainty.

It is generally clear if an author is using "risk" in this special sense. More confusion arises when authors use the phrase "risk perception," as in studies of what technologies or threats people see as more or less risky. Some authors seem to mean "perception of *a* risk" in a situation, as one might perceive an injustice, a joke, or a lesson. Different people would be expected to perceive different things. Other authors seem to use the phrase to mean "perception of *the* risk," with the implication that there really is some objective degree of risk in the situation, a "right answer," as in perceptions of distance or speed. For these authors the study of risk perception naturally focuses on how accurate (or, more commonly, inaccurate) risk perceptions are, while their colleagues in risk communication study how accuracy could be improved. The two groups react quite differently to such puzzles as the lay public's perception that nuclear power is a highly risky technology while experts think of it as low risk (see Slovic, Chapter 29, this volume). The first group tends to see the experts as in error, pursuing an overly narrow view of what constitutes risk. The second group sees the lay public as in error, needing more information, persuasion, or education. The gap is more than mere academic bickering: As Slovic notes, a difference of this sort as to the perceived riskiness of nuclear waste disposal seems quite likely to bring the nuclear power industry to a halt.

Of the following chapters, probably Zeckhauser and Viscusi (Chapter 27) come closest to the objectivist view of risk and to normative statements as to how it should be dealt with. (They are, after all, economists!) To these authors human fallibility in risk assessment and reduction is central. We overestimate some risks, underestimate others, pay vastly more for reducing some risks than others, treat risks differently when they flow from actions rather than inactions, and so on. As a nation we lack an overall risk management system, and thus end up with disjointed policies that implicitly value the saving of a single life thousands of times more highly in one context than another. Human mistakes and misdeeds (e.g., in our eating and driving habits) are the source of much of our avoidable risk.

Fischhoff, Bostrom, and Quadrel (Chapter 28), take a middle road. People need to understand the risks as well as the benefits of their choices. They also need to understand their limits as risk assessors, and the limits on the expert advice they are offered. Fischhoff et al. read the evidence as giving grounds for concern as to our abilities to assess risk. We are overly affected by the familiar litany of cognitive heuristics and biases (anchoring, availability, overconfidence, and the like); we are insensitive to the rate at which risk increases with repeated exposures. An especially interesting section of this chapter sketches a new approach to the expert–layperson problem. Rather than simply note the disparity in risk estimates, Fischhoff et al. summarize a series of studies that examined the mental models of each group and explored their differences. This approach suggests novel ways of improving communication between experts and lay people.

The final chapter, by Slovic (Chapter 29), picks up the key role of trust between the lay and expert groups (see also Lopes, 1991). Slovic notes the puzzle that, despite the real lowering of many risks over the past 20 years, many people feel more exposed to hazards than they ever were. They also feel disinclined to trust risk analysts, risk communication, or the technology of risk assessment itself. Slovic traces the psychological, political, and institutional context of this growing distrust, using the nuclear power industry as his example. As he notes, echoing the words of Abraham Lincoln, trust is asymmetric: It takes a long string of examples to build it up, and only one counterexample to tear it down. Once torn down, as the public's seems to be in the expert assessments of the risks of nuclear waste disposal, it is difficult to see just how it can be rebuilt.

### References

Lopes, L. L. (1991). Risk perception and the perceived public. In D. W. Bromley (Ed.), *The social response to environmental risk* (pp. 57–74). Boston: Kluwer.

# 27   Risk within Reason

*Richard J. Zeckhauser and W. Kip Viscusi*

Society's system for managing risks to life and limb is deeply flawed. We overreact to some risks and virtually ignore others. Often too much weight is placed on risks of low probability but high salience (such as those posed by trace carcinogens or terrorist action); risks of commission rather than omission; and risks, such as those associated with frontier technologies, whose magnitude is difficult to estimate. Too little effort is spent ameliorating voluntary risks, such as those involving automobiles and diet. When the bearers of risk do not share in the costs of reduction, moreover, extravagance is likely.

Part of the problem is that we rely on a mix of individual, corporate, and government decision to respond to risk. Our traditional coordinating mechanisms – markets and government action – are crippled by inadequate information, costly decision-making processes, and the need to accommodate citizens' misperceptions, sometimes arising from imbalances in media attention.

Risk can never be entirely eliminated from life, and reductions come at a price (in dollars, forgone pleasures, or both). Our current muddled approach makes it difficult to reach wise, well-informed decisions as to the preferred balance of risk and cost. Some large risks we ignore; some small ones we regulate stringently. Worse, our overreaction to very small risks impedes the kind of technological progress that has historically brought dramatic improvements in both health and material well-being. In addition, we are likely to misdirect our efforts, for example, by focusing on risks that command attention in the political process, such as newly identified carcinogens, rather than those where the greatest gains in well-being are available, such as individual life-style choices (1).

Our regulatory efforts focus too much on equipment and physical processes, too little on human error and venality. We may set stringent emission standards, which impose high costs per unit of environmental quality gained, yet ignore the haphazard operation of nuclear weapons plants.

Evidently willing to expend substantial resources to reduce risk, our society seems reluctant to look closely at the bargains it has struck. Unless we correct imbalances in the cost effectiveness of our risk management policies, we will continue to pay more than we should for health gains that are less than we could achieve.

The success of risk management policies should be judged in terms of their effect on expected utility, the only well-developed prescriptive framework for choice under uncertainty. This method assigns each potential outcome a value (utility) on a cardinal scale, weights these values by their probability of occurrence, and then adds them together to produce an expected utility, a summary measure of the attractiveness of an action (2). Although in practice the choices made by human beings under uncertainty frequently do not conform to the prescriptions of expected-utility theory, given time to reflect most people would accept the theory's axioms.

The formulation of risk policy should then begin by asking what outcomes would result from well-functioning market processes if individuals behaved so as to maximize their own expected utility. What level of adverse side effects from pharmaceuticals would be acceptable if we knew the risk and could take the time and effort to make sound decisions?

To provide the best possible basis for policy decisions, our hypothetical market should be open to future generations. If our great-grandchildren could compensate the present generation for preserving resources and the environment, what environmental decisions would we make today? Such a thought experiment should guide our efforts to bequeath posterity an efficient mix of technological capabilities, environmental quality, and cultural attainments.

### Human Fallibility in Responses to Risks

Decisions involving risks illustrate the limits of human rationality, as a substantial literature documents (3–6). Perhaps the most fundamental problem is that individuals have great difficulty comprehending extremely low-probability events, such as differentiating a risk of $10^{-7}$ from $10^{-5}$, a risk 100 times as large. When assessing such risks, even scientists may not appreciate how much greater the payoff is that comes from addressing the larger probability.

The numerous decision-making problems that arise with respect to small probabilities are individually of little consequence. Expected welfare loss from any single error may well be negligible. Aggregated, however, low-probability events make up a large part of an individual's risk level. Even truly substantial risks, such as the chance of death from a stroke (roughly 1 in 2,000 annually averaged over the population), are usually influenced by a myriad of decisions, each of which has only a small probabilistic impact on our longevity. Systematic errors in these decisions might have an enormous cumulative effect.

*Mistakes in Estimation.* Whereas people generally overestimate the likelihood of low-probability events (death by tornado), they underestimate higher risk levels (heart disease or stroke) (5). We are particularly likely to overestimate previously unrecognized risks in the aftermath of an unfavorable outcome (6). Such perceptional biases account for the emotional public response to such events as Three Mile Island or occasional incidents of deliberate poisoning of foodstuffs or medicines.

Risk perceptions may also be affected by the visibility of a risk, by fear associated with it, and by the extent to which individuals believe they can exercise control over it (3, 5). Consider the greenhouse effect, for example: although global warming is a prime concern of the Environmental Protection Agency (EPA), it ranks only 23rd among the U.S. public's environmental concerns (7). The high risk of automobile fatality – car accidents kill 1 in 5,000 Americans each year (8) – might perhaps be reduced significantly if drivers, informed with a more realistic sense of what they can and cannot do to control the risk, drank less alcohol and wore seat belts more often.

Because experience tells us little about low-probability risks, we resort to correlated indicators that pose less serious problems. Record high temperatures of 1988, for example, may or may not have been signals of an impending greenhouse effect (9). Unfortunately, such signals are seldom as timely or clear-cut as canaries in the coal mine. Adverse events may occur without a warning; witness the San Francisco earthquake. When a warning does sound, moreover, it may bear little relation to the magnitude, likelihood, or nature of a problem. Proper forest management, for example, should not be contingent on a dramatic fire, such as the one in Yellowstone National Park.

*Distortions in Monetary Valuation.* Economic valuations are distorted by misweighting of risks. From an expected-utility perspective, for example, individuals generally place too high a value on preventing increases in a risk from its current level [the so-called status quo bias or reference risk effect (10, 11)]. Such biases are reflected in government policy. Products causing rare forms of cancer especially arouse public concern; new technologies are often regulated much more strictly than old technologies and familiar risks (12). Although man-made carcinogens are carefully controlled, policy often tolerates much higher levels of natural carcinogens. Because of this imbalance, we pay more dollars for our products and end up with greater risks to our lives.

Studies of consumers show that many individuals would be willing to pay a premium for the assured elimination of a risk (11), as the Russian roulette problem illustrates. Consider two alternative scenarios for a forced round of play. In the first, you have the option to purchase and remove one bullet from a gun that has three bullets in its six chambers. How much would you pay for this reduction in risk? (Assume you are unmarried, with no children.) In the second situation, the gun has only a single bullet. How much would you pay to buy back this bullet? From an economic standpoint, you should always be willing to pay at least as much and typically more in the first situation since there is some chance you will be killed by one of the remaining bullets, in which case money is worthless (or worth less) (13). However, experiments find respondents are typically willing to pay more when a single bullet is in the gun, because its removal will ensure survival (11, 13, 14).

The Chilean grape scare provides an example of a risk that does not lend itself to statistical estimation or scientific assessment. Neither the government nor consumers could estimate how much consumers' risk was increased by the discovery of traces of cyanide in two Chilean grapes in Philadelphia (15). When precise scientific judgments concerning probabilities are elusive, concerns about regret (16) are likely to be significant. If societal norms were flouted, regret would be greater still. (Few of us would leave a baby sleeping alone in a house while we drove off on a 10-minute errand, even though car-crash risks are much greater than home risks.) With hindsight, one is frequently able to identify why an individual or society should have known certain risk estimates were far too low, as we learned when riots followed Hurricane Hugo and a highway collapsed during the San Francisco earthquake. Regret is less of an issue when consequences cannot be tied back to a particular risk exposure or a particular decision maker.

The valuation of a risk is likely to depend on how the risk is generated. We tolerate voluntarily assumed risks more than those over which we have no control, such as environmental hazards. We regard acts of commission as much more serious than acts of omission. In pharmaceutical screening, for example, the Food and Drug Administration (FDA) worries more about introducing harmful new drugs than about missing opportunities for risk reduction offered by new pharmaceutical products (17).

*Agency Dilemmas.* Problems of risk perception and valuation may become entangled with so-called agency problems. What rules apply when one individual or organization (the agent) makes risk decisions on behalf of another (the principal)? Should the agent replicate shortcomings in the principal's decision-making capabilities? Suppose there is 1 chance in 10,000 that a drug will have adverse consequences as severe as those of thalidomide. If the drug offers significant health benefits, it may be wise for society to permit even this high risk. Approving the drug, moreover, might generate information useful in revising the original risk assessment, so that the decision can later be reversed or amplified if appropriate. Yet in practice, the FDA (society's agent) would probably not make such a decision, because of its bias against accepting new risks (17).

Society's pattern of lopsided trade-offs between errors of omission and commission persists for at least two reasons. First, apart from people's levels of risk, their consumption of information is relevant. When a federal agency demonstrates that it will not take chances with individual health, that reassurance alone enhances individual welfare. Conversely, a perception that the government tolerates risks to the public might be more damaging than the risks themselves. Second, it is easier to observe the costs of bad drugs that are approved than to assess the forgone benefits of good drugs that were not introduced. [However, potential beneficiaries, such as the users of saccharin and people with acquired immunodeficiency syndrome (AIDS), sometimes put substantial pressure on the FDA to compromise normally stringent procedures for approving food additives and drugs (18, 19)].

How should we proceed once we admit that individuals do not correctly react to many risks? We might ask the government to make many more decisions. It is not clear, however, that the government is well equipped to compute certain risks accurately or to make sensible decisions once that information is obtained. Alternatively, we could shift decision-making authority to those best qualified to make particular kinds of choices. Here, however, the problem arises that the preferences of those making a decision might not be the same as those affected by it. A third possibility would be to develop processes enabling both agents and principals to participate in risk-related decisions, but there is little evidence that such processes would produce convergence. Finally, we might try to improve individuals' decision-making skills by providing them, for example, with expert-certified information, much as accounting firms verify the accuracy of reported financial data.

*The Informational Approach.* Society's objective should be to foster informed consumer choice. With respect to cigarette smoking, for example, this may not be the same thing as seeking a smoke-free society. (Note that research linking aflatoxin and cancer risks (20) has not moved the Surgeon General to call for a peanut butter-free society.) Politically, of course, the passive smoking concern may be a trump card, so that the actual magnitude of the risk imposed on others becomes irrelevant.

Hazard warnings are often used to convey risk information. Congress has mandated labels for cigarettes, artificial sweeteners, and alcoholic beverages. Federal agencies impose labeling requirements for consumer products, workplace risks, and pesticides. Informational efforts work in conjunction with market forces rather than attempting to supersede them.

Individuals may have difficulty processing risk information, however (6). Overambitious information efforts may outstrip decision-making capabilities (for example, California Proposition 65 (21), which requires warnings for products that expose consumers to annual risks of cancer of 1 in 7 million). The dangers are underreaction, overreaction, and nonreaction – a complete dismissal of the risk information effort. Sound decisions are unlikely to result. Indeed, the supposition of informed consent is called into question.

More general human cognitive limitations also work against detailed informational efforts. If a warning label contains more than a handful of items, or if warnings proliferate, problems of information overload arise (6).

In a democratic society one should hesitate to override the legitimate preferences of segments of the population, taking care not to dismiss diversity of taste as mere nonrational choice (22). Where there is broad consensus on a rational course of action, however, and either the cost of providing information is high or individuals cannot process the information adequately, mandatory requirements may be preferable to risk information efforts. Laws requiring the use of seat belts are one possible example.

Individuals often fail to interpret risks or value their consequences accurately. Government efforts may escape some of these biases, but are often thrown off course by political pressures and agency losses. The consequence is that our risk portfolio enjoys no legitimacy and satisfies no one. The first step toward a remedy is to develop a broad-based understanding of the nature of risk.

### Reason and Information about Risk

Information on risk is generated through several mechanisms. The most salient source is scientific research, but information can also be gained through experience, and knowledge of such information can be increased by distributing it more widely.

*Risk, Uncertainty, and Ignorance.* It is helpful to distinguish among risk, uncertainty, and ignorance. In the situation of risk, we know the states of the world that may prevail (a flipped coin will show one of two faces) and the precise probability of each state (heads and tails are equally likely). In the case of uncertainty, the precise probabilities are not known. With ignorance, we may not even be able to define what states of the world are possible.

The real world is rife with uncertainty. Even if we can make direct environmental measurements (for example, for atmospheric pollution), interpretation of our observations may be problematic (9). Does an unusually high temperature this year indicate an upward trend, or does it represent random variation around an unchanging mean?

As our technological capabilities grow and economic activity imposes further strains on the environment, we will increasingly find ourselves in situations of ignorance. As we enter apparently benign but uncharted territory, we cannot be confident that if there were threats, we would detect them. Many individual decisions, as well as scientific risk analyses, are afflicted by ignorance (5). California studies of transportation safety in the event of an earthquake, for example, failed to capture the full range of effects that may have led to the highway damage experienced in October 1989 (23). Under conditions of ignorance, the potential for bad societal decisions is particularly great. Conceivably, for example, environmental releases of genetically engineered organisms might alter the current ecological balance in ways we cannot anticipate (24).

Some observers insist that we simply cannot take such risks; others argue for weighing potential benefits the activity might bring against hypothetical disasters. In many areas, fundamental scientific research may shed light on what states of the world may prevail and with what probability. But while we wait, we must decide (if only negatively, by default) on the basis of our limited information whether to deploy experimental drugs that might save lives, innovative organisms that might preserve threatened ecosystems, and controversial technologies such as nuclear power, which reduces the environmental risks from reliance on fossil fuels but creates another class of hazards.

*Learning about Risks.* Information can often be acquired by another party without destroying its productive value for those who already possess it. Small countries, for example, make use of the information generated by large countries, say in drug regulation. Since generating information is often a costly process, there can be a temptation to hold back from making the effort, in the hope of a free ride. Society has designed various mechanisms to promote the development of information: governments support research and development, and they issue patents to protect the private value of information. Information on risk levels, however, cannot be patented. Without government participation, too little will be produced.

Risk information may be generated through experience. An employee can observe the injuries suffered by his co-workers in various jobs. Since the annual odds that a typical worker will experience an injury leading to one lost day of work per year are 3 in 100, even an individual observer will find some basis for making inferences about risk. In many cases, unfortunately, society may never learn how risky a process is, because the process changes before we get enough experience. With an estimated $10^{-7}$ annual risk, it would take years of widespread observation even to learn whether the risk is an order of magnitude higher or lower than we initially believed. In addition, carcinogenic risks are often coupled with long time lags and multiple causal factors, so that precise inferences are not possible.

In such situations it is rarely feasible to await the outcome of direct observations. One strategy would be to look instead for symptoms of high levels of risk. Thus, to assess whether we have underestimated the probability of a nuclear meltdown, we might ascertain whether our component estimates of the probability of a pipe break or human error were substantially too low.

Alternatively, we can look to parallel risk estimates to see whether they have been proven too high or too low, which would tell us about potential biases in risk-estimation technology.

*Resolving Discrepancies.* Discrepancies in probabilistic beliefs provide an economic rationale for betting, and in many important instances, markets for such bets exist. Beliefs about economic prospects are exercised every day in markets for stocks and bonds, foreign exchange, and commodity futures (25). The scientific debate over cold fusion might have been resolved more rapidly if the participants had made similar bets, thus providing information to each other and to bystanders.

Other societal mechanisms are also used to resolve informational differences. Adversary processes such as those of the judicial system, or a science court with an expert on each side, can air opposing viewpoints, but unlike markets, they will not reveal the weight of opinion on the two sides.

*Markets and Their Absence.* Markets generate information used by the world at large, not just by those who trade. Assessments of risk may be adjusted through market processes, but only to the extent that they are reflected in prices. After a disaster in one chemical plant, for example, investors may hastily unload all chemical company stocks. If their implicit valuation of chemical company risk is too pessimistic, more realistic appraisers will find bargains and bid up share prices to an appropriate level. In a more mundane fashion, futures prices tell decision makers the expected future price of oil, and insurance premiums reveal information about assessed levels of risk.

For many important risk decisions, however, market mechanisms are not useful means of conveying risk information. Whereas a poorly operated business will lose its ability to produce for the market, no one will take over decision making for an adult who underinvests in his own health. Poaching on the poor decisions of others – a critical factor ensuring efficient production in economic markets – is simply not possible.

Many informational asymmetries are not resolved successfully through markets. Firms may have better notions of the risks posed by their products or employment than do the individuals who bear these risks, and individual purchasers of insurance policies may be better informed than the firm about the likely claims they will make under these policies. Ideally, everyone would have an incentive to convey information honestly and truthfully. In reality, however, a firm marketing a potentially hazardous good in a world with a capricious tort system may have too much to lose by informing consumers of the risky characteristics of its products.

*Making the Most of Uncertainty.* Information is valuable when it accurately represents the risks posed. For one-time-only decisions, from the standpoint of Bayesian decision making, the mean assessment of the probability of each outcome is all that matters, for that gives the likelihood with which the outcome will be received. For example, suppose that with option I there is a 10% chance that a 0.01 risk is imposed and a 90% chance that no risk is imposed; with option II, there is a 100% chance of a 0.002 risk. Option I should be preferred, since its mean risk $(0.1 \times 0.01 + 0.9 \times 0 = 0.001)$ is lower than for option II (26).

In situations of learning and sequential decision, the precision of the estimate also matters. Paradoxically, imprecisely known probabilities are more favorable. Suppose you must choose between two alternative medical treatments. Therapy A is known to cure half the patients to whom it is applied. Therapy B is an experimental treatment that is equally likely to be either perfect or worthless. In each case, the probability of a cure is 0.5. In cases of single trial, the two options are equally attractive.

With two patients in sequential trials, however, the correct strategy is to pursue B. If the first patient recovers, give the second the same treatment; otherwise switch to A. With this strategy, on average 1.25 of two patients will recover, as opposed to only one out of two if the better known treatment A is chosen at the outset. [This is equivalent to the simplest version of the classic two-armed bandit problem (27).] In any choice between a certain and an uncertain risk of an adverse outcome, if the initial mean value for the probability is the same, the uncertain risk is preferable when learning and adaptive behavior after experience are possible.

Now suppose the experimental treatment is treatment C, which will turn out to be either a total failure or a 90% cure (with both possibilities equally likely). Trying C rather than A will be preferable [offering an expected 1.13 cures (28)], but now the first patient will face unfavorable odds with experimental treatment C (0.45 rather than 0.5 with A). If randomization is not possible, or if the first patient objects, perhaps even after a lottery is conducted, ethical norms would require offering him treatment A. This argument has been illogically extended to suggest that even if experimental treatment C looks better than established treatment A, we may find out it was worse, and we should therefore stick with A. In the medical context, patient interest provides an antidote to such misconceptions. Many experimental technologies are not blessed with such a counterweight.

*Regulatory Efforts and Misplaced Conservatism.* Governmental efforts at developing risk information are not guided by the formal statistical properties of the risk but rather by administrative procedures incorporating various types of "conservatism." Although risk assessment biases may operate in both directions (29), most approved procedures tend to overstate the actual risk (30). In regulating toxic substances, for example, results from the most sensitive animal species are often used, and government agencies such as the EPA routinely focus on the upper end of the 95% confidence interval as the risk level, rather than use the mean of the distribution. A series of such conservative assumptions – for example, on exposure or focusing on the most sensitive humans – can overstate the mean probability of an unfavorable outcome by several orders of magnitude.

If lives are at stake, should we not be conservative when risk estimates are known to be uncertain? In fact, conservatism of this nature is undesirable for three reasons. First, these conservative biases often are not uniform across risks, so that comparative risk judgments may be in error. If we focus on reducing risks for which standard errors are large with respect to their level, then we will save fewer expected lives than if we were guided by the mean of our probability distribution on the risk level. In effect, society will be curtailing the wrong risks, ones that offer less expected health improvement than other available options, for the resources and benefits forgone. The bias that results will cut against new technologies and innovative products. Second, stringent regulation of uncertain risks destroys opportunities for learning, ignoring the lesson of the medical treatment example above. Third and most fundamental, tilting risk assessments in a conservative direction confuses the informational and decision aspects of research about risks (30). A conceptually sound form of conservatism would have the decision maker (not the risk estimator) adjust the weights on the consequences. Adjusting the probabilities amounts to lying to ourselves about what we expect.

## Toward Reasonable Risk Policies

Restrictions on a risky activity, such as exposure limits or restrictions in use, should be based on the relative gains and losses of the activity as compared with its alternatives. In thinking about these trade-offs, one should remember that improvements in mortality and morbidity have come primarily from technological progress and a higher standard of living, not from government regulation or private forbearance (31). A dramatic case in point is that of postwar Japan, where mortality rates have fallen for all age groups. Over the period 1955 to 1975, with a rapid rise in the standard of living, mortality rates for men aged 65 to 69 fell 32% and men aged 25 to 29 had a 64% drop (32). Sustained economic development also seems to be the principal factor in explaining mortality gains in the United States. In contrast, risk regulation policies often provide few major dividends (33).

It is useful to think about risk-averting policy in terms of the rates of trade-off involved, such as the cost per expected life saved. Using this lives-saved standard of value highlights the most effective means of promoting our risk-reduction objective (34). The cost-effectiveness of existing regulations ranges widely, from $200,000 per life saved for airplane cabin fire protection to as much as $132 million per life saved for the 1979 regulation of diethyl stilbestrol (DES) in cattlefeed (35). These wide discrepancies reflect differences among agencies in their risk–cost balancing as well as differences in the character of risk-reducing opportunities. The Federal Aviation Administration has traditionally undervalued lives, looking only at lost earnings, whereas food additive regulations and EPA ambient air quality standards are set without consideration of cost. Elimination of such interagency imbalances would foster better control of risks at less cost.

The fundamental policy question is how far to proceed with lifesaving expenditures. Economists are accused, sometimes with justification, of concluding too quickly that policy choice to promote the saving of lives is merely a question of setting an appropriate price. In contrast, society often is insensitive to the trade-offs that must be made. Indeed, 80% of respondents polled 2 months after the Exxon *Valdez* oil spill indicated a willingness to pursue greater environmental protection "regardless of cost" (36). Ultimately, however, society must decide how much of a resource commitment it will make.

*Learning from Market Outcomes.* Market outcomes provide a natural starting point for obtaining information on how risk reduction policies are valued by their beneficiaries. Health risks are important components of goods and services sold on markets, providing an approach to valuation. Wage differentials for high-risk occupations imply a value of several million dollars for each expected death in the workplace (37).

Market data for many risk outcomes are not available, in part because government policies are largely directed at situations in which the market is believed not to function effectively, or at all. Thus, we have little price information to guide us when deciding, for example, whether society's resources would be better used to reduce rates of birth defects, to promote better nutrition, or to reduce oil spills from tankers.

The policies for which no market reference is possible are the very ones in which current practice may be farthest from the optimum. How much, for example, is it worth to prevent a low-level risk of genetic damage? Such valuation questions have received little careful consideration. When risks are received collectively, as when a sewage treatment plant or prison is placed in a community, little is learned about valuation, since compensation is rarely paid (38). The result has been severe inequity for the unfortunate few, and a democratic society that cannot find places to site essential though noxious facilities.

*Finding Appropriate Roles.* The government's responsibility in generating and using risk information involves structuring a decision process in which individuals and societal institutions work together. Policy choice in a democratic society is, however, complicated by discrepancies between lay and expert opinion. In some situations, the government must decide whether to intervene to overcome apparent limitations on individual choices. But it can be difficult to distinguish irrationality from legitimate citizen preferences. Are people who do not wear seat belts irrational? What about those who wolf down animal fats? Analogous questions arise with respect to policy emphasis. To what extent should the government focus on risks that are of particular concern to its citizens, who may be misinformed and subject to severe errors in perceptions and valuation of risk? Government agencies, subject to political pressures, may find it difficult to set their course in the direction indicated by dispassionate analysis of risks and overall benefits to society.

As science advances and our ability to detect risks improves, our opportunities for influencing risks have proliferated. To date we have proceeded haphazardly, responding to each risk in turn, whether it arises from a new technology, is revealed by scientific investigation, or is catapulted to prominence by media attention. This is not a sensible strategy for making balanced decisions across the entire spectrum of risks.

We need to acknowledge that risks to life and limb are inherent in modern society – indeed in life itself – and that systematic strategies for assessing and responding to risks are overdue. Such strategies will involve significant reassignment of decision-making responsibilities. Individuals should do more for themselves, paying greater attention, for example, to their diets and driving habits. Governments should focus less on microscopic contingencies, and more on human mistakes and misdeeds, the source of far greater risks.

### References and Notes

1   The role of life-style is discussed by V. Fuchs, *Who Shall Live? Health, Economics, and Social Choice* (Basic Books, New York, 1974), particularly pp. 52–54. He assesses the stark differences in mortality between high-living Nevada and sober Utah.

2   Under certainty, a mere ranking of outcomes is sufficient to determine the best choice. Choices under uncertainty require a more refined, cardinal metric to decide, for example: Is A preferred to a 50–50 chance of B or C? In most choice situations the probabilities are neither objectively defined nor easily estimated from data; subjectively estimated probabilities must guide action. L. J. Savage [in *The Foundations of Statistics* (Wiley, New York, 1954)] presents a careful axiomatic approach for combining the concepts of subjective probability and expected utility into a complete prescriptive basis for rational choice.

3   H. Kunreuther et al., *Disaster Insurance Protection* (Wiley, New York, 1978); A. Tversky and D. Kahneman, *Science* 211, 453 (1981); P. Slovic, ibid. 236, 280 (1987).

4   M. J. Machina, *Science* 236, 537 (1987).

5   B. Fischhoff et al., *Acceptable Risk* (Cambridge Univ. Press, Cambridge, 1981).

6   W. K. Viscusi and W. A. Magat, *Learning about Risk: Consumer and Worker Responses to Hazard Information* (Harvard Univ. Press, Cambridge, MA, 1987).

7   R. H. Baxter and F. W. Allen, "Assessing Environmental Risks: The Public's Views Compared with Those of the Environmental Protection Agency," Annual Conference of the American Association for Public Opinion Research, 20 May 1989, cited in the *New York Times*, 22 May 1989, p. B7.

8   National Safety Council, *Accident Facts* (National Safety Council, Chicago, IL, 1985), p. 15.

9   S. H. Schneider, *Science* 243, 771 (1989); L. Roberts, ibid. 242, 1010 (1988); R. A. Kerr, ibid. 243, 891 (1989); For a general assessment of risk and uncertainty, see R. Wilson and E. A. C. Crouch, ibid. 236, 267 (1987).

10  W. Samuelson and R. Zeckhauser, *J. Risk Uncertainty 1*, 7 (1988).

11  W. K. Viscusi, W. A. Magat, and J. Huber [*Rand J. Econ. 18*, 465 (1987)] report an experiment involving household chemicals in which there is a reference risk effect and a premium for certain elimination of the risk.

12  P. Huber, *Regulation 7*, 23 (1983).

13  Let $p$ be the initial probability of survival, $q$ be the increased probability of survival, purchased at cost $Z$, $U(Y)$ be the utility of income if alive, where $U'(Y) > 0$, and $U(\text{Death}) = 0$, independent of income. Assuming expected utility maximization, by definition $Z$ satisfies $pU(Y) + (1 - p)U(\text{Death}) = (p + q)U(Y - Z) + (1 - p - q)U(\text{Death})$, or setting $U(\text{Death}) = 0, pU(Y) = (p + q)U(Y - Z)$. Totally differentiating, one has

$$\frac{dZ}{dp} = \frac{U(Y - Z) - U(Y)}{(p + q)U'(Y - Z)} < 0.$$

14  D. Kahneman and A. Tversky explain a range of anomalies with prospect theory, including this problem, which they attribute to Zeckhauser. They find that where normative theory uses probabilities, humans use decision weights that are not linearly related to them [D. Kahneman and A. Tversky, *Econometrica 47*, 263 (1979)].

15  "Grape scare may blight Chilean's dream," *Wall Street Journal*, 17 March 1989, p. B12.

16  D. Bell, *Operations Res. 30*, 961 (1982).

17  H. Grabowski and J. Vernon, *The Regulation of Pharmaceuticals* (American Enterprise Institute, Washington, DC, 1983).

18  W. Booth, *Science 241*, 1426 (1988).

19  For example, the drug gancyclovir, used to treat a blindness-threatening eye infection suffered by one in four AIDS victims, was approved for use although it had not completed full clinical testing. In "Progress and placebos" [*Wall Street Journal* (29 June, 1989, p. A14)] it was observed that we had some difficulties counterbalancing the political-force approach to drug (and risk) regulation: "Should families of Alzheimer's patients follow the AIDS precedent, busing in about 1,000 of their demented parents to roam the agency's grounds outside of Washington for the benefit of television?"

20  B. N. Ames, R. Magaw, L. S. Gold, *Science 236*, 271 (1987).

21  L. Roberts, ibid. *243*, 306 (1989).

22  The requirement that motorcyclists wear helmets, despite their known preferences, is justified because it copes with a significant financial externality (that is, high medical treatment costs and liability costs imposed on others). It also saves lives at reasonable cost.

23  T. Egan ["Building codes: Designs for last quake, not next," *New York Times*, 22 October 1989, p. 26] reported "'The collapse came as a horrible surprise to us all,' said Robert J. Gore, assistant director of the California Department of Transportation.... The Bay Bridge lost a 250 ton section in the earthquake and Mr. Roberts (chief structural engineer for the State Transportation Department) said the standards for it had proved primitive. The collapse was due to 2 million pounds of force shearing off anchor bolts, he said. 'That's far in excess of what anyone would have calculated,' he said."

24  L. Roberts, *Science 243*, 1134 (1989); ibid., p. 1141.

25  A prominent theory – the so-called efficient markets hypothesis – holds that publicly available information about a firm will be transmitted rapidly into market outcomes as the stock price fully adjusts to reflect the influence of this information [E. Fama,

L. Fisher, M. Jensen, R. Roll, *Int. Econ. Rev. 10*, 1 (1969)]. K. J. Arrow [*Econ. Inquiry 20*, 1 (1982)] cites empirical evidence of futures markets, indicating that the operation of these markets may be imperfect.

26  J. Pratt, H. Raiffa, R. Schlaifer, *Introduction to Statistical Decision Theory* (McGraw-Hill, New York, 1965).

27  D. A. Berry and B. Fristedt, *Bandit Problems: Sequential Allocation of Experiments* (Chapman and Hall, London, 1985).

28  When C is bad, 0.5 person is saved on average. When C is good, 90% of the trials succeed and 1.9 people are saved on average; 10% of the trials fail and after the switch to A, 0.5 persons is saved on average. The expected value is 1.13.

29  L. Roberts, *Science 243*, 1553 (1989); L. B. Lave, ibid. *236*, 291 (1987); L. Lave, Ed., *Quantitative Risk Assessment in Regulation* (Brookings Institution, Washington, DC, 1982).

30  A. Nichols and R. Zeckhauser, *Regulation 10*, 13 (1986).

31  A. Wildavsky, *Searching for Safety* (Transaction Publishers, New Brunswick, NJ, 1988).

32  Data provided by Ministry of Health and Welfare, Japan.

33  The President's Council of Economic Advisers recently concluded that "In many cases, government control of risk is neither efficient nor effective." [*Economic Report of the President* (U.S. Government Printing Office, Washington, DC, 1987), p. 207.]

34  If very good information is available, one can use the more refined measure of cost per quality-adjusted life year (QALY) saved, thus taking into account both the number of person-years gained and their quality [R. J. Zeckhauser and D. S. Shepard, *Law Contemp. Probl. 39*, 5 (1976)].

35  J. F. Morrall, *Regulation 10*, 30 (1986).

36  A New York Times/CBS News Poll asked people if they agreed with the statement "Protecting the environment is so important that requirements and standards cannot be too high, and continuing environmental improvements must be made regardless of cost." Seventy-four percent of the public supported the statement in April 1989, shortly after the Exxon *Valdez* spill, while 80% agreed with it 2 months later. The *Times* concluded that "Public support for greater environmental efforts regardless of cost has soared since the Exxon *Valdez* oil spill in Alaska" ["Concern for environment," *New York Times*, 2 July 1989, p. 18].

37  W. K. Viscusi, *Risk by Choice* (Harvard Univ. Press, Cambridge, MA, 1983).

38  Little heed has been paid to innovative suggestions, such as the proposal of M. O'Hare, L. Bacow, and D. Sanderson [*Facility Siting and Public Opposition* (Van Nostrand Reinhold, New York, 1983)] that communities submit negative bids for accepting noxious facilities.

# 28    Risk Perception and Communication

*Baruch Fischhoff, Ann Bostrom, and*
*Marilyn Jacobs Quadrel*

Many health risks are the result of deliberate decisions by individuals consciously trying to get the best deal possible for themselves and for those important to them. Some of these choices are private ones, such as whether to wear bicycle helmets and seatbelts, whether to read and follow safety warnings, whether to buy and use condoms, and how to select and cook food. Other choices involve societal issues, such as whether to protest the siting of hazardous waste incinerators and half-way houses, whether to vote for fluoridation and "green" candidates, and whether to support sex education in the schools.

In some cases, single choices can have a large effect on health risks (e.g., buying a car with airbags, taking a dangerous job, getting pregnant). In other cases, the effects of individual choices are small, but can accumulate over multiple decisions (e.g., repeatedly ordering broccoli, wearing a seatbelt, using the escort service in parking garages). In still other cases, choices intended to affect health risks do nothing at all or the opposite of what is expected (e.g., responses to baseless cancer scares, adoption of quack treatments).

To make such decisions wisely, individuals need to understand the risks and the benefits associated with alternative courses of action. They also need to understand the limits to their own knowledge and the limits to the advice proffered by various experts. In this chapter, we review the research base for systematically describing a person's degree of understanding about health risk issues. We also consider some fundamental topics in designing and evaluating messages that are intended to improve that understanding. Following convention, we call these pursuits risk perception and risk communication research, respectively. In practice, the beliefs and messages being studied might deal with the benefits accompanying a risk, with the individuals and institutions who manage it, or with the broader issues that it raises (e.g., who gets to decide, how equitably risks and benefits are distributed).

### The Role of Perceptions about Risk Perceptions in Public Health

The fundamental assumption of this chapter is that statements about other people's understanding must be disciplined by systematic data. People can be hurt by inaccuracies in their risk perceptions. They can also be hurt by inaccuracies in what various risk managers believe about those perceptions. Those managers might include physicians, nurses, public health officials, legislators, regulators, and engineers – all of whom have some say in what risks are created, what is communicated about them, and what role laypeople have in determining their fate.

If their understanding is overestimated, then people may be thrust into situations that they are ill-prepared to handle. If their understanding is underestimated, then people may be disenfranchised from decisions that they could and should make. The price of such misperceptions of risk perceptions may be exacted over the long run, as well as in individual decisions. The outcomes of health risk decisions partly determine people's physical and financial resources. The processes of health risk decisions partly determine people's degree of autonomy in managing their own affairs and in shaping their society.

In addition to citing relevant research results, the chapter emphasizes research methods. One conventional reason for doing so is improving access to material that is scattered over specialist literatures or part of the implicit knowledge conveyed in professional training. A second conventional reason is to help readers evaluate the substantive results reported here, by giving a feeling for how they were produced.

A less conventional reason is to make the point that method matters. We are routinely struck by the strong statements made about other people's competence to manage risks, solely on the basis of anecdotal observation. These statements appear directly in pronouncements about, say, why people mistrust various technologies or fail to "eat right." Such claims appear more subtly in the myriad of health advisories, advertisements, and warnings directed at the public without any systematic evaluation. These practices assume that the communicator knows what people currently know, what they need to learn, what they want to hear, and how they will interpret a message.

Even the casual testing of a focus group shows a willingness to have those (smug) assumptions challenged.[1] The research methods presented here show the details needing attention and, conversely, the pitfalls to casual observation. The presentation also shows the limits to such research, in terms of how far current methods can go and how quickly they can get there. In our experience, once the case has been made for conducting behavioral research, it is expected to produce results immediately. That is, of course, a prescription for failure, and for undermining the perceived value of future behavioral research.

## Overview

*Organization.* The following section, Quantitative Assessment, treats the most obvious question about laypeople's risk perceptions: Do they understand how big risks are? It begins with representative results regarding the quality of these judgments, along with some psychological theory regarding reasons for error. It continues with issues in survey design, which focus on how design choices can affect respondents' apparent competence. Some of these methodological issues reveal substantive aspects of lay risk perceptions.

The next section, Qualitative Assessment, shifts the focus from summary judgments to qualitative features of the events to which they are attached. It begins with the barriers to communication created when experts and laypeople unwittingly use terms differently. For example, when experts tell (or ask) people about the risks of drinking and driving, what do people think is meant regarding the kinds and amounts of "drinking" and of "driving"? The section continues by asking how people believe that risks "work," on the basis of which they might generate or evaluate control options.

The next section provides a general process for developing communications about health risks. That process begins with identifying the information to be communicated, based on the descriptive study of what recipients know already and the formal analysis of what they need to know to make informed decisions. The process continues by selecting an appropriate format for presenting that information. It concludes with explicit evaluation of the resulting communication (followed by iteration if the results are wanting). The process is illustrated with examples taken from several case studies, looking at such diverse health risks as those posed by radon, Lyme disease, electromagnetic fields, carotid endarterectomy, and nuclear energy sources in space.

*Exclusions.* We do not address several issues that belong in a full account of their own, including the roles of emotion, individual differences (personality), culture, and social processes in decisions about risk. This set of restrictions suits the chapter's focus on how individuals think about risks. It may also suit a public health perspective, where it is often necessary to "treat" populations (with information) in fairly uniform ways. Access to these missing topics might begin with Refs. 27, 32, 36, 49, 66, 68, 71, 72.

## Quantitative Assessment

### Estimating the Size of Risks

A common presenting symptom in experts' complaints about lay decision making is that "laypeople simply do not realize how small (or large) the risk is." If that were the case, then the mission of risk communication would be conceptually simple (if technically challenging): Transmit credible estimates of how large the risks are (32, 49, 60, 68). Research suggests that lay estimates of risk are, indeed, subject to biases. Rather less evidence clearly implicates these biases in inappropriate risk decisions, or substantiates the idealized notion of people waiting for crisp risk estimates so that they can run well-articulated decision-making models. Such estimates are necessary, but not sufficient, for effective decisions.

In one early attempt to evaluate lay estimates of the size of risks, Lichtenstein et al. (40) asked people to estimate the number of deaths in the United States from 30 causes (e.g. botulism, tornados, motor vehicle accidents).[2] They used two different response modes, thus allowing them to check for the consistency of responses. One task presented pairs of causes; subjects chose the more frequent and then estimated the ratio of frequencies. The second task asked subjects to estimate the number of deaths in an average year; subjects were told the answer for one cause, in order to give an order-of-magnitude feeling (for those without a good idea for how many people live or die in the United States in an average year). The study reached several conclusions that have been borne out by subsequent studies:

*Internal Consistency.* Estimates of relative frequency were quite consistent across response mode. Thus, people seemed to have a moderately well-articulated internal risk scale, which they could express even in unfamiliar response modes.

*Anchoring Bias.* Direct estimates were influenced by the anchor given. Subjects told that 50,000 people die from auto accidents produced estimates two to five times higher than those produced by subjects told that 1000 die from electrocution. Thus, people seem to have less of a feel for absolute frequency, rendering them sensitive to the implicit cues in how questions are asked (51).

*Compression.* Subjects' estimates showed less dispersion than did the statistical estimates. In this case, the result was an overestimation of small frequencies and an underestimation of large ones. However, the anchoring bias suggests that this pattern might have changed with different procedures, which would make the compression of estimates the more fundamental result.

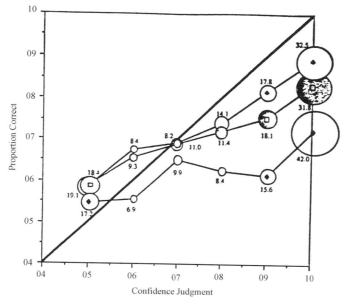

Figure 28.1. Calibration curves for adults (top, white: $N = 45$), not-at-risk teens (middle, dark: $N = 43$), and at-risk teens (bottom, white: $N = 45$). Each point indicates the proportion of correct answers among those in which subjects expressed a particular confidence level; the size of each circle indicates the percentage of answers held with that degree of confidence. (*Source:* 1990, Ref. 52)

*Availability Bias.* At any level of statistical frequency, some causes of death consistently received higher estimates than others. These proved to be causes that are disproportionately visible (e.g., as reported in the news media, as experienced in subjects' lives). This bias seemed to reflect a general tendency to estimate the frequency of events by the ease with which they are remembered or imagined – while failing to realize what a fallible index such availability is (32, 65).

*Miscalibration of Confidence Judgments.* In a subsequent study (21), subjects were asked how confident they were in their ability to choose the more frequent of the paired causes of death. They tended to be overconfident. For example, they had chosen correctly only 75% of the time when they were 90% confident of having done so. This result is a special case of a general tendency to be inadequately sensitive to the extent of one's knowledge (38, 72).

Figure 28.1 shows typical results from such a calibration test. In this case, subjects expressed their confidence in having chosen the correct answer to two-alternative questions regarding health behaviors [e.g., alcohol is (a) a depressant; (b) a stimulant]. The two curves reflect a group of middle-class adults and some of their adolescent children, recruited through school organizations.[3]

### Response Mode Problems

One recurrent obstacle to assessing or improving laypeople's estimates of risk is reliance on verbal quantifiers. It is hard for them to know what experts mean when a risk is described as "very likely" or "rare" – or for experts to evaluate lay perceptions expressed in those terms. Such terms mean different things to different people, and even to the same person in different contexts (e.g., likely to be fatal versus likely to rain, rare disease versus rare Cubs pennant), sometimes even within communities of experts (3, 39, 67).

The Lichtenstein et al. study (40) could observe the patterns reported above because it used an absolute response scale. As noted, it provided anchors to give subjects a feeling for how to answer. Doing so improved performance by drawing responses to the correct range, within which subjects were drawn to higher or lower values depending on the size of the anchor. Although most conclusions were relatively insensitive to these effects, they left no clear answer to the critical question of whether people overestimate or underestimate the risks that they face.

*Perceived Lethality.* A study by Fischhoff and MacGregor (19) provides another example of the dangers of relying on a single response mode to describe behavior. They used four different response modes to ask about the chances of dying, given that one was afflicted with each of various maladies (e.g., how many people die out of each 100,000 who get influenza; how many people died out of the 80 million who caught influenza last year). Again, there was strong internal consistency across response modes, whereas absolute estimates varied over as much as two orders of magnitude. A follow-up study reduced this range by providing an independent basis for eliminating the response mode that produced the most discrepant results (e.g., subjects were least able to remember statistics reported in that format – estimating the number of survivors for each person who succumbed to a problem).

*Perceived Invulnerability.* Estimating the accuracy of risk estimates requires not only an appropriate response mode, but also credible statistical estimates against which responses can be compared. The studies just described asked about population risks in situations where credible statistical estimates were available. Performance might be different (poorer?) for risks whose magnitude is less readily calculated. Furthermore, people may not see these population risks as personally relevant.

As a partial way to avoid these problems, some investigators have asked subjects to judge whether they are more or less at risk than others in more or less similar circumstances (63, 69). They find that most people in most situations see themselves as facing less risk than average others (which could, of course, be true for only half a population). A variety of processes could account for such a bias, including both cognitive ones (e.g., the greater availability of the precautions that one takes) and motivational ones (e.g., wishful thinking). To the extent that this bias exists in the world outside the experiment and interview, such a bias could prompt unwanted risk taking (e.g., because warnings seem more applicable to other people).[4]

### Defining Risk

These studies attempt to measure risk perceptions under the assumption that people define "risk" as the probability of death. Anecdotal observation of scientific practice shows that "risk" means different things in different contexts (8, 23). For some analysts, risk is expected loss of life of expectancy; for others, it is expected probability of premature fatality (with the former definition placing a premium on deaths among the young). Some of the apparent disagreement between experts and laypeople regarding the magnitude of risks in society may be due to differing definitions of risk (20, 62).

*Catastrophic Potential.* One early study asked experts and laypeople to estimate the "risk of death" faced by society as a whole from 30 activities and technology (62). The experts' judgments could be predicted well from statistical estimates of average-year fatalities – as could the estimates of lay-people given that specific definition. Lay estimates of "risk" were more poorly correlated with average-year fatalities. However, much of the residual variance could be predicted by their estimates of catastrophic potential, the ability to cause large numbers of deaths in a nonaverage year. Thus, casual observation had obscured the extent to which experts and laypeople agreed about routine death tolls (for which scientific estimates are relatively uncontroversial) and disagreed about the possibility of anomalies (for which the science is typically weaker).

Sensing that there was something special about catastrophic potential, some risk experts have suggested that social policy give extra weight to hazards carrying that kind of threat. One experimental study has, however, found that people may not care more for many lives lost in a single accident than for the same number of lives lost in separate incidents (61).[5] The critical factor in catastrophic potential is not how the deaths are grouped, but the possibility of discovering that a technology is out of control. Such "surprise potential" is strongly correlated with catastrophic potential in people's judgments (and, presumably, in scientific estimates). However, the two features represent rather different ethical bases for distinguishing among risks.

*Dimensions of Risk.* Recognizing that correlated features can confuse the interpretation of risk behaviors, investigators have looked extensively at the patterns of correlations among features (1, 22, 60). Overall, they have found a remarkably robust picture, typically revealing two or three dimensions of risk, which capture much of the variation in judgments of up to 20 aspects of risk. The general structure of this "risk space" is relatively similar across elicitation method, subject population (e.g., experts versus laypeople), and risk domain. Core concepts in these dimensions include how well a risk is understood and how much of a feeling of dread it evokes. The placement of individual hazards in the space does vary with individual and with group, in ways that can predict judgments of risk management policies (e.g., how tightly a technology should be regulated). Relatively little is known about the role of these dimensions in individual risk decisions.

*Risk Comparisons.* The multidimensional character of risk means that hazards that are similar in many ways may still evoke quite different responses. This fact is neglected in appeals to accept one risk, because one has accepted another that is similar to it in some ways (8, 18). The most ambitious of these appeals present elaborate lists of hazards, the exposure to which is adjusted so that they pose equivalent risks (e.g., both one tablespoon of peanut butter and 50 years of living at the boundary of a nuclear power plant create a one-in-a-million risk of premature death). Recognizing that such comparisons are often perceived as self-serving, the Chemical Manufacturers Association (6) commissioned a guide to risk comparisons, which presents such lists, but with the attached caution, WARNING! USE OF DATA IN THIS TABLE FOR RISK COMPARISON PURPOSES CAN DAMAGE YOUR CREDIBILITY.[6]

## Qualitative Assessment

### Event Definitions

Scientific estimates of risk require detailed specification of the conditions under which it is to be observed. For example, a fertility counselor estimating a woman's risk of an unplanned pregnancy would consider the amount of intercourse, the kinds of contraceptive used (and the diligence with which they are applied), her physiological condition (and that of her partner), and so on. If laypeople are to make accurate assessments, then they require the same level of detail. That is true whether they are estimating risks for their own sake or for the benefit of an investigator studying risk perceptions.

When such investigators omit needed details, they create adverse conditions for subjects. To respond correctly, subjects must first guess the question and then know the answer to it. Consider, for example, the question, "What is the probability of pregnancy with unprotected sex?" A well-informed subject who understood this to mean a single exposure would be seen as underestimating the risk by an investigator who intended the question to mean multiple exposures.

Such ambiguous events are common in surveys designed to study public perceptions of risk. For example, a National Center for Health Statistics survey (70) question asked, "How likely do you think it is that a person will get the AIDS virus from sharing plates, forks, or glasses with someone who had AIDS?" Even if the survey had not used an ambiguous response mode (very likely, unlikely, etc.), it would reveal relatively little about subjects' understanding of disease risks. For their responses to be meaningful, subjects must spontaneously assign the same value to each missing detail, while investigators guess what subjects decided.

We asked a relatively homogeneous group of subjects what they thought was meant regarding the amount and kind of sharing implied by this question (after they had answered it) (16). These subjects generally agreed about the kind of sharing (82% interpreted it as sharing during a meal), but not about the amount (a single occasion, 39%; several occasions 20%; routinely, 28%; uncertain, 12%). A survey question about the risks of sexual transmission evoked similar disagreement. We did not study what readers of the survey's results believed about subjects' interpretations.

### Supplying Details

Aside from their methodological importance, the details that subjects infer can be substantively interesting. People's intuitive theories of risk are revealed in the variables that they note and the values that they supply. In a systematic evaluation of these theories, Quadrel (52) asked adolescents to think aloud as they estimated the probability of several deliberately ambiguous events (e.g., getting in an accident after drinking and driving, getting AIDS through sex).

These subjects typically wondered (or made assumptions) about numerous features. In this sense, subjects arguably showed more sophistication than the investigators who created the surveys from which these questions were taken or adapted. Generally speaking, these subjects were interested in variables that could figure in scientific risk analyses (although scientists might not yet know what role each variable plays). There were, however, some interesting exceptions. Although subjects wanted to know the "dose" involved with most risks, they seldom asked about the amount of sex in one question about the risks of pregnancy and in another question about the risks of HIV transmission. They seemed to believe that an individual either is or is not sensitive to the risk, regardless of the amount of the exposure. In other cases, subjects asked about variables without a clear connection to risk level (e.g., how well members of the couple knew one another).

In a follow-up study, Quadrel (52) presented richly specified event descriptions to teens drawn from the same populations (school organizations and substance abuse treatment homes). Subjects initially estimated the probability of a risky outcome on the basis of some 20 details. Then, they were asked how knowing each of three additional details would change their estimates. One of those details had been provided by subjects in the preceding study; two had not. Subjects in this study responded to the relevant detail much more than to the irrelevant ones. Thus, at least in these studies, teens did not balk at making judgments regarding complex stimuli and revealed consistent intuitive theories in rather different tasks.

### Cumulative Risk – A Case in Point

As knowledge accumulates about people's intuitive theories of risk, it will become easier to predict which details subjects know and ignore, as well as which omissions they will notice and rectify. In time, it might become possible to infer the answers to questions that are not asked from answers to ones that are – as well as the inferences that people make from risks that are described explicitly to risks that are not. The invulnerability results reported above show the need to discipline such extrapolations with empirical research. Asking people about the risks to others like themselves is not the same as asking about their personal risk. Nor need reports about others' risk levels be taken personally.

One common, and seemingly natural, extrapolation is between varying numbers of independent exposures to a risk. Telling people the risk from a single exposure should allow them to infer the risk from whatever multiple they face; asking subjects what risk they expect from one amount should allow one to infer what they expect from other amounts. Unfortunately, for both research and communication, teens' insensitivity to the amount of intercourse (in determining the risks of pregnancy or HIV transmission) proves to be a special case of a general problem. Several reviews (9, 48) have concluded that between one third and one half of sexually active adolescents explain not using contraceptives with variants of, "I thought I (or my partner) couldn't get pregnant." Another study (59) found that adults greatly underestimated the rate at which the risk of contraceptive failure accumulates through repeated exposure, even after eliminating (from the data analysis) the 40% or so of subjects who saw no relationship between risk and exposure. One corollary of this bias is not realizing the extent to which seemingly small differences in annual failure rates (what is typically reported) can lead to large differences in the cumulative risk associated with continued use.

After providing practice with a response mode designed to facilitate the expression of small probabilities, Linville et al. (41) asked college students to estimate the risks of HIV transmission from a man to a woman as the result of 1, 10, or 100 cases of protected sex. For one contact, the median estimate was .10, a remarkably high value according to public health estimates (14, 33). For 100 contacts, however, the median estimate was .25, a more reasonable value. Very different pictures of people's risk perceptions would emerge from studies that asked just one of these questions or the other. Risk communicators could achieve quite different effects if they chose to describe the risk of one exposure and not the other. They might create confusion if they chose to communicate both risks, thus leaving recipients to reconcile the seeming inconsistency.

### Mental Models of Risk Processes

*The Role of Mental Models.* These intuitive theories of how risks accumulate were a by-product of research intended to improve the elicitation and communication of quantitative probabilities. Such research can serve the interests of individuals who face well-formulated decisions in which estimates of health risks (or benefits) play clearly defined roles. For example, a home owner poised to decide whether to test for radon needs estimates of the cost and accuracy of tests, the health risks of different radon levels, the cost and efficacy of ways to mitigate radon problems, and so on (64).

Often, however, people are not poised to decide anything. Rather, they just want to know what the risk is and how it works. Such substantive knowledge is essential for following an issue in the news media, for participating in public discussions, for feeling competent to make decisions, and for generating options among which to decide. In these situations, people's objective is to have intuitive theories that correspond to the main elements of the reigning scientific theories (emphasizing those features relevant to control strategies).

The term *mental model* is often applied to intuitive theories that are elaborated well enough to generate predictions in diverse circumstances (24). Mental models have a long history in psychology (7, 50). For example, they have been used to examine how people understand physical processes (26), international tensions (43), complex equipment (57), energy conservation (34), and the effects of drugs (31).

If these mental models contain critical bugs, they can lead to erroneous conclusions, even among otherwise well-informed people. For example, not knowing that repeated sex increases the associated risks could undermine much other knowledge. Bostrom et al. (5) found that many people know that radon is a colorless, odorless, radioactive gas. Unfortunately, some also associate radioactivity with permanent contamination. However, this widely publicized property of high-level waste is not shared by radon. Not realizing that the relevant radon by-products have short half-lives, home owners might not even bother to test (believing that there was nothing that they could do, should a problem be detected).

*Eliciting Mental Models.* In principle, the best way to detect such misconceptions would be to capture people's entire mental model on a topic. Doing so would also identify those correct conceptions upon which communications could build (and which should be reinforced). The critical threat to capturing mental models is reactivity, i.e., changing respondents as a result of the elicitation procedure. One wants neither to induce nor to dispell misconceptions, either through leading questions or subtle hints. The interview should neither preclude the expression of unanticipated beliefs nor inadvertently steer subjects around topics (13, 24, 28).

Bostrom et al. (5) offer one possible compromise strategy, which has been used for a variety of risks (2, 42, 47). Their interview protocol begins with very open-ended questions: They ask subjects what they know about a topic, then prompt them to consider exposure, effects, and mitigation issues. Subjects are asked to elaborate on every topic mentioned. Once these minimally structured tasks are exhausted, subjects sort a large stack of diverse photographs, according to whether each seems related to the topic, and explain their reasoning as they go.

Once transcribed, the interviews are coded into an expert model of the risk. This is a directed network, or influence diagram (29), which shows the different factors affecting the magnitude of the risk. The expert model is created by iteratively pooling the knowledge of a diverse group of experts. It might be thought of as an expert's mental model, although it would be impressive for any single expert to produce it all in a single session following the open-ended interview protocol. Figure 28.2 shows the results of coding one subject's interview into the expert model for radon. The subject's concepts were characterized as correct, incorrect, peripheral (technically correct, but only distantly related to the topic), background (referring to general principles of science), evaluative, and nonspecific (or vague).

### Creating Communications

#### Selecting Information

The first step in designing communications is to select the information that they should contain. In many existing communications, this choice seems arbitrary, reflecting some expert or communicator's notion of "what people ought to know." Poorly chosen information can have several negative consequences, including both wasting recipients' time and being seen to waste it (thereby reflecting insensitivity to their situation). In addition, recipients will be judged unduly harshly if they are uninterested in information that, to them, seems irrelevant. The Institute of Medicine's fine and important report, *Confronting AIDS* (30), despaired after a survey showed that only 41% of the public knew that AIDS was caused by a virus. Yet one might ask what role that information could play in any practical decision (as well as what those subjects who answered correctly meant by "a virus").

The information in a communication should reflect a systematic theoretical perspective, capable of being applied objectively. Here are three candidates for such a perspective, suggested by the research cited above:

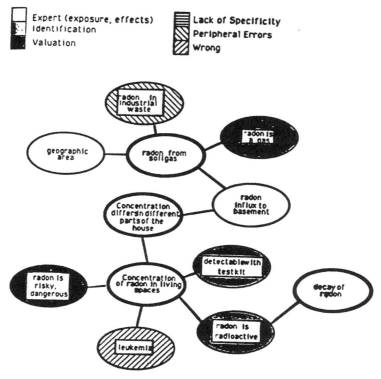

Figure 28.2.   One subject's model of processes affecting radon risk, elicited with an open-ended interview protocol. (*Source:* Bostrom et al., Ref 5.)

*Mental Model Analysis.* Communications could attempt to convey a comprehensive picture of the processes creating (and controlling) a risk. Bridging the gap between lay mental models and expert models would require adding missing concepts, correcting mistakes, strengthening correct beliefs, and deemphasizing peripheral ones.

*Calibration Analysis.* Communications could attempt to correct the critical "bugs" in recipients' beliefs. These are defined as cases where people confidently hold incorrect beliefs that could lead to inappropriate actions (or lack enough confidence in correct beliefs to act on them).

*Value-of-Information Analysis.* Communications could attempt to provide the pieces of information that have the largest possible impact on pending decisions. Value-of-information analysis is the general term for techniques that determine the sensitivity of decisions to different information (46).

The choice among these approaches would depend on, among other things, how much time is available for communication, how well the decisions are formulated, and what scientific risk information exists. For example, calibration analysis might be particularly useful for identifying the focal facts for public service announcements. Such facts might both grab recipients' attention and change their behavior. A mental model analysis might be more suited for the preparation of explanatory brochures or curricula.

Merz (45) applied value-of-information analysis to a well-specified medical decision, whether to undergo carotid endarterectomy. Both this procedure, which involves scraping out an artery that leads to the head, and its alternatives have a variety of possible positive and negative effects. These effects have been the topic of extensive research, which has provided quantitative risk estimates of varying precision. Merz created a simulated population of patients, who varied in their physical condition and relative preferences for different health states. He found that knowing about a few, but only a few, of the possible side effects would change the preferred decision for a significant portion of patients. He argued that communications focused on these few side effects would make better use of patients' attention than laundry lists of undifferentiated possibilities. He also argued that his procedure could provide an objective criterion for identifying the information that must be transmitted to insure medical informed consent.

### Formatting Information

Once information has been selected, it must be presented in a comprehensible way. That means taking into account the terms that recipients use for understanding individual concepts and the mental models they use for integrating those concepts. It also means respecting the results of research into text comprehension. That research shows, for example, that comprehension improves when text has a clear structure and, especially, when that structure conforms to recipients' intuitive representation of a topic; that critical information is more likely to be remembered when it appears at the highest level of a clear hierarchy; and that readers benefit from "adjunct aids," such as highlighting, advanced organizers (showing what to expect), and summaries. Such aids might even be better than full text for understanding, retaining, and being able to look up information. Fuller treatment than is possible here can be found in Refs. 12, 25, 35, 54, 58.

There may be several different formats that meet these general constraints. Recently, we created two brochures that presented clear but different structures to explain the risks of radon (4). One was organized around a decision tree, which showed the options facing home owners, the probabilities of possible consequences, and the associated costs and benefits. The second was organized around a directed network, in effect, the expert model of the mental model studies. Both were compared with the Environmental Protection Agency's (EPA) widely distributed (and, to EPA's great credit, heavily evaluated) *Citizen's Guide to Radon* (65a), which uses primarily a question-and-answer format, with little attempt to summarize or impose a general structure. All three brochures substantially increased readers' understanding of the material presented in them. However, the structured brochures did better (and similar) jobs of enabling readers to make inferences about issues not mentioned explicitly and to give explicit advice to others.

### Evaluating Communications

Effective risk communications can help people to reduce their health risks, or to get greater benefits in return for those risks that they take. Ineffective communications not only fail to do so, but also incur opportunity costs, in the sense of occupying the place (in recipients' lives and society's functions) that could be taken up by more effective communications. Even worse, misdirected communications can prompt wrong decisions by omitting key information or failing to contradict misconceptions, create confusion by prompting inappropriate assumptions or by emphasizing irrelevant information, and provoke conflict by eroding recipients' faith in the communicator. By causing undue alarm or complacency, poor communications can have greater public health impact than the risks that they attempt to describe. It may be no more acceptable to release an untested communication than an untested drug. Because communicators' intuitions about recipients' risk perceptions cannot be trusted, there is no substitute for empirical validation (17, 20, 49, 55, 60).

The most ambitious evaluations ask whether recipients follow the recommendations given in the communication (37, 68). However, that standard requires recipients not only to understand the message, but also to accept it as relevant to their personal circumstances. For example, home owners without the resources to address radon problems might both understand and ignore a communication about testing; women might hear quite clearly what an "expert" is recommending about how to reduce their risk of sexual assault, yet reject the political agenda underlying that advice (15). Judging the effectiveness of a program by behavioral effects requires great confidence that one knows what is right for others.

A more modest, but ethically simpler, evaluation criterion is ensuring that recipients have understood what a message was trying to say. That necessary condition might prove sufficient, too, if the recommended action is, indeed, obviously appropriate, once the facts are known. Formal evaluations of this type seem to be remarkably rare, among the myriad of warning labels, health claims and advisories, public service announcements, and operating instructions that one encounters in everyday life and work.

Evaluating what people take away from communications faces the same methodological challenges as measuring ambient risk perceptions. To elaborate slightly on a previous section, the evaluator wants to avoid reactivity, changing people's beliefs through the cues offered by how questions and answers are posed; illusory expertise, restricting the expression of inexpert beliefs; and illusory discrimination, suppressing the expression of inconsistent beliefs.

For example, as part of an ambitious program to evaluate its communications regarding the risks of radon, the EPA (10) posed the following question: "What kinds of problems are high levels of radon exposure likely to cause? a. minor skin problems; b. eye irritations; c. lung cancer." This question seems to risk inflating subjects' apparent level of understanding in several ways. Subjects who know only that radon causes cancer might deduce that it causes lung cancer. The words "minor" and "irritation" might imply that these are not the effects of "high levels" (of anything). There is no way to express other misconceptions, such as that radon causes breast cancer and other lung problems, which emerged with some frequency in our open-ended interviews (5).

In principle, open-ended interviews provide the best way to reduce such threats. However, they are very labor intensive. The stakes riding on many risk communications might justify that investment. Realistically speaking, the needed time and financial resources are not always available. As a result, open-ended, one-on-one interviews are better seen as necessary stepping stones to structured questionnaires, suitable for mass administration. Those questionnaires should cover the critical topics in the expert model, express questions in terms familiar to subjects, and test for the prevalence of misconceptions. Worked examples can be found in Ref. 4.

### Conclusion

Risk perception and risk communication research are complicated businesses, perhaps as complicated as assessing the magnitude of the risks that they consider. A chapter of this length can, at best, indicate the dimensions of complexity and the directions of plausible solutions. In this treatment, we have emphasized methodological issues because we believe that these topics often seem deceptively simple to those not trained in them. Because we all talk and ask questions in everyday life, it seems straightforward to do so regarding health risks. Unfortunately, there are many pitfalls to such amateurism, hints to which can be found in those occasions in life where we have misunderstood or been misunderstood, particularly when dealing with strangers on unfamiliar topics.

Research in this area is fortunate in being able to draw on well-developed literatures in such areas as cognitive, health, and social psychology; survey research; psycholinguistics; psychophysics; and behavioral decision theory.

It is unfortunate in having to face the particularly rigorous demands of assessing and improving beliefs about health risks. These often involve complex and unfamiliar topics, surrounded by unusual kinds of uncertainty, for which individuals and groups lack stable vocabularies. Health risk decisions also raise difficult and potentially threatening trade-offs. Even the most carefully prepared and evaluated communications may not be able to eliminate the anxiety and frustration that such decisions create. However, systematic preparation can keep communications from adding to the problem. At some point in complex decisions, we "throw up our hands" and go with what seems right. Good risk communications can help people get further into the problem before that happens.

Health risk decisions are not just about cognitive processes and cooly weighed information. Emotions play a role, as do social processes. Nonetheless, it is important to get the cognitive part right, lest people's ability to think their way to decisions be underestimated and underserved.

### Notes

1   Focus groups are a popular technique in market research. In them, survey questions, commercial messages, or consumer products are discussed by groups of laypeople. Although they can generate unanticipated alternative interpretations, focus groups create a very different situation than that faced by an individual trying to make sense out of a question, message, or product (44).

2   The "people" in this study were members of the League of Women Voters and their spouses. Generally speaking, the people in the studies described here have been students paid for participation (hence, typically older than the proverbial college sophomores of some psychological research) or convenience samples of adults recruited through diverse civic groups (e.g., garden clubs, PTAs, bowling leagues). These groups have been found to differ more in what they think than in how they think. That is, their respective experiences have created larger differences in specific beliefs than in thought processes. Fuller treatment of sampling issues must await another opportunity.

3   In other studies comparing individuals drawn from these groups (53), we have also observed little difference in their respective response patterns. These studies suggest that any differences in their risk behaviors cannot be attributed to differences in the sorts of judgments considered in this chapter. If that is the case, and if such adults and teens do differ in their risk behaviors, then it may reflect differences in the benefits that they get from the behaviors (or in the risks and benefits of alternative behaviors).

4   In a recent study (53), we derived judgments of relative risk from judgments of the absolute degree of risk that people assigned to themselves and to target others (a close friend, an acquaintance, a parent, a child). On a response scale that facilitated expressing very low probabilities, subjects assigned a probability of less than 1 in 10 million about 10% of the time and a probability of less than 1 in 10,000 about one third of the time. The events involved "a death or injury requiring hospitalization over the next five years" from sources like auto accidents, drug addiction, and explosions. Here, too, middle-class adults and adolescents responded similarly, despite the common belief that teens take risks, in part, because of a unique perception of invulnerability (11).

5   When accidents involving large numbers of fatalities are easy to imagine, catastrophic potential can be rated high because of availability, even when estimates of average-year fatalities are relatively low, as was the case for nuclear power in this study.

6   The guide also offers advice on how to make risk comparisons, if one feels the compulsion, along with examples of more and less acceptable comparisons. Although the advice is logically derived from risk perception research, it was not tested empirically. In such a test, we found little correlation between the predicted degree of acceptability and the acceptability judgments of several diverse groups of subjects (56).

### References

1   Arabie, P., Maschmeyer, C. 1988. Some current models for the perception and judgment of risk. *Org. Behav. Hum. Decis.* Proc. 41:300–29

2   Atman, C. 1990. *Network structures as a foundation for risk communication.* Doctoral diss. Carnegie Mellon Univ.

3   Beyth-Marom, R. 1982. How probable is probable? Numerical translation of verbal probability expressions. *J. Forecasting* 1:257–69

4   Bostrom, A., Atman, C., Fischhoff, B., Morgan, M. B. 1993. Evaluating risk communications: completing and correcting mental models of hazardous processes. Submitted.

5   Bostrom, A., Fischhoff, B., Morgan, M. G. Eliciting mental models of hazardous processes: a methodology and an application to radon. *J. Soc. Issues.* In press

6   Covello, V. T., Sandman, P. M., Slovic, P. 1988. *Risk Communication, Risk Statistics, and Risk Comparisons: A Manual for Plant Managers.* Washington, DC: Chem. Manuf. Assoc.

7   Craik, K. 1943. *The Nature of Explanation.* Cambridge: Cambridge Univ. Press

8   Crouch, E. A. C., Wilson, R. 1982. *Risk/Benefit Analysis.* Cambridge, Mass: Ballinger

9   Cvetkovich, G., Grote, B., Bjorseth, A., Sarkissian, J. 1975. On the psychology of adolescents' use of contraceptives. *J. Sex Res.* 11:256–70

10  Desvousges, W. H., Smith, V. K., Rink, H. H. III. 1989. *Communicating Radon Risk Effectively: Radon Testing in Maryland.* EPA 230-03-89-408. Washington, DC: US Environ. Prot. Agency, Off. Policy, Plan. Eval.

11  Elkind, D. 1967. Egocentrism in adolescence. *Child Dev.* 38:1025–34

12  Ericsson, K. A. 1988. Concurrent verbal reports on text comprehension: a review. *Text* 8:295–325

13  Ericsson, K. A., Simon, H. A. 1980. Verbal reports as data. *Psychol. Rev.* 87:215–51

14  Fineberg, H. V. 1988. Education to prevent AIDS. *Science* 239:592–96

15  Fischhoff, B. 1992. Giving advice: decision theory perspectives on sexual assault. *Am. Psychol.* 47:577–88

16  Fischhoff, B. 1989. Making decisions about AIDS. *In Primary Prevention of AIDS*, ed. V. Mays, G. Albee, S. Schneider, pp. 168–205. Newbury Park, Calif: Sage

17  Fischhoff, B. 1987. Treating the public with risk communications: a public health perspective. *Sci. Technol. Hum. Values* 12:13–19

18  Fischhoff, B., Lichtenstein, S., Slovic, P., Derby, S. L., Keeney, R. L. 1981. *Acceptable Risk.* New York: Cambridge Univ. Press

19  Fischhoff, B., MacGregor, D. 1983. Judged lethality: how much people seem to know depends upon how they are asked. *Risk Anal.* 3:229–36

20  Fischhoff, B., Slovic, P., Lichtenstein, S., 1983. The "public" vs. the "experts": perceived vs. actual disagreement about the risks of nuclear power. In *Analysis of*

*Actual vs. Perceived Risks*, ed. V. Covello, G. Flamm, J. Rodericks, R. Tardiff, pp. 235–49. New York: Plenum

21 Fischhoff, B., Slovic, P., Lichtenstein, S., 1977. Knowing with certainty: the appropriateness of extreme confidence. *J. Exp. Psychol. Hum. Percept. Perform.* 3:552–64

22 Fischhoff, B., Slovic, P., Lichtenstein, S., Read, S., Combs, B. 1978. How safe is safe enough? A psychometric study of attitudes towards technological risks and benefits. *Policy Sci.* 8:127–52

23 Fischhoff, B., Watson, S., Hope, C. 1984. Defining risk. *Policy Sci.* 17:123–39

24 Galotti, K. M. 1989. Approaches to studying formal and everyday reasoning. *Psychol. Bull.* 105:331–51

25 Garnham, A. 1987. *Mental Models as Representations of Discourse and Text.* New York: Halsted

26 Gentner, D., Stevens, A. L., eds. 1983. *Mental Models.* Hillsdale, NJ: Erlbaum

27 Heimer, C. A. 1988. Social structure psychology, and the estimation of risk. *Annu. Rev. Soc.* 14:491–519

28 Hendrickx, L. C. W. P. 1991. *How versus how often: the role of scenario information and frequency information in risk judgment and risky decision making.* Doctoral Diss., Rijksuniversiteit Groningen

29 Howard, R. A. 1989. Knowledge maps. *Manage. Sci.* 35:903–22

30 Inst. of Med. 1986. *Confronting AIDS.* Washington, DC: Natl. Acad. Press

31 Jungermann, H., Shutz, H., Thuring, M. 1988. Mental models in risk assessment: informing people about drugs. *Risk Anal.* 8:147–55

32 Kahneman, D., Slovic, P., Tversky, A., eds. 1982. *Judgment Under Uncertainty: Heuristics and Biases.* New York: Cambridge Univ. Press

33 Kaplan, E. H. 1989. What are the risks of risky sex? *Oper. Res.* 37:198–209

34 Kempton, W., 1987. Variation in folk models and consequent behavior. *Am. Behav. Sci.* 31:203–18

35 Kintsch, W. 1986. Learning from text. *Cogn. Instr.* 3:87–108

36 Krimsky, S., Plough, A. 1988. *Environmental Hazards.* Dover, Mass: Auburn

37 Lau, R., Kaine, R., Berry, S., Ware, J., Roy, D. 1980. Channeling health: a review of the evaluation of televised health campaigns. *Health Educ. Q.* 7:56–89

38 Lichtenstein, S., Fischhoff, B., Phillips, L. D. 1982. Calibration of probabilities: state of the art to 1980. See Ref. 32

39 Lichtenstein, S., Newman, J. R. 1967. Empirical scaling of common verbal phrases associated with numerical probabilities. *Psychon. Sci.* 9:563–64

40 Lichtenstein, S., Slovic, P., Fischhoff, B., Layman, M., Combs, B. 1978. Judged frequency of lethal events. *J. Exp. Psychol. Hum. Learn. Mem.* 4:551–78

41 Linville, P. W., Fischer, G. W., Fischhoff, B. Perceived risk and decision making involving AIDS. 1993. In *The Social Psychology of HIV Infection*, ed. J. B. Pryor, G. D. Reeder. Hillsdale, NJ: Erlbaum. In press

42 Maharik, M., Fischhoff, B. 1992. The risks of nuclear energy sources in space: Some activists' perceptions. *Risk Anal.* 12:383–92

43 Means, M. L., Voss, J. F., 1985. Star wars: a developmental study of expert and novice knowledge studies. *J. Mem. Lang.* 24:746–57

44 Merton, R. F. 1987. The focussed interview and focus groups. *Public Opin. Q.* 51:550–66

45 Merz, J. F. 1991. *Toward a standard of disclosure for medical informed consent: development and demonstration of a decision – analytic methodology.* Ph.D. diss. Carnegie Mellon Univ.

46    Merz, J. F., Fischhoff, B., 1990. Informed consent does not mean rational consent: cognitive limitations on decision-making. *J. Legal Med.* 11:321–50
47    Morgan, M. G., Florig, H. K., Nair, I., Cortes, C., Marsh, K., Pavlosky, K. 1990. Lay understanding of power-frequency fields. *Bioelectromagnetics.* 11:313–35
48    Morrison, D. M. 1985. Adolescent contraceptive behavior: a review. *Psychol. Bull.* 98:538–68
49    Natl. Res. Counc. 1989. *Improving Risk Communication.* Washington, DC: Natl. Acad. Press
50    Oden, G. C. 1987. Concept, knowledge, and thought. *Annu. Rev. Psychol.* 38:203–27
51    Poulton, E. C. 1989. *Bias in Quantifying Judgment.* Hillsdale, NJ: Erlbaum
52    Quadrel, M. J. 1990. *Elicitation of adolescents' perceptions: qualitative and quantitative dimensions.* Ph.D. diss. Carnegie Mellon Univ.
53    Quadrel, M. J., Fischhoff, B., Davis, W. 1993. Adolescent invulnerability. *Am. Psychol.* In press
54    Reder, L. M. 1985. Techniques available to author, teacher, and reader to improve retention of main ideas of a chapter. In *Thinking and Learning Skills: Vol. 2. Research and Open Questions*, ed. S. F. Chipman, J. W. Segal, R. Glaser, pp. 37–64. Hillsdale, NJ: Erlbaum
55    Rohrmann, B., 1990. *Analyzing and evaluating the effectiveness of risk communication programs.* Unpubl. Univ. of Mannheim
56    Roth, E., Morgan, G., Fischhoff, B., Lave, L., Bostrom, A. 1990. What do we know about making risk comparisons? *Risk Anal.* 10:375–87
57    Rouse, W. B., Morris, N. M. 1986. On looking into the black box: prospects and limits in the search for mental models. *Psychol. Bull.* 100:349–63
58    Schriver, K. A. 1989. *Plain language for expert or lay audiences: designing text using protocol aided revision.* Pittsburgh: Commun. Design Cent., Carnegie Mellon Univ.
59    Shaklee, H., Fischhoff, B. 1990. The psychology of contraceptive surprises: judging the cumulative risk of contraceptive failure. *J. Appl. Psychol.* 20:385–403
60    Slovic, P. 1987. Perceptions of risk. *Science* 236:280–85
61    Slovic, P., Fischhoff, B., Lichtenstein, S. 1984. Modeling the societal impact of fatal accidents. *Manage. Sci.* 30:464–74
62    Slovic, P., Fischhoff, B., Lichtenstein, S. 1979. Rating the risks. *Environment* 21:14–20, 36–39
63    Svenson, O. 1981. Are we all less risky and more skillful than our fellow drivers? *Acta Psychol.* 47:143–48
64    Svenson, O., Fischhoff, B. 1985. Levels of environmental decisions. *J. Environ. Psychol.* 5:55–68
65    Tversky, A., Kahneman, D. 1973. Availability: a heuristic for judging frequency and probability. *Cogn. Psychol.* 4:207–32
65a   US Environ. Prot. Agency Off. of Air and Radiat., US Dep. of Health and Hum. Serv., Cent. for Dis. Control. 1986. *A Citizen's Guide to Radon: What It Is and What to Do About It*, OPA-86-004
66    von Winterfeldt, D., Edwards, W., 1986. *Decision Analysis and Behavioral Research.* New York: Cambridge Univ. Press
67    Wallsten, T. S., Budescu, D. V., Rapoport, A., Zwick, R., Forsyth, B. 1986. Measuring the vague meanings of probability terms. *J. Exp. Psychol. Gen.* 115:348–65
68    Weinstein, N. 1987. *Taking Care: Understanding and Encouraging Self-Protective Behavior.* New York: Cambridge Univ. Press
69    Weinstein, N. D. 1980. Unrealistic optimism about future life events. *J. Pers. Soc. Psychol.* 39:806–20

70  Wilson, R. W., Thornberry, O. T. 1987. Knowledge and attitudes about AIDS: pro-
    visional data from the National Health Interview Survey, August 10–30, 1987. *Adv.
    Data*, No. 146
71  Yates, J. F., ed. 1992. *Risk Taking*. Chichester: Wiley
72  Yates, J. F. 1989. *Judgment and Decision Making*. Englewood Cliffs, NJ: Prentice Hall

# 29    Perceived Risk, Trust, and Democracy

*Paul Slovic*

### Introduction

My objective in this chapter is to examine the interplay between several remarkable trends within our society pertaining to the perception and management of risk.

The first of these trends is the fact that during a 20-year period during which our society has grown healthier and safer on average and spent billions of dollars and immense effort to become so, the American public has become more – rather than less – concerned about risk. We have come to perceive ourselves as increasingly vulnerable to life's hazards and to believe that our land, air, and water are more contaminated by toxic substances than ever before.

A second dramatic trend – that I believe is closely related to the first – is the fact that risk assessment and risk management (like many other facets of our society) have become much more contentious. Polarized views, controversy, and overt conflict have become pervasive. Frustrated scientists and industralists castigate the public for behaviors they judge to be based on irrationality or ignorance. Members of the public feel similarly antagonistic toward industry and government. A desperate search for salvation through risk-communication efforts began in the mid-1980s – yet, despite some localized successes, this effort has not stemmed the major conflicts or reduced much of the dissatisfaction with risk management.

Early studies of risk perception demonstrated that the public's concerns could not simply be blamed on ignorance or irrationality. Instead, research showed that many of the public's reactions to risk could be attributed to a sensitivity to technical, social, and psychological qualities of hazards that were not well modeled in technical risk assessments (e.g., qualities such as uncertainty in risk assessments, perceived inequity in the distribution of risks

This chapter originally appeared in *Risk Analysis*, 1993, *13*, 675–682. Copyright ©1993 by Plenum Publishing Corp. Reprinted by permission.

and benefits, and aversion to being exposed to risks that were involuntary, not under one's control, or dreaded). The important role of social values in risk perception and risk acceptance thus became apparent.[1]

More recently, another important aspect of the risk-perception problem has come to be recognized. This is the role of trust. In recent years there have been numerous articles and surveys pointing out the importance of trust in risk management and documenting the extreme distrust we now have in many of the individuals, industries, and institutions responsible for risk management. This pervasive distrust has also been shown to be strongly linked to risk perception and to political activism to reduce risk.[2–6]

In this chapter I shall look beyond current perceptions of risk and distrust and attempt to explain how they came to be this way. My explanation begins with the idiosyncrasies of individual human minds, befitting my background as a psychologist. However, individual psychology is not fully adequate to account for risk perception and conflict. A broader perspective is necessary, one that includes the complex mix of scientific, social, political, legal, institutional, and psychological factors operating within our society's risk-management system.

## The Importance of Trust

Everyone knows intuitively that trust is important for all forms of human social interaction. Perhaps because it is such a familiar concept, its importance in risk management has not been adequately appreciated. However, numerous recent studies clearly point to *lack of trust* as a critical factor underlying the divisive controversies that surround the management of technological hazards.[7–21]

To appreciate the importance of trust, it is instructive to compare those risks that we fear and avoid with those we casually accept. Starr[22] has pointed to the public's lack of concern about the risks from tigers in urban zoos as evidence that acceptance of risks is strongly dependent on confidence in risk management. Similarly, risk-perception research[23] documents that people view *medical* technologies based on use of radiation and chemicals (i.e., x-rays and prescription drugs) as high in benefit, low in risk, and clearly acceptable. However, they view *industrial* technologies involving radiation and chemicals (i.e., nuclear power, pesticides, industrial chemicals) as high in risk, low in benefit, and unacceptable. Although x-rays and medicines pose significant risks, our relatively high degree of trust in the physicians who manage these devices makes them acceptable. Numerous polls have shown that the government and industry officials who oversee the management of nuclear power and nonmedical chemicals are not highly trusted.[3,6,18,24]

During the past several decades, the field of risk assessment has developed to impart rationality to the management of technological hazards. Risk assessment has its roots in epidemiology, toxicology, systems analysis, reliability theory, and many other disciplines. Probably more than $1 billion has been spent to conduct innumerable animal bioassays and epidemiological studies to assess the human health consequences of exposure to radiation and chemicals and to develop probabilistic risk analyses for nuclear reactors, dams, hazardous waste treatment, and other engineered facilities. The Environmental Protection Agency, the Nuclear Regulatory Commission, and numerous other government agencies have made risk assessment the centerpiece of their regulatory efforts.[25–27]

It is now evident that public perceptions and acceptance of risk from nuclear and chemical technologies are not much influenced by technical risk assessments. Nowhere is this phenomenon more dramatically illustrated than in the unsuccessful struggle, across many years, to dispose of the accumulating volume of spent fuel from the nation's commercial nuclear reactors. The Department of Energy's program to establish a national repository has been stymied by overwhelming public opposition, fueled by public perceptions that the risks are immense and unacceptable.[6] These perceptions stand in stark contrast to the prevailing view of the technical community, whose risk assessments assert that nuclear wastes can be disposed of safely in an underground repository (see Table 29.1). Public fears and opposition to nuclear-waste disposal plans can be seen as a "crisis in confidence," a profound breakdown of trust in the scientific, governmental, and industrial managers of nuclear technologies. It is clear that the Department of Energy and the U.S. Congress have not adequately appreciated the importance of (dis)trust in the failure of the nuclear-waste program, nor have they recognized the implications of this situation.[6,21] Analogous crises of confidence can be demonstrated in numerous controversies surrounding exposures to chemicals. Again, risk assessment, in these situations based primarily on toxicology, is often impotent when it comes to resolving conflict about chemical risks.[28]

Because it is impossible to exclude the public in our uniquely participatory democracy, the response of industry and government to this crisis of confidence has been to turn to the young and still primitive field of risk communication in search of methods to bring experts and laypeople into alignment and make conflicts over technological decisions easier to resolve [see, e.g., William Ruckelshaus' stirring speeches on this topic,[26,29] the National Academy of Sciences report on risk communication,[30] and the Chemical Manufacturer's Association communication manual for plant managers[31]]. Although attention to communication can prevent blunders that exacerbate conflict, there is rather little evidence that risk communication has made any significant contribution to reducing the gap between technical risk assessments and public perceptions or to facilitating decisions about nuclear waste or other major sources of risk conflict. The limited effectiveness of risk-communication efforts can be attributed to the lack of trust. If you trust

Table 29.1.

---

The following comments reflect expert viewpoints on the risks from nuclear-waste disposal and the public's perceptions of these risks.

"Several years ago . . . I talked with Sir John Hill, . . . chairman of the United Kingdom's Atomic Energy Authority. 'I've never come across any industry where the public perception of the problem is so totally different from the problems as seen by those of us in the industry . . . ,' Hill told me. In Hill's view, the problem of radio-active waste disposal was, in a technical sense, comparatively easy." (L. J. Carter, *Nuclear Imperatives and Public Trust*. Resources for the Future, Inc., Washington, D.C., 1987, p. 9)

"Nuclear wastes can be sequestered with essentially no chance of any member of the public receiving a non-stochastic dose of radiation. . . . Why is the public's perception of the nuclear waste issue at such odds with the experts' perception?" (A. M. Weinberg, *Public Perceptions of Hazardous Technologies and Democratic Political Institutions*. Paper presented at Waste Management '89, Tucson, Arizona, 1989, pp. 1–2)

"The fourth major reason for public misunderstanding of nuclear power is a grossly unjustified fear of the hazards from radioactive waste . . . there is general agreement among those scientists involved with waste management that radioactive waste disposal is a rather trivial technical problem." (B. L. Cohen, *Before It's Too Late: A Scientist's Case for Nuclear Energy*. Flenum, New York, 1983, p. 119)

"The risk is as negligible as it is possible to imagine . . . It is embarrassingly easy to solve the technical problems, yet impossible to solve the political ones." (H. W. Lewis, *Technological Risk*. W. W. Norton, New York, 1990, pp. 245–246)

---

the risk manager, communication is relatively easy. If trust is lacking, no form or process of communication will be satisfactory.[32] Thus, trust is more fundamental to conflict resolution than is risk communication.

### Creation and Destruction of Trust

One of the most fundamental qualities of trust has been known for ages. Trust is fragile. It is typically created rather slowly, but it can be destroyed in an instant – by a single mishap or mistake. Thus, once trust is lost, it may take a long time to rebuild it to its former state. In some instances, lost trust may never be regained. Abraham Lincoln understood this quality. In a letter to Alexander McClure he observed: "If you *once* forfeit the confidence of your fellow citizens, you can *never* regain their respect and esteem" (italics added).

The asymmetry between the difficulty of creating trust and the ease of destroying it has been studied by social psychologists within the domain of interpersonal perception. For example, Rothbart and Park[33] had people rate 150 descriptive traits (adventurous, gentle, lazy, trustworthy, etc.) in terms of the number of relevant behavioral instances necessary to establish or disconfirm the trait. Favorable traits (like trustworthiness) were judged to be hard to acquire (many behavioral instances needed) and easy to lose. Unfavorable traits were judged to be easier to acquire and harder to lose. The number of behavioral instances required to disconfirm a negative quality (e.g., dishonesty) was greater than the number required to disconfirm a positive trait. As Abraham Lincoln might have predicted, trustworthiness stood out among the 150 traits as requiring a relatively large number of confirming instances to establish the trait and a relatively small number of relevant instances to disconfirm it. (Note that data here were *judgments* of the number of instances that would be required as opposed to data documenting the number of instances that actually confirmed or disconfirmed a trait.)

The fact that trust is easier to destroy than to create reflects certain fundamental mechanisms of human psychology that I shall call "the asymmetry principle." When it comes to winning trust, the playing field is not level. It is tilted toward distrust, for each of the following reasons:

1. Negative (trust-destroying) events are more visible or noticeable than positive (trust-building) events. Negative events often take the form of specific, well-defined incidents such as accidents, lies, discoveries of errors, or other mismanagement. Positive events, while sometimes visible, more often are fuzzy or indistinct. For example, how many positive events are represented by the safe operation of a nuclear power plant for one day? Is this one event? Dozens of events? Hundreds? There is no precise answer. When events are invisible or poorly defined, they carry little or no weight in shaping our attitudes and opinions.

2. When events do come to our attention, negative (trust-destroying) events carry much greater weight than positive events. This important psychological tendency is illustrated by a study in which my colleagues and I asked 103 college students to rate the impact on trust of 45 hypothetical news events pertaining to the management of a large nuclear power plant in their community.[34] Some of these events were designed to be trust increasing, such as:

- There have been no reported safety problems at the plant during the past year.
- There is careful selection and training of employees at the plant.
- Plant managers live nearby the plant.
- The county medical examiner reports that the health of people living near the plant is *better* than the average for the region.

Other events were designed to be trust decreasing, such as:

- A potential safety problem was found to have been covered up by plant officials.
- Plant safety inspections are delayed in order to meet the electricity production quota for the month.
- A nuclear power plant in another state has a serious accident.
- The county medical examiner reports that the health of people living near the plant is *worse* than the average for the region.

The respondents were asked to indicate, for each event, whether their trust in the management of the plant would be increased or decreased upon learning of that event. After doing this, they rated how strongly their trust would be affected by the event on a scale ranging from 1 (very small impact on trust) to 7 (very powerful impact on trust).

The percentages of Category 7 ratings, shown in Figure 29.1, dramatically demonstrate that negative events are seen as far more likely to have a powerful effect on trust than are positive events. The data shown in Table 29.2 are typical. The negative event, reporting plant neighbors' health as *worse* than average, was rated 6 or 7 on the impact scale by 50.0% of the respondents. A matched event, reporting neighbors' health to be *better* than average was rated 6 or 7 by only 18.3% of the respondents.

There was only one event perceived to have any substantial impact on increasing trust. This event stated that: "An advisory board of local citizens and environmentalists is established to monitor the plant and is given legal authority to shut the plant down if they believe it to be unsafe."

This strong delegation of authority to the local public was rated 6 or 7 on the impact scale by 38.4% of the respondents. Although this was a far stronger showing than for any other positive event, it would have been a rather average performance in the distribution of impacts for negative events.

The reasons for the greater impact of trust-destroying incidents are complex, and I shall not discuss them here except to note that the importance of an event is at least in part related to its frequency (or rarity). An accident in a nuclear plant is more informative with regard to risk, than is a day (or even a large number of days) without an accident. Thus, in systems where we are concerned about low-probability/high-consequence events, problematic events will increase our perceptions of risk to a much greater degree than favorable events will decrease them.

3. Adding fuel to the fire of asymmetry is yet another idiosyncracy of human psychology – sources of bad (trust-destroying) news tend to be seen as more credible than sources of good news. For example, in several studies of what we call "intuitive toxicology,"[35] we have examined people's confidence in the ability of animal studies to predict human health effects from chemicals. In general, confidence in the validity of animal studies is not particularly high. However, when told that a study has found that a chemical is

Local board authority to close plant
Evacuation plan exists
On-site government inspector
Rewarded for finding problems
Responsive to any sign of problems
Effective emergency action taken
Local advisory board established
Public encouraged to tour plant
Mandatory drug testing
No problems for five years
Hold regular public hearings
Employees carefully trained
Conduct emergency training
Community has access to records
Serious accident is controlled
Health nearby is better than average
Monitor radioactive emissions
Employees informed of problems
Neighbors notified of problems
No evidence of withholding information
Contribute to local charities
Employees closely supervised
Try to meet with public
Managers live nearby
Operates according to regulations
No problems in past year
Record keeping is good

*TRUST INCREASING*

Don't contribute to local charities
No public hearings
Little communication with community
Emergency response plans not rehearsed
Officials live far away
Poor record keeping
Accident occurs in another state
Accused of releasing radiation
Denied access to records
Employees not informed of problems
Delayed inspections
Public tours not permitted
Health nearby worse than average
Official lied to government
Serious accident is controlled
No adequate emergency response plan
Plant covered up problem
Employees drunk on job
Records were falsified

*TRUST DECREASING*

60%    40%    20%    0%    20%    40%    60%

**Percent Very Powerful Impact**

Figure 29.1. Differential impact of trust-increasing and trust-decreasing events. Note: Only percentages of Category 7 ratings (very powerful impact) are shown here.

carcinogenic in animals, people express considerable confidence in the validity of this study for predicting health effects in humans. Regulators respond like the public. Positive (bad news) evidence from animal bioassays is presumptive evidence of risk to humans; negative evidence (e.g., the chemical was not found to be harmful) carries little weight.[36]

4. Another important psychological tendency is that distrust, once initiated, tends to reinforce and perpetuate distrust. This occurs in two ways. First, distrust tends to inhibit the kinds of personal contacts and experiences that are necessary to overcome distrust. By avoiding others whose motives or actions we distrust, we never get to see if these people are competent, well-meaning, and trustworthy. Second, initial trust or distrust colors our

Table 29.2. *Judged Impact of a Trust-Increasing Event and a Similar Trust-Decreasing Event*[a]

| | Impact on Trust | | | | | | |
| --- | --- | --- | --- | --- | --- | --- | --- |
| | Very Small 1 | 2 | 3 | 4 | 5 | 6 | Very Powerful 7 |
| Trust-increasing event The county medical examiner reports that the health of people living near the plant is *better* than average | 21.5 | 14.0 | 10.8 | 18.3 | 17.2 | 16.1 | 2.2 |
| Trust-decreasing event The county medical examiner reports that the health of people living near the plant is *worse* than average | 3.0 | 8.0 | 2.0 | 16.0 | 21.0 | 26.0 | 24.0 |

[a] Cell entries indicate the percentage of respondents in each impact rating category.

interpretation of events, thus reinforcing our prior beliefs. Persons who trusted the nuclear power industry saw the events at Three Mile Island as demonstrating the soundness of the "defense in depth" principle, noting that the multiple safety systems shut the plant down and contained most of its radiation. Persons who distrusted nuclear power prior to the accident took an entirely different message from the same events, perceiving that those in charge did not understand what was wrong or how to fix it and that catastrophe was averted only by sheer luck.

### "The System Destroys Trust"

Thus far, I have been discussing the psychological tendencies that create and reinforce distrust in situations of risk. Appreciation of those psychological principles leads us toward a new perspective on risk perception, trust, and conflict. Conflicts and controversies surrounding risk management are not due to public irrationality or ignorance but, instead, can be seen as expected side effects of these psychological tendencies, interacting with our remarkable form of participatory democratic government, and amplified by certain powerful technological and social changes in our society. The technological change has given the electronic and print media the capability (effectively utilized) of informing us of news from all over the world – often right as it happens. Moreover, just as individuals give greater weight and attention to negative events, so do the news media. Much of what the media reports is bad (trust-destroying) news.[37] This is convincingly demonstrated by Koren and Klein,[38] who compared the rates of newspaper reporting of two studies, one providing bad news and one good news, published back to back in the March 20, 1991 issue of the *Journal of the American Medical Association*. Both studies examined the link between radiation exposure and cancer. The bad news study showed an increased risk of leukemia in white men working at the Oak Ridge National Laboratory. The good news study failed to show an increased risk of cancer in people residing near nuclear facilities. Koren and Klein found that subsequent newspaper coverage was far greater for the study showing increased risk.

The second important change, a social phenomenon, is the rise of powerful special interest groups – well-funded (by a fearful public) and sophisticated in using their own experts and the media to communicate their concerns and their distrust to the public in order to influence risk policy debates and decisions.[39] The social problem is compounded by the fact that we tend to manage our risks within an adversarial legal system that pits expert vs. expert, contradicting each other's risk assessments and further destroying the public trust.

The young science of risk assessment is too fragile, too indirect, to prevail in such a hostile atmosphere. Scientific analysis of risks cannot allay our fears of low-probability catastrophes or delayed cancers unless we trust the system. In the absence of trust, science (and risk assessment) can only feed distrust, by uncovering more bad news. A single study demonstrating an association between exposure to chemicals or radiation and some adverse health effect cannot easily be offset by numerous studies failing to find such an association. Thus, for example, the more studies that are conducted looking for effects of electric and magnetic fields or other difficult-to-evaluate hazards, the more likely it is that these studies will increase public concerns, even if the majority of these studies fail to find any association with ill health.[40,41] In short, such risk-assessment studies tend to increase perceived risk.

### Where Next? Risk and Democracy

Although the study of risk perception and trust has not yet led to a solution to our risk-management problems, it appears to be leading to a more adequate diagnosis of the root causes of risk concerns and risk conflicts. As we begin to understand the complexity of risk conflicts, we recognize the need for new approaches to risk management. The road branches in two very different directions.[42] One direction leads toward less public participation and more centralized control. One might call this the French model. France leads the world in the percentage of electricity generated by nuclear power (73% in 1991, compared to 21% for the U.S.). France, like the United States, was rocked by strong antinuclear protests during the late 1970s, but the state acted forcefully to repress these protests and the antinuclear movement never gained favor with the political parties in power. Today, surprisingly, the perception of risk from nuclear power remains extremely high in France – as high as in the United States, according to national surveys my colleagues and I recently conducted in both countries. However, French citizens, while recognizing that they have little control over risks to their health and safety, have a high degree of trust in their government and in the experts who design and operate nuclear power plants. Americans, in contrast, combine their similarly high degree of perceived risk with a distrust of government, science, and industry and a belief that they do have some ability to control risks. In fact, the American system does provide individual citizens and citizen groups considerable freedom to intervene in administrative proceedings, to question expert judgments of government agencies, and to force changes in policy through litigation.[43]

Political scientists have recognized that, in a climate of strong distrust, the French approach, in which policy formation and implementation is not accessible to public intervention, is expedient.[44] Campbell,[45] for example, argues that formal democratic institutions providing political access to nuclear critics may be fundamentally incompatible with commercial success of nuclear power.

What works in France, however, is unlikely to be achievable in the United States. The French nuclear power program is run by the state, not private industry. Electricité de France has long had a strong reputation for being competent and putting service above profits. The French have a tradition of looking to a scientific elite for guidance in policy matters. Jasper,[46] noting that the word as well as the image of a "technocrat" arose in France, observed that "Perhaps no other political system provides as large a role for people to exercise power on the basis of technical training and certification" (p. 83).

America, since Thomas Jefferson, has had a different approach to democracy, and it is not surprising that attempts to restrict citizens' rights to intervene directly in national risk-management policies have been vigorously opposed. A recent example is the unsuccessful attempt in Congress to strip the state of Nevada of its rights to issue environmental and safety permits for nuclear waste studies at Yucca Mountain.[47]

Given that the French approach is not likely to be acceptable in the United States, restoration of trust may require a degree of openness and involvement with the public that goes far beyond public relations and "two-way communication" to encompass levels of power sharing and public participation in decision making that have rarely been attempted.[48–50] Even this, however, is no guarantee of success.[51,52] In many situations, we may have to recognize that relationships are so poisoned that trust and conflict resolution cannot realistically be achieved in the short run. The bitter conflict over the proposed nuclear waste repository in Nevada is a prime example of such a situation. To preserve the form of democracy we value so highly, we will need to develop ways to work constructively in situations where we cannot assume that trust is attainable.[15]

We have a long way to go in improving our risk-management processes. Although we have expended massive amounts of time, money, and resources on scientific studies designed to identify and quantify risks, we have failed to expend the effort needed to learn how to manage the hazards that science is so good at identifying. Gerald Jacob[53] frames the challenge well in the context of nuclear waste disposal, and his words are also relevant to many other risk problems:

While everyone can appreciate that complex, highly sophisticated engineering is required to safely store nuclear materials for thousands of years, few have appreciated the political requirements necessary to design and implement such a solution. While vast resources have been expended on developing complex and sophisticated technologies, the equally sophisticated political processes and institutions required to develop a credible and legitimate strategy for nuclear waste management have not been developed. The history of high-level radioactive waste management describes repeated failure to recognize the need for institutional reform and reconstruction (p. 164).

Some may view the analysis in this chapter as a depressing one. I do not. Understanding the root causes of social conflict and recognizing the need to create better risk-management processes are essential first steps toward improving the situation. It is far more depressing, in my view, to fail to understand the complex psychological, social, cultural, and political forces that dictate the successes and failures of risk management.

### References

1   P. Slovic, "Perception of Risk," *Science 236*, 280–285 (1987).
2   R. J. Bord and R. E. O'Connor, "Risk Communication, Knowledge, and Attitudes: Explaining Reactions to a Technology Perceived as Risky," *Risk Analysis 10*, 499–506 (1990).
3   J. Flynn, W. Burns, C. K. Mertz, and P. Slovic, "Trust as a Determinant of Opposition to a High-Level Radioactive Waste Repository: Analysis of a Structural Model," *Risk Analysis 12*, 417–430 (1992).
4   H. C. Jenkins-Smith, *Culture, Trust, Ideology and Perceptions of the Risks of Nuclear Wastes: A Causal Analysis* (Paper prepared for the Annual Meeting of the Society for Risk Analysis, San Diego, California, December 6–9, 1992).
5   A. H. Mushkatel and K. D. Pijawka, *Institutional Trust, Information, and Risk Perceptions: Report of Findings of the Las Vegas Metropolitan Area Survey, June 29–July 1, 1992* (NWPO-SE-055-92) Carson City, Nevada, Nevada Nuclear Waste Project Office, 1992).
6   P. Slovic, J. Flynn, and M. Layman, "Perceived Risk, Trust, and the Politics of Nuclear Waste," *Science 254*, 1603–1607 (1991).

7   D. A. Bella, "Engineering and Erosion of Trust," *Journal of Professional Issues in Engineering 113*, 117–129 (1987).

8   D. A. Bella, C. D. Mosher, and S. N. Calvo, "Establishing Trust: Nuclear Waste Disposal," *Journal of Professional Issues in Engineering 114*, 40–50 (1988).

9   D. A. Bella, C. D. Mosher, and S. N. Calvo, "Technocracy and Trust: Nuclear Waste Controversy," *Journal of Professional Issues in Engineering 114*, 27–39 (1988).

10  G. Cvetkovich and T. C. Earle, *Social Trust and Value Similarity: New Interpretations of Risk Communication in Hazard Management* (Paper presented for the Annual Meeting of the Society for Risk Analysis, San Diego, California, December 6–9, 1992).

11  M. R. English, *Siting Low-Level Radioactive Waste Disposal Facilities: The Public Policy Dilemma* (New York, Quorum, 1992).

12  J. Flynn and P. Slovic, "Nuclear Wastes and Public Trust," *Forum for Applied Research and Public Policy 8*, 92–100 (1993).

13  W. Freudenburg, *Risk and Recreancy: Weber, the Division of Labor, and the Rationality of Risk Perceptions* (unpublished manuscript, Department of Rural Sociology, University of Wisconsin, Madison, 1991).

14  B. B. Johnson, *Trust in Theory: Many Questions, Few Answer* (Paper presented for the Annual Meeting of the Society for Risk Analysis, San Diego, California, December 6–9, 1992).

15  R. Kasperson, D. Golding, and S. Tuler, "Social Distrust as a Factor in Siting Hazardous Facilities and Communicating Risks," *Journal of Social Issues 48*, 161–187 (1992).

16  F. N. Laird, "The Decline of Deference: The Political Context of Risk Communication," *Risk Analysis 9*, 543–550 (1989).

17  J. V. Mitchell, "Perception of Risk and Credibility at Toxic Sites," *Risk Analysis 12*, 19–26 (1992).

18  K. D. Pijawka and A. H. Mushkatel, "Public Opposition to the Siting of the High-Level Nuclear Waste Repository: The Importance of Trust," *Policy Studies Review 10*, 180–194 (1992).

19  S. Rayner and R. Cantor, "How Fair Is Safe Enough? The Cultural Approach to Societal Technology Choice," *Risk Analysis 7*, 3–9 (1987).

20  O. Renn and D. Levine, "Credibility and Trust in Risk Communication," in R. E. Kasperson and P. J. M. Stallen (eds.), *Communicating Risks to the Public* (Dordrecht, Kluwer Academic, 1991), pp. 175–218.

21  U. S. Department of Energy, *Draft Final Report of the Secretary of Energy Advisory Board Task Force on Radioactive Waste Management* (Washington, D.C., December 1992).

22  C. Starr, "Risk Management, Assessment, and Acceptability," *Risk Analysis 5*, 97–102 (1985).

23  P. Slovic, "Perception of Risk from Radiation," in W. K. Sinclair (ed.), *Proceedings of the Twenty-Fifth Annual Meeting of the National Council on Radiation Protection and Measurements. Vol 11: Radiation Protection Today: The NCRP at Sixty Years* (Bethesda, Maryland, NCRP, 1990), pp. 73–97.

24  D. B. McCallum, S. L. Hammond, L. A. Morris, and V. T. Covello, *Public Knowledge and Perceptions of Chemical Risks in Six Communities* (Report no. 230-01-90-074, Washington, D.C., U.S. Environmental Protection Agency, 1990).

25  S. Levine, "Probabilistic Risk Assessment: Identifying the Real Risks of Nuclear Power," *Technology Review 87*, 40–44 (1984).

26  W. D. Ruckelshaus, "Science, Risk, and Public Policy," *Science 221*, 1026–1028 (1983).

27    U. S. Nuclear Regulatory Commission (USNRC), *Safety Goals for Nuclear Power Plant Operation* (USNRC Report NUREG-0880, Washington, D.C., May 1983).

28    J. D. Graham, L. C. Green, and M. J. Roberts, *In Search of Safety: Chemicals and Cancer Risk* (Cambridge, Massachusetts, Harvard, 1988).

29    W. D. Ruckelshaus, "Risk in a Free Society," *Risk Analysis 4*, 157–162 (1984).

30    National Research Council (NRC), *Improving Risk Communication* (Washington, D.C., National Academy Press, 1989).

31    V. T. Covello, P. M. Sandman, and P. Slovic, *Risk Communication, Risk Statistics, and Risk Comparisons: A Manual for Plant Managers* (Washington, D.C., Chemical Manufacturers Association, 1988).

32    J. Fessendon-Raden, J. M. Fitchen, and J. S. Heath, "Providing Risk Information in Communities: Factors Influencing What Is Heard and Accepted," *Science Technology and Human Values 12*, 94–101 (1987).

33    M. Rothbart and B. Park, "On the Confirmability and Disconfirmability of Trait Concepts," *Journal of Personality and Social Psychology 50*, 131–142 (1986).

34    P. Slovic, J. Flynn, S. Johnson, and C. K. Mertz, "*The Dynamics of Trust in Situations of Risk*" (Report no. 93-2, Eugene, Oregon, Decision Research, 1993).

35    N. Kraus, T. Malmfors, and P. Slovic, "Intuitive Toxicology: Expert and Lay Judgments of Chemical Risks," *Risk Analysis 12*, 215–232 (1992).

36    E. Efron, *The Apocalyptics* (New York, Simon & Schuster, 1984).

37    J. Lichtenberg and D. MacLean, "Is Good News No News?" *The Geneva Papers on Risk and Insurance 17*, 362–365 (1992).

38    G. Koren and N. Klein, "Bias Against Negative Studies in Newspaper Reports of Medical Research," *Journal of the American Medical Association 266*, 1824–1826 (1991).

39    *Wall Street Journal*, "How a PR Firm Executed the Alar Scare," pp. A1–A3 (October 3, 1989).

40    D. MacGregor, P. Slovic, and M. G. Morgan, "*Perception of Risks from Electromagnetic Fields: A Psychometric Evaluation of a Risk-Communication Approach*" (Report no. 92-6, Eugene, Oregon, Decision Research, 1992).

41    M. G. Morgan, P. Slovic, I. Nair, D. Geisler, D. MacGregor, B. Fischhoff, D. Lincoln, and K. Florig, "Powerline Frequency Electric and Magnetic Fields: A Pilot Study of Risk Perception," *Risk Analysis 5*, 139–149 (1985).

42    D. Fiorino, "Technical and Democratic Values in Risk Analysis," *Risk Analysis 9*, 293–299 (1989).

43    S. Jasanoff, *Risk Management and Political Culture* (New York, Russell Sage Foundation, 1986).

44    J. F. Morone and E. J. Woodhouse, *The Demise of Nuclear Energy? Lessons for a Democratic Control of Technology* (New Haven, Connecticut, Yale University, 1989).

45    J. L. Campbell, *Collapse of an Industry: Nuclear Power and the Contradictions of U.S. Policy* (Ithaca, New York, Cornell University Press, 1988).

46    J. M. Jasper, *Nuclear Politics: Energy and the State in the United States, Sweden, and France* (Princeton, New Jersey, Princeton University Press, 1990).

47    T. Batt, "Nevada Claims Victory in Yucca Deal," *Las Vegas Review-Journal* (July 23, 1992), pp. 1A–3A.

48    J. Flynn, R. Kasperson, H. Kunreuther, and P. Slovic, "Time to Rethink Nuclear Waste Storage," *Issues in Science and Technology 8*, 42–48 (1992).

49    H. Kunreuther, T. D. Aarts, and K. Fitzgerald, "Siting Noxious Facilities: A Test of the Facility Siting Credo," *Risk Analysis 13*, 301–318 (1993).

50    D. H. Leroy and T. S. Nadler, "Negotiate Way Out of Siting Dilemmas," *Forum for Applied Research and Public Policy 8*, 102–107 (1993).

51  R. J. Bord, "The Low-Level Radioactive Waste Crisis: Is More Citizen Participation the Answer?" in M. A. Burns (ed.), *Low-Level Radioactive Waste Regulation: Science, Politics, and Fear* (Chelsea, Michigan, Lewis, 1988), pp. 193–213.

52  D. Nelkin and M. Pollak, "Public Participation in Technological Decisions: Reality or Grand Illusion?" *Technology Review*, 55–64 (August/September 1979).

53  G. Jacob, *Site Unseen: The Politics of Siting a Nuclear Waste Repository* (Pittsburgh, Pennsylvania, University of Pittsburgh, 1990).

# Part X

# Research Methods

In one sense a special section on research methods for JDM researchers is unnecessary. Our problems are not fundamentally different from those of social science in general, so we share the same basic pool of methodology. Further, every JDM paper can be read for its methodological lessons as well as its substantive findings, so that the reader who has reached this point in the book has probably acquired a working knowledge of much of the JDM methodology. However, though each of the three chapters included in this section could have been included in another section, they are grouped here because the methodological issues they raise seem especially pertinent.

The first chapter (Fischhoff, Chapter 30) is, perhaps, the most substantively important of the three. It tackles head-on a fundamental issue for the JDM view: the assumption that we prefer some future states over others and know enough about these future preferences to guide our current choices. The assumption seems reasonable, even trivial, when the choice is familiar and immediate (e.g., Would you like ketchup with your fries?). It seems much less reasonable when the outcomes are distant and unfamiliar (e.g., Under what medical circumstances would you wish to have your doctor turn off the machinery that is keeping you alive?). The evidence, as Fischhoff reviews it, suggests that we should be much more careful than we currently are in our assumptions about how well-developed and internally coherent our values are in particular contexts. Respondents generally answer our questions, however foolish they are. The answers we get will be useful only if they tap the respondent's value system appropriately. (Note, once again, the traps terminology can lead us into. The procedure for assessing someone's values is referred to as "value elicitation." The strong implication is that the values are in there, simply waiting to be popped out by the clever researcher. The implication is, in many cases, simply wrong, as Fischhoff's chapter shows.)

Juslin, in Chapter 31, considers an important methodological point, inadvertent bias in task selection, and the effect this may have had on a large body of research in overconfidence. A common demonstration of overconfidence uses what are called "almanac questions," the sorts of general knowledge

515

questions whose answers can be found in almanacs. Subjects are asked to guess the answers and to rate their confidence that they are correct. Over dozens of such studies, researchers have found a tendency for subjects to express more confidence than is justified by their accuracy – for example, they give complete certainty to groups of answers of which they only got 75% right. Juslin's study suggests that these findings can be explained, at least in part, by the researchers having inadvertently selected "tricky" items, questions to which subjects would think, wrongly, they knew the answers. If nothing else, his study strongly reminds us of the importance of Brunswik's insistence that we must give proper attention to the task environment as well as the subject's responses if we are to understand what is going on.

The final chapter, by Bar-Hillel and Ben-Shakar (Chapter 32) on graphology, is included partly just for fun, but also as a prototype research problem. As the authors note, the practice of graphology – attempting to assess someone's personality from a sample of his or her handwriting – flourishes, despite its theoretical implausibility and its complete lack of substantiating evidence. Our interest here is not in why people believe in graphology's validity. It is in thinking about how one might design a convincing empirical study. After all, JDM researchers often face claims of expertise in important judgments, from radiologists diagnosing cancer in X-rays to gamblers predicting the performance of a racehorse. Why not, say, graphologists judging a trait for honesty? Suppose this distal variable is reflected in a set of imperfect cues in a person's handwriting. How might one collect a set of handwriting samples from people of known but variable honesty, but otherwise comparable on education and so on? (Maybe convicted felons and college students?) How might one recruit putatively expert judges? How would one conduct the experiment and analyze the data? It's an interesting design challenge for the careful JDM researcher. The only drawback, in my view, would be the very high likelihood of negative results!

# 30 Value Elicitation: Is There Anything in There?

*Baruch Fischhoff*

Taken all together, how would you say things are these days – would you say that you are very happy, pretty happy, or not too happy?
— National Opinion Research Center (NORC), 1978

Think about the last time during the past month that you were tired easily. Suppose that it had been possible to pay a sum of money to have eliminated being tired easily immediately that *one* time. What sum of money would you have been willing to pay?
— Dickie, Gerking, McClelland, & Schulze, 1987, p. 19 (Appendix 1)

In this task, you will be asked to choose between a certain loss and a gamble that exposes you to some chance of loss. Specifically, you must choose either: Situation A. One chance in 4 to lose $200 (and 3 chances in 4 to lose nothing). OR Situation B. A certain loss of $50. Of course, you'd probably prefer not to be in either of these situations, but, if forced to either play the gamble (A) or accept the certain loss (B), which would you prefer to do?
— Fischhoff, Slovic, & Lichtenstein, 1980, p. 127

600 people are ill from a serious disease. Physicians face the following choice among treatments: Treatment A will save 200 lives. Treatment B has 1 chance in 3 to save all 600 lives and 2 chances in 3 to save 0 lives. Which treatment would you choose, A or B?
— Tversky & Kahneman, 1981, p. 454

This chapter originally appeared in *American Psychologist*, 1991, 46, 835–847. Copyright © by American Psychological Association. Reprinted by permission.

## Problematic Preferences

### A Continuum of Philosophies

A critical tenet for many students of other people's values is that "If we've got questions, then they've got answers." Perhaps the most ardent subscribers to this belief are experimental psychologists, survey researchers, and economists. Psychologists expect their "subjects" to behave reasonably with any clearly described task, even if it has been torturously contrived in order to probe esoteric theoretical points. Survey researchers expect their "participants" to provide meaningful answers to items on any topic intriguing them (or their clients), assuming that the questions have been put into good English. Economists expect "actors" to pursue their own best interests, thereby making choices that reveal their values, in whatever decisions the marketplace poses (and economists choose to study).

This chapter examines this *philosophy of articulated values* both in its own right and by positioning it on a continuum of philosophies toward value formation and measurement. At the other end of this continuum lies what might be called the *philosophy of basic values*. It holds that people lack well-differentiated values for all but the most familiar of evaluation questions, about which they have had the chance, by trial, error, and rumination, to settle on stable values. In other cases, they must derive specific valuations from some basic values through an inferential process.

Perhaps the clearest example of this latter perspective might be found in the work of decision analysts (Raiffa, 1968; von Winterfeldt & Edwards, 1986; Watson & Buede, 1988). These consultants lead their clients to decompose complex evaluation problems into basic dimensions of concern, called *attributes*. Each attribute represents a reason why one might like or dislike the possible outcomes of a decision. For example, the options facing someone in the market for a car are different vehicles (including, perhaps, none at all), whose attributes might include cost, style, and reliability.

The relative attractiveness (or unattractiveness) of different amounts of each attribute is then captured in a *utility function*, defined over the range of possible consequences (e.g., Just how much worse is breaking down once a month than breaking down twice a year?). After evaluating the attributes in isolation, the decision maker must consider their relative importance (e.g., Just how much money is it worth to reduce the frequency of repairs from annual to biennial?). These trade-offs are expressed in a multiattribute utility function. Having done all of this, the consequences associated with specific actions are then evaluated by mapping them into the space spanned by that function.

Between the philosophies of articulated values and basic values, lie intermediate positions. These hold that although people need not have answers to all questions, neither need they start from scratch each time an evaluative question arises. Rather, people have stable values of moderate complexity, which provide an advanced starting point for responding to questions of real-world complexity. Where a particular version of this perspective falls on the continuum defined by the two extreme philosophies depends on how well developed these partial perspectives are held to be.

Each of these philosophies directs the student of values to different sets of focal methodological concerns. For example, if people can answer any question, then an obvious concern is that they answer the right one. As a result, investigators adhering to the articulated values philosophy will worry about posing the question most germane to their theoretical interests and ensuring that it is understood as intended. On the other hand, if complex evaluations are to be derived from simple evaluative principles, then it is essential that the relevant principles be assembled and that the inferential process be conducted successfully. That process could fail if it required too much of an intellectual effort and, also, if the question were poorly formulated or inadequately understood. If people have thought some about the topic of an evaluation question, then they have less far to go in order to produce a full answer. Yet, even if people hold such partial perspectives, there is still the risk that they will miss some nuances of the question and, as a result, overestimate how completely they have understood it and their values regarding the issues that it raises.

### A Choice of Paradigms

The effort to deal with these different worries in a systematic fashion has led to distinct research paradigms (Kuhn, 1962). Each such paradigm offers a set of methods for dealing with its focal worries, along with empirical tests of success in doing so. Each has evolved some theory to substantiate its approach. As paradigms, each is better suited to answering problems within its frame of reference than to challenging that frame. Thus, for example, the articulated values paradigm is better at devising additional ways to improve the understanding of questions than at determining whether understanding is possible.

This is, of course, something of a caricature. Many investigators are capable of wearing more than one hat. For example, survey researchers have extensively studied the properties of the *don't know* response (T. Smith, 1984). Still, when one is trying to get a survey (or experiment or economic analysis) out the door, it is hard to address these issues at length for every question. It may be easier to take *no answer* for an answer in principle than in practice. At the other extreme, it may be unprofitable for a consulting decision analyst to deal with situations in which the answer to a complex evaluation question is there for the asking, without the rigamarole of multiattribute utility elicitation.

Table 30.1. *Risk of Misdiagnosis*

| Assumption Made | Proper Assumption | | |
|---|---|---|---|
| | *Articulated Values* | *Partial Perspectives* | *Basic Values* |
| Articulated values | — | Get incomplete values<br>Inadvertently impose perspectives | Get meaningless values<br>Impose single perspective |
| Partial perspectives | Promote new perspectives<br><br>Distract from sharpening | — | Impose multiple perspectives<br>Exaggerate resolvability |
| Basic values | Shake confidence<br>Distract from sharpening | Discourage<br>Distract from reconciliation | — |

*Note:* Above diagonal: misplaced precision, undue confidence in results, missed opportunity to help. Below diagonal: needless complication, neglect of basic methodology, induced confusion.

To the extent that studies are conducted primarily within a single paradigm, it becomes critical to choose the right one. Table 30.1 summarizes the costs of various mismatches between the assumed and actual states of people's values. Above the diagonal are cases in which more is expected of people than they are prepared to give. The risk here is misplaced precision, reading too much into poorly articulated responses and missing the opportunity to help people clarify their thinking. Below the diagonal are cases in which too little is expected of people. The risk here is misplaced imprecision, needlessly complicating the task and casting doubt on already clear thinking.

The choice of a paradigm ought to be driven by the perceived costs and likelihoods of these different mismatches. Thus, one might not hire a survey researcher to study how acutely ill individuals evaluate alternative medical procedures, nor might one hire a philosopher to lead consumers through the intricacies of evaluating alternative dentifrices. Evaluation professionals should, in turn, devote themselves to the problems most suited to their methods.

Yet it is in the nature of paradigms that they provide clearer indications of relative than of absolute success. That is, they show which applications of the set of accepted methods work better, rather than whether the set as a whole is up to the job. After describing these paradigms in somewhat greater detail, I will consider some of the specific processes by which work within them can create an exaggerated feeling for the breadth of their applicability.

As a device for doing so, I will highlight how each paradigm might interpret several sets of potentially puzzling results, namely those produced by
the studies posing the four evaluation questions opening this article. In each
case, two apparently equivalent ways of formulating the question produced
rather different evaluations. Assuming that the studies were competently
conducted, an articulated values perspective would hold that if the answers
are different, then so must the questions have been. Any inconsistency is in
the eye of the beholder, rather than in the answers of the respondents.

A basic values philosophy leads to quite a different interpretation: If their
responses are buffetted by superficial changes in question formulation, then
people must not know what they want. As a result, none of the evaluations
should be taken seriously. At best, they reflect a gut level response to some
very general issue. According to the intermediate, partial perspectives philosophy, each answer says something about respondents. However, neither
should be taken as fully representing their values.

### A Sample of Problems

*Happiness.* Surveys sometimes include questions asking respondents to evaluate the overall state of their affairs. Answers to these questions might
be used, for example, as barometers of public morale or as predictors of
responses on other items (i.e., for statistical analyses removing individual mood as a covariate). In reviewing archival data, Turner and Krauss
(1978) discovered the apparent inconsistency revealed in Figure 30.1. Two respected survey organizations, asking virtually identical happiness questions,
produced substantially different proportions of respondents evaluating their
situation as making them *very happy.* If the temptation of naive extrapolation
is indulged, then quite different societies seem to be emerging from the two
surveys (happinesswise, at least).[1]

After a series of analyses carefully examining alternative hypotheses,
Turner and Krauss (1978) concluded that the most likely source of the response pattern in Figure 30.1 was differences in the items preceding the happiness question. In the NORC survey, these items concerned family life; in
the Survey Research Center (SRC) survey (Campbell, Converse, & Rodgers,
1976), they were items unrelated to that aspect of personal status.[2]

If respondents have fully articulated values, then different answers imply
different questions. Inadvertently, the two surveys have created somewhat
different happiness questions. Perhaps Happiness$_1$ (from the NORC survey)
emphasizes the role of family life, whereas Happiness$_2$ (from the SRC survey)
gives respondents more freedom in weighting the different facets of their
lives.

From the opposing perspective, the same data tell quite a different story.
If a few marginally related questions can have so great an impact, then
how meaningful can the happiness question (and the responses to it) be?

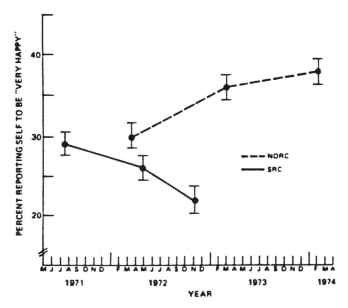

Figure 30.1. Trends in Self-Reported Happiness, 1971–1973. (*Note:* Estimates are derived from sample surveys of noninstitutionalized population of the continental United States, aged 18 and over. Error bars demark ±1 standard error around sample estimate. NORC = National Opinion Research Center; SRC = Survey Research Center. Questions were "Taken all together, how would you say things are these days – would you say that you are very happy, pretty happy, or not too happy?" (NORC); and "Taking all things together, how would you say things are these days – would you say you're very happy, pretty happy, or not too happy these days?" (SRC). (*Source:* From Turner & Martin, 1984. Copyright © 1984 by the Russell Sage Foundation. Reprinted by permission.)

Conceivably, it is possible to take all things together and assess the happiness associated with them. However, as long as assessments depend on the mood induced by immediately preceding questions, that goal has yet to be achieved.

According to the partial perspectives philosophy, the two responses might be stable. However, neither should be interpreted as a thoughtful expression of respondents' happiness. Achieving that would require helping respondents generate and evaluate alternative perspectives on the problem, not just the one perspective that happens to have been presented to them.

*Headache.* According to Executive Order 12291 (Bentkover, Covello, & Mumpower, 1985), cost–benefit analyses must be conducted for all significant federal actions. Where those actions affect the environment, that often requires putting price tags on goods not customarily traded in any marketplace. For regulations governing ozone levels, one such good is a change in the rate of subclinical health effects, such as headaches and shortness of breath. In order to monetize these consequences, resource economists have conducted surveys asking questions like the second example in the set of quotations at the beginning of this article (Cummings, Brookshire, & Schulze, 1986; V. K. Smith & Desvousges, 1988).

In Dickie et al.'s (1987) survey, people who reported having experienced being tired easily estimated that they would be willing to pay $17, on average, to eliminate their last day of feeling tired easily. Later in the same survey, the interviewer computed the overall monthly cost of eliminating each respondent's three most serious ozone-related health effects. This was done by multiplying how much people reported being willing to pay to eliminate the last occurrence of each effect by the number of reported episodes per month, then summing those products across symptoms. Respondents were then asked, "On a monthly basis is [__] what you would be willing to pay to eliminate these three symptoms?" (p. 20, Appendix 1). If respondents recanted, they were then asked what monthly dollar amount they would pay for the package. The markedly reduced dollar amount that most subjects provided was then prorated over the individual health effects. By this computation, respondents were now willing to pay about $2 to eliminate a day of being tired easily.

From a regulatory perspective, these strikingly different estimates indicate markedly different economic benefits from reducing ozone levels. (Indeed, the Office of Management and Budget [A. Carlin, personal communication, 1987] has seriously criticized the Dickie et al., 1987, study as a basis for revising regulations under the Clean Air Act.) From an articulated values perspective, they imply that the two questions must actually be different in some fundamental ways. For example, people might be willing to pay much more for a one-time special treatment of their last headache than for each routine treatment. From a basic values perspective, these results indicate that people know that symptomatic relief is worth something, but have little idea how much (even after an hour of talking about health effects). As a result, respondents are knocked about by ephemeral aspects of the survey, such as the highly unusual challenge to their values embodied by the request to reconsider. The investigators in this study seem to have adopted a partial perspectives philosophy. They treat respondents' values seriously, but not seriously enough to believe that respondents have gotten it right the first time. Rather, respondents need the help provided by showing them the overall implications of their initial estimates (Furby & Fischhoff, 1989).

*Gamble.* In samples of people shown the third example (Fischhoff et al., 1980), most people have preferred the gamble to the sure loss. However, they reverse this preference when the sure loss is described as an insurance premium, protecting them against the potentially greater loss associated with the gamble (Fischhoff et al., 1980; Hershey & Schoemaker, 1980). This difference is sufficiently powerful that it can often be evoked within subject, in successively presented problems.

From an articulated values perspective, the appearance of equivalence in these two versions of the problem must be illusory. Observers who see inconsistency in these responses must simply have failed to realize the differences. Perhaps, as a matter of principle, people refuse both to accept sure losses and to decline insurance against downside risks. In that case, these seemingly superficial differences in description evoke meaningful differences in how people judge themselves and one another. People want both to preserve a fighting chance and to show due caution. How they would respond to a real-world analog of this problem would depend on how it was presented.[3]

From a basic values perspective, these results show that people know that they dislike losing money, but that is about it. They cannot make the sort of precise trade-offs depicted in such analytical problems. As a result, they cling to superficial cues as ways to get through the task.

In this case, some subsidiary evidence seemingly supports the intermediate perspective. When both versions are presented to the same person, there is an asymmetrical transfer effect (Poulton, 1968, 1989). Specifically, there are fewer reversals of preference when the insurance version comes first than when it comes second. This suggests that viewing the sure loss as an insurance premium is a relevant perspective, but not one that is immediately available. By contrast, respondents do realize, at some level, that premiums are sure losses. Studies of insurance behavior show, in fact, some reluctance to accept that perspective. For example, people prefer policies with low deductibles, even though they are financially unattractive. Apparently, people like the higher probability of getting some reimbursement, so that their premium does not have to be viewed as a sure loss (Kunreuther et al., 1978).

*Disease.* About two thirds of the subjects responding to the fourth problem (Tversky & Kahneman, 1981) have been found to prefer Treatment A, with its sure saving of 200 lives. On the other hand, about the same portion prefer the second treatment when the two alternatives are described in terms of the number of lives that will be lost. In this version, Treatment A now provides a sure loss of 400 lives, whereas Treatment B gives a chance of no lives lost at all.

Applying the alternative philosophies to interpreting these results is straightforward. One difference in this case is that there is not only some independent evidence but also some theory to direct such interpretations. The discrepancies associated with the three previous problems were discovered, more or less fortuitously, by comparing responses to questions that happened to have been posed in slightly different ways. In this case, the discrepancies were generated deliberately. Kahneman and Tversky (1979) produced the alternative wordings as demonstrations of their *prospect theory*, which predicts systematic differences in choices as a function of how options are described, or *framed*. The shift from gains (i.e., lives saved) to losses is one such framing difference.

Prospect theory embodies a partial perspectives philosophy. It views these differing preferences as representing stable derivations of intermediate complexity from a set of basic human values identified by the theory. The sources of these differences seem ephemeral, however, in the sense that people would be uncomfortable living with them. Adopting an articulated values philosophy here would require arguing that people regard the different frames as meaningfully different questions – and would continue to do so even after thoughtful reflection.

In the absence of a theoretical account (such as prospect theory) or converging evidence (such as the asymmetrical transfer effect with the sure-loss–premium questions), one's accounting of seemingly inconsistent preferences becomes a matter of opinion. Those opinions might reflect both the particulars of individual problems and the general orientation of a paradigm. The next section describes these paradigms. The following section considers how they could sustain such different views on the general state of human values.

### The Paradigms

However the notion of *paradigm* is conceptualized (Lakatos & Musgrave, 1970), it is likely to involve (a) a focal set of methodological worries, (b) a corresponding set of accepted treatments, (c) a theoretical basis for justifying these treatments and directing their application, and (d) criteria for determining whether problems have been satisfactorily addressed. Table 30.2 characterizes the three paradigms in these terms. This section elaborates on some representative entries in that table.

#### *Philosophy of Articulated Values*

Investigators working within this paradigm have enormous respect for people's ability to articulate and express values on the most diverse topics. Indeed, so great is this respect that investigators' worrying often focuses on ensuring that evaluative questions are formulated and understood exactly as intended. Any slip could evoke a precise, thoughtful answer to the wrong question (Fischhoff & Furby, 1988; Mitchell & Carson, 1989; Sudman & Bradburn, 1982).

A hard-won lesson in this struggle involves recognizing the powerful influence that social pressures can exert on respondents (DeMaio, 1984). As a result, investigators take great pains to insulate the question–answerer relationship from any extraneous influences, lest those become part of the question. To prevent such complications, interviewers and experimenters stick to tight scripts, which they try to administer impassively in settings protected from prying eyes and ears. Lacking the opportunity to impose such control, economists must argue that marketplace transactions fortuitously

Table 30.2. *Three Paradigms for Eliciting Values*

| Worry | Treatment | Theoretical Base | Test of Success |
|---|---|---|---|
| **Assumption: People know what they want about all possible questions (to some degree of precision)** | | | |
| Inappropriate default assumptions (for unstated part of question) | Examine interpretation, specify more, manipulate expectations | Nonverbal communication, experimenter–interviewer effects, psycholinguistics | Full specification, empathy with subjects |
| Inappropriate interpretation of stated question | Use good English, consensual terms | Survey technique, linguistics | Sensible answers, consensual interpretation of terms |
| Difficulty in expressing values | Choose correct response mode | Psychometrics, measurement theory | Consistency (reliability of representation) |
| Strategic response | Proper incentives, neutral context | Microeconomics, demand characteristics | Sensible answers, nonresponse to "irrelevant" changes |
| **Assumption: People have stable but incoherent perspectives, causing divergent responses to formally equivalent forms** | | | |
| Deep consistency in methods across studies (failing to reveal problem) | "Looking for trouble": multiple methods in different studies; "asking for trouble": open-ended questions | Framing theory, new psychophysics, multiple disciplines, anthropology | Nonresponse to irrelevant changes |

| | | | |
|---|---|---|---|
| Eliciting values incompletely (within study) | Multiple methods within study, open ended | Same as above, counseling skills | Inability to elicit more |
| Inability to reconcile perspectives | Talking through implications | Normative analysis, counseling skills | Unpressured consistent response to new perspectives |
| **Assumption: People lack articulated values on specific topic (but have pertinent basic values)** | | | |
| Pressure to respond | Measure intensity, allow no response, alternative modes of expression | Survey research, social psychology | Satisfaction, stability among remainder |
| Instability over time | Accelerate experience | Attitude formation, behavioral decision theory | Stable convergence |
| Inability to relate | Client-centered process | Normative (re)analysis | Full characterization |
| Undetected insensitivity | Ask formally different questions | Normative analysis | Proper sensitivity |

have these desirable properties, in order to justify interpreting purchase decisions as reflecting just the value of the good and not the influences, say, of advertising or peer pressure.

At first blush, this protectiveness might seem somewhat paradoxical. After all, if people have such well-articulated preferences, why do they need to be shielded so completely from stray influences? The answer is that the investigator cannot tell just which stray influence will trigger one of those preferences. Indeed, the more deeply rooted are individuals' values, the more sensitive they should be to the nuances of how an evaluation problem is posed.

For example, it is considered bad form if the demeanor of an interviewer (or the wording of a question) suggests what the investigator expects (or wants) to hear. Respondents might move in that direction (or the opposite) because they aim to please (or to frustrate). Or they might be unmoved by such a hint because they are indifferent to the information or social pressure that it conveys. Because a hint becomes part of the evaluation question, its influence is confounded with that of the issues that interested the investigator in the first place.

Unfortunately, the logical consistency of this position can border on tautology, inferring that a change is significant from respondents' sensitivity to it and inferring that respondents have articulated values from their responses to changes in questions now known to be significant. Conversely, responding the same way to two versions of a task means that the differences between them are not irrelevant and that people know their own minds well enough not to be swayed by meaningless variations.

The potential circularity of such claims can be disrupted either by data or by argument. At the one extreme, investigators can demonstrate empirically that people have well-founded beliefs on the specific questions that they receive. At the other extreme, they can offer theoretical reasons why such beliefs ought to be in place (bolstered, perhaps, by empirical demonstrations in other investigations). Developing these data and arguments in their general form has helped to stimulate basic research into nonverbal communication, interviewer effects, and even the psycholinguistics of question interpretations (e.g., Jabine, Straf, Tanur, & Tourangeau, 1984; Rosenthal & Rosnow, 1969; Turner & Martin, 1984).

Within this paradigm, the test of success is getting the question specified exactly the way that one wants and verifying that it has been so understood. A vital service that professional survey houses offer is being able to render the questions of diverse clients into good English using consensual terms. This very diversity, however, ensures that there cannot be specific theory and data for every question that they ask. As a result, the test of success is often an intuitive appeal to how sensible answers seem to be. The risks of circularity here, too, are obvious.[4]

Assuming that respondents have understood the question, they still need to be able to express their (ready) answer in terms acceptable to the investigator. The great edifice of psychometric theory has evolved to manage potential problems here by providing elicitation methods compatible with respondents' thought processes and investigators' needs (Coombs, 1964; Nunnally, 1968). The associated tests of success are, in part, external – the ability to predict responses to other tasks – and, in part, internal – the consistency of responses to related stimuli. The risk in the former case is that the theoretical tie between measures is flawed. The risk in the latter case is that respondents have found some internally consistent way to respond to questions asked within a common format and varying in obvious ways (Poulton, 1989).

Perhaps surprisingly, the main concern of early contingent valuation investigators was not that respondents would have difficulty expressing their values in dollar terms. On the contrary, they feared that subjects would be able to use the response mode all too well. Knowing just what they want (and how to get it), subjects might engage in strategic behavior, misrepresenting their values in order to shift to others the burden of paying for goods that they value (Samuelson, 1954). In response, investigators developed sophisticated tasks and statistical analyses. Applications of these methods seem to have allayed the fears of many practitioners (Brookshire, Ives, & Schulze, 1976).[5]

### Philosophy of Basic Values

From the perspective of the philosophy of basic values, people's time is very limited, whereas the set of possible evaluative questions is very, very large. As a result, people cannot be expected to have articulated opinions on more than a small set of issues of immediate concern. Indeed, some theorists have argued that one way to control people is by forcing them to consider an impossibly diverse range of issues (e.g., through the nightly news). People who think that they can have some opinion on every issue find that they do not have thoughtful opinions on any issues (Ellul, 1963). The only way to have informed opinions on complex issues is by deriving them carefully from deeply held values on more general and fundamental issues (Rokeach, 1973).

Taking the headache question as an example, a meaningful answer is much more plausible from someone who has invested time and money in seeking symptomatic relief, which can serve as a firm point of reference for evaluating that special treatment. (Economists sometimes call these *averting behaviors* [Dickie et al., 1987].) Otherwise, the question seems patently unanswerable – and the wild discrepancies found in the research provide clear evidence of respondents' grasping at straws.

From the perspective of this paradigm, the existence of such documented discrepancies means that not all responses can be taken seriously. As a result, investigators adhering to it worry about any aspects of their methodology that might pressure respondents to produce unthoughtful evaluations. In this regard, an inherent difficulty with most surveys and experiments is that there is little cost for misrepresenting one's values, including pretending that one has them. By contrast, offering no response may seem like an admission of incompetence. Why would a question have been posed if the (prestigious?) individuals who created it did not believe that one ought to have an answer? With surveys, silence may carry the additional burden of disenfranchising onself by not contributing a vote to public opinion. With psychological experiments, it may be awkward to get out, or to get payment, until one has responded in a way that is acceptable to the experimenter.

One indication of the level of perfunctory responses in surveys may be seen in the repeated finding (Schuman & Presser, 1981) that explicitly offering a *don't know* option greatly increases the likelihood of subjects offering no opinion (e.g., from 5% to 25%). Yet even that option is a rather crude measure. Respondents must determine how intense a degree of ignorance or indifference *don't know* implies (e.g., Does it mean absolutely, positively having no idea?). Investigators must, then, guess at how respondents have interpreted the option.

Hoping to say something more about the intensity of reported beliefs, survey researchers have conducted a lively debate over alternative statistical analyses of seemingly inconsistent attitudes (e.g., Achen, 1975; Converse, 1964). Its resolution is complicated by the difficulty of simultaneously evaluating questions and answers (Schuman & Presser, 1981; T. Smith, 1984). For example, one potential measure of value articulation is the stability of responses over time. When people say different things at different times, they might just be responding randomly. However, they might also have changed their underlying beliefs or settled on different interpretations of poorly worded questions. Changes in underlying opinions may themselves reflect exogenous changes in the issues addressed by the question (e.g., "My headaches are worse now than the last time I was asked") or endogenous changes in one's thinking (e.g., "I finally came to realize that it's crazy to be squirreling money away in the bank rather than using it to make myself less miserable").

A striking aspect of many contingent valuation studies is the high rate of refusals to provide acceptable responses among individuals who have already agreed to participate in the study (Cummings et al., 1986; Mitchell & Carson, 1989; Tolley et al., 1986). These protest responses take several forms: simply refusing to answer the evaluation question, offering to pay $0 for a good that one has admitted to be worth something, and offering to pay what seems to be an unreasonably high amount (e.g., more than 10% of disposable income for relieving a headache). For investigators under contract to monetize environmental goods, these responses are quite troublesome.[6] For investigators who have the leisure to entertain alternative perspectives, these responses provide some insight into how respondents having only basic values cope with pressure to produce more. It is perhaps a testimony to the coerciveness of interview situations how rarely participants say *don't know*, much less try to bolt (as they have in these contingent valuation studies).

The term *protest response* implies hostility toward the investigator. Some of that emotion may constitute displaced frustration with one's own lack of articulated values. The investigator's "crime" is forcing one to confront not knowing exactly what an important good is worth. Perhaps a more legitimate complaint is that investigators force that confrontation without providing any help in its resolution.

As mentioned, investigators within the articulated values paradigm provide no help as a matter of principle. Elicited values are intended to be entirely those of the respondent, without any hint from the questioner. This stance might also be appropriate to investigators in the basic values paradigm in cases in which they want to know what is in there to begin with when an issue is first raised. However, basic values investigators might also be interested in prompting the inferential process of deriving specific values from general ones. That might be done nondirectively by leaving respondents to their own devices after posing an evaluative question and promising to come back later for an answer. In the interim, respondents can do whatever they usually do, such as ruminate, ask friends, listen to music, review Scripture, or experiment. Such surveys might be thought of as accelerating natural experiences, guided by descriptive research into how people do converge on values in their everyday life.

Alternatively, investigators can adopt a multiply directive approach. They can suggest alternative positions, helping respondents to think through how those positions might or might not be consistent with their basic values. Doing so requires a normative analysis of alternative positions that might merit adoption. That might require adding professions like economics or philosophy to the research team. Surveys that present multiple perspectives are, in effect, respondent centered, more akin to decision analysis than to traditional question-centered social research, with its impassive interviewers bouncing stimuli off objectified respondents. Studies that propose alternative perspectives incur a greater risk of sins of commission, in the sense of inadvertently pushing subjects in one of the suggested directions, and a reduced risk of sins of omission, in the sense of letting respondents mislead themselves by incompletely understanding the implications of the questions that they answer.

As shown in the discussion of the questions opening this chapter, a clear hint that people have only basic values to offer is when they show undue sensitivity to changes in irrelevant features of a question. It can also be suggested by undue *in*sensitivity to relevant features. Figure 30.2 shows the

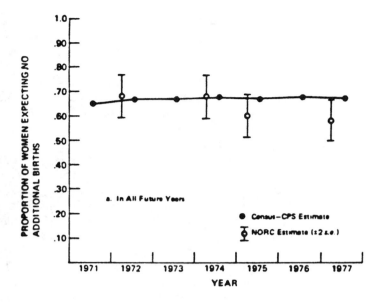

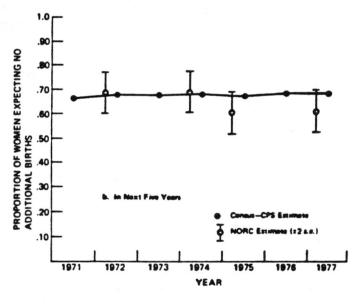

Figure 30.2. Estimates of fertility expectations of American Women: Proportion of women expecting no further children in (a) in all future years, and (b) in the next five years. (*Source:* Turner & Martin, 1984. *Note:* Samples included only married women aged 18–39; sample sizes in each year were approximately 4,000 (Census–CPS) and 220 (NORC). CPS = Current Population Survey; NORC – National Opinion Research Center. Copyright © 1984 by the Russell Sage Foundation. Reprinted by permission.)

proportion of women who reported that they expect no additional births, either in all future years (top panel) or in the next five years (lower panel).[7] In each panel, there was considerable agreement between responses elicited by two respected survey houses. So, here is a case in which all of the irrelevant differences in procedures (e.g., interviewers, sampling, preceding questions) had no aggregate effect on responses. Across panels, however, there is a disturbing lack of difference. If there are women who intend to give birth after the next five years, then the curves should be lower in the top panel than in the lower one. Although the investigators took care to specify time period, respondents either did not notice or could not make use of that critical detail.

An analogous result in contingent valuation research was Tolley et al.'s (1986) finding that people were willing to pay as much for 10 days worth as for 180 days worth of a fixed improvement in atmospheric visibility. Even more dramatic is Kahneman and Knetsch's (Kahneman, 1986) finding that respondents to a phone survey were willing to pay equal amounts to preserve the fisheries in one Ontario lake, in several Ontario lakes, and in all of the lakes in Ontario. These results could, of course, reflect articulated values based on utility functions that flattened out abruptly after 10 days and one lake. More likely, they reflect a vague willingness to pay a little money for a little good.

### Philosophy of Partial Perspectives

By adopting an intermediate position, individuals working within the partial perspectives paradigm must worry about the problems concerning both extremes. On the one hand, they face the risk of inadequately formulated and understood questions, preventing respondents from accessing those partially articulated perspectives that they do have. On the other hand, investigators must worry about reading too much into expressions of value produced under pressure to say something.

These worries may, however, take on a somewhat different face. In particular, the existence of partial perspectives may give a deceptive robustness to expressions of value. Thus, investigators using a single method may routinely elicit similar responses without realizing the extent to which their success depends on the method's ability to evoke a common perspective. That fact may be obscured further when a family of related methods produces similar consistency. It takes considerable self-reflection for investigators to discern the structural communalities in methods that seem to them rather different. Speculative examples might include a tendency for surveys to emphasize hedonic rather than social values by asking respondents for their personal opinions, or for experimental gambles to encourage risk taking because participants cannot leave with less than they went in with,[8] or to discourage emotional involvement because the scientific setting seems to call for a particularly calculating approach. Discovering the perspectives that it inadvertently imposes on itself is part of the continuing renewal process for any scientific discipline. In the social sciences, these perspectives may also be imposed on the people being studied, whose unruly behavior may, in turn, serve as a clue to disciplinary blinders (e.g., Furby, 1986; Gergen, 1973; Gilligan, 1982; Wagenaar, 1989).

Research methods may create consistent response sets, as well as evoke existing ones (Tune, 1964). When asked a series of obviously related questions on a common topic, respondents may devise a response strategy to cope with the experiment. The resulting responses may be consistent with one another, but not with responses in other settings. Indeed, those investigations most concerned about testing for consistency may also be the most vulnerable to generating what they are seeking. Think, for example, of an experiment eliciting evaluations for stimuli representing all cells of a factorial design in which each factor is a different outcome attribute. Why not come up with some simple rule for getting through the task?

For example, Poulton (1968, 1989) has conducted detailed secondary analyses of the quantitative estimates elicited in psychophysics experiments in an effort to capture the subjective intensity of physical stimuli (e.g., sweetness, loudness). He argued that the remarkable internal consistency of estimates across stimulus dimensions (Stevens, 1975) reflects the stability of investigators' conventions in setting up the details of their experiments. Although subjects have no fixed orientation to such unfamiliar forms of evaluation, they do respond similarly to structuring cues such as the kind of numbers to be used (e.g., integers vs. decimals) and the place of the standard stimulus in the range of possibilities.[9] The (nontrivial) antidotes are what might be called *looking for trouble* and *asking for trouble* – eliciting values in significantly different ways and using sufficiently open-ended methods to allow latent incoherence to emerge.

Economists hope to reduce these problems by discerning people's values from the preferences revealed in market behavior. Such actions ought to be relatively free of pressures to respond. After all, you don't have to buy. Or do you? Even if choices are voluntary, they can only be made between options that are on offer and with whatever information respondents happen to have. For example, you may hate ranch style homes but have little choice other than to choose one that makes the best of a bad situation in some locales. In that case, the preferences thereby revealed are highly conditional. Furthermore, even if the choice sets are relatively open and well understood, they may be presented in ways that evoke only a limited subset of people's values. By some accounts, evoking partial perspectives is the main mission of advertising (by other accounts, it is just to provide information). Some critics have argued that some perspectives (e.g., the value of possessing material goods) are emphasized so effectively that they change from being imposed perspectives to becoming endorsed ones.[10]

If one wants to predict how people will behave in situations presenting a particular perspective, then one should elicit their values in ways evoking that perspective.[11] If one wants to get at all their potentially relevant perspectives, then more diverse probing is needed. This is the work of many counselors and consultants. Although some try to construct their clients' subjective problem representation from basic values (along the lines of decision analysis), others try to match clients with general diagnostic categories. Each category then carries prognoses and recommendations. As mentioned, the counselor stance is unusual in social research. Like any direct interaction, it carries the risk of suggesting and imposing the counselor's favored perspective. Presumably, there is a limit to how quickly people can absorb new outlooks. At some point, they may lose cognitive control of the issue, wondering perhaps, "Whose problem is it, anyway?"

### How Could They Think This Way?

Described in its own right, any paradigm sounds like something of a caricature. Could proponents really believe that one size fits all when it comes to methodology? Surely, decision analysts realize that some values are already so well articulated that their decomposition procedures will only induce confusion. Surely, survey researchers realize that some value issues are so important and so unfamiliar in their details that respondents will be unable to resist giving uninformed answers to poorly understood questions. Surely they do. Yet, equally surely, there is strong temptation to stretch the envelope of applications for one's favored tools.

Some reasons for exaggerating the applicability of one's own discipline are common to all disciplines. Anyone can exaggerate the extent to which they are ready for a challenge. Each discipline has an intact critique of its competitors. People who ask questions know what they mean and also know how they would answer. What might be called anthropology's great truth is that we underestimate how and by how much others see the world differently than we do. Paradigms train one to soldier on and solve problems, rather than to reflect on the whole enterprise.

The inconsistent responses opening this chapter present an interesting challenge for that soldiering. As shown in the discussion of those results, each paradigm has a way to accommodate them. Yet investigators in the basic values paradigm seem much more comfortable with such accommodation. They seem more ready to accept the results as real (i.e., produced from sound, replicable studies) and much more ready to see the results as common. Basic values investigators sometimes seem to revel in such discrepancies (e.g., Hogarth, 1982; Nisbett & Ross, 1980), whereas articulated values investigators seem to view them as bona fide, but still sporadic, problems (e.g., Schuman & Presser, 1981).[12] Insight into these discrepant views about discrepancies can be gained by examining the institutional and methodological practices of these paradigms.

### Interest in Discrepancies

Basic values investigators would like to believe that there are many robust discrepancies "out there in the world" because they serve a vital purpose for this kind of science. Discovering a peculiar pattern of unexpected results has been the starting point for many theories (Kahneman & Tversky, 1982). McGuire (1969) has gone so far as to describe the history of experimental psychology as the history of turning artifacts into main effects. For example, increased awareness of experimenter effects (Rosenthal, 1967) stimulated studies of nonverbal communication (e.g., Ekman, 1985). In fact, some critics have argued that psychology is so much driven by anomalies that it tends to exaggerate their importance and generality (Berkeley & Humphreys, 1982). Anomalies make such a good story that it is hard to keep them in focus, relative to the sometimes unquirky processes that produce them (Fischhoff, 1988).

### Interest in Order

On the other hand, articulated values investigators are more interested in *what* people think than in *how* they think. For those purposes, all these quirks are a major headache. They mean that every question may require a substantial development effort before it can be asked responsibly, with elaborate pretesting of alternative presentations. The possibility of anomalies also raises the risk that respondents cannot answer the questions that interest the investigators – at least without the sort of interactive or directive elicitation that is anathema within this paradigm.

Of course, investigators in this paradigm are concerned about these issues. Some of the most careful studies of artifacts have come from survey researchers (e.g., Schuman & Presser, 1981). Classic examples of the effort needed to tie down the subjective interpretation of even seemingly simple questions may be found in the U.S. Department of Commerce studies of how to ask about employment status (Bailar & Rothwell, 1984). However, every research program with resource constraints is limited in its ability to pursue methodological nuances. When those nuances could represent fatal problems, then it is natural to want to believe that they are rare.

For survey research houses, these constraints are magnified by the commercial pressures to keep the shop open and running at a reasonable price. To some extent, clients go to quality and will pay for it. However, there is a limit to the methodological skepticism that even sophisticated clients will tolerate. They need assurance that investigators have the general skill needed to create workable items out of their questions. Clients might know, at some level, that "different questions might have produced different answers" (according to the strange wording that quality newspapers sometimes append to survey results). However, they still need some fiction of tractability.

### Ability to Experiment

A further constraint on articulated values scientists is their theoretical commitment to representative sampling. The expense of such samples means that very few tests of alternative wording can be conducted. Conversely, it means that many discrepancies (like the happiness questions) are only discovered in secondary analyses of studies conducted for other purposes. As a result, there are typically confounding differences in method that blur the comparison between questions.

By contrast, basic values scientists are typically willing to work with convenience samples of subjects. As a result, they can run many tightly controlled experiments, increasing their chances of finding discrepancies. Multiple testing also increases the chances of finding differences by chance. If they are conscientious, these scientists should be able to deal with this risk through replications (which are, in turn, relatively easy to conduct). This indifference to sampling might reflect a self-serving and cavalier attitude. On the other hand, it may be the case that *how* people think might be relatively invariant with respect to demographic features that are known to make a big difference in *what* they think.

### Precision of Search

The theories that basic values scientists derive to account for discrepancies are not always correct. When they are, however, they allow investigators to produce inconsistent responses almost at will. Much of experimental psychology is directed at determining the precise operation of known effects. For example, at the core of prospect theory is a set of framing operations designed to produce inconsistencies. The prevalence of phenomena under laboratory conditions has, of course, no necessary relationship to their prevalence elsewhere. Some extrapolation of prevalence rates from the lab to the world would, however, be only natural (Tversky & Kahneman, 1973). Furthermore, continuing absorption with a phenomenon should sharpen one's eagerness and ability to spot examples. Investigators who want and expect to see a phenomenon are likely to find it more often than investigators who do not. It would be only natural if the confirmation offered by such anecdotal evidence were overestimated (Chapman & Chapman, 1969).

The theoretical tools for seeking nuisance effects in an articulated values study would likely be more poorly defined. For example, the question might be posed as generally as "How common are order effects?" Given the enormous diversity of questions whose order might be reversed, the answer is, doubtless, "very low" in the domain of all possible questions. However, with questions of related content, order effects might be much more common (Poulton & Freeman, 1966). Moreover, questions are more likely to appear in surveys with somewhat related ones, rather than with completely related ones – even in amalgam surveys pooling items from different customers. Without a theory of relatedness, researchers are in a bind. Failure to find an order effect can just be taken as proof that the items were not related.[13]

### Criterion of Interest

Surveys are often conducted in order to resolve practical questions, such as which candidate to support in an election or which product to introduce on the market. As a result, the magnitude of an effect provides the critical test of whether it is worthy of notice. Unless it can be shown to make a difference, who cares? Laboratory results come from out of this world. If they cannot be mapped clearly onto practical problems, then they are likely to seem like curiosities. The psychologists' criterion of statistical significance carries little weight here. Survey researchers, with their large samples, know that even small absolute differences can reach statistical significance.

On the other hand, not all survey questions have that direct a relationship to action. One can assess the effects of being off by 5% in a preelection poll or a product evaluation, as a result of phrasing differences. However, in many other cases, surveys solicit general attitudes and beliefs. These are widely known to be weak predictors of behavior (Ajzen & Fishbein, 1980). As a result, it may be relatively easy to shrug off occasional anomalies as tolerable. Discrepancies should become more important and, perhaps, seem more common as the questions driving research become sharper. The discrepancies associated with contingent valuation studies have come under great scrutiny recently because of their enormous economic consequences. Changes in wording can, in principle, mean the difference between success and failure for entire companies or industries.

### Thinking about Lability

How common are artifacts? is an ill-formed question, insofar as there is no clear universe over which the relative frequency of instances can be defined. Nonetheless, investigators' intuitive feeling for overall frequency must determine their commitment to their paradigms and their ability to soldier on in the absence of definitive data. Understanding the nature and source of one's own disciplinary prejudices is essential for paradigms to be used wisely and to evolve. Understanding other disciplines' (more and less legitimate)

Table 30.3. *Conditions Favorable to Articulated Values*

| |
|---|
| Personally familiar (time to think) |
| Personally consequential (motivation to think) |
| Publicly discussed (opportunity to hear, share views) |
| Uncontroversial (stable tastes, no need to justify) |
| |
| Few consequences (simplicity) |
| Similar consequences (commensurability) |
| Experienced consequences (meaningfulness) |
| Certain consequences (comprehensibility) |
| |
| Single or compatible roles (absence of conflict) |
| Diverse appearances (multiple perspectives) |
| Direct relation to action (concreteness) |
| Unbundled topic (considered in isolation) |
| |
| Familiar formulation |

prejudices is necessary for collaboration. Implicit assumptions about the nature of human values seem to create a substantial divide among the social sciences. If they were to work together, the focal question might shift from how well articulated are values to where are they well articulated. Table 30.3 offers one possible set of conditions favorable to articulated values. Turner (1981) offered another. It might be informative to review the evidentiary record of discrepancies and nondiscrepancies in the light of such schemes.

### Notes

1  The two questions did differ slightly in their introductory phrase. One began "taken all together," the other "taking all things together." Only the bravest of theoreticians would try to trace the pattern in Figure 30.1 to this difference.

2  Subsequent research (Turner, 1984; Turner & Martin, 1984) has shown a somewhat more complicated set of affairs – which may have changed further by the time this chapter is printed and read. Incorporating the most recent twists in this research would change the details but not the thrust of the discussion in the text.

3  Thus, these results would lead one to expect lower renewal rates on insurance policies were subscribers to receive periodic bills for sure losses, rather than for premiums.

4  One is reminded of the finding that undetected computational errors tend to favor investigators' hypotheses. A nonmotivational explanation of this trend is that one is more likely to double-check all aspects of procedure, including calculations, when results are surprising (Rosenthal & Rosnow, 1969).

5  The processes by which these fears were allayed might be usefully compared with the processes by which psychology convinced itself that it knew how to manage the effects of experimenter expectations (Rosenthal, 1967).

6   In actual studies, investigators sometimes just throw out protest responses. At times, they adjust them to more reasonable values (e.g., reducing high values to 10% of disposable income).

7   This is a question of prediction, rather than of evaluation, except in the sense that intentions to have children reflect the perceived value of having them.

8   The need to protect human subjects poses this constraint. Even without it, there would be problems getting people to risk their own money in a gamble contrived by some, possibly mistrusted, scientist.

9   Many contingent valuation studies have elicited values by asking subjects questions such as "Would you pay $1, $2, $3, . . . ?" until they say no. One might compare the implicit structuring of this series of questions with that achieved by "Would you pay $10, $20, $30, . . . ?" or by moving down from $100 in $1 increments.

10  This is just the tip of the iceberg regarding the methodological difficulties of inferring values from observed market behavior (Campen, 1986; Fischhoff & Cox, 1985; Peterson, Driver, & Gregory, 1988). In many cases, technical difficulties make inferring values from behavior an engaging fiction.

11  Fischhoff (1983) considered some of the difficulties of predicting which frames are evoked by naturally occurring situations.

12  This observation was sharply drawn by Professor Robert Abelson at a meeting of the National Research Council Panel on Survey Measure of Subjective Phenomena (Turner & Martin, 1981). This section of my chapter is, in large part, an attempt to work up the pattern that he highlighted.

13  A related example – for which I have unfortunately misplaced the reference and must rely on memory – is the finding that people respond more consistently to items on a common topic when those are grouped in a survey than when the questions are scattered. An (expensive) attempt to replicate this finding took as its common topic attitudes toward shop stewards, and found nothing. That could mean that the first result was a fluke or that *shop stewards* is not a meaningful concept of the sort that could induce consistent attitudes when brought to people's attention.

### References

Achen, C. H. (1975). Mass political attitudes and the survey response. *American Political Science Review, 69*, 1218–1231.

Ajzen, I., & Fishbein, M. (1980). *Understanding attitudes and predicting social behavior.* Englewood Cliffs, NJ: Prentice-Hall.

Bailar, B. A., & Rothwell, N. D. (1984). Measuring employment and unemployment. In C. F. Turner & E. Martin (Eds.), *Survey measure of subjective phenomena* (pp. 129–142). New York: Russell Sage Foundation.

Bentkover, J., Covello, V., & Mumpower, J. (Eds.). (1985). *Benefits assessment: The state of the art.* Amsterdam: Reidel.

Berkeley, D., & Humphreys, P. (1982). Structuring decision problems and the "bias" heuristic. *Acta Psychologica, 50*, 201–250.

Brookshire, D. S., Ives, C. C., & Schulze, W. D. (1976). The valuation of aesthetic preferences. *Journal of Environmental Economics and Management, 3*, 325–346.

Campbell, A., Converse, P., & Rodgers, W. (1976). *The quality of American life: Perceptions, evaluations, and satisfaction.* New York: Russell Sage Foundation.

Campen, J. T. (1986). *Benefit, cost, and beyond.* Cambridge, MA: Ballinger.

Chapman, L. J., & Chapman, J. P. (1969). Genesis of popular but erroneous psychodiagnostic observations. *Journal of Abnormal Psychology, 74*, 271–280.

Converse, P. E. (1964). The nature of belief systems in mass politics. In D. E. Apter (Ed.), *Ideology and discontent*. Glencoe, NY: Free Press.

Coombs, C. H. (1964). *A theory of data*. New York: Wiley.

Cummings, R. D., Brookshire, D. S., & Schulze, W. D. (Eds.). (1986). *Valuing environmental goods: An assessment of the Contingent Valuation Method*. Totowa, NJ: Rowman & Allenheld.

DeMaio, T. J. (1984). Social desirability and survey measurement: A review. In C. F. Turner & E. Martin (Eds.), *Survey measure of subjective phenomena* (pp. 257–282). New York: Russell Sage Foundation.

Dickie, M., Gerking, S., McClelland, G., & Schulze, W. (1987). *Improving accuracy and reducing costs of environmental benefit assessments: Vol. 1. Valuing morbidity: An overview and state of the art assessment* (USEPA Cooperative Agreement No. CR812954-01-2). Washington, DC: U.S. Environmental Protection Agency.

Ekman, P. (1985). *Telling lies*. New York: Norton.

Ellul, J. (1963). *Propaganda*. New York: Knopf.

Fischhoff, B. (1983). Predicting frames, *Journal of Experimental Psychology: Learning, Memory, and Cognition, 9*, 103–116.

Fischhoff, B. (1988). Judgment and decision making. In R. J. Sternberg & E. E. Smith (Eds.), *The psychology of human thought* (pp. 153–187). New York: Wiley.

Fischhoff, B., & Cox, L. A., Jr. (1985). Conceptual foundation for benefit assessment. In J. D. Bentkover, V. T. Covello, & J. Mumpower (Eds.), *Benefits assessment: The state of the art* (pp. 51–84). Amsterdam: Reidel.

Fischhoff, B., & Furby, L. (1988). Measuring values: A conceptual framework for interpreting transactions with special reference to contingent valuation of visibility. *Journal of Risk and Uncertainty, 1*, 147–184.

Fischhoff, B., Slovic, P., & Lichtenstein, S. (1980). Knowing what you want: Measuring labile values. In T. Wallsten (Ed.), *Cognitive processes in choice and decision behavior* (pp. 117–141). Hillsdale, NJ: Erlbaum.

Furby, L. (1986). Psychology and justice. In R. L. Cohen (Ed.), *Justice: Views from the social sciences* (pp. 153–203). New York: Plenum.

Furby, L., & Fischhoff, B. (1989). *Specifying subjective evaluations: A critique of Dickie et al.'s interpretation of their contingent valuation results for reduced minor health symptoms* (U.S. Environmental Protection Agency Cooperative Agreement No. CR814655-01-0). Eugene, OR: Eugene Research Institute.

Gergen, K. J. (1973). Social psychology as history. *Journal of Personality and Social Psychology, 26*, 309–320.

Gilligan, C. (1982). *In a different voice: Psychological theory and women's development*. Cambridge, MA: Harvard University Press.

Hershey, J. R., & Schoemaker, P. J. H. (1980). Risk taking and problem context in the domain of losses: An expected utility analysis, *Journal of Risk and Insurance, 47*, 111–132.

Hogarth, R. M. (Ed.). (1982). *New directions for methodology of the social sciences: Question framing and response consistency*. San Francisco: Jossey-Bass.

Jabine, T. B., Straf, M. L., Tanur, J. M., & Tourangeau, R. (Eds.). (1984). *Cognitive aspects of survey methodology: Building a bridge between disciplines*. Washington, DC: National Academy Press.

Kahneman, D. (1986). Comment. In R. D. Cummings, D. S. Brookshire, & W. D. Schulze (Eds.), *Valuing environmental goods: An assessment of the Contingent Valuation Method*. Totowa, NJ: Rowman & Allenheld.

Kahneman, D., & Tversky, A. (1979). Prospect theory. *Econometrica, 47*, 263–292.

Kahneman, D., & Tversky, A. (1982). On the study of statistical intuitions. *Cognition, 11*, 123–141.

Kuhn, T. S. (1962). *The structure of scientific revolution.* Chicago: University of Chicago Press.

Kunreuther, H., Ginsberg, R., Miller, L., Sagi, P., Slovic, P., Borkin, B., & Katz, N. (1978). *Disaster insurance protection: Public policy lessons.* New York: Wiley.

Lakatos, I., & Musgrave, A. (Eds.). (1970). *Criticism and the growth of scientific knowledge.* Cambridge, England: Cambridge University Press.

McGuire, W. J. (1969). Suspiciousness of experimenter's intent. In R. Rosenthal & R. L. Rosnow (Eds.), *Artifact in behavioral research.* San Diego, CA: Academic Press.

Mitchell, R. C., & Carson, R. T. (1989). *Using surveys to value public goods: The Contingent Valuation Method.* Washington, DC: Resources for the Future.

National Opinion Research Center. (1978). *General Social Surveys, 1972–1978: Cumulative codebook.* Chicago: Author.

Nisbett, R. E., & Ross, L. (1980). *Human inference: Strategies and shortcomings of social judgment.* Englewood Cliffs, NJ: Prentice-Hall.

Nunnally, J. C. (1968). *Psychometric theory* (2nd ed.). New York: McGraw-Hill.

Peterson, G. L., Driver, B. L., & Gregory, R. (Eds.). (1988). *Amenity resource valuation: Integrating economics with other disciplines.* State College, PA: Venture.

Poulton, E. C. (1968). The new psychophysics: Six models for magnitude estimation. *Psychological Bulletin, 69*, 1–19.

Poulton, E. C. (1989). *Bias in quantifying judgments.* London: Erlbaum.

Poulton, E. C., & Freeman, P. R. (1966). Unwanted asymmetrical transfer effects with balanced experimental designs. *Psychological Bulletin, 66*, 1–8.

Raiffa, H. (1968). *Decision analysis.* Reading, MA: Addison-Wesley.

Rokeach, M. (1973). *The nature of human values.* New York: Free Press.

Rosenthal, R. (1967). Covert communication in the psychological experiment. *Psychological Bulletin, 67*, 356–367.

Rosenthal, R., & Rosnow, R. L. (Eds.). (1969). *Artifact in behavioral research.* San Diego, CA: Academic Press.

Samuelson, P. (1954). The pure theory of public expenditure. *Review of Economics and Statistics, 36*, 387–389.

Schuman, H., & Presser, S. (1981). *Questions and answers.* San Diego, CA: Academic Press.

Smith, T. (1984). Nonattitudes: A review and evaluation. In C. F. Turner & E. Martin (Eds.), *Survey measure of subjective phenomena* (pp. 215–256). New York: Russell Sage Foundation.

Smith, V. K., & Desvousges, W. H. (1988). *Measuring water quality benefits.* Boston: Kluwer-Nijhoff.

Stevens, S. S. (1975). *Psychophysics: Introduction to its perceptual, neural, and social prospects.* New York: Wiley.

Sudman, S., & Bradburn, N. M. (1982). *Asking questions: A practical guide to questionnaire design.* San Francisco: Jossey-Bass.

Tolley, G. et al. (1986). *Establishing and valuing the effects of improved visibility in the eastern United States* (USEPA Grant No. 807768-01-0). Washington, DC: U.S. Environmental Protection Agency.

Tune, G. S. (1964). Response preferences: A review of some relevant literature. *Psychological Bulletin, 61*, 286–302.

Turner, C. F. (1981). Surveys of subjective phenomena: A working paper. In D. Johnson (Ed.), *Measurement of subjective phenomena.* Washington, DC: U.S. Government Printing Office.

Turner, C. F. (1984). Why do surveys disagree? Some preliminary hypotheses and some disagreeable examples. In C. F. Turner & E. Martin (Eds.), *Surveying subjective phenomena* (pp. 159–214). New York: Russell Sage Foundation.

Turner, C. F., & Krauss, E. (1978). Fallible indicators of the subjective state of the nation. *American Psychologist, 33*, 456–470.

Turner, C. F., & Martin, E. (Eds.). (1981). *Surveys of subjective phenomena*. Washington, DC: National Academy Press.

Turner, C. F., & Martin, E. (Eds.). (1984). *Surveying subjective phenomena*. New York: Russell Sage Foundation.

Tversky, A., & Kahneman, D. (1973). Availability: A heuristic for judging frequency and probability. *Cognitive Psychology, 5*, 207–232.

Tversky, A., & Kahneman, D. (1981). The framing of decisions and the psychology of choice. *Science, 211*, 453–458.

von Winterfeldt, D., & Edwards, W. (1986). *Decision analysis and behavioral research*. New York: Cambridge University Press.

Wagenaar, W. A. (1989). *Paradoxes of gambling behavior*. London: Erlbaum.

Watson, S., & Buede, D. (1988). *Decision synthesis*. New York: Cambridge University Press.

# 31 The Overconfidence Phenomenon as a Consequence of Informal Experimenter-Guided Selection of Almanac Items

*Peter Juslin*

During the last 2 decades an accumulating body of research has been concerned with *calibration* of subjective probabilities. Calibration measures the extent to which the subjective probabilities provided by an assessor are realized in terms of the corresponding relative frequencies. Thus, according to this norm 60% of the propositions assigned a probability of .6 should turn out to be true, 70% of the propositions assigned a probability of .7, and so forth. Empirical research in this area has suggested at least two principal findings (for reviews see Lichtenstein, Fischhoff, & Phillips, 1982; Wallsten & Budescu, 1983; and O'Connor, 1989). (1) The overconfidence phenomenon: While expert judgments elicited in naturalistic settings often are well calibrated (Murphy & Brown, 1985; Yates & Curley, 1985; Keren, 1987; Wallsten & Budescu, 1983), lay people's assessment of the accuracy of their general knowledge has been characterized by overconfidence. In the spirit of the cognitive bias research program (see Kahneman, Slovic, & Tversky, 1982) this has often been interpreted as evidence for a general overconfidence bias. (2) The hard-easy effect: Overconfidence increases with the objective difficulty of the general knowledge items (almanac items), where objective difficulty is assessed in terms of the percentage of correct answers. For item samples with a high proportion correct underconfidence has been observed (Lichtenstein & Fischhoff, 1977).

The purpose of the present chapter is to challenge this view of the overconfidence phenomenon and to argue for an ecological approach to realism of confidence in general knowledge. People are regarded as well-calibrated to their everyday environments and the overconfidence phenomenon is seen as a pseudo-phenomenon due to the experimenter's informal selection of almanac items, rather than as a consequence of biased cognition. These claims will be substantiated by empirical data. . . .

This chapter originally appeared in *Organizational Behavior and Human Decision Processes*, 1994, *57*, 226–246. Copyright © by Academic Press Inc. Reprinted by permission.

*The Purpose of the Experiment*

The purpose of the experiment was to provide a test of the hypothesis that overconfidence, poor calibration, and poor resolution are consequences of the informal selection of almanac items. If we were able to "debias" the selection of items and select items in a way that allows the sample cue validities, $Sv$, to remain representative of the ecological cue validities, $Ev$, we would expect overconfidence to disappear and people to reveal good calibration. On the other hand, items selected in order to differentiate between more and less knowledgeable subjects should lead to the observation of overconfidence and poor calibration.

More specifically, the following two conditions were compared. (a) In the random selection condition the objects to be compared in the almanac items were selected randomly from a natural environment, a procedure unlikely to create systematic distortions in the $Sv$s. (b) In the informal selection condition a number of human "selectors," instructed to select items that differentiate between subjects high and low in knowledge, selected the almanac items. The potential "universe" of items that could be constructed was the same in both conditions. The almanac items involve comparisons in regard to six target variables that describe the world countries. There is a naturally defined set of objects (i.e., the world countries) that delimit a natural environment. Our hypotheses can thus be formulated.

> (H1) In the random selection condition we expect the overconfidence phenomenon to disappear, and people to reveal good calibration and high resolution.
> (H2) In the informal selection condition we expect a more traditional calibration curve, characterized by substantial overconfidence, low resolution, and poor calibration.

Finally, in order to illustrate the effects of deleting items with extreme solution probabilities a third hypothesis is added.

> (H3) If items with extreme $c_i$ ($c_i$ close to 1.0 or 0) are deleted in the random selection condition, a procedure that "simulates" the informal selection of items, the over/underconfidence score should change in the direction of overconfidence.

## Method

*Subjects*

Twelve subjects, 7 males and 5 females, with an average age of 23 years, performed the informal selection of almanac items. Twenty subjects, 10 males and 10 females, with an average age of 26 years, participated as subjects in the calibration study. All subjects were undergraduate university students and paid at a rate of 60 SEK (about 10 US dollars) per hour.

### Materials

The almanac items were of the half-range format. The subjects selected the answer believed to be the correct one and rated confidence on a scale with six alternatives (50%, 60%, 70%, 80%, 90%, 100%) that followed each item. The scale was anchored with the labels "Random" (50%) and "Absolute certainty" (100%). The items required the subjects to make comparative judgments in regard to six target variables. The target variables were latitudes ("Which city is farther north?"), population of capitals ("Which capital has more inhabitants?"), population of countries ("Which country has a larger population?"), mean life expectancy ("In which country does the population have a higher mean life expectancy?"), area ("Which country has a larger area?"), and population density ("Which country has more inhabitants per $km^2$?"). The 164 countries of the world provided the basis for the item construction.

*The Random Selection Condition.* For each target variable 20 pairs of countries were randomly selected from the pool of 13,366 possible pairwise comparisons that can be constructed on the basis of the 164 countries. This made up a total of 120 items.

*The Informal Selection Condition.* Twelve subjects performed the informal selection of almanac items. The selectors were formed in six pairs, one pair for each target variable. The rationale given to the selectors was that selection of good general knowledge items is a difficult task and that the research project needed help with the selection from persons not involved in the project. No reference was made to calibration or realism of confidence. The written instruction given to the selectors contained the following passage.

The items should be good general knowledge items. That is, the items should provide a test of the knowledge of the subjects, and in a general sense conform to your own standards for what is a good general knowledge item.

Each pair of selectors was equipped with the appropriate statistics, and with a World atlas. The statistics were presented in tables taken in their original shape from the United Nations Demographic Yearbook (1988) or the Swedish Statistical Yearbook (1990). It was stressed that the selection process should be cooperative and that each selected item should conform to the standards of both selectors. In this way each item had to pass the "censorship" of two selectors in order to be included in the sample. Each pair of selectors produced 20 items, making up a total of 120 informally selected items. The selectors spent between 40 and 60 min on the selection task.[1]

*Presentation of the Items to the Subjects in the Calibration Study.* The items were presented to the subjects by means of an interactive computer program (Geocal), implemented on an IBM PS/30. The items appeared one at a time on the computer screen. Each item was first presented along with two answer alternatives. After the subject had selected his/her answer by typing "a" or "b" on the keyboard, the confidence scale appeared below the question. The subject selected a confidence level. Finally, the program asked the subject to confirm his/her choice of answer and level of confidence, now appearing at the bottom of the screen. If the subject was not satisfied with his/her responses the cycle could be reentered for correction. The confirmation made by the subject triggered the program to enter the next item.

### Design and Procedure

The study was similar to a within-subjects design with method for item selection as the equivalent of an independent variable. In contrast to a real experiment, however, we are not investigating the causal impact of different treatments, but rather the consequence of creating different reference classes for evaluating the performance of the subjects. The order of the two conditions was counterbalanced across subjects. The subjects in the calibration study were first presented with a written instruction on how to use the confidence scale and the computer program. They were briefly introduced to the concept of calibration. The subjects were tested individually and worked through the item samples at their own pace. Between the two conditions the subjects had a break that ranged between 30 min and 3 hr, depending on the preferences of the subjects. The total time required to complete both conditions ranged between 65 and 180 min, with a mean of 80 min.

### Results

The calibration curves for the two conditions are shown in Figure 31.1. The calibration curve for the random selection condition falls quite close to the identity line, with a slight tendency toward underconfidence for the lower confidence levels. For the informal selection condition we have a calibration curve with a pronounced deviation from the identity line. As is the case with most published calibration curves based on almanac items, the general tendency is toward overconfidence.

These observations are confirmed by the probabilistic measures presented in Table 31.1. As expected the mean and the variance of confidence were similar in both conditions, while proportion correct $\bar{c}$ and resolution $s_c^2$ were lower in the informal selection condition.

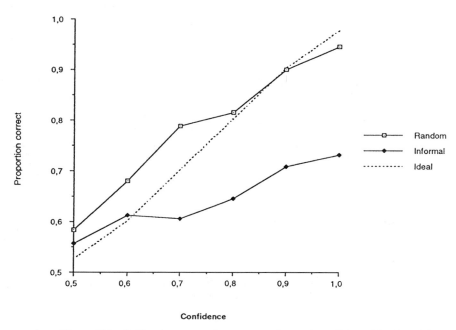

Figure 31.1. Calibration curves for two experimental conditions. The dotted line represents perfect calibration.

The random selection condition is superior in regard to all measures. Miscalibration is four times larger in the informal selection condition, while the resolution $s_c^2$ achieved is less than 20% of the corresponding figure for the random selection condition. As expected, the informal selection condition produced substantial and significant overconfidence (Wilcoxon signed rank

Table 31.1. *Probabilistic Measures for the Two Experimental Conditions*

|  | Selection Procedure | |
| --- | --- | --- |
| Measures | *Random* | *Informal* |
| $N$ | 2400 | 2400 |
| $\bar{x}$ | .722 | .705 |
| $s_x^2$ | .0339 | .0320 |
| $\bar{c}$ | .762 | .628 |
| $s_c^2$ | .0189 | .0037 |
| $(\bar{x} - \bar{c})$ | −.040 | .076 |
| Calibration | .0047 | .0203 |

test, two-tail: $T_{20} = 12$, $p < .01$). The underconfidence observed for the random selection condition also reached significance (Wilcoxon signed rank test, two-tail: $T_{20} = 12.5$, $p < .01$). For each subject an over/underconfidence score, a calibration score, and a resolution score were computed separately for each condition. The hypothesis that the over/underconfidence scores for the two conditions came from the same population of observations was rejected (Wilcoxon signed rank test, one-tail: $T_{20} = 0$, $p < .01$). That is, 20 of 20 subjects had a larger $(x - c)$ in the informal selection condition.

The individual differences were considerable, with some subjects exhibiting substantial underconfidence in both conditions, while other subjects were overconfident in both conditions. The over/underconfidence score ranged between $-0.14$ and $.04$ in the random selection condition, and from $-0.07$ to $.16$ in the informal selection condition. The product–moment correlation between the over/underconfidence scores obtained in the two conditions was $r_{20} = .697$, $p < .01$.

The differences in calibration and resolution were also significant (Wilcoxon signed rank test, one-tail: Calibration; $T_{20} = 47$, $p < .05$ : $s_c^2$; $T_{20} = 30$, $p < .01$). We conclude that the hypothesis, that overconfidence, poor calibration, and poor resolution are consequences of informal selection of almanac items, is supported by the experimental data.

*Item-specific Computations.* For each item the mean confidence judgment $\bar{x}_i$ and the proportion of the subjects that solved the item correctly $c_i$ (the solution probability) were computed. These item-specific computations are shown separately for each condition in Figure 31.2. As was hypothesized, items with a $c_i$ close to 1.0, i.e., items where the modal cue(s) used by the subjects led to the correct answer, were less frequent in the informal selection condition (7 items with $c_i = 1.0$ vs 20 in the random selection condition). Further, items where the modal cues led to the wrong answer (items with a $c_i$ below .5) are more frequent in the informal selection condition (35 vs 21 in the random selection condition). An $(\bar{x} - c)$ score was computed separately for each item. The hypothesis that the 120 items in the random selection condition and the 120 items in the informal selection condition were drawn from the same population of items was rejected (Mann–Whitney test; one-tail: $z = 6.32$, $p < .01$).

*A "Simulation" of the Informal Selection.* It has been suggested that the informal selection in part reflects a tendency to avoid items with extreme $c_i$ (close to 1.0 or 0). Consequently, we should be able to simulate this aspect of the informal selection procedure by deleting all items with a $c_i > .9$ or $c_i < .1$ in the random selection condition. This was expected to change the underconfidence observed for the random selection condition in the direction of overconfidence. This expectation was confirmed. The observed underconfidence of $-0.04$ changed into an overconfidence of 0.04. This demonstration

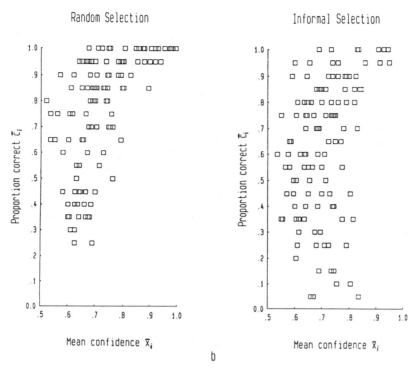

Figure 31.2. Item-specific computations for the two experimental conditions.

should, however, be viewed with caution. The effect may in part reflect the fact that no items with a $c_i = .1$ or $c_i < .1$ were encountered in the random selection condition, something that may be due to sampling error. On the other hand, the absence of items with a $c_i = .1$ or $c_i < .1$ supports the conjecture that these items are encountered very rarely when the objects of judgment have been randomly selected from a natural environment (note that there are five items with $c_i = .1$ or $c_i < .1$ in the informal selection condition: see Figure 31.2).

*Further Data from Random Samples of Items.* Table 31.2 reports three studies where data have been collected by means of paper and pencil tests in group settings. The three (independent) item samples in Table 31.2 were formed in accordance with the procedure used for the random selection condition. Consequently, these data provide further evidence relevant to our first hypothesis: People should be quite well calibrated when the objects of judgment have been randomly selected from a natural environment.

The instructions, and the subject population, were the same as those described under Method. In Table 31.2 the average age of the subject sample

Table 31.2. *Probabilistic Measures for Three Studies Where Samples of Items Have Been Produced by Random Selection Procedures*

| | | Samples | |
|---|---|---|---|
| | Study 1 | Study 2 | Study 3 |
| Format | CA | TF | TF |
| $n$(items) | 120 | 60 | 60 |
| $n$(Ss) | 30 | 16 | 30 |
| Age | 26 | 23 | 24 |
| F/M | 19/11 | 18/14 | 20/12 |
| $N$ | 3600 | 960 | 1920 |
| $\bar{x}$ | .74 | .71 | .70 |
| $s_x^2$ | .0416 | .0341 | .0295 |
| $\bar{c}$ | .78 | .73 | .71 |
| $s_c^2$ | .0194 | .0212 | .0082 |
| $(\bar{x} - \bar{c})$ | −.040 | −.016 | −.016 |
| Calibration | .0070 | .0040 | .0071 |

*Note:* CA, choice of answer, the subjects selects answers; TF, true–false, the subjects assigns truth values; $n$(items), number of items in the item sample; $n$(Ss), number of subjects in the subject group; $N$, total number of responses; Age, average age of the subjects; F/M, number of females/number of males.

is denoted "Age," the proportion of females and males is denoted "F/M," "$n$(items)" refers to the number of items, and "$n$(Ss)" refers to number of subjects. For item samples denoted with CA (Choice of Answer) the item format was the ordinary half-range, forced-choice format presented under Method. However, the item format for item samples marked with TF (True–False) was somewhat different. Each item consisted of a proposition that compared two objects (i.e., countries or capitals) in regard to a target variable. The subjects first indicated whether they believed the proposition to be true or false. Thereafter confidence in this judgment was assessed on an ordinary half-range confidence scale. A TF item thus had the following form.

> 00. France has more inhabitants than Afghanistan.
> Truth-value: ——

| 50% | 60% | 70% | 80% | 90% | 100% |
|---|---|---|---|---|---|
| RANDOM | | | | | CERTAINTY |

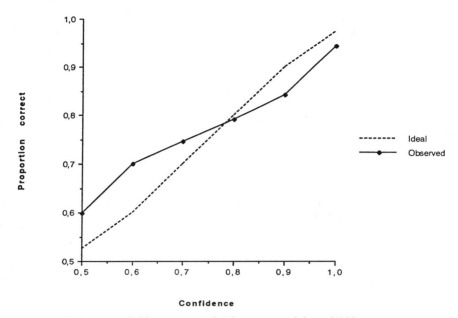

Figure 31.3. Calibration curve for the aggregated data of Table 31.2.

In Study 1 and Study 2 the almanac items involved latitude comparisons and mean life expectancy comparisons, while the almanac items in Study 3 concerned population size of countries and population size of capitals. As can be seen from Table 31.2, all three samples have over/underconfidence scores quite close to zero. The average over/underconfidence across the three samples is −.024. The corresponding average calibration score is .0060. In order to provide measures that can be better compared to those in Table 31.1 in regard to content, the data in Table 31.2 were aggregated into one calibration curve (see Figure 31.3).

The measures for this calibration curve were: $\bar{x} = .724$, $s_x^2 = .0374$, $\bar{c} = .755$, $s_c^2 = .0166$, over/underconfidence $= -.031$, Calibration $= .0055$. If we compare with Table 31.1 we see that the aggregated data from Table 31.2 provide an almost exact replication of the data reported for the random selection condition.

In order to get some points of reference it may be useful to compare the data presented in Table 31.2 with the data reported by Lichtenstein and Fischhoff (1977). This study reported data from altogether 15 conditions (easy vs hard tasks, best, middle and worst subjects) based on three experiments with general knowledge items of the two-alternative, half-range format. Overconfidence (10 conditions) ranged from .03 to .25 with an average of .12, and underconfidence from −.02 to −.06 with an average of −.04. The average over/underconfidence across all 15 samples was .067. The corresponding mean value across the samples in Table 31.2 is $-.024$. The calibration scores in Lichtenstein and Fischhoff (1977) ranged from .005 to .086 with an average of .024. The corresponding average calibration score across the samples in Table 31.2 is .0060. The $s_c^2$ in Lichtenstein and Fischhoff range between .003 and .017, with a mean of .0106. The mean of the $s_c^2$ in Table 31.2 is .0166.

In brief, the over/underconfidence and calibration scores reported in the study by Lichtenstein and Fischhoff (1977) are considerably poorer than the corresponding scores in Table 31.2. The argument of the present chapter is that this poor performance reflects the informal procedures used for item selection (e.g., post hoc divisions of the items into hard and easy on the basis of outcome), rather than biased cognition.

## Discussion

According to an ecological approach to realism of confidence we need to distinguish between two aspects of cue-based inferences. The first aspect is the objective effectiveness of the cue(s) in the subject's natural environment (the $Evs$), and in a specific item sample (the $Svs$). The second aspect is the "subjective" effectiveness of the cue(s) (the $Ivs$). The $Ivs$ are generated from the subject's knowledge structures and reflects the subject's beliefs about his environment. It is stressed that the $Ivs$ are formed by experience of the $Evs$ that hold in the subject's natural environment, while calibration is evaluated on the basis of the $Svs$ that hold for specific experimental samples of items. A minimum requirement for the observation of good calibration is that the $Svs$ remain representative of the $Evs$ in the subject's natural environment. Thus, the approach outlined here provides a hypothesis in regard to the descriptive aspect of the reference class problem.

The ecological approach can explain both the overconfidence phenomenon observed in studies with almanac items and the good calibration observed when the objects of judgment are selected randomly from a natural environment, something that no previous account can accomplish (e.g., that of Koriat, Lichtenstein, & Fischhoff, 1980). The overconfidence phenomenon is explained as a consequence of the procedures involved in the creation of traditional almanac items, rather than as the result of a cognitive bias. The results presented here support this interpretation of the overconfidence phenomenon and indicate that general procedures for debiasing overconfidence may be unwarranted. Further, a highly related account of the hard–easy effect reported by Lichtenstein and Fischhoff (1977) is provided, an explanation that received support in a recent study (Juslin, 1993a). Very similar views on the overconfidence phenomenon and the hard–easy effect have recently and independently been developed by Gigerenzer et al. (1991).

The hypothesis that the overconfidence phenomenon to a large extent reflects the creation of a biased reference class due to the informal selection of almanac items should, of course, not be taken to mean that people never are overconfident. On the contrary, real states of over- or underconfidence become more interesting once these selection effects are eliminated. Further, the conclusions suggested here are, at present, restricted to confidence in answers to almanac items. Future research will also have to account for the existence of large individual differences, a neglected problem in regard to both measurement and psychological theory.

The answer to the normative issue that has been implicit in the research presented here conforms to the *Principle of Behavior-Research Isomorphy* formulated by Brunswik (1952), implying that research should focus where behavior focuses. This principle suggests that if we believe that the subjects "aim" at calibration to a natural environment ($R_j$), their performance should be evaluated in terms of a set of tasks that allow the $Svs$ to remain representative of the $Evs$. For many kinds of predictions (e.g., weather forecasts), performed professionally by experts, there is a reference class defined by an environment of natural concern to both "producers" and "consumers" of these forecasts. When calibration is evaluated in terms of this reference class we are likely to approximate the $R_j$ of the forecasters. In the present study we tried to approximate $R_j$ by applying random sampling procedures on the basis of a natural set of objects. However, we do not know the actual range of the cues used for the solution of many kinds of almanac items, e.g., concerning sport or historical events. Consequently, the reference class problem, and the principle of behavior-research isomorphy, provides a serious challenge to calibration research based on general knowledge items.

The present chapter has mainly discussed the external validity of the overconfidence phenomenon. The external validity of a number of other conclusions based on informally selected almanac items may also be questioned. For instance, a number of studies have attempted to relate probabilistic performance to the knowledge and intelligence of the subjects (Lichtenstein & Fischhoff, 1977; Wright & Ayton, 1987) and to various personality traits of the subjects (Wright & Phillips, 1979). Some studies have compared the over/underconfidence and calibration scores for different conditions, often with the purpose of debiasing overconfidence (e.g., Koriat et al., 1980; Allwood and Montgomery, 1987; Arkes, Christensen, Lai, & Blumer, 1987), while other studies have compared general knowledge tasks with predictions (Wright & Wisudha, 1982; Wright, 1982; Ronis & Yates, 1987; Keren 1985). The conclusions of these studies may be restricted to sets of informally selected items and may not generalize to everyday decision making.

### Note

1   Informal discussions with the selectors after the selection session supported the expectations about the process of item selection. That is, "trivial" items were avoided and there was a preference for "interesting" facts.

## References

Allwood, L. M., & Montgomery, H. (1987). Response selection strategies and realism of confidence judgments. *Organizational Behavior and Human Decision Processes, 39,* 365–383.

Arkes, H. R., Christensen, C., Lai, C., & Blumer, C. (1987). Two methods of reducing overconfidence. *Organizational Behavior and Human Decision Processes, 39,* 133–144.

Brunswik, E. (1952). *The conceptual framework of psychology.* Chicago: Univ. of Chicago Press.

Gigerenzer, G., Hoffrage, U., & Kleinbölting, H. (1991). Probabilistic mental models: A Brunswikian theory of confidence. *Psychological Review,* in press.

Kahneman, D., Slovic, P., & Tversky, A. (1982). *Judgments under uncertainty: Heuristics and biases.* New York: Cambridge Univ. Press.

Keren, G. (1987). Facing uncertainty in the game of bridge: A calibration study. *Organizational Behavior and Human Decision Processes, 39,* 98–114.

Koriat, A., Lichtenstein, S., & Fischhoff, B. (1980). Reasons for confidence. *Journal of Experimental Psychology: Human Learning and Memory, 6,* 107–118.

Lichtenstein, S., & Fischhoff, B. (1977). Do those who know more also know more about how much they know? *Organizational Behavior and Human Performance, 20,* 159–183.

Lichtenstein, S., Fischhoff, B., & Phillips, L. D. (1982). Calibration of probabilities: The state of the art to 1980. In D. Kahneman, P. Slovic, & A. Tversky (Eds.), *Judgments under uncertainty: Heuristics and biases* (pp. 306–334). New York: Cambridge Univ. Press.

Murphy, A. H., & Brown, B. G. (1985). A comparative evaluation of objective and subjective weather forecasts in the United States. In G. Wright (Ed.), *Behavioral decision making* (pp. 329–359). New York: Plenum Press.

O'Connor, M. (1989). Models of human behavior and confidence in judgment: A review. *International Journal of Forecasting, 5,* 159–169.

Ronis, D. L., & Yates, J. F. (1987). Components of probability judgment accuracy: Individual consistency and effects of subject matter and assessment method. *Organizational Behavior and Human Decision Processes, 40,* 193–218.

Yates, J. F., & Curley, S. P. (1985). Conditional distribution analyses of probabilistic forecasts, *Journal of Forecasting, 4,* 61–73.

Wallsten, T. S., & Budescu, D. V. (1983). Encoding subjective probabilities: A psychological and psychometric review. *Management Science, 29,* 152–173.

Wright, G. (1982). Changes in the realism and distribution of probability assessments as a function of question type. *Acta Psychologica, 52,* 165–174.

Wright, G., & Ayton, P. (1987). Task influences on judgmental forecasting. *Scandinavian Journal of Psychology, 28,* 115–127.

Wright, G., & Phillips, L. D. (1979). Personality and probabilistic thinking: An exploratory study. *British Journal of Psychology, 70,* 295–303.

Wright, G., & Wisudha A. (1982). Distribution of probability assessments for almanac and future event questions. *Scandinavian Journal of Psychology, 23,* 219–224.

# 32 The A Priori Case against Graphology: Methodological and Conceptual Issues

*Maya Bar-Hillel and Gershon Ben-Shakhar*

*Motivation for Testing*

From time immemorial, people have wondered about the true nature of their fellow men, and have looked for cues that would reveal that nature to them. On the simple level, we size people up on the basis of their appearance, voice, etc. At the other end of the scale lies the domain of psychological testing.

Psychological tests come in many shapes and colors. They can differ as to goal (e.g., achievement versus aptitude), scope (describing the entire person versus predicting only one trait), by elicitation method (e.g., projective techniques versus questionnaires), by evaluation method (e.g., holistic intuitive evaluation versus closed scoring manuals), etc. But their common denominator is the desire to uncover or discover an unobservable truth about another from more readily available and observable behavior samples.

It is hardly necessary to explain the motivation for such endeavors. On the personal level, knowledge about others has important implications for one's own behavior and decisions. In modern industrialized societies, the ability to diagnose and predict people's behavior and their enduring patterns of traits and characteristics, acquires immense economic and societal significance that transcends the personal level.[1] Selection and classification of people for allocation of resources and duties (e.g., jobs, educational opportunities, therapeutic interventions, etc.) can be made immeasurably more efficient – or more congenial and fair – if the abilities and qualities of the potential candidates can be assessed or predicted.

Prevalent methods of psychological testing typically require information which can be obtained at most within a few hours, and which is relatively easily accessible. Methods relying on information that can be assessed even without the knowledge or cooperation of the testee are even more desirable.

From B. Nevo (Ed.), *Scientific Aspects of Graphology: A Handbook*, 1986. Courtesy of Charles C Thomas, Publisher, Ltd, Springfield, Illinois.

556

## *Two Domains of Psychological Testing*

Psychological tests can be loosely divided into tests of ability and tests of personality. In ability testing, the prototype of which is the IQ test, the first systematic attempt of modern times, undertaken by the French educator, Alfred Binet, at the turn of the century, was successful. Binet's idea was simple: If you want to detect intellectual brightness or dullness, ask questions of the kind that you think bright people are more likely than dull people to answer correctly, and score people by their success with such questions. This basic idea still characterizes much of intelligence testing.

This success story is in marked contrast with the story of personality testing. Whereas validity coefficients for ability tests typically range around .4 to .6, personality tests seldom enjoy validities of over .2 to .3.[2] Yet the attempts to assess personality systematically have a history even longer than that of intelligence assessment. Some methods are encountered today only in tales of old, as in the biblical story of Gideon selecting warriors according to how they drank water from a flowing stream (Judges, Ch. 7, Verses 1–8). These stories may have no basis in fact, but the methods they describe highlight a truth that still holds today: anyone can, and many do, invent their own idiosyncratic personality test.

A small inventory that we drew shows an amazing variety both of established and of esoteric "tests," some of which seem to have little to recommend them beyond the fact that they obviously show individual differences among people. The tests are based on: time and place of birth (astrology and numerology), line patterns on the palm (palmistry), patterns of bumps on the skull (phrenology), body characteristics (somatotype theory), patterns in externally produced configurations of cards (Tarot readings), color preferences (Luscher color test), dreams, word associations, responses to representational or abstract visual stimuli (e.g., the Thematic Apperception Test), free-hand drawings (e.g., Draw-a-Person tests, etc.), patterns of individual differences in responses to ability tests (e.g., IQ tests), etc. To this list might be added commonsensical cues such as biographical details, as well as style of dress, manner of speech, etc. Indeed, the limit to what can potentially be used as a guide to the inner self seems to be set largely by the limits of imagination – and audacity.[3]

Various kinds of rationale underlie personality tests. Some seem to be based on face validity – the judgment that test items really measure what they are supposed to. Typical here are, for example, the various pulp magazine questionnaires designed for self-diagnosis of psychological properties such as assertiveness, femininity, extroversion, etc.

Other tests are based on some notion of representativeness (Nisbett & Ross, 1980): the items may not be sampled directly from the content universe of interest, but they bear some kind of resemblance to it. Typically, the information gathered by these tests lends itself readily to description by adjectives suitable to or suggestive of personality description as well, and so when the test results show property X, it is taken as an indication that the subject has property X.

Other tests are simply based on the empirical observation that certain traits convey. Thus, if individuals that are independently known to differ on some dimension of interest (e.g., normal versus psychotic; extrovert versus introvert; career oriented versus family oriented; etc.) are found to respond in a systematically different manner to some questions or tasks, then the latter differences can be exploited for diagnostic purposes when the former are not known. Such, for example, is the rationale underlying the Minnesota Multiphasic Personality Inventory (MMPI), or the Strong Vocational Interest Blank. For example, "Masculinity-femininity measures traditionally have been constructed empirically so that on each item the response scored 'masculine' is the one that is endorsed by most males while the one scored 'feminine' is the one favored verbally by the majority of females" (Mischel, 1976, p. 141).

Naturally, tests can combine more than one rationale.

From a strictly scientific point of view, of course, the acid test for any proposed personality test is to put it to an empirical test. To be valid, it is not sufficient that a test be based on an appealing rationale. It has also actually to work.[4] It is extremely difficult to generate the kind of evidence that conclusively and rigorously demonstrates a test's validity. Decades of research have led to the conclusion that some of these difficulties are inherent in the construct being assessed by these tests – i.e., personality. This has led to skepticism about the very possibility of the naive kind of personality assessment that is based on the model of ability testing. The case of graphology can serve very nicely to demonstrate some of these issues and difficulties.

## What Is Graphology?

### Various Uses of Handwriting Analysis

Handwriting analysis is carried out for many purposes besides character assessment. In the forensic sciences it may be used to establish the identity of the writer, or the authenticity of the sample: in the medical sciences it may be used to diagnose drug effects (e.g., Hirsch, Jarvik, & Abramson, 1956; Legge, Steinberg, & Summerfield, 1964) or intoxication (e.g., Rabin & Blair, 1953); for the developmental sciences, writing provides a fascinating example of an acquired finely tuned motor skill; etc. The present chapter, however, pertains solely to attempts to predict behavior or derive personality descriptions from such analysis, and we shall limit the term "graphology" (as contrasted with the more general term "handwriting analysis") to this specific endeavor. Our critique of this endeavor should not be taken as an indictment of other forms of handwriting analysis, any more than a validation of handwriting analysis for those purposes should be taken as evidence for its validity as a personality test.

### Two Meanings of "Graphology"[5]

Personality assessment by graphology can be taken to refer both to the principle of the endeavor (i.e., the potential use of handwriting analysis for personality assessment), and to the actual field as defined by the manuals and practices of its adherents and experts. This distinction is important, since there is no single dominant theory or method of graphology, nor a central textbook. Hence, it is entirely possible, in principle, that one graphological theory be highly valid while another is not, or even that all existing graphological systems be invalid although the potential for a valid system is hidden in the features of handwriting. Our discussion will not be addressed to any specific graphological method, but rather will deal largely with issues relevant to the enterprise in its entirety. Nonetheless, the absence of a general consensus among graphologists is noteworthy, since it is one of the methodological concerns in this area. It reflects the state of the art, and has direct bearing on some of the issues which we shall consider. Thus, this chapter will combine a methodological critique of graphology as it is standardly practiced with an outline of the methodological concerns facing any graphological – or other – attempt at personality assessment.

Since graphology can, in principle, proceed via the extraction of any kind of information from any kind of handwritten text, it is instructive to list those aspects of graphology that characterize most prevalent methods, so that we shall have something concrete to examine.

### Input

In general, graphologists prefer handwritten samples that were not generated specifically for the purpose of being analyzed, and are spontaneous and expressive rather than the result of copying some text or of writing down from memory some standard text such as a poem or a pledge of allegiance. They prefer several samples produced at various times and under various circumstances to a single specimen, and a text of some length. They require a writing tool that is sensitive to factors such as pressure and speed, such as a pen, and caution against analyzing a photostatic handwritten sample. They are happier with a sample that includes the writer's signature. Advance knowledge of the writer's sex and age is deemed crucial and many require, in addition, information about the writer's nationality, and a brief medical and educational history. Handedness seems to be required too, though many manuals neglect to list it. Other information does not seem to be a firm prerequisite, but graphologists appreciate some background social and cultural facts about the writer, and in practice often know much more than that, including the reason that the graphological analysis is sought.

Some of these requirements are self-explanatory. Naturally, if pressure and speed are important graphological cues, one wants them maximally reflected in the handwritten sample; other cues might have different implications if they are standard in the writer's graphological community, or are idiosyncratic. However, the request for age and sex is rather odd, because rarely have we seen graphological manuals stratified according to these variables.[6]

### Output

The typical graphological analysis addresses itself in a global fashion to all aspects of the writer's personality, and its result is usually presented in the form of a free-style characterization of the entire personality. The methods whereby graphologists work vary a great deal, and need not concern us here.

### The A Priori Case for Graphology: Face Validity

On the face of it, handwriting analysis looks like an excellent candidate for personality assessment. Unlike palmistry, astrology, etc., the analysis relies on an actual sample of individual behavior. Indeed, the behavior is self-generated and expressive of its producer (Allport & Vernon, 1933).

Handwriting is also very rich in features and attributes which afford it the requisite scope for expressing the richness of personalities. Indeed, handwriting is as unique as personalities. Moreover, people can be more or less similar on various dimensions of handwriting, just as they can be more or less similar on various dimensions of personality. Like personality, handwriting exhibits both individual differences and shared structure.

Furthermore, handwriting is a stable characteristic of the individual (Fluckinger, Tripp, & Weinberg, 1961) which nevertheless shows development over time. It more or less retains its recognizable identity across writing media – not only pen versus pencil, but also page versus blackboard and even, to a lesser extent, mirror writing, writing with the nondominant hand, etc. Since these employ totally different muscles, it has led to some calling handwriting "brainwriting" (e.g., Saudek, 1929). Similarly, changes in writing circumstances (e.g., taking a dictation, copying a text, writing a complex essay, jotting down a shopping list), and in moods of the writer, seldom hinder us from recognizing a familiar handwriting, even if it underwent some changes due to these changing circumstances. This allows handwriting to reflect persisting cross-situational components of personality as well as those that are more occasional and transient. From a pragmatic point of view, just about anyone who is likely to undergo a personality test can write. A sample of handwriting is obtainable cheaply and quickly, and does not even require the consent or cooperation of the contributor. And, if handwriting analysts are to be believed, attempts to alter one's handwriting in order to foil the analyst are seldom successful, because the skilled analyst can either detect the attempt at deceit, or even see through it (Osborn, 1929). Finally, graphology seems not to be limited in terms of what it can divulge about the inner person. It claims to be able to detect attributes for which no other tests exist – most notably, honesty. Indeed, handwriting allegedly divulges the whole personality.

## Reexamining the A Priori Case for Graphology

The previous section highlighted various factors that argue, on a priori grounds, for the suitability of handwriting as a basis for personality assessment. There are, however, serious flaws in the a priori case for graphology. In this section we wish to point them out, and question both graphology's claim that handwriting potentially reveals the writer's personality, and graphologists' claim that state-of-the-art graphology has already figured out the key to the correspondence between personality features and those of handwriting. Some of the points we shall raise are based on circumstantial evidence. They are offered, however, not as proof of the invalidity of graphology, but just to emphasize that its apparent a priori advantages are no substitute for an empirical validation.

1. *How plausible is the connection between personality and handwriting?* With respect to some traits, a connection is quite plausible. For example, sloppy handwriting suggests a sloppy writer; stylized calligraphy indicates some artistic flair; bold, energetic script conjures an image of a bold, energetic personality; etc. To the extent that these inferences are valid, they are relatively easy to explain. Writing sloppily is an actual behavioral instance of sloppiness, artistic flair may well mean, among other things, an inclination to adopt a stylized handwriting, and a high level of energy would naturally find expression in one's motor movements, writing included. Such inferences are commonsensical and would seem to require no particular expertise.

We hasten to clarify that we are not asserting that any such connections actually exist, merely that we would not be arguing the case against graphology if its claims were restricted to the assertion of such connections. But graphology claims to be able to derive from handwriting much more – traits such as honesty, insight, leadership, vulnerability, responsibility, warmth, analytical capacity, musicality, sadistic inclinations, promiscuity, loyalty, etc. What reason is there to believe that traits such as these find any kind of expression in any graphological features? With respect to some, there is even no reason to believe that they are expressed in any kind of motor movement – and features of the body movement are only loosely correlated with writing movements, if at all (Allport & Vernon, 1933). Indeed, if a correspondence were to be empirically found between graphological features and such traits, it would be a major theoretical challenge to account for it. Other correspondences posited by some graphologists would, if they actually existed, be nothing short of miraculous. For examples: Sadism is expressed by sharply pointed end strokes (Friedenhain, 1959); suicidal tendencies are expressed by a signature and stroke that turns back upon the capital initial, crossing over it (Singer, 1969); the angular writer can be expected to be "firm, strong-minded, hard, uncompromising, tense, and tending to lack in ability to 'feel' " (Patterson, 1976); pregnancy can be detected from the way a woman writes letters with "bellies," such as the Hebrew Gimel (Koren, 1983); etc.

To be sure, science often makes use of signs whose relationship to what they indicate is far from intuitively obvious: spectograms, carbon dating, etc. But these relationships are anchored in theory and sustained by evidence, rather than being based exclusively on common association or representation (see Nisbett & Ross, 1980, on folk medicines). None of the examples above was supported by research.

2. *Are there enough constraints in graphological analysis?* The very richness of handwriting can be its downfall, especially if one compounds it by analyzing several different samples from the writer. Unless the graphologist makes firm commitments to the nature of the correspondence between handwriting and personality, one can find ad hoc corroboration for any claim. Moreover, when adopting an empiricist approach, one can then always find some variable on which some difference between two distinct populations (as defined by some trait) is significant.

3. *How robust is the connection between personality and handwriting features?* Graphologists' insistence on one particular writing instrument to the exclusion of others, on several writing samples taken at different times rather than just one, and on original texts rather than copied texts or photostats, is curious in the light of claims of relative constancy, especially since the a priori intuitions supporting graphology which were listed above operate on a much wider range of texts than those graphologists find acceptable. It may well be the case that some handwriting samples reflect personality better than others, but the insistence on particular kinds of handwriting samples is not supported by any account of why personality factors would express themselves in one and not in another, or by empirical demonstrations that these differences really do make a difference. As matters stand presently, it appears that from a graphological viewpoint, handwriting is actually extremely sensitive to extraneous influences that have nothing to do with personality.

4. *Is there consensus among graphologists?* A survey of expository books on graphology show a great deal of idiosyncracy and divergence. For example, the "modern" trend seems to be an increased reliance on global, holistic features of the handwriting, but many still use something akin to a "dictionary" of signs with fixed meanings. The absence of reliability between graphologists sets severe limitations on the validity coefficients that can be obtained.

None of the proposed methods are based on serious research. Clearly, it is not sufficient to establish the plausibility of some connections between handwriting and personality; the specific details of the nature of this connection must be worked out.

## "Mission Impossible": Why All Personality Tests Have Low Validities

In the previous section, we focused critically on some of the factors that seem to favor graphology, on a priori grounds, as compared to other popular methods of personality prediction, giving it some "scientific" plausibility. In the present section, we wish to focus on some of the factors that impede any personality test from having high predictive accuracy. These have nothing to do with the specific nature of the graphological enterprise, but they do apply to graphology as an instance of a general class. If the previous sections focussed on the suitability of handwriting as a means for personality assessment, the present section focusses on the end toward which personality tests are geared, namely the prediction of behavior, pointing out the obstacles to this goal.

### Traits versus Situations

Personality traits are not directly observable. Rather, they are constructs inferred from behavior. One of their chief functions is to serve as a way of organizing and systematizing an individual's various behaviors in a manner that accounts for differences among people and enables prediction within people. Although most psychological theories – including naive ones (i.e., those of laypeople) – assume that people behave more or less consistently over situations and time, a vast amount of empirical research has shown that there is less consistency in behavior than these theories would lead us to expect (e.g., Mischel, 1976). Since

behavior is situation-specific – [i.e.,] more dependent on the nature of the specific situation in which it occurs than on enduring traits or response tendencies in the person . . . [then] it is not very useful to characterize people in broad trait terms ("impulsive," "dependent," and so on) because individuals show variability and discrimination in their behavior. Whether a person acts impulsively depends to a great extent on the particular conditions she or he confronts. (Hilgard, Atkinson, & Atkinson, 1983, p. 413).

In other words, it is not possible to predict with much accuracy how a person would behave in a new situation from knowing how the person has behaved previously. Indeed, "it has been found that normal people tend to show considerable variability in their behavior even across seemingly similar conditions" (Mischel, 1976, p. 159). The fact that people tend to overattribute the causes of others' behavior to their dispositions and underattribute them to situational forces was labelled the fundamental attribution error by Ross (1977; 1978).

It follows from the above that if we wish to predict how people will behave in a certain situation, it is helpful to know how they have previously behaved in the same sort of situation. This is the approach taken today by assessment centers. This approach brings candidates for some position or job to a center where their performance is intensively and individually watched under conditions which attempt to simulate those under which they will actually be operating in the position or job. Although this prediction method is considerably more costly and time-consuming than standard personality tests, it reflects the growing realization that shortcuts simply fail to do the job. Whether or not a paper and pencil questionnaire – or a face-to-face interview – or analysis of projective tests opens a window to the real underlying personality, revealing the real inner self, it does not allow the prediction of actual behavior – which, ultimately, is the real variable of interest – with anything approaching satisfactory accuracy.

In a sense, graphological analysis is a move in exactly the opposite direction from the principle guiding assessment centers. It is an attempt to infer from how people behave in a single context – and one which is not a prototypical behavioral context – what kind of people they really are. It relies on a supreme article of faith that the characteristics of such behavior, as they are expressed in handwriting features, are indicative of the personality as a whole, and therefore of the entire range of an individual's behavior. It is a holographic notion of personality, and flies in the face of much of the evidence in the field.

The reasons why cross-situational behavioral consistency is so low have been discussed at length elsewhere (e.g., Mischel, 1976; Nisbett & Ross, 1980). Here we shall briefly mention a few.

First, behaviors and personality traits do not correspond one-to-one. Indeed, the same trait can cause a whole range of different behaviors and even opposing ones (e.g., some shy people when in a party shrink from social contact, withdrawing quietly, while others might drink a lot to overcome shyness, becoming loud and boisterous). And many different traits, even contrasting ones, can result in the same behavior (e.g., some of those who are loud and boisterous in a party are uninhibited extroverts, while others are timid introverts covering up and overcompensating). Second, two different people, even when put in the same situation extensionally and even if they (are assumed to) possess the same trait, may behave differently, if the situation assumes a different subjective or phenomological meaning for them. Third, some traits are applicable to a person without there even being much of an expectation of cross-situational consistency. For example, it is sufficient that a person be occasionally dishonest, or occasionally original, to deserve the trait name (Tversky, 1985). Fourth, traits may designate latent dispositions that are not realized in behavior because of lack of opportunity, incentive, etc. Thus, "inability to withstand temptation" would only manifest itself in the presence of temptation of sufficient magnitude.

Reasons such as this make it difficult to infer from traits what a person's behavior would be like, even assuming that the traits are correctly diagnosed and applied. The person reading a graphological character analysis, however, has a distinct sense that an integrated, whole personality has been put together, and that he now actually knows the person described. Moreover, it might give one a sense of being able to account for and explain observed behaviors. At the same time, however, it is of little help in predicting behavior.

This may explain the reluctance of many graphologists to have their work evaluated against specific behavioral or other observable criteria. Most graphologists, for example, decline to predict the sex of the writer from the handwriting, insisting that handwriting only reveals psychological, rather than biological, gender (e.g., Crépieux-Jamin, 1926). While common sense would agree that some women are masculine and some men are effeminate, it would be somewhat perverse to argue against the presumption that most women must be feminine and most men masculine. That would seem to render the terms rather empty of empirical content (recall the quote from Mischel, 1976, which we quoted above). Furthermore, even laypeople can diagnose a writer's sex from handwriting correctly about 70% of the time (e.g., Goodenough, 1945), whereas the diagnosis of "dominance" versus "nondominance" (often taken to be the equivalent of masculinity-femininity) is no better than chance (e.g., Eisenberg, 1938; Middleton, 1939). It would therefore seem reasonable to expect graphologists to be willing – and able – to predict a writer's sex from handwriting. That they refuse to do so reflects, under a charitable interpretation, their preference for predicting deep-lying unobservables to their observable correlates and perhaps even a disavowal of the relevance of behavioral criteria to the evaluation of their assessments.

## Why Does Graphology Appear to Work?

The popular appeal of graphology rests on two bases. One is its face validity, or the a priori factors favoring it. The other is the fact that people who have had some experience with graphological analysis are usually positively impressed. In other words, graphology "works." This is called personal validation and is, subjectively, an extremely powerful evidential source. Unfortunately, a sense of personal validation is rather easy to impart, and by means that have little if anything to do with true validity. Indeed, many of these means are no more than cheap gimmicks. Hyman (1977) lists some of these tricks and methods. Prior to becoming a cognitive psychologist, Hyman himself enjoyed a brief career as a cold reader (i.e., a character reader who has little if any advance information about the client prior to the actual reading). This puts him in a position to combine his personal experience and familiarity with the tricks of the trade with insights anchored in psychological research.

### The Barnum Effect

One powerful way to make strangers believe that you know all about them is to give them a character reading composed of certain statements that – though vague, contradictory, or universally true – are considered by just about all people to be uniquely descriptive of themselves. Indeed, in one study (Forer, 1949), people who thought that a certain personality sketch was written specially for them by a psychologist on the basis of a personality test gave the sketch a rating of over 4 on a 5-point scale ranging from 1 (poor fit), to 5 (perfect fit). In fact, the sketch given all of them was the same standard and uniform one. This effect has since been replicated in scores of classrooms in many countries and over many years, including by one of the present authors, who does it routinely in Introductory Psychology classes with much the same results (see also Hyman, 1977; Snyder and Shenkel, 1975).

Synder did a series of studies which uncovered some of the factors that enhance this effect (Snyder, 1974; Snyder and Shenkel, 1975). An important factor is that the client be prepared in advance to believe that the reading is done uniquely for him or her, using a method of some repute, or one in the validity of which the client is a priori willing to believe. Hyman (1977) developed a recipe for the ideal stock spiel. It consisted of a combination of "about 75% desirable items, but ones which were seen as specific, and about 25% undesirable items, but ones which were seen as general. The undesirable items had the apparent effect of making the spiel plausible" (p. 31). Many, however (e.g., Freud, 1933), have noted that telling the client what he or she wants to hear is very effective, even without adding the subtle touch of not being totally complimentary. Flattery, it has often been observed, will get you everywhere. When clients voluntarily solicit the opinion of a character reader, some of the important conditions are automatically met. (The "Barnum effect" takes its name from a quote from P. T. Barnum of Barnum and Bailey's Circus fame, that "there's a sucker born every minute.")

### "Cold Reading"

The stock spiel, effective as it is, can be improved upon if the reader has an opportunity to interact with the client and is sufficiently sensitive and observant. It is then possible to give a reading which not only sounds uniquely descriptive of the client, but actually is, since it incorporates specific elements picked up before or during the reading. One effective method is to begin with vague generalities and let the client's reactions direct you to truth. Typically, the naive client will not only steer you in the right direction, but will be actively engaged in interpreting whatever the reader is saying in a manner that would make it meaningful and sensible in terms of the client's personal history and concerns.

### Graphological Character Readings

Hyman does not list graphology in his paper, but it is easy to see how his tips can be readily applied by the graphologists who in addition, enjoy other advantages that enhance personal validation and that do not typically accrue to cold readers. First, they often have "hot" – namely, truly relevant and diagnostic – information prior to their character reading, for example, when a graphologist is asked by some firm to assess the suitability of candidates for potential employment on the basis of handwritten autobiographical sketches submitted by the candidates. Such sketches can lead to predictions of modest validity simply by virtue of the bio-data they contain, as well as other non-graphological attributes of the text (see e.g., Ben-Shakhar, Bar-Hillel, & Flug, 1985). Indeed, an autobiographical sketch is the typical handwritten sample used in these circumstances. The client may well receive a sense of personal validation – from output that has little, if anything, to do with graphological analysis, though that is what it purports to be.

Second, large-scale clients of graphologists, such as firms and organizations, are seldom in a position to evaluate the reading given by the graphologists against the truth. In other words, a criterion may be completely unavailable, for many reasons: some candidates are simply rejected at the graphologist's recommendations, other predictions have no clear observable correlates, etc. Even here, however, clients can get a sense of personal validation simply because a proficient graphologist can give a reading that simply sounds good. The character sketch may be rich or credible or familiar enough that it checks not with any specific piece of reality but simply with one's notion of what people are like.

### Why Does Personal Validation Work?

Graphology, we have argued, appears to work because personal validation is mistakenly substituted for empirical validation, although it is an illusory and fallacious validity measure. Why, however, does personal validation work? Hyman argues persuasively that the astute cold reader goes beyond reliance on people's gullibility or suggestibility. On the contrary, the cold reader enlists their active intelligence as problem solvers and as natural inference makers to assist him. A

reading succeeds just because it calls upon the normal processes of comprehension that we ordinarily bring to bear in making sense out of any form of communication. The raw information in a communication is rarely, if ever, sufficient in itself for comprehension. A shared context and background is assumed. Much has to be filled in by inference. The good reader, like anyone who manipulates our perceptions, is merely exploiting the normal processes by which we make sense out of the disorderly array of inputs that constantly bombard us. (Hyman, 1977, p. 33)

It is precisely when someone deliberately tries to distort our perceptions and inferences that the need to distrust naive intuition and arm oneself with proper methodological safeguards becomes essential. The validity of graphology cannot be left to the judgment of uninformed and undisciplined intuition since, unfortunately, the field has been infiltrated by malicious manipulators, as well as by those who are as much victims of the fallacy of personal validation as their clients. Stripped of the veneer of personal validation and of naive a priori considerations, graphology cannot at present claim the status of a scientifically based method of personality assessment. Happily for its proponents, however, this status is not inherent, but can be acquired by merit. Science need not, should not, and cannot, prove the impossibility of the graphological enterprise. It is graphology that needs to establish its feasibility and status as a scientific enterprise.

### Notes

1   For example, Schmidt, Hunter, McKenzie, & Muldrow (1979) estimated the economic value of valid procedures for selecting computer programmers at hundred of millions of dollars per year, based on a job life expectancy of 10 years and present market conditions. There is every reason to believe that the figures may be as high with respect to other occupations as well.
2   It is more appropriate to evaluate correlations in terms of percentage of explained variance, obtained by squaring the correlation. Hence, the former is four times as good as the latter, not two.
3   Shortly after Ronald Reagan became president of the USA, a journalist asked him why he always kept a jar of multicolored jelly beans on his desk. The president answered that he used it as a kind of personality test on some of his visitors. He would offer them some of the candy, and observe their response. Some took a handful, some took a single candy, and some took none at all; some chose only beans of one color, or avoided those of one color, while others were less discriminating; some chewed the candies slowly, others sucked on them; etc.
4   There are also difficulties inherent in tests that work empirically without any theoretical understanding of how it is that they do, but this is usually a temporary state of affairs, and we shall not be concerned with it here.
5   The term "graphology" should be kept distinct from the term "graphoanalysis," which is the trademarked name of a particular American school of graphology.
6   It could also serve merely to guide – or ensure – the graphologist in making judgments that are age and sex appropriate, or to protect the graphologist from the need to predict so readily verifiable – or refutable – a variable.

### References

Allport, G. W., & Vernon, P. E. (1933). *Studies in expressive movement*. New York: The Macmillan Company.

Ben-Shakhar, G., Bar-Hillel, M. & Flug, A. (1985). A validation study of graphological evaluation in personnel selection. In B. Nevo (ed.) *Scientific aspects of graphology: A handbook.*

Crépieux-Jamin, J. (1926). *The psychology of the movements of handwriting* (translated and arranged by L. K. Given-Wilson). London: Routledge.

Eisenberg, P. (1938). Judging expressive movement: I. Judgments of sex and dominance feelings from handwriting samples of dominant and non-dominant men and women. *Journal of Applied Psychology, 22,* 480–486.

Fluckiger, F. A., Tripp, C. A. & Weinberg, G. H. (1961). A review of experimental research in graphology, 1933–1960. *Perceptual and Motor Skills, 12,* 67–90.

Forer, B. R. (1949). The fallacy of personal validation: A classroom demonstration of gullibility. *Journal of Abnormal and Social Psychology, 44,* 118–123.

Freud, S. (1933). *New introductory lectures on psychoanalysis.* New York: W. W. Norton.

Friedenhain, (1959). F. *Write and reveal.*

Goodenough, F. L. (1945). Sex differences in judging the sex of handwriting. *Journal of Social Psychology, 22,* 61–68.

Hilgard, E., Atkinson, R. & Atkinson, R. (1983). *Introduction to psychology* (8th edition). New York: Harcourt, Brace & Jovanovitch.

Hirsch, M. W., Jarvik, M. E. & Abramson, H. A. (1956). Effects of LSD-25 and six related drugs on handwriting. *Journal of Psychology, 41,* 11–22.

Hyman, R. (1977). "Cold reading": How to convince strangers that you know all about them. *The Zeletic,* 18–37.

Koren, A. (1983). *Graphology.* Tel Aviv: Massada. (in Hebrew).

Legge, D., Steinberg, H. & Summerfield, A. (1964). Simple measures of handwriting as indices of drug effects. *Perceptual and Motor Skills, 18,* 549–558.

Middleton, W. C. (1939). The ability of untrained subjects to judge dominance from handwriting samples. *Psychological Record, 3,* 227–238.

Mischel, W. (1976). *Introduction to personality.* New York: Holt, Rinehart and Winston.

Nisbett, R. E. & Ross, L. (1980). *Human inference: Strategies and shortcomings of social judgment.* Englewood Cliffs, N.J.: Prentice Hall.

Osborn, A. S. (1929). *Questioned documents.* (2nd edition). Albany: Boyd Printing Company.

Patterson, J. (1976). *Interpreting handwriting.* New York: David McKay Company.

Rabin, A. & Blair, H. (1953). The effects of alcohol on handwriting. *Journal of Clinical Psychology, 9,* 284–287.

Ross, L. (1977). The intuitive psychologist and his shortcomings: Distortions in the attribution process. In L. Berkowitz (ed.) *Advances in experimental social psychology 10,* New York: Academic Press.

Ross, L. (1978). Some afterthoughts on the intuitive psychologist. In L. Berkowitz (ed.) *Cognitive theories in social psychology.* New York: Academic Press.

Saudek, R. (1929). *Experiments with handwriting.* New York: Morrow.

Schmidt, F. L., Hunter, J. E., McKenzie, R. C. & Muldrow, T. W. (1979). Impact of valid selection procedure on work-force productivity. *Journal of Applied Psychology, 64,* 609–626.

Singer, E. (1969). *The graphologist's alphabet.* London: Duckworth & Co.

Snyder, C. R. (1974). Why horoscopes are true: The effects of specificity on acceptance of astrological interpretations. *Journal of Clinical Psychology, 30,* 577–580.

Snyder, C. R. & Shenkel, R.J. (1975). The P. T. Barnum effect. *Psychology Today, 8*(3), 52–54.

Tversky, A. (1985). Personality traits: Scope and attribution (unpublished manuscript).

# Part XI

# Critiques and New Directions I

It is tempting to use these final sections of the book to wrap things up, tie everything together, and suggest a synthesis of JDM research to date. In our view this would be misleading. Neat overviews work best when work in a field is finished, even dead, and JDM research is neither. If nothing else the chapters thus far must have left the reader with a glimpse of the energy and tumult of the field, of the fierceness of the arguments and debates, and of the very different approaches and theoretical positions taken by different researchers. It would be simply misleading to try to comb out these differences into a set of bland, neutral summaries of particular topics.

Instead, the chapters in this and the following section were selected for their efforts to identify emerging themes in the field and to sketch out directions for new work. The first two chapters in this section were written in the early 1980s, when the heuristics and biases research program was at its height. Jungermann (Chapter 33) organizes his essay around the problematic but crucial notion of rationality. With a little deliberate exaggeration, he groups researchers into two groups. He labels as "pessimists" those whose work implies that human beings are deeply flawed in their JDM processes. The "optimists," in contrast, interpret this work as flawed or, at least, unrepresentative of the real world in which real human skills are learned and exercised. The optimists tend to be more impressed with evidence of excellent human performance in appropriate environments and tasks (and, of course, when the evidence is appropriately interpreted). He usefully reminds us of Simon's (1978) distinction between *substantive* rationality, which is to do with getting it right in the real world, and *procedural* rationality, which is to do with thinking coherently about a matter. Hammond (1996) has recently developed a similar distinction in his discussion of consistency and coherence in evaluating decision processes (see Chapter 3).

Edwards and von Winterfeldt (Chapter 34) fall firmly in the "optimist" camp, though with interesting wrinkles. Their critique of the heuristics and biases research (to which they refer as "cognitive illusions") is searching. The authors, working decision analysts, obviously encounter clients making

571

errors and experiencing cognitive difficulties – indeed, they would be out of business if they did not! They argue, however, that human decision performance, appropriately aided by tools and analytical assistance, can be very good. Their discussion of intuition and intellectual tools is especially interesting. Note, however, that the authors have shifted Jungermann's question significantly, from an interest in unaided human performance to a focus on human performance aided by some very smart analysts, powerful computers, and a variety of sophisticated tools. Presumably we might perform pretty well with such aid, pretty poorly without it.

New research has also grown from critiques of the old. Gigerenzer and Goldstein (Chapter 35) take up a challenge originally proposed by Simon (1956) under the terminology of "bounded rationality": Given that humans have significant limits in acquiring and using information, how well do they do compared to optimal models that face no such limits? Gigerenzer and Goldstein propose a number of very simple models of choice processes, which they describe as "fast and frugal" – they use very little information, so they can operate very quickly. The surprising result is that, at least in some carefully chosen task environments, these very simple models do very well indeed. Though other researchers have provided examples of this sort (e.g., Connolly, 1980; Thorngate, 1980), Gigerenzer and Goldstein provide the best developed and most psychologically plausible demonstrations of just how effective these "satisficing" algorithms can be.

The final chapter of this section, by Hilton and Slugoski, similarly takes up and greatly extends existing research critiques. Numerous authors have criticized specific heuristics and biases findings by arguing that the subjects might not have understood the problem as the experimenters intended. Hilton and Slugoski move beyond these ad hoc criticisms to a quite general case. They argue that one can best understand the exchange between an experimenter and a subject as a conversation. They use a set of rules that the English philosopher Grice suggested as being implicitly understood and generally followed by everyone engaged in conversation. For example, we all understand that the statement that "John tried to clean his room" implies that he failed – otherwise the speaker would have said simply that "John cleaned his room." Grice's rules provide a wonderfully powerful tool with which to reexamine puzzling experimental data and with which to redesign new and clarifying studies. The paper also provides yet another of the connections between JDM research and apparently unrelated scholarly work elsewhere, in this case the philosophy of language.

### References

Connolly, T. (1980). Uncertainty, action and competence: Some alternatives to omniscience in complex problem-solving. In S. Fiddle (Ed.), *Uncertainty: Behavioral and social dimensions*. New York: Praeger.

Hammond, K. R. (1996). *Human judgment and social policy*. New York: Oxford University Press.

Simon, H. A. (1956). Rational choice and the structure of the environment. *Psychological Review, 63*, 129–138.

Simon, H. A. (1978). Rationality as process and as product of thought. *American Economic Review, 68*, 1–16.

Thorngate, W. (1980). Efficient decision heuristics. *Behavioral Science, 25*, 219–225.

# 33   The Two Camps on Rationality

*Helmut Jungermann*

## The Status of the Rationality Concept

If one postulates that people are generally *rational*, one meets today usually objection or, at best, scepticism; biases, errors and faults are described and illustrated to prove that the postulate has little empirical justification. If one declares a person *irrational*, however, one equally will meet usually protest from this person; he or she will explain that there were good reasons for the judgment or decisions questioned. The contradiction might be due to the words "generally" and "usually" in the above statements: People are not *always* rational and people will not *always* claim to be rational. However, the present debate about the quality of human judgment and decision indicates that the controversy is not only about generalizations and exceptions (e.g., Einhorn & Hogarth, 1981; Nisbett & Ross, 1980; Cohen, 1979; Kahneman & Tversky, 1982a; Edwards, 1983; Fischhoff, 1983; Berkeley & Humphreys, 1982; Phillips, 1983). The participants in this debate tend to avoid the term "rationality" because it is overloaded with many connotations, but just for that reason I find it useful as an umbrella under which most contributions fit fairly well; they all treat one or another definition or meaning of rationality.

Rationality is not a genuine term of scientific psychology but rather a concept of philosophy and economics. The most common, and in this context most relevant, definition says that an action is rational if it is in line with the values and beliefs of the individual concerned; or more precisely, if it is "logical" or "consistent" as stated in a set of axioms. This definition specifies rational behavior normatively. Empirical research can study whether actual human behavior is rational in the sense that it obeys the norm.

To measure human behavior with a normative yardstick is not the rule but rather the exception in cognitive psychology. In the psychology of *perception*,

This chapter originally appeared in Scholz, R. W. (Ed.). *Decision Making under Uncertainty* (pp. 63–86). Amsterdam: Elsevier, 1983. Copyright © 1983 by Elsevier Science Publishers B.V. (North Holland). Reprinted by permission.

for instance, the physical world is taken as a standard when perceptual illusions are investigated. Normally, however, the physical stimuli are used to provoke responses; one tries to understand and explain these responses and they are not evaluated as "deviant from" or "consistent with" something. The psychology of *language* worked for some time on the assumption that human language could be evaluated with the linguistic yardstick of an ideal speaker or hearer. But this assumption turned out to be not very helpful in understanding actual human language, and research began to focus on psychological models like semantic networks. Finally, the psychology of *thinking* used, and to some extent still uses, formal logic as a yardstick for the study of deductive reasoning. But not only is this merely a small area within the psychology of thinking, the approach itself has increasingly been disputed as mistaken. Similarly to the development in psycholinguistics, the focus has been directed increasingly on the content rather than on the formal characteristics of thinking. In all these areas of research, the use of a physical or logical yardstick plays only a minor role today or has been abandoned altogether.

In the psychology of *judgment and decision*, on the other hand, normative models have been the most important research tools since its beginnings in the late fifties. Research has been primarily concerned with studying, explaining, and interpreting discrepancies between predictions derived from normative models and actual judgments and decisions. The most prominent models of judgment are probably Bayes' theorem and the multiattribute utility models, and the normative model of decision is the SEU model. Most research is still oriented toward these models and the debate about the quality of human judgment and decision is still centered around the idea of rationality embodied in these models.

In a somewhat exaggerated manner, I will distinguish two camps in this debate, one that points to the deficiency and one that argues for the efficiency of human judgment and decision. The *pessimists*, as I will call the members of the first camp, claim that judgment and decision making under uncertainty often show systematic and serious errors, due to in-built characteristics of the human cognitive system. Violations of rationality, particularly of the SEU model, are interpreted as true deficits of the decision maker. The *optimists* of the other camp claim that judgment and decision are highly efficient and functional even in complex situations. Observed violations of rationality axioms are interpreted as unjustified evaluations based on inappropriate theoretical assumptions or empirical approaches on the part of the researcher. In the following, I will describe the approach to rationality taken in both camps, each of which has various factions, and discuss some points that make the debate so complicated and, sometimes, obscure. The description cannot be as differentiated as the approaches are, of course, but I hope that it is essentially correct; the interested reader is referred to the original sources.

## The Pessimists: Biases Are in People

Since Simon (1955) proposed the concept of "bounded rationality," the strongest attacks against human rationality came from Tversky and Kahneman (e.g., 1974), Slovic (1972), Janis and Mann (1977), and Nisbett and Ross (1980). The general tendency of this research was that human judgment and decision making ability and capacity is indeed limited, leading to violations of rationality principles. There are three variants in this camp in explaining these violations: As results of *judgmental biases*, of *representational faults*, and of *coping defects*.

### Judgmental Biases

The most extensive and influential work of interest in this context has been the research of Tversky and Kahneman on probabilistic thinking. While in the sixties Peterson and Beach (1967) in their review came to the conclusion that people form and revise their beliefs according to the normative principles of statistics, Tversky and Kahneman (e.g., 1974) offered a different conception: Judgments of probabilities are often severely biased because people in many situations rely on heuristics which, although generally efficient, can sometimes lead to systematic errors. For example, people often judge the probability of an event according to the *representativeness* of the event for the underlying population or for the generating process. However, "this approach to the judgment of probability leads to serious errors, because similarity or representativeness is not influenced by several factors that should affect judgments of probability" (Tversky & Kahneman, 1974, p. 1124). Such factors are, for instance, base rates, sample size and the reliability of information. Another heuristic people use is the saliency or *availability* of information, i.e., how easily instances of the event whose probability is to be assessed can be retrieved from memory. Since ease of retrieval is also influenced by other factors than the actual frequency of the event (e.g., recent occurrence) the use of this heuristic can likewise result in systematic judgmental errors. Other heuristics described in this research are "anchoring and adjustment" and "simulation" (for a collection of the most important papers on biases and heuristics see the recent book by Kahneman, Slovic, & Tversky, 1982).

Judgmental biases may produce inconsistent decisions. Such inconsistencies would then not reflect violations of assumptions of the model (e.g., SEU model) but rather incorrect input. However, the discussion has mostly been restricted to the quality of the judgment itself. The judgment is compared to a standard like relative frequency or the inference based on a statistical model for which the researcher has defined the relevant data (e.g., what the base rates are). In both cases, deficiency means deviation of the judgment from some "objective" quantity, and the "objectivity" is rooted in the real world, or rather the researcher's view of the real world. The implicit notion of rationality, then, is not consistency but realism; it is less *formal* rationality that is questioned than *substantive* rationality: People use cognitive inference and retrieval strategies which often lead to (in the researcher's view) substantively incorrect judgments about the world.

*Implicitly*, this meaning of rationality pervades the discussion on biases and heuristics in probabilistic thinking. It is interesting to find it made *explicit* with respect to judgments which are equally important for decision making but much less debated, namely, utility judgments (March 1978). Tversky and Kahneman (1981) question the rationality of utility judgments that turn out to have been unrealistic anticipations of satisfaction at the time when the consequences actually incur. But biases and heuristics in the judgment of utility are still unexplored, maybe due to the lack of a yardstick like relative frequency it offers for probability judgments. A different approach is needed here, maybe taking the work of Ainslie (1975) on preferences as a function of time delay of satisfaction and the economic approach to "rational expectations" as a starting point. Rationality in this sense, i.e., as realism, certainly comes close to the meaning of this term in common sense: We often call hopes and fears "irrational" which we consider as extremely unrealistic. The question, of course, is who is to define reality.

### Representational Faults

A more recent argument against rationality, raised by the same group of researchers, concerns the effect of different frames for the decision problem on people's decision making behavior (Tversky & Kahneman, 1981; cp. also Payne, 1982). A striking example is the experiment in which a majority of subjects behaved risk averse when they had to decide between two options that were formulated in terms of lives saved, but behaved risk seeking when the options were formulated in terms of lives lost – although the (expected) values of the options were in both cases indentical. This violation of rationality, i.e., of the SEU model, is interpreted by the assumption that people code the possible outcomes as gains and losses rather than as final states, and the framing of the options induces in one case coding in terms of gains and in the other case coding in terms of losses, i.e., it induces subjects to focus on different parts of their utility functions. Since the utility functions are different below and above the reference point, apparently inconsistent preferences result. Coding outcomes in terms of gains and losses is, according to Kahneman and Tversky (1979), only one of several cognitive mechanisms which people use to edit, or represent, decision problems before the options will be evaluated, and these operations can also lead to violations of rationality. Other editing mechanisms are, for instance, the segregation of riskless components of prospects and the cancellation of components which are shared by two prospects.

The representational errors resulting from the application of such mechanisms are likened to perceptual illusions (Tversky & Kahneman, 1981). This implies the assumption that there exists one and only one correct representation of the problem, as there exists only one veridical representation of the physical world. Inconsistent preferences are understood as results of a deficient perception and interpretation of the decision problem.

It is interesting to note that with this argument, the context for discussing rationality is being enlarged. Previously, the domain of theoretical and empirical research was judgment and evaluation only, but *not* the cognitive activities which forego these steps, e.g., how the problem structure is generated. Only recently, interest has shifted to these early phases of the decision making process (e.g., Pitz, Sachs, & Heerboth, 1980; Jungermann, von Ulardt, & Hausmann, 1983), but this research has not been generally linked to the discussion about the deficiency/efficiency of judgment and decision.

### Coping Defects

The third attack on rationality comes from Janis and Mann (1977), who look at people's decision making behavior from a motivational perspective. They distinguish various coping patterns that people use in handling stress of decision situations, and only one of them corresponds to the rational behavior as explicated in decision theory. The other four patterns lead to defective decision making. For example, if the coping pattern is "defensive avoidance," the person escapes the decisional conflict by procrastinating, shifting responsibility to someone else, or constructing wishful rationalizations to bolster the least objectionable alternative, remaining selectively inattentive to corrective information. Although these patterns, as Mann and Janis (1982) concede, can occasionally be adaptive in saving time and effort, they often lead to defective decision making. "Deficiency" is here not directly defined in relation to some normative model, e.g., the SEU model, but more generally by the failure of people "to assimilate and combine information relating to outcome expectations and values" (p. 347) and particularly "to make use of the resources available to them for engaging in effective search for and appraisal of alternatives – within the limits of their cognitive capabilities and within limits imposed by powerful social constraints" (p. 346). In a large number of experimental studies, Janis and Mann (1977) have collected evidence for these coping defects, and they have tried to identify the conditions under which people exhibit different types of information processing behavior in decision situations.

Thus, Janis and Mann also emphasize the deficiences of human judgment and decision, but in their perspective, the sources are motivational, not cognitive in nature: "We see man not as a cold fish, but as a warm-blooded mammal, not as a rational calculator always ready to work out the best solution but as a reluctant decision maker – beset by conflicts, doubts, and worry, struggling with incongruous longings, antipathies, and loyalties..."(1977, p. 15). This latter statement illustrates that, although the focus is explicitly on decision making under stress, the authors tend to generalize their theory to human decision making in general.

A similar approach, though from a cognitive standpoint, has been taken by Dörner, who examined how people operate in highly complex and dynamic situations (e.g., Dörner, 1983; Dörner, Kreuzig, Reither, & Stäudel, 1983). In one of the studies, for instance, he used a computer model of a little town and had the subjects reign over this town as mayor for 10 simulated years in interaction with the computer. Having to cope with such ill-defined problems, subjects often apparently use a number of heuristic procedures which might be considered deficient. Dörner et al. do not compare the observed behavior with normative models of judgment and decision, however, but rather check whether the subjects' behavior meets certain demands of the situation. For example, requirements resulting from characteristics of the aspired goal are often managed by "redefining" or "forgetting" the final goal, by thematic vagabonding (e.g., swinging from one area of pursuit to another), or by encapsulation (e.g., sticking obstinately to a theme irrespective of the changing situation). Although the deficiencies displayed in these experiments are probably largely due to cognitive overload, some of the heuristics might well be used also in less complex situations.

In summary, the members of this camp view human judgment and decision making as deficient in several respects: Judgments are sometimes systematically biased, due to the use of heuristics; decisions are sometimes inconsistent, due to errors in the representation of the problem; and information search and combination is often defective, due to motivational factors. Mostly, this deficiency is not seen simply as a consequence of cognitive overload in highly complex or unfamiliar situations, but as rooted in mechanisms working within the human information processing system itself. People are prone to violate principles of rationality. A key assumption of at least the cognitive variants described is that there is a reliable and valid yardstick for the evaluation of judgment and decision, namely, the objective reality, and consequently that there is some kind of objectively veridical mode of information processing which is mapped in the respective normative model.

### The Optimists: Biases Are in the Research

In the last few years, a kind of counter-movement has developed. The members of this new camp partly question the validity of the other camp's findings, and partly emphasize the implicit rationality of human judgment and decision behavior. The biases, they argue, are not in human behavior but in the analysis of this behavior in the other camp (Berkeley & Humphreys, 1982). Interestingly enough, a leading representative of this camp has been a founder of the other camp with his research on conservatism in human information processing (Edwards, 1968); other researchers I include in this camp are Beach and Mitchell (1978), Einhorn and Hogarth (1981), Berkeley and Humphreys (1982), and Phillips (1983). Three theoretical arguments are raised in particular, which I will call the *meta-rationality* argument, the *continuity* argument and the *structure* argument.

### The Meta-Rationality Argument

The essence of this argument is that decision behavior which violates principles of rationality, as, for instance, the principle of maximizing subjectively expected utility, can be described as perfectly rational if the cognitive *costs* of being rational are taken into account. To illustrate the point, when somebody wants to buy a book at the train station for a long ride, he will probably not check all available books in order to find the best of all but he will look at a few and then buy the first that he finds reasonably attractive. This person can be described as working on the satisficing principle, i.e., as not behaving fully rational from a SEU model perspective. But to many people, that is counterintuitive. They would probably call a person nonrational if he *would* check all books in the store. With finite time and resources available, it is not rational to spend infinite effort on the exploration of all potential consequences of all options. Rather, the decision costs are weighed against the potential benefits resulting from the application of a decision strategy, and this may lead to violations of SEU model rationality which are, however, perfectly rational.

This point has been made by various authors (e.g., Miller & Starr, 1967; Einhorn & Hogarth, 1981; Janis & Mann, 1977; Hogarth, 1980; Montgomery & Svenson, 1976; cp. Payne, 1982). It is most explicitly and clearly represented in the contingency model of Beach and Mitchell (1978). In this model it is assumed that people make meta-decisions between the various decision strategies they have in their repertoire. Strategies differ with respect to the cognitive effort required and the probability with which they lead to an optimal solution (i.e., SEU maximizing, satisficing, elimination-by-aspects, coin flipping). Strategy selection is seen as contingent upon a (cost/benefit) compromise between the decision maker's desire to make the best decision and his or her negative feelings about investing time and effort in the decision making process. The strategy that is perceived as yielding the maximum net gain is the one selected. The specific choice depends on characteristics of the situation (e.g., familiarity of the problem, time pressure) and of the subject (e.g., knowledge, ability). Various hypotheses derived from this model have been experimentally investigated and have generally been confirmed (e.g., Christensen-Szalanski, 1978; McAllister, Mitchell, & Beach, 1979; Christensen-Szalanski, 1980).

The rationality cost, i.e., the cognitive effort associated with each strategy, is not formalized in Beach and Mitchell's (1978) model. For the comparison of multidimensional alternatives, Johnson (1979) has proposed a process model which allows the computation of the number of mental operations required. A similar method has been proposed by Shugan (1980). In both models it is assumed, however, that the researcher knows the number of attributes. For more simple strategies, a formal approach might be more difficult.

In the model of Beach and Mitchell (1978), maximizing of subjectively expected utility is only one of several available strategies, each of which may be chosen rationally as the best strategy under the given conditions, even coin flipping. Violations of "classical" rationality are considered as errors that the subject anticipates and, more important, tolerates. People are global maximizers with local inconsistencies (Elster, 1979). Renunciation of cognitive effort might not only result, however, from the calculation that the costs outweigh the expected benefits but also from the knowledge that *the very act of deliberating* can modify the character for the worse, and in ways judged even more important, through the stultifying effects on spontaneity" (Elster, 1979, p. 40). Thus, to save spontaneity, which in itself has a value, a person might rationally select a strategy possibly leading to violations of SEU rationality.

### The Continuity Argument

The core of this argument is the conceptualization of judgment and decision as moments in a continuous process. They sometimes may appear biased or deficient if treated or tested as discrete events, while they might in fact be very functional when considered as moments in a continuous and changing environment (Hogarth, 1981). An experiment by Ronen (1973), described in Hogarth (1981), can serve as an illustration: Subjects had to choose between two options with identical (positive) payoffs and probabilites of success. The outcomes were dependent on the results of two sequential events. In one option, there was a higher probability of success in the first step and a lower probability in the second step, while it was the other way around with the alternative option. Since the SEUs of the two options were equal, rationality would imply indifference. However, subjects preferred the option with the higher probability in the first step. Hogarth (1981) provides the following explanation: If people are used to a changing environment, they might give less weight to the probability of the second step since the situation might have changed when this phase has been reached; it might be attractive to stay in the game as long as possible, and therefore to choose the option with the higher probability of success in the first phase.

More generally, many experiments on probabilistic information processing have excluded the possibility of feedback and redundancy which, however, is characteristic of the environment and thus relevant for judgment and decision. Models have been tested under the assumption of a stable environment, while subjects might have operated under the assumption of a changing environment. A number of biases, demonstrated with the discrete approach, can be interpreted as indicators of cognitive mechanisms and strategies which are actually very functional in a continuous environment. Hogarth (1981) discusses several assumptions underlying prescriptive models which explicitly do not take this continuity into account, e.g., the *existence of a stable time horizon*. An example given by Tversky and Kahneman (1973) for the use of availability resulting in a biased judgment is reinterpreted by Hogarth (p. 206) with the argument that in the specific experimental situation under time pressure, the application of this heuristic could be considered as very functional: People use the cues which are most available first, because in normal life one can expect to have a chance to correct such a judgment. It is therefore important to specify under which conditions the application of a heuristic is functional and under which it is not. Another assumption discussed is the *stability of preferences and goals* which may be wrong for various reasons (March, 1978): First, preferences develop over time. Choices imply, however, anticipations of future preferences, i.e., preferences at the time when the consequences occur (a point I discussed earlier). Secondly, preferences are formed by experiences, and these experiences are often sought actively by people, sometimes in order to know more about their preferences. Thirdly, preferences are usually characterized by a high degree of ambiguity. Such ambiguity can be functional, because the person is open for further information and saves mental energy to clarify the ambiguity. Other assumptions discussed are the *stationarity of probabilistic processes*, the *independence of judgmental effects on consequences*, and the *abstraction from the competition character of action*. The continuity argument is raised by Hogarth (1981) not only against the contention of judgmental biases but also against the contention of representational errors.

The attack on the pessimists' camp can take two forms. Demonstrations of deficient judgment and decision can either be attributed to inadequate assumptions of the model, like fixed time horizons; the observed behavior was in fact efficient and functional, the model was wrong. Or one can claim that the experimental situations used for testing the model had a very low ecological validity and that therefore biases and errors were possibly artifacts, encouraged by the researcher.

### The Structure Argument

The third argument against the other camp has been raised in particular by Berkeley and Humphreys (1982) and Phillips (1983). The claim is that demonstrations of cognitive deficiency are questionable due to the neglect of the subjects' internal structural representation of the problem. The characterization of the observed behavior as biased rests on the assumption that the subjects share the experimenter's understanding of the problem structure. A common understanding of the problem structure can be assumed to be established by the use of process tracing methods or through the experimental instructions; or it can be assumed to exist a priori because of the objective nature of the task, as illustrated by Tversky and Kahneman (1981) in their use of the analogy of perception.

As an example, Berkeley and Humphreys (1982) discuss the problem presented to subjects by Tversky and Kahneman (1981) in which two options are formulated either in terms of lives lost or in terms of lives saved. In the first case, subjects behaved risk averse, in the second case they behaved risk prone, interpreted by Tversky and Kahneman as inconsistent preferences since "it is easy to see that the two problems are effectively identical" (p. 453). Berkeley and Humphreys question this interpretation because the "uncertainty, concerning human agency in affecting subsequent states of the world, is left unresolved" (p. 222) in Tversky and Kahneman's formulation of the problem. Berkeley and Humphreys offer a different structural representation the subjects might have developed in order to resolve this uncertainty which would result in preferences perfectly consistent with SEU theory. A similar reasoning is found in Hogarth (1981) and Phillips (1983).

The second approach, in which the problem structure is imposed under the assumption of a common understanding, does not investigate experimental data in their own right as products of the subjects' reasoning, but compares them with data resulting from the application of a normative model to the problem in question, "the assumption being that the model represents the basis for rational choice (or inference) in the presented problem" (Berkeley & Humphreys, 1982, p. 230). Two implications of this assumption are questioned by the authors: First, the naturalization of small worlds, which means the exclusion of the subjects' individual "goal-closing" of his or her large world into the small world of the experimental moment and presenting the observed departures from veridicality as *cognitive* rather than motivational biases (p. 233). Second, the utilization of normative models as ideal types, i.e., as standards of comparison with the intuitive model of the subject; this requires, however, the investigation of whether there is a common understanding of the way in which the problem universe is to be goal-closed and thus does not permit imposition of a problem structure (p. 234).

This argument, then, focuses on the structural representation of the task and its significance for the interpretation of judgments and decisions. The representation depends strongly, however, on the context within which it is developed. Different contexts evoke different knowledge – elements and structures of knowledge – and thus will often lead to different behaviors. Each behavior might be consistent within the given context although inconsistent with some behavior toward the same task in a different context. The description of behavior as deficient or nonrational is not justified if it is not invariant over multiple contexts; to the contrary, invariant behavior would be deficient.

Two views are still possible here: One can go as far as Phillips (1983) and argue phenomenologically that there is no criterion for defining some "objective" problem representation as implied in Tversky and Kahneman's (1981) analogy between judgmental errors and perceptual illusions. Or one can assume such a criterion but conclude that "task representation may be of more importance in defining errors than the rules they (the people) use within that representation" (Einhorn & Hogarth, 1981, p. 60), e.g., if one considers the case of a paranoid person. In both views, however, the problem of structure is essential for a discussion of deficiency/efficiency.

In summary, the members of this camp challenge the view that human judgment and decision is cognitively deficient. They question this conclusion with different arguments: Because an important parameter has been neglected, namely, the cost of a decision strategy; because judgments and decisions are treated as discrete events and not as moments in a continuous process; and because no attention has been paid to the internal structural representation of the problem as the person- and context-dependent basis of judgment and decision. The emphasis in all three positions is less on demonstrating efficiency of human behavior than on studying more carefully under what conditions people show which kind of behavior, and not "too easily to adopt a crude view of human rationality" (Slovic, 1972).

### Résumé and Outlook

It seems that the history of research on human judgment and decision making in the last 30 years represents a typical example of scientific progress. Against the once dominant model of rational man, the camp I have called pessimistic formed and questioned this conception by demonstrating deficiencies in judgment and decision. Now after this camp has ruled decision research for many years, it comes under attack by a new group that I have called optimistic which points to weaknesses in the former concepts and suggests even more differentiated perspectives of judgment and decision. Both camps have gained their impetus from the critique of the respective prevailing conception. Some of the criticisms, particularly of the optimists' camp against the pessimists' camp, have already been mentioned in the previous section. However, I will briefly sum up these points and add those more general arguments which have been exchanged between the two camps more recently.

The critique of the pessimists' position focuses on the following points: First, the experiments are of low ecological validity in the sense that they do not represent the majority of situations in which people have to give judgments and make decisions. Second, the experiments were designed such that biases and errors are not surprising since the situations and problems were taken out of any real life context. Third, important parameters like cognitive effort have not been accounted for in the models used as yardsticks.

Fourth, whether subjects cognitively represented the problem in the way the researcher assumed is rarely investigated. A more general, fifth argument is that this research has focused too much on errors rather than on the cognitive processes per se; not only is it hard to define what errors are, they also constitute atypical behavior samples.

The rejoinder of the pessimists' camp is: First, meta-theories on the selection of strategies according to cognitive effort considerations are methodologically more or less immune to charges of "irrationality"; any behavior that violates the SEU model can be "rationalized" by referring to some higher level of rationality. Second, demonstrations of differences between the experimental and real world situations do not prove that these differences matter. Third, speculations that subjects might have represented a problem cognitively differently than the researchers do not prove that they have done so. Fourth, the focus on errors is justified because (a) "they expose some of our intellectual limitations and suggest ways of improving the quality of our thinking," (b) they "often reveal the psychological processes and the heuristic procedures that govern judgment and inference," and (c) they "help the mapping of human intuitions by indicating which principles of statistics or logic are non-intuitive or counter-intuitive" (Kahneman & Tversky, 1982a, p. 124). Clearly, these are defensive arguments but therefore not less reasonable than the offensive arguments of the authors. It is not to be expected that this camp will capitulate as easily under the attack as did the "rational man" when that concept was besieged by today's defenders.

As Heraclit said, war is the father of all and the king of all. The theoretical and empirical work in both camps as well as the dispute between them has generated many data, insights, and ideas. The understanding of judgment and decision making has been dependent and differentiated and has opened new, more comprehensive research perspectives. I will characterize briefly some essential aspects of the present state of the debate and of the direction future research might take.

For almost all arguments, the theoretical point of reference is still the SEU model or some variant of it (e.g., prospect theory), despite some harsh critique (e.g., Fischhoff, Goitein, & Shapira, 1982). While one side provides evidence that people do not behave as the model predicts, the other side demonstrates that with different theoretical assumptions or experimental settings the same behavior might not violate the model at all. Pitz said (in 1977) that "models based upon some variant of expected value theory have the attraction of being familiar and easy to work with, and inertia is one of the strongest forces in nature" (p. 421); another reason is probably that the SEU model is hard to falsify since "with sufficient ingenuity, one can always find something that a particular decision maker has maximized in a particular situation" (Fischhoff et al., 1982, p. 317). Pitz also said that "until a well developed, systematic alternative to the normative model is available, it is likely that new approaches will have no more lasting success than did Gestalt psychology" (1977, p. 421). This still seems to be a fairly valid description of the present situation. However, that no real alternative has been offered might also be taken as an indicator of the strength of the model as a core of theories of judgment and decision. The wide use of expectancy-value models also in other areas of psychology, particularly in motivation research, is a further indicator (cp. Feather, 1982).

The issue is not anymore what the limitations of the human cognitive system are. All approaches assume that there are boundaries for rationality in situations of cognitive overload due to the capacity and processing limits of the system. The issue is how people form judgments and make decisions, and particularly whether they operate rationally *within* the constraints. While one side focused on errors, biases, and fallacies, the other side considers this a theoretically questionable and also too negative approach. In this view, research on judgment and decision making has been driven too much by a concern for errors relative to a normative standard the validity of which one can doubt with good arguments (Einhorn & Hogarth, 1981).

The focus on errors has recently been defended by Kahneman and Tversky (1982a) by pointing toward various advantages of this approach (see above). Kahneman and Tversky also argue that "the emphasis on the study of errors is characteristic of research on human judgment, but it is not unique to this domain: we use illusions to understand the principles of normal perception and we learn about memory by studying forgetting" (1982a, p. 123). I don't quite agree, for two reasons: First, because, although illusions are a subject of interest in the psychology of perception, the *emphasis* has certainly not been on errors. Second, memory research is not interested in errors *as such* but uses them as a dependent variable for testing models about storing or retrieval of information, i.e., about the "normal" memory processes and structures; researchers on memory do not demonstrate errors in their research, as do many researchers on judgment and decision. However, the recent discussion of the issue seems to have led to some rapprochement of positions. Kahneman and Tversky concede that "although errors of judgment are but a method by which some cognitive processes are studied, the method has become a significant part of the message" (1982a, p. 124), and they accentuate stronger than before, e.g., that the notion of judgmental heuristics should "provide a common account for both correct and incorrect judgments" (1982b, p. 325). If it is agreed, then, that "theoretically it is necessary to understand *all* reasoning data, regardless of their conformity to a normative rule system" (Evans, 1982, p. 319), the study of errors becomes a question of research strategy. Kahneman and Tversky, in their reply to Evans, argue that "errors may sometimes be more informative than correct judgments, which can be produced *either* by an initial valid intuition *or* by a subsequent correction" (1982b, p. 325).

Another important progress is to be seen in the now generally accepted conceptualization of judgment and decision as parts of a multistage cognitive process. Actually, activities that precede the "moment of decision" seem presently to be the prevailing object of theoretical and empirical work – in particular the acquisition and processing of information, or, in other terms, the generating and structuring of knowledge. Some work on predecisional cognitive processes is already available (cp. Einhorn & Hogarth, 1981), but new questions have come up. For instance, what are the implications of using the "conversational paradigm" (Berkeley & Humphreys, 1982; Kahneman & Tversky, 1982a)? How can we elicit or infer the cognitive representation of problems? We need theories of problem representation that explain the use and the results of particular judgmental and decision making strategies. There is also increasing interest in post-decisional processes, particularly the implementation of decisions (cp. Gasparski, 1980). Again, research has focused primarily on "errors," i.e., on the phenomenon that people often do not implement their mental decisions due to motivational and emotional factors (e.g., Sjöberg, 1980; Elster, 1979). Elster has analyzed the various strategies that people use to overcome this "weakness of will," interfering between decision and action (using Ulysses as a prominent example who bound himself to the mast in order not to give in to the temptation by the sirens). He put this problem in the context of the rationality debate: "Man often is not rational, and rather exhibits *weakness of will*. Even when not rational, man knows that he is irrational and can *bind himself* against the irrationality. This second-best or imperfect rationality takes care both of reason and passion. What is lost, perhaps, is the sense of adventure" (Elster, 1979, p. 111).

A final lesson to be learned from the debate might be that one should avoid the term rationality in psychology at all. Obviously, the concept is used with different meanings; it is certainly no longer defined exclusively by formal coherence and consistency. An alternative way of handling this difficulty is, however, to distinguish explicitly various meanings of the term. Besides formal rationality, concepts like substantive rationality and procedural rationality might be useful for a theory of judgment and decision (Simon, 1978). *Substantive* rationality captures an important aspect of the term as it is used in common language, namely, how realistic, correct, adequate some judgment or decision is with respect to the real world – the paranoid with his perfectly consistent beliefs and values provides an example. Rationality is not only a question of whether a choice is in line with a person's belief and preferences, but also a question of what sort of preferences and beliefs the person holds, a point elaborated also by Einhorn and Hogarth (1981). Differently stated, a decision might be consistent (and thus formally rational), but the judgments that provide the input for the decision might be very poor (and thus the choice might be substantively not rational). *Procedural* rationality can be linked to substantive rationality easily if one asks what information is searched for and used by a person to form values and beliefs, whether the person tried hard enough to anticipate future consequences of current actions and future preferences for those consequences, etc. What Janis and Mann (1977) describe as "vigilant information processing" might be considered one aspect of this kind of rationality. Particularly in a social context, when decisions have to be justified, procedural rationality can be much more important than substantive matters about which agreement often cannot be reached.

My conclusion from the debate between the two camps with respect to the rationality problem is threefold: *First*, we should be liberal (which does not mean vague) in our use of the rationality concept. The different meanings that I have briefly described (and others, cp. March, 1978) are all useful tools in analyzing judgment and decision processes. *Second*, we may use the concept in its prescriptive sense legitimately in situations where prescription is asked for, like in decision aiding or in decision training. Criteria for defining rationality in a prescriptive sense can be taken from our knowledge about the real world, from our intellectual system, and from the social consensus – however relative these criteria are in a historical or cultural sense. *Third*, we should use the concept in descriptive research more cautiously because it too easily entices us to label all behavior that does not meet the criteria as deviant or deficient, as errors, biases, or whatever. I subscribe to Kahneman and Tversky's balanced advice that we "should avoid overly strict interpretations, which treat reasonable answers as errors, as well as to overly charitable interpretations, which attempt to a rationalize every response" (1982a, p. 124). *Finally*, the recognition of the conditionality of normative models on assumptions about the environment as well as the cognitive representation of that environment, most convincingly elaborated by Einhorn and Hogarth (1981) and Payne (1982), is in my opinion the synthesis emerging from the debate between the (pessimistic) thesis and the (optimistic) antithesis. Implicitly or explicitly, it is agreed to by members of both camps.

### References

Ainslie, G. (1975). Specious reward: A behavioral theory of impulsiveness and impulse control. *Psychological Bulletin, 82*, 463–496.

Beach, L. R., & Mitchell, T. R. (1978). A contingency model for the selection of decision strategies. *Academy of Management Review, 3*, 439–449.

Berkeley, D., & Humphreys, P. (1982). Structuring decision problems and the "bias heuristic." *Acta Psychologica, 50*, 201–252.

Christensen-Szalanski, J. J. J. (1978). Problem-solving strategies: A selection mechanisms, some implications, and some data. *Organizational Behavior and Human Performance, 22*, 307–323.

Christensen-Szalanski, J. J. J. (1980). A further examination of the selection of problem-solving strategies: The effects of deadlines and analytic aptitudes. *Organizational Behavior and Human Performance, 25*, 107–122.

Cohen, L. J. (1979). On the psychology of prediction: Whose is the fallacy? *Cognition, 7*, 385–407.

Dörner, D. (1983). Heuristics and cognition in complex systems. In R. Groner, M. Groner, & W. F. Bischof (Eds.), *Methods of heuristics* (pp. 89–107). Hillsdale, NJ: Erlbaum.

Dörner, D., Kreuzig, H. W., Reither, F., & Stäudel, T. (Hrsg.). (1983). *Lohhausen*. Bern/Stuttgart/Wien: Hans Huber.

Edwards, W. (1968). Conservatism in human information processing. In B. Kleinmuntz (Ed.), *Formal representation of human judgement*. New York, Wiley.

Edwards, W. (1983). Human cognitive capabilities, representativeness, and ground rules for research. In P. C. Humphries, O. Svenson, & A. Vari (Eds.), *Analyzing and aiding decision processes* (pp. 507–513). Amsterdam: North Holland.

Einhorn, H. J., & Hogarth, R. M. (1981). Behavioral decision theory: Processes of judgment and choice. *Annual Review of Psychology, 32*, 53–88.

Elster, J. (1979). *Ulysses and the sirens*. Cambridge: Cambridge University Press.

Evans, J. St. B. T. (1982) On statistical intuitions and inferential rules: A discussion of Kahneman and Tversky. *Cognition, 12*, 319–323.

Feather, N. T. (Ed.). (1982). *Expectations and actions*. Hillsdale, NJ: Erlbaum.

Fischhoff, B. (1983). Reconstructive criticism. In P. C. Humphries, O. Svenson, & A. Vari (Eds.), *Analyzing and aiding decision processes* (pp. 507–513). Amsterdam: North Holland.

Fischhoff, B., Goitein, B., & Shapira, Z. (1982). The experienced utility of expected utility approaches. In N. T. Feather (Ed.), *Expectations and actions* (pp. 315–339). Hillsdale, NJ: Erlbaum.

Gasparski, W. (Ed.). (1980). *Decision making and action: Report*. Warsaw: Polish Academy of Sciences.

Hogarth, R. M. (1980). *Judgment and choice: The psychology of decision*. Chichester: Wiley.

Hogarth, R. M. (1981). Beyond discrete biases: Functional and dysfunctional aspects of judgmental heuristics. *Psychological Bulletin, 90*, 197–217.

Janis, I. L., & Mann, L. (1977). *Decision making: A psychological analysis of conflict, choice, and commitment*. New York: Free Press.

Johnson, E. J. (1979). *Deciding how to decide: The effort of making a decision*. Unpublished manuscript, University of Chicago, Graduate School of Business.

Jungermann, H., von Ulardt, I., & Hausmann, L. (1983). The role of the goal for generating action. In P. C. Humphries, O. Svenson, & A. Vari (Eds.), *Analyzing and aiding decision processes* (pp. 507–513). Amsterdam: North Holland.

Kahneman, D., Slovic, P., & Tversky, A. (Eds.). (1982). *Judgment under uncertainty: Heuristics and biases*. Cambridge: Cambridge University Press.

Kahneman, D., & Tversky, A. (1979). Prospect theory: An analysis of decision under risk. *Econometrica, 47*, 263–291.

Kahneman, D., & Tversky, A. (1982a). On the study of statistical intuitions. *Cognition, 11*, 123–141.

Kahneman, D., & Tversky, A. (1982b). A reply to Evans. *Cognition, 12*, 325–326.

Mann, L., & Janis, I. L. (1982). Conflict theory of decision making and the expectancy-value approach. In N. T. Feather (Ed.), *Expectations and actions* (pp. 341–364). Hillsdale, NJ: Erlbaum.

March, J. G. (1978). Bounded rationality, ambiguity, and the engineering of choice. *Bell Journal of Economics, 9*, 587–608.

McAllister, D. W., Mitchell, T. R., & Beach, L. R. (1979). The contingency model for the selection of decision strategies: An empirical test of the effects of significance, accountability, and reversibility. *Organizational Behavior and Human Performance, 24*, 228–244.

Miller, D. W., & Starr, M. K. (1967). *The structure of human decisions*. Englewood Cliffs, NJ: Prentice-Hall.

Montgomery, H., & Svenson, O. (1976). On decision rules and information processing strategies for choices among multiattribute alternatives. *Scandinavian Journal of Psychology, 17,* 283–291.

Nisbett, R. E., & Ross, L. (1980). *Human inference: Strategies and shortcomings of human judgment.* Englewood Cliffs, NJ: Prentice-Hall.

Payne, J. W. (1982). Contingent decision behavior. *Psychological Bulletin, 92,* 382–402.

Peterson, C. R., & Beach, L. R. (1967). Man as an intuitive statistician. *Psychological Bulletin, 68,* 29–46.

Phillips, L. D. (1983). A theoretical perspective on heuristics and biases in probabilistic thinking. In P. C. Humphries, O. Svenson, & A. Vari (Eds.), *Analyzing and aiding decision processes* (pp. 507–513). Amsterdam: North Holland.

Pitz, G. (1977). Decision making and cognition. In H. Jungermann & G. de Zeeuw (Eds.), *Decision making and change in human affairs* (pp. 403–424). Dordrecht: Reidel.

Pitz, G. F., Sachs, N. J., & Heerboth, J. (1980). Procedures for eliciting choices in the analysis of individual decisions. *Organizational Behavior and Human Performance, 26,* 396–408.

Ronen, J. (1973). Effects of some probability displays on choices. *Organizational Behavior and Human Performance, 9,* 1–15.

Shugan, S. M. (1980). The cost of thinking. *Journal of Consumer Research, 7,* 99–111.

Simon, H. A. (1955). A behavioral model of rational choice. *Quarterly Journal of Economics, 69,* 99–118.

Simon, H. A. (1978). Rationality as process and as product of thought. *American Economic Review, 68,* 1–16.

Sjöberg, L. (1980). Volitional problems in carrying through a difficult decision. *Acta Psychologica, 45,* 123–132.

Slovic, P. (1972). From Shakespeare to Simon: Speculations – and some evidence – about man's ability to process information. *Oregon Research Institute Monograph, 12*(2).

Tversky, A., & Kahneman, D. (1973). Availability: A heuristic for judging frequency and probability. *Cognitive psychology, 5,* 207–232.

Tversky, A., & Kahneman, D. (1974). Judgment under uncertainty: Heuristics and biases. *Science, 185,* 1124–1131.

Tversky, A., & Kahneman, D. (1981). The framing of decisions and the rationality of choice. *Science, 221,* 453–458.

# 34 On Cognitive Illusions and Their Implications

*Ward Edwards and Detlof von Winterfeldt*

Psychologists, and a few others, have been producing a literature on systematic errors in human performance of inference and decision-making tasks. The topic is large and complex, and the literature is unmanageable. The focus on human error in general is a folkway of psychology, particularly of experimental psychology (see Edwards, 1983). The fact that human beings sometimes make systematic intellectual errors is clearly a topic for psychological research, whereas the fact that other human beings under other circumstances can produce right answers to the same questions is ordinarily the subject matter of some other discipline, usually the one that discovered how to find the right answers. The motivation for the greater part of the research we will discuss has been clearly described by Kahneman and Tversky.

There are three related reasons for the focus on systematic errors and inferential biases in the study of reasoning. First, they expose some of our intellectual limitations and suggest ways to improve the quality of our thinking. Second, errors and biases often reveal the psychological processes that govern judgment and inference. Third, mistakes and fallacies help the mapping of human intuitions by indicating which principles of statistics or logic are non-intuitive or counterintuitive. (1982, p. 124)

This research strategy has led to many insights into human information-processing abilities and limits . . . .

This chapter explores four kinds of intellectual tasks: probability assessment and revision, decision making, intuitive physics, and logic and mental arithmetic. We call the kinds of errors with which this chapter deals "cognitive illusions." The first half of that phrase emphasizes the intellectual nature of the tasks; the second is intended to suggest that these phenomena

This chapter is a revised version of a paper that appeared in the *Southern California Law Review*, 1986, *59*(2), 401–451. Copyright © 1986 by Southern California Law Review. Reprinted by permission.

are quite similar to a variety of perceptual illusions extensively studied by psychologists....

Our main topic is human cognitive competence. The publication of paper after paper about easily predictable human intellectual errors is bound to produce in some of their readers the impression that such errors are both widespread and inevitable. The main intent of this chapter, aside from reviewing some of the literature, is to explore the extent to which that impression may be justified; that is, to try to find a meaningful perspective, in the light of this research, from which to assess what to expect from people faced with difficult intellectual tasks.

A thorough review of the literature requires a book, not a chapter. Fortunately, such a book appeared in 1982: *Judgment under Uncertainty: Heuristics and Biases*, edited by Daniel Kahneman, Paul Slovic, and Amos Tversky. In a slightly earlier book, Hogarth (1980) defined at least 27 sources of bias or error in judgment and decision making. A number of older sources have also reviewed the aspects of this literature that are concerned with probability assessment and decision making. We are not familiar with any reviews of the research on intuitive physics. Extensive reviews of errors in mental arithmetic can be found in the literature of educational psychology but are directed almost entirely to errors made by children as they relate to instruction and learning. One or two are cited later.

## The Research Paradigm for Finding Cognitive Illusions

*Webster's Third New International Dictionary* defines *illusion* as, among other things, "the state or fact of being intellectually deceived or . . . misled." The cognitive illusions fit the definition exactly.

The elements of every cognitive illusion are the same.

1. A formal rule that specifies how to determine a correct (usually, *the* correct) answer to an intellectual question. The question normally includes all information required as input to the formal rule.
2. A judgment, made without the aid of physical tools, that answers the question.
3. A systematic discrepancy between the correct answer and the judged answer. (Random errors do not count.)

Sometimes it takes two or three questions to demonstrate the presence of a cognitive illusion; the principle is the same.

This exposition of cognitive illusions will use relatively simple examples and demonstrations, usually taken verbatim from the early experiments that identified them. It will then speculate about possible intuitive remedies, using whatever relevant experimental and applied literature we know of. We consider it self-evident that by far the best remedy for such errors is to use the formal rules that lead to the right answers rather than unaided intuition to answer questions to which they apply.

Though our background is in psychology, our profession is decision analysis. This means that we set out to use a combination of formal analytic tools, psychological skills, and tricks of our trade to help people and organizations make valid inferences and wise decisions. Decision analysis is an applied discipline, and we are appliers as well as researchers. Our focus on helping people and organizations to act wisely in the presence both of irreducible uncertainties and of values that must be traded off against one another in making decisions dominates the expository part of this chapter.

## Cognitive Illusions in Probability and Inference

The research on probability assessment and inference to be discussed here grows out of the Bayesian point of view about those topics (see, e.g., Edwards, Lindman, & Savage, 1963). Those familiar with that viewpoint should skip the highly condensed précis that follows.

A probability is a number between 0 and 1. Probabilities describe propositions about events; for expository convenience we shall discuss only finite sets of events, though the generalization to infinite sets is straightforward. Probabilists agree that probabilities are in some sense measures of uncertainty. Bayesians hold that the sense is quite straight-forward: A probability is an appropriate description of your (or our, or someone's) uncertainty about the truth of a proposition asserting that the event will happen, or perhaps that it has happened. This means that probabilities describe *opinions* about the truth or falsity of propositions about events. Because an opinion must be some person's opinion, and because it describes the person as well as the proposition that the opinion is about and the event to which the proposition refers, such probabilities are usually called "personal." The term *subjective* is also often used; we avoid it, both because in a technical sense many personal probabilities are not very subjective, for there can be little disagreement about them, and because many scientists, not including us, find that word pejorative.

A major competitor to the Bayesian position is the frequentistic view. Frequentists hold that probabilities are the limiting values that relative frequencies approach as the number of observations of a random variable increases without limit. Although Bayesians would often regard information about relative frequencies as crucial to forming their opinions, they disagree with frequentists both about how such relative frequencies should be used to estimate probabilities and about what to do when relative frequencies are unavailable or even unimaginable. Bayesian and frequentistic approaches lead to quite different conclusions about the rules for statistical inference, and statisticians of these persuasions have engaged in running arguments since the early 1960s.

An important consequence of our Bayesian position is that it is entirely meaningful to assess the probability of a unique event. How likely is it, for you, that the 20th president of the United States was a Republican? He either was or was not, and no relative frequency seems relevant. But unless you are better informed about 19th-century presidents than we are, you are not sure whether he was or was not. You do have relevant information. You probably know that the 20th president served after Lincoln and before Theodore Roosevelt and that the Republican party existed and was quite successful during that period. You may be unsure what number would best describe the degree of uncertainty you feel about that assertion, but on the basis of the information you now have you would surely regard .5 as an underestimate. As the example illustrates, one way of finding out your probability that a proposition is true is to ask you. Psychologists have studied procedures for asking such questions and the merit of the resulting answers extensively; we review a bit of the relevant literature later.

Opinions change in the light of evidence. Let $P(H)$ be your opinion about how likely hypothesis $H$ is before you receive datum $D$, and let $P(H|D)$ be your opinion about $H$ now that you know $D$. Then

$$P(H|D) = P(D|H)P(H)/P(D).$$

This equation is one of the many ways of writing Bayes's theorem. $P(D|H)$, the probability that the datum would be observed if the hypothesis were true, is its essence. The denominator, $P(D)$, is an unimportant normalizing constant that forces the values of $P(H|D)$ to sum to 1 over the set of hypotheses being considered. If, for example, you are considering $H$ and not-$H$, then

$$P(D) = P(D|H)P(H) + P(D|\text{not-}H)P(\text{not-}H).$$

Bayes's theorem is trivial and uncontroversial; it is simply a consequence of the fact that the probabilities of an exhaustive set of mutually exclusive events must sum to 1. Its importance results from the fact that it is a normatively optimal rule for thinking; it tells you exactly how much you should revise your prior opinions (represented as $P(H)$) in the light of relevant new evidence (represented as $P(D|H)$ and $P(D|\text{not-}H)$) to form your posterior opinions (represented as $P(H|D)$). That is, it is one of the rules for getting the right answer specified by the cognitive illusions paradigm. Indeed, it is an especially significant one, because the task of revising opinions in the light of new evidence, sometimes called by such names as inference, diagnosis, or trial by jury, is of very considerable human importance.

### Conservatism

In the late 1950s, mostly as a result of Savage's work (1954), psychologists became aware of Bayes's theorem and of its importance as a normative rule for inference. The cognitive illusions paradigm had been invented much earlier, but this seemed to be an especially attractive context in which to apply it.

Phillips, Hays, and Edwards (1966) did the first study. In an unnecessarily complex task they found that no subject revised opinions nearly so much as the optimal Bayesian rule required. This inability has come to be called conservatism in probabilistic inference. Phillips and Edwards (1966) thereupon developed the simplest task they could invent that still embodies the basic Bayesian idea, the bookbag-and-pokerchips task. A subject is presented with two bookbags. One contains, for example, 70% red chips and 30% blue chips; the other has the opposite composition. One bag is chosen at random, so that the prior probability of the predominantly red bag is .5. Then a sample is taken with replacement, generating, for example, six red chips and four blue chips. The subjects are asked to provide posterior probabilities or odds in favor of the bag favored by the data. Typical responses in the above example are .6–.7, quite different from the normatively correct .84. The finding, strong and robust in experiments like these, has been that human inference is routinely conservative.

Early explanations of this phenomenon included response bias (people do not like to respond with extreme numbers), misperception (people underestimate the diagnostic impact of the data), and misaggregation (people perceive the impact of a single datum correctly but fail to aggregate properly the joint impact of several data). (See Edwards, Phillips, Hays, & Goodman, 1968; Wheeler & Edwards, 1975.) These explanations, together with the orderly nature of the conservatism phenomenon, led to relatively straightforward designs of tasks and procedures to avoid conservatism. Two are of particular interest. A system called PIP (for Probabilistic Information Processing; see Edwards, 1962; Edwards et al., 1968) separated the two tasks of assessing the diagnostic impact of particular data and aggregating diagnostic impacts into posterior opinions, assigning the former to human judgment and the latter to Bayes's theorem. Another way to reduce conservatism is to use response modes that call for responses in the midst of, rather than far away from, the numerical representations of the information to be aggregated (Eils, Seaver, & Edwards, 1977).

In the 1970s, the conservatism literature encountered a host of criticisms that challenged both the previous explanations and the corrective mechanisms they suggested. (For examples, see Beach, Wise, & Barclay, 1970; Kahneman & Tversky, 1972; Marks & Clarkson, 1972; Slovic & Lichtenstein, 1971; Vlek & Wagenaar, 1979.) The crux of many of these criticisms was that the Bayesian inference task is too complex for unaided human performance and consequently that subjects asked to perform Bayesian tasks seek and find simplifying strategies. A number of such strategies were suggested and explored in experiments, but none seemed to explain a broad range of studies of Bayesian tasks successfully.

A more general criticism, not only of conservatism experiments but of other experiments on probability assessment, also arose in the 1970s. Its essence is that laboratory experiments use contrived inference problems of types that occur rarely outside the laboratory and are misleading in their structure (Navon, 1978; Winkler & Murphy, 1973). In particular, real-world inference problems usually involve unreliable source data and conditional dependencies among data and among intermediate hypotheses. (Two data are conditionally independent, given a hypothesis, if the probability of either, given the hypothesis, is unaffected by knowledge that the other occurred. In symbols, if $D_i$ and $D_j$ are two data, then

$$P(D_i|H) = P(D_i|H,D_j)$$

for all values of $i$ and $j$ and for all hypotheses being considered. Conditional independence is so demanding a requirement on the relationships among data and hypotheses that it virtually never describes anyone's opinions except in the special contexts of laboratory experiments and other statistical inferences based on random sampling.)

We now believe that simple cures for conservatism are probably less useful than detailed structuring of actual inference problems to reflect facts of life such as the unreliability of many data and the existence of complex, conditionally dependent inference structures. Such structures call for disaggregated judgments of probabilities, but the appropriate combination rules for these probabilities are much more demanding than the simple single-stage formulation of Bayes's theorem.

### Ignoring Base Rates

Bayes's theorem specifies that proper inference from fallible evidence should combine that evidence with prior probabilities, that is, the opinions the person making the inference held before the new evidence became available (see Edwards et al., 1963). Often, though not always, the relevant prior information takes the form of base rates. Before you get close enough to the approaching blonde to recognize eye color, you may consider it likely that she has blue eyes, simply because so many blondes do. In recent years, a number of experiments have called into question whether people actually use base rates in probability judgments.

The seminal study of neglect of base rate was done by Kahneman and Tversky. One group of subjects was given the following cover story:

A panel of psychologists have interviewed and administered personality tests to 30 engineers and 70 lawyers, all successful in their respective fields. On the basis of this information, thumbnail descriptions of the 30 engineers and 70 lawyers have been written. You will find on your form five descriptions, chosen at random from the 100 available descriptions. For each description, please indicate your probability that each person described is an engineer, on a scale from 0 to 100. (1973, p. 241).

Subjects in another large group were given the same story except that it referred to 30 lawyers and 70 engineers. Both groups were then presented with five descriptions. For example:

Jack is a 45-year-old man. He is married and has four children. He is generally conservative, careful, and ambitious. He shows no interest in political and social issues and spends most of his free time on his many hobbies, which include home carpentry, sailing, and mathematical puzzles.

On the basis of this description, the subjects were expected to judge the probability that Jack is a lawyer (or, for some subjects, an engineer). The data indicate that base rates did not make much difference, although when the same subjects were asked what their judgment would be in the absence of the personality description, they indicated that they would in fact use the base rates. Kahneman and Tversky concluded that in the presence of specific individuating evidence, prior probabilities, by which they meant base rates, are ignored.

This neglect of base rates has been replicated in a number of studies using various stimuli, including some in which the numerical diagnosticity could be inferred, thus providing the ingredients for a straight-forward Bayesian calculation. (See, e.g., Bar-Hillel, 1980; Carroll & Siegler, 1977; Hammerton, 1973; Lyon & Slovic, 1976.) Although these studies generally supported the existence of a base-rate fallacy, they also showed that base rates are sometimes taken into account: when the link between base rate and target event is causal, when base rates appear relevant, when the base rates relate to individuating information, and when both diagnostic and base-rate information are essentially statistical.

This body of experimental evidence combines with a number of real-world observations to generate a picture of a robust phenomenon. The seminal paper about the real-world consequences of that neglect was written by Meehl and Rosen (1955). Dershowitz (1971) and McGargee (1976) have called attention to the consequences of failure to consider base rates in judicial contexts. Lykken (1975) noted the contribution of that failure to misinterpretations of lie detector tests. Oskamp (1965) complained of it in connection with interpreting case studies. Eddy (1982), in a very stimulating article, showed how not only medical doctors but also their teachers and textbooks fall into the base-rate trap.

Bar-Hillel (1980) put all this evidence and thought together in a most orderly and persuasive way. She summed it up as follows:

People integrate two items of information only if both seem to them equally relevant. Otherwise, high relevance information renders low relevance information irrelevant. One item of information is more relevant ... than another if it somehow pertains to it more specifically.

She suggests that this can happen in two ways:

(1) the dominating information may refer to a set smaller than the overall population to which the dominated items refer ... (2) the dominating information may be causally linked to the judged outcome, in the absence of such a link on behalf of the dominated information. This enhances relevance because it is an indirect way of making general information relate more specifically to individual cases.

Thus, Bar-Hillel sees the Tversky–Kahneman findings about causality as a special case of her more general principle of relevance.

In real-world applications of Bayesian inference models, one constructs a problem structure that appropriately reflects the statistical properties of the environment and that meets the analytic requirements of the Bayesian model. We believe that appropriate structures go a long way toward avoiding the base-rate bias. In almost every experimental situation that we reviewed, a little help in structuring the inference problem would have enormously improved the subjects' performance (or shown that subjects had, indeed, a different problem structure in mind). One part of problem structuring is to identify classes of hypotheses and events that are useful for decision making and that allow discrimination among data. Often such classes are constructed so that the prior distribution is relatively flat; that is, the hypotheses being considered are a priori fairly close to being equally likely. (If a prior distribution is very steep, one often tries to find subdivisions of the high-probability hypothesis.) Flat or gently sloping priors can be ignored. The structuring process also decomposes the problem in a way that highlights the separate relevance of priors, diagnostic information, reliability information, and their dependencies. This decomposition alone should enhance the inference maker's awareness of base rates, priors, diagnosticities, and their interlinkages.

In addition, we are convinced from everyday experience that professionals working at their professions make extensive use of base rates. Doctors routinely make diagnoses of upper respiratory ailments on the basis of history and physical data combined with base-rate information. Lawyers concerned with criminal defense routinely assess statements by their clients on the basis of base rates. Accountants use base-rate information in deciding what to explore carefully in audits. And so on. In a sense, sophisticated awareness of and use of base rates is a key element of what we mean by expertise.

Once the problem is appropriately structured, the simplest way to avoid the base-rate fallacy is by modeling priors explicitly, assessing likelihoods or likelihood ratios, and using Bayes's theorem to aggregate. Subjects thus would never be asked to aggregate base rates and diagnostic information intuitively. But sometimes intuitive aggregation cannot be avoided, and if Bar-Hillel's explanation is correct, aggregation of two nonequally relevant items of information can lead to distortions when done in the head. In such a case, the literature suggests the following strategies.

First, if both diagnostic information and base-rate information are essentially statistical, their statistical nature and interlinkages should be stressed. Second, if both can be related causally to the target event, the causal chains should be pointed out for both. Third, one could provide individuating information about base rates (as is usually implicit in diagnostic information). Fourth, Nisbett and Borgida (1975) suggested and Nisbett, Borgida, Crandall, and Reed (1976) demonstrated that one can make the base-rate information more dramatic and less abstract by using a few concrete examples instead of a set of descriptive statistics. All of these strategies essentially attempt to put base-rate and diagnostic information on an equal footing. Of course, the same strategies apply if two pieces of information of the same kind (e.g., two pieces of base-rate information; two pieces of diagnostic information) have different degrees of relevance.

### Ignoring Sample Size

A series of experiments by Tversky and Kahneman (1971, 1973, 1974) showed that subjects tend to ignore the sample size when constructing subjective sampling distributions and that even experienced and statistically trained psychologists fail to appreciate the power (or lack of power) of a small sample test. The result is what they call a human "belief in the law of small numbers." Tversky and Kahneman argue that this effect is due to the representativeness heuristic according to which a sample that is similar in features to the population is considered to be more likely than one that is dissimilar. Similarity thus can override other considerations like sample size.

In a particularly striking demonstration, Kahneman and Tversky (1972) asked subjects to construct sampling distributions for the mean height of 10, 100, and 1000 males drawn randomly from a population with mean 170 cm (the variance was not specified explicitly). Subjects gave individual probability estimates for five equal 5 cm intervals between 160 cm and 185 cm, plus estimates of the probabilities that the respective means would fall below 160 cm or above 185 cm. Sampling theory would, of course, prescribe that the variance of the subjective sampling distributions decrease with $N$. However, in Kahneman and Tversky's experiment, the median sampling distributions were, in fact, constant across $N$. Thus subjects appeared to be insensitive to sample size. Kahneman and Tversky (1972) report similar results for binomial sampling distributions, as well as for simpler questions about the probability that the proportion of elements in a sample would exceed a specified amount. For example, when subjects were asked to judge the probability that a random sample of newborn babies would contain at least 60% males, 56% of them gave the same answer independently of whether the sample was generated in a large hospital (large daily $N$) or a small hospital (small daily $N$), and the rest split evenly between the two hospitals.

These findings apply to sophisticated as well as naive subjects. Mathematical psychologists, trained in statistics, were found to be too confident in the replicability of statistically significant results. For example, they thought that a sample of 10 subjects is very likely to reproduce a result that was previously found to be significant with 20 subjects at the .05 level (Tversky & Kahneman, 1971).

Where the "law of small numbers" occurs, several precautions can be taken against it. One, as usual, is an appropriate problem structure, decomposing samples, data, and hypotheses to avoid judgments prone to the bias. This is especially true for the confidence judgments about samples, which can be structured and modeled in various ways (see, e.g., the two structures that Tversky and Kahneman, 1981, propose to construct a normative model for the significance test replication – there are many more of this sort). The findings by Bar-Hillel indicate that it is important to discuss with the experts and decision makers the nature of the sampling process, in particular considering replacement versus nonreplacement, proportions of samples to populations, and the effect of sample sizes on sample statistics. Especially important is a search for reasonable hypotheses about parent populations, given particular samples. One of the first things experts and inference makers may do, when faced with questions about the likelihood of a sample, is to generate hypotheses that make the data likely. If the sample makes the hypotheses about the population proposed by experiment or scenario seem absurd, it is entirely predictable that subjects will consider others. Every model of a data-generating process should be judged on its merits; none ever deserves unlimited credence. For a detailed discussion of such issues, see Edwards et al. (1963).

### Nonregressive Prediction

When experts or statistically unskilled human subjects have to predict a variable $y$ from knowledge of another variable $x$, and the correlation between $x$ and $y$ is less than perfect, traditional statistical models require that estimate to be regressive. In the extreme, if there is a zero correlation between the variables, the conditional estimate of $y$ given $x$ should coincide with the unconditional mean of $y$. The higher the correlation, the closer the estimate should fall to the 45-degree line (assuming standardized variables) in the graph of $y$ as a function of $x$. Normative regressiveness of prediction makes several assumptions about the nature of the prediction task, but these are general enough so that, in most situations, predictions of imperfectly correlated variables should be regressive.

Several studies have found that subjects instead tend to predict by matching the dependent to the independent variable and do not sufficiently account for the lack of perfect correlation. Kahneman and Tversky (1973) found this effect when asking subjects to predict a student's grade point average given information about aptitude test scores. In this task, as in others, subjects showed marked lack of regressiveness. As with the base-rate and the sample-size biases, Kahneman and Tversky attribute nonregressiveness to the representativeness heuristic in that "the degree of confidence one has in a prediction reflects the degree to which the selected outcome is more representative of the input than are other outcomes" (1973, p. 249).

Several other studies found nonregressive prediction in a variety of settings (see, e.g., Jennings, Amabile, & Ross, 1982; Nisbett & Ross, 1980). These studies also included findings that subjects typically overestimate the amount of covariation between two variables; in other words, they have "illusions of reliability and validity" (see, e.g., Chapman & Chapman, 1967, 1969). This illusion is stronger when covariation is estimated on theoretical grounds and prior expectations, smaller when based on data (Jennings et al., 1982).

Real-world evidence also suggests nonregressiveness. Teachers of statistics often find the notion of regressive estimates to be difficult to teach. Statistically experienced psychologists often cling to arguments about test validities in spite of contrary statistical evidence. Less sophisticated social scientists interpret regressive data as meaningful effects.

Kahneman and Tversky (1979) propose a heuristic procedure to correct nonregressive predictions. It consists of five steps. The first is to identify the reference class (the relevant population). The second is to assess the distribution of $y$ in that class. (Some of the language of the paper suggests, appropriately, that several different distributions should be assessed conditional on several different values of $x$ or of the $x$ vector.) The third is to obtain an estimate of the correlation between $x$ and $y$, preferably by statistical means. The fourth is to correct the intuitive estimate of $y$ by means of a computation based on that correlation. Kahneman and Tversky (1979) do not expect that suggestion to lead to immediate acceptance of the revised estimate; instead, they hope that it can be used as a basis for persuasion.

### Overconfidence

You would like any probability assessment to have two characteristics that relate to the outside world. One is obvious: You would like it to be extreme. An assessment close to 1 or 0 is far more useful guidance about what to expect, and therefore what to do, than an assessment near .5. The same thought for continuous distributions is that you would like probability density functions to be as peaked as possible.

The other property you would like probability assessment to have is called calibration, and it is much subtler than extremeness. You cannot assess the calibration of any single assessment. But if you have a number of probability assessments all of .6, then you would feel better about them if about 60% of the propositions so assessed turned out true and the other 40% turned out false than if, say, 10% or 90% turned out true. The same thought for any continuous distribution over a parameter is that you would like the area of the density function between any two cutoff points to correspond to the relative frequency with which the true value of the parameter falls between them.

Calibration and extremeness pull in opposite directions. Consider a weather forecaster who must every day specify a probability of rain. One way to proceed would be to inspect records, note that last year it rained on 60% of all days in that city, and so make each day's assessment for this year 60%. Such assessments (called climatological in meteorology) are likely to be well calibrated, because the percentage of rainy days changes relatively little from year to year. But they would be almost useless, because they do not differentiate among days.

The alternative of saying either that it will rain or that it will not rain is better, but not much. It makes no distinction between days on which you think it a bit more likely than not that it will rain and days on which you can see the puddles accumulating in the street while you formulate your forecast.

In order to balance the inward pull of the desire for good calibration against the outward pull of the desire for extremeness, you must use the evidence at hand – exactly what the weather forecasters do.

Research evidence about calibration is abundant but singularly hard to understand. Lichtenstein, Fischhoff, and Phillips (1982) have done an exceptionally good job of reviewing the experimental studies, which reach back all the way to Adams (1957). Most of the numerous experiments they review show excessively high assessments of probabilities over .5.

An important conclusion from Lichtenstein et al.'s review is that people are much less likely to be overconfident about easy probability judgments than about difficult ones. Pitz (1974) found that very difficult judgments produce most overconfidence. Lichtenstein and Fischhoff (1977), asking subjects to discriminate between such stimuli as drawings made by Asian or European children, found essentially no calibration at all; virtually any response meant about .5. Using various other stimuli and manipulations that made the discriminations easier, they found much better performance. Indeed, Lichtenstein and Fischhoff (1980) found underconfidence for easy judgments, as have several others. A particularly encouraging finding by Koriat, Lichtenstein, and Fischhoff (1980) is that respondents are less overconfident even on difficult questions if asked to write down reasons why the answer they prefer might be wrong.

Response modes may help reduce overconfidence, at least in the continuous case. Numerous studies have shown that probability distributions over continuous variables elicited using the fractile method are far too tight (see, e.g., Alpert & Raiffa, 1969; for reviews, see Lichtenstein, Fischhoff, & Phillips, 1977, 1982). Seaver, von Winterfeldt, and Edwards (1978) used direct probability assessment methods to construct continuous probability distributions and found that overconfidence and excessive tightness vanished.

Expertise helps too, even in experiments. Sieber (1974) and Pitz (1974) both found good calibration for students taking tests on the subject matter of courses they were then taking – about which they might be assumed to be fairly expert. However, Lichtenstein and Fischhoff (1977) found that graduate students in psychology did no better on psychology-related items than on general knowledge items. Perhaps expertise needs to be more specific than that.

Yet another conclusion implicit in the literature that Lichtenstein et al. review is that subtle verbal and other methodological issues may well have a lot to do with how such experiments come out, even though they mean nothing about the intellectual content of the task. A happy fourth conclusion suggested by some of the studies they review is that training in and experience at probability estimation can improve matters.

The facts that easy assessment tasks produce better calibration than difficult ones and that both training in probability estimation and experience at it improve performance help to explain other findings. Zlotnick (1968) found relatively good calibration for intelligence analysts, hampered primarily by a tendency to overestimate the probabilities of occurrence of dire events. That finding about overestimating the probability of dire events is widely reported in the real-assessments literature. The standard and plausible interpretation of it is that it is a by-product of utilities associated with the job. An intelligence analyst, or a doctor, would much rather warn of a dire event and later be proven wrong than to miss it in the first place.

Ludke, Stauss, and Gustafson (1977), in a study focused primarily on response modes, found relatively high quality of performance in calibration terms as well as others for all response modes studied; the respondents were trained medical personnel answering questions about familiar physiological topics like blood pressure. Lusted et al. (1980), reporting a very large field study of probability assessments by emergency room attending physicians, found generally good calibration except for the warning effect mentioned above. DeSmet, Fryback, and Thornbury (1979) also report good performance by medical respondents.

But the world's probability assessment championship clearly belongs to weather forecasters. Murphy and Winkler (1974, 1977a, 1977b) find average deviations of only .028 from perfect calibration for credible interval temperature forecasts. U.S. weather forecasters have been making probabilistic forecasts of rain since 1965. Figure 34.1 from Murphy and Winkler (1977a) shows the calibration data for 24,859 judgments made in Chicago during the four years ending June 1976. The number associated with each point is

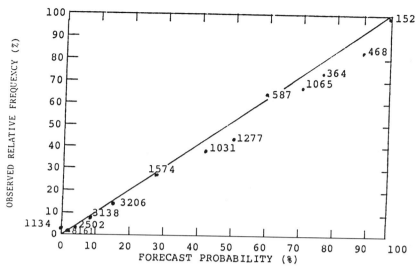

Figure 34.1.  Calibration curve for weather forecasters. (*Source:* Murphy & Winkler, 1977a).

the number of observations it represents. A. H. Murphy (personal communication, SPUDM, 1983) reports data that are even better. He believes that forecasters learn to do better with experience, and other data support that belief. Among numerous reasons why weather forecasters are so good are: (a) they make forecasts every day; (b) they get event feedback each day about yesterday's forecast; (c) they get numerical feedback via a rule called the Brier score, an example of a class of numerical rules that make it optimal to report one's true opinion as one's probability estimate; and (d) to some extent their Brier scores bear on promotion and pay.

In sum: These data seem to us to argue that substantive expertise helps probability assessment by making the task easy rather than hard. Expertise about probability assessment helps too, probably because the proficient and experienced probability estimator simply understands better what such estimates mean. Feedback both of outcomes and of scoring rule information helps. And, given these conditions, probability assessors can be expected to do a good job.

But these conditions are rare. Short of putting them in place, can anything be done? Not much.

### Hindsight

Two cognitive illusions have been cleverly studied by Fischhoff (1975, 1976; Fischhoff & Beyth, 1975); they are called the hindsight illusions. Fischhoff (1980) summarizes them as follows:

In hindsight, people consistently exaggerate what could have been anticipated in foresight. They not only tend to view what has happened as being inevitable, but also to view it as having appeared "relatively inevitable" before it happened. People believe that others should have been able to anticipate events much better than was actually the case. They even misremember their own predictions so as to exaggerate in hindsight what they knew in foresight.

These phenomena seem to be a probabilistic version of "I told you so." Fischhoff's studies leave no doubt about their reality.

Of all cognitive illusions, the hindsight illusions would seem to be easiest to correct: Simply make and write down the probability estimate before the event occurs or before the estimator learns the answer. But Fischhoff was motivated by the plight of the historian, condemned to look backward at events that have already occurred and to wonder what chance, if any, they had of occurring otherwise. (See Fischhoff, 1980, for a detailed discussion of these problems.) Writing history is an exercise in hindsight. Are the hindsight illusions an inevitable occupational disease for historians?

Perhaps. Still, the Bayesian position may have something to contribute. A formulation like "Twenty-four hours before the battle started, how probable was it that Napoleon would lose at Waterloo?" is at worst nonsense and at best incomplete, because it specifies neither whose the probability is nor the information on which it is based. The question "Twenty-four hours before the battle started, how probable did Napoleon consider it to be that he would lose at Waterloo?" is at least well framed; historians might try to answer it. To do so, they would have to find out what Napoleon then knew about his own past record of successes and failures and about the state of his enemies' forces, and what scenarios he was considering about how the battle would go. This strips the problem down to at least potentially manageable size. The sunken wall, for example, is irrelevant; Napoleon did not know it was there. Thus formulated, the apparent inevitabilities of history look less inevitable.

Proper formulation of the probability question is not necessarily a cure. Fischhoff's studies imply that the historian's post hoc point of view fairly well assures the first bias. They are silent about what would happen if the historian were to try to see the world the way Napoleon saw it on the spot – admittedly an extraordinarily difficult exercise of imagination.

### Debiasing

Von Winterfeldt and Edwards (1986) say,

Assessing uncertainties that may control significant decisions is serious business, and should be done in the right atmosphere. The analyst should work either one-on-one or in a small group .... Classroom settings are inappropriate .... [The respondent] should understand the techniques to be used, as much as time and other limits permit.... Good elicitation practice is never to rely on only one way of asking. Instead, ask the same or related questions in various ways, looking for inconsistencies. If you find some, be glad. They can be fed back to the respondent, who must then be asked to think some more, in order to get rid of them. Anything that promotes hard thought and insight helps.... We recognize some idealism in this set of prescriptions. Time, respondent patience, or cost may not permit. If they do, the enhanced accuracy may not be worth while.... Our advice has two purposes: to specify standards of skilled performance for an analyst, and to provide a check-list against which to assess the conditions of experimental studies that conclude that respondents do a poor job of uncertainty assessment. We are not very impressed with evidence that performance is poor unless the analyst went to great pains to try to help the respondent do well.

   Virtually none of the experimental literature so far reviewed conforms to these criteria. Indeed, the criteria are inconsistent with the part of the cognitive illusions paradigm that calls for intuitive, unaided judgments. Because much of that literature has in various ways argued that people make systematic errors in assessing uncertainties, it is natural to dismiss such studies by saying "Oh, they didn't do it right." But a number of studies have in fact tried out, one by one, some of the ways of improving elicitation procedures explicit or implicit in this chapter. Fischhoff (1982) has written an extraordinarily thoughtful and insightful review of such studies in the context of overconfidence and the hindsight biases.
   Consider Table 34.1, taken from Fischhoff (1982). Fischhoff's proposed list of debiasing strategies bears a very close resemblance indeed to the rules for probability estimation we have proposed already and to some that emerged from our discussion of calibration. One omission compared with our list is the idea of convergent operations: asking the same or related questions in such a way as to elicit inconsistencies and then using these inconsistencies as stimuli to reelicitation. The omission is major, because it is the most important thing a decision analyst does during probability elicitation. A second major omission is that Fischhoff rules out significant computational assistance. Still, Fischhoff's list is a very serious attempt to examine methodological deficiencies of probability elicitation experiments.
   Fischhoff proceeds to review a rather large number of studies that attempt to correct one or another of the faults he lists by using one or more of the strategies he lists. His review is both detailed and discouraging. Such corrections, at the level of intensity at which they have been tried, on the whole do very little to correct the two biases he examines. The two most effective procedures seem to be to make the task easier (or, equivalently, to enhance the substantive abilities and information that the respondent brings to it) and to teach probability estimation skills. The review seems to us to slight somewhat the earlier literature on effects of response modes.
   Fischhoff's summing-up is a gem of balanced thought. One point it makes is especially important to the perspective taken by this chapter. We have

Table 34.1. *Debiasing Methods According to Underlying Assumption*

| Assumption | Strategies |
|---|---|
| **Faulty tasks** | |
| Unfair tasks | Raise stakes |
| | Clarify instructions/stimuli |
| | Discourage second-guessing |
| | Use better response modes |
| | Ask fewer questions |
| Misunderstood tasks | Demonstrate alternative goal |
| | Demonstrate semantic disagreement |
| | Demonstrate impossibility of task |
| | Demonstrate overlooked distinction |
| **Faulty judges** | |
| Perfectible individuals | Warn of problem |
| | Describe problem |
| | Provide personalized feedback |
| | Train extensively |
| Incorrigible individuals | Replace them |
| | Recalibrate their responses |
| | Plan on error |
| **Mismatch between judges and task** | |
| Restructuring | Make knowledge explicit |
| | Search for discrepant information |
| | Decompose problem |
| | Consider alternative situations |
| | Offer alternative formulations |
| Education | Rely on substantive experts |
| | Educate from childhood |

*Source:* Fischhoff, 1982.

assumed all along that probability assessments are important enough that one should work hard to get them right.

[T]he relative validity of casual and work-hard laboratory experiments depends upon the real world situations to which their results are to be extrapolated. Each has its place. Understanding the laboratory–world match requires good judgment in characterizing both contexts. For example, work-hard situations are not necessarily synonymous with important situations. People may not work hard on an important problem unless they realize both the centrality of a judgment to the problem's outcome and the potential fallibility of that judgment. (Fischhoff, 1982, p. 441)

Probability judgments are often not central to important decision problems of which they are a part. And, clearly, the overwhelming majority of our uncertainties bear either on trivial decisions or on no decisions at all. In a sheer numerical sense, instances in which it is important to get the measurement of uncertainty just right are quite rare, and the kinds of uncertainty judgments studied in typical experiments are much more common, though still rare.

## Anchoring

When people are asked to generate an estimate, they frequently anchor on an obvious or convenient number (e.g., the mean, the mode) and then adjust upward or downward if there is a reason to believe that the correct number should be moved in either direction. In many situations that strategy works well, in particular when anchors are finely graded over the scale of estimates. Diamond evaluation is an example. The four standard dimensions for such evaluations are cut, color, clarity, and carats. Carats are, of course, easily measured on a balance. Diamond experts disagree about whether cut should be evaluated by a complex formula based on physical measurements or by intuitive judgments. But all agree that color and clarity must be assessed judgmentally. The training process uses many exemplars; the judgment reduces to assessing the similarity of the new diamond to remembered or currently available exemplars.

In other situations, anchoring and adjustment can lead to misjudgments. Slovic, Fischhoff, and Lichtenstein (1977) reviewed a number of studies showing the effect. Tversky and Kahneman (1974) argued that in probability judgments people frequently underadjust and thereby produce predictable biases in their numerical estimates.

Bar-Hillel (1973) and J. J. Cohen (1972) show that the probability of compound events is typically overestimated, and this seems to be an anchoring effect. People anchor on one event and fail to appreciate that multiplying two probabilities less than 1 by each other will produce a number less than either of them.

The previously discussed overconfidence bias has also been interpreted as an anchoring and adjustment bias (see, e.g., Slovic & Lichtenstein, 1971). By centering judgments around some median or modal value, subjects may attempt to find fractiles that are not sufficiently far removed from the anchor values.

In decision analytic practice, the key to reducing anchoring and adjustment biases is the use of multiple anchors and convergent validation techniques. When assessing continuous probability distributions, for example, one may begin by identifying the mean, the mode, and the plausible range of the random variable. In addition, the analyst could use two different assessment techniques: fractiles and direct probability estimation. The inevitable inconsistencies should lead to insights, discussions, and resolution. Sometimes an analyst may have a suspicion that respondents will anchor on some value like the most likely value or on a very low or very high value. In that case it is good practice to provide respondents with "counter-anchors" to "break" their intuitive anchors. In other cases it is useful to construct probabilities over different random variables, which can be formally related but invite anchors that produce divergent assessments.

### Retrieval and Scenario-based Availability

Tversky and Kahneman (1973) presented a number of studies concerned with the effect of various kinds of availability of instances or answers on judgments. Because we are trying to categorize instances according to the nature of the normative principle that leads to the right answer, rather than according to the underlying psychological mechanism, we shall discuss only some of those studies here, along with others conducted since.

The form of availability we discuss here has been called a bias, but the name may be inappropriate. Subjects tend to estimate a higher probability for those events for which they can easily generate or recall instances. The most familiar real-world examples are those in which extensive publicity about some atrocious crime or unusual kind of disaster much enhances lay assessment of how probable the event is. Every light-plane pilot knows that the true statement "The most dangerous part of the flight is the drive to and from the airport" is shocking and objectionable to most nonpilots, because plane crashes are normally publicized whereas automobile crashes, except for unusual ones, are not.

Tversky and Kahneman (1973) asked subjects to state whether words that begin with $R$ are more or less likely in the English language than those that have an $R$ as the third letter. Most subjects said that words that begin with an $R$ are more likely. The statistical fact is the reverse. Words that begin with $R$ are easier to recall or generate than words that have an $R$ in the third place. One interpretation of availability is that people overassess the probability of easily retrieved events and fail to recognize that is an error.

An even more complex collection of problems arises when judgments of probability must be based on scenarios about the future. This form of probability assessment has been formalized by the technical device known as "fault trees," which attempts to assess the probability of a low-probability event by drawing out a schematic of all the ways in which that event may occur and assessing the likelihood of each. (For a full technical presentation, see Green & Bourne, 1972; for the most famous application, see U.S. Nuclear Regulatory Commission, 1975.) The method is in extensive use. Anxieties about its validity among the engineers who developed it seem to focus primarily on whether its assumptions are satisfied. A much more dramatic set of possible problems is implied by a study by Fischhoff, Slovic, and Lichtenstein (1978), which showed that experienced automobile mechanics, asked to deal with various representations of the possible reasons why a car might not start, did not recognize the omission of major branches of the fault tree. Kahneman and Tversky (1982) have discussed other problems with simulations as bases for probability assessment.

## Evidence for Successful Statistical Intuitions in Inductive Reasoning

Rather recently, a countercurrent to the line of research summarized so far has begun to appear. By far the best summary of its thinking and content is contained in an important paper by Nisbett, Krantz, Jepson, and Kunda (1983).

The authors, starting from the premise that some intuitive judgments that should depend on statistical principles do and some do not, attempt to explore what problem and respondent characteristics favor the use of statistical principles. They note the important work of Piaget and Inhelder (1941/1975), which shows that children develop statistical intuitions as they grow older and that understanding of the behavior of physical objects that obviously behave randomly emerges as a function of age. They suggest that, here as elsewhere in development, the development of the individual to some extent resembles the development of human understanding in general. They identify three task variables that can influence the ease with which adults can think statistically: the degree to which the random nature of the data-generating device or process is visible and obvious, familiarity with the randomness of a sequence of events resulting from past experience with it or comparable sequences, and cultural prescriptions to reason statistically (e.g., the incessant baseball season bombardment with statistical information, implying random variability, about aspects of individual and team performance).

They conducted some very stimulating experiments. In one, subjects were far more willing to generalize from a very small number of consistent instances about what seems to be a nonrandom process (electrical conductivity of a metal) than about an obviously more variable one (obesity of a Pacific island dweller). Another showed that enumeration of a sample space and recognition that a subset of observations from it was in fact a sample made that sample less important and thus enhanced the importance of other conflicting information. Yet another showed that experienced athletes and actors were more likely to recognize that a poor performance could be random than inexperienced ones. They conclude from these and other arguments and data that

some of our subjects showed . . . an appreciation of the statistical principles that in previous work other subjects failed to appreciate. It seems more reasonable to explain [this success] by saying that they are more skilled at statistical reasoning than the other subjects than by saying that they saw through the experimenters' tricks . . . . We see a powerful argument in the work we have reviewed for the role of cultural evolution. It does not require unusual optimism to speculate that we are on the threshold of a profound change in the way that people reason inductively.... Most people today appreciate entirely statistical accounts of sports events, accident rates, and the weather.... Will our own descendants differ as much from us as we do from Bernoulli's contemporaries? (Nisbett et al., 1983, pp. 360–362)

These conclusions are perhaps an even more dramatic message of hope than the one we are offering. Our emphasis on understanding and expertise is like that of Nisbett, Krantz, Jepson, and Kunda, as is our recognition of gradual emergence of inductive skills during maturation and education. We think of decision analysis as a technique that can help hone those skills when they are lacking and needed. If we take the argument about cultural evolution seriously, we might look for the disappearance of decision analysts. There is precedent. At one time, professional scribes wrote for those who could not. Later, professional arithmeticians served the needs of merchants deficient in arithmetical skill. Both professions have disappeared.

### Other Classes of Cognitive Illusions

#### Violations of SEU

There are many axiomatic treatments of decision making. The axioms purport to be, and usually are, rules of behavior that no one would wish to violate if the stakes are high. Most such sets of axioms lead to a simple theorem, known as the SEU model. SEU stands for Subjectively Expected Utility, and the model simply asserts that, from various alternative actions available, one either should or does choose the one that has the largest SEU. In the preceding sentence "should" applies if the model is considered as normative or prescriptive; "does" applies if the model is considered as descriptive of actual behavior. The distinction, here and elsewhere in this essay, is far more slippery than it appears. People often do what they should do. Because under general though not universal circumstances the SEUs of the available options can be discovered (this is a major function of almost all decision analyses), one way in which people can behave wisely if the stakes are high enough to justify the effort is to discover the SEUs of the actions available to them (perhaps with the help of a decision analyst) and to maximize SEU deliberately. In special circumstances other rules for decision making are appropriate; examples include the famous minimax rule for some kinds of games and the less famous but more often applicable rule of avoiding gambler's ruin. Such rules can be interpreted as ways of maximizing SEUs in the situations to which they apply.

An expectation of anything is simply a weighted average. In this case the numbers being averaged are utilities. A utility is a subjective measure of the attractiveness of a possible outcome to the decision maker(s). Most actions can have various outcomes, depending on what chance or Nature or any other agency beyond the decision maker's control may do as a result of or after the action. These possible outcomes have personal probabilities. Take the utility of each possible outcome, multiply it by the probability that outcome will occur, sum these products over an exhaustive set of mutually exclusive outcomes, and you have an SEU.

Few thinkers about decision making have questioned the normative appropriateness of maximizing SEU, though some have questioned the feasibility of implementing the normative rule. But many theorists and experimenters have questioned whether people in fact do so and have sought and found contexts in which they do not. The literature is large, and we cannot do justice to it here. See von Winterfeldt and Edwards (1986) for a chapter-length discussion.

*Labile Values.* An assumption implicit in both normative and descriptive versions of the SEU model is that decision makers know what they would like to maximize. Fischhoff, Slovic, and Lichtenstein (1980) have challenged that assumption, arguing that phrasing and response mode variations have substantial effects on value judgments. A number of experiments support this view – but its implications for the SEU model are unclear because the status of the model is unclear. If it is taken to mean that people in fact routinely make decisions that maximize SEU, then it is clearly wrong, as a long history of experimentation and argument shows. The decision analytic position is that people can be helped to maximize SEU by suitable elicitation and computations. The fact that the numbers obtained depend to some extent on the method used to elicit them by no means implies that they cannot or should not be the basis for decisions. The practice of decision analysis is inherently iterative, and procedures that produce inconsistencies are valuable as incentives to more iteration and harder thought (see Fischer, 1979). Various studies in which decision analytic techniques have been used to elicit utilities and various methods have been used to validate the numbers thus elicited have been generally encouraging; see von Winterfeldt and Edwards (1996) for a review . . . .

## Reflections on the Cognitive Illusions

### Making Sense of Cognitive Illusions

We have found it extraordinarily difficult to make sense of the cognitive illusions, and this essay and others related to it have been through many previous unsuccessful versions. Several thoughts seem to have helped us.

1. The paradigm of cognitive illusions has been difficult to get into sharp focus, perhaps in part because the work with which we have been most familiar has concentrated on intellectual tasks that lie at or beyond the limits

of ability of most adults. It has been very helpful to think about intuitive arithmetic and intuitive physics – both easier tasks, at least in the forms in which we have thought about them. Obviously, both arithmetical and physical tasks can easily be devised that are well beyond the reach of adult human intuition. The point is that intuitively easy tasks of these kinds can also be devised. We know of no intuitively easy version of Bayesian inference. It has been helpful to us to be able to consider a full range of task difficulty.

2. We started out believing that we knew what the word *intuition* means. We also started out believing that a *cognitive process* is a fixed method of doing intellectual business. Both ideas now seem absurd. We can find no agreed-on definition of intuition in the literature, and we found that we ourselves disagreed about what the word means. Cognitive researchers better acquainted than we with the literature of developmental psychology helped us to understand that cognitive processes are not givens. They develop and change over time as a function of maturation, experience, and training.

Research on cognitive processes as it is normally done using adult subjects gives the appearance of reporting static processes for two reasons: because we like to describe those processes by means of static models, and because the time periods of such studies are normally short relative to the periods over which development and learning take place. Consequently, such experiments study "snapshots," pictures of how the cognitive process being studied works at a given level of development and training.

These two lines of thought have helped us. Many cognitive psychologists interested in cognitive illusions in adults say that they study them in order to learn more about intuitive cognitive processes; we quoted Kahneman and Tversky to that effect earlier. It is very helpful to recognize that, as Hammond and his colleagues put it, "Intuition is what analysis is not" (Hammond, Hamm, Grassia, and Pearson, 1984, p. 2), and that cognitive processes are responsive to maturation, experience, and education, even if we do try to capture them by means of static models that imply the contrary.

3. Yet another crucial recognition has been that the notion of intellectual effort is central to understanding thought. Because "intellectual effort" is a thoroughly subjective concept, experimentalists have tended to use objectively measurable stand-ins for it; the most common of these are incentives.

4. The notion of intellectual tools is important. Decision analysis is a collection of intellectual tools. Only recently did we come to think about the relation of intellectual tools to physical tools that implement them. Intellectual tools, we feel, are used if the user knows that they exist, knows how to use them, and considers it worthwhile to make the intellectual effort. If they are useful they become embodied in physical tools. Often, after the embodiment has occurred, the former user of an intellectual tool delegates the task performed by it to the physical tool and may even forget how to use the intellectual tool.

The topic of intellectual tools relates to expertise. Experts become expert in the use of intellectual tools as well as acquiring factual knowledge. They may use physical tools to implement the intellectual ones; experts on Bayesian statistics, though they have no difficulty recognizing a Bayesian problem, may need a hand calculator or even a computer to get the right answer.

If an experiment requires its subjects to perform a task that even an expert would need physical tools to perform but forbids their use, that fact at least implies that getting the answer right is not important enough to require a major intellectual effort....

## Summary

A cognitive illusion arises when (a) some formal rule specifies a (usually *the*) correct answer to an intellectual question, (b) human subjects, usually naive and always working without tools, are asked to perform the task intuitively, and (c) systematic discrepancies appear between the intuitive and the correct answers. This research paradigm has a 100-year history but has been extensively used since 1968 to study human probability assessment, inference, and risky decision making. This chapter reviews a number of familiar and less familiar cognitive illusions and attempts to examine what they do and do not imply about human intellectual competence in general.

When performing intuitively Bayesian probabilistic inferential tasks, human beings seem routinely to modify their opinions less than they should on the basis of the evidence and to make less use of base-rate information than they should. They also sometimes pay less attention than they should to the diagnostic implications of varying sample size.

Predictions typically should be regressive and very often are not. Probability assessments should be well calibrated and sometimes are when the probabilities are low. Many probabilities of over .5 are overassessed; the evidence about the effect of expertise, both about the topic at hand and about probability assessment, is conflicting. In hindsight, people tend to consider what actually happened as more inevitable than it was.

In assessing uncertain continuous quantities, people tend to use an anchoring-and-insufficient-adjustment procedure, which causes the probabilities of rare events to be underestimated.

Much research designed to improve intuition by such techniques as encouraging people to "work hard" or by raising the stakes has had generally discouraging results. Researchers have, however, been able to find both stimuli and forms of expertise that seem conducive to good performance in probability assessment.

Research on risky decision making has clearly shown that people do not maximize Subjectively Expected Utility (SEU) in choosing among gambles. This may be because of labile values or for other reasons, including in particular the fact that gambles can be packaged in various ways, and different packages lead to different relations of the gamble to the reference events with which it is compared.

Children make many mistakes in understanding simple physical principles, such as conservation of volume or number. Adults have been shown to make more sophisticated mistakes in understanding less obvious and familiar (but no less ubiquitous) physical principles.

Cognitive illusions can also be demonstrated in intuitive performance of problems in logic and arithmetic.

Exploration of arithmetic problems turns out to be helpful in understanding the cognitive illusions because they vary continuously in difficulty from obvious to very hard. Exploration of a sequence of such problems suggests at least four different interpretations of the notion of intuition: immediate and correct apprehension, a good approximation, intuitive knowledge of method for solving the problem but not of the solution, and intuitive ability to verify answers. Such exploration also raises the question of the boundaries of cognition. Are tasks performed with the aid of physical tools cognitive? Are tasks performed with the aid of more than one mind cognitive? Many aids to cognition (e.g., the decimal system) are taught to schoolchildren and so come to reside in the head; many also are designed into physical tools designed to facilitate cognitive work. Aids that once resided in the head may cease to do so as physical tools make them more accessible. The whole issue of how good human intuitive performance is may be more or less irrelevant to the broader question of human intellectual competence, because if the problem is important and the tools are available people will use them and thus get right answers. Indeed, this is the main difference between experimenters and subjects in experiments on the cognitive illusions.

### References

Adams, J. K. (1957). A confidence scale defined in terms of expected percentages. *American Journal of Psychology, 70*, 432–436.

Alpert, M., & Raiffa, H. (1969). *A progress report on the training of probability assessors.* Unpublished manuscript, Harvard University, Graduate School of Business Administration, Cambridge.

Bar-Hillel, M. (1973). On the subjective probability of compound events. *Organizational Behavior and Human Performance, 9*, 396–402.

Bar-Hillel, M. (1980). The base rate fallacy in probability judgments. *Acta Psychologica, 44*, 211–233.

Beach, L. R., Wise, J. A., & Barclay, S. (1970). Sample proportion and subjective probability revisions. *Organizational Behavior and Human Performance, 5*, 183–190.

Carroll, J. S., & Siegler, R. S. (1977). Strategies for the use of base rate information. *Organizational Behavior and Human Performance, 19*, 392–402.

Chapman, L. J., & Chapman, J. P. (1967). Genesis of popular but erroneous psychodiagnostic observations. *Journal of Abnormal Psychology, 72*, 193–204.

Chapman, L. J., & Chapman, J. P. (1969). Illusory correlation as an obstacle to the use of valid psychodiagnostic signs. *Journal of Abnormal Psychology, 74*, 271–280.

Cohen, J. J. (1972). A case for risk–benefit analysis. In H. J. Otway (Ed.), *Risk vs. benefit: Solution or dream?* (Rep. LA-4860-MS). Los Alamos: Los Alamos Scientific Laboratory.

Dershowitz, A. (1971). Imprisonment by judicial hunch. *American Bar Association Journal, 57*, 560–564.

deSmet, A. A., Fryback, D., & Thornbury, J. R. (1979). A second look at the utility of radiographic skull examination for trauma. *American Journal of Radiology, 132*, 75–99.

Eddy, D. M. (1982). Probabilistic reasoning in clinical medicine: Problems and opportunities. In D. Kahneman, P. Slovic, & A. Tversky (Eds.), *Judgment under uncertainty: Heuristics and biases*. Cambridge: Cambridge University Press.

Edwards, W. (1962). Dynamic decision theory and probabilistic information processing. *Human Factors, 4*, 59–73.

Edwards, W. (1983). Human cognitive capabilities, representativeness, and ground rules for research. In P. C. Humphries, O. Svenson, & A. Vari (Eds.), *Analyzing and aiding decision processes* (pp. 507–513). Amsterdam: North Holland.

Edwards, W., Lindman, H., & Savage, L. J. (1963). Bayesian statistical inference for psychological research. *Psychological Review, 70*, 193–242.

Edwards, W., Phillips, L. D., Hays, W. L., & Goodman, B. C. (1968). Probabilistic information processing systems: Design and evaluation: *IEEE Transactions on Systems Science and Cybernetics, SSC-4*, 248–265.

Eils, L., Seaver, D., & Edwards, W. (1977). *Developing the technology of probabilistic inference: Aggregation by averaging reduces conservatism* (Research Rep. 77-3). Los Angeles: University of Southern California, Social Science Research Institute.

Fischer, G. W. (1979). Utility models for multiple objective decisions: Do they accurately represent human preferences? *Decision Sciences, 10*, 451–479.

Fischhoff, B. (1975). Hindsight ≠ foresight: The effect of outcome knowledge on judgment under uncertainty. *Journal of Experimental Psychology: Human Perception and Performance, 1*, 288–299.

Fischhoff, B. (1976). Attribution theory and judgment under uncertainty. In N. H. Harvey, W. J. Ickes, & R. F. Kidd (Eds.), *New directions in attribution research* (pp. 421–452). Hillsdale, NJ: Erlbaum.

Fischhoff, B. (1980). For those condemned to study the past: Reflections on historical judgment. In R. A. Shweder & D. W. Fiske (Eds.), *New directions for methodology of social and behavioral science: No. 4. Fallible judgment in behavioral research* (pp. 79–93). San Francisco: Jossey-Bass.

Fischhoff, B. (1982). Debiasing. In D. Kahneman, P. Slovic, & A. Tversky (Eds.), *Judgment under uncertainty: Heuristics and biases* (pp. 422–444) Cambridge: Cambridge University Press.

Fischhoff, B., & Beyth, R. (1975). "I knew it would happen": Remembered probabilities of once-future things. *Organizational Behavior and Human Performance, 13*, 1–16.

Fischhoff, B., Slovic, P., & Lichtenstein, S. (1978). Fault trees: Sensitivity of estimated failure probabilities to problem representation. *Journal of Experimental Psychology: Human Perception and Performance, 4*, 330–344.

Fischhoff, B., Slovic, P., & Lichtenstein, S. (1980). Knowing what you want: Measuring labile values. In T. Wallsten (Ed.), *Cognitive processes in choice and decision behavior* (pp. 117–141). Hillsdale, NJ: Erlbaum.

Green, A. E., & Bourne, A. J. (1972). *Reliability technology.* New York: Wiley–Interscience.

Hammerton, M. (1973). A case of radical probability estimation. *Journal of Experimental Psychology, 101*, 252–254.

Hammond, K. R., Hamm, R. M., Grassia, J., & Pearson, T. (1984). *Direct comparison of intuitive, quasi-rational, and analytical cognition* (Rep. No. 248). Boulder: University of Colorado, Center for Research on Judgment and Policy.

Hogarth, R. M. (1980). *Judgment and choice: The psychology of decision*. Chichester: Wiley.

Jennings, D. L., Amabile, T. M., & Ross, L. (1982). Informal covariation assessment: Data-based versus theory-based judgments. In D. Kahneman, P. Slovic, & A. Tversky (Eds.), *Judgment under uncertainty: Heuristics and biases*. Cambridge: Cambridge University Press.

Kahneman, D., Slovic, P., & Tversky, A. (Eds.). (1982). *Judgment under uncertainty: Heuristics and biases*. Cambridge: Cambridge University Press.

Kahneman, D., & Tversky, T. (1972). Subjective probability: A judgment of representativeness. *Cognitive Psychology, 3*, 430–454.

Kahneman, D., & Tversky, T. (1973). On the psychology of prediction. *Psychological Review, 80*, 237–251.

Kahneman, D., & Tversky, A. (1979). Intuitive prediction: Biases and corrective procedures. *TIMS Studies in Management Sciences, 12*, 313–327.

Kahneman, D., & Tversky, A. (1982). On the study of statistical intuitions. *Cognition, 11*, 123–141.

Koriat, A., Lichtenstein, S., & Fischhoff, B. (1980). Reasons for confidence. *Journal of Experimental Psychology: Human Learning and Memory, 6*, 107–118.

Lichtenstein, S., & Fischhoff, B. (1977). Do those who know more also know more about how much they know? The calibration of probability judgments. *Organizational Behavior and Human Performance, 20*, 159–183.

Lichtenstein, S., & Fischhoff, B. (1980). Training for calibration. *Organizational Behavior and Human Performance, 26*, 149–171.

Lichtenstein, S., Fischhoff, B., & Phillips, L. D. (1982). Calibration of probabilities: The state of the art in 1980. In D. Kahneman, P. Slovic, & A. Tversky (Eds.), *Judgment under uncertainty: Heuristics and biases*. Cambridge: Cambridge University Press.

Lichtenstein, S., Fischhoff, B., & Phillips, L. D. (1977). Calibration of probabilities: The state of the art. In H. Jungerman & G. de Zeeuw (Eds.), *Decision making and change in human affairs* (pp. 275–324). Dordrecht: Reidel.

Ludke, R. L., Stauss, F. Y., & Gustafson, D. H. (1977). Comparison of methods for estimating subjective probability distributions. *Organizational Behavior and Human Performance, 19*, 162–179.

Lusted, L. B., Roberts, H. V., Edwards, W., Wallace, P. L., Lahiff, M., Loop, J. W., Bell, R. S., Thornbury, J. R., Seale, D. L., Steele, J. P., & Fryback, D. G. (1980). *Efficacy of x-ray procedures*. American College of Radiology.

Lykken, D. T. (1975). The right way to use a lie detector. *Psychology Today, 8(10)*, 56–60.

Lyon, D., & Slovic, P. (1976). Dominance of accuracy information and neglect of base rates in probability estimation. *Acta Psychological, 40*, 287–298.

Marks, D. F., & Clarkson, J. K. (1972). An explanation of conservatism in the bookbag-and-pokerchips situation. *Acta Psychologica, 36*, 145–160.

McGargee, E. I. (1976). The prediction of dangerous behavior. *Criminal Justice and Behavior, 3*, 3–22.

Meehl, P. E., & Rosen, A. (1955). Antecedent probability and the efficiency of psychometric signs, patterns, or cutting scores. *Psychological Bulletin, 52*, 194–216.

Murphy, A. H., & Winkler, R. L. (1974). Probability forecasts: A survey of National Weather Service forecasters. *Bulletin of the American Meteorological Society, 55*, 1449–1453.

Murphy, A. H., & Winkler, R. L. (1977a). Can weather forecasters formulate reliable forecasts of precipitation and temperature? *National Weather Digest, 2*, 2–9.

Murphy, A. H., & Winkler, R. L. (1977b). The use of credible intervals in temperature forecasting: Some experimental results. In H. Jungermann & G. de Zeeuw (Eds.), *Decision making and change in human affairs* (pp. 45–56). Dordrecht: Reidel.

Navon, D. (1978). The importance of being conservative: Some reflections on human Bayesian behavior. *British Journal of Mathematical and Statistical Psychology, 31,* 33–48.

Nisbett, R. E., & Borgida, E. (1975). Attribution and the psychology of prediction. *Journal of Personality and Social Psychology, 32,* 932–943.

Nisbett, R. E., Borgida, E., Crandall, R., & Reed, H. (1976). Popular induction: Information is not necessarily informative. In J. S. Carroll & J. W. Payne (Eds.), *Cognition and social behavior* (pp. 113–133). Hillsdale, NJ: Erlbaum.

Nisbett, R. E., Krantz, D. H., Jepson, C., & Kunda, Z. (1983). The use of statistical heuristics in everyday inductive reasoning. *Psychological Review, 90,* 339–363.

Nisbett, R. E., & Ross, L. (1980). *Human inference: Strategies and shortcomings of human judgment.* Englewood Cliffs, NJ: Prentice-Hall.

Oskamp, S. (1965). Over-confidence in case-study judgments. *Journal of Consulting Psychology, 29,* 261–265.

Piaget, J., & Inhelder, B. (1975). *The origin of the idea of chance in children.* New York: Norton. (Original work published 1941.)

Phillips, L. D., & Edwards, W. (1966). Conservatism in a simple probability inference task. *Journal of Experimental Psychology, 72,* 346–357.

Phillips, L. D., Hays, W. L., & Edwards, W. (1966). Conservatism in complex probabilistic inference. *IEEE Transactions on Human Factors in Electronics, 7,* 7–18.

Pitz, G. (1974). Subjective probability distributions for imperfectly known quantities. In L. W. Gregg (Ed.), *Knowledge and cognition* (pp. 29–41). New York: Wiley.

Savage, L. J. (1954). *The foundations of statistics.* New York: Wiley.

Seaver, D. A., von Winterfeldt, D., & Edwards, W. (1978). Eliciting subjective probability distributions on continuous variables. *Organizational Behavior and Human Performance, 21,* 379–391.

Sieber, J. E. (1974). Effects of decision importance on the ability to generate warranted subjective uncertainty. *Journal of Personality and Social Psychology, 30,* 688–694.

Slovic, P., Fischhoff, B., & Lichtenstein, S. (1977). Behavioral decision theory. *Annual Review of Psychology, 28,* 1–39.

Slovic, P., & Lichtenstein, S. (1971). Comparison of Bayesian and regression approaches to the study of information processing in judgment. *Organizational Behavior and Human Performance, 6,* 649–744.

Tversky, A., & Kahneman, D. (1971). Belief in the law of small numbers. *Psychological Bulletin, 76,* 105–110.

Tversky, A., & Kahneman, D. (1973). Availability: A heuristic for judging frequency and probability. *Cognitive Psychology, 5,* 207–232.

Tversky, A., & Kahneman, D. (1974). Judgment under uncertainty: Heuristics and biases. *Science, 185,* 1124–1131.

Tversky, A., & Kahneman, D. (1981). The framing of decisions and the rationality of choice. *Science, 221,* 453–458.

United States Nuclear Regulatory Commission (1975). *Reactor safety study: An assessment of accident risks in U.S. commercial nuclear power plants* (NUREG-75/014). Washington, DC: Nuclear Regulatory Commission.

Vlek, C., & Wagenaar, W. A. (1979). Judgment and decision under uncertainty. In J. A. Michon, E. G. Eijkman, & L. F. W. DeKlerk (Eds.), *Handbook of Psychonomics II* (pp. 253–345). Amsterdam: North Holland.

von Winterfeldt, D., & Edwards, W. (1986). *Decision analysis and behavioral research*. Cambridge: Cambridge University Press.

Wheeler, G. E., & Edwards, W. (1975). *Misaggregation explains conservative inference about normally distributed populations* (Research Rep. 75–11). Los Angeles: University of Southern California, Social Research Institute.

Winkler, R. L., & Murphy, A. H. (1973). Experiments in the laboratory and in the real world. *Organizational Behavior and Human Performance, 10,* 252–270.

Zlotnick, J. (1968). A theorem for prediction. *Foreign Service Journal, 45,* 20.

# 35    Reasoning the Fast and Frugal Way: Models of Bounded Rationality

*Gerd Gigerenzer and Daniel G. Goldstein*

Organisms make inductive inferences. Darwin (1872) observed that people use facial cues, such as eyes that waver and lids that hang low, to infer a person's guilt. Male toads, roaming through swamps at night, use the pitch of a rival's croak to infer its size when deciding whether or not to fight (Krebs & Davies, 1987). Stock brokers must make fast decisions about which of several stocks to trade or invest when only limited information is available. The list goes on. Inductive inferences are typically based on uncertain cues: the eyes can deceive, and so can a tiny toad with a deep croak in the darkness.

How does an organism make inferences about unknown aspects of the environment? There are three directions in which to look for an answer. From Pierre Laplace to George Boole to Jean Piaget, many scholars have defended the now classical view that the laws of human inference are the laws of probability and statistics (but less so logic, which does not deal as easily with uncertainty). Indeed, the Enlightenment probabilists derived the laws of probability from what they believed to be the laws of human reasoning (Daston, 1988). Following this time-honored tradition, contemporary research in psychology, behavioral ecology, and economics assumes standard statistical tools to be the normative and descriptive models of inference and decision making. Multiple regression, for instance, is both the economist's universal tool (McCloskey, 1985) as well as a model of inductive inference in multiple cue learning (Hammond, 1990) and clinical judgment (Brehmer, 1994); Bayes' theorem is a model of how animals infer the presence of predators or prey (Stephens & Krebs, 1986) as well as of human reasoning and memory (Anderson, 1990). This Enlightenment view that probability theory and human reasoning are two sides of the same coin crumbled in the early nineteenth century, but has remained strong in psychology and economics.

In the last 25 years, this stronghold came under attack by proponents of the heuristics-and-biases program who concluded that human inference is systematically biased and error-prone, suggesting that the laws of inference are quick-and-dirty heuristics and not the laws of probability (Kahneman, Slovic, & Tversky, 1982). This second perspective appears diametrically opposed to the classical rationality of the Enlightenment, but this appearance is misleading. It has retained the normative kernel of the classical view; for example, a discrepancy between the dictates of classical rationality and actual reasoning is what defines a "reasoning error" in this program. Both views accept the laws of probability and statistics as normative, but they disagree about whether humans can stand up to these norms.

Many experiments have been conducted to test the validity of these two views, identifying a host of conditions under which the human mind appears more rational or irrational. But most of this work has dealt with simple situations, such as Bayesian inference with binary hypotheses, one single piece of binary data, and all the necessary information conveniently laid out for the subject (Gigerenzer & Hoffrage, 1995). In many real-world situations, however, there are multiple pieces of information, which are not independent, but redundant. Here, Bayes' theorem and other "rational" algorithms quickly become mathematically complex and computationally intractable – at least for ordinary human minds. These situations make neither of the two views look promising. If one would apply the classical view to such complex real-world environments, this would suggest that the mind is a Laplacean Demon (Wimsatt, 1976), carrying around the collected works of Kolmogoroff, Fisher, or Neyman, and simply needs a memory jog like the slave in Plato's *Meno*. On the other hand, the heuristics-and-biases view of human irrationality would lead us to believe that humans are hopelessly lost in the face of real-world complexity, given their supposed inability to reason according to the canons of classical rationality, even in simple laboratory experiments.

There is a third way to look at inference, focusing on the psychological and ecological, rather than on logic and probability theory. This view questions classical rationality as a universal norm, and thereby questions the very definition of "good" reasoning on which both the Enlightenment and the heuristics-and-biases views were built. Herbert Simon, possibly the best-known proponent of this third view, proposed looking for models of "bounded rationality" instead of classical rationality. Simon (1956, 1982) argued that information-processing systems typically need to "satisfice" rather than "optimize." Satisficing, a blend of sufficing and satisfying, is a word of Scottish origin which Simon uses to characterize algorithms that successfully deal with conditions of limited time, knowledge, or computational capacities. His concept of satisficing postulates, for instance, that an organism would choose the first object (a mate, perhaps) which satisfies its aspiration level, instead of the intractable sequence of taking the time to survey all possible alternatives, estimating probabilities and utilities for the possible outcomes associated with each alternative, calculating expected utilities, and choosing the alternative which scores highest.

Let us stress that Simon's notion of bounded rationality has two sides, one cognitive and one ecological. As early as in *Administrative Behavior* (1945), he emphasized the cognitive limitations of real minds as opposed to the omniscient Laplacean Demons of classical rationality. As early as in his *Psychological Review* paper entitled "Rational choice and the structure of the environment" (1956), he emphasized that minds are adapted to real-world environments. The two go in tandem: "Human rational behavior is shaped by a scissors whose two blades are the structure of task environments and the computational capabilities of the actor" (Simon, 1990, p. 7). For the most part, however, theories of human inference have focused exclusively on the cognitive side, equating the notion of bounded rationality with the statement that humans are limited information processors, period. In a Procrustean-bed fashion, bounded rationality became almost synonymous with "heuristics and biases," thus paradoxically reasserting classical rationality as the normative standard for both "biases" and "bounded rationality" (for a discussion of this confusion see Lopes, 1992). Simon's insight, that the minds of living systems should be understood relative to the environment in which they evolved rather than to the tenets of classical rationality, has had little impact so far in research on human inference. Simple psychological algorithms which were observed in human inference, reasoning, or decision making were often discredited without a fair trial, since they looked so stupid by the norms of classical rationality. For instance, when Keeney and Raiffa (1993) discussed the lexicographic ordering procedure they had observed in practice – a procedure related to the class of satisficing algorithms we propose in this chapter – they concluded that this procedure "is naively simple" and "will rarely pass a test of 'reasonableness'" (p. 78). They did not report such a test. We shall.

Initially, the concept of bounded rationality was only vaguely defined, often as that which is not classical economics, and one could "fit a lot of things into it by foresight and hindsight," as Simon (1992, p. 18) himself put it. We wish to do more than oppose the Laplacean Demon view. We strive to come up with something positive that could replace this unrealistic view of mind. What are these simple, intelligent algorithms capable of making near-optimal inferences? How fast and how accurate are they? In this chapter, we propose a class of models which exhibit bounded rationality in both of Simon's senses. These satisficing algorithms operate with simple psychological principles that satisfy the constraints of limited time, knowledge, and computational might, rather than those of classical rationality. At the same time, they are designed to be fast and frugal without a significant loss of inferential accuracy since the algorithms can exploit the structure of environments.

The chapter is organized as follows. We begin by describing the task the cognitive algorithms are designed to address, the basic algorithm itself, and the real-world environment on which the performance of the algorithm will be tested. Next, we report on a competition in which a satisficing algorithm competes with "optimal" algorithms at making inferences about a real-world environment. The "optimal" algorithms start with an advantage: they use more time, information, and computational might to make inferences. Finally, we study variants of the satisficing algorithm which make faster inferences and get by with even less knowledge.

### Task

We deal with inferential tasks in which a choice must be made between two alternatives on a quantitative dimension. Consider the following example:

Which city has a larger population?
(a) Hamburg
(b) Cologne

Two-alternative choice tasks occur in various contexts in which inferences need to be made with limited time and knowledge, such as in risk assessment during driving (e.g., exit the highway now or stay on), treatment allocation decisions (e.g., who to treat first in the emergency room: the 80-year old heart attack or the 16-year-old car accident?), and financial decisions about whether to buy or sell in the trading pit. Inference concerning population demographics, such as city populations of the past, present, and future (e.g., Brown & Siegler, 1993), is of importance to people working in urban planning, industrial development, and marketing. Population demographics, which is better understood than, say, the stock market, will serve us later as a "drosophila" environment that allows us to analyze the behavior of satisficing algorithms.

We study two-alternative choice tasks in situations where a person has to make an inference based solely on knowledge retrieved from memory. We refer to this as *memory-based inference*, as opposed to *menu-based inference*. Memory-based inference involves search in declarative knowledge and has been investigated in studies of, inter alia, confidence in general knowledge (e.g., Juslin, 1994; Sniezek & Buckley, 1993), the effect of repetition on belief (e.g., Hertwig, Gigerenzer, & Hoffrage, 1995), hindsight bias (e.g., Fischhoff, 1977), quantitative estimates of area and population of nations (Brown & Siegler, 1993), and autobiographic memory of time (Huttenlocher, Hedges, & Prohaska, 1988). Studies of menu-based inference, on the other hand, involve making inferences from information presented by an experimenter (e.g., Hammond, Hursch, & Todd, 1964). In the tradition of Ebbinghaus' nonsense-syllables, attempts are often made here to prevent individual knowledge from impacting upon the results by using problems about hypothetical referents instead of actual ones. For instance, in celebrated judgment and decision-making tasks, such as the Cab problem and the Linda problem, all the relevant information is provided by the experimenter, and individual knowledge about cabs and hit-and-run accidents, or feminist bank tellers, is considered of no relevance (Gigerenzer & Murray, 1987). As a consequence, limited knowledge or individual differences in knowledge play a small role in menu-based inference. In contrast, the satisficing algorithms proposed in this chapter perform memory-based inference, they use limited knowledge as input and, as we will show, can actually profit from missing information.

Assume that a subject does not know or cannot deduce the answer to the Hamburg–Cologne question, but needs to make an inductive inference from related real-world knowledge. How is this inference derived? How can we predict choice (Hamburg or Cologne) from a person's state of knowledge?

## Theory

The cognitive algorithms we propose are realizations of a framework for modeling memory-based inferences, the theory of probabilistic mental models (for short, PMM theory; see Gigerenzer, Hoffrage, & Kleinbölting, 1991; Gigerenzer, 1993). PMM theory assumes that inferences about unknown states of the world are based on probability cues (Brunswik, 1955). The theory relates three visions: (i) inductive inference needs to be studied with respect to natural environments, as emphasized by Egon Brunswik and Herbert Simon; (ii) inductive inference is carried out by satisficing algorithms, as emphasized by Simon; and (iii) inductive inferences are based on frequencies of events in a reference class, as proposed by Hans Reichenbach and other frequentist statisticians. PMM theory accounts for choice and confidence, but only choice is addressed in this chapter.

The major thrust of the theory is that it substitutes the canon of classical rationality with simple, plausible psychological mechanisms of inference – mechanisms that a mind can actually carry out under limited time and knowledge, and that could have possibly arisen through evolution. Most traditional models of inference, from linear multiple regression models to Bayesian models to neural networks, try to find some optimal integration of all information available – every bit of information is taken into account, weighted, and combined in a computationally expensive way. The family of algorithms in PMM theory does not implement this classical ideal. Search in memory for relevant information is reduced to a minimum, and there is no integration (but rather a substitution) of pieces of information. These satisficing algorithms dispense with the fiction of the omniscient Laplacean Demon who has all the time and knowledge to search for all relevant information, to compute the weights and covariances, and then to integrate all this information into an inference.

*Limited Knowledge*

A PMM is an inductive device that uses limited knowledge to make fast inferences. Different from "mental models" of syllogisms and deductive inference (Johnson-Laird, 1983), which focus on the logical task of truth preservation and where knowledge is irrelevant (except for the meaning of connectives and other logical terms), PMMs perform intelligent guesses about unknown features of the world. To make an inference about which of two objects $a$ or $b$ has a higher value, knowledge about a reference class $R$ is searched, with $a,b \in R$. In our example, knowledge about the reference class "cities in Germany" could be searched. The knowledge consists of probability cues $C_i (i = 1, \ldots, n)$ and the cue values $a_i$ and $b_i$ of the objects for the $i$th cue. For instance, when making inferences about populations of German cities, the fact that a city has a professional soccer team in the major league ("Bundesliga") may come to a person's mind as a potential cue. That is, when considering pairs of German cities, if one city has a soccer team in the major league and the other does not, then the city with the team is likely, but not certain, to have the larger population.

Limited knowledge means that the matrix of objects by cues has missing entries (that is, objects, cues, or cue values may be unknown). Figure 35.1 models the limited knowledge of a person. She has heard of three German cities, $a$, $b$, and $c$, but not of $d$ (represented by three positive and one negative recognition values). She knows some facts (cue values) about these cities with respect to five binary cues. For a binary cue, there are two cue values, "positive" (e.g., the city has a soccer team), or "negative" (it does not). "Positive" refers to a cue value that signals a higher value on the target variable (for example, having a soccer team is correlated with high population). Unknown cue values are shown by a question mark. Since she has never heard of $d$, all cue values for object $d$ are by definition unknown.

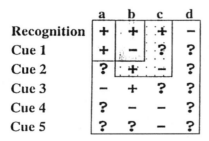

|  | a | b | c | d |
|---|---|---|---|---|
| **Recognition** | + | + | + | − |
| **Cue 1** | + | − | ? | ? |
| **Cue 2** | ? | + | − | ? |
| **Cue 3** | − | + | ? | ? |
| **Cue 4** | ? | − | − | ? |
| **Cue 5** | ? | ? | − | ? |

Figure 35.1. Illustration of bounded search through limited knowledge. Objects $a$, $b$, and $c$ are recognized; object $d$ is not. Cue values are positive (+) or negative (−); missing knowledge is shown by question marks (?). Cues are ordered according to their validities. To infer whether $a$ is greater than $b$, the Take The Best algorithm looks up the cue values only in the darker shaded space; to infer whether $b$ is greater than $c$, search is bounded to the lighter shaded space. The other cue values are not looked up.

People rarely know all information on which an inference could be based, that is, knowledge is limited. We model limited knowledge in two respects: (i) a person can have incomplete knowledge of the objects in the reference class (e.g., she recognizes only some of the cities), and/or (ii) limited knowledge of the cue values (facts about cities). For instance, a person who does not know all of the cities with soccer teams may know some cities with positive cue values (e.g., Munich and Hamburg certainly have teams), many with negative cue values (e.g., Heidelberg and Potsdam certainly do not have teams), and several cities for which cue values will not be known.

### The Take The Best Algorithm

The first satisficing algorithm presented is called the *Take The Best* algorithm, because its policy is "take the best, ignore the rest." It is the basic algorithm in the PMM framework. Variants which work faster or with less knowledge will be described later. We explain the steps of the Take The Best algorithm for binary cues (the algorithm can be easily generalized to many-valued cues), using Figure 35.1 for illustration.

The Take The Best algorithm assumes a subjective rank order of cues according to their validities (as in Figure 35.1). We call the highest ranking cue the "best" cue. The algorithm is shown in the form of a flow diagram in Figure 35.2.

1. *Recognition principle:* The recognition principle is invoked when the mere recognition of an object is a predictor of the target variable (population). The recognition principle states: if only one of the two objects is recognized, then choose the recognized object. If neither of the two objects is recognized, then choose randomly between them. If both of the objects are recognized, then proceed to step 2.

*Example:* If a subject in the knowledge state shown in Figure 35.1 is asked to infer which of city *a* and city *d* has more inhabitants, the inference will be "city *a*," since the subject has never heard to city *d* before.

2. *Search for the values of the best cue*: For the two objects, retrieve the cue values of the best cue from memory.
3. *Discrimination rule*: Decide whether the cue discriminates. The cue is said to discriminate between two objects if one has a positive cue value and the other does not. The four shaded knowledge states in Figure 35.3 are those in which a cue discriminates.
4. *Cue substitution principle*: If the cue discriminates, then stop searching for cue values. If the cue does not discriminate, go back to step 2 and continue with the next best cue until a cue that discriminates is found.
5. *Maximizing rule for choice*: Choose the object with the positive cue value. If no cue discriminates, then choose randomly.

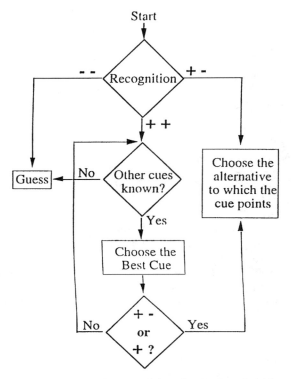

Figure 35.2. Flow diagram of the Take The Best algorithm.

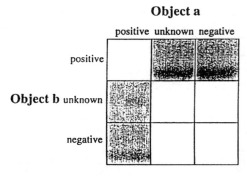

Figure 35.3. Discrimination rule. A cue discriminates between two alternatives if one has a positive cue value and the other does not. The four discriminating cue value combinations are shaded.

*Examples:* Suppose the task is judging which of city $a$ or $b$ is larger (Figure 35.1). Both cities are recognized (step 1), and search for the best cue results with a positive (+) and a negative (−) cue value for cue 1 (step 2). The cue discriminates (step 3), and search is terminated (step 4). The system makes the inference that city $a$ is larger (step 5).

Suppose now the task is judging which of city $b$ or $c$ is larger. Both cities are recognized (step 1) and search for the cue values of the best cue results in the negative cue value on object $b$ for cue 1, but the corresponding cue value for object $c$ is unknown (step 2). The cue does not discriminate (step 3), so search is continued (step 4). Search for the next best cue results with positive (+) and a negative (−) cue values for cue 2 (step 2). This cue discriminates (step 3), and search is terminated (step 4). The system makes the inference that city $b$ is larger (step 5).

The features of this algorithm are: (i) search extends through only a portion of the total knowledge in memory (as shown by the shaded parts of Figure 35.1), and is stopped immediately when the first discriminating cue is found, (ii) the algorithm does not attempt to integrate information, but uses cue substitution instead, and (iii) the total amount of information processed is contingent on each task (pair of objects) and varies in a predictable way between individuals with different knowledge. This fast and computationally simple algorithm is a model of "bounded rationality" (Simon, 1982) rather than of classical rationality. There is a close parallel with Simon's concept of "satisficing": the Take The Best algorithm stops search after the first discriminating cue is found, just as Simon's satisficing algorithm stops search after the first option which meets an aspiration level.

The algorithm is anything but a standard statistical tool for inductive inference: it does not use all available information, is noncompensatory, nonlinear, and variants of it can violate transitivity. Thus it differs from standard linear tools for inference such as multiple regression, as well as from nonlinear neural networks which are compensatory in nature. The Take The Best algorithm is noncompensatory because only the best discriminating cue determines the inference or decision; no combination of other cue values can override this decision. In this way, the algorithm does not conform to the classical economic view of human behavior (e.g., Becker, 1976) where, under the assumption that all aspects can be reduced to one dimension (such as money), there exists always a trade-off between commodities or pieces of information. That is, the algorithm violates the Archimedian Axiom which implies that for any multidimensional object $a(a_1, a_2, \ldots, a_n)$ preferred to $b(b_1, b_2, \ldots, b_n)$, where $a_1$ dominates $b_1$, this preference can be reversed by taking multiples of any one or a combination of $b_2, b_3, \ldots, b_n$. As we shall see, variants of this algorithm also violate transitivity, one of the cornerstones of classical rationality (McClennen, 1990).

*Empirical Evidence*

Despite their flagrant violation of the traditional standards of rationality, the Take The Best algorithm and other models from the framework of PMM theory have been successful in integrating various striking phenomena in memory-based inference and predicting novel phenomena, such as the confidence-frequency effect (Gigerenzer et al., 1991) and the less-is-more effect (Goldstein, 1994; Goldstein & Gigerenzer, 1995). PMM theory seems to be the only existing process theory of the overconfidence bias that successfully predicted conditions under which overestimation occurs, disappears, and inverts to underestimation (Gigerenzer et al., 1991; Gigerenzer, 1993; Juslin, 1993, 1994; Juslin, Winman, & Persson, 1995; but see Griffin & Tversky, 1992). Similarly, the theory predicts when the hard–easy effect occurs, disappears, and inverts – predictions which have been experimentally confirmed by Hoffrage (1994) and by Juslin (1993). The Take The Best algorithm also explains why the popular confirmation bias explanation of the overconfidence bias (Koriat, Lichtenstein, & Fischhoff, 1980) is not supported by experimental data (Gigerenzer et al., 1991, pp. 521–522).

Unlike earlier accounts of these striking phenomena in confidence and choice, the algorithms in the PMM framework allow for predictions of choice based on each individual's knowledge. Goldstein and Gigerenzer (1995) have shown that the recognition principle predicted individual subjects' choices in about 90 to 100% of all cases – even when subjects were taught information (negative cue values for the recognized objects) which suggested doing otherwise. Among the evidence for the empirical validity of the Take The Best algorithm are the tests of a bold prediction, the less-is-more effect, which postulates conditions under which people with little knowledge make better inferences than those who know more. This surprising prediction has been experimentally confirmed. For instance, U.S. subjects score slightly more correct inferences about German city populations (about which they know little) than about U.S. cities, and vice versa for German subjects (Gigerenzer, 1993; Goldstein 1994; Goldstein & Gigerenzer, 1995; Hoffrage, 1994). PMM theory has been applied to other situations where inferences have to be made under limited time and knowledge, such as rumor-based stock market trading (DiFonzo, 1994). A general review of the theory and the evidence is presented in McClelland and Bolger (1994), which concludes that "ecological models, and PMM theory (Gigerenzer et al., 1991) in particular, provide the most coherent account of how individuals realize subjective probability judgments, and afford the most satisfactory explanation of calibration performance with general-knowledge items" (p. 478).

The reader familiar with the original algorithm presented in Gigerenzer et al. (1991) will have noticed that we have simplified the discrimination rule.[1] In the present version, search is already terminated if one object has a positive cue value and the other does not, whereas in the earlier version search was terminated only when one object has a positive value and the other a negative one (compare Figure 3 in Gigerenzer et al. with the present Figure 35.3). This change follows empirical evidence that subjects tend to use this faster, simpler discrimination rule (Hoffrage, 1994).

This chapter does not attempt to provide further empirical evidence. For the moment, we assume the model is descriptively valid and investigate how accurate this satisficing algorithm is in drawing inferences about unknown aspects of a real-world environment. Can an algorithm based upon simple psychological principles which violate the norms of classical rationality make a fair number of accurate inferences?

## The Environment

We tested the performance of the Take The Best algorithm on how accurately it made inferences about a real-world environment. The environment was the set of all cities in Germany with more than 100,000 inhabitants (83 cities after German reunification), with population as the target variable. The model of the environment consisted of 9 binary ecological cues, and the actual 9 × 83 cue values.

Each cue has an associated validity, which is indicative of its predictive power. The *ecological validity* of a cue is the relative frequency with which the cue correctly predicts the target, defined with respect to the reference class (e.g., all German cities with more than 100,000 inhabitants). For instance, if one checks all pairs in which one city has a soccer team but the other city does not, one finds that in 87% of these cases the city with the team also has the higher population. This value is the ecological validity of the soccer team cue. The validity $v_i$ of the $i$th cue is:

$$v_i = p(t(a) > t(b) \mid a_i \text{ is positive and } b_i \text{ is negative}),$$

where $t(a)$ and $t(b)$ are the values of objects $a$ and $b$ on the target variable $t$, and $p$ is a probability measured as a relative frequency in $R$.

The ecological validity of the 9 cues ranged over the whole spectrum: from .51 (only slightly better than chance) to 1.0 (certainty), as shown in Table 35.1. A cue with a high ecological validity, however, is not often useful if its discrimination rate is small.

Table 35.1 also shows the discrimination rates for each cue. The discrimination rate of a cue is the probability that a cue will discriminate between two randomly chosen objects from the reference class. The discrimination rate is a function of the distribution of the cue values and the number $N$ of objects in the reference class. Let the relative frequencies of the *positive* and *negative* cue values be $x$ and $y$ respectively. Then the discrimination rate $d_i$

Table 35.1. *Cues, Ecological Validities, and Discrimination Rates*

| Cue | Ecological Validity | Discrimination Rate |
|---|---|---|
| National capital (is the city the national capital?) | 1.0 | .02 |
| Exposition site (was the city once an exposition site?) | .91 | .25 |
| Soccer team (does the city have a team in the major leagues?) | .87 | .30 |
| Intercity train (is the city on the Intercity line?) | .78 | .38 |
| State capital (is the city a state capital?) | .77 | .30 |
| License plate (is the abbreviation only one letter long?) | .75 | .34 |
| University (is the city home to a university?) | .71 | .51 |
| Industrial belt (is the city in the industrial belt?) | .56 | .30 |
| East Germany (was the city formerly in East Germany?) | .51 | .27 |

of the $i$th cue is:

$$d_i = \frac{2x_i y_i}{1 - \frac{1}{N}},$$

as an elementary calculation shows. Thus, if $N$ is very large, the discrimination rate is approximately $2x_i y_i$.[2] The larger the ecological validity of a cue, the better the inference. The larger the discrimination rate, the more often a cue can be used to make an inference. In the present environment, ecological validities and discrimination rates are negatively correlated. The redundancy of cues in the environment, as measured by pairwise correlations between cues, ranges between $-.25$ and $.54$, with an average absolute value of $.19$.[3]

### The Competition

The question of how well a satisficing algorithm performs in a real-world environment has rarely been posed in research on inductive inference. The present simulations seem to be the first to test how well simple satisficing algorithms do compared to standard integration algorithms which require more knowledge, time, and computational power. This question is important for Simon's postulated link between the cognitive and the ecological: if the simple psychological principles in satisficing algorithms are tuned to ecological structures, then these algorithms should not fail outright. We propose a competition between various inferential algorithms. The contest will go to the algorithm which scores the highest proportion of correct inferences in the shortest time.

### Simulating Limited Knowledge

We simulated subjects with varying degrees of knowledge about this environment. Limited knowledge can take two forms. One is limited recognition of objects in the reference class. The other is limited knowledge about the cue values of recognized objects. To model limited recognition knowledge, we simulated subjects who recognized between 0 and 83 German cities. To model limited knowledge of cue values, we simulated 6 basic classes of subjects, who knew 0, 10, 20, 50, 75, or 100% of the cue values associated with the objects they recognized. Combining the two sources of limited knowledge resulted in $6 \times 84$ types of subjects each having different degrees and kinds of limited knowledge. Within each type of subject, we created 500 simulated individuals, who differed randomly from one another in the particular objects and cue values they knew. All objects and cue values known were determined randomly within the appropriate constraints, that is, a certain number of objects known, a certain total percentage of cue values known, and the validity of the recognition principle (as explained in the following paragraph).

The simulation needed to be realistic in the sense that the simulated subjects could invoke the recognition principle. Therefore, the sets of cities the simulated subjects knew had to be carefully chosen so that the recognized cities were larger than the unrecognized ones a certain percentage of the time. We performed a survey to get an empirical estimate of the actual covariation between recognition of cities and city populations. Let us define the *validity* $v_r$ of the recognition principle to be the probability, in a reference class, that one object has a greater value on the target variable than another, in the cases where the one object is recognized and the other is not:

$$v_r = p(t(a) > t(b) | a_r \text{ is positive and } b_r \text{ is negative}),$$

where $t(a)$ and $t(b)$ are the values of objects $a$ and $b$ on the target variable $t$, $a_r$ and $b_r$ are the recognition values of $a$ and $b$, and $p$ is a probability measured as a relative frequency in $R$.

In a pilot study of 26 undergraduates at the University of Chicago, we found that the cities they recognized (within the 83 largest in Germany) were larger than the cities they did not recognize in about 80% of all possible comparisons. We incorporated this value into our simulations by choosing sets of cities (for each knowledge state, that is, for each number of cities recognized) where the known cities were larger than the unknown cities in about 80% of all cases. Thus, the cities known by the simulated subjects had the same relationship between recognition and population as did those of

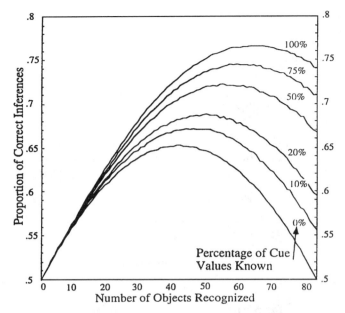

Figure 35.4. Correct inferences about the population of German cities (two-alternative choice tasks) by the Take The Best algorithm. Inferences are based on actual information about the 83 largest cities and 9 cues for population. Limited knowledge of the simulated subjects is varied across two dimensions: (i) the number of cities recognized (*x*-axis), and (ii) the percentage of cue values known (the six curves).

the human subjects. Let us first look at the performance of the Take The Best algorithm.

### Testing the Take The Best Algorithm

We tested how well subjects using the Take The Best algorithm did at answering real-world questions of the kind, "Which city has more inhabitants? (a) Heidelberg (b) Bonn." Each of the 500 simulated subjects in each of the 6 × 84 types was tested on the exhaustive set of 3,403 city pairs resulting in a total of 500 × 6 × 84 × 3,403 tests, that is, about 858 million.

The curves in Figure 35.4 show the average proportion of correct inferences for each proportion of objects and cue values known. The *x*-axis represents the number of cities recognized, and the *y*-axis shows the proportion of correct inferences that the Take The Best algorithm drew. Each of the 6 × 84 points that make up the six curves is an average proportion of correct inferences taken from 500 simulated subjects who each made 3,403 inferences.

When the proportion of cities recognized is zero, then the proportion of correct inferences is at chance level (.5). Up to half of all cities recognized, performance increases at all levels of knowledge about cue values. The maximum percentage of correct inferences is around 77%. The striking result is that this maximum is not achieved when subjects know all cue values of all cities, but rather when they know less. This result shows the ability of the algorithm to exploit limited knowledge, that is to do best when not everything is known. Thus, the Take The Best algorithm produces what we call the "less-is-more" effect. At any level of limited knowledge of cue values, learning more German cities will eventually cause a decrease in proportion correct. Take, for instance, the curve where 75% of the cue values are known, and the point where the simulated subjects recognize about 60 German cities. If these subjects learn about the remaining German cities, their proportion correct will decrease. The rationale behind the less-is-more effect is the recognition principle, and it can be understood best from the curve which reflects 0% of total cue values known. Here, all decisions are made on the basis of the recognition principle or by guessing. On this curve, the recognition prinicple comes into play most when half of the cities are known, so it takes on an inverse U-shape. The mode of this curve moves to the right with increasing knowledge about cue values. Note that even when a subject knows everything – all cue values of all cities – there are states of limited knowledge in which the subjects would make more accurate inferences. We are not going to discuss the conditions of this counterintuitive effect and the supporting experimental evidence here (see Goldstein & Gigerenzer, 1995). Our focus is on how much better integration algorithms can do in making inferences.

### Integration Algorithms

We have asked several colleagues in the fields of Statistics and Economics to devise decision algorithms that would do better than the Take The Best algorithm. The five integration algorithms we simulated and pitted against the Take The Best algorithm in a competition were among those suggested by our colleagues. These competitors include "proper" and "improper" linear models (Dawes, 1979; Lovie & Lovie, 1986). These algorithms, in contrast to the Take The Best algorithm, have the following two features in common: they search for all pieces of information (cue values) available, and they integrate all this information.

#### Contestant One: Tallying

Let us start with a simple integration algorithm: tallying of positive evidence (Goldstein, 1994). In this algorithm, the number of positive cue values for each object is tallied across all cues ($i = l, \ldots, n$) and the object with the largest number of positive cue values is chosen. Integration algorithms are not based (at least explicitly) on the recognition principle. For this reason, and to make the integration algorithms as strong as possible, we allow all the integration algorithms to make use of recognition information (the positive and negative recognition values, see Figure 35.1). Integration algorithms treat recognition as a cue like the nine ecological cues in Table 35.1. That is, in the competition, the number $n$ of cues is thus equal to ten (since recognition is included). The decision criterion for tallying is:

$$\text{If } \sum_{i=1}^{n} a_i > \sum_{i=1}^{n} b_i \quad \text{then choose city } a$$

$$\text{If } \sum_{i=1}^{n} a_i < \sum_{i=1}^{n} b_i \quad \text{then choose city } b$$

$$\text{If } \sum_{i=1}^{n} a_i = \sum_{i=1}^{n} b_i \quad \text{then guess}$$

The assignments of $a_i$ and $b_i$ are:

$$a_i, b_i = \begin{vmatrix} 1 \text{ if the } i\text{th cue value is positive } (+) \\ 0 \text{ if the } i\text{th cue value is negative } (-) \\ 0 \text{ if the } i\text{th cue value is unknown } (?) \end{vmatrix}$$

Let us compare cities $a$ and $b$, from Figure 35.1. By tallying the positive cue values, $a$ would score 2 points and $b$ would score 3. Thus tallying would choose $b$ to be the larger, in opposition to the Take The Best algorithm which would infer that $a$ is larger. Variants of tallying, such as the "frequency of good features heuristic" have been discussed in the decision literature (Alba & Marmorstein, 1987; Payne, Bettman, & Johnson, 1993).

### Contestant Two: Weighted Tallying

Tallying treats all cues alike, independent of cue validity. Weighted tallying of positive evidence is identical with tallying except that it weights each cue according to its ecological validity $v_i$. The ecological validities of the cues appear in Table 35.1. We set $v_i$ of the recognition cue to .8, which is the empirical average determined by the pilot study. The decision rule is as follows:

$$\text{If } \sum_{i=1}^{n} a_i v_i > \sum_{i=1}^{n} b_i v_i \quad \text{then choose city } a$$

$$\text{If } \sum_{i=1}^{n} a_i v_i < \sum_{i=1}^{n} b_i v_i \quad \text{then choose city } b$$

$$\text{If } \sum_{i=1}^{n} a_i v_i = \sum_{i=1}^{n} b_i v_i \quad \text{then guess}$$

Note that weighted tallying needs more information than both tallying and the Take The Best algorithm, namely, quantitative information about ecological validities. In the simulation, we provided the real ecological validities to give this algorithm its best chance.

Calling again on the comparison of objects $a$ and $b$ from Figure 35.1, let us assume that the validities would be .8 for recognition and .9, .8, .7, .6, .51 for cues 1 through 5. Weighted tallying would thus assign 1.7 points to $a$ and 2.3 points to $b$. Thus weighted tallying would also choose $b$ to be the larger.

Both tallying algorithms treat negative information ("$-$") and missing information ("?") identically. That is, they consider only positive evidence. The following algorithms distinguish between negative and missing information and integrate both positive and negative information.

### Contestant Three: Unit-Weight Linear Model

The unit-weight linear model is a special case of the equal-weight linear model (Huber, 1989), and has been advocated as a good approximation of weighted linear models (Dawes, 1979; Einhorn & Hogarth, 1975). The decision criterion for unit-weight integration is the same as for tallying – only the assignment of $a_i$ and $b_i$ differs:

$$a_i, b_i = \begin{vmatrix} 1 \text{ if the } i\text{th cue value is positive} \\ -1 \text{ if the } i\text{th cue value is negative} \\ 0 \text{ if the } i\text{th cue value is unknown} \end{vmatrix}$$

Comparing objects $a$ and $b$ from Figure 35.1 would assign 1 point to $a$ and 1 point to $b$ and thus choose randomly. This simple linear model corresponds to Model 2 in Einhorn and Hogarth (1975, p. 177) with the weight parameter set equal to 1.

### Contestant Four: Weighted Linear Model

This model is like the unit-weight linear model except that the values of $a_i$ and $b_i$ are multiplied by their respective ecological validities. The decision criterion is the same as with weighted tallying. The weighted linear model (or some variant of it) is often viewed as an "optimal" rule for preferential choice, under the idealization of independent dimensions or cues (e.g., Keeney & Raiffa, 1993; Payne, Bettman, & Johnson, 1993).

Comparing objects $a$ and $b$ from Figure 35.1, would assign 1.0 points to $a$ and .8 points to $b$ and thus choose $a$ to be the larger.

### Contestant Five: Multiple Regression

The weighted linear model reflects the different validities of the cues, but not the dependencies between cues. Multiple regression creates weights that reflect the covariances between predictors or cues, and is commonly seen as an "optimal" way to integrate various pieces of information into an estimate (e.g., Brunswik, 1955; Hammond, 1966). One-layer neural networks using the delta rule determine their "optimal" weights by the same principles as multiple regression does (Stone, 1986). The delta rule carries out the equivalent of a multiple linear regression from the input patterns to the targets.

The optimal weights for the multiple regression could simply be calculated from the full information about the nine ecological cues. To make multiple regression an even stronger competitor, we also provided information about which cities the simulated subjects recognized. Thus the multiple regression used nine ecological cues and the recognition cue to generate its weights. Since the weights for the recognition cue depend on which cities are recognized, we calculated $6 \times 500 \times 84$ sets of weights: one for each simulated subject. Unlike any of the other algorithms, regression had access to the actual city populations (even for those cities not recognized by the hypothetical subject) in the calculation of the weights. During the quiz, each simulated subject used the set of weights provided to it by multiple regression to estimate the populations of the cities in the comparison.

There was a missing-values problem in computing these $6 \times 84 \times 500$ sets of regression coefficients, since most simulated subjects did not know certain cue values, for instance, the cue values of the cities they did not recognize. We strengthened the performance of multiple regression by substituting unknown cue values with the average of the cue values the subject knew for the given cue.[4] This was done both in creating the weights and in using these weights to estimate populations. Unlike traditional procedures where weights are estimated from one half of the data, and inferences based on these weights are made for the other half, the regression algorithm had access to all the information on all the cities (except, of course, the unknown cue values) – more information than was given to any of the competitors. In the competition, multiple regression, and to a lesser degree, the weighted linear model, approximate the ideal of the Laplacean Demon.

### Results

*Speed*

The Take The Best algorithm is designed to enable quick decision making. Compared to the integration algorithms, how much faster does it draw inferences, measured by the amount of information searched in memory? For instance, in Figure 35.1, the Take The Best algorithm would look up four cue values (including the recognition cue values) to infer that $a$ is larger than $b$. None of the integration algorithms uses limited search; thus they always look up all cue values.

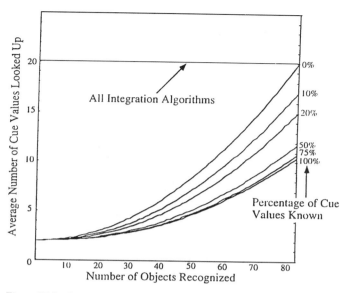

Figure 35.5. Amount of cue values looked up by the Take The Best algorithm and by the competing integration algorithms depending on the number of objects known (0–83) and the percentage of cue values known.

Figure 35.5 shows the amount of cue values retrieved from memory by the Take The Best algorithm for various levels of limited knowledge. The Take The Best algorithm reduces search in memory considerably. Depending on the knowledge state, this algorithm needed to search for between 2 (the number of recognition cue values) and 20 (the maximum possible) cue values. For instance, when a subject recognizes half of the cities and knows 50% of their cue values, then on average only about 4 cue values (that is, one fifth of all possible) are searched for. The average across all simulated subjects was 5.9, which is less than a third of all available cue values.

### Accuracy

Given that it searches only for a limited amount of information, how accurate is the Take The Best algorithm compared to the integration algorithms? We ran the competition for all states of limited knowledge shown in Figure 35.4. We first report the results of the competition in the case where each algorithm achieves its best performance: when 100% of the cue values are known. Figure 35.6 shows the results of the simulations, carried out in the same way as those in Figure 35.4.

To our surprise, the Take The Best algorithm drew as many correct inferences as any of the other algorithms, and more than some. This holds across the entire range of recognition knowledge. The curves for Take The Best,

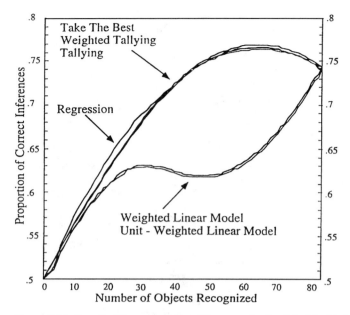

Figure 35.6. Result of the competition. The curve for the Take The Best algorithm is identical with the 100% curve in Figure 35.4. The results for proportion correct have been smoothed by a running median smoother to lessen visual noise between the lines.

multiple regression, weighted tallying, and tallying are so similar that there are only slight differences between them. Weighted tallying performed about as well as tallying, and the unit-weighted linear model performed about as well as the weighted linear model – demonstrating that the previous finding that weights may be chosen in a fairly arbitrary manner, as long as they have the correct sign (Dawes, 1979), is generalizable to tallying. The two integration algorithms which make use of both positive and negative information, unit-weight and weighted linear models, made considerably fewer correct inferences. By looking at the lower-left and upper-right corners of the graph, it can be seen that all competitors do equally well with a complete lack of knowledge, or with complete knowledge. They differ when knowledge is limited. Note that some algorithms can make more correct inferences when they do not have complete knowledge: a demonstration of the less-is-more principle mentioned earlier.

What is the result of the competition across all levels of limited knowledge? Table 35.2 shows the result for each level of limited knowledge of cue values, averaged across all levels of recognition knowledge. (Table 35.2 also reports the performance of two variants of the Take The Best algorithm, which we will discuss later: the Minimalist and the Take The Last algorithm.) The values in the 100% column of Table 35.2 are the values in Figure 35.6

Table 35.2. *Results of the Competition: Average Proportion of Correct Inferences*

| Algorithm | Percentage of Cue Values Known[a] | | | | | |
|---|---|---|---|---|---|---|
| | *10%* | *20%* | *50%* | *75%* | *100%* | *Average* |
| Take The Best | 0.621 | 0.635 | 0.663 | 0.678 | 0.691 | 0.658 |
| Weighted tallying | 0.621 | 0.635 | 0.663 | 0.679 | 0.693 | 0.658 |
| Regression | 0.625 | 0.635 | 0.657 | 0.674 | 0.694 | 0.657 |
| Tallying | 0.620 | 0.633 | 0.659 | 0.676 | 0.691 | 0.656 |
| Weighted linear model | 0.623 | 0.627 | 0.623 | 0.619 | 0.625 | 0.623 |
| Unit-weight linear model | 0.621 | 0.622 | 0.621 | 0.620 | 0.622 | 0.621 |
| **PMM Variant Algorithms** | | | | | | |
| Minimalist | 0.619 | 0.631 | 0.650 | 0.661 | 0.674 | 0.647 |
| Take The Last | 0.619 | 0.630 | 0.646 | 0.658 | 0.675 | 0.645 |

[a] Values are rounded, averages are computed from the unrounded values.

averaged across all levels of recognition. The Take The Best algorithm makes as many correct inferences as one of the competitors (weighted tallying), and more than the others. Since it is also the fastest, the competition goes to the Take The Best algorithm.

To our knowledge, this is the first time that it has been demonstrated that a satisficing algorithm like the Take The Best algorithm can draw as many correct inferences about a real-world environment as integration algorithms, across all states of limited knowledge. The dictates of classical rationality would have led one to the expect the integration algorithms to do substantially better than the satisficing algorithm.

Two results of the simulation can be derived analytically. First and most obvious is that if knowledge about objects is zero, then all algorithms perform at a chance level. Second, and less obvious, if all objects and cue values are known, then tallying produces as many correct inferences as the unit-weight linear model. This is because, under complete knowledge, the score under the tallying algorithm is an increasing linear function of the score arrived at in the unit-weighted linear model.[5] The equivalence between tallying and unit-weight linear models under complete knowledge is an important result. It is known that unit-weight linear models can sometimes perform about as well as optimal linear models (that is, models with weights that are chosen in an optimal way, such as in multiple regression). The equivalence implies that, under complete knowledge, merely counting pieces of positive evidence can do as well as optimal linear models. This result clarifies one condition under which searching only for positive evidence, a strategy that has been sometimes labeled "confirmation bias" or "positive search bias," can be a reasonable and efficient inferential strategy (Tweney & Walker, 1990).

Why do the unit-weighted and weighted linear models perform markedly worse under limited knowledge of objects? The reason is the simple and bold recognition principle. Algorithms which do not exploit the recognition principle in environments where recognition is strongly correlated with the target variable pay the price with a considerable number of wrong inferences. The unit-weighted and weighted linear models use recognition information and integrate it with all other information, but do not follow the recognition principle, that is, they sometimes choose unrecognized cities over recognized ones. Why is this? In the environment, there are more negative cue values than positive ones, and most cities have more negative cue values than positive ones. From this it follows that when a recognized object is compared to an unrecognized object, the (weighted) sum of cue values of the recognized object will often be smaller than that of the unrecognized object (which is $-1$ for the unit-weight model, and $-.8$ for the weighted linear model). Here the unit-weight and weighted linear models often make the inference that the unrecognized object is the larger one, due to the overwhelming negative evidence for the recognized object. Such inferences contradict the recognition principle. Tallying algorithms, in contrast, have the recognition principle built in implicitly. The reason is that since they ignore negative information, the tally for an unrecognized object is always zero, and thus is always smaller than the tally for a recognized object, which is at least one (for tallying, or $.8$ for weighted tallying, due to the positive value on the recognition cue). Thus, tallying algorithms always arrive at the inference that a recognized object is larger than an unrecognized one.

Note that this explanation of the different performances puts the full weight in a psychological principle (the recognition principle) explicit in the Take The Best algorithm, as opposed to the statistical issue of how to find optimal weights in a linear function. In order to test this explanation, we re-ran the simulations for the unit-weighted and weighted linear models under the same conditions, but replacing the recognition cue by the recognition principle. The simulation showed that the recognition principle accounts for all the difference.

### Can Satisficing Algorithms Get by Using Even Less Time and Knowledge?

The Take The Best algorithm produced a surprisingly high proportion of correct inferences, compared to more computationally expensive integration algorithms. Making correct inferences despite limited knowledge is an important adaptive feature of an algorithm, but being right is not the only thing that counts. In many situations, time is limited, and acting fast can be as important as being correct. For instance, if you are driving on an unfamiliar highway and you have to decide in an instant what to do when the road forks, your problem is not necessarily making the best choice, but simply making a quick choice. Pressure to be quick is also characteristic for certain types of verbal interactions, such as press conferences where a fast answer indicates competence, or commercial interactions such as having telephone service installed, where the customer has to decide in a few minutes which of a dozen calling features to purchase. These situations comprise the dual constraints of limited knowledge and limited time. The Take The Best algorithm is already faster than any of the integration algorithms, since it performs only a limited search and does not need to compute weighted sums of cue values. Can it be made even faster? It can, if search is guided by the recency of cues in memory rather than by cue validity.

### The Take The Last Algorithm

The Take The Last algorithm first tries the cue which discriminated the last time, and, if this cue does not discriminate, then tries the cue which discriminated the time before the last, and so on. The algorithm differs from the Take The Best algorithm in Step 2, which is now reformulated as Step 2':

> 2'. *Search for the cue values of the most recent cue*: For the two objects, retrieve the cue values of the cue used most recently. If it is the first judgment and there is no discrimination record available, retrieve the cue values of a randomly chosen cue.

Thus, in Step 4 the algorithm goes back to Step 2'. Variants of this search principle have been studied as the "Einstellung effect" in the water jar experiments (Luchins & Luchins, 1994), where the solution strategy of the most recently solved problem is tried first on the subsequent problem. This effect has also been noted in physician's generation of diagnoses for clinical cases (Weber, Böckenholt, Hilton, & Wallace, 1993).

This algorithm does not need a rank order of cues according to their validities; all that needs to be known is the direction in which a cue points. Knowledge about the rank order of cue validities is substituted by a memory of which cues were last used. Note that such a record can be built up independently of any knowledge about the structure of an environment, and neither needs, nor uses, any feedback about whether inferences are right or wrong.

### The Minimalist Algorithm

Can reasonably accurate inferences be achieved with even less knowledge? What we call the Minimalist algorithm needs neither information about the rank ordering of cue validities nor the discrimination history of the cues. In its ignorance, the algorithm picks cues in a random order. The algorithm differs from the Take The Best algorithm in Step 2, which is now reformulated as Step 2″:

2″. *Random search:* For the two objects, retrieve the cue values of a randomly chosen cue.

The Minimalist algorithm does not necessarily speed up search, but it tries to get by with even less knowledge than any other algorithm.

### Results

*Speed*

How fast are the fast algorithms? The simulations showed that, for each of the two variant algorithms, the relationship between amount of knowledge and the number of cue values looked up had the same form as for the Take The Best algorithm (Figure 35.5). That is, unlike the integration algorithms, the curves are concave and the number of cues searched for is maximum when knowledge of cue values is lowest. The average number of cue values looked up was lowest for the Take The Last algorithm (5.29) followed by the Minimalist algorithm (5.64) and the Take The Best algorithm (5.91). As knowledge becomes more and more limited (on both dimensions: recognition and cue values known), the difference in speed becomes smaller and smaller. The reason why the Minimalist algorithm looks up fewer cue values than the Take The Best algorithm is that cue validities and cue discrimination rates are negatively correlated (Table 35.1); therefore, randomly chosen cues tend to have larger discrimination rates than cues chosen by cue validity.

*Accuracy*

What is the price to be paid for speeding up search, or reducing the knowledge of cue orderings and discrimination histories to nothing? We tested the performance of the two algorithms on the same environment as all other algorithms. Figure 35.7 shows the proportion of correct inferences which the Minimalist algorithm achieved. For comparison, the performance of the Take The Best algorithm with 100% of cue values known is indicated by a dotted line. Note that the Minimalist algorithm performs surprisingly well. The maximum difference appears when knowledge is complete and all cities are recognized. In these circumstances, the Minimalist algorithm does about 4 percentage points worse than the Take The Best algorithm. On average, the proportion of correct inferences is only 1.1 percentage points less than the best algorithms in the competition (Table 35.2).

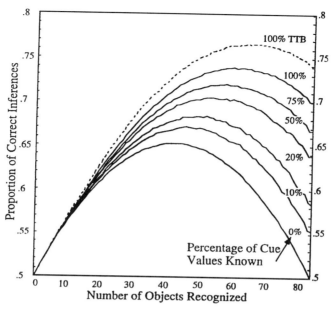

Figure 35.7. Performance of the Minimalist algorithm. For comparison, the performance of the Take The Best (TTB) algorithm is shown as a dotted line for the case where 100% of cue values are known.

The performance of the Take The Last algorithm is similar to Figure 35.7, and the average number of correct inferences is shown in Table 35.2. The Take The Last algorithm is faster, but scores slightly less than the Minimalist algorithm. The Take The Last algorithm has an interesting ability which fooled us in an earlier series of tests where we used a systematic (as opposed to a random) method for presenting the test pairs, starting with the largest city and pairing it with all others, and so on. An integration algorithm such as multiple regression cannot "find out" that it is being tested in this systematic way, and its inferences are accordingly independent of the sequence of presentation. However, the Take The Last algorithm found out and won this first round of the competition, outperforming the other competitiors by some 10 percentage points. How did it exploit systematic testing? Recall that it tries first the cue that discriminated the last time, if this one does not discriminate, it proceeds with the cue that discriminated the time before the last time, and so on. In doing so, when testing is systematic in the way described, it tends to find, for each city that is being paired with all smaller ones, the group of cues for which the larger city has a positive value. Trying these cues first increases the chances of finding a discriminating cue that points in the right direction (toward the larger city). We learned our lesson, and re-ran the whole competition with randomly ordered of pairs of cities.

## Discussion

The competition showed a surprising result: the Take The Best algorithm drew as many correct inferences about unknown features of a real-world environment as any of the integration algorithms, and more than some of them. Two further simplifications of the algorithm – replacing knowledge about the rank orders of cue validities by a memory of the discrimination history of cues (the Take The Last algorithm), or dispensing with both (the Minimalist algorithm) – showed a comparatively small loss in correct inferences, and only when knowledge about cue values was high.

To the best of our knowledge, this is the first inference competition between satisficing and "optimal" algorithms in a real-world environment. The result is of importance for encouraging research that focuses on the power of simple psychological mechanisms, that is, on the design and testing of satisficing algorithms. The result is also of importance as an existence proof that cognitive algorithms capable of successful performance in a real-world environment do not need to satisfy the classical norms of rational inference. The classical norms may be sufficient, but are not necessary, for good inference in real environments. . . .

### Can Reasoning Be Rational and Psychological?

At the beginning of this chapter, we pointed out the common opposition between the rational and the psychological, which emerged in the nineteenth century after the breakdown of the classical interpretation of probability (Gigerenzer et al., 1989). Since then, rational inference is commonly reduced to logic and probability theory, and psychological explanations are called upon when things go wrong. This division of labor is, in a nutshell, the basis on which much of the current research on judgment under uncertainty is built. As one economist from Princeton put it, "either reasoning is rational or it's psychological" (Gigerenzer, 1994). Can not reasoning be both rational and psychological?

We believe, that after 40 years of toying with the notion of bounded rationality, it is time to overcome the opposition between the rational and the psychological and to reunite the two. The PMM family of cognitive algorithms provides precise models that attempt to do so. They differ from the Enlightenment's unified view of the rational and psychological in that they focus on simple psychological mechanisms which operate under constraints of limited time and knowledge and are supported by empirical evidence. The single most important result in this chapter is that simple psychological mechanisms operating in these algorithms can yield as many (or more) correct inferences in less time than the standard statistical linear models which are traditionally equated with rational inference. The demonstration that a fast and frugal satisficing algorithm won the competition defeats the widespread view that only "optimal" algorithms can be accurate. Models of inference do not have to forsake accuracy for simplicity. The mind can have it both ways.

### Notes

1  We also now use the term "discrimination rule" instead of "activation rule."
2  For instance, if $N = 2$, and one cue value is positive and the other negative ($x_i = y_i = .5$), $d_i = 1.0$. If $N$ increases with $x_i$ and $y_i$ held constant, then $d_i$ decreases and converges to $2x_i y_i$.
3  There are various other measures of redundancy besides pairwise correlation. The important point is that whatever measure of redundancy one uses, the resultant value does not have the same meaning for all algorithms. For instance, all that counts for the Take The Best algorithm is what proportion of correct inferences the second cue adds to the first in the cases where the first cue does not discriminate, and how much the third cue adds to the first two in the cases where they do not discriminate, and so on. If a cue discriminates, search is terminated, and the degree of redundancy in the cues which were not included in the search is irrelevant. Integration algorithms, in contrast, integrate all information, and thus always work with the total redundancy in the environment (or knowledge base). For instance, when deciding among objects $a$, $b$, $c$, and $d$ in Figure 35.1, the cue values of cues 3, 4, and 5 do not matter from the point of view of the Take The Best algorithm (since search is terminated before reaching cue 3). However, the values of cues 3, 4, and 5 affect the redundancy of the ecological system, from the point of view of all integration algorithms. The lesson is that the degree of redundancy in an environment depends on the kind of algorithm that operates on the environment. One needs to be cautious in interpreting measures of redundancy without reference to an algorithm.
4  If no single cue value was known for a given cue, then the missing values were substituted by .5. This value was chosen because it is the midpoint of 0 and 1, which are the values used to stand for negative and positive cue values, respectively.
5  The proof for this is as follows. The tallying score $t$ for a given object is the number $n^+$ of positive cue values, as defined above. The score $u$ for the unit weight linear model is $n^+ - n^-$, where $n^-$ is the number of negative cue values. Under complete knowledge, $n = n^+ + n^-$, where $n$ is the number of cues. Thus $t = n^+$ and $u = n^+ - n^-$. Since $n^- = n - n^+$, by substitution into the formula for $u$ we find that $u = n^+ - (n - n^+) = 2t - n$.

### References

Alba, J. W., & Marmorstein, H. (1987). The effects of frequency knowledge on consumer decision making. *Journal of Consumer Research, 14*, 14–26.

Anderson, J. R. (1990). *The adaptive character of thought*. Hillsdale, NJ: Erlbaum.

Armelius, B., & Armelius, K. (1974). The use of redundancy in multiple-cue judgments: Data from a suppressor-variable-task. *American Journal of Psychology, 87*, 385–392.

Becker, G. (1976). *The economic approach to human behavior*. Chicago: The University of University Press.

Brehmer, B. (1994). The psychology of linear judgment models. *Acta Psychologica, 87*, 137–154.

Breiman, L., Friedman, J. H., Olshen, R. A., & Stone, C. J. (1993). *Classification and regression trees*. New York: Chapman & Hall.

Brown, N. R., & Siegler, R. S. (1993). Metrics and mappings: A framework for understanding real-world quantitative estimation. *Psychological Review, 100*, 511–534.

Brunswik, E. (1955). Representative design and probabilistic theory in a functional psychology. *Psychological Review, 62*, 193–217.

Darwin, C. (1965 (original published in 1872)). *The expressions of the emotions in man and animal*. Chicago: The University of Chicago Press.

Daston, L. J. (1988). *Classical probability in the Enlightenment*. Princeton, NJ: Princeton University Press.

Dawes, R. M. (1979). The robust beauty of improper linear models. *American Psychologist, 34*, 571–582.

DiFonzo, N. (1994). *Piggybacked syllogisms for investor behavior: probabilistic mental modeling in rumor-based stock market trading*. Ph.D. dissertation, Temple University.

Einhorn, H. J., & Hogarth, R. M. (1975). Unit weighting schemes for decision making. *Organizational Behavior and Human Performance, 13*, 171–192.

Fischhoff, B. (1977). Perceived informativeness of facts. *Journal of Experimental Psychology: Human Perception and Performance, 3*, 349–358.

Gigerenzer, G. (1993). The bounded rationality of probabilistic mental models. In K. I. Manktelow & D. E. Over (Eds.), *Rationality: Psychological and philosophical perspectives* (pp. 284–313) London: Routledge.

Gigerenzer, G. (1994). Why the distinction between single-even probabilities and frequencies is relevant for psychology (and vice versa). In G. Wright & P. Ayton (Eds.), *Subjective probability* (pp. 129–161). New York: Wiley.

Gigerenzer, G., & Hoffrage, U. (1995). How to improve Bayesian reasoning without instruction: Frequency formats. *Psychological Review, 102*, 684–704.

Gigerenzer, G., & Hoffrage, U., & Kleinbölting, H. (1991). Probabilistic mental models: A Brunswikian theory of confidence. *Psychological Review, 98*, 506–528.

Gigerenzer, G., & Murray, D. J. (1987). *Cognition as intuitive statistics*. Hillsdale, NJ: Erlbaum.

Gigerenzer, G., Swijtink, Z., Porter, T., Daston, L., Beatty, J., & Krüger, L. (1989). *The empire of chance: How probability changed science and everyday life*. Cambridge: Cambridge University Press.

Goldstein, D. G. (1994). *The less-is-more effect in inference*. M. A. thesis, The University of Chicago.

Goldstein, D. G., & Gigerenzer, G. (1995). *The recognition principle and the less-is-more effect*. Unpublished manuscript.

Griffin, D., & Tversky, A. (1992). The weighing of evidence and the determinants of confidence. *Cognitive Psychology, 24*, 411–435.

Hammond, K. R. (1966). *The psychology of Egon Brunswik*. New York: Holt, Rinehart & Winston.

Hammond, K. R. (1990). Functionalism and illusionism: Can integration be usefully achieved? In R. M. Hogarth (Ed.), *Insights in decision making*, Chicago: The University of Chicago Press.

Hammond, K. R., Hursch, C. J., & Todd, F. J. (1964). Analyzing the components of clinical inference. *Psychological Review, 71*, 438–456.

Hertwig, R., Gigerenzer, G., & Hoffrage, U. (1995). The reiteration effect in hindsight bias. Manuscript submitted for publication.

Hoffrage, U. (1994). *Zur Angemessenheit subjektiver Sicherheits-Urteile: Eine Exploration der Theorie der probabilistischen mentalen Modelle*. Ph.D. dissertation, Universität Salzburg.

Huber, O. (1989). Information-processing operators in decision making. In H. Montgomery & O. Svenson (Eds.), *Process and structure in human decision making* (pp. 3–21). New York: Wiley.

Huttenlocher, J., Hedges, L., & Prohaska, V. (1988). Hierarchical organization in ordered domains: Estimating the dates of events. *Psychological Review, 95*, 471–484.

Johnson-Laird, P. N. (1983). *Mental models*. Cambridge, MA: Harvard University Press.

Juslin, P. (1993). An explanation of the hard-easy effect in studies of realism of confidence in one's general knowledge. *European Journal of Cognitive Psychology, 5*(1), 55–71.

Juslin, P. (1994). The overconfidence phenomenon as a consequence of informal experimenter-guided selection of almanac items. *Organizational Behavior and Human Decision Processes, 57*, 226–246.

Juslin, P., Winman, A., & Persson, T. (1995). Can overconfidence be used as an indicator of reconstructive rather than retrieval processes? *Cognition, 54*, 99–130.

Kahneman, D., Slovic, P., & Tversky, A. (Eds.). (1982). *Judgment under uncertainty: Heuristics and biases*. Cambridge: Cambridge University Press.

Keeney, R. L., & Raiffa, H. (1993). *Decisions with multiple objectives*. Cambridge: Cambridge University Press.

Koriat, A., Lichtenstein, S., & Fischhoff, B. (1980). Reasons for confidence. *Journal of Experimental Psychology: Human Learning and Memory, 6*, 107–118.

Krebs, J. R., & Davies, N. B. (1987). *An introduction to behavioral ecology* (2nd ed.). London: Blackwell.

Lopes, L. L. (1992). Three misleading assumptions in the customary rhetoric of the bias literature. *Theory & Psychology, 2*, 231–236.

Lopes, L. L. (1994). Psychology and economics: Perspectives on risk, cooperation, and the marketplace. *Annual Review of Psychology, 45*, 197–227.

Lovie, A. D., & Lovie, P. (1986). The flat maximum effect and linear scoring models for prediction. *Journal of Forecasting, 5*, 159–168.

Luchins, A. S., & Luchins, E. H. (1994). The water jar experiments and Einstellung effects: I. Early history and surveys of textbook citations. *Gestalt Theory, 16*, 101–121.

McClelland, A. G. R., & Bolger, F. (1994). The calibration of subjective probabilities: Theories and models 1980–1994. In G. Wright & P. Ayton (Eds.), *Subjective probability* (pp. 453–482). Chichester: Wiley.

McCloskey, D. N. (1985). *The rhetoric of economics*. Madison: University of Wisconsin Press.

Simon, H. A. (1945). *Administrative behavior: A study of decision-making processes in administrative organization*. New York: The Free Press.

Simon, H. A. (1956). Rational choice and the structure of the environment. *Psychological Review, 63*, 129–138.

Simon, H. A. (1982). *Models of bounded rationality*. Cambridge, MA: MIT Press.

Simon, H. A. (1990). Invariants of human behavior. *Annual Review of Psychology, 41*, 1–19.

Simon, H. A. (1992). *Economics, bounded rationality, and the cognitive revolution*, Aldershot Hants, UK: Elgar.

Sniezek, J. A., & Buckley, T. (1993). Decision errors made by individuals and groups. In N. J. Castellan (Ed.). *Individual and group decision making*. Hillsdale, NJ: Erlbaum.

Stephens, D. W., & Krebs, J. R. (1986). *Foraging theory*. Princeton, NJ: Princeton University Press.

Stone, G. O. (1986). An analysis of the delta rule and the learning of statistical associations. In D. Rumelhart, J. McClelland, & the PDP Research Group (Eds.), *Parallel Distributed Processing: Explorations in the microstructure of cognition*. Cambridge, MA: MIT Press.

Tweney, R. D., & Walker, B. J. (1990). Science education and the cognitive psychology of science. In B. F. Jones & L. Idol (Eds.), *Dimensions of thinking and cognitive instruction* (pp. 291–310) Hillsdale, NJ: Erlbaum.

Weber, U., Böckenholt, U., Hilton, D. J., & Wallace, B. (1993). Determinants of diagnostic hypothesis generation: Effects of information, base rates, and experience. *Journal of Experimental Psychology: Learning, Memory, & Cognition, 19,* 1151–1164.

Wimsatt, W. C. (1976). Reductionism, levels of organization, and the mind-body problem. In G. G. Globus, G. Maxwell, & I. Savodnik (Eds.), *Consciousness and the brain: A scientific and philosophical inquiry* (pp. 199–267). New York: Plenum.

# 36 Judgment and Decision Making in Social Context: Discourse Processes and Rational Inference

*Denis J. Hilton and Ben R. Slugoski*

Reasoning from ordinary language is shaped by the nature of social interaction and conversation (Austin, 1962; Grice, 1975; Searle, 1969). These higher-level assumptions can determine what we attend to, which memories we search, and what kinds of inference we draw. Consider the way in which the word *family* can be differentially interpreted according to context and thus lead to seemingly inconsistent judgments being expressed in a conversational exchange (cf. Strack, Martin, & Schwarz, 1988):

> Q. "How is your family?"
> A. "Fairly well, thank you."

A married man might reply this way if he considers that his wife has recently been saddened by the loss of a close friend, but that his two children are in good form. Here the respondent interprets *family* to mean *the wife and kids*.

Suppose, however, that you had first asked this man about his wife and then his family. The exchange might have run as follows:

> Q. "How is your wife?"
> A. "Not too good, I'm afraid"
> Q. "And how is your family?"
> A. "Extremely well, thank you!"

In this case, the respondent would normally feel bound to interpret *family* as *the kids*, since he will have already given information about his wife and

This chapter was specially prepared for this book. This is a revised version of D. J. Hilton (1995), "The social context of reasoning: Conversational inference and rational judgment," *Psychological Bulletin, 118,* 248–271. Readers are directed to the original for a more extensive consideration of the issues. We are grateful to Dr. Terry Connolly for his editorial stewardship.

will not wish to burden the questioner with redundant information that she already has. So he gives an answer about his family that is seemingly inconsistent with his earlier answer.

From one perspective, giving different answers to the same question asked on different occasions may seem irrational. We might suppose, for example, that he is unable to activate the same representation of the concept *my family* on the two occasions owing to defective or biased memory-retrieval processes. This kind of argument is familiar from much research on rational judgment. Thus, irrationality is often demonstrated experimentally through producing different responses to the same question asked in different contexts, such as the study of framing effects on risky choice (Tversky & Kahneman, 1981) and preference reversals (Payne, Bettman, & Johnson, 1992), or through question-order effects on responses in survey research (Schuman & Presser, 1981).

Attributing irrationality to the respondent in the above case, however, may be premature. Norms of rational communication (e.g., Grice, 1975) require a speaker to cooperate with a hearer by not burdening him or her with redundant information. Specifically, in the case where the hearer has just been told about the health of the speaker's wife, one can argue that interlocutors are entitled to assume that the reference to *family* meant *just the kids*, rather than the *wife and kids*. This interpretation of the word *family* is conversationally rational in the context of the previous exchange about the health of the speaker's wife. The context-dependent interpretation of the word *family* would thus absolve the speaker of the charge of cognitive inconsistency. Rather, he has cooperatively and rationally altered his answers to the question as a function of the interactional context.

Recognition of conversational constraints on utterance interpretation and inference may thus have important implications for experimental psychologists. No psychological experiment or investigation takes place in a social vacuum. All experiments and surveys are forms of social interaction between experimenter and participant, which invariably involve communication through ordinary language. Thus, survey and experimental researchers who attribute inconsistent or normatively errorful responses to cognitive shortcomings may be in danger of committing an attribution error, that is, of misattributing patterns of inferential behavior to features of the person, and overlooking how it is constrained by its interpersonal context.

Theories of judgment should therefore include a front-end component that determines how the incoming message is interpreted in its context. This may remove many anomalies in the interpretation of respondents' behavior. It has been a perennial problem for students of judgment and reasoning to determine whether a "mistake" is caused by faulty reasoning about the information given or by application of correct reasoning procedures to "incorrect" or "irrelevant" information that a respondent has incorporated in her representation of the reasoning problem (Henle, 1962; Johnson-Laird,

1983). Conversational assumptions often require us to go beyond the information explicitly given in an utterance. Thus, the final judgment may often be highly rational given the respondent's use of these assumptions in forming a representation of the reasoning task.

We therefore begin by reviewing some of the logical and linguistic properties of conversational inference with particular reference to the question of rationality in research on judgment and reasoning. We show how these logico-linguistic properties may be moderated by inferences about the social context of communication, and particularly the hearer/respondent's attributions about the speaker/experimenter (e.g., the speaker's knowledge, intentions, group membership). This attributional model generates predictions about the ways in which conversational inference may affect the representation of judgment and reasoning tasks. We apply the model to the analysis of experiments on reasoning drawn from social psychology, cognitive psychology, and decision research and show that the attributional model of conversational inference organizes phenomena found in these diversified literatures within a common framework. Importantly, the framework can also help elucidate which biases are *not* susceptible of explanation in conversational terms. We conclude by discussing methodological implications and directions for future research.

## Properties of Conversational Inference

### The Inductive Nature of Conversational Inference

Conversational inference is itself a form of judgment under uncertainty. Hearers have to make hypotheses about the speaker's intended meaning on the basis of what is explicitly said. For example, most hearers routinely go beyond the information given in the utterance "I went to the cinema last night" to infer that the speaker meant to convey that she saw a film last night. The additional information conveyed in this way by the speaker is termed a *conversational implicature* (Grice, 1975). Grice thus argued that to understand a speaker's full meaning, the listener must both understand the meaning of the sentence itself ("what is said") and what it conveys in a given context ("what is implicated").

Conversational inference thus shares some important properties with inductive inference (Levinson, 1983). First it is *ampliative*, that is, the conclusion contains more information than the premises. The inference that the speaker went to the cinema and saw a film contains more information than the assertion that she just went to the cinema. Consequently, the conclusions of both conversational and inductive inference are both *defeasible*, that is, they can be canceled by the addition of new information. The speaker may cancel the implicature that he or she saw a film at the cinema last night by saying, "I went to the cinema last night, but couldn't get in."

Table 36.1. *Grice's Cooperative Principle and the Maxims of Conversation*

The Cooperative Principle

  Make your contribution such as is required, at the stage at which it occurs,
  by the accepted purpose or direction in which you are engaged.

The Maxim of Quality
  Try to make your contribution one that you believe to be true, specifically:
      1. Do not say what you believe to be false.
      2. Do not say that for which you lack adequate evidence.

The Maxim of Quantity
      1. Make your contribution as informative as is required for the current
         purposes of the exchange.
      2. Do not make your contribution more informative than is required.

The Maxim of Relation
  Make your contributions relevant.

The Maxim of Manner
      1. Avoid obscurity.
      2. Avoid ambiguity.
      3. Be brief.
      4. Be orderly.

*Source:* Grice (1975).

Grice's (1975) Cooperative Principle (CP) and its derivative maxims are detailed in Table 36.1. This scheme describes a form of rational communication in which the maximum amount of valuable information is transmitted with the least amount of encoding and decoding effort. The CP and the subordinate maxims seem to correspond to important psychological dimensions as well as the tensions between them to produce important logical and linguistic consequences.

### Attributional Bases of Conversational Inference

Grice's (1975) assumption of cooperativeness and the corresponding maxims of conversation depend on the hearer making certain default attributions about the speaker. In particular, the assumption of cooperativeness presupposes that utterances are produced by an intentional agent who wishes to cooperate with us and has the ability to realize this intention. We argue that each set of conversational maxims imply certain kinds of attributions about the speaker (see Table 36.2).

The *maxim of quality* concerns the likely truth-value of an utterance. Thus, if the hearer attributes properties such as sincerity, reliability, and knowledgeability to the speaker, then the hearer may well consider the probable truth-value of an utterance to be high. If, on the other hand, the hearer

Table 36.2. *Assumed Characteristics of Message and Speaker Implied by Grice's Logic of Conversation*

| Assumption/Maxim of Conversation | Message Characteristics | Characteristics Attributed to Speaker |
|---|---|---|
| Cooperativeness | Observes four maxims (see below) | Intentional Helpful Sincere Honest |
| Quality | Truth-value probability | Reliable Competent |
| Quantity | Informativeness | Mutual knowledge Group membership |
| Relation | Goal relevance | Interactional goals |
| Manner | Clarity | Knowledge of language |

considers the speaker to be insincere, unreliable, or unknowledgeable, then the hearer may well consider the probable truth of the utterance to be low.

The *maxim of quantity* concerns the perceived informativeness of an utterance. Speakers should not burden hearers with information they are already likely to know. What speakers and hearers take for granted may in part depend on perceptions of class membership. Competent members of Western society do not need to be told why a customer who ate a good meal with good service in a restaurant left a big tip. From their own world knowledge they are able to make the necessary bridging inferences (Clark & Haviland, 1977; Schank & Abelson, 1977). Thus hearers will often go beyond the information given in making inferences, since they assume that relevant information that they are likely to know has already been omitted.

The *maxim of relation* enjoins speakers to mention information that is relevant to the goals of the interaction. Hearers are entitled to assume that any relevant information that they are not likely to know will have been included. They are also entitled to assume that information that has been included is relevant. Otherwise why mention it? One problem for experimental research is that psychologists routinely violate this assumption by introducing information precisely because it is irrelevant to the judgment task in hand (e.g., Nisbett, Zukier, & Lemley, 1981). If hearers (participants) continue to attribute essentially cooperative intentions to speakers (experimenters), then they are liable to be misled by the information given.

The *maxim of manner* enjoins speakers to be brief, orderly, clear, and unambiguous. Departures from these submaxims are often motivated by considerations of tact or politeness (Brown & Levinson, 1987) and hence may signal status and intimacy differentials between the speaker and recipient (see, e.g., Slugoski, 1995; Slugoski & Turnbull, 1988). Adherence to these prescriptions also depends on the speaker's control of the language. Hearers may take this into account in interpreting an utterance. For example, a German tourist in England might conceivably ask a passerby for directions to "the Townhouse" when she meant "the Town Hall." Rather than direct the tourist to the nearest renovated Georgian residence, a cooperative hearer might attribute the speaker's unclarity to her inexperience in British English and direct her to the Town Hall. Usually such misunderstandings in conversation can be corrected through discussion. However, such opportunities for repair do not exist in experimental and survey research. Consequently, experimenters may not notice ambiguities in their response formats, which are systematically reinterpreted by participants, thus leading to systematic biases in the results obtained. This seems to have been the case in much basic attribution research (Hilton, 1990b; Turnbull & Slugoski, 1988).

Grice (1975) also noted that there may be *clashes* between two or more of the maxims, such that it may be impossible fully to meet one maxim without breaching the other(s). For example, when required to make judgments under uncertainty, respondents often will find themselves unable both to be completely certain (maxim of quality) as well as maximally informative (maxim of quantity) and will resolve the conflict by finding a principled balance between the two. Thus, Tversky and Kahneman (1983) considered the possibility that the conjunction "error" observed in their studies – that is, the tendency to treat the likelihood of a conjunction, $P(A \& B)$, as more probable than its least typical constituent – to result from their participants' tendency to assign probabilities to the alternatives in terms of their highest expected value, that is, some product of truthfulness *and* informativeness. Although Tversky and Kahneman rejected this interpretation of their results, Mosconi and Macchi (1996) recently showed that in a pragmatic context such as the courtroom, a person who provides the more inclusive class as an answer (e.g., "the accused is blond") is perceived as being evasive or "reticent" relative to the one who provides the included class (e.g., "the accused is blond and has a moustache"), and indeed the latter answer was judged "more probable" than the former. Another example might be the tendency for people to prefer mentioning basic-level categories (Rosch, 1978) over their subordinate (informative but unlikely) or superordinate (likely but uninformative) classes in identification tasks (Tversky & Kahneman, 1983). Note that both of these examples assume that cooperative speakers try to be informative, not just true.

### Attributions about the Speaker and the Choice of Rational Interpretations

A major criterion for attributing rationality is consistency (Strawson, 1952). Below, we show how rational interpretations of utterances are selected because they are consistent with the conversational context, and specifically beliefs about the speaker. We begin with an example of how attributions about the speaker might guide interpretations of the quantifier "some."

As noted above, the trade-off between the maxims of quality and quantity implies that speakers should try to be as informative as possible without running the (undue) risk of being false. Thus, the interpretations hearers choose may in large part depend on attributions they have made about the speaker's knowledge of and interests in the topic under discussion. For example:

1. "Some of the policemen beat up the protester."

This statement could convey one of two different implicatures, either:

2. "Some of the policemen beat up the protester" (but the speaker knows that not all of them did).

or

3. "Some of the policemen beat up the protester" (but the speaker does not know whether all of them did).

Levinson (1983) characterizes the first implicature as a *K*-implicature (because the speaker *knows* that the stronger assertion is not the case) and the second a *P*-implicature (because the stronger assertion is *possible*, owing to the speaker's lack of relevant knowledge). One may reasonably surmise that the hearer is more likely to draw the *K*-implicature if he or she considers the speaker to be very knowledgeable about the topic (e.g., an eyewitness who was there) than not (e.g., a person reporting the incident at second or third hand).

In some circumstances, however, the hearer may not draw the *K*-implicature even if he or she assumes that the speaker is indeed knowledgeable about the event. Such would be the case if the speaker were a police spokesman at a press conference who wished to limit perceptions of police brutality in a critical public. The spokesman may not want to tell lies, thus observing the maxim of quality, but may only commit himself to the weakest possible statement about police aggression that is consistent with evidence known to the public. If the hearer attributes noncooperativeness of this kind to the speaker, then the hearer may assume that the spokesman may be seeking to avoid committing himself to stronger statements that would be relevant, but damaging to presentational goals that the police force might have.

It is not difficult to think of other factors that might affect the interpretation of such statements. For example, if the hearer knows that the speaker is a foreigner with a limited control of English and not know words such as *a few* or *many*, which the speaker might reasonably have used to specify the proportion of policemen involved, then the hearer might treat *some* as being vague, and consistent with either a low or high proportion of policemen (see Moxey & Sanford, 1987; Politzer, 1993 for further discussions of pragmatic interpretation of quantifiers).

*Consistency in Interpretation and Reasoning*

In experimental tasks, there are thus two major stages in arriving at a judgment from the information given, both of which require the participant to make rational choices. The first comprises interpreting the task. Here the participant chooses the most *rational interpretation* using the criterion of consistency with higher-order assumptions about conversation and knowledge about the discourse context, and specifically attributions about the speaker. The second stage involves applying a *normative model of reasoning* to the representation thus formed, for example, by applying Bayes's theorem to a belief updating problem, Mill's method of difference to a causal problem, and so on. A schematic diagram of this two-stage process is given in Figure 36.1.

Most research on judgment and reasoning has focused on the second stage of rational inference. As will be seen below, anomalies found in experiments on judgment and reasoning have typically been attributed to inadequate understanding of normative models of inference, such as Bayes's rule, Mill's method of difference, *modus tollens*, and so on. Less attention has been paid to the first stage, however, wherein apparently irrational judgments may be due to interpretations made at the conversational inference stage.

We thus argue that participants enter the experimental and survey situation with prior expectations about the experimenter. Manipulating participants' perceptions of the experimenter or survey researchers' cooperativeness, intentionality, authority, and knowledge should affect the interpretations made and thus the final judgments that are produced. In addition, the general assumption of cooperativeness may cause information normally thought of as "incidental" to the experimental task, such as response scales, to be treated as relevant. Below, we review evidence that supports these claims. First, this provides support for the attributional model of conversational inference by showing how information about source characteristics changes output judgments. Even where task interpretations have not been directly assessed, this at least offers prima facie evidence that participants may be applying Grice's maxims of conversation to the interpretation of experimental messages. And second, in so doing, this also calls into question the classification of some of these participants' responses as errors.

## Attributions about the Experimenter and Rational Inference

There is general evidence that experiments may be regarded as social interactions in which the participants' attributions about the experimenter affect their behavior. Social psychological research quite clearly suggests that participants attribute serious purposes even to patently absurd experiments (Orne, 1962) and behave in a highly cooperative manner in response to some very questionable experimental demands when they view the experimenter

**PROCESSES**                          **CRITERIA OF RATIONALITY**

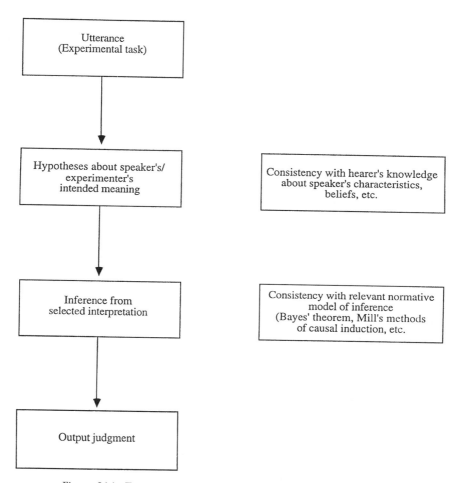

Figure 36.1. Two-stage resolution of uncertainty: Utterance interpretation and judgment.

as being authoritative, but reduce this compliance when the experimenter is perceived as lacking in authority (Milgram, 1974). It is also well known that source attributes such as expertise, credibility, and prior attitude affect participants' responses to experimental attempts at belief change (e.g., McGuire, 1968). In sum, we may surmise that adult experimental participants and survey respondents are generally compliant and treat the experimenter as authoritative and cooperative.

*Intentional and "Random" Presentations of Information
in Base-rate Experiments*

One of the most widely known studies on decision making has been the "engineers and lawyers" problem introduced by Kahneman and Tversky (1973; Tversky & Kahneman, 1974), which has almost invariably been used to support the claim that people are poor decision makers. Their basic finding was that participants were more likely to rely on individuating information about the target than on base-rate information. For example, participants in some conditions were told that the target person "shows no interest in political and social issues and spends most of his free time on his many hobbies, which include home carpentry, sailing, and mathematical puzzles." They were then presented with base-rate information indicating that the target person came from a sample of 100 people, which included either 30 or 70 engineers, depending on the experimental condition. The participants predicted that the target person is probably an engineer, regardless of which base rate they had been given. Kahneman and Tversky attributed this underuse of base-rate information to the operation of the *representativeness heuristic*, that is, participants based their decision about the probability that the target was an engineer on the similarity of the target to their stereotype of engineers.

However, recent evidence suggests that the "underuse of base-rate information" is restricted to "word problems" in which the base-rates are presented verbally. Thus, studies that present base-rate information on-line to participants in the form of learning trials show that participants can use the information appropriately when making judgments (Christensen-Szalanski & Beach, 1982; Medin & Edelson, 1988). Other studies that require participants to make judgments in which they have prior real-world experience or expertise also find no tendency to underutilize base-rate information. For example, participants appropriately use their own implicit knowledge about the base-rate of diseases when judging the probability of a doctor's prediction that they will suffer from that illness (Wallsten, Fillenbaum, & Cox, 1986; Weber & Hilton, 1990). Doctors make appropriate adjustments for the base-rate probability of illnesses in a diagnosis task where they deploy implicit knowledge about symptom-group associations (e.g., weight loss in young girls suggests anorexia, weight loss in old men suggests cancer) in medium-fidelity diagnosis tasks (Fox, 1980; Weber, Bockenholt, Hilton, & Wallace, 1993), whereas they fail to use explicitly presented base-rate information in a medical prognosis task presented in the form of a verbal vignette (Eddy, 1982). Consequently, people's use of the representativeness heuristic may be governed by contextual factors, such as the assumptions they make about verbally presented base-rate information.

In fact, participants' use of base-rate information has been shown to be affected by various pragmatic factors. Krosnick, Li, and Lehman (1990) noted that participants always read individuating information first and base-rate information second in Kahneman and Tversky's (1973) procedure and other similar ones. Consistent with Grice's (1975) third submaxim of manner – "Be orderly" – they hypothesized that the order of presentation of information may have served as a cue to participants to weight the initial information more and the later information less. Consistent with this reasoning they found that participants used the base-rate information more when it was presented first. Krosnick et al. (1990) also took memory measures and were able to rule out the hypothesis that the greater weighting of earlier information was due to enhanced recall at the time of judgment.

If participants were indeed using order of presentation as a cue to determine the intended relevance of the information, then the significance of the cue should be invalidated if the subject believes that it has not been intentionally produced by the experimenter. And this indeed appears to be the case; Krosnick et al. (1990) found that the order effect disappeared when participants were told that the order of presentation had been randomly determined.

Ginossar and Trope (1987, Experiment 6) presented the engineers and lawyers problem to participants as if the information had been generated as part of a card game. Framing the description as having been produced by a "game of chance" would undermine the assumption that the information was produced as part of an intentional communication. Consistent with the attributional model, participants were more likely to use base-rate information in this condition.

Schwarz, Strack, Hilton, and Naderer (1991) employed a related manipulation that undermines the assumption of intentionality. They told participants that the individuating information either had been produced by a panel of psychologists or statisticians who had conducted the original set of interviews with the sample of engineers and lawyers, or had been drawn randomly from the psychologists' or statisticians' files by a computer. In all cases, participants were given the personality description that is "representative" of an engineer and were told that there were 30 engineers in the sample of 100. When told in the psychology condition that the individuating information had been given them by a human researcher, participants on average estimated the probability that the target was an engineer was .76, replicating Kahneman and Tversky's (1973) original findings. However, when told that it had been drawn at random from the psychologist's file by a computer, participants' average estimate was .40, in line with the normative use of base-rate information.

On the other hand, in the "statistics" condition, participants were more likely to weight individuating information when it was drawn at random by a computer from a larger sample of descriptive information (.74) than when it was written by a nonspecified "researcher" (.55). One possible explanation is that random sampling is a valued procedure in a statistics framework, and participants therefore attached greater significance to the "representative" (i.e., randomly selected) information here. Although this explanation is post hoc, it does underscore the importance of attention to participants' inferences about the particular expertise and credibility possessed by the source of information. Grice's (1975) maxim of quality enjoins speakers not to say what they know to be false, or at least not to say what they lack adequate evidence for. Consequently, varying the credibility of the speaker should affect the weight attached to the speaker's messages. Ginossar and Trope (1987, Experiment 5) varied the credibility of the source of information in the engineers and lawyers problem. They found that participants rated the personality description as having the highest probability of being true when the source was a trained psychologist ($M = .78$), lowest when the source was a palm reader ($M = .31$), and intermediate when the source was a beginning interviewer ($M = .59$).

### The Assumed Relevance of Nondiagnostic Information: Accountability and the Activation of Conversational Norms

Although Grice's (1975) maxim of relation prescribes that speakers should include only relevant information, experimenters routinely violate this assumption by deliberately including information that is meant to be irrelevant to the task in hand. A clear example of this is the "dilution" effect studied by Nisbett et al. (1981). They found that participants rationally used information about a target person such as IQ or effort that is diagnostic of that person's grade point average. However, when the description included irrelevant information (age, hair color, etc.), participants made less use of the diagnostic information. From the point of view of probability theory, there is no rational reason for this, as the diagnostic information is still as predictive when presented with nondiagnostic information as when presented alone. Nisbett et al. (1981) posited an intrapsychic explanation in terms of the representativeness heuristic owing to the dilution of the diagnostic information with irrelevant nondiagnostic information, which reduced the perceived similarity of the target person to the target category.

As Tetlock, Lerner, and Boettger (1996) point out, however, the effect is also consistent with an explanation in terms of rational processes of conversational inference. Participants may assume that all the information that they are given, whether diagnostic or nondiagnostic, is mentioned because it is relevant. They may therefore weight all the information as diagnostic. On the assumption that nondiagnostic information is weighted negatively, the dilution effect would be observed. Such an effect would be removed if participants believed that the information had been presented without conscious design.

Tetlock et al. therefore presented the information to participants as having been screened for its relevance (thus activating conversational norms), randomly sampled from a computer database (deactivation of conversational norms), and with no information about the conversational relevance of the information. Half the participants were subjected to an accountability manipulation, being told that they would have to explain their decision to others when the experiment was over. This manipulation has been extremely successful in attenuating biases in judgment usually attributed to heuristics, presumably by inducing more cognitive effort (see Tetlock, 1992, for a review).

Tetlock et al. (1996) found that the accountability manipulation led to more use of the nondiagnostic information in the conditions where conversational norms had been activated or no information either way had been given. This is consistent with participants' belief that the nondiagnostic information must be relevant (otherwise it would not have been mentioned) and the accountable participants' wish to perform well in the judgment task by making maximum use of information that they presume has been guaranteed by the maxim of relevance. These results replicate the findings of Tetlock and Boettger (1989) and suggest that participants' default assumption is that conversational rules are operative in the experiment. Significantly, when conversational norms have been deactivated, they were less likely to use the nondiagnostic information, and thus exhibit the dilution effect. Compared to nonaccountable participants in this condition, accountable ones were actually less likely to fall prey to this error, further reinforcing the view that the dilution effect is attributable to the unreciprocated respect participants have for conversational norms in this particular experimental paradigm.

### Conversational Inference and the Effect of Leading Questions on Memory

One of the best-known *framing* effects concerns the effect of leading questions on memory. In a classic experiment, Loftus and Palmer (1974) showed that the presuppositions loaded into questions about an automobile accident affected participants' memory about that accident. Thus, if participants were asked how fast a car was going when it *smashed* into a truck, they were more likely to give a higher estimate of the speed of the car in a subsequent memory test than if they had been asked how fast the car had been going when it *hit* the truck. These findings were consistent with other results, which showed that participants were inclined to falsely accept presuppositions associated with descriptions of scenes, even when those presuppositions were not actually true of the scenes described (Hornby, 1972, 1974).

However, the effect of leading questions on memory may occur only in social settings where the CP is assumed to hold valid, such as psychology experiments. Participants may have assumed that the experimenter in Loftus and Palmer's (1974) study was cooperative and thus uncritically accepted the presuppositions loaded in the question. In a test of this interpretation, Dodd and Bradshaw (1980) found no effect of leading questions on memory as compared to a control condition when the source was specified as "a lawyer representing a defendant," although they were able to replicate the original result when the source of the leading question was the experimenter, as in Loftus and Palmer's original procedure.

Dodd and Bradshaw's (1980) results are thus consistent with the suggestion that when the leading question was attributed to an adversative source, such as a defending lawyer in an American court, participants suspended the assumption of cooperativeness and were thus not vulnerable to biasing effects of leading questions. Interestingly, participants were still vulnerable to biasing effects from the recall probes about the speed of the car, which varied the descriptive cues used ("How fast was the car going when it hit/collided with/smashed"... etc.). The recall probes all emanated from the same source (the experimenter) regardless of experimental condition, however, and thus may still have been treated as being guaranteed by the assumption of cooperativeness and used to infer the speed of the vehicle. Consequently, although the Loftus and Palmer (1974) results are typically discussed as demonstrating the effect of cognitive biases on memory, they may plausibly be attributed to the operation of conversational assumptions, which guide reconstructive inferences about the speed of the car.

### Part–Whole Contrasts and the Conjunction Fallacy

Strack et al. (1988) reasoned that if a specific question precedes a general one that logically includes it, hearers will interpret the general question to exclude the information already mentioned in the first question. Suppose a survey respondent is asked about satisfaction with her life in general; she is likely to report her global satisfaction with her personal and professional life. If, however, she is asked first about her professional life and then about her life in general, she will treat "life in general" as referring to nonprofessional parts of her life if she wishes to respect the maxim of quantity and give her questioner new information.

Dulany and Hilton (1991) applied this logic to the analysis of Tversky and Kahneman's (1983) conjunction fallacy task. In the best known version of this task, participants read a detailed description of a target person, which runs as follows:

> Linda is 31 years old, single, outspoken, and very bright. She majored in philosophy. As a student she was deeply concerned with issues of discrimination and social justice, and also participated in antinuclear demonstrations.

Participants are then asked to check which one of the following two alternatives is most probable:

> Linda is a bank teller (T)
> Linda is a bank teller and is active in the feminist movement (T & F)

Tversky and Kahneman (1983) report that 85% of participants rate the conjunction of constituents (T & F) as more probable than the single constituent (T). This "conjunction effect" is considered a fallacy since a conjunction of two constituents cannot be more probable than one of the constituents alone. This is because the logic of extensional sets requires that the class of people who are bank tellers and feminists be a subset of the class of people who are bank tellers. Tversky and Kahneman argue that people make this error in probability judgment because they are guided by the representativeness heuristic, which finds the conjunction (T & F) to be more similar to the *model* (i.e., the target description of Linda) than the constituent (T) alone and is therefore judged as more probable. As support, they note that very few participants commit the conjunction fallacy in the *no-model* condition where minimal information about the target ("Linda is 31 years old") is presented, because this fails to activate the representativeness heuristic.

Several researchers have argued from conversational principles that participants interpret "Linda is a bank teller" (T) to mean "Linda is a bank teller who is not active in the feminist movement" (T & *not* F) in this context (Morier & Borgida, 1984; Politzer & Noveck, 1991). If so, the judgment that T is more probable than T & F is no longer a fallacy, since T is implicitly read as indicating another kind of conjunction, namely T & *not-F*. Based on an analysis of attribution processes in conversational inference, Dulany and Hilton (1991) sought to predict the conditions under which participants would draw the absolving interpretation of "Linda is a bank teller." They argued that the rich information given to the participant in the model condition may justify the inference that the experimenter knows a lot about the target. The participant may reason that if the experimenter knows a lot about the target, Linda, then the reason he neglected to say that Linda is not active in the feminist movement is because he knows this not to be the case, thus conveying a K-implicature that Linda is *not* active in the feminist movement. By contrast, in the no-model condition, the participant may reason that the experimenter neglected to say that Linda is a bank teller because he or she does not know whether this is the case or not, thus implying the P-implicature that it is logically possible that Linda either may or may not be a bank teller. The P-implicature corresponds to the extensional interpretation of the constituent that would imply that the conjunction effect is indeed a logical fallacy. Dulany and Hilton (1991) found that participants did in fact draw more K-implicatures in the model condition as predicted. Thus, they were most likely to make interpretations that would absolve them of charges of fallacious reasoning in just those conditions where they were most likely to judge the conjunction as more probable than the constituent. When interpretations were controlled for, a greatly reduced fallacy rate of 25 to 30% was found.

Tversky and Kahneman (1983) acknowledged that participants may be interpreting $T$ to mean $T$ & $not$-$F$ and sought to deal with this problem by developing a *direct* version of the task in which the extensional nature of the conjunct was explicitly stated. Thus, they asked participants to judge the probability of "Linda is a bank teller whether or not she is active in the feminist movement." However, this phrasing is also unsatisfactory as it could be reinterpreted as "Linda is a bank teller even if she is active in the feminist movement," in much the same way as "We will go to the zoo tomorrow *whether or not* it rains" can be interpreted as "We will go to the zoo tomorrow *even if* it rains." Following Grice's maxim of manner, Dulany and Hilton (1991) developed a less ambiguous version of the direct test and found less than half the conjunction fallacies obtained by Tversky and Kahneman (1983). Thus, it seems that ambiguities in the wording used may have led Tversky and Kahneman to overestimate the number of conjunction fallacies committed.

In a closely related analysis, Politzer and Noveck (1991) show how changes to the linguistic structure of the conjunction task that preserve its logical form also reduce error rates. In one of their problems, participants were told that Daniel was a bright high school student and were then asked to judge the probability of the following three predictions about his performance in further studies:

> Daniel entered medical school ($M$)
> Daniel dropped out of medical school for lack of interest (presupposed $M$ & $D$)
> Daniel graduated from medical school (presupposed $M$ & $G$)

In the above case, the constituent *Daniel entered medical school* is presupposed by his later dropping out or graduating. Following the conjunction rule, the implicit conjunctions should be judged as less probable than the constituent. In fact, 30% of participants did judge the one of the conjunctions (*presupposed M & D* or *presupposed M & G*) to be more probable than the constituent ($M$), thus committing the fallacy.

The Daniel problem resembles Tversky and Kahneman's (1983) Linda problem in terms of the class inclusion relations between the alternatives, but differs in that these class inclusion relations are not suggested explicitly. However, it is possible to change the Daniel problem such that these relations are expressed explicitly through the connective *and*, as below:

Daniel entered medical school (*M*)
Daniel entered medical school and dropped out for lack of interest
    (*M & D*)
Daniel entered medical school and graduated (*M & G*)

Politzer and Noveck (1991) argue that, as in the Linda problem, the use of *and* will force the implicature that the constituent implies a conjunction (either *M & not-D* or *M & not-G*). In this explicit condition, 53% of the participants rated one the conjunctions (*M & D* or *M & G*) as more probable than the constituent (*M*). Politzer and Noveck (1991) thus claim that making the inclusion relation explicit through the use of the connective *and* actually worsens performance, thus casting doubt on Tversky and Kahneman's (1983) claim that "people are not accustomed to the detection of nesting among events, even when the relations are clearly displayed" (p. 304). Equally, they observe that the increase in the error rate produced by the introduction of *and* seems to contradict Tversky and Kahneman's (1983) view that "the conjunction fallacy is not restricted to esoteric interpretations of the connective *and*" (p. 303).

Unlike Dulany and Hilton (1991), Politzer and Noveck (1991) did not assess how their manipulation of the explicitness of the class inclusion relation might have affected the implicature drawn from the constituent. Nevertheless, although much remains to be done to elucidate how the response alternatives used in conjunction tasks are interpreted (see Adler, 1991; Fiedler, 1988; Hertwig & Gigerenzer, 1996; Mosconi & Macchi, 1996; Wolford, Taylor, & Beck, 1990, for alternative approaches), enough already seems to have been done to illustrate the value of using conversational pragmatics to analyze these issues.

## The Relevance of "Incidental" Information

Grice's (1975) maxim of relation enjoins speakers to be relevant. Speakers should not mention irrelevant information. Thus, hearers are entitled to assume that all the information given to them is relevant to the task in hand, and, according to the maxim of quality, not misleading in any way. However, experimenters often include "irrelevant" information that may in fact be used by participants to interpret their experimental task. As will be shown below, such "irrelevant" information may be conveyed through the kinds of dependent measures used or through interpretations of the independent variables that were not intended by the experimenter.

### *Relevance, Accessibility, and the Wason Selection Task*

Of all the means yet devised for demonstrating human irrationality, none has been quite so successful as the Selection Task introduced by Peter Wason. This putative test of conditional reasoning presents participants with four cards (e.g., "A," "D," "4," "7") together with a rule to be tested ("If there is a vowel on one side, then there is an even number on the other side"). It has consistently been found that participants tend to choose the rule-confirming card ("4") over one of the two potentially rule-falsifying cards ("7") (see Evans, 1982, for a review). Following the earliest accounts (Wason, 1968; Wason & Johnson-Laird, 1972), psychologists have typically interpreted participants' performance as evidence for a pervasive "confirmation bias" operative in human inference; that is, when faced with the task of testing an hypothesis or belief, people prefer to look for evidence that will support their hypothesis/belief rather than subject it to risk of refutation (see e.g., Evans, 1982; Klayman & Ha, 1987). In fact, the subsequent discovery of many content and contextual factors mediating the basic effect has resulted in a much more complex picture implicating a host of other cognitive mechanisms, for example, the availability (Pollard, 1982) and representativeness (Kahneman & Tversky, 1972; Slugoski, Shields, & Dawson, 1993) heuristics, biconditional inference rule (Wyer & Srull, 1989), pragmatic reasoning schemas (Cheng & Holyoak, 1985), and even an evolved "cheater-detector" algorithm (Cosmides, 1989). Nevertheless, the upshot remains that, at least with regard to the original, abstract version of the task, people's judgments can reliably be shown to depart from a logically valid rule of deductive inference (*modus tollens*) in favor of an invalid rule (*modus ponens*).

According to Sperber, Cara, and Girotto (1995), participants' typical performance on the Selection Task reflects no more than the standard processes of discourse comprehension. Drawing on Sperber and Wilson's (1986) Relevance Theory, they note that it is quite rational for people to attempt to take into account all of the information given by the experimenter on the presumption of its relevance to the performance of the task. Participants apply their intuitive assessments of relevance based on two criteria – anticipated information yield and processing cost – which together determine choice of card or cards. According to the model, typical performance (choice of "A" and "4" cards) is explained by the fact that there are few cognitive consequences (little information yield) associated with the stated rule (the rule is artificial and arbitrary, and its validity is of little personal utility). Hence, assessments of relevance will be based almost entirely on considerations of economy. Since both "vowel" and "even number" are stated in the rule, the experimenter may be assumed by the participant to have done so in the expectation that their joint occurrence is relevant to the solution of the task. Otherwise, why would the speaker have made this information salient and hence easily accessed at the time of judgment? That is, participants are rationally justified in choosing the "A" and "4" cards because they are generally correct in using the most easily accessed information from a speaker's utterance as a cue to its relevance for *any* act of utterance interpretation. Sperber et al. (1995) supported their analysis with four experiments showing, across a variety of content domains, that manipulations of accessibility and information yield can result in normatively correct as well as incorrect response patterns. Echoing our own position, they concluded that, "All you have to do to make people appear irrational is to devise an experiment where their intuitions of relevance go the wrong way. Psychologists too may be subject to illusions of relevance. The strong sense among them that the Selection Task results are highly relevant to our understanding of the human mind may have been . . . precisely such an illusion" (p. 90).

### *Transparency of Reference and Employment of Base-rate Information*

Grice's maxim of manner exhorts speakers to be clear and unambiguous. Using methods similar to those of Dulany and Hilton (1991), Macchi (1995) showed that participants use base-rate information in response to questions that clarify the nature of the judgment required. In one of her experimental tasks, adapted from the suicide problem of Tversky and Kahneman (1982), participants were informed that 80% of a population of young adults were married whereas 20% were single. They were also told that the percentage of deaths by suicide is three times higher among single individuals than among married individuals. Macchi suggests that the phrasing "three times higher" is ambiguous between the percentage of all suicides (implying that 75% of deaths are singles whereas 25% are marrieds) and the percentage among singles as opposed to the percentage among marrieds. It is an empirical question as to which interpretation is more likely to be preferred here, and a normative question for the rules of conversation to decide which is more rational. In any case, participants' median response (3:1) is entirely consistent with the former interpretation. Participants thus appear not to use the base-rate information about the proportion of marrieds and singles in the population in making their judgments.

Noting that this effect may be due to a misunderstanding, Macchi rephrased this item of information as "30% of single individuals and 10% of married individuals commit suicide," which has the merit of being unambiguous and clear, and coherent with the manner of describing the base-rate information, which was also expressed in percentages. In this condition, participants used the base-rate information appropriately.

Macchi also showed that similar changes in discourse structure that add no information but simply clarify the relationship between supersets and subsets produce similar variations in use of base-rate information in Tversky and Kahneman's (1982) suicide problem. In particular, she showed that the manipulation of causal relevance that induced use of base-rate information may have done so because it manipulated discourse structure by explicitly mentioning both the superset (young adults) and the subset (suicides) in the same question. A similar superset–subset phrasing of a logically similar but noncausal problem involving books and paperbacks likewise induced use of base-rate information, whereas a question that referred explicitly to the subset but not the superset did not induce corresponding use of base-rate information. As noted above with other paradigms, an effect (the use of base-rate information) may have been misattributed to a cognitive factor (causal relevance) when in fact it is attributable to discourse processes.

## Implications of Conversational Inference for Attributions of Rationality

The larger issue addressed in this chapter has been the attribution of rationality or irrationality to human judgments. We have argued that in many cases, judgments that have been or could be considered irrational may be in fact be considered rational if prior processes of conversational inference are taken into account. These shape the representation of the task used by the experimental or survey respondent. According to the logic of conversation, participants may interpret what is said to them in particular ways and be justified in adding extra premises that seem to be relevant in interpreting what is said. The inductive nature of conversational inference – its ampliativeness and defeasibility – poses a general problem for the metaphysical assumptions of workers interested in assessing errors in human judgment. This is because such workers normally assume that the correct answer can be determined by applying a normative model to the explicitly given data set, such as Bayes's rule for probabilistic inference tasks (Tversky & Kahneman, 1974).

In what Rommetveit (1978) termed the "negative rationality" perspective, errors are defined by deviations from the predictions of the normative model. The inference task is thus essentially *deductive* in nature; given the premises the "correct" answer can be deduced. However, according to conversational inference it is rational to *add to*, *elaborate*, or *reinterpret* the information given, subject to Gricean assumptions. Consequently, the overall experimental task, of forming a representation of the information given and of reasoning from that representation, also becomes inductive in nature. In assessing the overall rationality of the participant's resonse, the experimenter has to take the rationality of his or her interpretation of the task into account, as well as the rationality of his or her reasoning processes.

The inductive nature of conversational inference suggests that many of the experimental results that have been attributed to faulty reasoning may be reinterpreted as being due to rational interpretations of experimenter-given information. However, the attributional model of conversational inference does *not* imply that participants never make bona fide errors of reasoning. Rather, better specification of these inference processes should enable researchers to identify cases where mistakes may be attributable to conversationally guided interpretations of the judgment task, as opposed to cases where mistakes are due to genuine errors of reasoning. Below, we consider how the present framework can help classify errors more clearly, either by explicitly controlling respondents' assumptions about the conversational relevance of information or by assessing the representations built up on the basis of such assumptions.

*Controlling for Conversational Inference in the Identification of Errors of Reasoning*

It may therefore be that many patterns of judgment that have been classified as "errors" appear quite rational when systematic and normal processes of conversational inference are taken into account. However, the approach also allows us to deem as irrational "errors" that cannot be explained by processes of conversational inference. For example, Tversky and Kahneman (1974) report that numerical anchors produced randomly by a roulette wheel biased subsequent estimates of the number of African countries in the U.N. Since randomness prevents the attribution of intentionality to the number given as an anchor, such an effect can only be the result of a cognitive bias. Likewise, Tetlock's (1985) finding that anchoring effects are reduced by making participants accountable for their judgments are consistent with the "heuristics" view that the effect can be reduced with incentives inducing more cognitive effort.

## Conclusions

Judgments about the intended meaning of utterances are themselves judgments under uncertainty. The inferred intended meaning is likely to be affected by the hearer's perceptions about the speaker. The implication for psychological experiments on rationality is that respondents' answers may deviate from what might be expected from a normative model, not because of an individual's cognitive shortcomings, but because of his or her application of consensually shared rules of conversational inference.

Like previous work on experimental demand effects, the attributional model of conversational inference predicts that source characteristics will affect the experimental respondent's performance. However, previous work on source effects has focused on how respondents comply with experimental demands by, for example, detecting the experimenter's hypothesis and producing the desired behavior (Orne, 1962; Rosenthal & Rubin, 1978). The present approach focuses on how respondents *deviate* from the judgments predicted by the normative model considered relevant by the experimenter, by using rules of conversational inference quite different from those assumed by the experimenter.

Understanding conversational inference may help clarify the question as to which normative model is appropriate in a given situation. Thus, various writers have addressed the question of whether the experimental tasks used are truly representative of real-life decision tasks (e.g., Funder, 1987; Hogarth, 1981; Tetlock, 1985). Sometimes it can be suggested that an alternative normative model of judgment can describe participants' patterns of reasoning, as when Cohen (1979, 1981) suggested a Baconian model of judgment as an alternative to the Bayesian model used by Tversky and Kahneman (1974). One advantage of the conversational framework is, of course, that it can help identify how responses reflect one reasoning process rather than another by better specifying the implicit premises that the respondent derives from the information explicitly given. For example, Hilton (1990a, 1991) shows how laypeople's causal attributions can be seen to follow a normative model of causal inference, namely the analysis of variance, when the role of presupposed knowledge in completing the data-matrix necessary for the computation of an ANOVA or its equivalent is taken into account.

Recognition of the conversational context of the psychology experiment may thus enable researchers to better recognize the rationality of participants' judgments. It is also important to recognize, however, how processes of conversational inference may produce errors in real-world setting. This could happen in several ways. First, hearers may be inaccurate in their perceptions of speakers, thus causing them to misinterpret utterances. While this is a common source of miscommunication, it may be that some errors in social perception are systematic. For example, Fussell and Krauss (1992) suggest that hearers overestimate the mutual knowledge they share with speakers owing to the false-consensus effect. Second, as Levinson (1995) suggests, many reasoning heuristics may have evolved because they are adaptive in contexts of social interaction. For example, the expectation that errors of interpretation will be quickly repaired may be correct when we are interacting with a human being, but incorrect when managing a complex system such as an aircraft, a nuclear power plant, or an economy. The evolutionary adaptiveness of such an expectation to a conversational setting may explain why people are so bad at dealing with lagged feedback in other settings.

Recognition of linguistic and conversational factors may also have practical implications for facilitating statistical reasoning. Presentations of numerical information in terms of frequencies rather than probabilities (Fiedler, 1988; Gigerenzer & Hoffrage, 1995) or that make set–superset relations clear (Macchi, 1995) are likely to facilitate correct understanding of statistical problems. Clearly, newspapers and other media should take advantage of this.

Thus, the attributional model of conversational inference introduces a social dimension to the study of reasoning and inference. It suggests that no utterance is depersonalized, that all messages have a source, and that reasoning and inference processes typically operate on socially communicated information. However, it does by no means deny the importance of cognitive processes. Rather, it argues that the processes of inference, reasoning, and understanding are shaped by interpersonal assumptions even in supposedly "neutral" settings such as the laboratory experiment. Hence, it offers a view of reasoning and inference that better reflects the social context in which our judgments and decisions typically are elicited and deployed. As such, the generality of this approach can be gauged by the success with which it has been applied to understanding reasoning and judgment in a wide number of domains, such as children's cognitive development (Adler, 1984; Donaldson, 1982; Siegal, 1991; Siegal & Peterson, 1994), causal explanation processes (Hilton, 1990a, 1991; Turnbull & Slugoski, 1988), as well as attitude measurement and survey research (Schwarz & Strack, 1991; Tourangeau & Razinski, 1988).

### References

Adler, J. E. (1984). Abstraction is uncooperative. *Journal for the Theory of Social Behaviour, 14,* 165–181.

Adler, J. E. (1991). An optimist's pessimism: Conversation and conjunction. In E. Eells & T. Maruszewski (Eds.), Probability and rationality. *Poznan Studies in the Philosophy of the Sciences and Humanities, 21,* 251–282.

Austin, J. L. (1962). *How to do things with words.* Oxford, UK: Clarendon Press.

Brown, P., & Levinson, S. C. (1987). *Politeness: Some universals in language usage.* Cambridge: Cambridge University Press.

Cheng, P. W., & Holyoak, K. J. (1985). Pragmatic reasoning schemas. *Cognitive Psychology, 17,* 391–416.

Christensen-Szalanski, J. J., & Beach, L. R. (1982). Experience and the base-rate effect. *Organizational Behavior and Human Performance, 29,* 270–78.

Clark, H. H., & Haviland, S. E. (1977). Comprehension and the given-new contract. In R. O. Freedle (Ed.), *Discourse production and comprehension* (pp. 1–40), Norwood, NJ: Ablex.

Cohen, L. J. (1979). On the psychology of prediction: Whose is the fallacy? *Cognition, 8,* 385–407.

Cohen, L. J. (1981). Can human irrationality be experimentally demonstrated? *Behavioral and Brain Sciences, 4,* 317–330.

Cosmides, L. (1989). The logic of social exchange: Has natural selection shaped how humans reason? Studies with the Wason Selection Task. *Cognition, 31,* 187–276.

Dodd, D. H., & Bradshaw, J. M. (1980). Leading questions and memory: Pragmatic constraints. *Journal of Verbal Learning and Memory, 19,* 695–704.

Donaldson, M. (1982). Conservation: What is the question? *British Journal of Psychology, 73,* 199–207.

Dulany, D. L., & Hilton, D. J. (1991). Conversational implicature, conscious representation and the conjunction fallacy. *Social Cognition, 9,* 85–100.

Eddy, D. (1982). Probabilistic reasoning in clinical medicine: Problems and opportunities. In D. E. Kahneman, P. Slovic, & A. Tversky (Eds.), *Judgment under uncertainty: Heuristics and biases.* Cambridge: Cambridge University Press.

Evans, St. B. T. (1982). *The psychology of deductive reasoning.* London: Routledge & Kegan Paul.

Fiedler, K. (1988). The dependence of the conjunction fallacy on subtle linguistic cues. *Psychological Research, 50,* 123–129.

Fox, J. (1980). Decisions under the influence of memory. *Psychological Review, 87,* 190–211.

Funder, D. C. (1987). Errors and mistakes: Evaluating the accuracy of social judgment. *Psychological Bulletin, 101,* 75–90.

Fussell, S. R., & Krauss, R. M. (1992). Coordination of knowledge in communication: Effect of speakers' assumptions about what others know. *Journal of Personality and Social Psychology, 62,* 378–391.

Gigerenzer, G., & Hoffrage, U. (1995). How to improve Bayesian reasoning without instruction: Frequency formats. *Psychological Review, 102,* 684–703.

Ginossar, Z., & Trope, Y. (1987). Problem solving in judgment under uncertainty. *Journal of Personality and Social Psychology, 52,* 464–474.

Grice, H. P. (1975). Logic and conversation. In P. Cole & J. L. Morgan (Eds.), *Syntax and semantics. Vol. 3: Speech acts* (pp. 41–58). New York: Academic Press.

Henle, M. (1962). On the relation between logic and thinking. *Psychological Review, 69,* 366–378.

Hertwig, R., & Gigerenzer, G. (1996). The "conjunction fallacy" revisited: Polysemy, conversational maxims, and frequency judgments. Presented at the 3rd International Conference on Thinking, London, U.K.

Hilton, D. J. (1990a). Conversational processes and causal explanation. *Psychological Bulletin, 107,* 65–81.

Hilton, D. J. (1990b). Formal models of causal attribution: Conceptual, methodological and empirical issues. Unpublished manuscript.

Hilton, D. J. (1991). A conversational model of causal explanation. In W. Stroebe & M. Hewstone (Eds.), *European Review of Social Psychology, 2,* 51–81.

Hogarth, R. M. (1981). Beyond discrete biases: Functional and dysfunctional aspects of judgmental heuristics. *Psychological Bulletin, 90,* 197–217.

Hornby, P. A. (1972). The psychological subject and predicate. *Cognitive Psychology, 3,* 632–642.

Hornby, P. A. (1974). Surface structure and presupposition. *Journal of Verbal Learning and Verbal Behavior, 13,* 530–538.

Johnson-Laird, P. N. (1983). *Mental models.* Cambridge: Cambridge University Press.

Kahneman, D., & Tversky, A. (1972). Subjective probability: A judgment of representativeness. *Cognitive Psychology, 3,* 430–454.

Kahneman, D., & Tversky, A. (1973). On the psychology of prediction. *Psychological Review, 80,* 237–251.

Klayman, J., & Ha, Y.-W. (1987). Confirmation, disconfirmation, and information in hypothesis-testing. *Psychological Review, 94,* 211–222.

Krosnick, J. A., Li, F., & Lehman, D. (1990). Order effects and the underuse of base-rate information. *Journal of Personality and Social Psychology, 59,* 1140–1152.

Levinson, S. C. (1983). *Pragmatics.* Cambridge: Cambridge University Press.

Levinson, S. C. (1995). Interactional biases in human thinking. In E. Goody (Ed.), *Social intelligence and interaction.* Cambridge: Cambridge University Press.

Loftus, E. F., & Palmer, J. C. (1974). Reconstruction of automobile destruction. *Journal of Verbal Learning and Verbal Behavior, 13,* 585–589.

Macchi, L. (1995). Pragmatic aspects of the base-rate fallacy. *The Quarterly Journal of Experimental Psychology, 48*(1), 188–206.

McGuire, W. J. (1968). The nature of attitudes and attitude change. In G. Lindzey & E. Aronson (Eds.), *The handbook of social psychology* (Vol. 3, 2nd ed). Reading, MA: Addison Wesley.

Medin, D. L., & Edelson, S. (1988). Problem structure and the use of base-rate information from experience. *Journal of Experimental Psychology: General, 117,* 68–65.

Milgram, S. (1974). *Obedience to authority.* New York: Harper & Row.

Morier, D. M., & Borgida, E. (1984). The conjunction fallacy: A task-specific phenomenon. *Personality and Social Psychology Bulletin, 10*, 243–252.

Mosconi, G., & Macchi, L. (1996). Pragmatic factors in the conjunction fallacy. Presented at the 3rd International Conference on Thinking, London, U.K.

Moxey, L., & Sanford, A. J. (1987). Quantifiers and focus. *Journal of Semantics, 5*, 189–206.

Nisbett, R. E., Zukier, H., & Lemley, R. H. (1981). The dilution effect: Nondiagnostic information. *Cognitive Psychology, 13*, 248–277.

Orne, M. T. (1962). On the social psychology of the psychological experiment: With particular reference to demand characteristics and their implications. *American Psychologist, 17*, 776–783.

Payne, J. W., Bettman, J. R., & Johnson, E. J. (1992). Behavioral decision theory: A constructive processing perspective. *Annual Review of Psychology, 43*, 87–131.

Politzer, G. (1993). *La psychologie du raisonnement: Lois de la pragmatique et logique formelle.* Thèse pour le Doctorat d'Etat ès Lettres et Sciences Humaines. Université de Paris VIII, U.F.R. de Psychologie.

Politzer, G., & Noveck, I. (1991). Are conjunction rule violations the result of conversational rule violations? *Journal of Psycholinguistic Research, 20*, 83–102.

Pollard, P. (1982). Human reasoning: Some possible effects of availability. *Cognition, 12*, 65–96.

Rommetveit, R. (1978). On Piagetian cognitive operations, semantic competence, and message-structure in adult-child communication. In I. Markova (Ed.), *The social context of language.* Chichester, UK: Wiley.

Rosch, E. (1978). Principles of categorization. In E. Rosch & B. B. Lloyd (Eds.), *Cognition and categorization.* Hillsdale, NJ: Erlbaum.

Rosenthal, R., & Rubin, D. B. (1978). Interpersonal expectancy effect: The first 345 studies. *The Behavioral and Brain Sciences, 3*, 377–415.

Schank, R. C., & Abelson, R. P. (1977). *Scripts, plans, goals, and understanding: An enquiry into human knowledge structures.* Hillsdale, NJ: Erlbaum.

Schuman, H., & Presser, S. (1981). *Questions and answers in attitude surveys: Experiments on question form, wording and context.* New York: Academic Press.

Schwarz, N., & Strack, F. (1991). Context effects in attitude surveys. In W. Stroebe & M. Hewstone (Eds.), *European Review of Social Psychology* (Vol. 2). Chichester, UK: Wiley.

Schwarz, N., Strack, F., Hilton, D. J., & Naderer, G. (1991). Base-rates, representativeness and the logic of conversation. *Social Cognition, 9*, 67–84.

Searle, J. R. (1969). *Speech acts: An essay in the philosophy of language.* Cambridge: Cambridge University Press.

Siegal, M. (1991). *Knowing children: Experiments in conversation and cognition.* Hillsdale, NJ: Erlbaum.

Siegal, M., & Peterson, C. C. (1994). Children's theory of mind and the conversational territory of cognitive development. In C. Lewis & P. Mitchell (Eds.), *Children's early understanding of mind and the conversational territory of cognitive development.* Hove, UK: Erlbaum.

Slugoski, B. R. (1995). Mindless processing of requests? Don't ask twice. *British Journal of Social Psychology, 34*, 335–353.

Slugoski, B. R., Shields, H. A., & Dawson, K. A. (1993). Relation of conditional reasoning to heuristic processing. *Personality and Social Psychology Bulletin, 19*(2), 158–166.

Slugoski, B. R., & Turnbull, W. M. (1988). Cruel to be kind and kind to be cruel: Sarcasm, banter and social relations. *Journal of Language and Social Psychology, 7*, 101–121.

Sperber, D., & Wilson, D. (1986). *Relevance: Communication and cognition.* Oxford: Basil Blackwell.

Sperber, D., Cara, F., & Girotto, V. (1995). Relevance theory explains the selection task. *Cognition. 57*, 31–95.

Strack, F., Martin, L. L., & Schwarz, N. (1988). Priming and communication: Social determinants of information use in judgments of life satisfaction. *European Journal of Social Psychology, 18*, 429–442.

Strawson, P. F. (1952). *Introduction to logical theory*. London: Methuen

Tetlock, P. E. (1985). Accountability: The neglected social context of judgment and choice. *Research in Organizational Behavior, 7*, 297–332.

Tetlock, P. E. (1992). The impact of accountability on judgment and choice: Toward a social contingency model. In M. P. Zanna (Ed.), *Advances in experimental social psychology* (Vol. 25). New York: Academic Press.

Tetlock, P. E., & Boettger, R. (1989). Accountability: A social magnifier of the dilution effect. *Journal of Personality and Social Psychology, 57*, 388–398.

Tetlock, P. E., Lerner, J., & Boettger, R. (1996). The dilution effect: Judgmental bias, conversational convention, or a bit of both? *European Journal of Social Psychology, 26*, 914–934.

Tourangeau, R., & Razinski, K. (1988). Cognitive processes underlying context effects in attitude measurement. *Psychological Bulletin, 103*, 299–31.

Turnbull, W., & Slugoski, B. R. (1988). Conversational and linguistic processes in causal attribution. In D. J. Hilton (Ed.), *Contemporary science and natural explanation: Common-sense conceptions of causality*. Brighton, UK: Harvester.

Tversky, A., & Kahneman, D. (1974). Judgment under uncertainty: Heuristics and biases. *Science, 185*, 1124–1131.

Tversky, A., & Kahneman, D. (1981). The framing of decisions and the psychology of choice. *Science, 211*, 453–458.

Tversky, A., & Kahneman, D. (1982). Causal schemas in judgments under uncertainty. In M. Fishbein (Ed.), *Progress in social psychology* (Vol. 1). Hillsdale, NJ: Erlbaum.

Tversky, A., & Kahneman, D. (1983). Extensional versus intuitive reasoning: The conjunction fallacy in probability judgment. *Psychological Review, 90*, 293–315.

Wallsten, T. S., Fillenbaum, S., & Cox, J. A. (1986). Base-rate effects on the interpretations of probability and frequency expressions. *Journal of Memory and Language, 25*, 571–587.

Wason, P. C. (1968). Reasoning about a rule. *Quarterly Journal of Experimental Psychology, 20*, 273–281.

Wason, P. C., & Johnson-Laird, P. N. (1972). *The psychology of reasoning: Structure and content*. London: Batsford.

Weber, E. U., Böckenholt, U., Hilton, D. J., & Wallace, B. (1993). Clinical and base-rate information as determinants of diagnoses. *Journal of Experimental Psychology: Learning, Memory and Cognition, 19*, 1151–1164.

Weber, E. U., & Hilton, D. J. (1990). Context effects in the interpretation of probability words: The effects of base-rate and severity. *Journal of Experimental Psychology: Human Perception and Performance, 16*, 781–789.

Wolford, G., Taylor, H. A., & Beck, J. R. (1990). The conjunction fallacy? *Memory and Cognition, 18*, 47–53.

Wyer, R. S., & Srull, T. K. (1989). *Memory and cognition in its social context*. Hillsdale, NJ: Erlbaum.

# Part XII

# Critiques and New Directions II

Continuing the final group of chapters, in the first selection in this section, Kleinmuntz (Chapter 37) takes up a controversial practical question that has been central to JDM research since its inception. If you had to make an important prediction, judgment, or decision, would you do better trusting your intuition or a mechanical procedure of some sort (a formula, a computerized decision aid)? We have seen pieces of this continuing debate in earlier chapter (e.g., Dawes, Chapter 23; Hammond et al., Chapter 8, both this volume), but Kleinmuntz provides an overview so broad as to be almost a one-stop course in JDM. He notes the descriptive work on cognitive difficulties and poor task performance; he considers the normative rules and models, and how well they perform; and he surveys the evidence for hybrid systems in which human decision makers and mechanical decision aides interact. He draws his evidence both from lab studies and from a huge range of applications, from accounting to medicine, from management to polygraphy (lie detection). It is just this kind of interdisciplinary pursuit of an important practical and intellectual question that makes JDM such an exciting field.

Baron (Chapter 38) is concerned with some socially important judgments and decisions that have a pretty clear moral flavor to them. Should one, for example, launch a vaccination program that will save lives but will directly cause the deaths of some smaller number? Many people are reluctant to cause direct harm in this way, even if the indirect payoffs are better. Baron argues that such decisions violate our general rule of choice: Judge actions by their consequences (e.g., in the vaccination decision, by the number of lives saved). He therefore sees these "nonconsequential" choices as errors. Since not everyone agrees, Baron takes some care to build a philosophical justification of the general consequential rule. His chapter can thus be seen as an extension of the heuristics-and-biases idea of setting up a normative rule, observing that people depart systematically from it, and explaining the differences in terms of biases flowing from (in this case) overgeneralized application of generally useful rules. (This chapter also provides an

677

introduction to a wonderful journal, *Behavioral and Brain Sciences*, in which each article is accompanied by numerous short comments from others in the field and the author's response to them. It's a great way to get up to speed on interesting issues in the field, and the commentaries that accompanied Baron's article are well worth reading if you want to dig into this area further.)

As we saw earlier (Part IX) much of the experimental work on risk has been done with very simple, two-outcome gambles. Lopes (Chapter 39) has worked instead with multioutcome gambles, such as lotteries with many tickets, each printed with a different amount of money. This task shifts the subject's attention away from the individual payoffs and toward their overall pattern – whether they are mainly small with a few highs, all clustered around the middle, or whatever. Her studies using these multioutcome gambles have led her to a new theory of how people assess risk, based on their balancing of the desirability of a secure, low-end payoff ("security"), and the attraction of a chancy, high-end payoff ("potential"). Different people strike different balances, reflected in their target or "aspiration" levels. Lopes places her SP/A (security-potential/aspiration) theory in its historical context, showing how it parallels and contrasts with earlier examinations of risk over several hundred years. She also has some wise thoughts on the value of simple algebraic models and how best to construct them.

The last chapter (Connolly & Beach, Chapter 40) is intended to reinforce the message that JDM work is going on outside of the traditional SEU model and its variants. Some of this work is novel, some even flaky, and all of it is at quite early stages of development. It thus looks quite puny against the magnificent bulk of the SEU-type models, with several centuries of development behind them. The essay takes one of these novel approaches, Image Theory, and tries to identify the core issues it raises, the questions that will still need answering even if current versions of the theory are discarded. The authors see the core contrast between Image Theory and traditional models as being its attention to contextual connectedness, the embedding of the decision maker in a network of actions, plans, and values all potentially linked to one another. Traditional models tend to strip the world down to a choice, its likely direct consequences, and some evaluation of those consequences. Image Theory tries to restore the links: that actions are embedded in a network of other actions, and tie together into sequences we think of as strategies; that preferences are derived from networks of values that connect to one another (recall Keeney & McDaniels, Chapter 7, this volume); and that an effort to move around in such a network is likely to depend a lot more on detailed local knowledge (of oneself and of the world) than on any comprehensive overview of the whole tangled network. Purposive action, then, is seen as highly local, rather than a particular application of quite general decision skills. Where traditional approaches take a heroic, "have model, will travel" view of the decision maker, the Image Theory view is in many ways a more modest one. This seems an excellent issue on which to close the book: Will the next generation of decision theorists be more taken with the highly general or the deeply specific? Let us hope they will continue to find both as fascinating as we do.

# 37　Why We Still Use Our Heads Instead of Formulas: Toward an Integrative Approach

*Benjamin Kleinmuntz*

More than three decades ago, an article by Meehl (1957) asked, "When shall we use our heads instead of the formula?" He replied that if people have a formula, then they should use their heads only very, *very* seldom. *Heads* in the article's title refers to the processing of data clinically, subjectively, or intuitively; *formula* refers to its nonjudgmental, mathematical, statistical, or mechanical combination.

One purpose of this review is to extend Meehl's (1957) query beyond clinical psychology. Accordingly, it draws examples from medicine, polygraphy, engineering, finance, accounting, management, game playing, and revenue collection. Another objective is to explore the complexity of the question itself. This article addresses six main issues: (a) Cognition is flawed; (b) the flaws are remediable, given proper training and closer correspondence between intuition and task environments; (c) analytical reasoning, formulas, or both can improve thinking; (d) formulas can be used as a standard with which to compare cognition; (e) judgment can be aided when used together with formulas; and (f) there are cost–benefit trade-offs associated with using unaided as well as aided intuition.

Perhaps the most important objective of this critique is to raise an old issue that is again of contemporary interest. For, as Einhorn (1988) and Simon (1986) recently observed, increased access to computers and other decision supports invites new comparisons of human with machine intelligence. This being the case, it is timely to assess the pros and cons of using intuition with and without decision aids. Although this chapter begins on a divisive note – whether to use the head *or* the formula – it concludes by recommending that *both* be used. By so doing, I aspire to foster further research aimed at exploring how, when, and where using the head, the formula, or both will improve decisions.

This chapter originally appeared in *Psychological Bulletin*, 1990, *107*, 296–310. Copyright © 1990 by American Psychological Association. Reprinted by permission.

Before embarking on this inquiry, I simply want to note that in what follows the terms *prediction, forecasting, cognition, thought, inference, judgment, choice, diagnosis, decision making, intuition, reasoning,* and *problem* solving are often used interchangeably, although more careful distinctions have been made elsewhere (e.g., see Anderson & Reder, 1987; Billings & Scherer, 1988; Einhorn & Hogarth, 1982; Tversky, Sattah, & Slovic, 1988). In this chapter, such distinctions and precision are unnecessary.

### Statistical *or* Intuitive Judgment

#### Argument and Some Evidence for Formulas

One of the earliest calls for the scientific study of judgment came from Meehl's (1954) influential book, *Clinical Versus Statistical Prediction*. He argued that many judgments are best made statistically, not intuitively. He reviewed 20 empirical studies comparing the two prediction modes. Only once was intuition better than statistics. Meehl (1965) later increased this box-score tally to 51 studies, of which 33 favored the head; and 17 demonstrated "approximate equality" of the two approaches (see J. S. Wiggins, 1973, pp. 182–189). Using a somewhat different framework, Sawyer (1966) reviewed 45 studies. He found none in which clinical prediction excelled.

This form of scorekeeping, which became an integral part of the so-called clinical versus statistical prediction controversy, has all but subsided in intensity over the years, albeit with an occasional spontaneous recovery (e.g., Dawes, 1976, 1979, 1988; Einhorn, 1986; Goldberg, in press; Holt, 1978, 1986; B. Kleinmuntz, in press; Meehl, 1986; Sarbin, 1986). An early study in this debate, that by Goldberg (1965), was particularly important for the formula side. It provided strong evidence that in predicting a dichotomous diagnosis, a simple linear composite of five Minnesota Multiphasic Personality Inventory scales outperformed the best from among 13 clinicians (for decision rule alternatives to this formula, see Alexander & Kleinmuntz, 1962; Meehl & Dahlstrom, 1960). Other studies, using various mechanical modes of information processing, obtained similar results (e.g., see Dawes, 1971; Goldberg, 1969, 1971; Grebstein, 1963; B. Kleinmuntz, 1963; Sawyer, 1966). Thus, the evidence seemed clearly to favor the formula's use in personality assessment.

#### Counterargument but No Evidence for Heads

One of Meehl's challengers over the years has been Holt (1958, 1970, 1978, 1986). He has found Meehl's analysis of judgmental deficiency disconcerting. Holt believed that meaningful person assessment must involve subjectivity. Evidently, the clinician is necessary so as to perceive, integrate, synthesize, and hence intuit a theory of the person being assessed.

The evidence favoring such intuition, however, has been meager. For example, the one study that showed the head to be equally as good as, if not better than, the formula (e.g., Lindzey, 1965; see also Meehl, 1965) was properly criticized for its methodological flaws (e.g., Goldberg, 1968a). Its current status is that, at best, it can be considered a tie (see Dawes, 1976, 1979, 1988; Wiggins, 1973, p. 185). Holt's position, therefore, being devoid of empirical support, is untenable.

In any case, Meehl's (1957, 1967) view does not differ radically from Holt's. Meehl clearly stated that humans excel over formulas in selected predictive tasks. For example, he (1954, p. 24) illustrated this with the case of Professor X, for whom a prediction equation yields a .90 probability of going to the movie on a particular night. If Professor X, however, were to have just broken his leg, then the equation would not hold. The broken leg exemplifies the importance of special cases.

Writing on the topic recently, Meehl (1986) had this to say about intuition: "95% of the ordinary decisions made by working practitioners [in mental health settings] are not comparable in richness and subtlety to that of a good psychoanalytic hour" (p. 373). On behalf of the formula, he observed, "When you check out at a supermarket, you don't eyeball the heap of purchases and say to the clerk, 'Well it looks to me as if it's about $17.00 worth; what do you think?' The clerk adds it up" (p. 372). It seems, then, that Meehl is not the wicked actuary often portrayed by some on the "clinical" side.

### Controversy Fallout: Cognition at Center Stage

These polemics aside, however, Meehl's (1954, 1957, 1959, 1960, 1965, 1967, 1986) main contribution over the years has been to place judgment at center stage. He did not deal with it at a general philosophical level, nor did he provide just another tool for the statistical side. Rather, he provided a sound rationale and empirical evidence for the scientific scrutiny of judgment.

This facet of his argument inspired different kinds of studies. Some laboratories, for instance, became less concerned with the relative *accuracy* of the two methods than with what Meehl (1960) called "the cognitive activity of the clinician." This shifted the focus onto the inferential *process*. Hoffman (1960, 1968; see also Wiggins & Hoffman, 1968), for example, proposed linear, configural, and analysis of variance models to describe judgment. Hoffman did not claim that people actually combine information mathematically, nor did he claim that such models outperform humans; instead, he showed the models' descriptive and predictive powers. Perhaps more important, however, Hoffman modeled experts at their best.

Similarly, Hammond (1955) and his associates (e.g., Hammond, Hursch, & Todd, 1964; Hammond & Summers, 1965), somewhat influenced by Meehl but more so by Brunswik's (1952, 1955, 1956) lens model paradigm, also modeled judgment. Hammond and associates showed that the lens model can approximate one's weighting of the cues or predictors in a task. Furthermore, their scheme, with some modification (see Tucker, 1964), demonstrated that the formula captures the optimal or suboptimal use of available environmental cues. It does so by specifying the lower and upper limits of judgmental capability, given the cues of a decision problem. Lens modeling has been explored in a large variety of clinical and nonclinical contexts (e.g., Brady & Rappoport, 1973; Brehmer, 1972; Camerer, 1981; Dudycha & Naylor, 1966; Einhorn, Kleinmuntz, & Kleinmuntz, 1979; Hammond, 1965, 1978; Hammond, Summers, & Deane, 1973; Slovic & Lichtenstein, 1971; Szucko & Kleinmuntz, 1981) and is discussed extensively elsewhere (e.g., Hammond, Stewart, Brehmer, & Steinmann, 1975).

Thus, the study of judgment and cognition, which was once a concern only within clinical psychology, now extends beyond that narrow bound. It is evident in such diverse domains as, for instance, medicine (Blois, 1980; Einhorn, 1972, 1974; B. Kleinmuntz & Elstein, 1987), polygraphy (B. Kleinmuntz & Szucko, 1984; Lykken, 1981), security investment (Slovic, 1972), legal adjudication (Hastie, Penrod, & Pennington, 1983; Saks & Kidd, 1980; Wrightsman, 1987), auditing (R. H. Ashton, Kleinmuntz, Sullivan, & Tomassini, 1989), and management (Blattberg & Hoch, in press). More generally, its importance has been acknowledged in the judgment and decision literature at large (e.g., Arkes & Hammond, 1986; Edwards & von Winterfeldt, 1986; Fischhoff, 1987; Hogarth, 1987; Tversky & Kahneman, 1982). The concern about flawed intuition has also laid the groundwork for using heads in combination with formulas (Blattberg & Hoch, in press; Einhorn, 1972; Hogarth, 1978; Sawyer, 1966), as I indicate later.

In sum, then, I have now made five observations about judgment: (a) It is flawed, (b) it can be outperformed, (c) it can be modeled by formulas, (d) it is worthy of further study, and (e) it may be used in combination with formulas. How it is flawed, what can be done about it, and where and how it is useful in and of itself and in combination with formulas are addressed in the remainder of this chapter.

## Unaided Judgment

Some time ago, Simon (1955, 1956) introduced the concept of *bounded rationality*. This is the idea that cognition is limited vis-à-vis the economist's normative (or rational) model, by which Simon meant that people do not think rationally because doing so, he posited, requires excessive cognitive effort. Instead, they *satisfice*; that is, they set a criterion acceptance level and then use a simplifying decision strategy or heuristic to meet that level. The most important psychological statement and research on this topic thereafter, according to one source (Jungermann, 1986), have come from Tversky and Kahneman (e.g., 1974). Their work, along with that of others, found that people do not judge uncertainty according to the rules of probability and statistics. This is due, in the main, to their using heuristics that in turn lead to cognitive biases and limitations, some of which are discussed next.

*Cognitive Suboptimality*

A common way to demonstrate cognitive suboptimality in the laboratory has been to define a judgment or choice task, determine the optimal response, usually by comparing it with one obtained by applying a Bayesian model (Slovic & Lichtenstein, 1971; see also Edwards, 1968; Phillips & Edwards, 1966), and to observe the extent to which actual behavior deviates from the optimal response. Much of this research focuses on the limitations and errors of probabilistic thinking and is pessimistic about cognition. It also contains explanations for, and possible solutions to, these limitations. I illustrate these issues by arbitrarily discussing four biasing or limiting phenomena (out of a possible dozen or more). More complete reviews of these can be found in the so-called judgment and decision literature (e.g., Arkes & Hammond, 1986; R. H. Ashton et al., 1989; Einhorn & Hogarth, 1981; Hogarth, 1987; Kahneman, Slovic, & Tversky, 1982; D. N. Kleinmuntz, 1987; Pitz & Sachs, 1984; Slovic, Fischhoff, & Lichtenstein, 1977; Wright, 1985). The four phenomena are *illusory correlation, overconfidence, relevance of experience*, and *cognitive overload*.

The first of these, uncovered by Chapman and Chapman (1969), demonstrated how people's prior expectations of perceived relations bias inferences. Chapman and Chapman taught naive subjects to associate personality characteristics with human figure drawing cues. Most subjects indeed learned to see what they expected to see. The subjects also overestimated the frequency of the learned co-occurrences. One example is the association of large eyes with suspiciousness, an illusory correlation that has also become popular among experienced clinical psychologists (Chapman & Chapman, 1971; for a critique of these studies, see Hammond, 1986).

Another biasing phenomenon is overconfidence, which was identified by Oskamp (1962, 1965) among clinical psychologists whose confidence, but not necessarily diagnostic accuracy, increased when provided additional information about psychiatric cases. Worse yet, Holsopple and Phelan (1954) earlier reported that the most confident clinicians tend to be the least accurate (see also Arkes, 1981), a finding that has serious implications for unwary patients.

Generally, overconfidence can be assessed by keeping a box score of the frequency of predicted outcomes relative to their actual occurrence. According to Einhorn (1980b), this helps "calibrate" human judges by disclosing their forecasting accuracy. Unfortunately, very few experts bother to keep tallies of their performance, perhaps because of sloth, poor record-keeping habits, or, more likely, because they lack awareness of their past cognitive strategies. Evidence of this lack was found by Huesmann, Gruder, and Dorst

(1987). They demonstrated the inability of subjects to report hypnotically induced "forbidden" search strategies in memory. Yet subjects still used this information to solve problems. Similarly, Lewicki, Hill, and Bizot (1988) showed that although unconsciously acquired knowledge can facilitate performance, it cannot always be articulated. Hence, if people will not tally or cannot explicate their forecasting strategies, they cannot reconstruct them. Nor are recall and explication necessarily accurate (see Ericsson & Simon, 1980; Nisbett & Wilson, 1977).

Typical findings are that overconfident people overestimate how much they know, even about the easiest knowledge tasks. They are reasonably well calibrated when their announced odds are low (1:1–3:1), but are less so when their publicized odds are high. Furthermore, they are well calibrated for sports and weather forecasting (for a review of the forecasting literature, see Fischhoff & MacGregor, 1982, 1986; Lichtenstein & Fischhoff, 1977; MacGregor & Slovic, 1986; Murphy & Winkler. 1984; Pitz, 1974; Ronis & Yates, 1987; Yates & Curley, 1985; see also Fischhoff, Slovic, & Lichtenstein, 1977; Lichtenstein, Fischhoff, & Phillips, 1977, 1982; and Wright & Ayton, 1986). Most findings suggest that people tend to be overconfident and thus poorly calibrated for some events on some occasions but are well calibrated under certain circumstances and for some events. Other current research and discussions aimed at sorting out these events, occasions, and conditions appear in a wide variety of domains (e.g., Bazerman, 1983; Edwards & von Winterfeldt, 1986; Saks & Kidd, 1980; Slovic, 1982; Thaler, 1986).

The problem for most people is that overconfidence, as noted by Einhorn and Hogarth (1978), leads to overweighting of the importance of occurrences that confirm their hypotheses. This results in their ignoring or not collecting information that may be unfavorable to their hypotheses. This, in turn, impedes learning from environmental feedback, with its deleterious effect on future predictions (see Einhorn, 1980a; Goldberg, 1968b; see also Einhorn & Hogarth, 1981, and Hammond et al., 1973).

Regarding the relevance of experience for predictive accuracy, research suggests that experience alone may not be important (Garb, 1989; Goldberg, 1959, 1968b, 1970; B. Kleinmuntz & Szucko, 1982, 1984, 1987; Oskamp, 1962, 1965; Szucko & Kleinmuntz, 1981; Turner, 1966; Watson, 1967). In many decision settings, inexperienced practitioners, and even naive laboratory subjects, perform as well (or as poorly) as more experienced ones (Goldberg, 1959). These results, according to Brehmer (1980), are exactly what they should be, given that experience alone often yields little feedback information from which to learn (for an extensive review of the effects of cognitive feedback on multiple measures of performance, see Balzer, Doherty, & O'Connor, 1989).

Finally, research that has its roots in the information-processing psychology of Newell and Simon (1972) provides additional evidence suggesting that cognition is bounded. For example, studies by Kotovsky, Hayes, and

Simon (1985) found that memory capacity and cognitive processing capability in solving toy problems (e.g., Tower of Hanoi) are easily overloaded. Correct problem solution depends on learning to use appropriate decision rules for the problem at hand, which, in turn, calls for careful study of the features of complex problems *and* the capacities of the information processor.

## Cognitive Correctives

The emerging judgment and decision literature is attending increasingly to *debiasing*, which is aimed at identifying variables that contribute to poor judgment. By so doing, the hope is to control and eliminate systematic bias. Fischhoff (1980, 1982a, 1982b, 1987), for example, divided the putative biasing culprits as follows: those due to faulty tasks, those due to faulty judges, or mismatches between judges and tasks.

Regarding biases due to faulty tasks, Fischhoff (1980, 1982a) noted that experimenters possibly present subjects with unfair tasks (e.g., subjects did not care about, were confused by, became suspicious of, were unable to express what they knew about, or were given too many tasks). They also present confusing or carelessly designed tasks that overlook what subjects can or cannot do. Fischhoff's solutions are to clarify task instructions, use better response modes, and ask fewer questions.

Biases that arise because of faulty judges are traceable to the selection of subjects who are incorrigibly untrainable. This can be corrected in part by extended training programs with feedback. It would be best, however, not to select such subjects. When neither the task nor the judge is apparently at fault, Fischhoff (1980, 1982a) called for an examination of the person–task situation. He suggested selecting subjects with domain-specific expertise or restructuring tasks that permit the best use of existing cognitive skills.

In this context, Nisbett, Krantz, Jepson, and Kunda (1983) recommended the use of formal training in statistics as a corrective. Their recommendation originates in research showing that everyday inductive reasoning is roughly equivalent to using formal statistical principles. Similar advice is offered by others interested in having experts avoid common judgmental biases because once a bias is in place, its influence is difficult to control (e.g., see also Arkes, 1981; Chapman & Chapman, 1969; Christensen & Elstein, in press; Fischhoff, 1979; Politser, 1987; Wood, 1978).

From among these debiasing solutions, the easiest to implement is that of clarifying instructions to subjects. It may also be the most useful. For example, Svenson (1985) found that, among undergraduates challenged by complex laboratory judgment tasks designed to elicit their estimates of probable death risks of persons depicted in eight hypothetical cases, confusion over task requirements caused risk overestimation. Svenson also reported that systematic risk overestimation occurred when they failed to incorporate fully the relevant instructions. On the other hand, people who understood the task attained proper approximations of risk, a finding also reported by Dod (1988) in a study of physicians' risk preferences.

Hogarth (1981) has taken another approach in this regard. His contention is that behavioral decision research needs to focus on continuous prediction occurring in dynamic and complex task environments (see also Hogarth & Makridakis, 1981; Neisser, 1976). By adopting such a framework, laboratory researchers would more closely approximate real-world decision making. Using a simulated continuous and dynamic laboratory task environment, D. N. Kleinmuntz (1985, 1987) and D. N. Kleinmuntz and Thomas (1987) did indeed demonstrate that the use of this framework can lead to new insights about decision making.

Using a different research paradigm, Hammond, Hamm, Grassia, and Pearson (1987) proposed that there is a time for pure intuition and a time for quasi-rational and analytical reasoning. When to use which depends largely on a problem's task characteristics. Accordingly, Hammond et al. devised a cognitive continuum, ranging from intuition at one end to analysis at the other. They also conceptualized a corresponding range of task conditions. At the intuitive pole, the tasks require rapid, unconscious data processing that combines available information by simple averaging. It has low reliability but is moderately accurate. Analysis, the other end of the continuum, is relatively more slow, conscious, and deliberate, but its reliability and accuracy are higher. It entails aggregating information by using organizing principles that are more complicated than averaging. Hammond et al. (1987) do not claim that analytical reasoning is without error. It can produce extreme error. Nevertheless, the importance of their schema, which they tested empirically among a group of highway engineers, is that it permits detailed analyses of how error arises. They did so by facilitating comparisons of intuitive, quasi-rational, and analytical cognition under several task conditions and by closely adjusting the correspondence between the type of task presented (intuition inducing vs. analysis inducing) and the cognitive activity selected (intuition vs. analysis).

To summarize this review so far, I have argued that people are indeed not as good as they think they are at using their heads, but that they can be debiased in a variety of ways, can be formally trained to minimize error, and can be guided to make better decisions. Moreover, by modifying experimental environments so as to resemble real-world complex tasks, people's reasoning can be improved. Finally, by means of detailed analyses of when to use intuition versus more analytical thinking, people can reduce judgmental error.

Having summed up the discussion in this way, it is also noteworthy that there are some who argue for the limited generalizability of laboratory research to real-world decisions (e.g., Christensen-Szalanski & Beach, 1984; Christensen-Szalanski & Bushyhead, 1981; Ebbesen & Konečni, 1975, 1980; Fischhoff, 1987; Funder, 1987). Others, however, have shown that people can be adaptive even in laboratory settings (e.g., Klayman, 1984, 1988; Klayman & Ha, 1987; Paquette & Kida, 1988; Payne, Bettman, & Johnson, 1988; Reder, 1987; see also Payne, 1982). Still others have argued that although people can be stupid in experimental rooms, they function quite adequately in a cognitively complex world (e.g., Toda, 1962; see also Toda, 1980). The question now, given that rational reasoning is possible with proper training and under some conditions, is whether decision aids can improve thinking.

## Aided Judgment

So far I have noted that judgment can be outperformed by simple linear composites of predictors and how decisions can be modeled by a variety of regression approaches. This section focuses on three other types of formula. These are, in turn, the Bayesian, signal detection, and computer approaches.

### Bayesian View

An alternative to the algebraic and additive correlational schemes already encountered is the Bayesian paradigm. It has its recent roots in Savage's (1954, 1972) work on statistical decision theory. Savage was a pioneer in promoting the idea of formalizing subjective probability by combining data and beliefs about the data (see also Edwards, 1954, 1961, 1962, 1971; Edwards, Lindman, & Savage, 1963; Meehl & Rosen, 1955; Slovic & Lichtenstein, 1971). The Bayesian approach can help optimize predictions under uncertainty. It does so by offering a normative model of how people *should* think if they are to think optimally.

A well-known early example of its use in clinical psychology grew out of Rosen's (1954) psychometric efforts and difficulties at predicting suicide, an infrequent occurrence even among the psychiatrically hospitalized. Meehl and Rosen (1955), in a subsequent analysis, demonstrated that in predicting such rare events it is helpful to apply Bayes's rule. Their analysis showed that by incorporating appropriate base rates (i.e., prior probabilities), the Bayesian formula improves on unaided intuition. Moreover, Meehl and Rosen argued that a psychometric device, to be efficient, must outperform predictions based only on prior probability data – a seemingly obvious point, but one that is counterintuitive to practicing clinicians (see also Rorer & Dawes, 1982, on bootstrapping psychometric base rates and Grove, 1985, on why this procedure is not cost efficient in bootstrapping diagnoses).

### Decision Analysis

A formal technique that incorporates Bayes's theorem, decision analysis, is a more recent and elaborate decision support procedure. It adds two essential components to conventional Bayesian thinking (e.g., Edwards, 1971, 1977; Edwards et al., 1963; Hogarth, 1987, especially pp. 177–203; Howard, 1966; Keeney, 1982; Keeney & Raiffa, 1976; Raiffa, 1968). Stated here as questions, these are as follows: (a) What are the consequences of alternative actions? and (b) what are the uncertainties in the environment relevant to the actions and their consequences?

Decision analysis as a decision aid has been applied in a variety of non-clinical (e.g., Arkes & Hammond, 1986, pp. 4–7; Bell, Keeney, & Raiffa, 1977; Gardiner & Edwards, 1975; Kaufman & Thomas, 1977; Keeney, 1982; von Winterfeldt & Edwards, 1986) and clinical disciplines (e.g., Beck, 1986; Beck & Pauker, 1983; Pauker & Kassirer, 1987; Sisson, Schoomaker, & Ross, 1976; for critical and technical reviews, see Hershey & Baron, 1987; Hogarth, 1987, pp. 177–184; Politser, 1981, 1984; Politser & Fineberg, 1987). Decision analysis is useful because it decomposes complex problems, thus simplifying them. It often depicts graphically, in the form of decision trees, the courses of action open to the decision maker, the probabilities associated with their outcomes, and their corresponding consequences. These components are aggregated multiplicatively. Assuming the technique's correct application, decision analysis assists in making better decisions.

A critical assumption in applying this technique, of course, is that experts' preferences, beliefs, and likelihood functions are elicited accurately. Or, as Pitz (1974) reminded readers, "in any decision analysis, the [subjective] evaluation of uncertainty at each stage of the decision is critical to the final solution" (p. 41). The procedure is admittedly not free of subjectivity and, hence, of error.

According to D. N. Kleinmuntz (1990), it is important to identify and control such error potential (e.g., Fischhoff, 1980, 1982a; Hogarth, 1975; Lichtenstein et al., 1982; Wallsten & Budescu, 1983). It is also important to assess the accuracy of preference elicitation (Farquhar, 1984; Fischhoff, Slovic, & Lichtenstein, 1980; Hershey, Kunreuther, & Schoemaker, 1982). D. N. Kleinmuntz (1990) listed numerous corrective procedures that can then be applied to reduce the effects of error in decision-analytic models. The correctives include (a) using multiple assessments to check for consistency, (b) performing sensitivity analyses to modify probabilities and preferences for specific decisions, and (c) building error theories designed to predict, explain, and control the cumulative impact of error on inference and judgment.

### Signal Detectability

Signal detection research, also an outgrowth of statistical decision theory, was originally developed to help detect radar signals in air traffic control systems (e.g., Tanner & Swets, 1954). The idea was to evaluate observers' ability to detect simple sensory stimuli embedded in noise. A practical example would be a situation in which airplane "blips" must be identified on a radar screen. The signals, in this case, the blips, are observed against a background of noisy or extraneous echoes. The observation task is to discriminate between the two classes of events, signals and noise, a seemingly trivial task.

Decision accuracy, however, depends on the *decision criterion* used by observers. The criterion is influenced by cognitive threshold limitations and by various random and systematic biases that, in turn, cause deviations from discriminative optimality. Signal detection theory provides a normative standard with which to compare the precision of observers with their empirical performance. The technique can thus be used to improve detection performance because the comparison yields values that disclose differences between the inherent detectability of noisy signals and the ability to detect them. It has been used successfully in a wide variety of settings where an individual's or a diagnostic system's predictive accuracy must be evaluated (e.g., Lopes, 1982; Mowen & Linder, 1979; Swets, 1964, 1986, 1988; Szucko & Kleinmuntz, 1981, 1985).

### Information-Processing View

Unlike much of the judgment and decision research discussed so far, which has its roots in correlational or statistical decision theory, information-processing psychology views computer program statements as formalisms to represent intelligent problem solving. Its goal is to construct by modeling cognition what McCorduck (1979) called "machines who think." This view broadens the definition of formula to include more than mathematical or statistical approaches as decision support systems. It probably comes closest to Meehl's (1954, p. 38) idea that computers may someday replace thinking.

The computer's potential as a surrogate intelligent system, according to this view, is that its software statements can be used as elements of psychological theories. The idea of computer thinking received an important impetus from the work of Newell and Simon (1961, 1972). Over the years, they have argued and demonstrated (with several generations of information-processing languages) that people can articulate their reasoning by producing *thinking-aloud* protocols while solving problems. Computer thinking, however, has not yet realized its potential (see Reynolds, 1987, pp. 12–13, for a brief description of computer uses in psychology and computer science).

Perhaps the most important outgrowth of this view to date has been to cast the computer into a new and important role. For example, it has led to artificial intelligence, or AI, and expert systems research, which offers the possibility of the computer as a decision support. This expert systems use is described further in the next section on aided and unaided intuition. It will suffice here to indicate that it shares with other formulas the possibility of becoming a powerful tool for aiding thinking, and to note that expert systems are product-directed computer programs, whereas research in AI, generally, is more theory-directed (see Schank, 1984, pp. 32–38, for a clarification of this distinction).

To summarize this section on aided judgment, it is apparent that Bayesian and decision-analysis approaches can offer valuable decision supports if they are properly applied. The errors that arise are often identifiable and therefore controllable. Another decision aid, signal detectability, can also help evaluate and augment judgmental accuracy. Information-processing psychology, which proposes a descriptive modeling approach to thinking, can do likewise. It is also important to note that in applying these formulas, intuitive inputs and monitoring are essential. Therefore, it seems wise to consider the possibility of using the best of both approaches: decision support and judgment, as indicated in the following section.

### Statistical *and* Intuitive Judgment

Some years ago, Edwards (1962) and then Sawyer (1966) proposed that experts can contribute to predictive inference by providing judgments that could be aggregated mechanically. Following up on this idea, Einhorn (1972) demonstrated that when expert measurement and the formula are used together, the combination outperforms either method used alone. For example, he studied expert pathologists who predicted cancer survival. He found that their predictive accuracy was improved by using their heads as measuring devices and formulas as rules to combine the measurements.

Similarly, Blattberg and Hoch (in press) have shown this in a managerial context. In five different business forecasting situations, a 50% model plus a 50% manager solution outperformed either of these decision modes in isolation. Evidently, the improvement over unaided judgment was due to the formula's capitalizing on both the intuiter's "special case" insights (i.e., as in Meehl's, 1954, broken leg example) and the model's reliable combination of this information. A similar result was reported by Showers and Chakrin (1981) in revenue collection. They used the formula as a customer credit screen and the head to provide inputs to their credit evaluation procedures.

Yet another aggregating tack has been reported by Hogarth (1978). He proposed that the validity of expert judgment is enhanced by forming *staticized* groups (i.e., aggregating the opinions of two or more experts). Thus, he developed an analytical model that, given certain conditions, yields group validity data that suggest how many experts should be included in a staticized group. It can also help decide which expert(s) may be added or deleted in order to attain optimality. This and similar group models of judgment and problem solving have been tested in a variety of laboratory and real-world settings and have been found to be quite efficient at improving decision making (e.g., A. H. Ashton & Ashton, 1985; R. H. Ashton, 1986: Clemen, 1986; Clemen & Winkler, 1985, 1987; Davis, 1969; Hill, 1982; Libby & Blashfield,

1978; Makridakis & Winkler, 1983; Morris, 1983, 1986; Steiner, 1972; Winkler, 1986; Winkler & Makridakis, 1983).

*Bootstrapping* (see Dawes, 1971; Dawes & Corrigan, 1974) also provides an illustration of the combined use of heads and formulas. It is the phenomenon whereby a model of the person or persons outperforms the unaided intuition of the modeled person or persons. Essentially, its rationale is quite simple. Humans provide predictor inputs, assigning them their putative weights and monitoring the directions of the resulting predictions. The formula's contribution is its consistent decision-rule application and integration. This head–formula combination can work well (e.g., Bowman, 1963; Camerer, 1981; Dawes, 1971, 1988; Dawes & Corrigan, 1974; Hammond, 1955; Hoffman, 1960, 1968; Hogarth, 1978; B. Kleinmuntz, 1963). But there are problems.

One problem, as Slovic (1972) noted, is that modeling intuition can preserve and reinforce, and perhaps even magnify, existing cognitive biases. The assumption of bootstrapping, however, as well as that of most mechanical processing techniques, is that despite its inclusion of cognitive biases, the prediction formula invariably outperforms unaided intuition because the increased reliability attained by the formula outweighs any effects of bias and intuition (Robin Hogarth, personal communication, February 19, 1989).

Another problem with bootstrapping is that the judges being modeled may not be cognitively competent. B. Kleinmuntz and Szucko (1987), for example, found this to be the case among polygraphers thinking aloud while analyzing lie detection protocols. The difficulty was that the polygraphers were highly fallible. Their predictions were the equivalent of a crapshoot. Even so, as Arkes (personal communication, October 6, 1988) has indicated, the modeling of their reasoning should surpass their performance so long as they provide judgments with even an iota of validity. So it did in several earlier studies where it was shown with lens modeling and signal detection theory how and why polygraphers do not optimize their predictions with the information provided them (B. Kleinmuntz & Szucko, 1982, 1984; Szucko & Kleinmuntz, 1981, 1985).

Cognitive inputs are also important when using Bayes's formula. This is best articulated by such Bayesians as Savage (1972) and Edwards (1972). For example, Savage advocated the use of formal inference for medical diagnosis in combination with the human's "wonderful abilities to make such informal diagnoses, *for which there is sometimes no formal substitute yet available* – as when we recognize an odor or a face" (p. 134; emphasis added). In a similar vein, Edwards (1972) stated, "there are actually two intellectual steps in diagnosis after data collection is complete. One is the *judgment of the meaning* of each individual symptom; the other is the aggregation of the symptoms to reach a diagnosis" (pp. 140–141; see also Berger & Berry, 1988, and Dawes, 1988, on the importance of human judges). The italicized statements are intended to emphasize the importance of subjectivity even in formal procedures.

The entry of computers as decision supports is a relatively recent phenomenon. This expert systems use of computers is designed to perform highly specialized knowledge tasks. Toward this end, so-called knowledge engineers provide strategies and information to computers, by eliciting it either from experts or from textbooks, or both (e.g., Barr & Feigenbaum, 1981; Newell & Simon, 1972; Schank, 1984; Simon, 1979; Waterman, 1986).

Expert systems have been found to be especially useful in fields with shortages of qualified specialists. Their outperformance of humans is due to their ability to accumulate, organize, and codify large quantities of knowledge. Expert systems also decompose, formulate, and view new problems so that they are easy to solve. They do so by searching through a set of possible solutions, finding an efficient or acceptable one, and then modifying and permanently storing the engineered expertise. Once the knowledge and strategies have been acquired and stored, the computer becomes a reliable and swift aggregating tool.

Recent examples of specialties in which expert systems have been constructed as decision supports include analogical problem solving (Eliot, 1986), outer-space-station operation (Leinweber, 1987), legal reasoning (Wiehl, 1989), oncology protocol management (Shortliffe, 1986, 1987), general medical diagnosis (Barnett, Cimino, Hupp, & Hoffer, 1987), and emergency room prediction of myocardial infarction among chest pain patients (Goldman et al., 1988). Most of these systems use a combination of the expert's knowledge and other available information about how best to solve the problem at hand. Current work in the area focuses on doing a task analysis, in combination with the expert, and then designing a system that performs such tasks well. Edwards (personal communication, March 9, 1989) called these *competent* systems to suggest that such task-analysis-based systems can outperform experts, not just simulate them.

### Benefits and Costs of Combining Heads with Formulas

Given the apparent success of diverse formulas, when used alone or together with intuition, and considering the many pitfalls of unaided intuition, one may well ask, "Why are we still using our heads instead of formulas?" The answers to this query are many, depending on whom one asks.

#### Deluded Self-Confidence

A partial answer can be found in the example of de Dombal's research in internal medicine. Over a period of more than a dozen years, he and his coworkers (de Dombal, 1984b; de Dombal, Horrocks, & Walensley, 1975; and de Dombal, Leaper, Stanilaud, McCann, & Horrocks, 1972) developed computer-based Bayesian diagnostic systems of acute abdominal pain. These were quite successful in that by 1975, one of the system's early versions reached 91% accuracy, outperformed senior clinicians (de Dombal et al., 1975), and proved to be largely generalizable, especially when the prior probabilities were properly adjusted to match the local population. Its advantages over unaided judgment were clear.

Despite these virtues, however, de Dombal (1984a) did not recommend the system's routine use. He expressed reservations about its first-rate performance, particularly because human well-being was at risk. In such high-risk situations, he felt, decision makers should rely on their own, not a computer's, expertise. This self-confidence in human expertise has been confirmed in a laboratory study. Arkes, Dawes, and Christensen (1986), for example, have shown that the acceptability to users of a decision aid does not rest on whether it substantially outperforms unaided judgment. Rather, it depends on their *belief* that they have *real expertise* in a domain, thus inspiring confidence in the possibility of beating the odds. That such is the case has subsequently been demonstrated by de Dombal, who has written that he and his group "showed that throughout the UK doctors' performance levels were poor and could themselves improve with the aid of a computer-based decision support [and] a queue formed" (de Dombal, personal communication, March 21, 1989; see also Adams et al., 1986).

### Configural Complexities

Another argument often heard in favor of heads over formulas, particularly in clinical settings, is that clinical decisions entail integrating complex *patterns* of symptoms and signs. Presumably, these are due to their task environments being more ill-structured than those of game playing (e.g., see Abelson, 1985; Wilkinson, Gimbel, & Koepke, 1982). Meehl (1967) called these patterns "configurated functions" that are "visual gestalten [that] can be perceived without the percipient's knowing the underlying formula" (p. 597).

Complexity, however, also characterizes the problems encountered in game playing. Yet game-playing computer programs have been somewhat more successful and have met with greater acceptance than clinicians' computer programs. For example, Simon (1979) estimated that a good chess player needs to know some 1,300 chess piece and position patterns in order to play well; masters and grandmasters, some 50,000 or more such configurations. These estimates of the number of patterns and their complexity *seem* on a par with those existing in many cognitive tasks confronting clinicians. Why, then, have computers not been equally successful among clinical specialists?

Probably because the analogy between clinical information processing and game playing can be pushed too far. There are some similarities, but there are many more differences. Compared with the problems encountered in the clinical sciences, games are well structured and the moves and rules are clearly defined. Moreover, less is at risk if one loses. Clinical problems, *per contra*, are ill-structured. The "opponent" is nature, which carries with it more uncertainty and ambiguity than chess and other games. Also, as noted in the de Dombal example given earlier, the stakes are high if one loses, thus rendering the comparison with chess tenuous. What is needed in clinical settings, however, to carry the analogy further, is an international grand master program, one that beats the odds most of the time. Such convincing evidence may persuade even the most self-confident clinicians to abandon the use of unaided intuition.

### Costs and Availability of Decision Supports

Yet another reason for not using formulas with or without intuition is the costs. These can be computed, but not easily. One way is to compute the added error costs incurred in any of the three modes (i.e., formula vs. intuition vs. both used together). The time and effort invested in doing so can be considerable. Few people possess the financial resources or level of technical and experimental sophistication needed to test the quality of decision making.

Regarding the error possibilities themselves in using formulas, Fischhoff and Beyth-Marom (1983) noted that even Bayesian inference can be error-prone in several ways. First, judgmental and other cognitive biases and miscalculations can disrupt its proper application. Second, one can formulate the wrong hypotheses for particular predictions or actions to be taken. Third, as already noted earlier, one may err in eliciting beliefs and values before incorporating these into a decision analysis. Fourth, prior probabilities or likelihood functions can be estimated or observed incorrectly, or may be ignored altogether. Fifth, even if all the foregoing procedures are correct, one can use the wrong aggregation rule (i.e., averaging instead of multiplying) or apply the right one incorrectly. An evaluation of any of these possibilities can be time and labor intensive.

The other costs of using decision aids can occur in deciding which to use and when and how to use them, assuming one is available. Even here, people need to exercise good judgment; or, to phrase this in decision-analysis terms, the decision to use an aid is a large and difficult choice problem that must itself be decomposed. Thus, the use of an aid, including the decision to use one, requires a high degree of technical wherewithal about the assumptions underlying their proper application. This, too, can be costly, in terms of both time and money (e.g., see Fischhoff, 1980; Hogarth, 1987, p. 197; D. N. Kleinmuntz, 1987).

All of these cost considerations assume that decision support systems are readily available and appealing to prospective users, although most decision makers are unaware of their availability. When made aware of them, they may not use them, or may even oppose their implementation. Clinicians, for instance, or engineers, managers, and others considering the use of decision supports, are unfamiliar with many of the techniques discussed in this chapter. They need to have had contact with the literature on linear models, decision analysis, signal detection, or expert systems. Only a very few have. Even if they have read about these esoteric aids, according to Hogarth (1987, p. 199) "there are a number of resistances to such quantification." These resistances may be quite irrational and based on egocentric and emotional grounds. Moreover, only a few of the knowledgable users have the time or ability to design experiments to evaluate the decision support system's efficacy. This is, again, a difficult and costly undertaking. The dilemma leaves people no choice but to use their heads in deciding whether to use any system at all. In these instances, they usually end up using their heads instead of formulas.

Thus, in sum, one can see that despite the possible advantages of using decision supports, their implementation is often difficult. The difficulty is sometimes monetary, temporal, emotional, or technical. More often it is in the form of the unavailability of the aids and the means for their evaluation. Outside consultation, if affordable, may be necessary; but that, too, is often unavailable.

## Summary and Concluding Comments

The answer as to why people still use their heads, flawed as they may be, instead of formulas, is that for many decisions, inferences, choices, and problems there are as yet no available formulas. When formulas are available, their evaluation is not feasible, when used either alone or in combination with intuition. Coming full circle to the recognition that people may have to use their heads *instead* of, or *together* with, formulas while awaiting new decision support developments, I offer the following guidelines. All of these emerge from the review, but were not previously explicated as such. Meanwhile, the reader may take comfort in Payne et al.'s (1988; Payne, Bettman, & Johnson, 1990) findings, which show that although people's decisions are sometimes suboptimal, they can adapt in directions representing optimal efficiency–accuracy trade-offs:

1. People could delineate the types of decisions that do not easily lend themselves to intuition. For example, it is counterproductive to compute and assign optimal weights to cues. Nor should one attempt to apply decision rules in one's head. In these instances, it is advisable to use a calculator or an appropriate aggregating formula. Recall here Meehl's (1986) advice "not to eyeball the heap of purchases" (p. 372) at the supermarket checkout counter; just add it up.

2. Likewise, one could identify the types of decision problems that are not readily formalized. Meehl (1967), for example, noted that these include predictions that are open ended (i.e., the content of the criterion is created

rather than prespecified) and that deal with special cases. Other types include inferences that require as yet unarticulated decision rules or those that necessitate the intuitive development of a theory of the phenomena under observation. There are also judgments that need to be made or solved quickly if they are to be practical. Add to these the use of the head when available formulas are as yet unevaluated or unvalidated and when dealing with special cases as suggested by Meehl's (1954) broken leg example.

3. Using Guidelines 1 and 2, one could develop meta-rules that stipulate when to use the formulas, heads, or a mixture of both. This calls for familiarization with most available decision aids, as well as with situations for their use. An example of a meta-rule might be to use Blattberg and Hoch's (in press) equal weighting combination of 50% model and 50% expert. Further research may show other solutions to be more appropriate for specific classes of problems. Meanwhile, the 50:50 solution is appealing, first because it is simple. Second, it overcomes some of the resistance to decision supports because it provides experts with the opportunity to continue to participate in decisions. Finally, it has the demonstrated advantage of being invariably more accurate than using either formulas or heads alone.

4. It may be helpful, as well, to differentiate between types of decisions that involve backward rather than forward reasoning. Most clinical inference, for example, is characterized by backward reasoning in that diagnosticians often attempt to link observed effects to prior causes. Compared with this form of post hoc explanation, statistical prediction entails forward reasoning because it is concerned with forecasting future outcomes, given observed information. Whereas the former provides decision makers with many degrees of freedom, statistical reasoning soon confronts them with discrepancies between predicted and actual outcomes. Furthermore, clinical and statistical approaches rest on different assumptions about random error. The clinical side considers error a nuisance variable. The statistical approach, *per contra*, accepts error as inevitable, and in so doing makes less error in prediction in the long run (Einhorn, 1986; see also Einhorn, 1988; Einhorn & Hogarth, 1982, 1986).

5. Regardless of whether backward or forward inferences are made formally, intuitively, or both, one should record their accuracy during the course of a day, week, month, and so on. This entails careful documentation of the heuristics or formulas used for decisions – not an easy assignment. Then what is one to do? Garb's (1989) meta-rule is that when such box-score tallying is not feasible, or when unbiased feedback is unavailable, experts should use available decision aids rather than intuition.

6. Extreme confidence in one's predictive accuracy, particularly without the benefit of outcome feedback, should be a red flag suggesting that, in all likelihood, the predictions are flawed. A post hoc analysis of these predictions is advisable and may indeed identify where one has erred.

7. Considering that people tend to seek out confirming data once they have formulated an idea or hypothesis, researchers should follow Hogarth's (1987, p. 118) suggestion to systematically search for evidence that may disconfirm such a formulation. This is equally true for refuting a model's accuracy. It must be subjected to tests of falsifiability. Then and only then can an idea or a decision support system be refined and strengthened (G. F. Pitz, personal communication, December 5, 1988).

8. Given that intuition involves complex data processing, one should recognize that there are four ways to stray (e.g., see Hogarth, 1987, pp. 4–7): (a) selective perception, perhaps due to anticipatory biases; (b) imperfect information processing, possibly resulting from the same biases; (c) inaccurate calculations due to cognitive limitations; and (d) incorrect reconstructions of events because of biases, faulty memory, or both. An awareness of these possibilities, and the will to ferret them out, plus the determination to correct them, may lead to better decisions.

9. Because most probabilistic estimates have been shown to be systematically biased, constructing a rough scale of predictability may be helpful for a new class of events. Kahneman and Tversky (1979) have suggested that one could then check the new predictions and their outcomes against records of past ones for similar events.

10. Because formal decision aids are also error prone, one could test their before-and-after efficacy. This can be done by careful prior planning, empirical studies, requesting outside evaluative consultation, or a combination of all of these.

11. Wherever feasible, if a formula or aggregating rule is available, its cost efficiency should be tested with and without its use. If its application to simulated (i.e., Monte Carlo) or real-world data shows only slight improvement (or none), it should be discarded.

12. If the formula is an expert system, research might focus on a design that permits it to recognize its inability to solve certain decision problems. For, as Newell (cited in Wertheimer, 1985) observed, expert systems are "shallow; they don't know what they know and why they know it" (p. 29). Moreover, future research might do well also to teach expert systems to communicate their inabilities to users and, perhaps, even suggest alternative approaches to the problem at hand.

The guidelines are practical, but they hardly explain why only a select subset of clinicians and, more generally, experts are outstanding intuiters. Why is it, for instance, that some clinicians earn formidable reputations for their expertise, while others with equal training and experience do not? How come Kasparov, who retained his international grandmaster chess championship, will in all likelihood rely on his wits the next time around? He will probably do so opposite Karpov, not a computer. The task now, clearly, is to plan research that aids lesser mortals to become first-rate experts.

Researchers seem to be on the way to reaching that goal. One measure of this is the increased interest in studying expert–novice differences (e.g., Charness, 1981; Chi, Feltovitch, & Glaser, 1981; Larkin, McDermott, Simon, & Simon, 1980; Murakami, 1990; Shanteau, 1988). Another is the acceptance of decision support systems, which seems to be on the rise. One dramatic instance of the latter can be found in recent newspaper reports of Carnegie Mellon's Hitech and Deep Thought chess programs. Each uses heuristics and strategies that borrow liberally from its creator (Hans Berliner and Feng-Hsiung Hsu, respectively) and can now outwit them as well as some chess grandmasters. This is an interesting bootstrapping *tour de force*. It is also a fine example of how decision aids can work together with specialists who supply their inputs and monitor their outputs. Perhaps in the near future, tournament chess players, as well as other specialists, will show up for work accompanied by their decision support assistants. The likelihood of this possibility will increase as a function of more media exposure to such decision aids. Then prospective users and researchers as well as the public at large will be inured to their appearance in hitherto unusual places. In the interim, however, people will probably continue to rely more on their heads than on formulas.

### References

Abelson, R. P. (1985). A variance explanation paradox: When a little is a lot. *Psychological Bulletin, 97*, 129–133.

Adams, I. D., Chan, M., Clifford, P. C., Cooke, W. M., Dallos, V., de Dombal, F. T., Edwards, M. H., Hancock, D. M., Hewlett, D. J., McIntyre, N., Sommerville, P. G., Spiegelhalter, J. T., Wellwood, J., & Wilson, D. H. (1986). Computer aided diagnosis of acute abdominal pain: A multicentre study. *British Medical Journal, 293*, 800–804.

Alexander, L. B., & Kleinmuntz, B. (1962). Computer program for the Meehl-Dahlstrom MMPI profile rules. *Educational and Psychological Measurement, 22*, 193–199.

Anderson, J. R., & Reder, L. (1987). Effects of number of facts studied on recognition versus sensibility judgments. *Journal of Experimental Psychology: Learning, Memory, and Cognition, 13*, 355–367.

Arkes, H. R. (1981). Impediments to accurate clinical judgment and possible ways to minimize their impact. *Journal of Consulting and Clinical Psychology, 49*, 323–330.

Arkes, H. R., Dawes, R. M., & Christensen, C. (1986). Factors influencing the use of a decision rule in a probabilistic task. *Organizational Behavior and Human Decision Processes, 37*, 93–110.

Arkes, H. R., & Hammond, K. R. (Eds.). (1986). *Judgment and decision making: An interdisciplinary reader*. New York: Cambridge University Press.

Ashton, A. H., & Ashton, R. H. (1985). Aggregating subjective forecasts: Some empirical results. *Management Science, 31*, 1499–1508.

Ashton, R. H. (1986). Combining the judgments of experts: How many and which ones? *Organizational Behavior and Human Decision Processes, 38*, 405–414.

Ashton, R. H., Kleinmuntz, D. N., Sullivan, J. B., & Tomassini, L. A. (1989). Audit decision making. In A. R. Abdel-khalik & I. Solomon (Eds.), *Research opportunities in auditing: The second decade* (pp. 95–132). Sarasota, FL: American Accounting Association, Auditing Section.

Balzer, W. K., Doherty, M. E., & O'Connor, R. Jr. (1989). Effects of cognitive feedback on performance. *Psychological Bulletin, 106*, 410–433.

Barnett, G. O., Cimino, J. J., Hupp, J. A., & Hoffer, E. P. (1987). DX-plain: An evolving diagnostic decision-support system. *Journal of the American Medical Association, 258*, 67–74.

Barr, A., & Feigenbaum, E. A. (1981). *The handbook of artificial intelligence* (Vol. 2). Los Altos, CA: William Kaufmann.

Bazerman, M. (1983). Negotiator judgment. *American Behavioral Scientist, 27*, 211–218.

Beck, J. R. (1986). Laboratory decision science applied to chemometrics: Strategic testing of thyroid function. *Clinical Chemistry, 32*, 1701–1713.

Beck, J. R., & Pauker, S. G. (1983). The Markov process in medical prognosis. *Medical Decision Making, 3*, 419–458.

Bell, D. E., Keeney, R. L., & Raiffa, H. (1977). *Conflicting objectives in decisions*. New York: Wiley.

Berger, J. O., & Berry, D. A. (1988). Statistical analysis and the illusion of objectivity. *American Scientist, 76*, 159–165.

Billings, R. S., & Scherer, L. L. (1988). The effects of response mode and importance on decision making: Judgment versus choice. *Organizational Behavior and Human Decision Processes, 41*, 1–19.

Blattberg, R. C., & Hoch, S. J. (in press). Database models and managerial intuition: 50% model + 50% manager. *Management Science*.

Blois, M. S. (1980). Clinical judgment and computers. *New England Journal of Medicine, 303*, 192–197.

Bowman, E. H. (1963). Consistency and optimality in managerial decision making. *Management Science, 9*, 310–321.

Brady, D., & Rappoport, L. (1973). Policy-capturing in the field: The nuclear safeguards problem. *Organizational Behavior and Human Performance, 9*, 253–266.

Brehmer, B. (1972). Policy conflict as a function of policy differences and policy complexity. *Scandinavian Journal of Psychology, 13*, 208–221.

Brehmer, B. (1980). In one word: Not from experience. *Acta Psychologica, 45*, 223–241.

Brunswik, E. (1952). *The conceptual framework of psychology*. Chicago: University of Chicago Press.

Brunswik, E. (1955). Representative design and probabilistic theory. *Psychological Review, 62*, 193–217.

Brunswik, E. (1956). *Perception and the representative design of psychological experiments* (2nd ed.). Berkeley: University of California Press.

Camerer, C. (1981). General conditions for the success of bootstrapping models. *Organizational Behavior and Human Performance, 27*, 411–422.

Chapman, L. J., & Chapman, J. P. (1969). Illusory correlation as an obstacle to the use of valid psychodiagnostic signs. *Journal of Abnormal Psychology, 74*, 271–280.

Chapman, L. J., & Chapman, J. P. (1971, November). Test results are what you think they are. *Psychology Today*, pp. 18–22.

Charness, N. (1981). Search in chess: Age and skill difference. *Journal of Experimental Psychology: Human Perception and Performance, 7*, 467–476.

Chi, M. I. H., Feltovich, P. J., & Glaser, R. (1981). Categorization and representation of physics problems by experts and novices. *Cognitive Science, 5*, 121–152.

Christensen, C., & Elstein, A. E. (in press). Informal reasoning in the medical profession. In J. F. Voss, D. N. Perkins, & J. Segal (Eds.), *Informal reasoning and education*. Hillsdale, NJ: Erlbaum.

Christensen-Szalanski, J. J. J., & Beach, L. R. (1984). The citation bias: Fad and fashion in the judgment and decision literature. *American Psychologist, 35,* 75–78.

Christensen-Szalanski, J. J. J., & Bushyhead, J. B. (1981). Physician's use of probabilistic information in a real clinical setting. *Journal of Experimental Psychology: Human Perception and Performance, 7,* 928–935.

Clemen, R. T. (1986). Calibration and the aggregation of probabilities. *Management Science, 32,* 312–314.

Clemen, R. T., & Winkler, R. L. (1985). Limits for the precision and value of information from dependent sources. *Operations Research, 33,* 427–441.

Clemen, R. T., & Winkler, R. L. (1987). Calibrating and combining precipitation probability forecasts. In R. Vierte (Ed.), *Probability and Bayesian statistics* (pp. 97–110). New York: Plenum Press.

Davis, J. H. (1969). *Group performance.* Reading, MA: Addison-Wesley.

Dawes, R. M. (1971). A case study of graduate admissions: Application of three principles of human decision making. *American Psychologist, 26,* 180–188.

Dawes, R. M. (1976). Shallow psychology. In J. S. Carroll & J. W. Payne (Eds.), *Cognition and social behavior* (pp. 3–11). Hillsdale, NJ: Erlbaum.

Dawes, R. M. (1979). The robust beauty of improper linear models in decision making. *American Psychologist, 34,* 571–582.

Dawes, R. M. (1988). You can't systematize human judgment: Dyslexia. In J. Dowie & A. S. Elstein (Eds.), *Professional judgment: A reader in clinical decision making* (pp. 150–162). New York: Cambridge University Press.

Dawes, R. M., & Corrigan, B. (1974). Linear models in decision making. *Psychological Bulletin, 81,* 95–106.

de Dombal, F. T. (1984a). Clinical decision making and the computer: Consultant, expert, or just another test? *British Journal of Health Care Computing, 1,* 7–12.

de Dombal, F. T. (1984b). Future progress for computer aids as gastroenterologists. *Frontiers of Gastrointestinal Research, 7,* 186–198.

de Dombal, F. T. Horrocks, J. C., & Walensley, A. (1975). Computer-aided diagnosis and decision-making in the acute abdomen. *Journal of the College of Physicians of London, 9,* 211–223.

de Dombal, F. T., Leaper, D. J., Stanilaud, J. R., McCann, A. P., & Horrocks, J. C. (1972). Computer aided diagnosis of acute abdominal pain. *British Medical Journal, 2,* 9–18.

Dod, J. M. (1988). *Risk preferences among experienced and inexperienced physicians.* Unpublished doctoral dissertation, University of Illinois, Chicago, Illinois.

Dudycha, L. W., & Naylor, J. C. (1966). Characteristics of the human inference process in complex choice behavior situations. *Organizational Behavior and Human Performance, 1,* 110–128.

Ebbesen, E. B., & Konečni, V. J. (1975). Decision making and information in the courts: The setting of bail. *Journal of Personality and Social Psychology, 32,* 805–821.

Ebbesen, E. B., & Konečni, V. J. (1980). On the external validity of decision-making research: What do we know about decisions in the real world? In T. S. Wallsten (Ed.), *Cognitive processes in choice and decision behavior* (pp. 21–45). Hillsdale, NJ: Erlbaum.

Edwards, W. (1954). The theory of decision making. *Psychological Bulletin, 51,* 380–417.

Edwards, W. (1961). Behavioral decision theory. *Annual Review of Psychology, 12,* 473–498.

Edwards, W. (1962). Dynamic decision theory and probabilistic information processing. *Human Factors, 4,* 59–73.

Edwards, W. (1968). Conservatism in human information processing. In B. Kleinmuntz (Ed.), *Formal representation of human judgment* (pp. 17–52). New York: Wiley.

Edwards, W. (1971). Bayesian and regression models of human information process-ing – A myopic perspective. *Organizational Behavior and Human Performance, 6*, 639–648.

Edwards, W. (1972). N = 1. In J. A. Jacquez (Ed.), *Computer diagnosis and diagnostic methods* (pp. 139–151). Springfield, IL: Charles C Thomas.

Edwards, W. (1977). How to use multiattribute utility measurement for social decision making. *IEEE Transactions on Systems, Man and Cybernetics, SMC-7*, 326–340.

Edwards, W., Lindman, H., & Savage, L. J. (1963). Bayesian statistical inference for psychological research. *Psychological Review, 70*, 193–242.

Edwards, W., & von Winterfeldt, D. (1986). On cognitive illusions and their implications. In H. Arkes & K. R. Hammond (Eds.), *Judgment and decision making: An interdisciplinary reader* (pp. 642–679). Cambridge: Cambridge University Press.

Einhorn, H. J. (1972). Expert measurement and mechanical combination. *Organizational Behavior and Human Performance, 7*, 86–106.

Einhorn, H. J. (1974). Expert judgment: Some necessary conditions and an example. *Journal of Applied Psychology, 57*, 562–571.

Einhorn, H. J. (1980a). Learning from experience and suboptimal rules in decision mak-ing. In T. S. Wallsten (Ed.), *Cognitive processes in choice and decision behavior* (pp. 1–20). Hillsdale, NJ: Erlbaum.

Einhorn, H. J. (1980b). Overconfidence in judgment. In R. A. Shweder & D. W. Fiske (Eds.), *New directions for methodology of social and behavioral science: Fallible judgment in behavioral research* (pp. 1–16). San Francisco: Jossey-Bass.

Einhorn, H. J. (1986). Accepting error to make less error. *Journal of Personality Assessment, 50*, 387–395.

Einhorn, H. J. (1988). Diagnosis and causality in clinical and statistical prediction. In D. C. Turk & P. Salovey (Eds.), *Reasoning, inference and judgment in clinical psychology* (pp. 51–70). New York: Free Press.

Einhorn, H. J., & Hogarth, R. M. (1978). Confidence in judgment: Persistence of the illusion of validity. *Psychological Review, 85*, 395–406.

Einhorn, H. J., & Hogarth, R. M. (1981). Behavioral decision theory: Processes of judg-ment and choice. *Annual Review of Psychology, 32*, 53–88.

Einhorn, H. J., & Hogarth, R. M. (1982). Prediction, diagnosis, and causal thinking in forecasting. *Journal of Forecasting, 1*, 23–36.

Einhorn, H. J., & Hogarth, R. M. (1986). Judging probable cause. *Psychological Bulletin, 99*, 3–19.

Einhorn, H. J., Kleinmuntz, D. N., & Kleinmuntz, B. (1979). Linear regression *and* process tracing models of judgment. *Psychological Review, 86*, 465–485.

Eliot, L. B. (1986). Analogical problem-solving and expert systems. *IEEE Expert, 1*, 17–30.

Ericsson, K. A., & Simon, H. A. (1980). Verbal reports as data. *Psychological Review, 87*, 215–251.

Farquhar, P. H. (1984). Utility assessment methods. *Management Science, 30*, 1283–1300.

Fischhoff, B. (1979). Perceived informativeness of facts. *Journal of Experimental Psychology: Human Perception and Performance, 3*, 349–358.

Fischhoff, B. (1980). Clinical decision analysis. *Operations Research, 28*, 28–43.

Fischhoff, B. (1982a). Debiasing. In D. Kahneman, P. Slovic, & A. Tversky (Eds.), *Judg-ment under uncertainty: Heuristics and biases* (pp. 422–444). New York: Cambridge University Press.

Fischhoff, B. (1982b). For those condemned to study the past: Heuristics and biases in hindsight. In D. Kahneman, P. Slovic, & A. Tversky (Eds.), *Judgment under uncertainty: Heuristics and biases* (pp. 335–351). New York: Cambridge University Press.

Fischhoff, B. (1987). Judgment and decision making. In R. J. Sternberg & E. E. Smith (Eds.), *The psychology of human thought* (pp. 153–187). New York: Cambridge University Press.

Fischhoff, B., & Beyth-Marom, R. (1983). Hypothesis evaluation from a Bayesian perspective. *Psychological Review, 90*, 239–260.

Fischhoff, B., & MacGregor, D. (1982). Subjective confidence in forecasts. *Journal of Forecasting, 1*, 155–172.

Fischhoff, B., & MacGregor, D. (1986). Calibrating data bases. *Journal of the American Society for Information Science, 37*, 222–233.

Fischhoff, B., Slovic, P., & Lichtenstein, S. (1977). Knowing with certainty: The appropriateness of extreme confidence. *Journal of Experimental Psychology: Human Perception and Performance, 3*, 552–564.

Fischhoff, B., Slovic, P., & Lichtenstein, S. (1980). Knowing what you want: Measuring labile values. In T. S. Wallsten (Ed.), *Cognitive processes in choice and decision behavior* (pp. 117–141). Hillsdale, NJ: Erlbaum.

Funder, D. C. (1987). Errors and mistakes: Evaluating the accuracy of social judgment. *Psychological Bulletin, 101*, 95–90.

Garb, H. N. (1989). Clinical judgment, clinical training and professional experience. *Psychological Bulletin, 105*, 387–396.

Gardiner, P. C., & Edwards, W. (1975). Public values: Multiattribute utility measurement for social decision making. In M. Kaplan & S. Schwartz (Eds.), *Human judgment and decision processes* (pp. 1–37). New York: Academic Press.

Goldberg, L. R. (1959). The effectiveness of clinicians' judgments: The diagnosis of organic brain damage from the Bender-Gestalt Test. *Journal of Consulting Psychology, 23*, 25–33.

Goldberg, L. R. (1965). Diagnosticians vs. diagnostic signs: The diagnosis of psychosis vs. neurosis from the MMPI. *Psychological Monographs, 79*(9, Whole No. 602).

Goldberg, L. R. (1968a). Seer over sign: The first "good example"? *Journal of Experimental Research in Personality, 3*, 168–171.

Goldberg, L. R. (1968b). Simple models or simple processes? Some research on clinical judgments. *American Psychologist, 23*, 483–496.

Goldberg, L. R. (1969). The search for configural relationships in personality assessment: The diagnosis of psychosis vs. neurosis from the MMPI. *Multivariate Behavioral Research, 4*, 523–536.

Goldberg, L. R. (1970). Man versus model of man: A rationale plus some evidence for a method of improving on clinical inferences. *Psychological Bulletin, 73*, 422–432.

Goldberg, L. R. (1971). Five models of clinical judgment: An empirical comparison between linear and nonlinear representations of the human inference process. *Organizational Behavior and Human Performance, 6*, 458–479.

Goldberg, L. R. (in press). Human mind versus regression equation: Five contrasts. In D. Cicchetti & W. Grove (Eds.), *Festschrift in honor of Paul E. Meehl*. New York: Cambridge University Press.

Goldman, L., et al. (1988). A computer protocol to predict myocardial infarction in emergency department patients with chest pain. *New England Journal of Medicine, 318*, 797–803.

Grebstein, L. (1963). Relative accuracy of actuarial prediction, experienced clinicians, and graduate students in a clinical judgment task. *Journal of Consulting Psychology, 37*, 127–132.

Grove, W. (1985). Bootstrapping diagnoses using Bayes's theorem: It's not worth the trouble. *Journal of Consulting and Clinical Psychology, 53*, 261–263.

Hammond, K. R. (1955). Probabilistic functioning and the clinical method. *Psychological Review, 62,* 255–262.

Hammond, K. R. (1965). New directions in research in conflict resolution. *Journal of Social Issues, 21,* 44–66.

Hammond, K. R. (1978). Toward increasing competence of thought in public policy formation. In K. R. Hammond (Ed.), *Judgment and decision in public policy formation, AAAS selected symposium* (pp. 11–32). Boulder, CO: Westview Press.

Hammond, K. R. (1986). Generalization in operational contexts: What does it mean? Can it be done? *IEEE Transactions on Systems, Man and Cybernetics, SMC-16,* 428–433.

Hammond, K. R., Hamm, R. M., Grassia, J., & Pearson, T. (1987). Direct comparison of the efficacy of intuitive and analytic cognition in expert judgment. *IEEE Transactions on Systems, Man, and Cybernetics, SMC-17,* 753–770.

Hammond, K. R., Hursch, C. J., & Todd, F. J. (1964). Analyzing the components of clinical inference. *Psychological Review, 71,* 438–456.

Hammond, K. R., Stewart, T. R., Brehmer, R., & Steinmann, D. O. (1975). Social judgment theory. In M. F. Kaplan & S. Schwartz (Eds.), *Human judgment and decision processes* (pp. 271–312). New York: Academic Press.

Hammond, K. R., & Summers, D. A. (1965). Cognitive dependence on linear and non-linear cues. *Psychological Review, 72,* 215–224.

Hammond, K. R., Summers, D. A., & Deane, D. H. (1973). Negative effects of outcome feedback on multiple-cue probability learning. *Organizational Behavior and Human Performance, 9,* 30–34.

Hastie, R., Penrod, S. D., & Pennington, N. (1983). *Inside the jury.* Cambridge, MA: Harvard University Press.

Hershey, J. C., & Baron, J. (1987). Clinical reasoning and cognitive processes. *Medical Decision Making, 7,* 203–211.

Hershey, J. C., Kunreuther, H. C., & Schoemaker, P. J. H. (1982). Sources of bias in assessment procedures for utility functions. *Management Science, 28,* 936–954.

Hill, G. W. (1982). Group versus individual performance: Are N + 1 heads better than one? *Psychological Bulletin, 91,* 517–539.

Hoffman, P. J. (1960). The paramorphic representation of clinical judgment. *Psychological Bulletin, 57,* 116–131.

Hoffman, P. J. (1968). Cue-consistency and configurality in human judgment. In B. Kleinmuntz (Ed.), *Formal representation of human judgment* (pp. 53–90). New York: Wiley.

Hogarth, R. M. (1975). Cognitive processes and the assessment of subjective probability distributions. *Journal of the American Statistical Association, 70,* 271–289.

Hogarth, R. M. (1978). A note on aggregating opinions. *Organizational Behavior and Human Performance, 21,* 40–46.

Hogarth, R. M. (1981). Beyond discrete biases: Functional and dysfunctional aspects of judgmental heuristics. *Psychological Bulletin, 90,* 197–217.

Hogarth, R. M. (1987). *Judgement and choice: The psychology of decision* (2nd ed.). Chichester, UK: Wiley.

Hogarth, R. M., & Makridakis, S. (1981). The value of decision making in a complex environment: An experimental approach. *Management Science, 27,* 92–107.

Holsopple, J. G., & Phelan, J. G. (1954). The skills of clinicians in analysis of projective tests. *Journal of Clinical Psychology, 10,* 307–320.

Holt, R. R. (1958). Clinical and statistical prediction: A reformulation and some new data. *Journal of Abnormal and Social Psychology, 56,* 1–12.

Holt, R. R. (1970). Yet another look at clinical and statistical prediction: Or is clinical psychology worthwhile? *American Psychologist, 25,* 337–349.

Holt, R. R. (1978). *Methods in clinical psychology: Predictions and research* (Vol. 2). New York: Plenum Press.

Holt, R. R. (1986). Clinical and statistical prediction: A retrospective and would-be integrative perspective. *Journal of Personality Assessment, 50,* 376–386.

Howard, R. A. (1966). Decision analysis: Applied decision theory. In S. B. Hertz & J. Melese (Eds.), *Proceedings of the Fourth International Conference on Operations Research* (pp. 55–71). New York: Wiley.

Huesmann, L. R., Gruder, C. L., & Dorst, G. (1987). A process model of posthypnotic amnesia. *Cognitive Psychology, 19,* 33–62.

Jungermann, H. (1986). Two camps on rationality. In H. Arkes & K. R. Hammond (Eds.), *Judgment and decision making: An interdisciplinary reader* (pp. 627–641). New York: Cambridge University Press.

Kahneman, D., Slovic, P., & Tversky, A. (Eds.). (1982). *Judgment under uncertainty: Heuristics and biases.* New York: Cambridge University Press.

Kahneman, D., & Tversky, A. (1979). Prospect theory: An analysis of decisions under risk. *Econometrica, 47,* 263–291.

Kaufman, G. M., & Thomas, H. (Eds.). (1977). *Modern decision analysis: Selected readings.* Middlesex, UK: Penguin.

Keeney, R. L. (1982). Decision analysis: An overview. *Operations Research, 30,* 803–838.

Keeney, R. L., & Raiffa, H. (1976). *Decision with multiple objectives: Preferences and value tradeoffs.* New York: Wiley.

Klayman, J. (1984). Learning from feedback in probabilistic environments. *Acta Psychologica, 56,* 81–92.

Klayman, J. (1988). Cue discovery in probabilistic environments: Uncertainty and experimentation. *Journal of Experimental Psychology: Learning, Memory and Cognition, 14,* 317–330.

Klayman, J., & Ha, Y. W. (1987). Confirmation, disconfirmation, and hypothesis testing. *Psychological Review, 94,* 211–228.

Kleinmuntz, B. (1963). Personality test interpretation by digital computer. *Science, 139,* 416–418.

Kleinmuntz, B. (in press). Computerized clinicians: Developments and problems. In D. Cicchetti & W. Grove (Eds.), *Festschrift in honor of Paul E. Meehl.* Minneapolis: University of Minnesota Press.

Kleinmuntz, B., & Elstein, A. S. (1987). Computer modeling of clinical judgment. *Critical Reviews in Medical Informatics, 1,* 209–228.

Kleinmuntz, B., & Szucko, J. J. (1982). On the fallibility of lie detection. *Law and Society Review, 17,* 85–104.

Kleinmuntz, B., & Szucko, J. J. (1984). A field study of the fallibility of polygraphic lie detection. *Nature, 308,* 349–350.

Kleinmuntz, B., & Szucko, J. J. (1987). *Deception, lie detection, and the dynamics of legal decision making.* (Final project report submitted on Grant NES-83-19138). Washington, DC: National Science Foundation.

Kleinmuntz, D. N. (1985). Cognitive heuristics and feedback in a dynamic decision environment. *Management Science, 31,* 680–702.

Kleinmuntz, D. N. (1987). Human decision processes: Heuristics and task structure. In P. A. Hancock (Ed.), *Human factors psychology* (pp. 123–157). North Holland: Elsevier.

Kleinmuntz, D. N. (1990). Decomposition and the control of error in decision analytic models. In R. M. Hogarth (Ed.), *Insights in decision making: A tribute to Hillel J. Einhorn* (pp. 107–126). Chicago: University of Chicago Press.

Kleinmuntz, D. N., & Thomas, J. B. (1987). The value of action and inference in dynamic decision making. *Organizational Behavior and Human Decision Processes, 39*, 341–364.

Kotovsky, K., Hayes, J. R., & Simon, H. A. (1985). Why are some problems hard? Evidence from Tower of Hanoi. *Cognitive Psychology, 17*, 248–294.

Larkin, J. H., McDermott, J., Simon, D. P., & Simon, H. A. (1980). Expert and novice performance in solving physics problems. *Science, 208*, 1335–1342.

Leinweber, D. (1987). Expert systems in space. *IEEE Expert, 2*, 26–38.

Lewicki, P., Hill, T., & Bizot, E. (1988). Acquisition of procedural knowledge about a pattern of stimuli that cannot be articulated. *Cognitive Psychology, 20*, 24–37.

Libby, R., & Blashfield, R. K. (1978). Performance of a composite as a function of the number of judges. *Organizational Behavior and Human Performance, 21*, 121–129.

Lichtenstein, S., & Fischhoff, B. (1977). Do those who know more also know more about how much they know? The calibration of probability judgments. *Organizational Behavior and Human Performance, 2*, 159–183.

Lichtenstein, S., Fischhoff, B., & Phillips, L. D. (1977). Calibration of probabilities: The state of the art. In H. Jungermann & G. de Zeeuw (Eds.), *Decision making and change in human affairs* (pp. 275–324). Dordrecht, The Netherlands: Reidel.

Lichtenstein, S., Fischhoff, B., & Phillips, L. D. (1982). Calibration of probabilities: The state of the art to 1980. In D. Kahneman, P. Slovic, & A. Tversky (Eds.), *Judgment under uncertainty: Heuristics and biases* (pp. 306–334). New York: Cambridge University Press.

Lindzey, G. (1965). Seer versus sign. *Journal of Experimental Research in Personality, 1*, 17–26.

Lopes, L. (1982). Doing the impossible: A note on induction and the experience of randomness. *Journal of Experimental Psychology: Learning, Memory, and Cognition, 8*, 626–636.

Lykken, D. T. (1981). *A tremor in the blood: Uses and abuses of the lie detector*. New York: McGraw-Hill.

MacGregor, D., & Slovic, P. (1986). Perceived acceptability of risk as a decision-making approach. *Risk Analysis, 6*, 245–256.

Makridakis, S., & Winkler, R. L. (1983). Averages of forecasts: Some empirical results. *Management Science, 29*, 987–996.

McCorduck, P. (1979). *Machines who think: A personal inquiry into the history and prospects of artificial intelligence*. New York: W. H. Freeman.

Meehl, P. E. (1954). *Clinical versus statistical prediction: A theoretical analysis and a review of the evidence*. Minneapolis: University of Minnesota Press.

Meehl, P. E. (1957). When shall we use our heads instead of the formula? *Journal of Counseling Psychology, 4*, 268–273.

Meehl, P. E. (1959). A comparison of clinicians with five statistical methods of identifying psychotic MMPI profiles. *Journal of Counseling Psychology, 2*, 102–109.

Meehl, P. E. (1960). The cognitive activity of the clinician. *American Psychologist, 15*, 19–27.

Meehl, P. E. (1965). Seer over sign: The first good example. *Journal of Experimental Research in Personality Research, 1*, 29–32.

Meehl, P. E. (1967). What can the clinician do well? In D. N. Jackson & S. Messick (Eds.), *Problems in human assessment* (pp. 594–599). New York: McGraw-Hill.

Meehl, P. E. (1986). Causes and effects of my disturbing little book. *Journal of Personality Assessment, 50*, 370–375.

Meehl, P. E., & Dahlstrom, W. G. (1960). Objective configural rules for discriminating psychotic from neurotic MMPI profiles. *Journal of Consulting Psychology, 24*, 375–387.

Meehl, P. E., & Rosen, A. (1955). Antecedent probability and the efficiency of psychometric signs, patterns, or cutting scores. *Psychological Bulletin, 52,* 194–216.

Morris, P. A. (1983). An axiomatic approach to expert resolution. *Management Science, 29,* 24–32.

Morris, P. A. (1986). Observations on expert aggregation. *Management Science, 32,* 321–328.

Mowen, J. C., & Linder, D. E. (1979). Discretionary aspects of jury decision making. In L. E. Abt & I. R. Stuart (Eds.), *Social psychology and discretionary law* (pp. 219–239). New York: Van Nostrand.

Murakami, J. S. (1990). *Expert-novice differences in medical problem solving.* Unpublished master's thesis, University of Illinois at Chicago, Department of Psychology.

Murphy, A. H., & Winkler, R. L. (1984). Probability forecasting in meteorology. *Journal of the American Statistical Association, 79,* 489–500.

Neisser, U. (1976). *Cognition and reality: Principles and implications of cognitive psychology.* New York: W. H. Freeman.

Newell, A., & Simon, H. A. (1961). Computer simulation of human thinking. *Science, 134,* 2011–2017.

Newell, A., & Simon, H. A. (1972). *Human problem solving.* Englewood Cliffs, NJ: Prentice-Hall.

Nisbett, R. E., Krantz, D. H., Jepson, C., & Kunda, Z. (1983). The use of statistical heuristics in everyday inductive reasoning. *Psychological Review, 90,* 339–363.

Nisbett, R. E., & Wilson, T. D. (1977). Telling more than we can know: Verbal reports on mental processes. *Psychological Review, 84,* 231–259.

Oskamp, S. (1962). The relationship of clinical experience and training methods to several criteria of clinical prediction. *Psychological Monographs, 76*(Whole No. 547).

Oskamp, S. (1965). Overconfidence in case-study judgments. *Journal of Consulting Psychology, 29,* 261–265.

Paquette, L., & Kida, T. (1988). The effect of decision strategy and task complexity on decision performance. *Organizational Behavior and Human Decision Processes, 41,* 128–142.

Pauker, S. G., & Kassirer, J. P. (1987). Medical progress: Decision analysis. *New England Journal of Medicine, 316,* 250–258.

Payne, J. W. (1982). Contingent decision behavior. *Psychological Bulletin, 92,* 382–402.

Payne, J. W., Bettman, J. R., & Johnson, E. J. (1988). Adaptive strategy selection in decision making. *Journal of Experimental Psychology: Learning, Memory, and Cognition, 3,* 534–552.

Payne, J. W., Bettman, J. R., & Johnson, E. J. (1990). The adaptive decision maker: Effort and accuracy in choice. In R. M. Hogarth (Ed.), *Insights in decision making: A tribute to Hillel J. Einhorn* (pp. 129–153). Chicago: University of Chicago Press.

Phillips, L. D., & Edwards, W. (1966). Conservatism in a simple probability inference task. *Journal of Experimental Psychology, 72,* 346–357.

Pitz, G. F. (1974). Subjective probability distributions for imperfectly known quantities. In L. W. Gregg (Ed.), *Knowledge and cognition* (pp. 29–41). Hillsdale, NJ: Erlbaum.

Pitz, G. F., & Sachs, N. J. (1984). Judgment and decision: Theory and application. *Annual Review of Psychology, 35,* 139–163.

Politser, P. (1981). Decision analysis and clinical judgment: A reevaluation. *Medical Decision Making, 1,* 363–389.

Politser, P. E. (1984). Explanations of statistical concepts: Can they penetrate the haze of Bayes? *Methods of Information in Medicine, 23,* 99–108.

Politser, P. E. (1987). Medical education for a changing future: New concepts for revising texts. *Medical Education, 21*, 320–333.

Politser, P., & Fineberg, H. W. (1987). *Toward predicting the value of a medical decision analysis.* Paper presented at the International Symposium of Forecasting, Boston.

Raiffa, H. (1968). *Decision analysis: Introductory lectures on choices under uncertainty.* Reading, MA: Addison-Wesley.

Reder, L. M. (1987). Strategy selection in question answering. *Cognitive Psychology, 19,* 909–138.

Reynolds, J. H. (1987). *Computing in psychology: An introduction to programming methods and concepts.* Englewood Cliffs, NJ: Prentice-Hall.

Ronis, D., & Yates, J. F. (1987). Components of probability judgment accuracy: Individual consistency and effects of subject matter and assessment method. *Organizational Behavior and Human Decision Processes, 40*, 192–218.

Rorer, L. G., & Dawes, R. M. (1982). A base rate bootstrap. *Journal of Consulting and Clinical Psychology, 50*, 419–425.

Rosen, A. (1954). A detection of suicidal patients: An example of some limitations in the prediction of infrequent events. *Journal of Consulting Psychology, 18*, 397–403.

Saks, M. J., & Kidd, R. F. (1980). Human information processing and adjudication: Trial by heuristics. *Law and Society Review, 15*, 123–160.

Sarbin, T. R. (1986). Prediction and clinical inference: Forty years later. *Journal of Personality Assessment, 50*, 362–369.

Savage, L. J. (1954). *The foundations of statistics.* New York: Wiley.

Savage, L. J. (1972). Diagnosis and the Bayesian viewpoint. In J. A. Jacquez (Ed.), *Computer diagnosis and diagnostic methods* (pp. 131–138). Springfield, IL: Charles C Thomas.

Sawyer, J. (1966). Measurement and prediction, clinical and statistical. *Psychological Bulletin, 66*, 178–200.

Schank, R. C. (1984). *The cognitive computer: On language, learning, and artificial intelligence.* Reading, MA: Addison-Wesley.

Shanteau, J. (1988). Psychological characteristics and strategies of expert decision makers. *Acta Psychologica, 68*, 203–215.

Shortliffe, E. H. (1986). Update on ONCOCIN: A chemotherapy advisor for clinical oncology. *Medical Informatics, 11*, 15–21.

Shortliffe, E. H. (1987). Computer programs to support clinical decision making. *Journal of the American Medical Association, 258*, 61–66.

Showers, J. L., & Chakrin, L. M. (1981). Reducing uncollectible revenue from residential telephone customers. *Interfaces, 11*, 21–31.

Simon, H. A. (1955). A behavioral model of rational choice. *Quarterly Journal of Economics, 69*, 99–118.

Simon, H. A. (1956). Rational choice and the structure of the environment. *Psychological Review, 63*, 129–138.

Simon, H. A. (1979). Information processing models of cognition. *Annual Review of Psychology, 30*, 363–396.

Simon, H. A. (1986). Report of the research briefing panel on decision making and problem solving. *Research Briefings 1986, National Academy of Sciences.* Washington, DC: National Academy Press. (Reprinted in *Interfaces*, 1987, *17*, 11–31)

Sisson, J. C., Schoomaker, E. B., & Ross, J. C. (1976). Clinical decision analysis: The hazard of using additional data. *Journal of the American Medical Association, 236*, 1259–1263.

Slovic, P. (1972). Psychological study of human judgment: Implications for investment decision making. *Journal of Finance, 27*, 779–799.

Slovic, P. (1982). Toward understanding and improving decisions. In W. C. Howell & E. A. Fleishman (Eds.), *Human performance and productivity: Information processing and decision making* (Vol. 2, pp. 157–183). Hillsdale, NJ: Erlbaum.

Slovic, P., Fischhoff, B., & Lichtenstein, S. (1977). Behavioral decision theory. *Annual Review of Psychology, 28,* 1–39.

Slovic, P., & Lichtenstein, S. (1971). Comparison of Bayesian and regression approaches to the study of information processing in judgment. *Organizational Behavior and Human Performance, 6,* 649–744.

Steiner, I. D. (1972). *Group process and productivity.* New York: Academic Press.

Svenson, O. (1985). Cognitive strategies in a complex judgment task: Analysis of concurrent reports and judgments of cumulated risk over different exposure times. *Organizational Behavior and Human Decision Processes, 36,* 1–15.

Swets, J. A. (Ed.). (1964). *Signal detection and recognition by human observers: Contemporary readings.* New York: Wiley.

Swets, J. A. (1986). Form of empirical ROCs in discrimination and diagnostic tasks: Implications for theory and measurement of performance. *Psychological Bulletin, 99,* 181–198.

Swets, J. A. (1988). Measuring the accuracy of diagnostic systems. *Science, 240,* 1285–1293.

Szucko, J. J., & Kleinmuntz, B. (1981). Clinical versus statistical lie detection. *American Psychologist, 36,* 488–496.

Szucko, J. J., & Kleinmuntz, B. (1985). Psychological methods of truth detection. In C. P. Ewing, Jr. (Ed.), *Psychology, psychiatry, and the law: A clinical and forensic handbook* (pp. 441–466). Sarasota, FL: Professional Resource Exchange.

Tanner, W. P., Jr., & Swets, J. A. (1954). A decision-making theory of visual detection. *Psychological Review, 61,* 401–409.

Thaler, R. H. (1986). The psychology and economic conference handbook: Comments on Simon, on Einhorn and Hogarth, and on Tversky and Kahneman. *The Journal of Business, 59*(4, Part 2), S279–S284.

Toda, M. (1962). The design of a fungus eater: A model of human behavior in an unsophisticated environment. *Behavioral Science, 1,* 164–183.

Toda, M. (1980). What happens at the moment of decision? Meta decisions, emotions, and volitions, In J. Sjoberg, T. Tyszka, & J. A. Wise (Eds.), *Human decision making* (Vol. 2). Bodafors, Sweden: Doxa.

Tucker, L. R. (1964). A suggested alternative formulation in the developments by Hursch, Hammond, and Hursch and by Hammond, Hursch, and Todd. *Psychological Review, 71,* 528–530.

Turner, D. R. (1966). Predictive efficiency as a function of amount of information and level of professional experience. *Journal of Projective Techniques and Personality Assessment, 30,* 4–11.

Tversky, A., & Kahneman, D. (1974). Judgment under uncertainty: Heuristics and biases. *Science, 185,* 1124–1131.

Tversky, A., & Kahneman, D. (1982). Evidential impact of base rates. In D. Kahneman, P. Slovic, & A. Tversky (Eds.), *Judgment under uncertainty: Heuristics and biases* (pp. 153–160). New York: Cambridge University Press.

Tversky, A., Sattah, S., & Slovic, P. (1988). Contingent weighting in judgment and choice. *Psychological Review, 95,* 371–384.

von Winterfeldt, D., & Edwards, W. (1986). *Decision analysis and behavioral research.* Cambridge University Press.

Wallsten, T. S., & Budescu, D. V. (1983). Encoding subjective probabilities: A psychological and psychometric review. *Management Science, 29*, 151–173.

Waterman, D. A. (1986). *A guide to expert systems.* Reading, MA: Addison-Wesley.

Watson, C. G. (1967). Relationship of distortion to DAP diagnostic accuracy among psychologists at three levels of sophistication. *Journal of Consulting Psychology, 31*, 142–146.

Wertheimer, M. (1985). A gestalt perspective on computer simulations of cognitive processes. *Computers in Human Behavior, 1*, 19–33.

Wiehl, L. (1989, January 20). Computers assuming new notes at law firms. *New York Times*, p. 24.

Wiggins, J. S. (1973). *Personality and prediction: Principles of personality assessment.* Reading, MA: Addison-Wesley.

Wiggins, N., & Hoffman, P. J. (1968). Three models of clinical judgment. *Journal of Abnormal Psychology, 73*, 70–77.

Wilkinson, L., Gimbel, B. R., & Koepke, D. (1982). Configural self-diagnosis. In N. Hirschberg & L. G. Humphreys (Eds.), *Multivariate applications in the social sciences* (pp. 103–113). Hillsdale, NJ: Erlbaum.

Winkler, R. L. (1986). Expert resolution. *Management Science, 32*, 298–303.

Winkler, R. L., & Makridakis, S. (1983). The combination of forecasts: Some empirical results. *Journal of the Royal Statistical Society*, Series A(146, Part 2), 150–157.

Wood, G. (1978). The knew-it-all-along effect. *Journal of Experimental Psychology: Human Perception and Performance, 4*, 345–353.

Wright, G. (Ed.). (1985). *Behavioral decision making.* New York: Plenum Press.

Wright, G., & Ayton, P. (1986). Subjective confidence in forecasts: A response to Fischhoff and MacGregor. *Journal of Forecasting, 5*, 117–123.

Wrightsman, L. R. (1987). *Psychology and the legal system.* Monterey, CA: Brooks/Cole.

Yates, J. F., & Curley, S. P. (1985). Conditional distribution analyses of probabilistic forecasts. *Journal of Forecasting, 4*, 61–73.

# 38 Nonconsequentialist Decisions

*Jonathan Baron*

I want to defend an approach to the study of errors in decision making based on a comparison of decisions to normative models. I shall argue that this approach is a natural extension of the psychology of reasoning errors and that it has some practical importance. Decisions (and judgments) have consequences. By improving decisions, we might, on the average, improve the consequences. Many of the consequences that people often lament are the result of human decisions, such as those made by political leaders (and, implicitly, by those who elect them). If we can improve decision making, we can improve our lives.

Psychologists can make errors, too, but we can make errors of omission as well as errors of commission. If we fail to point out an error that should be corrected, the error continues to be made. Errors of commission have an extra cost. If we mistakenly try to change some pattern of reasoning that is not really erroneous, we not only risk making reasoning worse but we also reduce our credibility. Arguably, this has happened for many "pop psychologists." Still, we cannot wait for perfect confidence, or we will never act. Academic caution is not the only virtue.

The basic approach I shall take here (Baron 1985, 1988) is to consider three types of accounts or "models" of decision making. Normative accounts are those that specify a standard by which decision making will be evaluated. Descriptive accounts tell us how decision making proceeds in fact. Of particular interest are aspects of decision making that seem nonnormative. If we find such phenomena, we know there is room for improvement. Prescriptive accounts are designs for improving decision making. They can take the form of very practical advice for everyday decision making (Baron et al. 1991) or formal schemes of analysis (Bell et al. 1988). A systematic departure from a normative model can be called an error or a bias, but calling it this is of no use if the error cannot be corrected. Therefore, the ultimate standards are prescriptive. The prescriptive standards that we should try to find will represent the best rules to follow for making decisions, taking into account human limitations in following any standard absolutely. Normative standards are theoretical, to be appealed to in the evaluation of prescriptive rules or individual decisions.

In the rest of this chapter, I shall outline a normative model of decision making. I shall then summarize some departures from that model, mostly based on my own work and that of my colleagues. Most of these departures involve following rules or norms that agree with the normative model much of the time. Departures based on more pernicious rules (e.g., racist ones) doubtless occur too, but less often. I shall discuss the methodological implications of these departures for philosophy and psychology and their prescriptive implications for public policy and education.

### Consequentialism as a Normative Model

Here, I shall briefly defend a simple normative model according to which the best decisions are those that yield the best consequences for achieving people's goals. Goals are criteria by which people evaluate states of affairs, for example, rank them as better or worse. Examples of goals are financial security, maintenance of personal relationships, social good, or more immediate goals such as satisfying a thirst.

Various forms of consequentialism have been developed, including expected-utility theory and utilitarianism. I have defended these particular versions elsewhere (Baron 1993). For present purposes, consequentialism holds simply that the decision should be determined by all-things-considered judgments of overall expected goal achievement in the states to which those decisions immediately lead. In this simple form of consequentialism, the states are assumed to be evaluated holistically, but these holistic evaluations take into account probabilities of subsequent states and the distribution of goal achievement across individuals. Suppose, for example, that the choice is between government programs $A$ and $B$, each affecting many people in uncertain ways. If I judge that the state of affairs resulting from $A$ is, on the whole, a better one than that resulting from $B$ for the achievement of goals, then consequentialism dictates that I should choose $A$. It is irrelevant that program $B$ may, through luck, turn out to have been better. In sum, judgment of expected consequences should determine decisions.

To argue for this kind of consequentialism, I must ask where normative models come from, what their justification could be. I take the idea of a normative model to be an abstraction from various forms of behavior that I described at the outset, specifically those in which we express our endorsement of norms (in roughly the sense of Gibbard 1988), that is, standards of reasoning. The basic function of such endorsement is to induce others to conform to these norms. What reasons could we have for endorsing norms?

Self-interest and altruism give us such reasons. Self-interest gives us reason to endorse norms, such as the Golden Rule, with which we exhort others to help us or to refrain from hurting us. Altruism motivates the same norms: we tell people to be nice to other people. And altruism gives us reason to endorse norms for the pursuit of self-interest. We care about others so we want to teach them how to get what they want. Indirectly, advocacy of such norms helps the advocate to follow them, so we also have a self-interested reason to endorse them.

It might be argued that norms themselves can provide reasons for their own endorsement. For example, those who think active euthanasia should be either legal or illegal want others to agree with them. But in any inquiry about what norms we should endorse, it is important that we put aside the norms we already have, lest we beg the question. In thinking about my own normative standards, I put aside the goals that derive from those standards, although I must treat other people's goals as given when I think about what is best for *them*.

If goal achievement gives us reasons to endorse norms, then, other things being equal, we should endorse norms that help us achieve our goals (collectively, because our reasons are both altruistic and selfish). Other things *are* equal, I suggest, because we have no other reasons for endorsing norms. Goals are, by definition, the motives we have for doing anything. We need not decide here on the appropriate balance of goals of self versus others. This issue does not arise in the examples I shall discuss.

For example, consider two possible norms concerning acts and omissions that affect others. One norm opposes harmful acts. Another opposes both harmful acts and omissions, without regard to the distinction. The second norm requires people to help other people when the judged total harm from not helping exceeds that from helping. Harm includes everything relevant to goal achievement, including effort and potential regret. Which norm should I want others to follow? If others follow the first, more limited, norm, my goals will not be achieved as well, because I would lose the benefit of people helping me when the total benefits exceed the costs. I therefore have reason to endorse a norm that does not distinguish acts and omissions, and I have no reason to distinguish acts and omissions as such in the norms I endorse. Once I endorse this norm, those who accept it will want me to follow it, too, but if I hold back my endorsement for this reason, I will lose credibility (Baron 1993).

Suppose I have a goal opposing harmful action but not opposing harmful omission. This goal is not derived from my moral intuitions or commitments, which we have put aside. In this case, I would have reason to endorse the limited norm. The more people who have such a (nonmoral) goal, the more reason we all have to endorse this norm (out of altruism, at least). But consequentialism would not be violated, for adherence to the norm would in fact achieve people's nonmoral goals. Although this argument leads to a consequentialist justification for a norm distinguishing acts and omissions, the argument is contingent on a (dubious) assumption about human desires.

Consider the case of active versus passive euthanasia. Suppose we believe that there are conditions under which most people would want life-sustaining treatment withheld but would not want to be actively killed. Then, if we do not know what a patient wants, this belief would justify a distinction. However, if we know that the patient has no goals concerning the distinction, we have no reason to make it on the patient's behalf. (Likewise, the slippery-slope argument that active euthanasia will lead to reduced respect for life depends on a contingent fact that could be taken into account if it were true. The slippery slope could also go the other way: refraining from active euthanasia could lead to errors of misallocation of resources and the consequent neglect of suffering.) Our decision would depend on whether death itself was to be preferred, not on the way in which death comes about (assuming that the means of death have no other relevant consequences of their own for people's goals). In sum, we do not necessarily have any reason to want each other to honor a principle distinguishing acts and omissions.

Consider another example. Suppose a girl has a 10 in 10,000 chance of death from a disease. A vaccine will prevent that disease, but there is a 5 in 10,000 chance of death from its side effects. The girl should endorse a norm that tells you to give her the vaccine, assuming that this helps her achieve her goal of living. We would each want one another to act in this way, so we all have reason to endorse this norm. Following Hare (1963), I shall call this kind of argument a Golden Rule argument.

If you have a goal of not putting others at risk through acts in particular and if this inhibits you from vaccinating the girl, she is hurt. She has reason to discourage you from holding such goal. It is in her interest for your goals about your decisions to be concerned only with their consequences. Of course, altruistically, she might be concerned with your own goals about your decisions, so she might conclude that it is on the whole better for you not to vaccinate her. But she has no general reason – apart from what she knows about you in particular – to endorse a norm for you that prescribes nonvaccination. The norms we have selfish reason to endorse are those concerned only with consequences, because those are what affect us.

Even when we endorse norms out of altruism, we have no general reason to endorse a norm treating acts and omissions differently. You might have a goal of not causing harm to *yourself* through acts, so you might not vaccinate yourself. Such a goal would make it more harmful for me to force you to vaccinate yourself, for I would go against that goal. But I have no reason, altruistic or selfish, to endorse a norm that leads you to have such a goal if you do not already have it, for it will not help you achieve your other goals, or mine.

This kind of argument concerning the act–omission distinction differs from other approaches to this issue (see Kuhse 1987, for an enlightening review). Most of these are based on intuitions about cases as data to be accounted for (e.g., the articles in Fischer & Ravizza 1992). Yet it is just these intuitions that are at issue. I suggest that many of them arise from overgeneralizations, to which people – even those who become moral philosophers – become committed in the course of their development. In this case, for example, harmful acts are usually more intentional than harmful omissions, and hence, more blameworthy. But intention is not different in the cases just discussed. People continue to distinguish acts and omissions, however, even when the feature that typically makes them different is absent.

This same argument will apply to the other kinds of norms I shall discuss. In general, the function of normative models for decision making (as described earlier) is not served by any norms other than those that specify attaining the best consequences, in terms of goal achievement. And those norms should not encourage people to have any goals for decision making other than achieving the best consequences. We might be able to go farther than this, specifying norms for the analysis of decisions into utilities and probabilities, for example, but the examples discussed do not require such analysis. (Although the vaccination case involved probabilities, I simply assumed that anyone would judge a lower risk of death to be a better state of affairs: no trading off of probability and utility was required.)

The upshot of this argument is that we have reason to be disturbed, prima facie, when we find others making decisions that violate consequentialism. On further investigation, we might find that no better prescriptive norms are possible. But, unless this is true, these norms will lead to decisions that prevent us from achieving our goals as well as other decisions might. Our goals themselves, including our altruistic goals, therefore, give us reason to be concerned about nonconsequentialist decisions. What we do about this disturbance is another question, to which we might apply consequentialist norms.

## Departures from Consequentialism

I shall now present a few examples of possible violations of consequentialism. I hope these examples make it plausible that nonconsequentialist thinking exists and matters, even if each example is subject to one quibble or another.

### Omission and Status-Quo Bias

Ritov and Baron (1990) examined a set of hypothetical vaccination decisions like the one just described. We compared omission and commission as options within the same choice. In one experiment, subjects were told to imagine that their child had a 10 out of 10,000 chance of death from a flu epidemic, that a vaccine could prevent the flu, but the vaccine itself could kill some number of children. Subjects were asked to indicate the maximum overall death rate for vaccinated children for which they would be willing to vaccinate their child. Most subjects answered well below 9 per 10,000. Of the subjects who showed this kind of reluctance, the mean tolerable risk was about 5 out of 10,000, half the risk of the illness itself. The findings were the same when subjects were asked to adopt the position of a policymaker deciding for large numbers of children. When subjects were asked for justification, some said they would be responsible for any deaths caused by the vaccine, but they would not be (as) responsible for deaths caused by failure to vaccinate. When a Golden Rule argument was presented (Baron 1992), the bias was largely eliminated. Asch et al. (1993) and Meszaros et al. (1992) have found that the existence of this bias correlates with mothers' resistance toward pertussis vaccination (which may produce death or permanent damage in a very few children).

Other studies (Ritov & Baron 1992; Spranca et al. 1991) indicate a general bias toward omissions over acts that produce the same outcome. In one case used by Spranca et al. (1991), for example, subjects were told about John, a tennis player who thought he could beat Ivan Lendl only if Lendl were ill. John knew that Ivan was allergic to cayenne pepper, so, when John and Ivan went out to the customary dinner before their match, John planned to recommend to Ivan the house salad dressing, which contained cayenne pepper. Subjects were asked to compare John's morality in different endings to the story. In one ending, John recommended the dressing. In another ending, John was about to recommend the dressing when Ivan chose it for himself, and John, of course, said nothing. Of the 33 subjects tested, 10 thought that John's behavior was worse in the commission ending; no subject thought the omission was worse. Other studies (Baron & Ritov, in press; Ritov & Baron 1992; Spranca et al. 1991, Experiment 4) show that the bias toward omissions is not limited to cases in which harm (or risk) is the result, although the effect is greater when the decision leads to the worse of two possible outcomes (Baron & Ritov, in press).

Inaction is often confounded with maintaining the status quo; and several studies have shown an apparent bias toward the status-quo/omission option. People require more money to give up a good than they are willing to pay for the same good (Knetsch & Sinden 1984; Samuelson & Zeckhauser 1988; and, for public goods, Mitchell & Carson 1989). Kahneman et al. (1990) showed that these effects were not the result of wealth effects or other artifacts. They are, at least in part, true biases. Although Ritov and Baron (1992) found that this status-quo bias was largely a consequence of omission bias, Schweitzer (in press) found both omission bias without a status-quo option, and status-quo bias without an omission option. Baron (1992) and Kahneman et al. (1990) also found a pure status-quo bias. Status-quo bias, like omission bias, can result from overgeneralization of rules that are often useful, such as, "If it ain't broke, don't fix it."

It is clear that omission and status-quo bias can cause failures to achieve the best consequences, as we would judge them in the absence of a decision. Possible examples in real life are the pain and waste of resources resulting from the prohibition of active euthanasia (when passive euthanasia is welcomed), the failure to consider aiding the world's poor as an obligation on a par with not hurting them (Singer 1979), and the lives of leisure (or withdrawal from worldly pursuits) led by some who are capable of contributing to the good of others.

### Compensation

Compensation for misfortunes is often provided by insurance (including social insurance) or by the tort system. The consequentialist justification of compensation is complex (Calabresi 1970; Calfee & Rubin, in press; Friedman 1982), but, in the cases considered here, compensation should depend on the nature of the injury (including psychological aspects) and not otherwise on its cause or on counterfactual alternatives to it. (The compensation in these cases can help the victim, but it cannot punish the injurer or provide incentive for the victim to complain). Any departure from this consequentialist standard implies that some victims will be overcompensated or others undercompensated, or both.

Miller and McFarland (1986) asked subjects to make judgments of compensation. When a misfortune was almost avoided, more compensation was provided than when it was hard to imagine how it could have been avoided. A possible justification for this difference is that victims were more emotionally upset in the former case than in the latter. Ritov and Baron (1994), however, found the same sort of result when subjects understood that the victim did not know the cause of the injury or the alternatives to it. In all cases a train accident occurred when a fallen tree was blocking the tracks. Subjects judged that more compensation should be provided (by a special fund) when the train's unexpected failure to stop caused the injury than when the suddenness of the stop was the cause. The results were the same whether the failure was that of an automatic stopping device or of a human engineer.

These results can be partially explained in terms of norm theory (Kahneman & Miller 1986), which holds that we evaluate outcomes by comparing them to easily imagined counterfactual alternatives. When it is easy to imagine how things could have turned out better, we regard the outcome as worse. When subjects were told that the outcome would have been worse if the train had stopped (when it did not stop), or if the train had not stopped (when it did), they provided less compensation, as norm theory predicts. Likewise, they provided more compensation if the counterfactual outcome would have been better. But this information about counterfactuals did not eliminate the effect of the cause of the outcome. Hence, norm theory, while supported, is not sufficient to explain all the results. Another source could be overgeneralization of principles that would be applied to cases in which an injurer must pay the victim. The injurer is more likely to be at fault when a device fails or when the engineer fails to stop.

A similar sort of overgeneralization might be at work in another phenomenon, the person-causation bias. Here, subjects judge that more compensation should be provided by a third party when an injury is caused by human beings than when it is caused by nature (Baron 1992; Ritov & Baron, 1994). This result is found, again, when both the injurer (if any) and the victim are unaware of the cause of the injury or of the amount of compensation (Baron 1993), so that even psychological punishment is impossible. For example, subjects provided more compensation to a person who lost a job from unfair and illegal practices of another business than to one who lost a job from normal business competition (neither victim knew the cause). The same result was found for blindness caused by a restaurant's violation of sanitary rules versus blindness caused by a mosquito.

This effect might be an overgeneralization of the desire to punish someone. Ordinarily, punishment and compensation are correlated, because the injurer is punished by having to compensate the victim (or possibly even by the shame of seeing that others must compensate the victim). But when this correlation is broken, subjects seem to continue to use the same heuristic rule. This sort of reasoning might account in part for the general lack of concern about the discrepancy between victims of natural disease, who are rarely compensated (beyond their medical expenses), and victims of human activity, who are often compensated a great deal, even when little specific deterrence results because the compensation is paid by liability insurance.

### Punishment

Notoriously, consequentialist views of punishment hold that two wrongs do not make a right, so punishment is justified largely on the grounds of deterrence. Deterrence can be defined generally to include education, support for social norms, and so on, but punishment must ultimately prevent more harm than it inflicts. Again, I leave aside the question of how to add up harms across people and time. The simple consequentialist model put forward here implies that, normatively, our judgment of whether a punishment should be inflicted should depend entirely on our judgment of whether doing so will bring about net benefit (compared to the best alternative), whether or not the judgment of benefit is made by adding up benefits and costs in some way. (We might want to include here the benefits of emotional satisfaction to those who desire to see punishment inflicted. But we would certainly want to include deterrent effects as well.)

People often ignore deterrence in making decisions about punishment or penalties. Baron and Ritov (in press) asked subjects to assess penalties and compensation separately for victims of birth-control pills and vaccines (in cases involving no clear negligence). In one case, subjects were told that a higher penalty would make the company and others like it try harder to make safer products. In an adjacent case, a higher penalty would make the company more likely to stop making the product, leaving only less safe products on the market. Most subjects, including a group of judges, assigned the same penalties in both of these cases. In another test of the same principle, subjects assigned penalties to the company even when the penalty was secret, the company was insured, and the company was going out of business, so that (subjects were told) the amount of the penalty would have no effect on anyone's future behavior. Baron et al. (1993) likewise found that subjects, including judges and legislators, typically did not penalize companies differently for dumping hazardous waste, whether the penalty would make companies try harder to avoid waste or induce them to cease making a beneficial product. It has been suggested (e.g., Inglehart 1987) that companies have in fact stopped making beneficial products, such as vaccines, exactly because of such penalties.

Such a tendency toward retribution could result from overgeneralization of a deterrence rule. It may be easier for people – in the course of development – to understand punishment in terms of rules of retribution than in terms of deterrence. Those who do understand the deterrence rationale generally make the same judgments – because deterrence and retribution principles usually agree – so opportunities for social learning are limited. Other possible sources of a retribution rule may be a perception of balance or equity (Walster et al. 1978) and a generalization from the emotional response of anger, which may operate in terms of retribution (although it may also be subject to modulation by moral beliefs; see Baron 1992).

A second bias in judgments of punishment is that people seem to want to make injurers undo the harm they did, even when some other penalty would benefit others more. Baron and Ritov (1993) found that both compensation and penalties tended to be greater when the pharmaceutical company paid the victim directly than when penalties were paid to the government and compensation was paid by the government (in the secret-settlement case described earlier). Baron et al. (1993) found (unsurprisingly) that subjects preferred to have companies clean up their own waste, even if the waste threatened no one, rather than spend the same amount of money cleaning up the much more dangerous waste of a defunct company. Ordinarily, it is easiest for people to undo their own harm, but this principle may be overgeneralized.

Both of these biases can lead to worse consequences in some cases, although much of the time the heuristics that lead to them probably generate the best consequences. These results, then, might also be the result of over-generalization of otherwise useful heuristics.

### Resistance to Coerced Reform

Reforms are social rules that improve matters on the whole. Some reforms require coercion. In a social dilemma, each person is faced with a conflict between options: One choice is better for the individual and the other is better for all members of the group in question. Social dilemmas can be, and have been, solved by agreements to penalize defectors (Hardin 1968). Coercion may also be required to resolve negotiations (even though almost any agreement would be better for both sides than no agreement) or bring about an improvement for many at the expense of a few, as when taxes are raised for the wealthy. It is in the interest of most people to support beneficial but coercive reforms, and some social norms encourage such support, but other social norms may oppose reforms (Elster 1989).

To look for such norms, Baron and Jurney (1993) presented subjects with six proposed reforms, each involving some public coercion that would force people to behave cooperatively, that is, in a way that would be best for all if everyone behaved that way. The situations involved abolition of television advertising in political campaigns, compulsory vaccination for a highly contagious flu, compulsory treatment for a contagious bacterial disease, no-fault auto insurance (which eliminates the right to sue), elimination of lawsuits against obstetricians, and a uniform 100% tax on gasoline (to reduce global warming).

Most subjects thought things would be better on the whole if the reforms, as described, were put into effect, but many of *those* subjects said they would not vote for the reforms. Subjects who voted against proposals they saw as improvements cited several reasons. Three reasons played a major role in such resistance to reform, as indicated both by correlations with resistance (among subjects who saw the proposal as improvements) and by subjects indicating (both in yes-no and free-response formats) that these were the reasons for their votes: fairness, harm, and rights.

*Fairness* concerns the distribution of the benefits or costs of reform. People may reject a generally beneficial reform such as an agreement between management and labor, on the grounds that it allocates benefits or costs in a way that violates some standard of distribution.

*Harm* refers to a norm that prohibits helping one person by harming another, even if the benefit outweighs the harm and even if unfairness is otherwise not at issue (e.g., when those to be harmed are determined randomly). Whereas opposition to reform on the grounds of fairness compares reform to a reference point defined by the ideally fair result, opposition on the grounds of harm compares it to the status quo. One trouble with most reforms is that they help some people and hurt others. For example, an increased tax on gasoline in the United States may help the world by reducing $CO_2$ emissions, and it will help most Americans by reducing the budget deficit; but it will hurt those few Americans who are highly dependent on gasoline, despite the other benefits for them. The norm against harm is related to omission bias, because failing to help (by not passing the reform) is not seen as an equivalent to the harm resulting from action.

A *right*, in this context, is an option to defect. The removal of this right might be seen as a harm, even if, on other grounds, the person in question is clearly better off when the option to defect is removed (because it is also removed for everyone else).

Subjects cited all of these reasons for voting against coercive reforms (both in yes-no and open-ended response formats). For example, in one study, 39% of subjects said they would vote for a 100% tax on gasoline, but 48% of those who would vote against the tax thought it would do more good than harm on the whole. Subjects thus admitted to making nonconsequentialist decisions, both through their own judgment of consequences and through the justifications they gave. Of those subjects who would vote against the tax despite judging that it would do more good than harm, for example, 85% cited the unfairness of the tax as a reason for voting against it, 75% the fact that the tax would harm some people, and 35% the fact the tax would take away a choice that people should be able to make. (In other cases, rights were more prominent.) Removal of liberty by any means may set a precedent for other restrictions of freedom (Mill 1859); hence a consequentialist argument could be made against coercion even when a simple analysis suggests that coercion is justified. But no subject made this kind of argument. The appeals to the principles listed were in all cases direct and were written as though they were sufficient.

Baron (1993) obtained further evidence for the "do no harm" heuristic. Subjects were asked to put themselves in the position of a benevolent dictator of a small island consisting of equal numbers of bean growers and wheat growers. The decision was whether to accept or decline the final offer of the island's only trading partner, as a function of its effect on the incomes of the two groups. Most subjects would not accept any offer that reduced the income of one group to increase the income of the other, even if the reduction was a small fraction of the gain, and even if the group bearing the loss had a higher income at the outset. (It remains to be determined whether subjects think the subjective effect of the loss is greater than that of the gain.) The idea of Pareto efficiency (Pareto 1971) may have the same intuitive origin.

Additional evidence for the role of fairness comes from a number of studies in which subjects refuse to accept beneficial offers because the benefits seem to be unfairly distributed (Camerer & Loewenstein 1993; Thaler 1988).

In all of these studies of departures from consequentialism, it might be possible for someone who had made a nonconsequentialist decision to find a consequentialist justification for it, for example, by imagining goals or subtle precedent-setting effects. Yet, in all these studies, justifications are typically not of this form. Moreover, the question at issue is not whether a conceivable consequentialist justification can be found but, rather, whether subjects faced with a description of the consequences, divorced from the decisions that led to them, would judge the consequences for goal achievement in a way that was consistent with their decisions. It seems unlikely that they would do so in all of these studies.

### The Sources of Intuition

I have given several examples of possible nonconsequentialist thinking. My goal has been to make plausible the claim that nonconsequentialist decision rules exist and that they affect real outcomes. Before discussing what, if anything, should be done about these norms, we should consider whether they are really as problematical as I have suggested. One argument against my suggestion is that these norms have evolved through biological and cultural evolution over a long period of time; hence they are very likely the best we can achieve, or close to the best.

Like Singer (1981), I am skeptical. Although several evolutionary accounts can explain the emergence of various forms of altruism as well as various moral emotions such as anger (Frank 1985), I know of no such accounts of the specific norms I have cited. (I could imagine such an account for the norm of retribution, however, which might arise from a tendency to counterattack.) Any account that favors altruism would also seem to favor consequentialist behavior, and this would be inconsistent with nonconsequentialist norms. Even an account of anger as a way of making threats credible (Frank 1985) need not distinguish between anger at acts and omissions. Indeed, we are often angry with people for what they have failed to do.

Even if norms have an evolutionary basis, we still do not need to endorse them. As Singer (1981) points out in other terms, evolution is trying to solve a problem other than that of determining the best morality to endorse. A rule might engender its own survival without meeting the above criteria for being worthy of endorsement. For example, chauvinism might lead to its own perpetuation by causing nations that encourage it to triumph over those that do not, the victors then spreading their norms to the vanquished. Likewise, ideologies that encourage open-mindedness might suffer defections at higher rates than those that do not, leading to the perpetuation of a doctrine that closed-minded thinking is good (Baron 1991). Such mechanisms of evolution do not give us reason to endorse the rules they promote. As Singer points out, an evolutionary explanation of a norm can even undercut our attachment to it, because we then have an alternative to the hypothesis that we endorsed it because it was right.

Some have compared decision biases to optical illusions, which are a necessary side effect of an efficient design or adaptation (Funder 1987). Without a plausible account of how this adaptation works, however, acceptance of this argument would require blind faith in the status quo. More can be said, however. Unlike optical illusions (I assume), nonconsequentialist decision rules are not always used. In all the research I described, many or most subjects did not show the biases in question. Moreover, Larrick et al. (in press) found that those who do not display such biases are at least no worse off in terms of success or wealth than those who do. (Whether they are morally worse was not examined.) Nonconsequential decision making is not a fixed characteristic of our condition.

To understand where nonconsequentialist rules (norms) come from, we need to understand where *any* decision rules come from. I know of no deep theory about this. Some rules may result from observation of our biological behavioral tendencies, through the naturalistic fallacy. We observe, for example, that men are stronger than women and sometimes push women around, so we conclude that men ought to be dominant. Rules are also discovered by individuals (as Piagetian theorists have emphasized); they are explicitly taught (as social-learning theorists have emphasized) by parents, teachers, and the clergy; and they are maintained through gossip and other kinds of social interaction (Sabini & Silver 1981).

If people evolved to be docile, as proposed by Simon (1990), then we become attached to the rules that we are taught by others. These rules need have no justification for this attachment mechanism to work. Arbitrary rules can acquire just as much loyalty as well-adjusted rules. And, indeed, people sometimes seem just as attached to rules of dress or custom that vary extensively across cultures as they are to fundamental moral rules that seem to be universal (Haidt et al., in press).

Why would anyone invent or modify a rule and teach it to someone else? One reason is that the teachers benefit directly from the "students" following the rule, as when parents teach their children to tell the truth, help with the housework, or control their tempers. In some cases, these rules are expressed in a general form ("don't bother people," "pitch in and do your share"), perhaps because parents understand that children will be liked by others if they follow those rules. So parents teach their children to be good in part out of a natural concern with the children's long-run interests. Parents may also take advantage of certain opportunities for such instruction: a moral lesson may be more likely after a harmful act than after a failure to help (unless the help was specifically requested).

Often, such rules are made up to deal with specific cases, for example, "don't hurt people," in response to beating up a little brother. We can think of such rules as hypotheses, as attempts to capture what is wrong with the case in question. It is useful to express the rules in a more general form rather than referring to the specific case alone ("don't twist your brother's arm"). But such general rules are not crafted after deep thought. They are spur-of-the-moment inventions, although they do help control behavior for the better.

If the rule is badly stated, one corrective mechanism is critical thought about the rule itself (Singer 1981). To criticize a rule, we need to have a standard, a goal, such as the test suggested earlier: Is this a member of the set of rules that we benefit most from endorsing? We also need to have arguments about why the rule fails to achieve that standard as well as it could, such as examples (like those I gave earlier) where the rule leads to general harm. And we need alternative rules, although these can come after the criticism rather than before it.

In the absence of such critical thought, rules may attain a life of their own. They become overgeneralized (or the rules that might replace them in specific cases are undergeneralized, even if they are used elsewhere). Because of our docility, perhaps, and the social importance of moral rules, our commitments to these rules are especially tenacious. The retributive rule of punishment, "an eye for an eye," was originally a reform (Hommers, 1986), an improvement over the kind of moral system that led to escalating feuds. But when applied intuitively by a court to the cases of a child killed by a vaccine, without negligence, it is overgeneralized to a case where the rule itself probably does harm (Baron & Ritov 1993; Oswald 1989 makes a similar suggestion).

Critical thought about moral rules undoubtedly occurs. It may be what Piaget and his followers take to be the major mechanism of moral development. The sorts of experience that promote such thought may work because they provide counterexamples to rules that have been used so far. But critical thought is not universal. A principle such as "do no harm" may be developed as an admonition in cases of harm through actions. This principle may then be applied to cases in which harm to some is outweighed by much greater good to others, such as compulsory vaccination laws, fuel taxes, or free-trade agreements. The application may be unreflective. The principle has become a fundamental intuition, beyond question.

Such overgeneralization is well known in the study of learning. For example, Wertheimer (1959) noted that students who learn the base-times-height rule for the area of a parallelogram often apply the same rule inappropriately to roughly similar figures and fail to apply the rule when it should be applied, for example, to a long parallelogram turned on its side. Wertheimer attributed such over- and undergeneralization to learning without understanding. I have suggested (Baron 1988) that the crucial element in understanding is keeping the justification of the formula in mind, in terms of the purpose served and the arguments for why the formula serves that purpose. In the case of the base-times-height rule, the justification involves the goal of making the parallelogram into a rectangle, which cannot be done in the same way with, for example, a trapezoid.

Overgeneralization in mathematics is easily corrected. In morality and decision making, however, the rules that people learn arise from important social interactions. People become committed to these rules in ways that do not usually happen in schoolchildren learning mathematics. In this respect, overgeneralization also differs from mechanisms that have been proposed as causes of types of biases other than those discussed here, mechanisms such as the costs of more complex strategies, associative structures, and basic psychophysical principles (Arkes 1991).

A defense of overgeneralization is that preventing it is costly. Crude rules might be good enough, given the time and effort it would take to improve them. Moreover, the effort to improve them might go awry. People who reflect on their decision rules might simply dig themselves deeper into whatever hole they are in, rather than improving those rules. We might also be subject to self-serving biases when we ask whether a given case is an exception to a generally good rule (Hare 1981), such as in deciding whether an extramarital affair is really for the best (despite a belief that most are not).

These defenses should be taken seriously, but their implications are limited. They imply that we should be wary of trying to teach everyone to be a moral philosopher. They also suggest that prescriptive systems of rules might differ from normative systems (although they do not prove this – see Baron 1990). But they do not imply that simpler rules are more adequate as normative standards than full consequentialist analyses.

Moreover, some decisions are so important that the cost of thorough thinking and discussion pales by comparison to the cost of erroneous choices. I have in mind issues such as global environmental policy, fairness toward the world's poor, trade policy, and medical policy. In these matters, the thinking is often done by groups of people engaged in serious debate, not by individuals. Thus, there is more protection from error, and the effort is more likely to pay off. Many have suggested that utilitarianism and consequentialism are fully consistent with common sense or everyday moral intuition (e.g., Sidgwick 1907), but this may be more true in interpersonal relations than in thinking about major social decisions.

Finally, the cost of thinking (or the cost of learning) may be a good reason for not learning a more adequate rule, but not a good reason for having high confidence in the inadequate rules that are used instead. Yet many examples of the use of nonconsequentialist rules are characterized by exactly such confidence, to the point of resisting counterarguments (e.g., Baron & Ritov 1993). In some cases it might be best not to replace the nonconsequentialist rules with more carefully crafted ones but, rather, to be less confident about them and more willing to examine the situation from scratch. The carefully crafted rules might be too difficult to learn. In such cases we might say that overgeneralization is a matter of excessive rigidity in the application of good general rules rather than in the use of excessively general rules.

In this section, I have tried to give a plausible account of how erroneous intuitions arise in the development of individuals and cultures. Direct evidence on such development is needed. In the rest of this chapter, I explore some implications of my view for research and application. These implications depend in different ways on the probability that this view is correct. Some require only that it is possible.

### Intuition as a Philosophical Method

If intuitions about decision rules result from overgeneralization, then (as also argued by Hare 1981 and Singer 1981) these intuitions are suspect as the basic data for philosophical inquiry. Philosophers who argue that the act–omission distinction is relevant (e.g., Kamm 1986; Malm 1989) typically appeal directly to their own intuitions about cases. Unless it can be shown that intuitions are trustworthy, these philosophers are simply begging the question.

Rawls (1971) admits that single intuitions can be suspect, but he argues for a reflective equilibrium based on an attempt to systematize intuitions into a coherent theory. Such systematization need not solve the problem, however. For example, it might (although it does not do so for Rawls) lead to a moral system in which the act–omission distinction is central, a system in which morality consists mainly of prohibitions and positive duties play a limited role, if any (as suggested by Baron 1986).

Rawls's argument depends to some extent on an analogy between moral inquiry and fields such as modern linguistics, where systematization of intuition has been a powerful and successful method. The same method arguably underlies logic and mathematics (Popper 1962, Ch. 9). I cannot refute fully this analogical argument, but it is not decisive, only suggestive. I have suggested (along with Singer 1981) that morality and decision rules have an external purpose through which they may be understood, and that this criterion, rather than intuition, can be used as the basis of justification. Perhaps this idea can be extended by analogy to language, logic, and mathematics, but that is not my task here.

### Experimental Methodology

Experiments on decision biases often use between-subject designs (each condition given to different subjects) or other means to make sure that subjects do not compare directly the cases the experimenter will compare (such as separating the cases within a long series). The assumption behind such between-subject designs is that subjects would not show a bias if they knew what cases were being compared. All of the biases I have described above are within-subject. Subjects show the omission bias knowingly, for example, even when the act and omission versions are adjacent.

In between-subject designs, subjects may display biases that they would themselves judge to be biases. Such inconsistency seems to dispense with the need for a normative theory such as the consequentialist theory I have proposed, or expected utility theory. But without an independent check, we do not know that subjects would consider their responses to be inconsistent. Frisch (1993) took the trouble to ask subjects whether they regarded the two critical situations as equivalent – such as buying versus selling as ways of evaluating a good – and she found that they often did not. In other words, between-subject designs are not necessary to find many of the classic biases (including the status-quo effect described earlier), and subjects often disagree with experimenters regarding which situations are equivalent.

When we use within-subject designs, however, we cannot simply claim that subjects are making mistakes because they are violating the rules they endorse. When asked for justifications for their judgments, subjects in all the experiments I described earlier endorsed a variety of rules that are consistent with their responses. We therefore need a normative theory, such as the consequentialist theory I have outlined, if we are to evaluate subjects' responses.

Much the same normative theory seems to be implicit in most of the literature on framing effects and inconsistencies. Whether or not a factor is relevant to making a decision is a normative question, to which alternative answers can be given. For example, Schick (1991) argues that the way decision makers describe situations to themselves *is* normatively relevant to the decision they ought to make (even, presumably, if these descriptions do not affect consequences), because descriptions affect their "understanding" of the situation, and understandings are necessarily part of any account of decision making. Hence, framing effects do not imply error. If consequentialism is correct, though, Schick is wrong: consequentialism implies that understandings themselves can be erroneous (we might say). The attempt to bring in a consequentialist standard through the back door while ostensibly talking about inconsistency (Dawes 1988) and framing effects will not work. The standard should be brought in explicitly, as I have tried to do.

In sum, although between-subject designs are useful for studying heuristics, we may also use within-subject designs to evaluate subjects' rules against a normative standard such as consequentialism.

### Policy Implications

The examples I used to illustrate my argument are of some relevance to issues of public concern, as noted. I am tempted to offer evidence of psychological biases as ammunition in various battles over public policy. Tetlock and Mitchell (1993), however, correctly warn us against using psychological research as a club for beating down our political opponents. It is too easy, and it can usually be done by both sides. On the other hand, a major reason for studying biases is to discover where decisions need improvement, and if we researchers are going to reject all application to public or personal decision making, we might as well fold up our tents and move on to more useful activities. How should we draw the line between making too many claims and too few?

I do not propose to answer this question fully, but part of an answer concerns the way we make claims concerning public policy debates. I suggest that claims of biased reasoning be directed at particular *arguments* made by one side or the other, not at positions, and certainly not at individuals.

For example, one of the arguments against free-trade agreements is that it is wrong to hurt some people (e.g., those on both sides who will lose their jobs to foreign competition) to help others (e.g., those who will be prevented from losing their jobs because their products will be exported). This could be an example of omission bias, or the do-no-harm heuristic, which operates in much clearer cases and which, I have argued, is indeed an error in these clear cases. Now real trade negotiations are extremely complex, and they involve other issues characteristic of any negotiations, such as trying to get the best deal for everyone. So at most we could conclude that a particular part of the argument against free trade is a fallacy that has been found elsewhere in the laboratory. This does not imply that the other arguments opposing free trade are wrong or not decisive, or that the people who oppose free trade are any more subject to error than those who favor it.

With this kind of caution at least, the general program of research can be extended more broadly to other matters of policy that I have not discussed here, such as fairness in testing and selection for academic and employment opportunities, abortion, euthanasia, nationalism, the morality of sex, and so on. In all these kinds of cases, arguments for two (or more) sides are complex, but some of the arguments are probably erroneous. Psychology has a role to play in discovering fallacious arguments and pointing them out.

One discipline has concerned itself with exactly this kind of inquiry, the study of informal logic (e.g., Arnauld 1964; Johnson & Blair 1983; Walton 1989). This field, however, has not incorporated many of the advances in normative theory that have occurred since the time of Aristotle, and it has paid no attention to psychological evidence – sparse as it is – about which fallacies actually occur in real life.

### References

Arkes, H. R. (1991). Costs and benefits of judgment errors: Implications for debiasing. *Psychological Bulletin* 110:486–98.

Arnauld, A. (1964). *The art of thinking (Port Royal Logic)* (trans. by J. Dickoff & P. James; originally published in 1662). Bobbs-Merrill.

Asch. D., Baron, J., Hershey, J. C., Kunreuther, H., Meszaros, J., Ritov, I., & Spranca, M. (1993). Determinants of resistance to pertussis vaccination. Unpublished manuscript, Department of Psychology, University of Pennsylvania.

Baron, J. (1985). *Rationality and intelligence.* Cambridge University Press.

Baron, J. (1986). Tradeoffs among reasons for action. *Journal for the Theory of Social Behavior* 16:173–95.

Baron, J. (1988). *Thinking and deciding*. Cambridge University Press.

Baron, J. (1990). Thinking about consequences. *Journal of Moral Education* 19:77–87.

Baron, J. (1991). Beliefs about thinking. In: *Informal reasoning and education*, ed. J. F. Voss, D. N. Perkins, & J. W. Segal. Erlbaum.

Baron, J. (1992). The effect of normative beliefs on anticipated emotions. *Journal of Personality and Social Psychology* 63:320–30.

Baron, J. (1993). Heuristics and biases in equity judgments: A utilitarian approach. In: *Psychological perspectives on justice: Theory and applications*, ed. B. A. Mellers & J. Baron. Cambridge University Press.

Baron, J., Baron, J. H., Barber, J. P., & Nolen-Hoeksema, S. (1991). Rational thinking as a goal of therapy. *Journal of Cognitive Psychotherapy (special issue)* 4:293–302.

Baron, J., Gowda, R., & Kunreuther, H. (1993). Attitudes toward managing hazardous waste: What should be cleaned up and who should pay for it? *Risk Analysis* 13: 183–92.

Baron, J., & Jurney, J. (1993). Norms against voting for coerced reform. *Journal of Personality and Social Psychology*, 64, 347–355.

Baron, J., & Ritov, I. (1993). Intuitions about penalties and compensation in the context of tort law. *Journal of Risk and Uncertainty* 7:17–33.

Baron, J., & Ritov, I. (in press). Reference points and omission bias. *Organizational Behavior and Human Decision Processes*.

Bell, D. E., Raiffa, H., & Tversky, A., Eds. (1988). *Decision making: Descriptive normative, and prescriptive interactions*. Cambridge University Press.

Calabresi, G. (1970). *The costs of accidents: A legal and economic analysis*. Yale University Press.

Calfee, J. E., & Rubin, P. H. (in press). Some implications of damage payments for nonpecuniary losses. *Journal of Legal Studies*.

Camerer, C., & Loewenstein, G. (1993). Information, fairness, and efficiency in bargaining. In: *Psychological perspectives on justice: Theory and applications*, ed. B. A. Mellers & J. Baron. Cambridge University Press.

Dawes, R. M. (1988). *Rational choice in an uncertain world*. Harcourt Brace Jovanovich.

Elster, J. (1989). *The cement of society*. Cambridge University Press.

Fischer, J. M., & Ravizza, M. (1992). *Ethics: Problems and principles*. Holt, Rinehart & Winston.

Frank, R. F. (1985). *Passions within reason: The strategic role of the emotions*. Norton. Friedman, D. (1982). What is "fair compensation" for death or injury? *International Review of Law and Economics* 2:81–93.

Frisch, D. (1993). Reasons for framing effects. *Organizational Behavior and Human Decision Processes* 54:399–429.

Funder, D. C. (1987). Errors and mistakes: Evaluating the accuracy of social judgement. *Psychological Bulletin* 101:75–90.

Gibbard, A. (1988). Hare's analysis of "ought" and its implications. In: *Hare and critics: Essays on moral thinking*, ed. D. Seanor & N. Fotion. Clarendon Press.

Haidt, J., Koller, S. H., & Dias, M. G. (in press). Affect, culture, and morality, or, Is it wrong to eat your dog? *Journal of Personality and Social Psychology*.

Hardin, G. R. (1968). The tragedy of the commons. *Science* 162:1243–48.

Hare, R. M. (1963). *Freedom and reason*. Clarendon Press.

Hare, R. M. (1981). *Moral thinking: Its levels, method and point*. Clarendon Press.

Hommers, W. (1986). Ist "Voller Ersatz" immer "Adäquate Ersatz"? Zu einer Diskrepanz Regelungen des Gesetzbuches im EXODUS und der Adäquatheits-These der Equity-Theorie. *Psychologische Beiträge* 28:164–79.

Inglehart, J. K. (1987). Compensating children with vaccine-related injuries. *New England Journal of Medicine 316*:1283–88.

Johnson, R. H., & Blair, J. A. (1983). *Logical self-defense* (2nd ed.). McGraw-Hill Ryerson.

Kahneman, D., Knetsch. J. L., & Thaler, R. H. (1990). Experimental tests of the endowment effect and the Coase theorem. *Journal of Political Economy 98*:1325–48.

Kahneman, D., & Miller D. T. (1986). Norm theory: Comparing reality to its alternatives. *Psychological Review 93*:136–53.

Kamm, F. M. (1986). Harming, not aiding, and positive rights. *Philosophy and Public Affairs 15*:3–32.

Knetsch, J. L., & Sinden, J. A. (1984). Willingness to pay and compensation: Experimental evidence of an unexpected disparity in measures of value. *Quarterly Journal of Economics 99*:508–22.

Kuhse, H. (1987). *The sanctity of life doctrine in medicine: A critique*. Oxford University Press.

Larrick, R. P., Nisbett, R. E., & Morgan, J. N. (in press). Who uses the cost-benefit rules of choice? Implications for the normative status of economic theory. *Organizational Behavior and Human Decision Processes*.

Malm, H. M. (1989). Killing, letting die, and simple conflicts. *Philosophy and Public Affairs 18*:238–58.

Meszaros, J. R., Asch, D. A. Baron, J., Hershey, J. C., Kunreuther, H., & Schwartz, J. (1992). Cognitive influences on parents' decisions to forgo pertussis vaccination for their children. Unpublished manuscript, Center for Risk Management and Decision Processes, University of Pennsylvania.

Mill, J. S. (1859). *On liberty*. J. W. Parker.

Miller, D. T., & McFarland, C. (1986). Counterfactual thinking and victim compensation. *Personality and Social Psychology Bulletin 12*:513–19.

Mitchell, R. C., & Carson, R. T. (1989). *Using surveys to value public goods: The contingent valuation method*. Resources for the Future.

Oswald, M. (1989). Schadenshöhe, Strafe und Verantwortungsattribution. *Zeitschrift für Sozialpsychologie 20*:200–210.

Pareto, V. (1971). *Manual of political economy* (trans. A. S. Schweir; orginally published in 1909). A. M. Kelley.

Popper, K. R. (1962). *Conjectures and refutations: The growth of scientific knowledge*. Basic Books.

Rawls, J. (1971). *A theory of justice*. Harvard University Press.

Ritov, I., & Baron, J. (1990). Reluctance to vaccinate: Omission bias and ambiguity. *Journal of Behavioral Decision Making 3*:263–77.

Ritov, I., & Baron, J. (1992). Status-quo and omission bias. *Journal of Risk and Uncertainty 5*:49–61.

Ritov, I., & Baron, J. (1994). Judgments of compensation for misfortune: the role of expectation. *European Journal of Social Psychology, 24*, 525–539.

Sabini, J., & Silver, M. (1981). *Moralities of everyday life*. Oxford University Press.

Samuelson, W., & Zeckhauser, R. (1988). Status-quo bias in decision making. *Journal of Risk and Uncertainty 1*:7–59.

Schick, F. (1991). *Understanding action: An essay on reasons*. Cambridge University Press.

Schweitzer, M. E. (in press). Untangling the status-quo and omission effects: An experimental analysis. *Organizational Behavior and Human Decision Processes*.

Sidgwick, H. (1907). The methods of ethics (7th ed). Macmillan.

Simon, H. A. (1990). A mechanism for social selection and successful altruism. *Science 250*:1665–68.

Singer, P. (1979). *Practical ethics*. Cambridge University Press.

Singer, P. (1981). *The expanding circle: Ethics and sociobiology*. Farrar, Straus & Giroux.

Spranca, M., Minsk, E., & Baron, J. (1991). Omission and commission in judgment and choice. *Journal of Experimental Social Psychology 27*:76–105.

Tetlock, P. E., & Mitchell, G. (1993). Liberal and conservative approaches to justice: Conflicting psychological portraits. In: *Psychological perspectives on justice: Theory and applications*, ed. B. A. Bellers & J. Baron. Cambridge University Press.

Thaler, R. H. (1988). The ultimatum game. *Journal of Economic Perspectives 2*:195–206.

Walster, E., Walster, G. W., & Berscheid, E. (1978). *Equity: Theory and research*. Allyn & Bacon.

Walton, D. N. (1989). *Informal logic: A handbook for critical argumentation*. Cambridge University Press.

Wertheimer, M. (1959). *Productive thinking* (rev. ed.; originally published in 1945). Harper & Row.

# 39    Algebra and Process in the Modeling of Risky Choice

*Lola L. Lopes*

## Experiments on Histograms and Multioutcome Distributions

Early studies on probability and variance preferences introduced the idea that distributional characteristics of risky options might affect preferences. Coombs later followed up his interest in the higher moments of distributions with a theory of risk perception called *portfolio theory* (Coombs, 1975; Coombs & Huang, 1970; Coombs & Lehner, 1981). Although most of this research used two-outcome gambles, Coombs and Bowen (1971) presented subjects with multiple-play games represented as 25-outcome distributions. Each distribution was represented twice, once as a histogram plotting net outcome against probability, and again as a list pairing each of the 25 possible outcomes with its probability of occurrence.

More recently, I have used multioutcome gambles to study how people's perceptions of risk and preferences among options relate to distributional shapes (Lopes, 1984, 1987). Examples of the gambles are shown in Figure 39.1. Each display consists of a set of rows, at the left of which is an amount that might be won (or lost) and at the right of which is a row of tally marks representing probability. Subjects are instructed to think of the tally marks as lottery tickets, each one marked with the prize amount shown at the left. They are also told that each gamble has the same amount of prize money and tickets. Although the gambles have many possible outcomes, they are easy to understand because the shapes of the distributions are simple and the between-row spacing in a given gamble is roughly equal in terms of monetary outcome.

Schneider and Lopes (1986) used multioutcome gambles to study the influence of risk preference on the reflection effect. In the experiment, two groups of subjects were compared, one preselected for extreme risk aversion and the other for extreme risk seeking. The gamble preferences of the

```
200  I                130  |||||||||||||||||||||||||||||    200  |||||
187  II               115  ||||||||||||||||||||||          189  |||||
172  III              101  ||||||||||||||            178  |||||
157  IIII             86   |||||||||||              168  |||||
143  IIIII            71   |||||||             158  |||||
129  IIIIIII          57   |||||              147  |||||
114  IIIIIIIII        43   IIII              136  |||||
 99  IIIIIIIIIIIII    28   III               126  |||||
 85  IIIIIIIIIIIIIIIII 13  II               116  |||||
 70  IIIIIIIIIIIIIIIIIIIIIIII  0  I          105  |||||
                                              94  |||||
        Riskless            Short Shot        84  |||||
                                              74  |||||
200  IIIIIIIIIII                              63  |||||
186  IIIIIIIII                                52  |||||
172  IIIIIIII                                 42  |||||
159  IIIIIII                                  32  |||||
146  IIIII                                    21  |||||
132  III                                      10  |||||
119  I                439  I                   0  |||||
106  I                390  II
 93  I                341  III
 80  I                292  IIII            Rectangular
 66  III              244  IIIII
 53  IIIII            195  IIIIII
 40  IIIIIII          146  IIIIIIII
 26  IIIIIIII          98  IIIIIIIIIII
 13  IIIIIIIIII        49  IIIIIIIIIIIIIIIII
  0  IIIIIIIIII         0  IIIIIIIIIIIIIIIIIIIIIIIIIII

      Bimodal              Long Shot
```

Figure 39.1. Examples of multioutcome lotteries. The numbers represents amounts that might be won (or lost) and the tally marks represent lottery tickets (100 total). The expected values of all lotteries are $100.

two groups differed substantially across gain and loss conditions. When risk averse subjects chose among gains, their preferences were essentially as would be predicted by classical risk aversion (diminishing marginal utility) or by security-minded decumulative weighting. For losses, however, their preferences were neither strictly risk averse (security-minded) nor risk seeking (potential-minded). In contrast, the preferences of the risk-seeking subjects were essentially as predicted by increasing marginal utility or potential-minded decumulative weighting for losses, but their preferences among gains were neither strictly risk seeking (potential-minded) nor risk averse (security-minded). The complex pattern of results plus retrospective comments from subjects suggested that the two groups used the same choice processes but assessed the trade-off between avoiding bad outcomes and seeking good outcomes very differently.

## Choice Boards and Eye Movement Studies

Although the algebraic models (described in the original paper) were not intended to describe the processes of choice, when they are taken seriously as candidate models of process, they make many interesting and testable predictions. Perhaps the most important such prediction concerns whether the choice involves holistic evaluations of individual alternatives or dimensional (i.e., attribute-based) comparisons that move back and forth between alternatives.[1] Holistic evaluation is implied, for example, by the idea that people choose among risks by comparing the expected utilities of the alternatives, whereas dimensional comparisons are implied by the lexicographic semiorder (LS) model as well as by many other models that have been proposed for choice under risk (Payne, Bettman, & Johnson, 1990). Another important prediction concerns the amount of information that is used in the choice process. Holistic processes tend to call on all the available information, whereas dimensional processes usually shortcut search.

By far the most heavily used tool for studying information use is the choice board, in which information is offered to subjects in the form of an attribute-by-alternative array. Each cell in the array contains a single item of information that is hidden from sight until a subject "asks" to see it. Choice board studies have consistently suggested that as the number of alternatives increases, the proportion of information searched per alternative decreases. In addition, variability of search within alternatives increases. This suggests that as task load increases, subjects tend to increase their use of (dimensional) strategies that allow them to process alternatives more efficiently. In addition, subjects also adapt their strategies to time pressure and to structural variations in problems, such as whether outcome probabilities are relatively homogeneous or not.

Eye movements have also been used to study information acquisition in risky choice. Subjects in a study by Rosen and Rosenkoetter (1976) chose between two-outcome gambles displayed on a computer screen. Each gamble was described by three pieces of information: the amount to be won, the probability of winning, and the amount to be lost. The (complementary) probability of losing was not shown. Subjects also chose between analogous pairs not involving risk (vacations, gift packages). The main result was that the stimulus environment had a major influence on choice strategy. The predominant search pattern for gambles was holistic: about one-third of the transitions were intradimensional and two-thirds were interdimensional. In contrast, the two varieties of transition were split almost evenly for choices between gift packages containing varying quantities of theater ticketes, gasoline, and free groceries. Rosen and Rosenkoetter explained the predominance of holistic processing for gambles in terms of attribute interdependency. In their view, risk dimensions such as probability of winning or payoff have much less meaning in isolation than quantities of theater tickets, say, or gasoline.

Russo and Dosher (1983) also used eye movements to study risky choice. Their gambles were so-called "one outcome" gambles described only by probability of winning and payoff. Choice pairs were presented as $2 \times 2$ arrays. Unlike the previous eye movement study of Rosen and Rosenkoetter (1976), Russo and Dosher's data revealed a relatively even split between holistic and dimensional processing. One important task difference that may explain this is that dimensional strategies work well with one-outcome gambles. As Russo and Dosher pointed out, rough comparisons of gambles based on absolute dimensional differences come reasonably close to expected value computations but with considerably less effort.

## Verbal Protocols

As we have already seen (Slovic & Lichtenstein, 1968; Tversky, 1969), it was not uncommon for the researchers who pioneered the use of experimental methods for studying risky choice processes to look to subjects' retrospective verbal accounts for confirmation of their ideas. However, some researchers have asked subjects to provide on-line ("think-aloud") protocols during choice that have later been subjected to detailed analysis (see, e.g., Payne, Braustein, & Carroll, 1978; Payne, Laughhunn, & Crum, 1980). The results of such analyses have been useful as a source of converging data for validating conclusions drawn from experiments using other methods.

For example, Montgomery (1977) and Ranyard (1982) used protocols to study violations of transitivity. Montgomery's study used the same stimulus set as Tversky (1969) and supported the LS model. Ranyard's study differed in that it systematically varied the ranges on the probability and payoff dimensions. The results indicated that when either one of the ranges was large relative to the other, that dimension tended to dominate, but when differences on both dimensions were small, intransitivities occurred. The protocols in Ranyard's experiment also revealed that his subjects were paying attention to more of the information than Montgomery's subjects had seemed to use. This led Ranyard to suggest that the underlying choice rule is actually a nonlinear additive difference (NLAD) rule in which smaller differences receive less weight than larger differences.[2]

Other researchers have adapted protocol methods to settings in which choice times and comparison processes occur too quickly for on-line reporting. These methods ask subjects for retrospective accounts but move data collection closer to the choice process. For example, Russo and Dosher (1983) supplemented eye movement data with "prompted verbal protocols" in which real-time recordings of a subject's eye movements are replayed for the subject at the end of the experiment and subjects are asked to recall and report the thoughts that were occurring during the fixations. Alternatively, Lopes (1987) embedded occasional requests for written explication of the reasons for a current choice into the context of a larger choice set. Some of these protocols will be used for illustration in what follows.

## The Bridge between Process and Algebra

Our trek through the history of risky choice research has taken us across a variety of experimental terrains and up a series of theoretical peaks that may seem isolated and fundamentally unbridgeable. The isolation is more apparent than real, however, for there are points of connection everywhere – empirical outcroppings from which we can launch conceptual lines. In this section, we will examine four such lines, each one woven from several interrelated strands. The first connects the stepwise processes of lexicographic choice to the algebraic idea of decumulative weighting. The second contrasts several different algebraic approaches to modeling risk preference. The third discusses the relation between aspiration and conflict in risky choice, and the last shows how decumulative weighting and stochastic control can be incorporated into a single psychological model.

### *Lexicographic Processes and the Idea of Weighting*

Lexicographic choice is rooted in the idea of priority: in order to apply the process, one needs to know what one values and in what order of importance. Glimmerings of lexicographic processes have surfaced repeatedly in studies of risky choice, all suggesting that probabilities are more important than payoffs (Montgomery, 1977; Payne & Braunstein, 1971, 1978; Ranyard, 1982; Slovic & Lichtenstein, 1968; Tversky, 1969). Still, it is not easy to prioritize probability and payoff in isolation (Rosen & Rosenkoetter, 1976; Schoemaker, 1979). Schoemaker, for example, tried to get a context-free measure of the relative importance of probabilities and payoffs by displaying an "urn" of unknown content and asking subjects to judge its worth. Before responding, however, subjects could request either information about the proportion of winning balls in the urn or about how much would be won if a winning ball were drawn. Although subjects complied with the task, their context-free requests were unrelated to the relative importance they later placed on probabilities and payoffs when choosing among duplex bets.

To resolve the apparent inconsistency between Schoemaker's result and the more typical finding, it is useful to study the mechanisms that mediated the enhanced influence of probability in three of the earlier experiments. Recall that in Slovic and Lichtenstein's (1968b) seminal study of duplex bets, subjects appeared to set bids in a two-stage process, first using $P_W$ to determine whether a bet was attractive or not and then using $\$_W$ or $\$_L$ to establish a value. Given that the expected value of duplex bets reflects all four risk dimensions, why should subjects have given priority to probability when they decided whether or not a bet was attractive?

This question can be answered tentatively by examining the constraints in the task. Suppose that the subjects realized that all four dimensions contribute to attractiveness but did not know how to integrate them. They might have coped with the difficulty by looking for a one-dimensional cutting rule of the form "A gamble is attractive if it has the best level of X." Because $\$_W$ and $\$_L$ were already earmarked for use in the second stage, the only viable candidates for X would have been $P_W$ and $P_L$.[3] Between these, approximately two-thirds of the subjects appeared to use $P_W$ and one-third appeared to use

$P_L$, a difference that could have been driven by a relatively minor task variable such as left-to-right reading habits or a tendency to imagine spinning the win pointer before the lose pointer. In either case, however, subjects appeared to use probability information (either $P_W$ or $P_L$) to decide whether to accept an attractive bet (i.e., pay to play it) or to reject an unattractive bet (i.e., require payment to play it).

The study by Payne and Braunstein (1971) suggested that probabilities are also processed before payoffs when subjects choose between duplex bets. In their information processing model of the choice process, Payne and Braunstein proposed that subjects begin by determining the relation between $P_W$ and $P_L$.[4] If $P_W < P_L$ for both gambles, the most likely outcome is a loss. Given the unattractive situation, subjects choose so as to minimize $P_L$. If $P_W > P_L$ for both gambles, the most likely outcome is a win. Given the attractive situation, subjects maximize $\$_W$ if they can, or maximize $P_W$ if not. If $P_W = P_L$, the situation is intermediate. Depending on type, one subject might choose pessimistically, opting to minimize $P_L$; another might choose optimistically, opting to maximize $\$_W$ or $P_W$. Thus, probability provides an initial screen on attractiveness just as it did in Slovic and Lichtenstein's (1968) model of the bidding process. In the case of choice, however, attractiveness moderates the criterion that is used to differentiate between alternatives. When the alternatives are unattractive, the model applies a conservative rule aimed at reducing the probability of losing. When the alternatives are attractive, the model uses a less conservative approach focused on making the most of the opportunity for a win.

The studies of intransitivity by Tversky (1969) and others (Montgomery, 1977; Ranyard, 1982) also suggested that the relative attractiveness of (positive) two-outcome gambles is assessed initially in terms of probabilities, with payoffs figuring only secondarily. Thus, both choices and on-line protocols indicated that subjects choose conservatively when probability differences are large, opting for the gamble that gives them the smaller probability of losing. When probability differences are small, however, subjects switch their attention to payoffs, choosing the gamble with the more lucrative payoff.

Together, then, process models for three reasonably dissimilar tasks suggest that the apparently greater importance of probability information in risky choice is real and that it is driven by an inclination on the part of subjects to screen out gambles that offer an unacceptable probability of winning and to consider payoffs only for gambles that pass the initial screening. If this is so, however, we are left with explaining why Schoemaker's (1979) more direct assessment failed to confirm probability's enhanced relative importance. The explanation to be pursued here is that the extremely simple structure of the stimuli used in these older experiments has allowed the probability/payoff distinction to mask a more fundamental distinction. This is the difference between "worst-case" evaluations that are aimed at preventing bad outcomes and "best-case" evaluations that are aimed at exploiting opportunities for good outcomes.

The difference between the probability/payoff distinction and the worst-case/best-case distinction can be most easily appreciated with respect to multioutcome gambles. These gambles have many probabilities and many payoffs, making it difficult to imagine how a subject could use one class of information while ignoring the other. However, it is easy to demonstrate how subjects evaluating multioutcome gambles can focus selectively on achieving security (a worst-case perspective) or on making the most of the potential for a big win (a best-case perspective). For example, when unselected subjects are offered a choice between the short shot and the long shot in Figure 39.1, most appear to use security-minded (or worst-case) weighting process, comparing lottery tickets from the "bottom up"[5] and choosing so as to maximize the probability of winning a prize of some sort:

"I choose the [short shot] because there is only one chance of me losing and the best odds indicate a good chance of winning $71 or more. The [long shot] has too many opportunities to lose – it is too risky."

"I'd rather have greater chances of winning a little something than greater chances for nothing. The triple jackpot [in the long shot] doesn't make me want to go for it cuz the odds are too great."

When the probabilities of winning appear similar, however, the same subjects may switch to a "top-down" (potential-minded or best-case) comparison of maximum payoffs. A particularly illuminating protocol is the following one in which a subject who is usually very security-minded nervously reverses an initial preference for the bimodal gamble (see Fig. 39.1) after realizing that it and the long shot are actually similar in probability of winning:

"Chances of getting zero are greater in the [long shot]. On the other hand, there are better prizes in the [long shot] once you get a ticket with a prize. In fact, chances of getting a prize of less than 40 or 50 look about the same, and then the [long shot] has better prizes. I'm not sure I'm making a good decision here."

A process of the latter sort in which subjects switch from bottom-up (security-minded) to top-down (potential-minded) comparisons is functionally isomorphic to the "probabilities before payoffs" process that produces intransitivities in choices among two-outcome gambles. In other words, a subject who chooses the two-outcome gamble with the larger probability of winning is – by virtue of that very act – also opting for security. Likewise, a subject who chooses the gamble with the larger payoff is also opting for potential.

The same bottom-up before top-down comparison strategy also predicts the sorts of nonlinearities that underlie the Allais paradoxes. For example, if the process is applied to the constant ratio problem described earlier, bottom-up comparison of gambles A and B quickly reveals that the gambles differ on the very first (i.e., worst) "ticket": B gets nothing, whereas A gets $1 million, so A is preferred. In comparing C and D, the bottom-most tickets all yield zero so neither gamble is favored. When a top-down comparison is engaged, however, D is favored, as its $2 million greatly exceeds the $1 million offered by C. Thus, a generalized lexicographic process operating on a comparison principle of bottom-up before top-down yields aggregate patterns that can be described by cautiously hopeful decumulative weighting. The same generalized emphasis on applying bottom-up criteria before other criteria also appears in algebraic rules that explain the Allais paradoxes by hybridizing maximin and expected utility (e.g., Gilboa, 1986; Jaffray, 1986).

Obviously, strict lexicographic choice is unlikely to hold up when differences in outcomes are very small; but the rule can be relaxed through two different psychological processes. The first involves some sort of discrimination function that discounts small differences among outcomes. If the size of the discountable difference were a function of outcome magnitude, the function would imply diminishing sensitivity. The second process involves changes in attention to differences as the comparison moves up or down the distribution. A process of the latter sort is what is captured quantitatively by decumulative weighting functions. The latter process also generalizes the NLAD process described by Ranyard (1982) to the case of multioutcome gambles and is, therefore, also a generalization of the LS process described by Tversky (1969).

In summary, it appears almost certain that lexicographic processes figure in risky choice. In each instance, importance judgments that are captured algebraically by the idea of *weight* express themselves in individual choices by the *order* in which operations are carried out. Nonetheless, there is ambiguity concerning what exactly is prioritized by the lexicographic rule. Studies based on one-outcome bets or duplex bets tend to suggest that probabilities are processed before payoffs. Studies with multioutcome bets tend to suggest that bottom-up (security-minded) analysis precedes top-down (potential-minded) analysis. And both kinds of studies suggest that subjects attempt to guarantee an acceptable outcome (maximize the probability of winning) before concerning themselves with the larger payoffs. As we have already seen, one of these ambiguities is easily resolved: When a bottom-up before top-down process is applied to simple gambles, the result is identical to a probabilities before payoffs process. But the ambiguity between security weighting and maximizing the probability of winning does not disappear. Instead, it is sharpened in the domain of losses and provides the key to understanding why gain and loss decisions are so often asymmetrical, being neither identical across domains nor reflected.

### Risk Attitude in Process and Algebra

Although the pattern of preferences that we call "risk aversion" has provided the predominant focus for behavioral models of risky choice, there have been important exceptions such as Friedman and Savage's (1948) suggestion concerning the purchase of lottery tickets. But the lottery ticket issue pales in comparison to the interest that Kahneman and Tversky generated by their suggestion (1979; also Tversky & Kahneman, 1992) that the utility function is S-shaped about the status quo, being concave (risk averse) for gains but convex (risk seeking) for losses.

Before examining the empirical evidence for and against the S-shaped function, it is worthwhile to examine its psychological rationale and to compare it with the Bernoullian rationale for a concave utility function. According to Tversky and Kahneman, the S-shaped function reflects a psychophysical principle of diminishing sensitivity by which "the impact of a change diminishes with the distance from the reference point" (1992, p. 303). Although diminishing sensitivity applies symmetrically to losses and to gains, Tversky and Kahneman also incorporate a principle of loss aversion into their utility function by which "losses loom larger than corresponding gains" (1992, p. 303). Loss aversion is needed to account for the fact that people typically reject gambles that give them a 50/50 chance at $\pm v$.

In psychophysics, sensitivity reflects the variance of responses to a stimulus of given intensity. Diminishing sensitivity corresponds to the case in which variance increases as a function of stimulus magnitude. As the concept is used by Tversky and Kahneman, it captures the intuition that – for either gains or losses – a difference of a constant magnitude (say $100) seems subjectively smaller when it is applied to large magnitudes ($4,200 vs. $4,300, for instance) than when it is applied to small magnitudes ($200 vs. $300). The intuition is clearly valid. Whether it accounts for risk attitude is another matter.

Diminishing marginal utility can also be linked to psychophysics: this time, to the shape of the psychophysical function that relates the physical magnitude of a stimulus to its psychological magnitude. In Bernoulli's conception, increasing the asset level of a poor person by some objective increment $v$ produces a much greater increase in subjective well-being than would be gotten by increasing the asset level of a rich person by the same increment. This idea suggests a saturation phenomenon: Inputs to the system can increase indefinitely, but the output of the system cannot.

"Psychophysical shape" and "sensitivity" may seem to be different names for the same thing, but the two are empirically and conceptually distinct. For example, just-noticeable-differences increase (i.e., sensitivity decreases) as a function of stimulus magnitude for both brightness and line length, but the psychophysical function for brightness is concave, whereas the function for line length is linear. Thus, although it is possible that diminishing marginal utility and diminishing sensitivity both play a role in people's evaluations of gamble outcomes, it is not possible for the utility function to be both Bernoullian and S-shaped.

For reasons of history, Bernoulli's function was the first to face empirical scrutiny. It was also the first to fail, most obviously because people do buy lottery tickets and are also willing to take risks in order to avoid losses

(Fishburn & Kochenberger, 1979; Williams, 1966). But the Bernoullian failure did not ensure that the S-shaped function succeeded when it was tested empirically. In fact, evidence from three different kinds of experiments suggests the contrary.

Reflection studies compare people's preferences among gambles involving gains with their preferences among corresponding gambles in which the outcomes are losses. In general, S-shaped utility predicts that the preference order should be reversed (reflected) across the two domains.[6] In many cases, however, studies that have tested the reflection hypothesis across parametric variations of probability and value have found that preferences among gain gambles demonstrate strong risk aversion, whereas preferences for losses are weaker (nearer to risk neutrality) or more variable than the corresponding pattern for risk aversion (Cohen, Jaffray, & Said, 1987; Hershey & Schoemaker, 1980; Schneider & Lopes, 1986; Weber & Bottom, 1989, Experiment 3; see also Luce, Mellers, & Chang, 1993).

In framing studies, the gambles that are presented in gain and loss frames are numerically the same, but outcomes are described in complementary terms that reflect different reference points. Thus, if a treatment may save some members of a doomed group, one may describe either the number who will be saved if the treatment is applied or the number who will die despite treatment. The original demonstrations of framing effects were shown in the work of Tversky and Kahneman (1981; also Kahneman & Tversky, 1982, 1984). Since then, however, there have been several systematic studies using a variety of different problems in which framing effects have been inconsistent. Although the predominant pattern for choice in the positive frame has been risk aversion, choices in the loss frame have tended to be variable across problems (Fagley & Miller, 1987; Maule, 1989; Miller & Fagley, 1991; Schneider, 1992) and people's expressed preferences for frames have not predicted their choices (Fischhoff, 1983).

The final approach to testing the S-shaped utility hypothesis focuses on its effects on higher-order phenomena. A study by Budescu and Weiss (1987) illustrate the type. The object was to test whether the sorts of intransitive cycles that were demonstrated by Tversky (1969) would be reflected if outcomes were switched from gains to losses. Three basic results were obtained. First, gain/loss reflection was supported. Second, the clear majority of subjects were either transitive in both domains or intransitive in both domains. Third – and contrary to expectation – intransitive cycles were not reflected.

Given the support for reflection across gain and loss choices, the lack of reflection for intransitive cycles was surprising. However, a closer look at the data suggests how it may have happened. For the most part, Budescu and Weiss's results are counts of the numbers of subjects who show particular effects. A subject who reversed his or her majority preferences across the 12 gain/loss comparisons was (properly) scored as confirming reflection. Whether the subject was equally consistent in the two domains is not generally indicated. The authors do, however, include raw data for one intransitive subject (Budescu & Weiss, 1987, Table 3, p. 192). Although this subject is risk averse for gains and risk seeking for losses by the majority rule, the subject's preferences are highly reliable for gain pairs (scores of 11/12, 12/12, 0/12, or 1/12 account for 10 out of 12 table entries) and much less reliable for loss pairs (none of the scores was more extreme than 10/12 or 2/12). Thus, although reflection occurred in terms of majority counts, the pattern for losses may have been less reliable, thus decreasing the likelihood that higher-order patterns (such as intransitivities) would be reflected in toto.

Although the most studied explanations for risk aversion have been based on the idea of convexity in the utility function, other alternatives exist. Yaari (1987) was the first to suggest that one could explain risk aversion without diminishing marginal utility by the use of a decumulative weighting function. Lopes (1990) later took a similar tack but preferred the cautiously hopeful function that also explains the purchase of lottery tickets. Other approaches (e.g., Allais, 1986; Quiggen, 1982; Tversky & Kahneman, 1992) have combined convexity with decumulative weighting. Despite the shifts in modeling strategy, however, most theories of risk taking either accept risk aversion as an empirical fact or base the shape of the utility function on psychological assumptions (diminishing marginal utility, diminishing sensitivity) that imply risk aversion at least for gains. Risk seekers have been out in the cold because no theories have provided a principled reason for expecting their existence.

With the growth of interest in decumulative weighting models, however, the situation could change. Not only is there a function (the potential-minded function) that can describe risk-seeking choices algebraically, the psychological basis of the function is also easily argued. One interpretation is that risk seekers are optimistic. Another is that they value opportunity (potential) over safety (security). In either case, the psychological mechanism can be operationalized as a top-down (or top-down before bottom-up) comparison sequence that affects the relative attention that is paid to bad and good outcomes.

The clearest evidence favoring such an attentional or value-directed concept is seen in the protocols of the subjects who consistently prefer riskier options. For illustration, here are the protocols of two subjects who preferred the long shot to the short shot (see Figure 39.1).

"The chance for winning nothing is small with the [short shot] but since the dollar amount in the [long shot] is attractive I run the risk of losing and go for the [long shot]."

"I'll take the added risks of losing it all or getting a lower number for the chance of the higher prizes."

Although these subjects are seemingly as aware of the bad outcomes in the long shot as the security-minded subjects who were profiled previously, they willingly trade security for the enhanced potential of the riskier gamble.

Although less is known about people who choose risky options than is known about people who choose safe options, there have been occasional suggestions of an individual difference factor involving the relative attention that people pay to preventing bad outcomes versus enabling good outcomes. In the Payne and Braunstein (1971) model described earlier, for instance, an individual difference factor intervenes whenever a gamble pair cannot be categorized as either attractive or unattractive. The factor determines whether the subject chooses to minimize $P_L$ (a security-based decision) or to maximize either $\$_W$ or $P_W$ (both potential-based decisions). Similarly, in a study of duplex bets incorporating protocols, Schoemaker (1979) found that of the 16 subjects who said that they focused solely on loss dimensions ($P_L$ or $\$_L$), 94% were risk averse in an unrelated coin flipping task. In contrast, of the 14 subjects who said that they focused solely on win dimensions ($P_W$ or $\$_W$), 57% were risk seeking in the coin flipping task.

In summary, there are several ways to describe when risks will be taken and who will take them. The popular hypothesis of the S-shaped utility function suggests that risk seeking will occur about as often and about as consistently for losses as risk aversion occurs for gains. The data, however, reveal a considerable asymmetry across the two domains in the strength and reliability of preferences. In contrast, theories that locate risk attitude in decumulative weighting functions (e.g., Yaari, 1987) do not distinguish between gains and losses. Although such theories may predict well for gains, they cannot handle the sometimes unreliable but still relatively high levels of risk seeking that occur for losses.

### Aspiration and Conflict

An alternate route to explaining risk seeking for losses is suggested by the observation that subjects are not only less predictable when choosing among losses, they also complain more often about the difficulties of choosing. The following, for example, are protocols from two subjects choosing between the rectangular and the short-shot loss lotteries (see Figure 39.1). Although they choose differently, both are conflicted.

"Another difficult one. I chose the [rectangular] lottery because the odds are equal on each dollar amount, whereas the [short shot] shows the odds in favor of a loss of $70 or more, and very good odds of losing $130. The [rectangular] seems to be a safer risk despite the potential for a higher loss, i.e., $200 max."

"Chances of losing ≤$100 are about the same for both, but [rectangular] has higher possible loss, so I picked [short shot]. I realize [short shot] give less chance of a very low loss, which reduces my certainty about choice."

Protocols such as these suggest that subjects facing losses are often torn between a desire to take the lottery offering the better chance of losing little or nothing and the inescapable fact that the lottery doing so is usually the more dangerous. The latter consideration is recognizable as the routine output of a bottom-up comparison process that focuses on the differences in the gambles' worst outcomes. Given either a security-minded or a cautiously hopeful weighting process, the choice should be settled immediately in favor of the short shot. In contrast, the apparent desire to lose little or nothing is reminiscent of the kinds of aspiration-driven risk taking that figure in bold play and other forms of stochastic control.

The existence and operation of aspiration levels in choice has long been acknowledged in the form of criteria that function as cutoffs in noncompensatory decision models. In the case of risky choice, however, aspiration levels have slipped in by the back door as kinks in the utility function (Friedman & Savage, 1948), utility functions with discrete steps (Simon, 1955), and shifts in the reference point defining gains and losses (Kahneman & Tversky, 1979). Thus, the idea of achieving an aspiration level has been folded into the idea of maximizing expected utility, a move that saves the expected utility model but only at the theoretical price of defining away the experience of conflict in risky choice.

SP/A (security-potential/aspiration) theory (Lopes, 1987, 1990) has pursued an alternative course by proposing that aspiration level functions as an additional basis for choice, one whose recommendations sometimes conflict with the recommendations of a decumulative comparison process. For illustration, consider a security-minded subject who has a modest aspiration level for gains (perhaps winning $50 or more) but who hopes to give up little or nothing (perhaps $50 or less) for losses. If this subject is presented with the rectangular and the short-shot gambles for gains (see Figure 39.1), both security and aspiration favor the short shot (upper left panel of Figure 39.2). Choice should be easy and unconflicted. For losses, however, security favors the short shot because it has a better worst outcome (−$130 vs. −$200), whereas aspiration favors the rectangular gamble because it offers the greater chance of losing less than $50 (25% vs. 10%). The result is psychological conflict, reduced confidence, and inconsistent choices. Thus, the theory predicts that security-minded subjects will demonstrate reliable security seeking for gains but will have mixed preferences for losses, exactly as Schneider and Lopes (1986) found with subjects preselected for extreme degrees of risk aversion.

The opposite pattern is predicted for potential-minded subjects. To see this, first consider the response of such subjects to losses (upper right panel of Figure 39.2). In this case it is assumed that potential-minded subjects (like everyone else) hope to lose little or nothing (perhaps $50 or less), which makes them favor the rectangular gamble. Because their top-down comparison process favors the same gamble, choice is easy and unconflicted. A pattern of consistent potential seeking for losses should result, exactly as Schneider and

## Short Shot Vs. Rectangular

**Security-Minded Pattern**

|  | Security | Aspiration |
|---|---|---|
| Gains | Short Shot | Short Shot |
| Losses | Short Shot | Rectangular |

**Potential-Minded Pattern**

|  | Potential | Aspiration |
|---|---|---|
| Gains | Rectangular | Short Shot |
| Losses | Rectangular | Rectangular |

## Short Shot Vs. Riskless

**Security-Minded Pattern**

|  | Security | Aspiration |
|---|---|---|
| Gains | Riskless | Riskless |
| Losses | Short Shot | Short Shot |

**Potential-Minded Pattern**

|  | Potential | Aspiration |
|---|---|---|
| Gains | Riskless | Riskless |
| Losses | Short Shot | Short Shot |

Figure 39.2. SP/A predictions of security-minded (left panels) and potential-minded (right panels) decision makers. SP/A predicts reversed preferences for these two types of decision makers for the short-short versus rectangular comparison and identical preferences for the short-shot versus riskless comparison.

Lopes (1986) found with subjects preselected for extreme risk seeking. For gains, however, potential continues to favor the rectangular gamble because of its high maximum. But aspiration level can produce a conflict if the subject adopts the goal of not coming up empty (say, winning $50 or more), a goal that is more likely met with the short shot. Thus, SP/A predicts mixed preferences for gains, as Schneider and Lopes (1986) also found.

SP/A theory also predicts the choices on which security-minded and potential-minded subjects agree. For example, offered the riskless and the short-shot gain lotteries (see Figure 39.1), both groups overwhelmingly prefer the riskless lottery (see lower left panel of Figure 39.2). Moreover, they do so for similar reasons, as can be seen in the following protocols, the first from a security-minded subject and the second from a potential-minded subject:

"The [riskless lottery] has (1) a higher jackpot and (2) greater chance of winning a larger amount *under* $100. I look at the highest amount I could lose rather than the highest amount I could win."

"I picked the [riskless lottery] because both the minimum and the maximum amounts are more, and because for both there's a good chance of getting around $100."

Although these subjects ordinarily disagree about gains, they agree here because the riskless gamble effectively satisfies each of their dominant criteria. Likewise, for losses, both groups of subjects strongly prefer the short shot (lower right panel of Figure 39.2) as can be seen in protocols given, respectively, by the same two subjects:

"[Took short shot because] (1) there is a greater chance of losing $130 or more with the [riskless lottery]. (2) There is a greater chance of losing less than $70 in the [short shot]."

"I pick the short shot because the maximum loss is less and because you may be able to hit as low as zero loss. No matter what, you lose $70 and possibly $200 in the [riskless] lottery – too much risk."

The reflection of preferences from gains to losses is complete and identical for both subjects because the recommendations of both the security (or potential) factor and the aspiration factor are reflected completely and identically for both groups.

The issue of when and how reflection occurs is interesting and depends critically on the distributional characteristics (that is, the "shapes") of the gambles being compared. To see this, recall for a moment the protocol from the ordinarily security-minded subject who convinced himself that choosing the long shot over the bimodal gamble was warranted by the fact that "chances of getting a prize of less than 40 or 50 look about the same [for both]." This is exactly the kind of shift that LS and NLAD models predict when probability differences are small. When the same subject was confronted with the two gambles defined as losses, however, the bimodal was chosen with dispatch:

"The bimodal has a lower ceiling with the same chances of paying $100 or less."

Although this subject reflected his preference from the long shot to the bimodal, he did not reflect his reasoning process. Instead, his routine bottom-up comparison process suggested that the bimodal and long shot gambles are similar in security for gains but are unequivocally dissimilar in security for losses.

Evidence of reflection across gains and losses has ordinarily been interpreted as evidence favoring an S-shaped utility function. But the S-shaped utility hypothesis also predicts reflection in reasoning, as Hershey and Schoemaker (1980) pointed out in their parametric comparison of subjects' choices for gains and losses. When they examined subjects' stated rationales, however, they found no evidence of reflectivity in reasoning. Similarly, the failure of Budescu and Weiss (1987) to find reflection in intransitive cycles suggests that the process that generates intransitivity for gains has a different result when it operates on losses.

The difference can be illustrated by revisiting the gambles used earlier to illustrate Tversky's (1969) transitivity experiment. Figure 39.3 shows the three gain gambles and corresponding loss gambles laid out schematically so that bad outcomes are on the bottom and good outcomes are on the top. The inequalities show how a person using the bottom-up before top-down comparison process might evaluate the various possible pairs. For gains, a bottom-up analysis would reveal that A and B are similar: there is only a small difference (4.1%) in the proportion of "tickets" resulting in zero and this occurs relatively "far up" in the comparison. If the person switches to

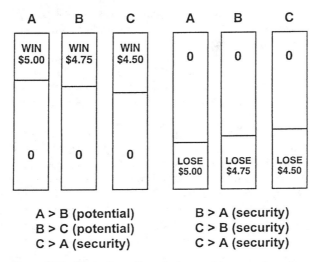

A > B (potential)    B > A (security)
B > C (potential)    C > B (security)
C > A (security)     C > A (security)

Figure 39.3. Illustration of how lexicographic processing of security and potential predicts intransitivity for gains but not for losses.

a top-down process, the result would favor A. A similar analysis would hold for B versus C. In the case of A versus C, however, the bottom-up process would discover a larger difference (8.2%) that also becomes evident sooner (i.e., nearer the bottom). Although a three-gamble sequence might not be long enough to elicit intransitivity from every subject, anyone using the proposed process would eventually switch from top-down (potential-driven) choices to bottom-up (security-driven) choices given longer sequences.

For losses, however, the situation is different. A bottom-up process would discover right away – with the very first "ticket" – that A is worse than B (−$5.00 < −$4.75), that B is worse than C (−$4.75 < −$4.50), and that A is worse than C (−$5.00 < −$4.50), and would consequently prefer B to A, C to B, and C to A. Thus, although the outcomes of the gambles have been reflected, the operations and recommendations of the comparison process have not. Whether a person is choosing between gains or between losses, the comparison process is still bottom-up before top-down, producing intransitivity for gains but transitivity for losses.

Of course, what Budescu and Weiss (1987) actually found when they looked at intransitivity for losses was a little more complicated than this. Their subjects' preferences displayed an unsystematic mixture of transitivity and intransitivity along with a reasonable amount of risk seeking. But this is exactly what one would expect when aspiration level is considered as it is in SP/A theory: although security alone might argue that C > B > A for losses, aspiration level pulls in the opposite direction because maximizing the probability of no loss argues that A > B > C.

*SP/A and Dual-Criterion Decision Making*

Having journeyed this far and constructed some bridges between distant theoretical viewpoints, it is time to take stock of our present surroundings. Although algebraic models and process models of risky choice seem miles apart conceptually, they can be easily reconciled by recognizing that algebraic models describe patterns of preference across option sets, whereas process models describe the sequence and content of comparison processes that underlie individual acts of choosing. What in algebra is expressed as "importance" or "weight" is expressed in process by temporal "priority" or by relative "attention." And what in process is expressed as strategy or criterion shift is expressed in algebra by nonlinearity. Although there is no conflict between algebraic and process descriptions, they are not the same thing.

SP/A theory represents the terminus (if only temporary) of my own intellectual meandering – back and forth, from algebra to process, from judgment to choice – over the last 20 years. It embodies a variety of process/algebra connections that have already been discussed. These include noncompensatory processes, lexicographic semiorders, attentional mechanisms, and aspiration levels on the process side, along with compensatory processes, nonlinear averaging, decumulative weighting, and stochastic control on the algebraic side. There remains, however, one additional feature that characterizes the theory: this is the fact that SP/A is a dual-criterion model.

If an algebraic expression for SP/A is written that covers everything discussed thus far, it would look something like this:

$$SP/A = F[SP, A] = F\left[ v_1 + \sum_{i=2}^{n} h(D_i)(v_i - v_{i-1}), \sum_{i=1}^{n} \alpha_i p_i \right].$$

The model states that there are two basic inputs to the choice process. The first input, SP, represents the aggregate effect of a comparison process that can be operationalized for most people as bottom-up before top-down. The weighting function ($h$), which transforms the decumulative probabilities ($D_i = \sum_{j=i}^{n} p_j$), captures the relative importance to the decision maker of avoiding bad outcomes (security) and achieving good outcomes (potential).

Because the SP process can be modeled algebraically with a cautiously hopeful weighting function, it can be classed with the family of weighted averaging models that evolved from the expected value criterion of the sixteenth century. However, it is important to remember that the SP term describes aggregate patterns of data across trials rather than behavior on single trials. Thus, someone who compares gambles lexicographically using only rough assessments of security and potential will produce patterns of choices that suggest cautiously hopeful weighting even though no decumulative weighted value is ever computed.

The second input, A, represents the aggregate effect of a process that evaluates risky options in terms of the likelihood that the payoff will exceed an aspiration level. The variable $\alpha_i$ (multiplying the individual values of $p_i$) takes a value between 1 and 0 depending on whether the associated $v_i$ meets the aspiration level. If the aspiration level is discrete, $\alpha_i$ is an index variable taking only the values 1 or 0; if the aspiration level is fuzzy, $\alpha_i$ will vary continuously between 1 and 0.

The A process is cousin at least to the concepts of bold play and stochastic control first studied by Dubins and Savage (1976). By including the stochastic control term in the model, SP/A theory challenges yet another of the basic elements underlying the expected value criterion, this being the idea that probabilities and outcomes are combined in the index of gamble value. Although combination of probability and value does occur in the bottom-up before top-down SP process, it does not occur in assessing whether the aspiration level will be met.

The function $F$ combines two inputs that are logically and mathematically distinct, much as Allais (1952/1979) proposed long ago. Because SP and A provide conceptually independent assessments of a gamble's attractiveness, one possibility is that $F$ is a weighted average in which the relative weights assigned to SP and A reflect their relative importance in the current decision environment. Another possibility is that $F$ is multiplicative. In either version, however, $F$ would yield a unitary value for each gamble, in which case SP/A would be unable to predict the sorts of intransitivities demonstrated by Tversky (1969) and others.

The existence of intransitivities suggests that the various inputs to the choice process may not be combined into a unitary value, in which case SP/A theory may also need to challenge the higher-order idea that a single index is sufficient to describe the value of a risky option. For example, SP and A (and even S and P) might be assessed sequentially and evaluated according to the sorts of context-sensitive lexicographic processes that figure in the LS and NLAD models proposed by Tversky (1969) and Ranyard (1982). Indeed, I called on a sequential process of just this sort in Figure 39.3 to "explain" the existence of intransitivities for gains in the Budescu and Weiss (1987) experiment.

Alternatively, it may be that SP and A assessments are themselves subject to context effects that depend on the particular pair of gambles being compared. Luce, Mellers, and Chang (1993), for example, recently showed that intransitivity can result if the process of choosing among gambles involves a "reference level" that itself changes as a function of the gambles being compared. Previous work with SP/A theory has also suggested that aspiration levels may be affected by the gambles in the immediate choice set (Lopes, 1987). For example, if one of the gambles offers a sure amount (such as the $70 minimum in the riskless lottery of Figure 39.1), that value is likely to serve as the aspiration level in evaluating an alternative gamble provided that no other aspiration level is operating.

As it stands, SP/A theory does not include a utility transformation. This is not because the concept of subjective value seems wrong or unnecessary. Instead, the omission signals some theoretical uneasiness at inserting a free function into the theory without knowing what purpose the function will serve. It seems at present that most experimental results involving "risk aversion" and "risk seeking" can be handled by SP/A theory without this additional complication. But even if new results suggest conclusively that something akin to utility needs to be considered, it remains to be seen whether that something extra should be diminishing marginal utility (as might be operating in problems that span very wide outcome ranges) or diminishing sensitivity (as might be operating if subjects evaluate gambles superficially without considering the impact of outcomes on living standards). A good case could be made for either logically, but data must show the way.

SP/A theory sprang from the desire to construct an algebraic model of risky choice that incorporates the subjective reality of the chooser. As experience with SP/A has accumulated, the model has demonstrated its ability to provide qualitative accounts of data that appear anomalous from more standard perspectives. For example, when Schneider and Lopes (1986) tested preselected groups of risk-averse and risk-seeking subjects on preferences for gain and loss lotteries, the results were highly complex across the two groups and failed to support any of the commonly proposed forms of utility function (concave, convex, or S-shape). In SP/A terms, however, the complexity in the data signaled a single difference between groups: whether the subjects were security-minded or potential-minded.

SP/A theory has also been able to explain differences in the degree to which decision makers experience conflict during the choice process and to account for seemingly anomalous patterns of risk preference such as those underlying the St. Petersburg paradox (Lopes, 1995), both forms of the Allais paradox, and both occurrences and nonoccurrences of intransitivity as observed by Budescu and Weiss (1987). That it does so without invoking either nonlinear utility or sign-dependent weighting functions (i.e., weighting functions that differ for gains and losses) testifies to the value of doing algebraic modeling with process in mind. Although there are limits to what we can learn about process experimentally, the descriptive successes of SP/A theory suggest that in exploring the psychological world of risky choice, it is simpler and more certain to travel from process to algebra than to go the other way around.

### Notes

1  Holistic processes are also called interdimensional, as search proceeds from dimension to dimension within a single alternative. Dimensional processes are also called intradimensional for obvious reasons.

2  The LS model is a special case of NLAD in which differences that do not exceed a threshold are strictly ignored. Under NLAD, smaller probability differences receive less weight than larger differences but are still traded off against payoff differences.

3   As it happens, each of these four rule variants is equivalent for the stimuli that Slovic and Lichtenstein used. The 9 attractive gambles under any of the variants yield a net expected value of $7, whereas the 18 unattractive gambles yield a net expected value of −$7.

4   In Payne and Braunstein's stimuli, there were only three possible relations: $P_W > P_L$ for both gambles, $P_W = P_L$ for both gambles, or $P_W < P_L$ for both gambles.

5   "Bottom" here refers to the bottom (low or bad end) of the distribution and not necessarily to the bottom of the display. Displaying lotteries with bad outcomes on top does not affect subjects' preferences (Schneider & Lopes, 1986).

6   Small differences in the slopes of the utility and weighting functions may cause there to be some pairs of gambles in which reflection is not predicted. Which gambles these are depends critically on the details of the two functions and would, therefore, differ from person to person. However, situations of nonreflection are uncommon and would tend to be restricted to particular sorts of gambles.

### References

Allais, M. (1979). The foundations of a positive theory of choice involving risk and a criticism of the postulates and axioms of the American School. In M. Allais & O. Hagen (Eds.), *Expected utility hypotheses and the Allais Paradox* (pp. 27–145). Dordrecht, Holland: Reidel. (Original work published 1952)

Allais, M. (1986). *The general theory of random choices in relation to the invariant cardinal utility function and the specific probability function.* Working Paper No. C4475. Centre d'Analyse Economique, École des Mines, Paris, France.

Budescu, D., & Weiss, W. (1987). Reflection of transitive and intransitive preference: A test of prospect theory. *Organizational Behavior and Human Decision Processes, 39,* 184–202.

Cohen, M., Jaffray, J.-Y., & Said, T. (1987). Experimental comparison of individual behavior under risk and under uncertainty for gains and for losses. *Organizational Behavior and Human Decision Processes, 39,* 1–22.

Combs, C. H. (1975). Portfolio theory and the measurement of risk. In M. F. Kaplan & S. Schwartz (Eds.), *Human judgment and decision processes.* New York: Academic Press.

Coombs, C. H., & Bowen, J. N. (1971). A test of VE-theories of risk and the effect of the central limit theorem. *Acta Psychologica, 35,* 15–28.

Coombs, C. H., & Huang, L. (1970). Tests of a portfolio theory of risk preference. *Journal of Experimental Psychology, 85,* 23–29.

Coombs, C. H., & Lehner, P. E. (1981). Evaluation of two alternative models for a theory of risk: I. Are moments of distributions useful in assessing risk? *Journal of Experimental Psychology: Human Perception and Performance, 7,* 1110–1123.

Dubins, L. E., & Savage, L. J. (1976). *Inequalities for stochastic processes: How to gamble if you must* (2nd ed.). New York: Dover.

Fagley, N. S., & Miller, P. M. (1987). The effects of decision framing on choice of risky versus certain options. *Organizational Behavior and Human Decision Processes, 39,* 264–277.

Fischhoff, B. (1983). Predicting frames. *Journal of Experimental Psychology: Learning, Memory, and Cognition, 9,* 103–116.

Fishburn, P. C., & Kochenberger, G. A. (1979). Two-piece von Newmann–Morgenstern utility functions. *Decision Sciences, 10,* 503–518.

Friedman, M., & Savage, L. J. (1948). The utility analysis of choices involving risk. *Journal of Political Economy, 56,* 279–304.

Gilboa, I. (1986). A combination of Expected Utility and Maximin Decision Criteria. Working Paper No. 12-86. Tel Aviv University.

Hershey, J. C., & Schoemaker, P. J. H. (1980). Prospect theory's reflection hypothesis: A critical examination. *Organizational Behavior and Human Performance, 25,* 395–418.

Jaffray, J.-Y. (1986). *Choice under risk and the security factor: An axiomatic model.* Unpublished manuscript. Laboratorie d'Econometrique, University Paris VI.

Kahneman, D., & Tversky, A. (1979). Prospect theory: An analysis of decision under risk. *Econometrica, 47,* 263–291.

Kahneman, D., & Tversky, A. (1982). The psychology of preferences. *Scientific American, 248,* 163–169.

Kahneman, D., & Tversky, A. (1984). Choices, values, and frames. *American Psychologist, 39,* 341–350.

Lopes, L. L. (1984). Risk and distributional inequality. *Journal of Experimental Psychology: Human Perception and Performance, 10,* 465–485.

Lopes, L. L. (1987). Between hope and fear: The psychology of risk. *Advances in Experimental Social Psychology, 20,* 255–295.

Lopes, L. L. (1990). Remodeling risk aversion. In G. M. von Furstenberg (Ed.), *Acting under uncertainty: Multidisciplinary conceptions* (pp. 267–299). Boston: Kluwer.

Lopes, L. L. (1995). When time is of the essence: Averaging, aspiration, and the short run. *Organizational Behavior and Human Decision Processes,* in press.

Luce, R. D., Mellers, B. A., & Chang, S.-J. (1993). Is choice the correct primitive? On using certainty equivalents and reference levels to predict choices among gambles. *Journal of Risk and Uncertainty, 6,* 115–143.

Maule, A. J. (1989). Positive and negative decision frames: A verbal protocol analysis of the Asian disease problem of Tversky and Kahneman. In H. Montgomery & O. Svenson (Eds.), *Process and structure in human decision making.* London: Wiley.

Miller, P. M., & Fagley, N. S. (1991). The effects of framing, problem variations, and providing rationale on choice. *Personality and Social Psychology Bulletin, 17,* 517–522.

Montgomery, H. (1977). A study of intransitive preferences using a think-aloud procedure. In H. Jungermann & G. dr Zeeuw (Eds.), *Decision making and change in human affairs* (pp. 347–362). Dordrecht, Holland: Reidel.

Payne, J. W., Bettman, J. R., & Johnson, E. J. (1990). The adaptive decision maker: Effort and accuracy in choice. In R. M. Hogarth (Ed.), *Insights in decision making: A tribute to Hillel J. Einhorn.* Chicago: University of Chicago Press.

Payne, J. W., & Braunstein, M. L. (1971). Preferences among gambles with equal underlying distributions. *Journal of Experimental Psychology, 87,* 13–18.

Payne, J. W., & Braunstein, M. L. (1978). Risky choice: An examination of information acquisition behavior. *Memory & Cognition, 6,* 554–561.

Payne, J. W., Braunstein, M. L., & Carroll, J. S. (1978). Exploring predecisional behavior: An alternative approach to decision research. *Organizational Behavior and Human Performance, 22,* 17–44.

Payne, J. W., Laughhunn, D. J., & Crum, R. (1980). Translation of gambles and aspiration level effects in risky choice behavior. *Management Science, 26,* 1039–1060.

Quiggin, J. (1982). A theory of anticipated utility. *Journal of Economic Behavior and Organization, 3,* 323–343.

Ranyard, R. (1982). Binary choice patterns and reasons given for simple risky choice. *Acta Psychologica, 52,* 125–135.

Rosen, L. D., & Rosenkoetter, P. (1976). An eye fixation analysis of choice and judgment with multiattribute stimuli. *Memory & Cognition, 4,* 747–752.

Russo, J. E., & Dosher, B. A. (1983). Strategies for multiattribute choice. *Journal of Experimental Psychology: Learning, Memory, and Cognition, 9*, 676–696.

Schneider, S. L. (1992). Framing and conflict: Aspiration level contingency, the status quo, and current theories of risky choice. *Journal of Experimental Psychology: Learning, Memory, and Cognition, 18*, 1040–1057.

Schneider, S. L., & Lopes, L. L. (1986). Reflection in preferences under risk: Who and when may suggest why. *Journal of Experimental Psychology: Human Perception and Performance, 12*, 535–548.

Schoemaker, P. J. H. (1979). The role of statistical knowledge in gambling decisions: Moment versus risk dimension approaches. *Organizational Behavior and Human Performance, 24*, 1–17.

Simon, H. H. (1955). A behavioral model of rational choice. *Quarterly Journal of Economics, 69*, 99–118.

Slovic, P., & Lichtenstein, S. (1968). Relative importance of probabilities and payoffs in risk taking. *Journal of Experimental Psychology Monograph, 78*, (No. 3, Pt. 2), 1–18.

Todhunter, I. (1865). *A history of the mathematical theory of probability from the time of Pascal to that of Laplace.* Bronx, NY: Chelsea.

Tversky, A. (1969). Intransitivity of preferences. *Psychological Review, 76*, 31–48.

Tversky, A., & Kahneman, D. (1981). The framing of decisions and the psychology of choice. *Science, 211*, 453–458.

Tversky, A., & Kahneman, D. (1992). Advances in prospect theory: Cumulative representation of uncertainty. *Journal of Risk and Uncertainty, 5*, 297–323.

Tversky, A., Sattath, S., & Slovic, P. (1988). Contingent weighting in judgment and choice. *Psychological Review, 95*, 371–384.

von Neumann, J., & Morgenstern, O. (1947). *Theory of games and economic behavior* (2nd ed.). Princeton, NJ: Princeton University.

Weber, E. U., & Bottom, W. P. (1989). Axiomatic measures of perceived risk: Some tests and extensions. *Journal of Behavioral Decision Making, 2*, 113–132.

Williams, C. A. (1966). Attitudes toward speculative risks as an indicator of attitudes toward pure risks. *Journal of Risk and Insurance, 33*, 577–586.

Yaari, M. E. (1987). The dual theory of choice under risk. *Econometrica, 55*, 95–115.

# 40    The Theory of Image Theory: An Examination of the Central Conceptual Structure

*Terry Connolly and Lee Roy Beach*

For some time decision researchers have known that the subjective expected utility (SEU) model and its near relatives offer only an imperfect description of how most humans make decisions. Despite vigorous attempts to improve descriptive accuracy, many researchers suspect that the remedies offered (e.g., inflected utility functions, nonprobabilistic weighting schemes, non-maximizing combination rules) are largely cosmetic, preserving the basic logic of the model only by the use of ad hoc expedients. Only recently has it become clear that this collective body of work, which we will call Traditional Decision Theory (TDT), is being seriously challenged by alternative theories which offer a different view of decision making than that provided by TDT.

TDT is the result of some three hundred years of work by many scholars, and is, by any standard, a major intellectual achievement. Because it is the dominant paradigm for thinking about decision making, challengers are required to offer a great deal before their claims and alternative views are taken seriously. As a result, such alternatives, inevitably embryonic, are liable to be rejected in their entirety at the first empirical set-back, even if complete rejection is not warranted. The purpose of this chapter is to outline the challenge to TDT, and to argue for giving alternatives to TDT the leeway to develop to their potential in spite of inevitable initial empirical failures.

Space limitations prevent any complete survey of all of the alternatives to TDT that have been proposed. We will concentrate our attention on one example, image theory (Beach, 1990, 1993; Beach & Mitchell, 1987, 1990). We will take the position that image theory (IT), in its current (1993) version, is exemplary of a class of theories each of which, though differing in specifics, shares a group of assumptions and orientations different from those of TDT.

Reprinted from J.-P. Caverni, M. Bar-Hillel, F. H. Barron, & H. Jungermann (Eds.), *Contributions to Decision Making I.* © Copyright 1995, pp. 83–96, with kind permission from Elsevier Science – NL, Sara Burgerhartstraat 25, 1055 KV Amsterdam, The Netherlands.

By clarifying which elements are specific to the current version of IT and which are generic to the class of theories, we hope to promote the survival of the class even if the current version of IT does not itself survive.

In what follows, we first give a brief description of the frontrunners among the challengers to TDT, and a somewhat fuller summary of the main points of IT. Next we explore the points of contrast between IT and TDT, emphasizing the types of phenomena each addresses, the assumptions each makes, and the contrasts of theory and prediction between the two. From this contrast we develop the foundations of a research agenda which will serve the survival and development of both IT and the other challenging theories.

### Some Nontraditional Decision Theories

There have recently appeared a number of descriptive models of decision making that depart markedly from the normative, economic logic of TDT. We are limited here to a brief description of the central idea of each of these theories; the interested reader is referred to Klein, Orasanu, Calderwood and Zsambok (1993) for more complete discussions.

*Recognition-Primed decision making* (Klein, 1989) states that the majority of "decisions" actually involve recognition of the situation as one for which the decision maker has a prepared course of action or a course of action that can be modified to suit the situation. Noble's (1989) *cognitive situation assessment* theory is similar in that the focus of the theory is on how the decision maker identifies the requirements of the situation and uses past experience as a source for ways of satisfying those requirements. In a similar vein, Lipshitz's (1989) theory of *argument-driven decision making* views decision making as relying on causal logic to derive reasonable ways of dealing with environmental demands. Pennington and Hastie's (1988) theory of *explanation-based decision making* fits well with the other theories except that it assumes that situation assessment involves elaboration of a story that incorporates the decision maker's knowledge about what led up to the present situation and the implications of that knowledge and that story for what will happen in the future. These four theories focus on the role of situation assessment, past experience, and causal thinking in decision making. None of these is an explicit part of TDT.

In a slightly different vein, Connolly's (1988; Connolly & Wagner, 1988) theory of *decision cycles* sees decision making as an incremental process in which the decision maker's view of the situation is refined as behavior is implemented, and behavior is modified thereby to better suit the demands of the situation; thus what may have been a "bad" decision to begin with is molded into a "good" decision in light of feedback. Montgomery's (1983) *search for dominance structure* model is a theory of post-decisional behavior in which the favored decision alternative is bolstered to become the clearly dominant alternative. Finally, Hammond's (1988) *cognitive continuum theory* considers the nature of, and implications of, intuitive and analytical processes in decision making. These last three theories emphasize the roles of cognitive processes in guiding and justifying decisions, and do so in a much richer way than is afforded by TDT.

## Image Theory

Image theory contains many of the elements of the theories briefly described above. It acknowledges that situation assessment is a prior condition for decision making; that past experience is fundamental, often making reflective decision making unnecessary; that causal reasoning often is central when decisions must be made; that intuition is a familiar component of decision making; and that feedback obtained in the course of implementation not only guides behavior but also leads to further decisions in support of goal attainment.

Image theory views the decision maker as a manager of knowledge and information who attempts to keep a reasonable degree of consistency among his or her images of what is right, what he or she is attempting to achieve, and what he or she is doing to promote those achievements. Together, these images encompass the decision maker's store of knowledge.

The labels for the images are: the value image (beliefs and values that define what is right), the trajectory image (the goal agenda describing what he or she is attempting to achieve), and the strategic image (the plans aimed at achievement of the goals on the trajectory image – plans are the blueprints that guide tactical behavior and that can be used to forecast the future that they will promote).

Not all of the decision maker's knowledge is relevant in every situation. Framing is the process by which a partition of the entire knowledge store is defined such that it contains those aspects of the three images that are relevant to the situation at hand. These relevant aspects of the images constitute standards against which the suitability of decision options are evaluated. The theory (Beach, 1990) describes how framing takes place.

There are two kinds of decisions, adoption decisions and progress decisions. These are made using either or both of two kinds of decision tests, the compatibility test or the profitability test. Adoption decisions can be further divided into screening decisions and choice decisions. Adoption decisions are about adoption or rejection of candidate goals or plans as constituents of the trajectory or strategic images. Screening consists of eliminating unacceptable candidates. Choice consists of selecting the most promising candidate from among the survivors of screening.

Progress decisions consist of assaying the compatibility ("fit") between the forecasted future if a given plan is implemented (or continues to be implemented) and the ideal future as defined by the trajectory image. Incompatibility triggers rejection of the plan and adoption of a substitute.

Failure to find a feasible substitute prompts reconsideration of the plan's goal.

The compatibility test assays the fit between a candidate goal or plan and the decision standards defined by those aspects of the three images that constitute the frame. It is a single mechanism, in contrast to the profitability test which is the decision maker's unique repertory of choice strategies for selecting the best option from among the survivors of screening by the compatibility test.

Image theory sees decision making proceeding in the following way: the decision maker frames the situation in terms of knowledge about how it arose and its place in the large perspective of events. If the situation requires decision making and the decision is one that has been made before, the decision maker probes memory to find a strategy for dealing with it, called a policy. If the decision is unique or if the former policy failed, the decision maker must consider the options (which are goals or plans), screen them using the compatibility test, and adopt the best survivor using the profitability test. If only one option is considered, and if it survives the compatibility test, it is the choice without having to evoke the profitability test. Similarly, if more than one option is considered and only one survives, it is the choice. If more than one option is considered and more than one survives, the profitability test is used to break the tie by selecting the best choice, where best is defined by the particular choice strategy that is used.

Progress decisions proceed in a different manner. Here the question is whether a given plan is forecasted to achieve its goal if implementation is continued. The key is the compatibility between those aspects of the trajectory image included in the frame and the forecast generated by running the plan fast-forward. Sufficient compatibility implies retention of the plan and its continued implementation. Insufficient compatibility implies cessation of implementation and replacement of the plan with one that is more promising – often only a slight modification of the original plan in light of the discrepancy between the trajectory image and the forecast. This process is engaged in periodically during implementation in order to monitor progress toward goal achievement.

Image theory research has focused strongly on adoption decisions – screening and choice (summarized in Beach, 1990, 1993). Dunegan (1993) has initiated research on progress decisions that shows promise and that is supportive of the image theory position. There has been limited research on the nature of images (Brown, Mitchell, & Beach, 1987; Beach, Smith, Lundell & Mitchell, 1988; Bissell & Beach, 1993). The theory has generated two books and 25 papers, of which 9 papers are empirical studies and the rest are elaborations of the theory and attempts to apply it to such areas as auditing, job search, management, consumer behavior, family planning, political decisions, and so on. In short, image theory is in its infancy and empirical testing has just begun.

## Contrasting Theoretical Concerns

To better understand the difference between the theoretical concerns of Image Theory (IT) and those of traditional decision theory (TDT), let us apply both to a concrete practical example. Suppose that you find yourself with an unexpected free afternoon in a city you know and like, with several hours to fill before your flight home. How will you spend your time? A walk seems appealing, and you are faced with a decision as to which favorite old haunts you will visit. How do TDT and IT approach the problem?

Note first that the problem, though not in the least exotic, is quite complex. It assumes that one wishes to act purposively – some possible afternoons would certainly be better than others – though no clear single purpose is specified. There are a variety of ways to have fun: the art gallery, the museum, a stroll through old town, a teashop, a view. Not all of these will be reachable in the time available, some will complement one another (the stroll followed by a rest at tea), others will compete (having tea at one place perhaps precludes coffee immediately afterwards somewhere else). Extensive knowledge is assumed of both the environment (the city and its delights) and oneself (one's tastes and their likely shifts as the afternoon unfolds, energy lags, hunger increases). More may be learned about both as the afternoon proceeds: previously unvisited parts of the city may offer new surprises; a new taste may be discovered at a market stand. There are uncertainties: Will it rain, will I get lost? And there are important contingencies: one road leads on to another, closing off the road not taken; one lunch precludes a second, while invigorating the traveler for a stroll rather than a book shop.

These complexities are noted primarily because they must all be ignored in a TDT formulation of the problem. If, following Korzybski, we recall that the map is not the territory, we should recall also that the decision tree is not the map. TDT abstracts the traveler's problem as a current choice between alternative paths which are attractive only because of the destinations to which they (may) later lead. Note how the complex intertwinings of streets, satisfactions, contingencies, and opportunities are simplified and packaged in the abstraction. Time is bifurcated into "Now," the time at which choice is made, and "Later," the time at which outcomes are experienced and evaluated. A road chosen now is treated only as a value-neutral path to a unitary "destination" or "outcome" – perhaps formulated as "Spend afternoon in Area A," "Spend afternoon in Area B," and so on. Any number of issues are treated as exogenous, or not treated at all: Why are these and only these options considered? Is the possibility of an earlier flight home considered? Why? Or why not? Is a destination equally liked or disliked regardless of the path by which it is approached? How long is the time-frame within which the afternoon's activities will be evaluated? How does one evaluate a "destination" when the activities it includes are themselves branched, capricious, opportunistic, unexpected? And so on.

None of this is intended as either comprehensive or novel as a critique of TDT. It is simply to try to recapture, for those of us long steeped in TDT, what a very strange abstraction is at its core. We assume that the root interest of decision theory, orthodox or heterodox, is with how people do, or better could, get around on the ground. The concern is with real roads, really taken or not, that lead to real destinations, satisfactory or not. TDT operates at two removes of abstraction from that real world: first the abstraction from territory to map, then the abstraction from map to decision tree. The brilliant achievements of TDT have been won at the level of the tree. It should not surprise us that the two-way path from world to tree and back is sometimes fraught with difficulties. To refer to these simply as issues of "framing" (Tversky & Kahneman, 1981) or "implementation" (Harrison, 1975) seems to diminish the conceptual distance that needs to be covered in moving from world to model and back.

It is at this basic, architectural level of theory that we see IT as most sharply confronting the orthodoxy of TDT. The core of IT is a richly interconnected network, embedding acts, actions, plans, projections of future outcome streams and other organized sequences of actions with purposes, objectives, principles and values. IT is thus highly contextualized – it addresses first the decision maker's understanding of the world, the actions he or she might take, their relationships to one another and to later consequences, and the linkages between these consequences and his or her value structure. For expositary and pedagogical reasons this network has generally been presented in terms of the three somewhat distinct "images," noted earlier: the Value Image, clustered around principles and purposes; the Strategic Image, clustered around actions and their organization; and the Trajectory Image, clustered around the intersection of action and purpose. But the central thrust of IT is to confront head-on the fact that actions, purposes, and goals are often richly interconnected. It is, perhaps, the empirical exception rather than the rule that the three elements are linked in the minimal sense captured in traditional decision trees. IT turns our attention to a network of connections, built up over time in the mind of the decision maker. Action selection is only marginally the result of conscious deliberation at the moment of decision. It is closer to an output of a production system in which complex responses are generated by discrete triggering conditions. The spirit is that of Simon's (1947) description of "programmed decisions" or Miller, Galanter, and Pribram's (1960) discussion of plans and actions.

The core contrast between TDT and IT, then, turns on two conceptual partitions. One partition divides what is thought to be "inside," what "outside" the decision maker. The second partition is between those matters that are specific to the focal decision, and those that are stored or relatively stable over time. To overdraw the contrast only slightly:

TDT treats the decision maker as somehow "owning" an abstract decision mechanism, something like an unlabeled decision tree, and the computational skills to analyze it. In making a specific decision, this general-purpose machine is first loaded with content relevant to the decision (option names, values, a selection rule, etc.) and the computations are done to select an action. The output of this process is then back-translated or "implemented" as a real action in the real world.

IT treats the decision maker as "owning" a context-specific network, slowly assembled over time, connecting values, preferences, goals, actions, plans, and strategies. In making a specific decision, this network is activated by either external stimuli (e.g., loss of status quo, presentation of a new possibility) or internal stimuli (e.g., discrepancy between actual and anticipated outcomes). This activation leads to search for the closest feasible path through the net, and new action choice.

Even this rather oversimplified contrast leads to a number of potentially testable empirical propositions. For example:

### 1. Typical Number of Options Considered by a Competent Decision Maker

TDT would predict many, IT few. (Note that the proposition concerns *competent* decision makers. A narrow search for options could be read as evidence either of an IT process or of an incompetent TDT process. Narrow search with good long-run effectiveness would thus be the crucial evidence.)

### 2. Extent of Deliberation, Speed of Decision

TDT would imply relatively extensive deliberation, since large amounts of information need to be processed. IT predicts much less processing at the moment of choice, since most of the relevant considerations in matching action to purpose have been previously embedded in the network connections.

### 3. Cross-Context Transferability of Decision Skills

TDT predicts that individuals capable of skilled decision making in one context are likely to excel similarly in different contexts: they own and operate excellent decision engines. IT predicts much less transfer, since the network is specific to a particular context – a given disease group for a physician, a given investment category for a stockbroker.

### 4. Reliance on Potentially Flawed Cognitive Processes

Given the enormous recent interest in cognitive biases, illusions, fallacies, and the like, it is worth noting that TDT appears heavily reliant on such inference-like processes, while IT is not. The latter may thus offer a more plausible account of good performance in real contexts than does TDT.

### 5. Implementation Concerns

TDT yields action choice only at the highly abstract, model level, and thus faces potential difficulties translating this abstract recommendation into action on the ground. IT, in contrast, is concerned throughout with recognizable, concrete actions and consequences, so problems of back-translation arise much less.

### 6. Locus of Subject-Matter Expertise

In TDT, subject-matter expertise is essentially "off-line," and distinct from decision making expertise. Indeed, the two types of expertise may well reside in different heads, with the decision maker acquiring subject-matter information from advisers or local experts as need arises. In IT, subject-matter expertise is central to the decision apparatus itself. It is difficult to imagine an IT decision maker delegating action selection to another person, even a high-priced decision analyst!

### 7. Linkage to Central Values and Principles

In TDT, action is linked to the decision maker's central values only indirectly, by means of an exogenous process by which values are made manifest as preferences over outcomes. In principle, as long as the decision maker can express preferences at the level of specific outcomes, issues of central, higher-level values need not arise. In contrast, IT explicitly links these higher-level values into the lower-level objectives, goals, and preferences, opening the possibility for a treatment of values endogenous to the decision process itself.

### 8. Articulability of Decision Process and Results

Interestingly, either a TDT or an IT mode of arriving at a choice can be articulated or defended, though the terms of doing so differ from one to the other. A TDT explanation stresses the comprehensiveness of the analysis, the conformity with canons of rationality, the extent of computations and sensitivity analyses, the care with which optimal action was selected. An IT explanation would stress more the linkages: between the action chosen and other actions contemplated or already in process; and between the action chosen and important goals, values, and objectives.

### 9. Selection of Research Subjects and Tasks

TDT, with its implicit assumption of the generic central process, is free to use essentially any convenient subjects and tasks. College students playing low-stakes gambles are a perfectly reasonable and cost-effective choice. IT, in contrast, requires tasks and subjects for whom there has been reasonable opportunity to develop the postulated issue-specific network interconnections. This does not exclude student subjects, of course – students do in fact choose apartments, friends, sexual practices, work habits and areas of study, and may well have developed something more than rudimentary connections among the elements involved. They probably do not, however, routinely gamble with million-dollar stakes at known odds. Their performance in such tasks will thus tell us little of interest to IT.

As these examples suggest, there is substantial empirical content to the contrast we are drawing between TDT and IT conceptualizations. (We would claim, indeed, that substantial empirical support favors the IT over the TDT predictions in many of these issues, but our purpose here is theoretical rather than empirical comparison between the two). In retrospect, it is perhaps unfortunate that the majority of IT research to date has concerned a relatively peripheral cluster of concerns, those associated with the screening of options into a short list of serious candidates. Such screening processes are, certainly, of real interest, but they do not bear on the central theoretical contrasts between IT and TDT. The latter is simply silent on the matter: Options are generally treated as "given" or, in some models, as the results of (costly) search. IT does, of course, make specific predictions as to how screening will proceed – that it will be done by EBA or negative lexicographic filters, ignoring differences on any above-threshold dimension; and that information used in screening is not reused in later choice. Much evidence consistent with such mechanisms has been generated (see Beach 1993 for review). However, IT's predictions in this area are not central to the network vs. tree issues sketched above; and the mechanisms, if established, could as easily be appropriated by TDT as an exogenous, predecision process as taken as evidence hostile to it.

It is time now to take up the more central IT issues: just how interconnected and organized is the hypothesized network of values, strategies, and goals in the mind of the competent decision maker? How is this net built up over time? Can alternative network structures yield equivalent performance in terms of successful choices? How broad are subject-matter domains? What elements do they include? Is the three-way division proposed in current versions of IT empirically supported, or is it merely an expository convenience? This line of inquiry is not much illuminated by research that takes, say, a value image and reduces it to a simple list. The guiding metaphor, after all, is that of the image. The items comprising it are not simply an ear, a nose, a mouth, an eye: they are a face, the elements organized, orderly, interconnected. These organizational issues have been central to psychology at least since the work of Bartlett (1932) on the importance of "active organization" in schemas. They have surfaced more recently in the decision making context in such work as that of Margolis (1987) on the role of patterns in cognition and thinking; in Pennington and Hastie's (1988) work on how stories are used to organize complex bodies of information, as in jury decisions; and in Jungermann's (1985) work on scenarios (stories about the future) in decision making. Future research on IT will need to address these issues of network scope, content, and organization more seriously if it is to live up to its central metaphor: the image.

## Conclusion

This essay has explored some of the central theoretical contrasts between Image Theory (IT) and Traditional Decision Theory (TDT). We have identified several such contrasts, and drawn from them a number of implications, some with real empirical content: number of options considered, generalizability of decision making skills, the importance of subject-matter expertise, and others. In each of these, the current version of IT, sketched earlier, makes specific predictions and will live or die on the empirical evidence.

We have not sought here to survey the empirical evidence to date (though we do believe it to be generally supportive of most predictions of current IT). Our purpose has been to anticipate the inevitable empirical setbacks, and to set out what is central to theories of the IT sort, what peripheral. We have identified several points of fundamental contrast between IT and TDT: the sorts of research that will illuminate each, the types of subjects and research tasks required. These are the seeds of an extensive research agenda.

We do not expect the current version of IT to survive unscathed. As particular predictions are sharpened and tested, we fully expect that IT will require major modification, even rethinking – as, indeed, TDT has been modified and refined in the empirical fires. What we have argued for here is precisely the scope that allows such refinement. IT represents not a single theory but a class of theories: less generic, more contextual, more networked, less deliberative, than TDT. Our hope is that the work of constructing an empirically justified theory of this sort will not be abandoned at the first empirical setback. What we now treat as TDT represents the flowering of several centuries of revision and refinement. We hope some of the same tolerance will be extended to the new theoretical efforts currently represented by IT.

### References

Bartlett, F. C. (1932). *Remembering: a study in experimental and social psychology*. Cambridge: Cambridge University Press.

Beach, L. R. (1990). *Image theory: Decision making in personal and organizational contexts*. Chichester, UK: Wiley

Beach, L. R. (1993). Image theory: Personal and organizational decisions. In G. A. Klein, J. Orasanu, R. Calderwood, & C. E. Zsambok (Eds.). (1993), *Decision making in action: Models and methods*. Norwood, NJ: Ablex Publishing Co.

Beach, L. R., & Mitchell, T. R. (1987). Image theory: Principles, goals and plans in decision making. *Acta Psychologica, 66*, 201–220.

Beach, L. R., & Mitchell, T. R. (1990). Image theory: A behavioral theory of decisions in organizations. In B. M. Staw & L. L. Cummings (Eds.), *Research in organizational behavior, 12*, Greenwich, CT: JAI Press.

Beach, L. R., Smith, B., Lundell, J., & Mitchell, T. R. (1988), Image theory: Descriptive sufficiency of a simple rule for the compatibility test. *Journal of Behavioral Decision Making, 1*, 17–28.

Bissell, B. L., & Beach, L. R. (1993). *Image theory: The role of the compatibility test in situational diagnosis.* Technical report 93-12, University of Arizona. Department of Management and Policy.

Brown, F., Mitchell, T. R., & Beach, L. R. (1987). *Images and decision making: The dynamics of personal choice.* Technical report # 87-1. Seattle: University of Washington, Department of Psychology.

Connolly, T. (1988). Hedge-clipping, tree-felling, and the management of ambiguity. In M. B. McCaskey, L. R. Pondy, & H. Thomas (Eds.). *Managing: the challenge of ambiguity and change.* New York: Wiley.

Connolly, T., & Wagner, W. G. (1988). Decision cycles. In R. L. Cardy, S. M. Puffer, & M. M. Newman (Eds.), *Advances in information processing in organizations (Vol. 3.)* 183–205. Greenwich, CT: JAI Press.

Dunegan, K. J. (1993). Framing, cognitive modes and image theory: Toward an understanding of a glass half-full. *Journal of applied Psychology, 78*, 491–503.

Hammond, K. R. (1988). Judgment and decision making in dynamic tasks. *Information and Decision Technologies, 14*, 3–14.

Harrison, E. F. (1975). *The managerial decision-making process.* Boston: Houghton Mifflin.

Jungermann, H. (1985). Inferential processes in the construction of scenarios. *Journal of Forecasting, 4*, 321–327.

Klein, G. A. (1989). "Recognition-primed decisions." In W. B. Rouse (Ed.), *Advances in man-machine system research, 5*, 47–92. Greenwich, CT: JAI Press.

Klein, G. A., Orasanu, J., Calderwood, R., & Zsambok, C. E. (Eds.) (1993). *Decision making in action: Models and methods.* Norwood, NJ: Ablex Publishing Co.

Lipschitz, R. (1989). *Decision making as argument driven action.* Boston: Boston University Center for Applied Social Science.

Margolis, H. (1987). *Patterns, thinking and cognition: A theory of judgment.* Chicago: University of Chicago Press.

Miller, G. A., Galanter, E., & Pribram, K. H. (1960). *Plans and the structure of behavior.* New York: Holt, Rinehart & Winston.

Montgomery, H. (1983). Decision rules and the search for dominance structure: Towards a process model of decision making. In P. Humphreys, O. Svenson, & A. Vari (Eds.), *Advances in psychology.* Amsterdam: North-Holland.

Noble, D. (1989). *Application of a theory of cognition to situation assessment.* Vienna. VA: Engineering Research Associates.

Pennington, N., & Hastie, R. (1988). Explanation-based decision making: Effects of memory structure on judgment. *Journal of Experimental Psychology: Learning, Memory and Cognition, 14* (3), 521–533.

Simon, H. A. (1947). *Administrative behavior.* New York: Macmillan. 1947.

Tversky, A., & Kahneman, D. (1981). The framing of decisions and the psychology of choice. *Science, 211*, 453–458.

# Author Index

# Subject Index

*Note:* Italicized page numbers refer to figures and tables.